THE ULTIMATE ENCYCLOPEDIA OF

SCIENCE FICTION

THIS IS A CARLTON BOOK

Copyright © Carlton Books
Limited 1996

This edition published 1996

10 9 8 7 6 5 4 3 2 1

ISBN 1 85868 188 X

Project Editor: Simon Kirrane
Editorial assisstant: Roland Hall
Designer: Norma Martin
Picture Research: Sarah Moule
Production: Garry Lewis

Printed and bound in Dubai

General Editor

David Pringle is editor and publisher of the monthly science-fiction magazine Interzone (a Hugo Award-winner in 1995). He is past-editor of Foundation: The Review Of Science Fiction (1980-86), and has written or edited many non-fiction books including six Interzone anthologies and Earth Is The Alien Planet: J. G. Ballard (1979), Science Fiction: The 100 Best Novels (1985), Imaginary People: A Who's Who Of Modern Fictional Characters (1987), Modern Fantasy: The 100 Best Novels (1988) and The St James Guide To Fantasy Writers (1995).

Other Contributors

David Langford is a freelance author and computer-software writer. He has written three novels and several non-fiction books, including The Third Millennium (with Brian Stableford, 1985). He is eleven-times Hugo Award-winner as best science-fiction fan-writer and for best fanzine (Ansible).

Brian Stableford is a novelist and critic of distinction in the science-fiction field. His many novels include Cradle Of The Sun (1969), Halcyon Drift (1972), The Realms Of Tartarus (1977), The Walking Shadow (1979), Journey To The Centre (1982), The Empire Of Fear (1988), The Werewolves Of London (1990) and Serpent's Blood (1995). His non-fiction works include The Third Millennium (with David Langford, 1985), Scientific Romance In Britain, 1890-1950 (1985) and The Way To Write Science Fiction (1989).

Paul Di Filippo is a novelist and highly-regarded short-storywriter who lives in Providence, Rhode Island, USA. He is a regular book reviewer for Asimov's Science Fiction magazine, and his first book, a collection of novellas entitled The Steampunk Trilogy, was published in 1995. Other books are forthcoming.

John Grant is a prolific writer of science-fiction, fantasy and non-fiction books. He worked for many years in publishing and has edited numerous reference books, including the Encyclopedia Of Walt Disney's Animated Characters (1987). He was Technical Editor of The Encyclopedia Of Science Fiction (Orbit, 1993), and his novels include the fantasies Albion (1991) and The World (1992).

Chris Gilmore is a freelance editor, critic and short-story writer; and is a regular book reviewer for Interzone magazine. He lives in Bedford.

THE ULTIMATE ENCYCLOPEDIA OF
SCIENCE FICTION

THE DEFINITIVE ILLUSTRATED GUIDE

General Editor: David Pringle
Hugo Award Winner

CARLTON

Contents

Foreword

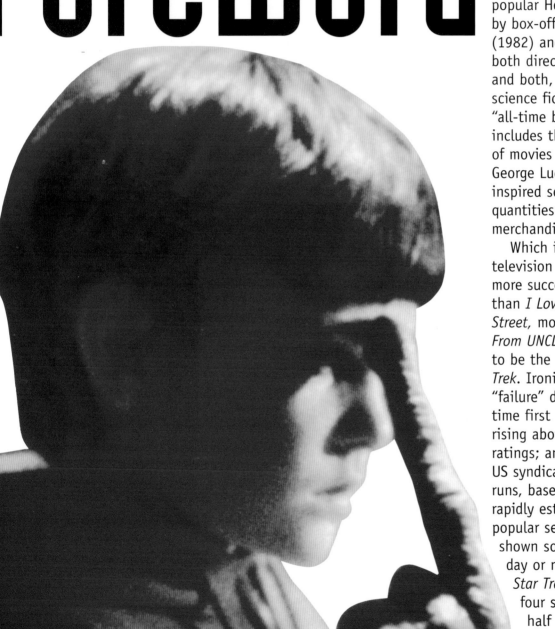

How popular and influential is science fiction? Some might judge it to be a minority taste; but consider the following:

Which are the most successful movies ever produced? The two most popular Hollywood films, measured by box-office receipts, are *E.T.* (1982) and *Jurassic Park* (1993), both directed by Steven Spielberg and both, as it happens, works of science fiction. The top ten list of "all-time box-office hits" also includes the famous *Star Wars* trilogy of movies (1977-83) produced by George Lucas; and these have inspired scores of books and vast quantities of comics, toys and other merchandise.

Which is the most famous television series ever produced — more successful, in global terms, than *I Love Lucy* or *Coronation Street,* more watched than *The Man From UNCLE*? The answer, surely, has to be the science-fiction series *Star Trek*. Ironically, it was adjudged a "failure" during its American prime-time first run (1966-69), never rising above 20th place in the ratings; and yet, when it went into US syndication (the system of re-runs, based on local TV stations), it rapidly established itself as the most popular series ever, constantly shown somewhere, at some hour of day or night, for 30 years now. *Star Trek* has inspired three or four spinoff TV series, more than half a dozen big-screen movies, countless weekend conventions attended by tens of thousands of people, and well over 200 associated books; and no end is in sight.

Which is the most famous radio drama ever broadcast? The answer is *The War Of The*

Worlds (1938), an adaptation of H. G. Wells's celebrated science-fiction novel of 1898, produced by Orson Welles and written by Howard Koch. The events that surrounded this radio production led to numerous newspaper reports and several books — and, decades later, to a TV movie, *The Night That Panicked America* (1975). The drama itself is still available on disc and tape, and has been re-broadcast around the world.

Which is the most famous fictional character to have emerged from comic strips or comic books? The answer, by a considerable margin, is Superman, the red-caped 'Man of Steel' from the planet Krypton. He was the invention of two teenage science-fiction fans (Jerry Siegel and Joe Shuster) who hawked their strip around various newspapers in the mid-1930s, without success, until eventually it was accepted by the company destined to evolve into DC Comics. The commercial success of the Superman comic book was so enormous, from 1939 onwards, that it virtually created an entire industry. It also led to cinema cartoons, serials, TV series, big-budget movies and much more.

Which is the most famous and influential English-language novel of the 20th century? That is a more difficult question to answer, as fame and influence are hard to quantify in literature. Yet there are few candidates more convincing than George Orwell's Nineteen Eighty-Four (1949), a work of political science fiction that not only sold in the millions (and is still selling strong) but inspired a powerful BBC TV dramatization (1954) and two subsequent large-screen films. No novel (with the possible exception of Joseph Heller's Catch-22) has been more frequently cited by politicians, newspaper leader-writers and assorted pundits. Orwell's phrases — Big Brother, Thought Police, Ministry of Truth, doublethink, and so on — have entered the language, and his masterpiece surely has more claim to be a book that has changed the world than has any other novel of the past hundred years.

We rest our case. Science fiction is the most significant mode of fiction of the century! This book aims to celebrate it, in all its variety.

David Pringle
Interzone   *May 1996*

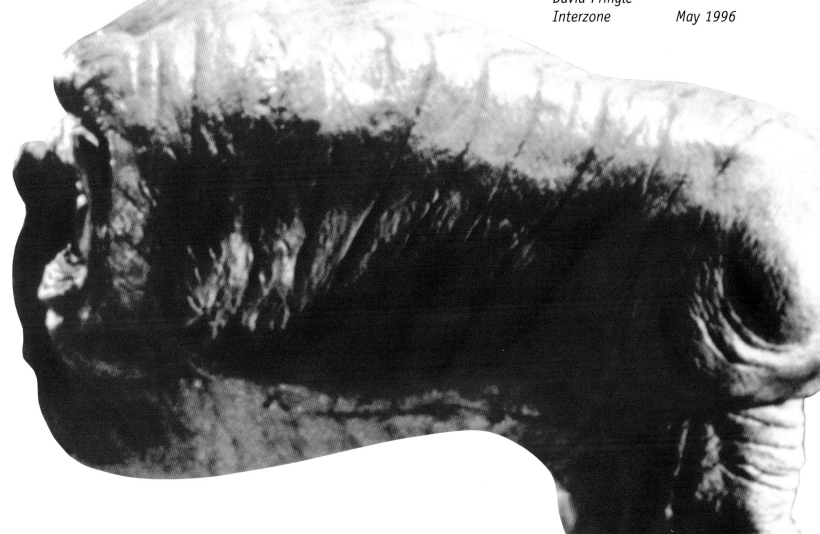

Introduction

From pulp magazines to satellite TV, science fiction has moved through many media. It also has a long prehistory, in writings from the Renaissance to the First World War...

§cience fiction gained its name in the American pulp magazines of the late 1920s, but the name didn't become a household term until the pulps were dying, in the early 1950s. (Around the same time, in the 1950s, the contraction "sci-fi" was coined, by analogy with "hi-fi" — but it has a derogatory ring for many people, and throughout this book we prefer to use the more neutral abbreviation "sf".) Pulp magazines were so called because they were printed on the roughest kind of wood-pulp paper and were aimed at the widest possible audience, a readership often viewed as "low-brow". Such magazines which published almost nothing but fiction — love stories, crime stories, western stories, war stories, foreign-legion and seafaring adventure stories, horror and fantasy stories, as well as sf — were a phenomenon of the first half of this century, and have long since been replaced by mass-market paperbacks, comics and television.

Decades ago, science fiction left the pulps and entered the newer media; it also invaded other forms of communication such as cinema and radio (themselves developments of the pulp era) and, much more recently, pop music, TV advertising, graphic novels, interactive computer games, CD-ROMs and the first glimmerings of virtual-reality systems. The pulps that nurtured sf — *Amazing Stories, Wonder Stories, Astounding Stories* and many others — are long gone (although the last of the trio just cited transformed itself into a small-format magazine, renamed *Analog*, which is still appearing in 1996). Nevertheless, the pulp magazines remain important to any understanding of modern popular sf because it was there, during the first half of the century, that the genre gained its present shape and variety of types.

For sf, viewed as a form of popular literature, is not so much a single genre as a cluster of overlapping sub-genres. The half-dozen or so most familiar story-types — let us call them "templates" — of science fiction include:

SPACE OPERA: a term used, by analogy with "horse opera" or "soap opera", for tales of interstellar heroics, usually involving mighty spacecraft and fearsome superweapons. E. E.

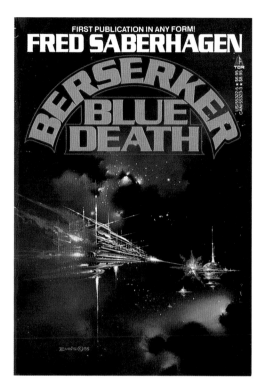

"Doc" Smith's *Lensman* novels are archetypal space opera, and the *Star Wars* films are more recent examples.

PLANETARY ROMANCE: a romantic adventure story set on a colourful alien planet, often involving an element of swordplay (or science-fictional equivalent). Edgar Rice Burroughs's A *Princess Of Mars* and its many sequels are the archetypes. Ursula Le Guin's *The Left Hand Of*

 GUNPLAY *Space Operas centres on spaceships, alien threat and, as here, doom-laden weapons*

Darkness is a much more sophisticated modern example.

FUTURE CITIES: tales of the high-tech urban future, usually involving some sort of rebellion, whether successful or failed, against an unpleasant tyranny. Examples range from H. G. Wells's *When The Sleeper Wakes* through George Orwell's *Nineteen Eighty-Four* to Frederik Pohl and C. M. Kornbluth's *The Space Merchants* and beyond. Movies such as *Blade Runner* and *RoboCop* belong to this mode.

DISASTER STORIES: narratives about the present-day or near-future world upset by major cataclysm, whether man-made or natural. Examples include John Wyndham's *The Day Of The Triffids*, J. G. Ballard's *The Drowned World* and Terry Nation's BBC television series *Survivors*.

ALTERNATIVE HISTORIES: stories set in an imaginary time-line which has diverged from our common history. Philip K. Dick's *The Man In The High Castle*, about a world in which the Germans and the Japanese won World War II, is a celebrated instance. Robert Harris's *Fatherland* is a recent bestseller on precisely the same theme.

HIGH-RISE HABITAT *FUTURE CITIES AS IN THIS SCENE FROM BLADE RUNNER, ARE OFTEN PLACES OF MENACE, MAN-MADE YET CURIOUSLY MINERAL AND IMPERSONAL. AGAINST SUCH SOUL-DESTROYING ANT-HILLS A LONE HERO OR A SMALL GROUP MAY REVOLT*

 CAMPFIRE TALES *Prehistory, as in this scene from* Quest for Fire, *is often a setting for* **SF**

PREHISTORICALS: tales set in the earth's remote past, usually incorporating modern scientific theories about prehistory. They range from William Golding's *The Inheritors* to the *Earth's Children* series of bestsellers by Jean M. Auel and movies such as *The Quest For Fire*.

Those templates underpin a great deal of popular science fiction. There are other story-forms — for example, time-travel and time-paradox narratives; tales of alien invasion; tales of supermen and new mental powers; and "comic infernos" which parody everything listed here — and there are numerous combinations and variations of all the types. The templates are discussed, along with common themes, motifs and buzz-words (Hard SF, New Wave SF, Cyberpunk, Steampunk, etc) in the following chapter of this book.

If we limit ourselves, for the moment, to a consideration of the six major templates described above, several features become apparent. Firstly, not all science fiction concerns space and space travel: Space Operas and Planetary Romances obviously have cosmic or interplanetary settings, but stories that conform to the other four templates are largely earthbound. Secondly, not all science fiction concerns the future: Future-City stories evidently look to the day after tomorrow, but Disaster

Stories usually are set in the present day (or near enough), while Prehistoricals are set in the distant past, and Alternative-History stories are set "sidewise in time". Thirdly, not all science fiction concerns machinery or technological artefacts: such items loom large in Space Operas and Future-City stories, but often they have no part to play in stories that conform to other templates.

So, science fiction is a varied form, rich in possible narratives and possible settings. What all its templates have in common, however, is that they generate stories which take us away from the here-and-now, away from the "mundane" and into radically *different* worlds or *altered* worlds. Thrillers that utilize occasional sf devices — a superweapon, for example, with which some villain holds the world to ransom — tend not to be regarded as true sf because they invariably return everything to the *status quo ante* at the end of the tale (that is, when the hero defeats the villain and destroys his weapon). In true science fiction, the pleasures are less conventional, less "normalizing" than those to be found in most crime fiction or, for that matter, in most romantic fiction. In sf, the world is almost always changed forever, and there can be no going back.

The reader may close the book and so return to everyday reality, but nevertheless an imaginative vista has been opened in his or her mind — be it the vista of a new planet, a wholly changed society, a lost world of the past, an historical possibility that never materialized, or a vision of the end of time. Once such imaginative perspectives have been revealed, through the medium of the best science fiction, the reader is changed — like it or not. This is the peculiar appeal of sf — it is about changed worlds; and it changes you, the reader and it is this aspect of sf that makes for such challeging literature.

Science Fiction, Utopia-and Fantasy

THE EVOLUTION OF SF HAS BEEN SUCH THAT IT CAN BE TRACED BACK IN HISTORY AND ONE OF THE MOST DURABLE FORMS IS THE UTOPIAN IDEAL

Although science fiction became a named genre as a result of stories appearing in the US pulps, it was not a new thing under the sun. A large public on both sides of the Atlantic was already familiar with the "extraordinary voyages" of Jules Verne (the first of which appeared in the 1860s) and the "scientific romances" of H. G. Wells (from the mid-1890s),

along with a wide range of other works that we would now regard as sf. Some of these late 19th-century and early 20th-century books were among the most popular of their day, but there was no generally agreed label for them. Tales of the future, interplanetary romances, fantasies of science, invention stories, pseudo-scientific fiction — descriptive terms like these were used

way (so-called "science fantasy"); yet the distinction remains crucial for all that.

Science fiction is, or generally attempts to be, rational. It conforms to the laws of nature, as we understand them; it adheres to the modern scientific world view. Hence the genre's name: the label would be pointless if there were not some element of "science" to be found in sf. The critic John Clute has defined sf briefly as a type of fiction which "argues for a changed world". Argument implies reason and realism, a scientific thinking-through: fantasy may also deal in changed worlds, but it doesn't *argue for* them — it simply gives them to us, as impossible wonders (a genie from a bottle, a statue which comes to life, an entire world where magic works and where elves and trolls and dragons and unicorns roam).

The writer J. G. Ballard attempted an equally brief definition when he said that sf is fiction inspired by science, whereas fantasy is fiction inspired by fiction. Fantasy, on the whole, shuffles traditional elements, images

by reviewers, sometimes interchangeably; but one of the commonest labels — and perhaps the most accurate — was "utopian fiction".

The word "utopia", coined by Thomas More, derives from Greek (outopos) and means "no place", although it may also be regarded as a pun with the simultaneous meaning of "good place" (eutopos). But whether it depicts good, bad or indifferent places, the fact is that all science fiction is, in a sense, about "no place". That is to say, it is about imaginary societies or worlds — places which do not exist, so far as we know, but which could exist, which might have existed, or which may one day exist.

Words like could and might and may indicate the other great quality of sf and utopian fiction — its "realism". It deals with non-existent other places and other times, other societies and other beings, but it does not deal in the downright impossible. Stories which frankly concern themselves with impossible things — magical, supernatural, arbitrary, wish-fulfilling events or places or entities — and which make these seem beguiling, even plausible for the duration of the tale, are generally known as fantasy; and it is important to draw a distinction between science fiction and fantasy. It is not always easy to perceive the difference in particular works: many authors have written in both modes and have sometimes even mixed the two in a deliberate

The Ancestry of Science Fiction

IS FUNDAMENTAL TO SF STORIES WHOSE HEROES SET OFF INTO THE GREAT WILDERNESS OF UNKNOWN SPACE, BOLDLY GOING WHERE NO HUMAN HAS GONE BEFORE

and notions derived from mythology and folk-tale, from hoary legends and religious traditions — all things which may be regarded, in Ballard's sense, as "fiction". Science fiction, by contrast, takes the real world as its starting point, the world revealed to us by reason, by observation, by experimentation, by thinking anew — all those activities which may be regarded as "science". This is not to say that sf writers always get their science right; all too frequently, they get it wrong in the details, but it is the attitude which counts, the effort to reason things through, the attempt to show how we may get from *here* (our mundane reality) to *there* (the changed world).

 THOMAS MORE, *SHARP-EYED INITIATOR OF THE UTOPIAN TRADITION, AND SO A REMOTE FOUNDER OF SF*

Even if it is anti-traditional, in the sense just described, science fiction has an ancestry: it was not born yesterday, and it has its own tradition. Literary critics, such as the late Northrop Frye, have distinguished between different kinds of prose fiction, from Ancient Greek times to the present. One great distinction they like to draw is between the novel and the romance. Novels deal realistically with the societies that surround us: they are generally about courtship and money and social class and individual ambition; they are, almost invariably, about "the comedy of manners", the ways in which people behave towards each other. Jane Austen's Pride And Prejudice is a perfect example; Kingsley Amis's The Old Devils is a more recent one. Romances, on the other hand, are essentially adventure stories set in distant times or exotic places: a hero is obliged to overcome various obstacles and villains before he wins through, finds the treasure, gains the heroine's hand, and so on. Rider Haggard's King Solomon's Mines is an example of what critics mean by romance (and Haggard himself used the term, always referring to his "novels" as romances); any of Ian Fleming's James Bond thrillers would serve as a more recent example. Most serious, or literary, fiction tends towards the novel, while most popular, or mass-market, fiction tends towards the romance.

Science fiction, however, does not fall easily into either category. It borrows from both, in large measures — realism and a respect for facts deriving from the novel, exoticism and psychological excitement deriving from the romance — but it does more: with its concern for the depiction of imaginary worlds, realistically but flamboyantly conceived, it is very much a fiction of intellectual ideas, almost at times a "discussion fiction". Neither the novel, in the pure sense, nor the romance has much time for ideas: they are too concerned, respectively, with character and with adventure. So perhaps sf's true parentage can be found in a third type of prose fiction, distinct from the novel and the romance. As it happens, Northrop Frye has described just such a third type, beginning in Ancient Greece, which fits sf extremely well. Recognition of sf's kinship with this third sort of fiction has been overlooked for various reasons, in part because one of the older, and less satisfactory, terms for sf — "scientific romance" — confuses the issue by identifying sf with one particular kind of fiction, the wrong kind.

Generically, science fiction is not a form of romance, as is often supposed (that way lies heroic fantasy of the Tolkien sort, rather than sf proper), nor is it a sub-form of the social novel. Rather, it is a descendant of the type of prose fiction sometimes referred to as Lucianic Satire (after Lucian of Samosata, a Greek writer of the 2nd century AD). Lucianic Satire — also commonly known as "Menippean Satire" after an earlier writer, Menippus, whose works are now lost — is a kind of fiction which tends to the fantastic but also puts a considerable emphasis on the discussion and dramatization of ideas. (Romance, by contrast, while also fantastic in tendency, has little interest in ideas, being instead an embodiment of archetypal human feelings and desires.) In Lucian's fictions, the ideas discussed, and frequently lampooned, were those of the Classical Greek philosophers, many of whom were exponents of early "science". Lucian himself was a sly, subtle and highly learned writer — with a wonderful sense of humour. He makes an appropriate father-figure for science fiction, even if nowadays we would define his stories as fantasy rather than sf (but exactly the kind of fantasy which appeals strongly to sf readers, the kind written recently by, say, Terry Pratchett).

It was another highly learned writer with a sense of humour, the Englishman Thomas More, who revived the Lucianic Satire for the modern world, and in doing so laid the foundation stone of science fiction. In 1516, More, aided and abetted by his fellow Renaissance humanists Erasmus and Peter Gilles (the first SF Writers' Workshop?), produced a book-length fiction called Utopia. With its ambiguous depiction of an unknown island where society is organized along more rational lines, this book took its inspiration partly from Lucian, some of whose

FOUNDING FATHERS *Columbus, discoverer of the New World, and Amerigo, may be seen as the inspirers of much utopian fiction and sf*

stories More had translated from the Greek, and from other ancient writers such as Plato, but also — and this point is crucial — from recent historical experience. More was writing barely two decades after the Italian-born Spanish navigators Cristoforo Colombo and Amerigo Vespucci had discovered a "new world" on the other side of the Atlantic. More's fictional sailor, Raphael Hythloday, is depicted as having sailed to America with Vespucci, and as having remained there to make his own great discovery after the real-life navigator returned to Europe.

Thus Thomas More added a post-Renaissance sense of realism to the lively genre of Lucianic Satire. If we regard the New World explorers of his day as the equivalents of 20th-century lunar astronauts, then More's was the principal fiction inspired by that experience — a marriage of philosophical tall tale and up-to-date speculative geography. More wrote in Latin, the lingua franca which made his work accessible to educated readers throughout Europe, and so did many of his followers in what came to be known as the "utopian" literary tradition, including the Englishman Joseph Hall (Mundus Alter Et Idem, 1605), the German Johann Valentin Andreae (Christianopolis, 1619), the Italian Tommaso Campanella (The City Of The Sun, 1623), the Englishman Francis Bacon (The New Atlantis, 1627) and the German Johannes Kepler (Somnium, 1634).

With those last two names we enter the era of modern science: Bacon was the first great propagandist for the "scientific method", and his utopian tale depicts a society (again on an island, off America) dedicated to systematic research and its technological fruits; Kepler was a major astronomer who advocated the then-forbidden heliocentric theory (that the earth orbited the sun, not vice versa) and his piece of fiction — written, significantly, after he had taught himself Greek in order to translate Lucian — took the form of an imaginary flight to the moon, copiously embellished with authoritative scientific detail.

Literary voyages to the moon, usually involving the discovery of some utopian or anti-utopian society there, came into vogue in the 17th century, the leading examples being the English The Man In The Moone by Francis Godwin (1638) and the French Histoire Comique Contenant Les Etats Et Empires De La Lune Et Du Soleil by Cyrano de Bergerac (1657-62; translated as Other Worlds). Cyrano's witty and inventive tale, or pair of tales, was probably the greatest Lucianic Satire of its century and one which consciously built on the example of its predecessors: Godwin's "spaceman" hero Domingo Gonsales recurs as a character, and there is also an appearance of utopographer Tommaso Campanella. (Such recursiveness, or genre self-referentiality, seems to be a common characteristic of the whole tradition right down to modern science fiction: Lucian's tales featured appearances by the satirist Menippus and others of the famous dead, while his lunar travellers in 'The True History' fly past the playwright Aristophanes' imaginary sky-city, the delightfully named Cloudcuckooland.)

SF in the 18th Century

THE 18TH CENTURY WAS A HEYDAY FOR SCIENCE FICTION, EVEN IF MANY PEOPLE WEREN'T AWARE OF THE FACT AT THE TIME

The greatest Lucianic Satire of the following century was undoubtedly Jonathan Swift's more earthbound Gulliver's Travels (1726). Like Thomas More, Swift combined scrupulous realism of surface detail with a fascination for ideas, much fantastic invention and a deep sense of irony. His Gulliver encounters no mythical creatures, but wholly new beings who are rationally (and savagely) described — the tiny people of Lilliput, the giants of Brobdingnag, the mad scientists of Laputa, the grotesque immortal Struldbruggs, the intelligent horses and brutish Yahoos of Houyhnhnm-land. Moreover, his new worlds reflect and comment on our world to devastating effect: Gulliver's bungled attempt to describe the "benefits" of gunpowder

SENSE AND SENSIBILITY *JONATHAN SWIFT MAY HAVE BEEN A MAN OF GOD, BUT NO ONE HAD AN EARTHIER SENSE OF HUMANKIND'S NATURE AND FAILINGS*

to the horrified queen of Brobdingnag is a case in point. Swift's importance for later science fiction cannot be overestimated. His influence on, for example, H. G. Wells was profound; and Swift himself was influenced by the writers of the Lucianic tradition who had gone before (the notes in a modern edition of Gulliver, the Penguin paperback of 1967, begin with this claim: "There are many passages in which he seems to be indebted to, among others, Lucian, Rabelais and Cyrano de Bergerac.")

Swift's great book — no one, apart from the makers of the recent TV mini-series starring Ted Danson, has ever seriously described it as a "novel" — spawned many emulations, among them such works as A Voyage To Cacklogallinia by Samuel Brunt (1727), featuring a voyage to the moon; A Trip To The Moon by Murtagh McDermot (1728), more lunar satire; Memoirs Of The Twentieth Century by Samuel Madden (1733), the first work of futurist satire, using the device of a package of letters which is transported back in time from the end of the 20th century; The Adventures Of Eovaai (or The

Unfortunate Princess) by Eliza Haywood (1736), containing what is perhaps the first depiction in fiction of an extra-terrestrial visitor; Gaudentio Di Lucca by Simon Berington (1737), in which the narrator finds a peace-loving civilization in central Africa; Nicolai Klimii Iter Subterraneum (A Journey To The World Underground) by Ludwig Holberg (1741), a celebrated hollow-earth satire translated from Latin into English in 1742, but not into its author's native Danish until many decades later; The Life And Adventures Of Peter Wilkins by Robert Paltock (1750), a fantastic imaginary voyage to the then-unexplored south, in which the hero discovers a race of winged people and transforms their society in a way that Gulliver was unable to achieve; and, perhaps most famously, Micromégas by Voltaire (Francois-Marie Arouet, 1752), a satirical conte philosophique in which two giants from other worlds visit the earth and comment on our foibles. All in all, it is a rich tradition of 18th-century Lucianic

Satire, or proto-science fiction.

The most important development in the utopian tradition towards the end of the 18th century was the discovery of the future; up until then most such works had been set in the present day, either in unexplored parts of the earth or on the moon (or sometimes the sun). The earth was fast shrinking, however, thanks to the voyages of Captain Cook and other mariners of the period. The annexation of the future as suitable territory for the "rational fantasies" of proto-sf was to be a development as momentous for the utopian genre as the discovery of scientific research and technology had been in Francis Bacon's day, 150 years earlier. A beginning was made in an anonymous British work called The Reign Of George VI, 1900-1925 (1763), which has been described by scholar Paul K. Alkon as "a fantasy of relentless conquest [with] the ambiguous distinction of initiating the genre of future warfare". But the real breakthrough came with L'An 2440 by Louis Sebastien Mercier (1771;

C.W.QUINNELL

· SIR · FRANCIS · BACON ·

imaginatively bolder than most of Verne's tales. Meanwhile, in Britain, the new vogue for ballooning produced works like The Aerostatic Spy; or, Excursions With An Air Balloon by "An Aerial Traveller" (1785). But the main initiatives in the proto-sf of succeeding decades remained with the French, heirs of the 18th-century Enlightenment, who followed up Mercier's book with a remarkable series of science-fictional "firsts": Les Posthumes (Posthumous Letters) by Restif de la Bretonne (1802), perhaps the earliest far-future cosmic voyage; Le Dernier Homme (The Last Man) by Jean-Baptiste Cousin de Grainville (1805), the first "dying earth" story; Le Roman De L'avenir (The Novel Of The Future) by Félix Bodin (1834), an early attempt

at a realistic novel of tomorrow complete with a built-in theory of sf — Bodin called it "littérature futuriste"; Napoléon Et La Conquête Du Monde (Napoleon And The Conquest Of The World) by Louis Geoffroy (1836; later republished as Napoléon Apocryphe), the first alternative history, in which Napoleon is imagined as conquering not only Europe and Asia but also the North Pole, with the help of much applied science; Le Monde Tel Qu'il Sera (The World As It Will Be) by Emile Souvestre (1846), the first futuristic dystopia; Star Ou Psi De Cassiopée (Star, Or Psi Cassiopeia) by C. I. Defontenay (1854), the first detailed evocation of an alien solar system; and Paris Avant Les Hommes (Paris Before Men) by Pierre Boitard (1861), the first prehistoric tale of ape-men. It adds up to an astonishing half-century of French imaginative creativity, culminating in the appearance of Jules Verne's debut novel in 1863.

SF in the 19th Century

THE FIRST HALF OF THE CENTURY BELONGED TO FRENCH WRITERS SUCH AS JULES VERNE, BUT THIS PERIOD ALSO SAW THE APPEARANCE OF MARY SHELLEY'S GOTHIC HORROR TALE, FRANKENSTEIN

translated as Memoirs Of The Year 2500). This book, avidly read throughout Europe despite persistent attempts to ban it, featured a narrator thrown forward in time by almost 700 years to discover a Paris transformed for the better by the application of reason, science and technology. The idea that one could build one's fictional utopia here, in one's home city, simply by displacing it into the future, was revelatory: no one had thought of it before.

Unsurprisingly, there were many attempts to emulate Mercier's achievement, particularly in Germany (whose literary historians describe such books as Zukunftsromane — "future novels"). Examples range from the anonymous Das Jahr 1850 (The Year 1850, 1777) to the fascinating Ini: Ein Roman Aus Dem 21. Jahrhundert (Ini: A Novel Of The 21st Century) by Julius von Voss (1810); this last, full of flying machines and other futuristic marvels, sounds very much like Jules Verne more than 50 years before his time — except that it is

Sometimes claimed as the "first" science-fiction novel is Mary Shelley's Gothic horror tale, Frankenstein, Or The Modern Prometheus (1818), about a Swiss student who builds an artificial man from bits and pieces of dead bodies and then suffers the moral consequences of his act. Despite the book's greatness, evidenced by its longevity in print and the vast number of stage, film and TV adaptations it has inspired, Frankenstein's claim to be the first sf novel seems weak in the light of all that has been said so far in

FRANKENSTEIN'S MONSTER *HERE PORTRAYED BY ROBERT DE NIRO, WAS THE SYMBOL OF ALL THAT WAS MENACING ABOUT 19TH-CENTURY SCIENCE*

fashionable hollow-earth theories of John Cleves Symmes); A Voyage To The Moon by Joseph Atterley (pseudonym of George Tucker, 1827); The Moon Hoax by Richard Adams Locke (1835), an apocryphal newspaper account of marvellous new discoveries on the moon, originally entitled 'Great Astronomical Discoveries Lately Made By Sir John Herschel At The Cape Of Good Hope' and swiftly republished in booklet form; Three

MASTER OF THE MACABRE *EDGAR ALLAN POE SAW THE POSSIBILITIES OF SCIENCE FICTION, BUT DID NOT LIVE TO DEVELOP THEM VERY FAR*

this introduction. Perhaps that claim is greater if stress is placed on the word novel: it is one of the first works which is both sf and a novel, with realistically depicted characters acting in a recognizable modern world. Most earlier sf works cited above are not so much novels as utopian tales, satires or fictionalized philosophical discussions — Lucianic Satires, in short.

With the dawn of the 19th century, and with Mary Shelley, the proto-sf tradition becomes more novelistic (as indeed do most other forms of literature: it was to be the "Age of the Novel"). Even with this qualification, though, it may be argued that a number of other sf "novels" preceded Frankenstein by some years. Von Voss's Ini of 1810, mentioned above, seems to have been one; a Dutch work, A Remarkable Aerial Voyage And Discovery Of A New Planet by Willem Bilderdijk (1813), has been claimed as another. After the consolidation of the Industrial Revolution in the early 19th century, and with the continuing spread through all ranks of

society of literacy and scientific ideas, the time was ripe for the development of a more modern science fiction.

Arguably, this did not come until the world-wide success of Jules Verne's novels after 1863, but — in addition to all the French books cited earlier — there were numerous harbingers. Early examples from America include Symzonia: A Voyage Of Discovery by "Adam Seaborn" (1820), about a utopian society situated inside our globe (based on the then-

Some Guidance to New Readers

Where to begin as a new reader of present-day sf? What to choose when you're confronted with a vast array of titles in a well-stocked book shop? Which authors to sample if you were keen on Asimov or Clarke or Heinlein 20 years ago but have a suspicion that "they don't write them like that any more"? As editor of a science-fiction magazine, I'm asked this sort of question frequently. You have to take into account who is doing the asking — young or old, male or female, "sophisticated" or "naive", a professional journalist or someone you've met at a party — but often I find myself giving some variant of the following answer:

If you're all at sea in book shop or library, you could do worse than head straight for the authors whose names begin with "B". For plain readers who want a good story with an upbeat ending, preferably one set in outer space or on another planet, I recommend the newer British writer Stephen Baxter, or the newer American writer Lois McMaster Bujold. Both are rising stars, with eager followings. Baxter is stronger on scientific background and the old-fashioned Sense of Wonder; Bujold is stronger on characterization and continuity from book to book; but each may offer enjoyment to the reader unversed in today's sf.

Stray backwards and forwards along the shelf and you'll find that group of heavyweight American writers jocularly known as the "Killer B's" — Greg Bear, Gregory Benford and David Brin. They can be more demanding — Benford, for example, is a professor of physics as well as a novelist — but they're all near the top of their field, and if you enjoyed Baxter and/or

Bujold you could give these guys a try. If you want writing with a more British flavour, try Iain Banks or Eric Brown. And there are other worthwhile Americans, ranging from John Barnes to Octavia Butler. By the time you've sampled all these B's you'll be well-grounded in some of the best contemporary sf, and able to find your way safely enough through the rest of the alphabet.

ONE TO LOOK OUT FOR *Lois Bujold is a new American sf novelist who writes gripping tales that give many readers value for their money.*

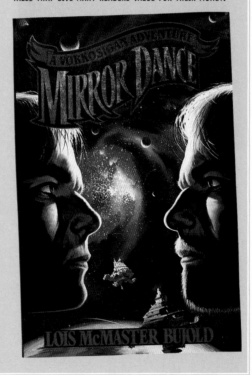

Hundred Years Hence by Mary Griffith (1836); and, of course, Edgar Allan Poe's Tales (originally collected in 1840 and 1845; a relevant modern selection is The Science Fiction Of Edgar Allan Poe edited by Harold Beaver, Penguin, 1976). Poe is generally regarded as the father of the modern horror story, but some of his tales are undeniably science-fictional, among them 'The Unparalleled Adventure Of One Hans Pfaall', about a balloon flight to the moon, and 'Mellonta Tauta', a satirical tale of the 29th century. Poe was to exert a great influence on Jules Verne, and later he was to be one of the

models on which Hugo Gernsback, the first sf magazine editor, was to found his conception of the genre (Gernsback's famous 1926 definition of what at first he called "scientifiction" was "the Jules Verne, H. G. Wells and Edgar Allan Poe type of story — a charming romance mingled with scientific fact and prophetic vision").

In Britain, other early sf novels include The Last Man by Mary Shelley (1826), a long tale about the world in decline after a great plague; The Mummy! by Jane Webb (1827), another lengthy romance of the future; Eureka: A Prophecy Of The Future by R. F. Williams (1837);

Heliondé; Or, Adventures In The Sun by Sydney Whiting (1855), which features a journey to the sun by a man in disembodied state (interestingly, the author quotes Lucian, and lists 25 earlier cosmic voyages in literature); The Air Battle: A Vision Of The Future by "Herrmann Lang" (1859); and The History Of A Voyage To The Moon by "Chrysostom Trueman" (1864), which has been described by critic Darko Suvin as "the missing link between Poe and both Verne and Wells ... in some ways astonishing for its time". But, despite such missing links, there is no doubt that it was Verne who made the greatest impact on the world's imagination: almost all his books were translated into English and most other languages, and some of them continue to be adapted as films, radio serials and TV mini-series. (This commentator's earliest sf memory of any kind is of a BBC radio version of Journey To The Centre Of The Earth, circa 1955.)

With Verne, we come to the end of the history of proto-sf and the beginning of sf proper. His second published novel, Journey To The Centre Of The Earth (1864) may be described as the first great "scientific romance", an enthralling story which involves not only an incredible journey through cave-systems beneath the earth but also detailed speculations on geology and palaeontology — and probably the first appearance in fiction of prehistoric animals. It was followed by From The Earth To The Moon (1865), less exciting than the previous book but a very Lucianic work, full of satire on American gun enthusiasts, and a sequel, Round The Moon (1870), which, for all its erroneous details, may still be cited as one of the most prophetic pieces of fiction ever written: Verne's astronauts blast off from Florida, successfully circumnavigate the moon, and splash down in the Pacific Ocean — just like the Apollo 8 crew almost a century later, at Christmas 1968. 20,000 Leagues Under The Sea (1870), the tale of the super-submarine Nautilus and its half-mad Captain Nemo, is another Verne masterpiece; and it was followed by dozens of other novels less well remembered but keenly read in their day.

By the 1870s, a wide general public was

aware of sf, in the guise of the Vernean "extraordinary voyage" or "invention story", and the French master of the form inspired numerous imitators which it would be tedious to list in full here (among them were a number of American dime novelists, notably Luis P. Senarens, whose works were directly ancestral to the early-20th-century pulp-magazine fiction).

In Britain and America, an older form of utopian and futuristic fiction continued to appear, not directly influenced by Verne, and in ever-greater quantities after 1870: among its highlights are The Battle Of Dorking by G. T. Chesney (1871), The Coming Race by Bulwer Lytton (1871), Erewhon, Or Over The Range by Samuel Butler (1872), Across The Zodiac: The Story Of A Wrecked Record by Percy Greg (1880), After London, Or Wild England by Richard Jefferies (1885), A Crystal Age by W. H. Hudson (1887), Looking Backward: AD 2000-1887 by Edward Bellamy (1888), A Strange Manuscript Found In A Copper Cylinder by James De Mille (1888), A Plunge Into Space by Robert Cromie (1890), Caesar's Column by Ignatius Donnelly (1890), Mizora: A Prophecy by Mary E. Bradley Lane (1890), News From Nowhere, Or An Epoch Of Rest by William Morris (1890) and The Angel Of The Revolution: A Tale Of The Coming Terror by George Griffith (1894).

All these, and many, many more examples of futuristic fiction were produced before the next great landmark in the development of the genre, the appearance of H. G. Wells's first novel, The Time Machine, in 1895.

The Wellsian Legacy

FEW PEOPLE CAN CLAIM TO HAVE HAD AS MUCH INFLUENCE ON SCIENCE FICTION AS THE NOVELIST H. G. WELLS, AUTHOR OF THE WAR OF THE WORLDS AND THE TIME MACHINE

With Wells, the scientific romance came of age. In his early books, notably The Time Machine, The Island Of Dr Moreau (1896) The War Of The Worlds (1898) and The First Men In The Moon (1901), he managed to produce a near-perfect blend of all that had gone before — utopia, anti-utopia, Swiftian satire, philosophical tale, Vernean adventure, scientific invention story — and in a fashion that seemed thoroughly modern. His career as a writer was long, stretching from the turn of the century until the Second World War, and it made him one of the best-known individuals in the world. Well-versed in literature (despite his humble origins, he seemed to have read everything, from Plato to Mary Shelley) as well as in science (he was, briefly, a biology student under the tutelage of Darwin's apostle, Thomas Henry Huxley), Wells was ideally placed, and ideally talented, to bring together the various currents of the sf tradition and to turn them into a mighty river of ideas which would flow from him to all the sf authors of the 20th century — not only the "post-Wellsian" British writers such as Aldous Huxley, Olaf Stapledon and George Orwell, but to foreigners like the Russian Yevgeny Zamyatin, the Frenchman Maurice Renard and the Czech Karel Capek, and, via Gernsback's Amazing Stories (which reprinted most of Wells's sf in its early years), to all the pulp-magazine writers of America.

Amazing Stories was founded by Hugo Gernsback in 1926 and a phenomenon which very quickly came to be called "science fiction" was born; and so this introduction comes full circle. The essays and shorter entries that fill this book tell the rest of the story, concentrating on modern sf from the 1920s to the present — not only in magazine and book form, but also in films and television, with some reference to radio, comics and other media. Science fiction is an ever-growing and complex form, and a significant one: at its most ambitious, sf's subject matter is nothing less than the human condition, humanity's place in space and time, the ultimate fate of intelligent life. At the same time, the genre is an entertainment medium of great flexibility and range: it is to be enjoyed — as, we hope, you will enjoy this book.

ALIEN INVASION *WELLS'S THE WAR OF THE WORLDS, HERE RELOCATED TO AMERICA FOR THE 1953 FILM, WAS ORIGINALLY A POWERFUL ANTI-IMPERIALIST FABLE.*

astounding STORIES

⊷◈⊶

A GUIDE TO THE MAJOR PLOT TEMPLATES WHICH SCIENCE FICTION

EMPLOYS IN ITS EXPLORATION OF TIME AND SPACE AND THE

IDEAS IT HAS GENERATED IN THE PROCESS

⊷◈⊶

templates

UNLIKE MOST POPULAR GENRES, SF CANNOT BE FORMULARIZED BUT ITS WRITERS CAN AND DO TAKE ADVANTAGE OF A NUMBER OF BASIC PATTERNS WITHIN WHICH THEIR IDEAS CAN BE DISPLAYED

Space Operas

The space opera template is fundamental to sf stories whose heroes set off into the great wilderness of unknown space, boldly going where no human has gone before and boldly doing what no human has ever done before. The term was coined by analogy with "soap opera" and "horse opera" as a sneering put-down, but it has been accepted and to some extent revalidated for stories built on a more ambitious scale than imaginatively-conservative tales of space travel, that merely celebrate the moment of release from our earthly imprisonment or try to anticipate the actual exploration of outer space.

Early space-tourists, like the loving couple featured in George Griffith's *A Honeymoon In Space* (1901), were limited to the solar system, but an important new phase in the evolution of sf was begun by the first writers to venture out into the galactic wilderness. Chief among these pioneers was E. E. "Doc" Smith in the Skylark series begun with *The Skylark Of Space* (1928). Edmond Hamilton's Interstellar Patrol series began in the same year with *Crashing Suns*. Jack Williamson's space operas matured with the field during a long career, extending from *The Legion Of Space* (1934) to *Lifeburst* (1984). These early adventurers delighted in writing exuberant tales of interstellar conflict, in which whole alien races were wiped out, entire planets devastated and stars exploded, but those who followed in their footsteps usually took care to avoid casual genocide and cosmic vandalism. "Doc" Smith's celebrated Lensman series, which he subsequently expanded into a seven-volume "History of Civilization", was

ASTOUNDING STORIES

OCTOBER 1937

20¢

REG. U. S. PAT. OFFICE

GALACTIC PATROL by EDWARD E. SMITH, Ph.D.

Out of Night
By
DON A. STUART

STAR WARS *The space operas of the 1930s took it for granted that the space battles of the future would be fought with magical rays*

written during the 1930s and 1940s, but still proved capable of delighting a new generation of readers when it was reprinted in the 1970s.

Stories of exploration and conquest were soon supplemented by novels, which took it for granted that humankind would eventually spread out to occupy most of the habitable planets in the galaxy and build a galactic empire. In its earliest versions, this was closely modelled on the Roman Empire: Isaac Asimov's Foundation series, whose original stories appeared between 1942 and 1950, provided the principal model. Towards the end of his life, Asimov added several more volumes to the series, which is now to be continued by other writers.

Many sf writers have used galaxy-spanning civilizations to good effect, often in long-running series. Poul Anderson's two series featuring the swashbuckling special agent Dominic Flandry and the cunning trader Nicholas van Rijn combine to form one of sf's most extensive adventures in future history. James Blish's *Cities In Flight* series (omnibus edition 1970) cleverly extrapolated Oswald Spengler's theory of cultural cycles to a galactic stage. Gordon R. Dickson's Dorsai series attempted to develop a system of ethics appropriate to galactic conquest. Cordwainer Smith's stories of *The Instrumentality Of Mankind* (omnibus edition 1994) introduced a poetic romanticism further developed by Samuel R. Delany in *Empire Star* (1966) and *Nova* (1968). E. C. Tubb's Dumarest series (1967-84) involved its hero in an endless quest for the lost homeworld of humankind. Iain M. Banks' Culture series, begun with *Consider Phlebas* (1987), drastically revised the politics of galactic civilization and modernized its technology. Stephen R. Donaldson's Gap series, begun with *The Gap Into Conflict: The Real Story* (1990), borrowed the structure and grandiosity of Wagner's Ring cycle in order to introduce a literal operatic dimension. The most famous cinematic interstellar empire is that featured in the *Star Wars* trilogy. On TV, *Star Trek*'s Federation and its rival cultures have undergone a gradual evolution of complexity: the painstaking diplomatic efforts of the various teams featured in its spin-off series contrast markedly with the shoot-first-and-ask-questions-later attitude of early space-opera heroes, although the demands of serial melodrama ensure that the shooting usually does start at some stage. The dramatic change in contemporary attitudes to war – greatly assisted by the experience of the Vietnam war – can be seen by comparing Robert A. Heinlein's *Starship Troopers* (1959) and Joe Haldeman's *The Forever War* (1974). Orson Scott Card's anachronistic *Ender's Game* (1985) was rapidly followed by several apologetic sequels in which the hero must do penance for his cavalier destruction of an alien spacefleet.

Primitive adventures in space opera are often dismissed nowadays, but modern works like *Santiago* (1986) by Mike Resnick and *Heart Of The Comet* (1986) by David Brin and Gregory Benford retain a nostalgic affection for the old-style sense of wonder. A similar nostalgia is lovingly displayed in a series of anthologies edited by Brian Aldiss: *Space Opera* (1974), *Space Odysseys* (1976) and *Galactic Empires* (1976). The ideas and themes of early space opera are mercilessly parodied in Douglas Adams's *The Hitch-Hiker's Guide To The Galaxy* and Grant Naylor's *Red Dwarf*, as they had earlier been in Harry Harrison's *Bill The Galactic Hero* (1965), but some of the leading writers in the sf field continue to produce more sophisticated accounts of multicultural galactic civilizations, in which human beings generally play a more modest role.

In David Brin's Uplift series, humans are newcomers to a well-established galaxy-wide culture, but they retain special status by virtue of having become a star-travelling species without outside assistance. Lois McMaster Bujold's light-hearted series featuring the exploits of physically-handicapped military genius Miles Vorkogisian have proved extremely popular, 'The Mountains Of Mourning' (1989), The *Vor Game* (1990), *Barrayar* (1991) and *Mirror Dance* (1994) all winning Hugo awards in recent years.

More earnest tales of the far frontiers of galactic culture like Vonda N. McIntyre's Starfarers series (begun 1989) and C. J. Cherryh's *Rimrunners* (1991) provide further emphatic evidence that space opera is no longer a male preserve. Female heroes are also far more common nowadays, as in Melissa Scott's Silence Leigh stories, collected in *The Roads Of Heaven* (1988) and Colin Greenland's endearingly old-fashioned Tabitha Jute trilogy, begun with *Take Back Plenty* (1990).

Although we now know that our galaxy is only one among many, relatively few sf writers have managed to find ways of embracing this larger stage. Modern cosmological accounts of the Big Bang and the "many worlds interpretation" of the uncertainties of quantum mechanics have, however, inspired a number of novels in which characters use the time-bending effects of travelling at light-speed to watch universes dying and being reborn; notable examples include *Tau Zero* (1970) by Poul Anderson and *The Singers Of Time* (1991) by Frederik Pohl and Jack Williamson.

Eloquent testimony to the dramatic extension of our scientific knowledge, and the possibilities inherent within it, is provided by Greg Bear's *Eon* (1985) and *Eternity* (1988), and by an extraordinarily ambitious series of novels by Greg Benford, which began with *In The Ocean Of Night* (1977) and recently reached its spectacular conclusion in *Sailing Bright Eternity* (1995), its six volumes taking in enormous vistas of space and time.

The universe beyond the solar system now seems a far stranger and more hostile place than it did in the days when "Doc" Smith and Edmond Hamilton imagined it as a giant playground for fanciful boys' games, but the prospect of exploring and colonizing the wilderness of stars still produces a powerful effect on the science-fictional imagination, and will doubtless continue to do so.

Planetary Romances

The planetary romance template involves characters in hectic adventures on another planet. It often features a long journey through a number of gaudily exotic environments, where many strange creatures and peculiar societies are to be found.

Early voyages to the moon or Mars, which culminated in encounters with utopian civilizations, cannot to be counted as planetary romances because their primary purpose was always satirical or educative, although many do have elements included purely for fun. The earliest authentic examples of this story-type include Hugh MacColl's *Mr Stranger's Sealed Packet* (1889) and Edwin Lester Arnold's *Lieut. Gulliur Jones – His Vacation* (1905), also known as *Gulliver Of Mars*.

However, it was the chronicle of John Carter's adventures on Mars set out in *A Princess Of Mars* (1917) by Edgar Rice Burroughs which first made planetary romance popular. Like many later writers in the tradition, Burroughs was to return to his favourite imaginary world time and time again, eventually extending the Barsoom series to 11 volumes. His work inspired imitations by several other writers for the non-specialist pulp magazines, including a series by Ralph Milne Farley begun with *The Radio Man* (1924) and a series by Otis Adelbert Kline begun with *The Planet Of Peril* (1929), both set on Venus. The sub-genre was still popular enough to generate further imitations in the paperback era, including John Norman's Gor series, Lin Carter's Callisto series and the Dray Prescot series by "Alan Burt Akers" (Kenneth Bulmer). David Lake's Xuma novels pay overt homage to the originals in a far more ironic manner.

Once science fiction had diversified into its own specialist magazines, writers began to pay more attention to the ecology of their alien worlds. Significant pioneering work in this vein was done by Stanley G. Weinbaum, in stories written in the early 1930s. The image of Burroughs's Mars – a world of red deserts and decadent civilizations – remained sufficiently powerful, though, to give rise to more sophisticated descendants in C. L. Moore's tales of Northwest Smith (1933-37), collected in *Scarlet Dream* (1981), and the work of Leigh Brackett, including the stories from the 1940s and 1950s collected in *The Coming Of The Terrans* (1967) and *Eric*

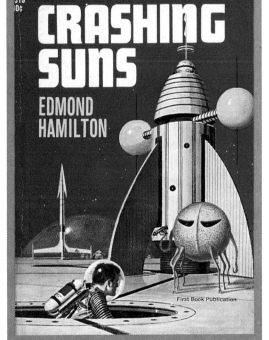

Red alert for the Interstellar Patrol
CRASHING SUNS
EDMOND HAMILTON
First Book Publication

 THE SUNSMASHER *EDMOND HAMILTON'S FONDNESS FOR BLOWING UP PLANETS AND STARS FORCED HIM ON TO THE GALACTIC STAGE IN THIS SERIES, BEGUN IN 1929*

John Stark: Outlaw Of Mars (1982). Brackett's Mars was further refined by Ray Bradbury in the haunting short stories combined to make up *The Martian Chronicles* (1950), also known as *The Silver Locusts*, but a new era of realism was ushered in by Arthur C. Clarke's *The Sands Of Mars* (1951). In recent times, lushly romantic depictions of Mars have only featured in calculatedly anachronistic works of sf, of which the best is Ian McDonald's *Desolation Road* (1988).

The versions of Venus employed by Farley and Kline were more temperate versions of Burroughs's Mars, but sf writers who used similar scenarios soon began to replace them with the conventional image of Venus as a cloud-shrouded planet mostly (or even entirely) covered by oceans. C. L. Moore's 'Clash By Night' (1943) was followed by *Fury* (1947), written in collaboration with her husband Henry Kuttner, but a different sequel was later provided by David A. Drake in *The Jungle* (1991). A watery Venus is also featured in C. S. Lewis's religious allegory *Perelandra* (1943). This phase of Venus's "imaginary history" was celebrated in the anthology *Farewell, Fantastic Venus!* (1968) edited by Brian Aldiss and Harry Harrison.

As it became less and less likely that the other worlds in the solar system could support life as we know it, planetary romances moved out into the galactic empire, often featuring "lost colonies" more-or-less cut off from the benefits of galactic civilization. Jack Vance became a prolific writer of such romances: *Big Planet* (1952) was the most memorable of his early works in that vein, while *The Languages Of Pao* (1958) showed that more sophisticated sf ideas could be usefully imported into the framework. Philip José Farmer also produced several notable examples, *The Green Odyssey* (1957) being the work which prompted critic Russell Letson to coin the term "planetary romance". Although Hal Clement's works belong to a more realistic school, *Mission Of Gravity* (1953) and *Cycle Of Fire* (1957) warrant consideration as unusually well-disciplined exercises in planetary romance.

Several modern sf writers have devoted many years and numerous volumes to the loving development of particular alien worlds. L. Sprague de Camp's Krishna series began in 1949 with 'The Queen Of Zamba' (also known as *Cosmic Manhunt* and *A Planet Called Krishna*) and presently extends as far as *The Swords Of Zinjaban* (1991), written in collaboration with Catherine Crook de Camp. Marion Zimmer Bradley's Darkover series began in 1958 with the magazine version of *The Planet Savers*, reached a terminus of sorts in *City Of Sorcery* (1985), and is still continuing in anthologies put together at the behest of the "Friends of Darkover". Frank Herbert's Dune series commenced serialization in 1963, eventually culminating in *Chapter House Dune* (1985). Anne McCaffrey's Pern series originated in the novella 'Weyr Search' (1968) and is still going strong in *The Dolphins Of Pern* (1994).

Such exercises as these have established "world-building" as one of the most important and problematic aspects of modern sf writing, with

TAKE ME TO YOUR LEADER *Early planetary romances were usually aimed at juvenile readers and the heroes always wore their school ties proudly*

chapters devoted to it in most guides for would-be sf writers. The kind of liberties which Edgar Rice Burroughs took are no longer considered sporting, and nowadays writers are expected to be moderately conscientious in designing the ecospheres of their alien worlds and in adapting human and alien societies to exotic environments. Such environments can, of course, offer new opportunities as well as limitations; dreams of flight are indulged in *Windhaven* (1981) by George R. R. Martin and Lisa Tuttle, while *Drowntide* (1987) by Sydney van Scyoc offers an account of the languid luxuries of underwater life. Donald Kingsbury's *Courtship Rite* (1982), also known as *Geta*, combines realism and romance very cleverly. Planets with eccentric orbits – which result in extreme and much-extended "seasons" – have been featured in several bold exercises of this kind, including Brian Aldiss's Helliconia trilogy (1982-5) and a series by Paul Park begun with *Soldiers Of Paradise* (1987). Robert Silverberg has undertaken numerous adventures in exotic world-building, carefully exploiting the romantic aspect of such endeavours in *The Face Of The Waters* (1991) and *The Kingdoms Of The Wall* (1992).

As sf became more realistic under the influence of John W. Campbell Jr's editorial manifesto, many writers of planetary romance moved into the marginal genre of science fantasy, where the deliberate mixing of sf and fantasy motifs helped them to sustain a zestful and vivid exoticism. The revival of the fantasy genre in the 1970s, as well as the common practice of filing fantasies and sf novels on the same shelves in bookshops, dramatically increased the scope for this kind of hybrid work. Notable recent examples include the Well World series by Jack Chalker, *The Snow Queen* (1980) by Joan D. Vinge, *Golden Witchbreed* (1983) by Mary Gentle, the two-volume 'Book Of Mana' (1993-94) by Ian Watson, *Alien Influences* (1994) by Kristine Kathryn Rusch and *Shadow's End* (1994) by Sheri S. Tepper. This marginal genre will continue to be exceptionally hospitable to planetary romances, but it is unlikely that even the most determinedly realistic exercises in world-building will ever abandon the element of romance, which adds colour and energy to their inventions.

September • 50 cents

analog
SCIENCE FACT — SCIENCE FICTION

A LIFE FOR THE STARS by James Blish
A story of the industrial cities of space

THE SKY'S NO LIMIT *In Blish's Okie series the cities of Earth flee economic depression by getting on their spindizzies and looking for work*

Contrasting images of future possibility were displayed in the rival cities of Frankville and Stahlstadt in *The Begum's Fortune* (1879) by Jules Verne, while frank hatred of what cities seemed to be becoming was expressed in Richard Jefferies's *After London* (1885), in which London has become a tract of poisoned land shunned by people who have reverted to a rural way of life. In the future cities of *Caesar's Column* (1890) by Ignatius Donnelly and *When The Sleeper Wakes* (1899) by H. G. Wells, the poor continue to live utterly wretched lives while the rewards of advanced technology are reserved for the super-rich. This kind of imagery was given striking visual expression in Fritz Lang's famous silent film *Metropolis* (1926).

Splendid visions of the city of the future as a marvellous assembly of imposing skyscrapers and soaring flyovers were commonplace in the artwork of the early sf magazines. Prolific illustrator Frank R. Paul was very

Future Cities

The future city template is employed in stories that revolve around the changes that continued progress has brought about; it often uses a conventional thriller plot or a tale of revolution against hi-tech oppressors. When sf writers speculate about the future of life on earth, their visions are inevitably dominated by images of the city; human history is largely the story of the founding and growth of cities – that is the meaning of the word "civilization".

When utopian writers first began to shift their ideal states into the future, they imagined the cities which they lived in remade and perfected according to their own desires. Paris is transformed in Louis-Sebastien Mercier's *Memoirs Of The Year Two Thousand Five Hundred* (1771), Boston in Edward Bellamy's *Looking Backward* (1888) and London in William Morris's *News From Nowhere* (1891). Such optimism was, however, far from universal: the cities which grew so rapidly in the wake of the industrial revolution included slums afflicted by disease, poverty and crime, and many writers of the time found the prospect of their further spread horrible to contemplate.

ALL MOD CONS *The futuristic cities of 1930s sf were replete with roomy edifices in which mere men were dwarfed by macho machinery*

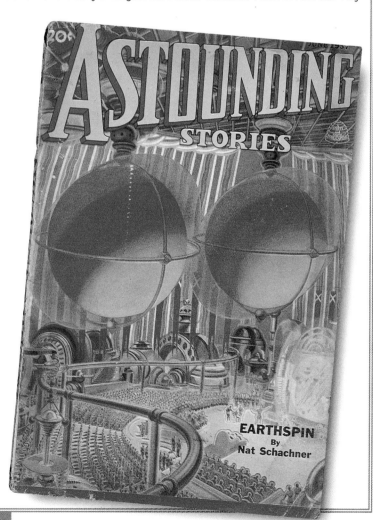

ASTOUNDING STORIES

EARTHSPIN
By
Nat Schachner

good at drawing wonderful cities, although his human beings always looked awkward. Such cities were often encased by huge crystal domes, emphasizing the opposition between urban and rural life. A particularly memorable example is the city of Diaspar, in Arthur C. Clarke's *Against The Fall Of Night* (1948), expanded as *The City And The Stars* (1956). The spectacular world-city of Trantor lay at the heart of Isaac Asimov's galactic empire from its beginning in the 1940s, but it was not described in detail until *Prelude To Foundation* (1988).

Even in pulp sf, Frank Paul's grandiose images were often juxtaposed with depictions of cities that had been reduced to ruins by all manner of catastrophes. These images of the wreckage of once-great civilizations were not merely an expression of anxiety; they also embodied the kind of nostalgic longing for escape to a simpler way of life which haunts many contemporary city-dwellers. E. M. Forster's 'The Machine Stops' (1909) is a classic hymn of hate against processes of mechanization which are seductive as well as oppressive. The series of stories collected in Clifford Simak's *City* (1952) describes a much more disciplined exodus from city life. More recent variations on the theme of hard-won escape to the wilderness include *Fahrenheit 451* (1953) by Ray Bradbury, *The Eye Of The Heron* (1978) by Ursula K. Le Guin and *Out On Blue Six* (1989) by Ian McDonald.

Even when there is no readily-available, rural alternative, futuristic sf often deals with rebellions against exaggerated versions of contemporary bugbears of city life. *The Space Merchants* (1953) and *Gladiator-at-Law* (1955) by Frederik Pohl and Cyril M. Kornbluth offer scathing accounts of urban environments spoiled by advertising and failed housing projects. The cities in Ken Bulmer's *The Ulcer Culture* (1969) and Storm Constantine's *The Monstrous Regiment* (1990) – both of which play host to sharp divisions between the haves and have-nots – are particularly extreme compendia of everything that is unpleasant about modern city life. The city is rarely seen as a liberating environment, although James Blish's *Cities In Flight* series (omnibus edition 1970) has cities like New York transforming themselves into huge interstellar spacecraft by courtesy of anti-gravity devices and air-imprisoning domes.

Many sf writers take it for granted that the cities of the future will have to increase their size continually in order to accommodate a steadily growing population, and that, no matter how big they become, they will still be cramped and crowded. It is often assumed that this constant expansion will necessitate the vertical extrapolation of living space, as tower-blocks get taller and taller. In *The World Inside* (1971), Robert Silverberg calls these super-skyscrapers Urbmons, while Philip K. Dick calls them Conapts and others prefer the term Arcology.

Not all accounts of life in such vast edifices are horror stories: *The Towers Of Utopia* (1975) by Mack Reynolds and *Oath Of Fealty* (1981) by Larry Niven and Jerry Pournelle take a more pragmatic view. Even future cities which possess their fair share of sleaziness can retain something of the charisma which worthy cities like Paris and Venice are deemed to possess. Edward Bryant's *Cinnabar* (1976), Terry Carr's *Cirque* (1977) and C.

J. Cherryh's Merovingen (in *Angel With The Sword*, 1985) are places where it would certainly be fun to live.

When sf writers try to track the possible futures of actual cities, they are usually careful to maintain a measure of civic pride, however quirky or apologetic. Earnest attempts to examine the futures of various American cities can be found in *The Time-Swept City* (1977) by Thomas F. Monteleone (Chicago), *Catacomb Years* (1979) by Michael Bishop (a domed urban nucleus centred on Atlanta), *The Years Of The City* (1984) by Frederik Pohl (New York), *Pacific Edge* (1990) by Kim Stanley Robinson (Los Angeles) and *Future Boston* (1994) edited by David Alexander Smith. Less optimistic accounts of future California are contained in Pat Murphy's *The City, Not Long After* (1989) and William Gibson's *Virtual Light* (1993), but they are not without a certain defiant affection, although the picture of the Los Angeles/San Francisco sprawl provided in Gibson's various accounts of a slightly more remote future are not so charitable.

The increasing automation of future cities is taken memorably to extremes in a number of stories in which the cities continue to survive and thrive after their inhabitants have returned to a more primitive existence. Such almost-deserted cities are featured in *Strength Of Stones* (1981) by Greg Bear and *The Silent City* (1981) by Elisabeth Vonarburg, while cities which have undergone much more dramatic self-transformations – by courtesy of nanotechnology run wild – are described in Kathleen Ann Goonan's *Queen City Jazz* (1994).

In TV and cinema sf, futuristic cities are understandably rather impressionistic, given that they have to be played by models or paintings. Future-set action films like *RoboCop* (1987) tend to take a pragmatic view, assuming that urban decay will continue to provide an abundant supply of derelict sites which can be shot up and blown up to spectacular effect. The advent of computer-generated special effects has, however, assisted in the compilation of some memorable imagery, budgets permitting. Ridley Scott's *Blade Runner* (1982) is particularly effective in conveying the impression of a future in which the trends affecting today's cities have all been continued.

Disasters

The disaster story template involves recording the progress of some terrible catastrophe, or the attempts of the survivors of some such catastrophe to preserve and rebuild civilization. Some of the earliest recorded stories include accounts of catastrophes which all-but-destroyed human civilization: the Biblical deluge is echoed in the mythology of the Greeks and the epic of Gilgamesh, while the prophetic Book of Revelations, with its elaborate description of a world-ending Apocalypse, is comparable to Norse anticipations of the Twilight of the Gods.

Apocalyptic visions enjoyed a brief literary vogue in the early years of the 19th century, the most notable being Mary Shelley's great-plague story *The Last Man* (1826) and Edgar Allan Poe's brief account of 'The

THE LAST MAN
M. P. SHIEL'S NOVEL DESCRIBES THE AWFUL ANGUISH OF THE SOLE INHERITOR OF A DEPOPULATED WORLD

Conversation Of Eiros And Charmion' (1839), but it was not until the end of the century that they became a consistently prominent feature of popular fiction. The cometary collisions popularized by French astronomer Camille Flammarion became briefly fashionable, but most writers preferred to describe events whose consequences were not quite so apocalyptic.

The gas cloud in Arthur Conan Doyle's *The Poison Belt* (1913) produced no long-lasting effect: it was there to teach readers a useful lesson in humility. The widespread perception that the world stood in dire need of some such lesson gave many subsequent disaster stories a distinctly ambivalent quality, which added a certain weight to the wanton delight many writers took in the contemplation of large-scale destruction.

The peculiar but defiant optimism which comes into play at the end of M. P. Shiel's *The Purple Cloud* (1901) is echoed, albeit in more subdued fashion, in many 20th-century disaster stories, especially those produced in Britain. After the Great War of 1914-18, there was an understandable upsurge in bitter parables arguing that modern men thoroughly deserved to lose all the gifts of civilization because of their stupid inability to refrain from warfare. These existed alongside numerous accounts of natural catastrophe which saw a return to a more primitive way of life as a not-entirely-unwelcome alternative to self-destruction.

Nordenholt's Million (1923) by J. J. Connington and *Deluge* (1928) and *Dawn* (1929) by S. Fowler Wright are early examples of this way of thinking, which eventually reached its extreme in such benign catastrophe stories as 'The Great Fog' (1944) by Gerald Heard and *The Story Of My Village* (1947) by H. de Vere Stacpoole.

Stories of natural catastrophe continued to play a more prominent role in British sf than in the American genre. John Wyndham built his reputation with *The Day Of The Triffids* (1951), later adapted for both cinema and TV, and *The Kraken Wakes* (1953). John Christopher's *The Death Of Grass* (1956) and *The World In Winter* (1962) are in the same tradition, which continued in *Greybeard* (1964) by Brian Aldiss, *The Inferno* (1973)

THE SURVIVAL OF THE FITTEST *JOHN CHRISTOPHER'S NOVEL DESCRIBES WITH CLINICAL PRECISION THE DISINTEGRATION OF THE SOCIAL AND MORAL ORDER*

by Fred and Geoffrey Hoyle, and the film *Dark Enemy* (1984), made by the Children's Film Unit.

Such tales often combine a bleak appreciation of the loss of civilized values with a nostalgic affection for the small-scale rural communities that the survivors must re-establish. The long-running TV series *The Survivors* (1975-77) steered a similarly careful course between grim realism and cosy romance. The ambivalence of the British disaster story was brought to a surreal peak of perfection by J. G. Ballard's accounts of the various metamorphoses of Earth and subsequent reconstructions of the human psyche in *The Drowned World* (1962), *The Drought* (1964) and *The Crystal World* (1966).

American disaster stories were always much more likely to be laid out as stark and straightforward tragedies, like *The Scarlet Plague* (1912) by Jack London, although 'The Metal Doom' (1932) by David H. Keller is a striking exception. *Earth Abides* (1949) by George R. Stewart is not without an element of romance, but it is in essence a book of lamentations, as is the film *The Day The Earth Caught Fire* (1961). 'Inconstant Moon' (1971) by Larry Niven, is a neat, modern tale in the same dark vein, about a vast solar flare which reveals itself to those it does not

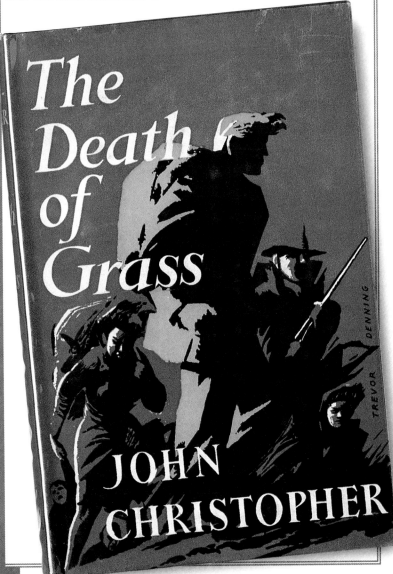

destroy by vividly brightening the face of the moon.

When American writers sought solace in the face of disaster, they were likely to find it in contemplating the virility and intelligence of the survivors. Such stories as *The Second Deluge* (1912) by Garrett P. Serviss, *Darkness And Dawn* (1914) by George Allan England and *When Worlds Collide* (1933) by Philip Wylie and Edwin Balmer take what comfort they can from this kind of winnowing process, becoming the pioneers of a rich tradition of American "survivalist fiction" – a tradition which has recently expanded into lifestyle fantasy on a spectacular scale. The tradition includes many stories of nuclear holocaust, but variants dealing with great plagues include *Some Will Not Die* (1961) by Algis Budrys and *The Time Of The Fourth Horseman* (1976) by Chelsea Quinn Yarbro. The survivalist tradition reached an extraordinary allegorical extreme in *The Stand* (1978; restored text 1990) by Stephen King, while faith in the ability of Americans to turn threatened disaster into wonderful opportunity reached an equally improbable extreme in David Brin's *Earth* (1990). A surreal disaster novel closer in spirit to the British tradition is Richard Kadrey's *Kamikaze l'Amour* (1995).

Given all this, it is hardly surprising that America has also produced some scathingly sarcastic apocalyptic satires, including *Greener Than You Think* (1947) by Ward Moore and *Cat's Cradle* (1963) by Kurt Vonnegut, although the funniest send-up of disaster stories – in which all imaginable apocalypses converge in a single climax – is *Earthdoom!* (1987) by British writers David Langford and John Grant. *Earthdoom!* parodies the disaster movies which enjoyed a considerable vogue in the 1970s; relatively few of these were sf but there is a sub-set concerned with alien importations and mutant monsters, extending from *The Andromeda Strain* (1971, based on a book by Michael Crichton) through David Cronenberg's *Rabid* (1976) and *The Kingdom Of The Spiders* (1977) to *The Swarm* (1978). Similar movies featuring plagues of vampires or zombies cannot really be considered sf in spite of their frequent attempts to put the blame on "radiation", although an exception might be made for such parodies as *Night Of The Comet* (1984).

Relatively little disaster fiction from other cultures has been translated into English, but there are two notable Japanese novels, both of which are concerned with the possible submersion of that nation: *Inter Ice Age 4* (1970) by Kobo Abe and *Japan Sinks* (1976) by Sakyo Komatsu.

HISTORY'S WORST NIGHTMARE *IMAGINING WHAT THE WORLD WOULD BE LIKE HAD THE OPPOSITION WON WORLD WAR II HELPS TO REMIND US HOW FORTUNATE WE ARE*

There has recently been a minor boom in cosmic disaster stories occasioned by the fashionability of the "Fermi paradox" (usually stated as "If we are not alone, where are they?"). Apocalyptic "explanations" of the failure of extra-terrestrial civilizations to make themselves evident include *Across The Sea Of Suns* (1984) by Gregory Benford and *The Forge Of God* (1987) by Greg Bear. The advent of AIDS and scares involving "mad cow disease" have injected sinister new life into alarmist plague stories, although many of these focus on the battle for containment rather than the destruction of civilization. Notable examples include Bruce Sterling's 'Sacred Cows' (1993) and the film *Outbreak* (1995). Innovative large-scale disasters are featured in *Sunstroke* (1993) by David Kagan, *Mother Of Storms* (1994) by John Barnes and *Ill Wind* (1995) by Kevin J. Anderson.

Alternative Histories

The alternative history template involves setting a story in a world which might have developed had some crucial event in history happened differently. Once sf writers had begun to use time travel as a device for exploring the future, the past was inevitably annexed to their imaginative territory – and all the pasts that might have been (with or without the interference of time-travellers) became available for exploration. Long before physicists invented the "many worlds interpretation" of the uncertainties of quantum mechanics, sf writers had imagined that all possible human histories might be held side-by-side in a vast system of parallel worlds, sometimes called a "multiverse".

The game of constructing alternative histories is, of course, often played by historians. A notable anthology of such essays is *If It Had Happened Otherwise* (1931), edited by J. C. Squire, also known as *If; Or, History Rewritten*. The first novels investigating alternative histories were French: in Louis-Napoléon Geoffroy's *Napoléon Apocryphe* (1836) Napoleon conquers the world, and in Charles Renouvier's *Uchronie* (1857) history is transformed because the decaying Roman Empire fails to embrace Christianity. Like Geoffroy, most of the English writers who became interested in alternative history used wars as their crucial turning-points. *Hallie Williams* (1900) by F. P. Williams was the first of numerous American works speculating on what might have happened had the Confederacy won the American Civil War; Ward Moore's *Bring The Jubilee* (1953) is the best-known sf novel on that theme.

Arthur Conan Doyle's 'The Death Voyage'

NEW YORK, MONDAY, MAY 7, 1945

THE ALLIES SURRENDER!

HITLER VICTORIOUS

Edited by
GREGORY BENFORD & MARTIN HARRY GREENBERG

BERKLEY · 0-425-10137-1 · [$5.25 CANADA] · $3.95 U.S.

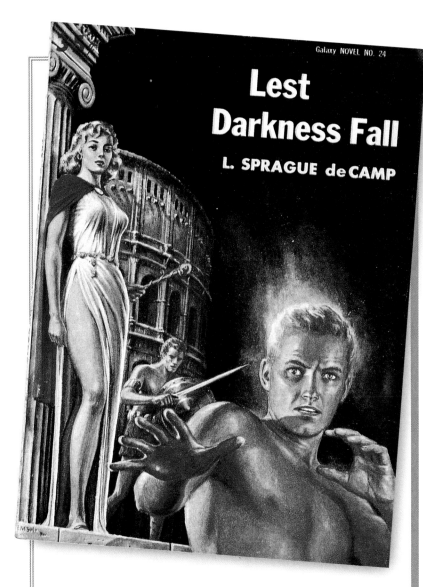

Galaxy NOVEL NO. 24

Lest Darkness Fall

L. SPRAGUE de CAMP

 HAD I KNOWN THEN WHAT I KNOW NOW... *L. SPRAGUE DE CAMP'S HERO HAS THE CHANCE TO REMAKE HISTORY, IF ONLY HE CAN FIGURE OUT WHAT REQUIRES CHANGING*

(1929) features an alternative ending to World War I, but it was World War II that became the favourite topic of alternative historians. Stories set in worlds where Hitler was victorious are numerous: they include *The Sound Of His Horn* (1952) by Sarban, *The Man In The High Castle* (1962) by Philip K. Dick, the film *It Happened Here* (1963), *Hitler Has Won* (1975) by Frederick Mullally, *SS-GB* (1978) by Len Deighton, the TV serial *An Englishman's Castle* (1978) by Philip Mackie, *Moon Of Ice* (1988) by Brad Linaweaver, and *Fatherland* (1992) by Robert Harris. An anthology of 11 such stories is *Hitler Victorious* (1986) edited by Gregory Benford and Martin H. Greenberg. *1945* (1995) by Newt Gingrich and William R. Fortschen also takes World War II as its crucial turning-point.

Pulp sf writers tended to deal with alternative worlds on a wholesale basis. In Murray Leinster's 'Sidewise In Time' (1934), time-slippages turn the earth's surface into a patchwork of alternative histories. Alternative worlds went to war in Jack Williamson's *The Legion Of Time* (1938), battling for the prize of existence – a notion further developed by Fritz Leiber in *Destiny Times Three* (1945) and the Change War series, which includes *The Big Time* (1958).

The idea of alternative histories competing for actuality was soon recomplicated by the introduction of police forces charged with keeping time-tracks safe from disruption. Isaac Asimov's *The End Of Eternity* (1955) features the totalitarian control of a single history, but Sam Merwin's *House Of Many Worlds* (1951), H. Beam Piper's Paratime series (begun with 'Time Crime' in 1955), Poul Anderson's 'Time Patrol' series (whose early stories are collected in *Guardians Of Time,* 1960) and John Brunner's *Times Without Number* (1962) are by no means so restrained. Simon Hawke's long-running Time Wars series, begun with *The Ivanhoe Gambit* (1984), uses the notion to comic as well as melodramatic effect. Even more extravagant conflicts across and between timelines are displayed in Keith Laumer's *Worlds Of The Imperium* (1962) and its sequels, Barrington J. Bayley's *The Fall Of Chronopolis* (1974), Jack Chalker's *Downtiming The Night Side* (1985), Frederik Pohl's *The Coming Of The Quantum Cats* (1986) and John Crowley's 'Great Work Of Time' (1989).

Pulp sf produced one classic account of a plausible alternative history in L. Sprague de Camp's *Lest Darkness Fall* (1939), in which a man thrown back to sixth-century Italy sets out to protect social progress against the effect of the Dark Ages. The argument of the book is that the most important agents of historical change are not battles and wars but relatively humble technological innovations whose consequences often pass unnoticed by contemporary commentators.

The effects of a suppression of the Industrial Revolution – usually as a result of Catholicism resisting the challenge of the Reformation – are investigated in several memorable novels, including *Pavane* (1968) by Keith Roberts and *The Alteration* (1976) by Kingsley Amis. Other novels playing with the history of the great religions include John Boyd's *The Last Starship From Earth* (1969), Harry Turtledove's series begun with *Agent Of Byzantium* (1987) and L. Neil Smith's *The Crystal Empire* (1986).

Some alternative histories reach back into the prehistoric mists to imagine alternative patterns of evolution. Examples include Harry Harrison's series begun with *West Of Eden* (1984), in which the dinosaurs never became extinct; the stories collected in Harry Turtledove's *A Different Flesh* (1988), in which Europeans reaching the New World find it inhabited by half-human "Sims"; and Brian Stableford's *The Empire Of Fear* (1989), in which a race of "vampires" has emerged from Africa to dominate Europe.

It is a matter of opinion whether worlds affected by more radical changes can be considered as alternative histories, but there are many fantasy novels which imagine history distorted by the fact that the magic people once believed in actually worked. Randall Garrett's Lord D'Arcy series, which comprises the novel *Too Many Magicians* (1967) and two collections, hypothesizes that the scientific revolution of the 17th century discovered laws of magic which facilitated the growth of "magical technology".

Alternative history stories have enjoyed a considerable boom in recent years, especially in America. Gregory Benford and Martin H. Greenberg followed up the success of *Hitler Victorious* with several more volumes:

Alternate Empires (1989), *Alternate Heroes* (1990), *Alternate Wars* (1991) and *Alternate Americas* (1992). These came out in parallel with another series edited by Mike Resnick, including *Alternate Kennedys* (1992), *Alternate Presidents* (1992) and *Alternate Warriors* (1993). ("Alternate history" has become the conventional term in American sf, although "alternative" is preferable on grammatical grounds.)

The reason for this dramatic upsurge in popularity is connected with the various ways in which Americans have recently been forced to re-evaluate their own history along with the myths which converted that history into a triumphant march of freedom, democracy and the frontier spirit. The voices of native Americans and black Americans, long condemned to cry in the wilderness, have made themselves heard and have prompted a guilt-stricken reappraisal of The Way The West Was Won – as well as the way the larger West continues to win the battle for cultural domination of the world.

The patterns of cause and effect that propel history forward are awesomely intricate and often hidden from the consciousness of the actors involved. The extrapolation of alternative histories has a useful purpose as well as a particular aesthetic appeal, raising and dramatizing important questions about how we came to be in the particular mess we are in, and how we might perhaps steer a way out of it. The scope for such stories is vast: the recent explosion of activity has only served to scratch the surface. The actual past may be dead and gone, but all the pasts that might have been remain wide open to imaginative exploration.

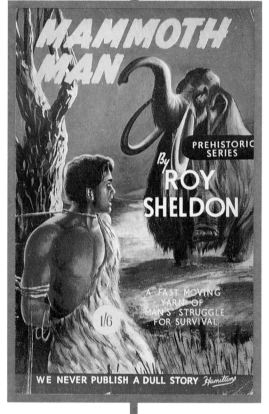

Prehistorical Romances

The prehistorical romance template tells the story of some discovery made in the very distant past, which was crucial to the process of elevating human beings above mere brutish existence and setting them on the path to civilization.

Some critics do not consider prehistorical romances to be sf, but our knowledge of the distant past is the product of a complex process of scientific deduction based on the analysis of fossils, fragments of bone and primitive tools. Stories based on speculations rising from these deductions are just as entitled to be considered science-based fictions as any

 WHEN MEN WERE NEARLY MEN... *A RARE 1950s VENTURE IN PREHISTORIC ROMANCE PSEUDONYMOUSLY WRITTEN BY BIOCHEMIST* **H. J. CAMPBELL**

extrapolative account of future technology or space exploration.

The steady scientific unravelling of the puzzle of the past had its most resounding impact in the late 19th century, when it succeeded in establishing an account of the origins of the human race which contrasted sharply with the account given in the Bible. This drastic revision of man's perceived place in nature was dramatized by numerous writers in the wake of the publication of Charles Darwin's *The Descent Of Man* (1871). The key question raised by these flights of fancy was exactly what qualities early humans possessed that enabled them to become spectacular winners in the struggle for existence. The obvious answer was, of course, intelligence, but opinions differed as to which product of intelligence first gave the ancestors of humankind a vital edge over their ape-like cousins.

In 'A Story Of The Stone Age' (1897), H. G. Wells envisaged the vital moment in human evolution as the production of a "new club", immediately employed as a means of murder. This view was to be echoed many times before being given spectacular visual form in Stanley Kubrick's film *2001: A Space Odyssey* (1968), in which the bone triumphantly flung up into the air by the apeman, who has realized its deadly usefulness, metamorphoses into a space station as the action leaps from past to future. The mastery of fire was represented as the crucial historical break in Stanley Waterloo's *The Story Of Ab* (1897) and J. H. Rosny the elder's *The Quest For Fire* (1909), the latter being the basis of the 1981 film. Jack London's *Before Adam* (1906) puts more emphasis on human communication and the consequent evolution of social co-operation.

The elder Rosny was a prolific writer of prehistorical romances, producing half a dozen more between 1892 and 1930, but only one other was translated into English. His influence prompted several other French writers to produce similar works, but the template was not much used in Britain until a number of writers, severely disenchanted with contemporary civilization, began producing works that glorified the virile simplicity of prehistoric races.

When Mankind Was Young (1927) by F. Britten Austin and *Allan And The Ice-Gods* (1927) by H. Rider Haggard are comparatively tentative early examples. In *Dream; Or The Simian Maid* (1929) and *The Vengeance Of Gwa* (1935; as by Anthony Wingrave) S. Fowler Wright suggested that modern man must be descended from the degraded rival species of his noble savages, but, in *Three Go Back* (1932) and 'The Woman Of Leadenhall Street' (1936; as by Lewis Grassic Gibbon), J. Leslie Mitchell assumed that our ancestors must have been powerful enough to see off the brutal

Neanderthalers before they were corrupted by civilization. In *The Inheritors* (1955), William Golding sided with Wright, making the supposedly gentle Neanderthalers his heroes; they live in relative harmony with nature until they are wiped out by our restlessly violent forebears. Golding took an equally cynical view of the unsociability of our ancestors in 'Clonk Clonk' (1971).

A similar glorification of prehistorical existence, even more extreme in its romanticism, is widespread in the works of Edgar Rice Burroughs, displayed most straightforwardly in *The Eternal Lover* (1914), also known as *The Eternal Savage*. Although other aspects of Burroughs's work were carried forward by pulp sf writers this was not, but his several tales of "lost worlds", in which prehistoric people co-exist with survivals from much earlier eras, may have combined with Arthur Conan

Doyle's *The Lost World* (1912) to convince Hollywood's film-makers that there was nothing wrong with movies in which our ancestors are constantly engaged in running battles with dinosaurs. D. W. Griffith's *Man's Genesis* (1911) had avoided this folly, but later movies in the vein of *One Million B.C.* (1940), *One Million Years B.C.* (1966) and *When Dinosaurs Ruled The Earth* (1969) revelled in it.

One of the most interesting imaginative products of scientific accounts of early man can be found in a number of works whose complex stories move from prehistory to modern times in order to provide a comprehensive account of the unfolding of human nature. These include *The Long Journey* (1908-22) by the Danish Nobel Prize-winner Johannes V. Jensen, *Chains* (1925) by the French writer Henri Barbusse and the 12-volume Testament Of Man series (1943-60) by the American Vardis Fisher. F. Britten Austin's *Tomorrow* (1930) is a more modest exercise in the same vein. Many of these works use the Biblical account of Adam's Fall to provide a set of symbols carefully echoed in their stories, which often involve some kind of metaphorical "expulsion from Eden". *The Sons Of The Mammoth* (1929) by the Soviet anthropologist V. G. Bogoraz is understandably unsympathetic to such attempts to allow the Book of Genesis to slip back into our accounts of man's origin by the back door.

The steady progress of physical anthropology has allowed more recent fictional images of prehistoric human life to become increasingly detailed and sophisticated, as in *Cook* (1981) by Tom Case, *No Enemy But Time* (1982) by Michael Bishop and *A Bone From A Dry Sea* (1993) by Peter Dickinson. The same information has been cleverly employed to enhance a remarkable revitalization of prehistorical romance in the best-selling novels of Jean Auel, which constitute the Earth's Children series, beginning with *The Clan Of The Cave Bear* (1980). The heroine of these novels is a Cro-Magnon girl raised by Neanderthalers, who imparts a progressive impetus to their culture. Auel imports a thoroughly modern preoccupation with civilized humankind's alienation from the natural world into her accounts of the complicated development of personal relationships in a world that contains more than one human species.

The enormous success of these novels has prompted the production of imitations, including a series by W. Michael Gear and Kathleen O'Neal Gear begun with *People Of The Wolf* (1991) and continued in *People Of The River* (1992), *People Of The Sea* (1993), etc. This fashionability looks set to endure for at least a few more years.

The origin of humankind is not the only topic of imaginative interest raised by the discoveries of palaeontologists; the other is the long reign and eventual

...AND WOMEN WERE NEARLY WOMEN *THE HEROINE OF S. FOWLER WRIGHT'S PSEUDONYMOUS PREHISTORIC ROMANCE FACES BRUTISH MASCULINITY IN THE RAW*

extinction of the dinosaurs. The difficulty of writing stories in which dinosaurs are characters has restricted most accounts of that era to tales of time travel, but one which almost qualifies as a prehistorical romance of the period in which mammals obtained their crucial edge over their reptilian cousins is John Taine's *Before The Dawn* (1934).

Time Travels

The time-travel template involves characters moving forward or back in time, and becoming actively involved in the making or remaking of history. The paradoxes generated by the extrapolation of such ideas are employed as ingenious convolutions of the plot rather than deflating reductions to mere absurdity.

The publication of H. G. Wells's *The Time Machine* (1895) was a crucial moment in the history of science fiction. Previously, explorations of the future and the distant past had mostly been limited to ambiguous dreams and hallucinations, like those visited upon Scrooge by the ghosts in Charles Dickens's *A Christmas Carol* (1843) and the timeslip experienced by the hero of Mark Twain's *A Connecticut Yankee At King Arthur's Court* (1889). The only other readily-available device was unnaturally long sleep, like that experienced by the hero of Edward Bellamy's *Looking Backward* (1888). Both of these methods were severely limited, the first by its implicit insubstantiality, and the second by virtue of the fact that its one-way traffic was very slow. Wells's time machine was frankly an impossibility, thinly excused by the clever deployment of jargon which made time a "fourth dimension", but it made the infinite vistas of past and future available to tourists who could move back and forth within them at the flick of a switch. Seemingly appalled by his own temerity, Wells never used such a device again, but others were ready and willing to follow in his footsteps.

Several early pulp sf writers were fascinated by the possibilities of time travel. John Taine's highly original *The Time Stream* was written in the early 1920s but not published until 1931; in the meantime, Ray Cummings undertook pioneering adventures in such novels as *The Man Who Mastered Time* (1924) and *The Shadow Girl* (1929). The ability of time-travellers to tie logical knots in cause-and-effect was quickly discovered and the opportunities for ingenious plot-construction exploited. Ralph Milne Farley's early experiments in this vein, begun with 'The Time Traveler' (1931), were collected in *The Omnibus Of Time* (1950).

ace book
F-174
40¢

One man's trip beyond Doomsday

FIRST THROUGH TIME

First Book Publication

By the prize-winning author of FIRST ON MARS
REX GORDON

The humble bicycle-like time machine of Wells's story was soon displaced by more capacious vessels, like those featured in John Russell Fearn's *Liners Of Time* (1935). Armoured time machines conveyed platoons of fighting men in Jack Williamson's *The Legion Of Time* (1938) – a notion ultimately taken to its extreme by Barrington J. Bayley's account of time-travelling fortresses in *The Fall Of Chronopolis* (1974).

The cavalier attitude of these time-hopping extravaganzas was soon undermined by sceptical objections. The language difficulties that time-travellers would face were dramatized by L. Sprague de Camp in 'The Isolinguals' (1937), while T. L. Sherred's 'E For Effort' (1947) argued that even the invention of a device to see into the past would inevitably precipitate a civilization-destroying war. It was, however, the marvellous ingenuity of time-loops which most entranced the sf writers of the 1940s, cunningly displayed in Robert A. Heinlein's 'By His Bootstraps' (1941) and Ross Rocklynne's 'Time Wants A Skeleton' (1941). Heinlein was later to provide the ultimate entanglement of cause and effect in 'All You Zombies...' (1959), whose central character becomes his own mother and father. The potential which time-travellers had to duplicate themselves repeatedly was eventually extended to absurd limits in David Gerrold's *The Man Who Folded Himself* (1973).

Instead of looping time back upon itself, other stories allowed history to unravel, vast populations or entire worlds disappearing in a trice by virtue of seemingly trivial alterations of the past, as in Nathan Schachner's 'Ancestral Voices' (1933) and Ray Bradbury's 'A Sound Of Thunder' (1952). The history-changing plans of time-travellers often went perversely awry, as in Poul Anderson's 'The Man Who Came Early' (1956) and L. Sprague de Camp's 'Aristotle And The Gun' (1958).

The quest for new plot twists inevitably ran into a problem of dwindling resources in the post-war years, but casually moved on to a larger stage in "time police" stories in which vast manifolds of alternative worlds were patrolled by secret armies of historical conservationists eager to stamp out paradoxes. Sf writers who have made particularly prolific use of time-knotting plots include Charles L. Harness, whose works in this vein extend from 'Time Trap' (1948) and *Flight Into Yesterday* (1949; also known as *The Paradox Men*) to *Krono* (1988) and *Lurid Dreams* (1990); and Robert

 LOOK OUT FUTURE, HERE I COME *THE BICYCLE-LIKE TIME MACHINE USED BY H. G. WELLS WAS SOON REPLACED BY SLICKER AND SLEEKER HIGH-TECH MODELS*

Silverberg, whose contributions range from *The Time-Hoppers* (1967) through the extraordinarily convoluted *Up The Line* (1969) to 'The Far Side Of The Bell-Shape Curve' (1982). The sub-genre lends itself both to slapstick comedy, as in Bob Shaw's *Who Goes Here?* (1977), and to deeply-felt sentimentality, as in *Time And Again* (1970) by Jack Finney and *A Rose For Armageddon* (1982) by Hilbert Schenck.

The opportunity to meet famous people from the past is another widely-exploited possibility of time travel. Shakespeare and Abraham Lincoln are among the favourites. The comic potential of such meetings is particularly tempting; even encounters with Christ tend to be conspicuously lacking in reverence. The Crucifixion is one of the prime targets of inquisitive time-travellers, featured in Michael Moorcock's *Behold The Man* (1969), Brian Earnshaw's *Planet In The Eye Of Time* (1968), Garry Kilworth's 'Let's Go To Golgotha' (1975) and Gore Vidal's *Live From Golgotha* (1992). Manly Wade Wellman took the "hunt-the-celebrity" game a step further when the timeslipped hero of *Twice In Time* (1940) became somebody famous – a notion cleverly recomplicated by Tim Powers in *The Anubis Gates* (1983).

Serial time-hopping has long been a staple of TV sf, most elaborately in the highly enterprising BBC saga of *Doctor Who* (begun in 1963) and – in a carefully formularized fashion – in the US series *The Time Tunnel* (1966) and *Quantum Leap* (begun 1989). Cinematic exercises were relatively unadventurous until the success of *The Terminator* (1984) and *Back To The Future* (1985). The latter's first sequel appeared in the same year as the blithely uninhibited comedy *Bill And Ted's Excellent Adventure* (1989), which recovered the impetus of Terry Gilliam's *Time Bandits* (1981) and took celebrity-hunting to an absurd extreme. *Millennium* (1989) is much weaker than the 1983 novel which John Varley developed from his long-delayed screenplay.

The time-distortion story, pioneered by Wells in 'The New Accelerator' (1901), was ingeniously carried forward by Eric Frank Russell's 'The Waitabits' (1955) and David I. Masson's 'Traveller's Rest' (1965). Examples of time-dislocation are featured in Charles Eric Maine's *The Isotope Man* (1957), Brian Aldiss's 'Man In His Time' (1965) and Eric Brown's 'The Time-Lapsed Man' (1988). There have been several accounts of time running in reverse, including *An Age* (1967), also known as *Cryptozoic!*, by Brian Aldiss, *Counter-Clock World* (1967) by Philip K. Dick and *Time's Arrow* (1991) by Martin Amis. Such gimmicks as these often shade into more thoughtful contemplations of the mysteries of time. J. W. Dunne's theoretical musings about time influenced a number of writers, including J. B. Priestley, whose several 'Time Plays' are the principal theatrical works relevant to the theme. Other works in a more meditative vein include 'The Voices Of Time' (1960), 'Chronopolis' (1960) and *The Crystal World* (1966) by J. G. Ballard, and *Chronolysis* (1980) by Michel Jeury.

The centenary of Wells's Time Machine was commemorated, in various ways, the most notable homage being paid by Stephen Baxter, who produced a brilliantly ingenious and adventurous sequel, *The Time Ships* (1995).

Alien Intrusions

The simplest of all the templates that are used in science fiction is that in which the normal course of the everyday world – or its near-future equivalent – is disrupted by intruders from elsewhere or elsewhen. This can, of course, happen on a massive scale, as in stories of extra-terrestrial invasion such as H. G. Wells's *The War Of The Worlds* (1898), but it is often a purely domestic affair in which the disturbing presence is limited and temporary.

Visitors from other worlds, or from the far future, are often employed as objective observers to pass judgment on the sins and follies of our society. Early examples include the winged Venusian of W. S. Lach-Szyrma's *Under Other Conditions* (1892) and the time-travelling anthropologist of Grant Allen's *The British Barbarians* (1895). Other exotic visitors to Britain, whose observations set human existence in a broader context, were featured in *The Clockwork Man* (1923) by E. V. Odle, *Proud Man* (1934) by Murray Constantine (Katharine Burdekin), *Saurus* (1938) by Eden Phillpotts and *The Flames* (1947) by Olaf Stapledon.

Wells's pioneering alien invasion story was part of a long series of anxious fantasies in which England is invaded; the trend was begun by George Chesney's *The Battle Of Dorking* (1871), a clever piece of propaganda for army reform and rearmament, and it continued in such works as *The Invasion Of 1910* (1906) by William le Queux and *When William Came* (1913) by H. H. Munro. Wells added extra spice to the formula by imagining that an invasion of the Earth by technologically-superior Martians might seem much the same to Englishmen as the European invasion of Tasmania had seemed to the Tasmanians who were about to be exterminated.

The USA was far less prone to anxieties about terrestrial invasion, although Philip Francis Nowlan's original Buck Rogers stories (1928-9) were set in a future America conquered by Asiatic invaders. American pulp sf writers were much more interested in exotic intruders.

Not all such stories were extravagant melodramas of inter-species conflict: 'Old Faithful' (1934) by Raymond Z. Gallun challenged the assumptions of alien-invasion fiction, while far subtler incursions were featured in *The Metal Monster* (1920) by A. Merritt, 'The Alien Intelligence' (1929) by Jack Williamson and 'The Arrhenius Horror' (1931) by P. Schuyler Miller. Nor were all such invasions launched from outer space; marauding armies might come from other dimensions, other times, or even from the atomic microcosm. Among the more bizarre invaders were Fredric Brown's 'The Waveries' (1945): a race of electrical energy-beings who hijacked terrestrial air-waves.

When they did not arrive with guns blazing, pulp sf's alien visitors often came bearing gifts – although these were sometimes deceptive – and they occasionally had important messages to deliver, which sometimes turned out to be bitter pills to swallow. Harry Bates's 'Farewell To The Master' (1940) lost its original sobering message when it was filmed as *The*

Day The Earth Stood Still (1951), but it gained another, reflecting contemporary anxieties about the nuclear threat. 1951 also produced the first film version of *The Thing*, based on John W. Campbell Jr's 'Who Goes There?' (1938).

These two films were the forerunners of a glut of cautionary movies running the whole gamut of Cold War anxieties, often to the point of naked paranoia. Others included *Invaders From Mars* (1953), *The Beast From 20,000 Fathoms* (1953), *It Came From Outer Space* (1953), George Pal's *The War Of The Worlds* (1954), *Godzilla* (1954), *Them!* (1954), *The Beast With A Million Eyes* (1955), *Invasion Of The Body Snatchers* (1956; based on Jack Finney's 1955 book *The Body Snatchers*), *It Conquered The World* (1956), *Fiend Without A Face* (1957) and *I Married A Monster From Outer Space* (1958). British TV manifested something of the same spirit in such thriller serials as the three Quatermass adventures (1953, 1955 and 1958-59), *The Trollenberg Terror* (1956-57) and *A For Andromeda* (1961), but US TV was surprisingly slow off the mark with such belated series as *The Outer Limits* (1963-65) and *The Invaders* (1967-68).

Benign intruders such as the ones featured in *The Day The Earth Stood Still* and *The Man From Planet X* (1951) were heavily outnumbered on screen by their menacing counterparts, but they were becoming much more common in print as many writers began to regret and repent the implicit xenophobia of much pulp sf. Arthur C. Clarke's *Childhood's End* (1953) is one of the most memorable "invasion" stories which subjected anti-alien prejudice to scathing condemnation; others include *The Dreaming Jewels* (1950) by Theodore Sturgeon and *A Mirror For Observers* (1954) by Edgar Pangborn.

Other stories stressed the strangeness of alien visitors, while hopefully insisting that productive communication might still be possible. This line of argument was extrapolated in numerous works of the next 20 years, ranging from *The Black Cloud* (1957) by Fred Hoyle through such works as *The Wanderer* (1964) by Fritz Leiber, *Nightwings* (1969) by Robert Silverberg, *The Byworlder* (1971) by Poul Anderson, *Trillions* (1971) by Nicholas Fisk, *The Gods Themselves* (1972) by Isaac Asimov and *Rendezvous With Rama* (1973) by Arthur C. Clarke to *And Having Writ...* (1978) by Donald R. Bensen and *Miracle Visitors* (1978) by Ian Watson. The *War Of The Worlds* type of alien invasion story came to seem rather old-fashioned during this period, fit only for sarcastic satires like Thomas M. Disch's *The Genocides* (1965).

In more recent times, there have been determined attempts to revive the full melodramatic potential of the alien incursion story, in such novels as *Footfall* (1985) by Larry Niven and Jerry Pournelle and such films as *Alien* (1979), *Predator* (1987), *They Live* (1988) and *Species* (1995).

However, these have had to sit alongside more fervent exercises in cinematic sentimentality than any seen before, such as *Close Encounters Of The Third Kind* (1977), *E.T.* (1982), *Starman* (1984; spin-off TV series 1986-87), *Cocoon* (1985) and *Batteries Not Included* (1987). They also co-exist with mildly satirical comedy films like *The Brother From Another Planet* (1984), *Earth Girls Are Easy* (1988) and *Meet The Applegates* (1990). TV

series attempting to update the alien menace include *V* (1983-85) and *The War Of The Worlds* (1988-90), although the latter was contemporaneous with the conscientiously anti-xenophobic *Alien Nation* series (1989-90).

By far the most successful recent use of a menacing alien incursion is to be found in *The X-Files* (begun 1994), which defines and exploits a thoroughly up-to-date species of paranoia with constant references to a sinister alien presence seemingly working hand-in-glove with secret government agencies. The series draws on well-publicized items of modern folklore, involving the continual abduction of human guinea pigs by UFO-based aliens and the supposed crash-landing of an alien spaceship in New Mexico in 1947. The best-known "non-fictional" extrapolations of this folklore are to be found in Whitley Strieber's *Communion* (1987), *Transformation* (1988) and *Majestic* (1989). The "Majestic incident" is also the inspiration behind Algis Budrys's wearily cynical novel *Hard Landing* (1994).

It is becoming rather difficult, in an age when alien incursions have become so commonplace, for books or films to discover any sense of profound and awe-inspiring strangeness in alien incursions, but a few noble attempts have been made by such films as *Repo Man* (1984) and such books as *The Divine Invasion* (1981) by Philip K. Dick, the trilogy by Damon Knight concluded with *A Reasonable World* (1991) and *Sarah Canary* (1991) by Karen Joy Fowler.

Mental Powers

The sf template which deals with new mental powers is a tale of uncomfortable discovery in which the capabilities of *Homo superior* are glimpsed. It is often a tale of difficult self-discovery and frequently involves children who know not what they are – at least to begin with.

The idea that certain human individuals living in our midst are gifted with special mental powers is very old. Such powers traditionally include the ability to read the thoughts of others, the ability to see the future and the ability to move inanimate objects by the power of the will. Seers and magicians were often valued members of tribal communities, but the Christian Church decided that, with the exception of miracles worked by saints, all such activities required demonic assistance, and were therefore evil.

After the Christian Church's long war to suppress witchcraft had petered out in the 18th century, however, the numbers of people laying claim to unusual mental powers began to increase again. These claims, which multiplied rapidly in the works of spiritualists, Theosophists and other occultists, were increasingly couched in pseudo-scientific jargon. A hundred years ago, they were taken seriously enough to draw many inquisitive scientists into such organizations as the Society for Psychical Research.

The quasi-scientific vocabulary developed by researchers into what would nowadays be called the "paranormal" was given modern form by J.

would be developed in the course of man's future evolution became commonplace in the early 20th century. Notable attempts to describe such evolved men include John Beresford's *The Hampdenshire Wonder* (1911), Olaf Stapledon's *Odd John* (1935), Stanley G. Weinbaum's *The New Adam* (1939) and A. E. Van Vogt's *Slan* (1940) – the last-named inspiring many other pulp sf stories in which people with new mental powers are harassed and persecuted by the less able humans they are destined to replace.

There was a "psi-boom" in the sf magazines of the early 1950s, when the idea that humankind was on the very brink of its next evolutionary leap was widespread. Most magazine sf writers were prepared to take the side of the persecuted supermen in the cause of progress: notable examples include Henry Kuttner's Baldy series, collected as *Mutant* (1953), and George O. Smith's *Highways In Hiding* (1956). There is, however, considerable ambivalence in such stories as James Blish's *Jack Of Eagles* (1952) and John Wyndham's *The Midwich Cuckoos* (1957), the latter being the basis of the films *Village Of The Damned* (1960) and *Children Of The Damned* (1963). *The Demolished Man* (1953) by Alfred Bester is a relatively rare attempt to imagine a society into which "espers" are usefully integrated.

During the Cold War, many sf writers were intrigued by the possibility of applying ESP to the business of espionage, as in Wilson Tucker's *Wild Talent* (1954) and the TV series *The Champions* (1968-9). Others – including John Brunner in *The Whole Man* (1964) and Roger Zelazny in *The Dream Master* (1966) – imagined its application to psychotherapy. Theodore Sturgeon was particularly preoccupied with ESP as a means of "healing" psychologically-damaged individuals; *The Dreaming Jewels* (1950) and *More Than Human* (1953) are classic works in this vein. Far less optimistic accounts of ESP-endowment are, however, offered by Joanna Russ in *And Chaos Died* (1970), Lester del Rey in *Pstalemate* (1971), Robert Silverberg in *Dying Inside* (1972) and Leigh Kennedy in *The Journal Of Nicholas The American* (1986).

An interesting sub-category of stories of mental evolution concentrates on intelligence-enhancement rather than on the development of quasi-supernatural powers. Poul Anderson's *Brain Wave* (1954) boldly attempts to describe a sudden wholesale leap in human and animal intelligence, while Daniel Keyes's 'Flowers For Algernon' (1959; expanded to novel length in 1966 and filmed

B. Rhine, an experimenter at Duke University whose pioneering exercise in parapsychology *Extra-Sensory Perception* (1934) popularized the acronym ESP. The alternative categorization of "psi-powers" was more enthusiastically taken up by pulp sf writers, although the term has lost its currency in recent times. ESP includes clairvoyance ("second sight"), telepathy (thought-reading) and precognition. Many modern sf stories also deal with a restricted kind of telepathy in which only feelings may be perceived, usually called "empathy". The remaining psi-powers include psychokinesis or telekinesis (moving objects by will power), levitation and teleportation (transporting one's own body by will power) and mind-control.

Most stories which take the paranormal for granted are more aptly classified as occult fiction, but those which try to extrapolate the ideas in a fairly rational manner certainly warrant consideration as sf. C. H. Hinton's two volumes of *Scientific Romances* (1886 and 1902) try to account for paranormal phenomena by invoking the fourth dimension. Muriel Jaeger's *The Man With Six Senses* (1927) carefully builds a case to demonstrate that an extra sense might be a curse rather than a blessing.

The notion that new mental powers

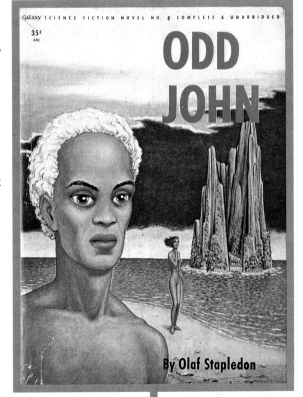

as *Charly* in 1968) remains one of the most effective and memorable of all short sf stories. Later attempts to depict enhanced intelligence include *Camp Concentration* (1968) by Thomas M. Disch, *Ability Quotient* (1975) by Mack Reynolds and *Beggars In Spain* (1993) and its sequel by Nancy Kress.

A particularly ambitious use of this kind of template features in stories where the acquisition of new mental powers creates messianic figures, as in J. D. Beresford's *What Dreams May Come...* (1941), Mack Reynolds's *Of Godlike Power* (1966) and Frank Herbert's first *Dune* trilogy (1965-76).

Sf stories dealing with precognition must deal with the apparent paradox of having "true" knowledge of the future which allows the future to be changed. C. J. Cherryh's 'Cassandra' (1978) is one of many stories to borrow inspiration from mythology and to depict precognition of a teasingly wayward kind, like that in Stephen King's *The Dead Zone* (1979). King's early work featured a wide range of similarly-wayward powers, like those possessed by *Carrie* (1974) and the unlucky *Firestarter* (1980); the author's success prompted some imitations, but scope for the use of such motifs as central themes is limited in the visual media, and precognition and psychokinesis are more frequently used in horror films than in sf.

Among the few sf films which put unusual mental powers centre-stage are *The Power* (1968; based on Frank M. Robinson's 1956 novel), *The Fury* (1978), David Cronenberg's *Scanners* (1980), *Dreamscape* (1984) and *Vibes* (1992). On the other hand, the inclusion of a single character with additional mental powers in a team of adventurers can be useful as a lever for moving plots along. The device is fruitfully employed in the British TV series *Blake's Seven* (1978-81) and *Star Trek: The Next Generation* (1987-94), the latter being mainly responsible for the recent fashionability of empaths. The ability of certain characters to draw upon the mind-enhancing power of the Force is crucial to the plot of *Star Wars* (1977), as well as to all its sequels and spin-offs.

Belief in ESP and other psi-powers is still widespread and many believers are convinced that there is abundant laboratory evidence to support their case, although non-believers point cynically to the complete absence of any technical or industrial applications. The psychological plausibility of telepathy and precognition so far outweighs any rational doubts about the possibility of such phenomena that they will certainly remain within sf's standard vocabulary of ideas.

Comic Infernos

The comic-inferno template involves distorting the world we know – either by projecting it into the future or displacing it to an alien location – in order to expose its absurdities. The oldest works of fiction we know, the tragedies of Greek drama, co-existed with "satyr-plays" which used similar methods to comic effect. So it has always been; all earnest literary forms

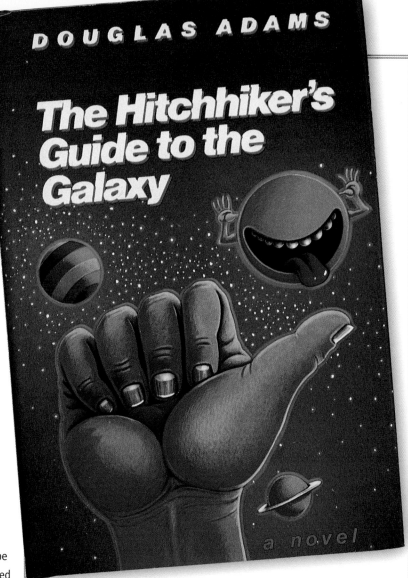

DON'T PANIC! THE HITCH-HIKERS GUIDE TO THE GALAXY *WAS IMMENSELY POPULAR IN BRITAIN ON THE RADIO, TELEVISION, AND AS A BOOK*

are shadowed by works which use their motifs to poke fun: it is from "satyr-play" that the modern word "satire" is derived.

Science fiction has adopted many ideas which once seemed so silly that they were never used for any reason except to poke fun – voyages to the moon were frequently employed in ludicrously exaggerated travellers' tales – and it is hardly surprising that it has given rise to comedies wilder and more excessive than any seen before. *The Hitch-Hiker's Guide To The Galaxy* and *Red Dwarf* are the most obvious modern examples.

Classic satires like Thomas More's *Utopia* (1516), Jonathan Swift's *Gulliver's Travels* (1726) and Voltaire's *Micromegas* (1750) extrapolate from the familiar to the unfamiliar in much the same way that sf does, and are thus sometimes acclaimed as important precursors. Modern satires which use the future as a stage for their exaggerations, such as Karel Capek's *R.U.R.* (1920), Aldous Huxley's *Brave New World* (1932) and Kurt Vonnegut's *Cat's Cradle* (1963), have been very influential within the field and are routinely co-opted into it by critics in search of respectability.

Similarly, such classic sf works as H. G. Wells's *The Time Machine* (1895) and *The First Men In The Moon* (1901) have satirical elements, and

Wells went on to write such heavy-handed satires as *Mr Blettsworthy On Rampole Island* (1928) and *The Autocracy Of Mr Parham* (1930).

Early pulp science fiction played host to the rather laboured satires of Stanton A. Coblentz, such as *The Sunken World* (1928), but a much breezier kind of comedy was introduced by Henry Kuttner in such works as the Galloway Gallegher series (1943-48), collected in *Robots Have No Tails* (1952), and Robert Bloch's adventures of Lefty Feep (1942-46), collected in *Lost In Time And Space With Lefty Feep* (1987).

Satirical sf took a giant step forward in the 1950s in the work of a number of writers associated with *Galaxy* magazine. These included Frederik Pohl and Cyril M. Kornbluth, who collaborated on a scathing satire on the world of advertising, *The Space Merchants* (1953), and dreamt up three absurd societies in *Search The Sky* (1954). Pohl's solo works in the same vein include 'The Midas Plague' (1954) and 'The Tunnel Under The World' (1955). Damon Knight, Robert Sheckley and William Tenn also wrote some fine satirical short fiction for *Galaxy*, although they were less successful at novel length. Fritz Leiber's *The Silver Eggheads* (1961) is in a similar vein.

In the 1960s, science-fictional satire became more stylish and even more pointed in such works as Brian Aldiss's *The Primal Urge* (1961) and *The Dark Light Years* (1964) and Thomas M. Disch's *The Genocides* (1965) and *Mankind Under The Leash* (1966). John Sladek's *The Reproductive System* (1968) was the first of several deft sf satires, reaching a high point in his two-volume novel *Roderick* (1980) and *Roderick At Random* (1983). A broader species of comedy existed, however, in the works of Ron Goulart, which grew steadily more slapdash after the pinnacle of *After Things Fell Apart* (1972).

By the late 1960s, sf satirists were often inclined to make sf itself one of their prime targets. The science-fiction community of fans and writers, regularly brought together by conventions, is parodied in *Dwellers Of The Deep* (1970) and *Gather In The Hall Of The Planets* (1971) by "K. M. O'Donnell" (Barry N. Malzberg), who was to carry the same crusade forward in bleakly mordant fashion in *Herovit's World* (1973) and *Galaxies* (1975), written under his own name. The covert assumptions of futuristic power fantasy were laid bare in *The Iron Dream* (1972) by Norman Spinrad. The wilder excesses of space opera were pilloried in Harry Harrison's *Star Smashers Of The Galaxy Rangers* (1973) and Brian Aldiss's *The Eighty-Minute Hour* (1974).

The rich Eastern European tradition of satirical writing, which produced the works of Karel Capek, Frigyes Karinthy's magnificently bizarre *Capillaria* (1921) and Mikhail Bulgakov's *The Fatal Eggs* (1924), extended into the sf

of such writers as Josef Nesvadba, some of whose stories are collected in *In The Footsteps Of The Abominable Snowman* (1970), and Stanislaw Lem, most notably the "robotic fairy tales" of *The Cyberiad* (1974).

The English-language traditions of satire were not nearly as hospitable to bizarre intrusions, and rarely strayed into science-fictional territory, although American satirists like Thomas Pynchon, John Barth and Thomas Berger all produced marginally relevant work and Kurt Vonnegut had to struggle hard to avoid classification as an sf writer. Also marginal to the genre are the works of Robert Anton Wilson, most notably the *Illuminatus* trilogy (1975), co-written with Robert Shea, which were cleverly adapted for the stage by UK comedian Ken Campbell's Science Fiction Theatre of Liverpool.

British satirists who have used science-fictional devices include Kingsley Amis, Snoo Wilson and Ben Elton, the last-named on a fairly extravagant scale in such novels as *Stark* (1989), *Gridlock* (1991) and *This Other Eden* (1993).

Satire has never been a strong point of cinematic sf, although *The Man In The White Suit* (1951), *Doctor Strangelove* (1963) and Woody Allen's *Sleeper* (1973) are notable exceptions. American TV has produced several popular comedy sf series, including *My Favourite Martian* (1963-66) and *Mork And Mindy* (1978-82), and *Alien Nation* (1989-90) retains a mild satirical element alongside its melodrama, but is devoid of any real cutting edge. The British media are much less inhibited: the TV version of Douglas Adams's cult radio show *The Hitch-Hiker's Guide To The Galaxy* (1981) and Rob Grant and Doug Naylor's *Red Dwarf* series (begun 1988) display a much livelier and wider-ranging comic imagination.

Before the book versions of Douglas Adams's *Hitch-Hiker* series (1979-84) became bestsellers, publishers had taken the view that sf comedy did not sell well – so much so that William Moy Russell's very amusing *The Barber Of Aldebaran* (1995) took 40 years to get into print – but, once its potential had been demonstrated, the floodgates opened.

Much of the resultant work made little or no distinction between sf and fantasy, blithely combining motifs from both genres; Terry Pratchett's bestselling tales of the Discworld were foreshadowed in *Strata* (1981) and continue to make clever use of an eye trained in science-fictional scepticism. Other contemporary sf humorists of note include Josephine Saxton, author of *Queen Of The States* (1986), and David Langford, author of the definitive book of sf parodies, *The Dragonhiker's Guide To Battlefield Covenant At Dune's Edge: Odyssey Two* (1988).

 MIRROR, MIRROR ON THE WALL WHO'S THE FAIREST ROBOT OF THEM ALL? *GALLOWAY GALAGHER'S MECHANICAL NARCISSIST WAS NO SNOW WHITE*

75464-095 95¢

LANCER SCIENCE FICTION LIBRARY
ROBOTS HAVE NO TAILS
MEET GALLEGHER, GENIUS AND INVENTOR—AND
THE WACKIEST HERO
IN THIS OR ANY WORLD!
Henry kuttner

With a new introduction by **C.L.Moore**

motifs

In a science fiction story, the central idea or image is the true "hero". Most such ideas are variations on a limited number of fundamental themes.

Alien Life

The imaginative construction of creatures radically different from those found on Earth began little more than a century ago. H. G. Wells set two important precedents with the monstrous Martians of *The War Of The Worlds* (1898) and the hyper-efficient hive-society of *The First Men In The Moon* (1901); American pulp sf made prolific use of both these models in tales which mostly took it for granted that anything that was alien was ripe for extermination.

Monstrous enemies of humankind were compounded in great number out of the repulsive characteristics of snakes, insects and slugs. The common practice of blowing up such creatures as spiders and centipedes to giant size – and the opportunities such images offered to the grateful illustrators of the pulp magazines – gave rise to the "bug-eyed monster" cliché often used as a put-down by people hostile to the genre. There were, however, friendlier aliens who were happy to assist in the human colonization of the galaxy; these usually resembled birds or the cuter kinds of furry mammals.

The representation of aliens entered a new phase in the ingenious tales of Stanley G. Weinbaum, who appreciated that weird aliens needed to be integrated into some kind of ecological order. Although pulp sf writers continued to invent ever more repulsive alien monsters – notable examples include those featured in A. E. van Vogt's *The Voyage Of The Space Beagle* (1950) and Robert A. Heinlein's *The Puppet Masters* (1951) – the main emphasis gradually shifted towards the possibility of establishing friendly communication. Murray Leinster's 'First Contact' (1945) lent its name to a whole sub-genre of sf.

Attempts to present more credible non-human aliens became more sophisticated after World War II, as colonialism went out of fashion and even the British Empire transformed itself into the British Commonwealth. The work of Hal Clement, who delighted in designing alien life adapted to very exotic environments, set new standards of amiability as well as ingenuity. At the same time, aliens began to feature in earnest philosophical fantasies like Clifford D. Simak's *Time And Again* (1951) and James Blish's *A Case Of Conscience* (1958). The cinema, however, remained extraordinarily fond of loathsomely monstrous aliens and still makes regular use of them in such movies as *Alien* (1979), *Predator* (1987) and *Species* (1995).

Modern sf which deals with conflict between humans and aliens –

however violent – is usually focused on the necessity of finding a way to get along together in a shared universe; TV's *Star Trek* and its various spin-off series are obsessed with this issue, as is *Babylon 5* (begun 1994). This is only to be expected in a world whose nations are trying desperately hard to form and maintain a viable global community.

The possibility that the alien might be beyond our understanding – as in such novels as Stanislaw Lem's *Solaris* (1961) – has come to seem more fearful than any mere ugliness of form. The search for extra-terrestrial intelligence (SETI) continues, its eager hopefulness reflected in such works as Carl Sagan's *Contact* (1985). The predominant anxiety of contemporary sf is that we might prove unworthy of admission to the galactic community.

Artificial Intelligence

The science-fictional ancestors of computers were "mechanical brains", first employed as story-devices in the 19th century. In pulp sf, they featured extensively in the work of John W. Campbell Jr, whose 'The Last Evolution' (1930) was the first of many stories to argue that machine

WHETHER YOU'RE A MAN OR A MACHINE, YOUR SOUL IS NOTHING BUT SOFTWARE So *IF YOU WANT ETERNAL LIFE YOU'D BETTER MAKE YOUR OWN PROVISION*

William Gibson's *Neuromancer* (1984) to launch cyberpunk – celebrated the awareness that machine evolution might soon run completely out of control. The idea that computer networks might make a spontaneous and unplanned leap to consciousness – perhaps with dire consequences for their users – is a significant element in the plots of Bruce Sterling's *Schismatrix* (1985) and Michael Swanwick's *Vacuum Flowers* (1987). The notion that human minds might one day be "downloaded" into machinery quickly became fashionable; the idea of afterlives being hawked as a commercial product of technology is extravagantly developed in such novels as Greg Bear's *Eon* (1985) and Greg Egan's *Permutation City* (1994).

The possibility that computers might eventually develop self-consciousness has been explored in several strangely sentimental stories tracking the mechanical "childhood" of individual machines. Notable examples include *When Harlie Was One* (1972) by David Gerrold, *The Adolescence Of P-1* (1977) by Thomas J. Ryan and *Valentina: Soul In Sapphire* (1984) by Joseph H. Delaney and Marc Stiegler. Greg Bear's *Queen Of Angels* (1990) also includes an uplifting account of the spontaneous genesis of machine self-awareness in an exploratory space-probe.

The idea that artificial intelligence is something that can be incorporated by design and kept under human control already seems rather passé, though; Gregory Benford's *Sailing Bright Eternity* (1995) has to go to extraordinary lengths to find a plausible role for organic intelligence in a cosmic scheme which is dominated by machine intelligence.

Cosmic Collisions

The notion that Earth might collide with a comet or a stray asteroid first became commonplace in the 19th century, when the idea that meteors were caused by cosmic debris burning in the atmosphere gained universal acceptance and astronomers realized how cluttered the solar system is. The French astronomer Camille Flammarion popularized the idea in numerous articles and offered an account of the world's reaction to news of an impending impact in *Omega: The Last Days Of The World* (1893-94). Different responses to similar news are featured in *The Day Of Uniting* (1926) by Edgar Wallace and *Death Requests The Pleasure* (1940) by Maurice Dekobra. The reappearance of Halley's comet in 1910 prompted the production in that year of the pioneering cosmic disaster movie *The Comet*.

The Tunguska explosion of 1908 remains the most famous meteor-strike of recent times – although some sf stories, including Ian Watson's *Chekhov's Journey* (1983) have offered more interesting explanations of that particular event. Sf novels featuring more destructive meteor-strikes include *A Torrent Of Faces* (1967) by James Blish and Norman L. Knight, and *Lucifer's Hammer* (1977) by Larry Niven and Jerry Pournelle. 'The Star' (1897) by H. G. Wells, *When Worlds Collide* (1933; filmed in 1951) by Philip

intelligence was the logical end-product of evolution. In Isaac Asimov's 'The Last Question' (1956), such a machine intelligence eventually becomes God.

Some sf writers welcomed the advent of computers on the grounds that they could help free human society from the irrationalities of human decision-making; Asimov's 'The Evitable Conflict' (1950), Mark Clifton and Frank Riley's *They'd Rather Be Right* (1957) and Algis Budrys's *Michaelmas* (1977) argue this case. Adherents of the opposing view offered accounts of the ways in which computers might become instruments of oppression, as in *The Shockwave Rider* (1975) by John Brunner, and accounts of computers with delusions of grandeur which stage their own coups d'état, as in *Colossus* (1966) by D. F. Jones. This dispute continues, equipped with increasingly graphic imagery in the work of the cyberpunk movement, which was inspired by the rapid evolution of computers in the real world.

Following the advent of the microprocessor, the huge and monolithic supercomputers of 1950s and 1960s sf were gradually replaced in the 1970s by a multitude of smaller machines, loosely aggregated into a worldwide network. The nearer futures of sf were soon teeming with primitive and unruly artificial intelligences, whose human users were often as ill-adjusted to society as the machines themselves.

Rudy Rucker's *Software* (1982) and *Wetware* (1988) – which helped

Wylie and Edwin Balmer, *The Wanderer* (1964) by Fritz Leiber and *Nemesis* (1989) by Isaac Asimov feature larger and even more disruptive cosmic visitors to the solar system. In *The Hopkins Manuscript* (1939) by R. C. Sherriff, the Moon crashes into the Earth. Arthur C. Clarke's *Rendezvous With Rama* (1973) begins with a meteor-strike which prompts the establishment of "Project SPACEGUARD" with a view to early detection and possible deflection of threatening objects. The film *Meteor* (1979) and Gregory Benford and William Rotsler's *Shiva Descending* (1980) both deal with such problems.

Cosmic collisions were further popularized by Immanuel Velikovsky's *Worlds In Collision* (1950) and its follow-ups, which offered a highly fanciful but supposedly non-fictional account of the recent history of the solar system, but sf writers disdainfully ignored this possible source of inspiration. They were by no means as inclined to ignore the more recent publicity given to the hypothetical asteroid-strike 65,000,000 years ago which – according to Luis and Walter Alvarez, in a paper published in 1980 – left a huge crater in the Gulf of Mexico and filled the atmosphere with enough dust to blot out the Sun for long enough to cause the mass extinction of the dinosaurs. Arthur Clarke wrote the first version of his own asteroid-deflection story, *The Hammer Of God* (1993) for *Time* magazine in 1992, and the longer version makes much of the lessons supposedly to be learned from this discovery. Other speculative theorists have suggested that the Ice Ages, which have afflicted Earth throughout its history, have all been the result of meteor-strikes, although a far more melodramatic variety of cosmic collision is proposed as an explanation by Charles Pellegrino in *Flying To Valhalla* (1994) and *The Killing Star* (1995), the latter written in collaboration with George Zebrowski.

Cutting-edge Technologies

Science-fiction writers have always tried to extrapolate the possibilities of newly emergent technologies. In the early 1940s, they wrote extensively about nuclear power; in the 1950s, about computers, and so on. At present, there are three main areas of current research which have seized the science-fictional imagination with a firm grip: genetic engineering (see below), nanotechnology and virtual reality.

Nanotechnology involves the building of machines which can operate on a molecular scale (a nanometre is 1/1,000,000,000 of a metre). Genetic engineering, which involves harnessing the molecular machinery of our own cell-nuclei, is a "domestication" of natural nanotechnology, but K. Eric Drexler argues in *Engines Of Creation: The Coming Era Of Nanotechnology* (1987) that we will soon be able to engineer inorganic machinery on the same scale.

Greg Bear's *Blood Music* (1985), involving the manipulation of genes to make tiny biocomputers which then run out of control, was one of the earliest sf stories to appreciate what fast-evolving molecular machines might be capable of. A similarly ambitious account of the transformation of the human condition by nanomachinery which remains under control is Marc Stiegler's 'The Gentle Seduction' (1989). More elaborate schemes are sketched out in *The Nanotech Chronicles* (1991) by Michael Flynn and *Assemblers Of Infinity* (1993) by Kevin J. Anderson and Doug Beason, while nanotechnological resurrection of the dead is featured in *Necroville* (1994) by Ian McDonald. Sophisticated "internal technologies" are not yet fully integrated into sf's stereotyped images of the near and far future, but they soon will be.

Virtual Reality technology currently involves people putting on headsets and "data-gloves", so that they can not only look into but also interact with a computer-generated "artificial world". Familiar applications include flight-simulators and various kinds of game-machines. Howard Rheingold's book *Virtual Reality* (1991) examines many of the current uses of such technology and their possible extrapolation, including the likelihood that the data-glove will evolve into a whole "data-suit" which will allow total immersion in such virtual worlds. Such immersion is a central theme in the sf of the cyberpunk movement.

Artificial worlds of experience appeared in sf long before the term "virtual reality" was coined, a significant early example being 'City Of The Living Dead' (1930) by Laurence Manning and Fletcher Pratt in which whole populations prefer living in VR to the real world – a common anxiety in sf. Significant sf novels in which people become trapped in virtual realities include *Octagon* (1981) by Fred Saberhagen, and Kim Newman's *The Night Mayor* (1989).

A more intensive extrapolation of VR applications can be found in *Chimera* (1993) by Mary Rosenblum. VR has understandably been a popular theme in the visual media, employed in such films as *Welcome To Blood City* (1977), *Tron* (1982) and *The Lawnmower Man* (1992), and in

 DAY OF THE DEAD IN IAN McDONALD'S NOVEL NANOTECHNOLOGY SECURES THE MEANS TO MAKE EVERYONE A ZOMBIE AND VOODOO MOVES INTO THE BOARDROOM

the TV series *Wild Palms* (1994), *Disclosure* (1995) and most recently *VR-5* (begun 1995).

Stories which combine both themes, integrating moderately sophisticated internal technologies and fast-evolving VR technologies into images of near-future society, include *Queen Of Angels* (1990) by Greg Bear, 'Inherit The Earth' (1995) by Brian Stableford and *Fairyland* (1995) by Paul J. McAuley.

Cyborgs

"Cyborg" is a contraction of "cybernetic organism", which refers to any fusion of flesh and machine. Medical cyborgs – people fitted with prosthetic limbs, artificial organs or coronary pacemakers – already exist in some profusion; exaggerated versions are featured in such works of fiction as Bernard Wolfe's *Limbo* (1952) and Martin Caidin's *Cyborg* (1972). The

 GUNSLINGERS *THE POSSIBILITIES OF CYBORGIZATION LEND NEW MEANING TO SUCH PHRASES AS "SIDEARMS", "DRESSED TO KILL" AND "ARMED TO THE TEETH"*

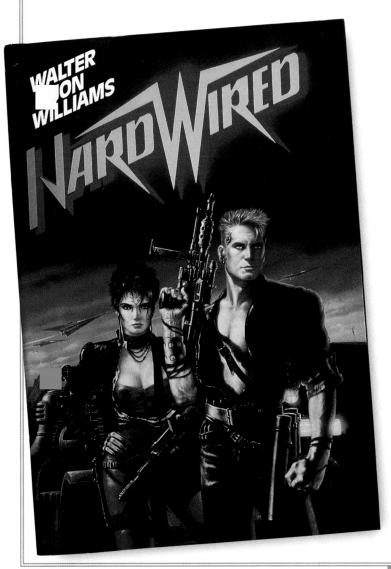

latter was the basis of the TV movie *The Six-Million Dollar Man* (1973) and its spin-off series (1974-8), which gave rise in its turn to *The Bionic Woman* (1976-8).

The first significant fictional cyborg was E. V. Odle's *The Clockwork Man* (1923), who had a clockwork mechanism built into his head to regulate his being and allow him to move across many dimensions. The early sf pulps often featured tales of human brains transplanted into mechanical bodies – a notion most thoughtfully developed in 'No Woman Born' (1944) by C. L. Moore. *Who?* (1958) by Algis Budrys, filmed by Jack Gold in 1974, addresses the problem of determining the identity of a person who no longer has a face or fingerprints.

Sf writers have made much of the idea of adapting cyborgs to the business of piloting spaceships. Introduced by Cordwainer Smith in 'Scanners Live In Vain' (1950), the theme was taken up by Thomas N. Scortia in 'Sea Change' (1956) and then by Anne McCaffrey, in the long series of stories begun with *The Ship Who Sang* (1961), which is currently being carried forward in collaboration with other writers. *Superluminal* (1983) by Vonda N. McIntyre and *The Forever Man* (1986) by Gordon R. Dickson are in the same tradition.

Stories dealing with the cyborgization of humans for the purpose of exploring other worlds include Arthur C. Clarke's 'A Meeting With Medusa' (1971), Frederik Pohl's *Man Plus* (1976), Kevin J. Anderson's *Climbing Olympus* (1994) and Mike Resnick's *A Miracle Of Rare Design* (1994). Barrington J. Bayley's *The Garments Of Caean* (1976) features two races of cyborgs adapted to the harsh environment of outer space itself.

Cyborgs adapted for armed combat are commonplace in sf: notable examples include 'Kings Who Die' (1962) by Poul Anderson, *A Plague Of Demons* (1965) by Keith Laumer and the various Doctor Who adventures which featured the cyborgized alien Daleks. The film *RoboCop* (1987) and its sequels introduce a dramatically-useful restraint into the image of the cyborg fighting-machine. The modification of humans, so that they may connect themselves more intimately with powerful computers, has become very fashionable in recent years and is a staple of cyberpunk fiction. Memorable imagery of this kind can be found in Bruce Sterling's *Shaper And Mechanist* series, Walter John Williams' *Hardwired* (1986), and Gwyneth Jones's *Escape Plans* (1986).

Philip K. Dick's novel *The Three Stigmata Of Palmer Eldritch* (1964) uses the eponymous cyborg as an archetype of evil and a symbol of an undesirable mechanization of human feeling. Similar anxieties are vividly displayed in David R. Bunch's surreal tales, collected in *Moderan* (1971) – in which humans shed their "fleshstrips" to live as recluses in their mechanized "strongholds" – and the remarkable Japanese film *Tetsuo* (1990).

Dinosaurs & other survivals

The dinosaurs which roamed the earth in such profusion before their disappearance 65,000,000 years ago have long exerted a powerful fascination over the human imagination. The possibility of finding some isolated enclave where they survive has been a popular theme of sf since Jules Verne's *Journey To The Centre Of The Earth* (1864), and the (very faint) hope of finding a few in the real world is maintained by such cherished items of folklore as the Loch Ness Monster. The only other prehistoric survivals with anything like the glamour of dinosaurs are a few of the early mammals exterminated by our ancestors, notably mammoths and sabre-toothed tigers. These were once widely featured in lost-race novels, but remained scarce for some time thereafter until they made a spectacular comeback in Jean Auel's best-selling prehistorical romances.

Arthur Conan Doyle's *The Lost World* (1912) was first filmed in 1925, establishing dinosaurs as favourite subjects of stop-motion animation; they were abundant on the island ruled by *King Kong* (1933) and were also to be found in the *Valley Of Gwangi* (1969). Edgar Rice Burroughs's trilogy *The Land That Time Forgot* (1924) was the basis for the film of the same name (1975) and *The People That Time Forgot* (1977). Burroughs also featured a dinosaur-inhabited island in the less earnest *The Cave Girl* (1925). Extra-terrestrial dinosaurs are featured in *A Journey In Other Worlds* (1894) by John Jacob Astor. Earthly dinosaurs evolve for a second time in *The Greatest Adventure* (1929) by John Taine and *Carnivores* (1993) by Penelope Banks Kreps, while intelligent dinosaurs who might have evolved had their forebears not been wiped out are featured in the series begun with *West Of Eden* (1984) by Harry Harrison.

The favourite dinosaur species of popular fiction has always been *Tyrannosaurus rex*, a favourite target for time-travelling hunters in such stories as 'A Gun For Dinosaur' (1956) and *Rivers Of Time* (1993) by L. Sprague de Camp and *The Dinosaur Hunters* (1966) by Henri Vernes. The favourite individual dinosaur is, however, the Japanese Gojira or Godzilla, who probably owed his original inspiration to *The Beast From 20,000 Fathoms* (1953). Godzilla's 20-year film career began in 1954 and extended through numerous sequels which transformed him by degrees into a curiously quixotic hero defending the Earth (or Japan, at least) from other less altruistic alien intruders. In this capacity, Godzilla was transferred to animated cartoons of a more primitive variety, accompanied by an infant counterpart. Such sentimentality reached its height in *Baby – The Secret Of The Lost Legend* (1985). A more general fascination with dinosaurs is gaudily displayed in James Gurney's art book *Dinotopia* (1992).

The idea that dinosaurs might be re-created by genetic engineers was popularized by Steven Spielberg's hugely successful film (1993) of Michael

Crichton's *Jurassic Park* (1990). The book's sequel borrowed the Conan Doyle title *The Lost World* (1995), presumably by way of paying homage, although it does not feature a lost world. Harry Adam Knight's *Carnosaur* (1984; filmed in 1994) is a more restrained exercise in the same vein.

The Dying Earth

In the 19th century, it was assumed that the sun's heat was a product of combustion and that the sun would therefore burn out, leaving the Earth to freeze. Images of this slow death can be found in Camille Flammarion's *Omega: The Last Days Of The World* (1893-4), H. G. Wells's *The Time Machine* (1895) and George C. Wallis's 'The Last Days Of Earth' (1901). William Hope Hodgson's *The Night Land* (1912) is bizarre as well as bleak, offering a phantasmagorical vision of a decadent world where frightful monsters gather to threaten the last remnants of humankind. Similar imagery is found in *The Amphibians* (1924) by S. Fowler Wright, later incorporated into *The World Below* (1929), which drew upon Wright's translation of Dante's *Inferno*.

A bolder fusion of the ornamentations of literary decadence with the idea of the earth grown old was contrived by Clark Ashton Smith in his tales of *Zothique* (1932-37; collected 1970). This depiction of a world made colourful by irredeemable corruption was echoed in Jack Vance's classic collection *The Dying Earth* (1950), whose sequels include *The Eyes Of The Overworld* (1966), *Cugel's Saga* (1983) and *Rhialto The Marvelous* (1984). *A Quest For Simbilis* (1974) by Michael Shea is set in the same world.

Decadent romanticism is also displayed, sometimes lavishly, in *Earth's Last Citadel* (1943) by Henry Kuttner and C. L. Moore, *Hothouse* (1962) and many other stories by Brian W. Aldiss, *The Jewels Of Aptor* (1962) by Samuel R. Delany, *Midsummer Century* (1972) by James Blish and *Earth In Twilight* (1981) by Doris Piserchia. It is taken to a calculatedly absurd extreme in Michael Moorcock's 'Dancers At The End Of Time' trilogy (1972-76), in which humans with godlike powers constantly seek diversion from the tedium of their limitless existence.

As well as bleak visions of the end of the human race such as Donald Wandrei's 'The Red Brain' (1927), John W. Campbell Jr's 'Twilight' (1934) and Raymond Z. Gallun's 'Seeds Of The Dusk' (1938), the sf pulps also

THRILLING WONDER STORIES
APRIL
Apr 40
16-1
15¢
CONQUEST BY FIRE
By WARD HAWKINS
FEATURING
ROAR OF THE ROCKET
A Complete Novel of The Spaceways
By OSCAR J. FRIEND
A THRILLING PUBLICATION

 TYRANNOSAURUS WRECKS *Long before the advent of Godzilla pulp sf writers had realised the potential of saurian versions of King Kong*

featured stories in which starfaring humankind outlasts the Earth – a notion boldly advanced in J. B. S. Haldane's essay 'The Last Judgement' (1927) but not reproduced in *Last And First Men* (1930), the far-ranging novel which Olaf Stapledon developed from that essay's seed. The omission was made good in Arthur C. Clarke's Stapledon-influenced *Against The Fall Of Night* (1948), which was revised as *The City And The Stars* (1956), although Gregory Benford's *Beyond The Fall Of Night* (1990) is a recent sequel to the original version. In Edmond Hamilton's 'Requiem' (1962), the Earth's death is a TV spectacular relayed to a galaxy-wide audience.

Stories of the dying earth featuring attempts to secure some kind of rebirth include Raymond Gallun's 'When Earth Is Old' (1951) and Clark Ashton Smith's 'Phoenix' (1954). The latter involves the re-ignition of a burnt-out sun – a notion brilliantly shorn of its anachronistic quality in Gene Wolfe's four-volume *Book Of The New Sun* (1980-83). Rebirth is also a significant theme in the far-future fantasies of Robert Silverberg, notably the surreal *Son Of Man* (1971).

The Elixir of Life

The elixir of life and the fountain of youth have always been key motifs of imaginative fiction, but so has the notion of the "tedious punishment": the curse of unbearable immortality imposed on Tantalus and the Wandering Jew. The ambivalence inherent in these two sets of myths is clearly evident in early sf, which is deeply suspicious of the value of extreme human longevity. In *The Inner House* (1888), Walter Besant argues that immortality would lead to personal and social sterility – an opinion echoed in *The Makropoulos Secret* by Karel Capek, 'Life Everlasting' (1934) by David H. Keller and *After Many A Summer Dies The Swan* (1939) by Aldous Huxley, but dismissed as mere cowardice by George Bernard Shaw in *Back To Methuselah* (1921) and *The Man Who Awoke* (1933) by Laurence Manning. Such stories as 'Live For Ever' (1954) by J. T. McIntosh and 'At Death's End' (1954) by James Blish found glorious opportunity in the possibility of life-extension, but 'World Without Children' (1951) by Damon Knight and *Drunkard's Walk* (1960) by Frederik Pohl were anxious that the advantages might well be outweighed by unanticipated disadvantages.

What does seem to be universally accepted is that the craving for more life that some people possess is so powerful that they would stop at

THE DYING EARTH

nothing to obtain it. Lurid accounts of the lengths to which such individuals might go can be found in *To Live Forever* (1956) by Jack Vance, *The Immortals* (1962) by James E. Gunn, *Bug Jack Barron* (1969) by Norman Spinrad, 'The Weariest River' (1973) by Thomas N. Scortia, *Welcome Chaos* (1983) by Kate Wilhelm and *Eternity* (1984) by Mack Reynolds and Dean C. Ing. The number of people who are willing to pay vast sums of money to be cryonically stored after death, in the hope that technological progress will one day permit their resurrection, provides further evidence relevant to this point.

Sf novels featuring immortal heroes usually assume that they would adapt to that state of being – ones who have done so are featured in Wilson Tucker's *The Time Masters* (1953), Clifford D. Simak's *Way Station* (1963), Roger Zelazny's *This Immortal* (1966) and Robert Heinlein's *Time Enough For Love* (1973) – but many are eventually driven to extremes in order to avoid boredom.

Raymond Z. Gallun's *The Eden Cycle* (1974), Michael Moorcock's tales of the 'Dancers At The End Of Time' and Robert Silverberg's *Sailing To Byzantium* (1985) take this view. Closer and more detailed analyses, such as those to be found in Octavia Butler's *Wild Seed* (1980), Pamela Sargent's *The Golden Space* (1982) and Poul Anderson's *The Boat Of A Million Years* (1989), often steer a middle course. Brian Stableford's many stories dealing with the theme – most notably 'Les Fleurs Du Mal' (1994) and 'Mortimer Gray's History Of Death' – are, however, unqualified in their enthusiasm.

Some stories of longevity suggest that the limited capacity of human memory would continually retire the more distant past to oblivion, and that this process would have both advantages and disadvantages. The notion is a background element in Kim Stanley Robinson's Mars trilogy (1992-6) but is brought into sharper focus in Michael Flynn's 'Melodies Of The Heart' (1994).

The Endangered Environment

It is only in the last 50 years that the importance and complexity of ecological issues have been appreciated, but anxiety quickly gave birth to pressure groups like Greenpeace and Friends of the Earth as well as political organizations like Europe's various green parties. W. H. Hudson's heartfelt fantasies about the urgent desirability of cultivating a new harmony between human life and the natural world, *A Crystal Age* (1887)

INDIAN SUMMER *IF IT DOESN'T END WITH A BANG OR A WHIMPER THE WORLD MAY LIVE TO ENJOY A GLORIOUSLY COLOURFUL AND LUSHLY DECADENT SENILITY*

THE SHEEP LOOK UP

JOHN BRUNNER
Author of STAND ON ZANZIBAR

 SHEEP IN GAS MASKS *JOHN BRUNNER'S ALARMIST NOVEL ARGUES THAT IF SOCIETY CAN'T MAKE A RAPID EWE-TURN WE'LL ALL BE WELL AND TRULY RAMMED*

and *Green Mansions* (1904), now seem remarkably prophetic; the precariousness of the human ecological situation has inevitably become a major theme of modern sf.

The possibility of a devastating "ecocatastrophe", first featured in such novels as A. G. Street's *Already Walks Tomorrow* (1938) and John Christopher's *The Death Of Grass* (1956), has now become so commonplace in tales of the future that the vast majority of stories regard some such crisis as inevitable. The principal bugbear of the 1960s was the population explosion, which was supplemented in the 1970s by environmental pollution, in the 1980s by the "greenhouse effect" and in the 1990s by the thinning of the ozone layer. The more extreme accounts of near-future ecocatastrophe include *The Sheep Look Up* (1972) by John Brunner, *The Nitrogen Fix* (1980) by Hal Clement, *Greenhouse* (1984) by Dakota James, *Nature's End* (1986) by Whitley Strieber and James Kunetka and *Hot Sky At Midnight* (1994) by Robert Silverberg.

Many ecocatastrophe stories exhibit a bitter irony, sometimes shading into black comedy; most sf writers feel that we will get no more than we

deserve if we drown in our own industrial excrement. Prescriptive works explaining how we might extract ourselves from the self-made mire are, however, rare. Ernest Callenbach's *Ecotopia* (1975) is an exceptional attempt to design an ecologically-viable utopia.

Following early precedents set by Stanley G. Weinbaum, genre sf writers eventually developed a sub-genre of "ecological puzzle stories" in which explorers of other worlds must figure out peculiar relationships which exist between the local plants and animals and flora. Examples include James H. Schmitz's 'Grandpa' (1955), Brian Aldiss's *Planetary Ecological Survey Team* (PEST) series (1958-62), Richard McKenna's 'Hunter Come Home' (1963) and John Boyd's *The Pollinators Of Eden* (1969).

Ecological puzzles frequently hold the key to problems which arise in sf stories about the colonization of other worlds, especially where the local ecosystems resist displacement by earthly crops. Examples include Mark Clifton's *Eight Keys To Eden* (1960), Frank Herbert's *Dune* (1965), and Michael Coney's *Syzygy* (1973). Attempts to re-establish lost ecological harmonies often take on mystical overtones, which are taken to various extremes in such works as Piers Anthony's *Omnivore* (1968), Somtow Sucharitkul's *Starship And Haiku* (1984) and Jacqueline Lichtenberg's *Dushau* (1985) and its sequels. Earth-based ecological mysticism, which often draws on exaggerated versions of James Lovelock's "Gaea hypothesis", is displayed in such works as Hilbert Schenck's *At The Eye Of The Ocean* (1980) – but extreme Gaea-worshippers come in for harsh criticism in such works as David Brin's *Earth* (1990).

Genetic Engineering

When biologists cracked the genetic code in the late 1950s, scientists became the potential masters of future evolution, as had been anticipated in such sf novels as *The Island Of Dr Moreau* (1896) by H. G. Wells and *Brave New World* (1932) by Aldous Huxley. The prospect had usually been considered horrific, although the prophetic essay which gave Huxley the idea – J. B. S. Haldane's *Daedalus, Or Science And The Future* (1923) – and Robert Heinlein's *Beyond This Horizon* (1942) were determinedly enthusiastic. James Blish's *Titan's Daughter* (1961; based on a 1952 novella) is somewhat ambivalent, but his *The Seedling Stars* (1956) pointed out that our ability to colonize alien worlds might well depend on our ability to adapt humans to exotic ways of life.

When genetic engineering became a real possibility, the first focus of interest was the idea of cloning people, developed in Ursula Le Guin's 'Nine Lives' (1969) and Pamela Sargent's *Cloned Lives* (1976), which explored the possible psychological consequences of growing up as part of a clone, and Ira Levin's *The Boys From Brazil* (1976), which suggested that re-creating Hitler might be more difficult than merely cloning him. Le Guin's *The Left Hand Of Darkness* (1969) scrupulously investigates an "alien" society created by means of a modest engineering of human sexuality.

The alarmist British TV series *Doomwatch* (1970-72) helped spread awareness of some of the implications of genetic engineering; its first episode – novelized as *Mutant-59* (1972) by Kit Pedler and Gerry Davis – concerned the disastrous escape of a bacterium engineered to metabolize plastic. Subsequent TV productions such as *First Born* (1989) and *Chimera* (1991; based on Stephen Gallagher's 1982 novel) have maintained the same hysterically anxious tone, and *The X-Files* (begun 1994) regularly attributes all manner of horrors to the results of secret experiments with "alien DNA".

A far more enthusiastic account of the possibilities of human engineering can be found in a loosely knit series of stories by Brian Stableford, whose early examples are collected in *Sexual Chemistry* (1991). These involve the gradual extension of the human lifespan, humankind's achievement of complete technical mastery of Earth's biosphere and the adaptation of humans for life in space – topics also addressed by Lois McMaster Bujold's *Falling Free* (1988). Greg Egan's short fiction, including many items collected in *Axiomatic* (1995), often deals with similar issues in a more suspicious fashion, as does James Patrick Kelly's *Wildlife* (1994).

Future societies which make extravagant (and sometimes highly eccentric) uses of genetic engineering are widely featured in the work of John Varley, in the Shaper And Mechanist stories of Bruce Sterling, which include the novel *Schismatrix* (1985), and in C. J. Cherryh's *Cyteen* (1988). As the products of biotechnology have an increasing impact on the real world, its possibilities are bound to be taken aboard virtually all science-fictional images of the future; the ethical and political questions which are thrown up by even the most elementary biotechnologies will inevitably take their place among the hottest issues in the genre.

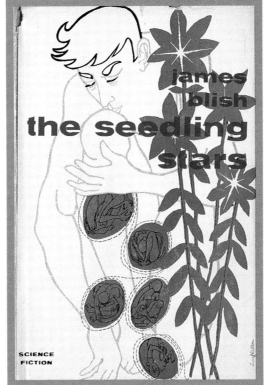

SCIENCE FICTION

james blish
the seedling stars

Nuclear War & Its Aftermath

When news of the bombing of Hiroshima was released in 1945, the editor of *Astounding SF*, John W. Campbell Jr, exultantly proclaimed that sf would have to be taken seriously from now on. Campbell's own first published story had been 'When The Atoms Failed' (1930), and he had been visited by government agents anxious about leaks in the Manhattan Project when he published Cleve Cartmill's 'Deadline' in 1944. Nuclear weapons had,

ALL CHANGE! JAMES BLISH'S PANTROPY SERIES SUGGESTED THAT THE CONQUEST OF THE UNIVERSE MIGHT REQUIRE AN UNLIMITED CAPACITY FOR ADAPTATION

however, been featured in sf even before his involvement; *The World Set Free* (1914) by H. G. Wells and *Public Faces* (1932) by Harold Nicolson are notable examples.

News of Hiroshima sparked off of a glut of apocalyptic fantasies in which civilization is destroyed and the survivors of atomic war must then contend with radioactive pollution on a massive scale. For 50 years, this has remained a powerful cause of real anxiety, reflected in such stories as 'Memorial' (1946) by Theodore Sturgeon, *Shadow On The Hearth* (1950) by Judith Merril, *The Long Loud Silence* (1952) by Wilson Tucker, 'Lot' (1953) by Ward Moore, *False Night* (1954) by Algis Budrys, *On The Beach* (1957; film version 1959) by Nevil Shute, *Z For Zachariah* (1975) by Robert C. O'Brien and *Warday* (1984) by Whitley Strieber and James W. Kunetka, as well as such films as *The War Game* (1965), *The Day After* (1983), *Testament* (1983) and *Threads* (1984). Further testimony to the strength of this anxiety is its extrapolation into such blackly satirical movies as *Dr Strangelove, Or How I Learned To Stop Worrying And Love The Bomb* (1963) and *The Bed-Sitting Room* (1969).

The more distant consequences of nuclear holocaust, in which societies struggling to recover from the holocaust continue to bear the curse of genetic mutation, are tracked in 'Coming Attraction' (1950) by Fritz Leiber, *The Chrysalids* (1955) by John Wyndham, *Twilight World* (1961) by Poul Anderson, *Davy* (1964) by Edgar Pangborn, *Dr Bloodmoney, Or How We Got Along After The Bomb* (1965) by Philip K. Dick, *Riddley Walker* (1980) by Russell Hoban and *The Postman* (1985) by David Brin. The classic *A Canticle For Leibowitz* (1960) by Walter M. Miller illustrates G. W. F. Hegel's famous dictum that those who fail to learn from history are condemned to repeat it. An ironic post-holocaust romanticism was popularized by the second and third films in the *Mad Max* series (1981 and 1985), having been foreshadowed in the 1969 film of Harlan Ellison's 'A Boy And His Dog' (1967).

Interesting alternative-history stories in which the bombing of Hiroshima does not happen include 'The Lucky Strike' (1984) by Kim Stanley Robinson and *The Proteus Operation* (1985) by James P. Hogan. Although the recent end of the Cold War has reduced the fear of nuclear war somewhat, the prospect still hangs over the world like the sword of Damocles. A scrupulous, satirical examination of the way in which responsibility for this state of affairs must be allocated can be found in James Morrow's harrowing *This Is The Way The World Ends* (1986), in which the "unadmitted" – people robbed of their chance to exist by nuclear war – put the destroyers of the world on trial and find everyone guilty, arguing that complacency equals complicity.

Overpopulation & Pollution

In his *Essay On The Principle Of Population As It Affects The Future Improvement Of Society* (1798), T. R. Malthus argued that human populations tended to increase exponentially, continually outgrowing their resources, and would always be subject to the "negative checks" of famine, war and plague.

Although a second edition of 1803 conceded that population-growth might also be limited by "moral restraint", Malthus clearly had little faith in that prospect and most modern sf writers agree with him. Malthusian anxieties made a big comeback in the 1960s, encouraged by such non-fictional exercises in alarmism as *The Population Bomb* (1968) by Paul Ehrlich and the Club of Rome's primitive computer-analysis of *The Limits To Growth* (1972), but the notion of institutionalized population control had already been introduced into sf in *Master Of Life And*

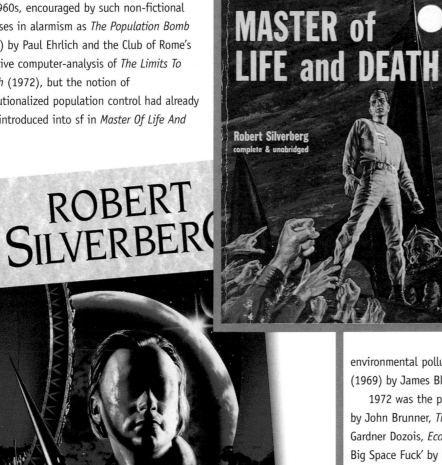

Death (1957) by Robert Silverberg.

Notable novels of the 1960s dealing with overpopulation include *The Eleventh Commandment* (1962) by Lester del Rey, *Make Room! Make Room!* (1966) by Harry Harrison, *A Torrent Of Faces* (1968) by James Blish and Norman L. Knight and the ambitious *Stand On Zanzibar* (1969) by John Brunner, which still ranks as the definitive sf treatment of the subject. Later treatments of the theme, accepting the inevitability of continued population increase, tend to be more contemplative; examples include *The World Inside* (1972) by Robert Silverberg and *334* (1972) by Thomas M. Disch. Confidence in moral restraint was so low that sf stories considering organized population control often envisaged Draconian methods, sometimes extending to mass murder; examples include *The Quality Of Mercy* (1965) by D. G. Compton, *Logan's Run* (1967) by William F. Nolan and George Clayton Johnson, and *Time Of The Fourth Horseman* (1976) by Chelsea Quinn Yarbro.

Another very successful alarmist work of the 1960s was Rachel Carson's *The Silent Spring* (1962), which argued that environmental pollution had entered a new phase by virtue of the widespread use of non-biodegradable substances which gradually built up fatal concentrations as they passed along the food-chain. This anxiety, added to fears about the polluting effects of nuclear waste from power-stations, seemed more urgent than anxieties about overpopulation, as is evident in such near-hysterical stories as 'Shark Ship' (1958) by C. M. Kornbluth – an early horror story in which the effects of overpopulation and environmental pollution are combined – and 'We All Die Naked' (1969) by James Blish.

1972 was the peak year for anti-pollution parables; *The Sheep Look Up* by John Brunner, *The End Of The Dream* by Philip Wylie, 'King's Harvest' by Gardner Dozois, *Ecodeath* by William Jon Watkins and E. V. Snyder, and 'The Big Space Fuck' by Kurt Vonnegut all appeared in that year. More sober treatments of the theme include *The Thinking Seat* (1970) by Peter Tate and 'To Walk With Thunder' (1973) by Dean McLaughlin.

In the past 20 years, overpopulation and pollution have frequently been merged into images of all-encompassing ecocatastrophe such as *O-Zone* by Paul Theroux (1986), *Nature's End* (1986) by Whitley Strieber and James W. Kunetka, *Earth* (1990) by David Brin and *Hot Sky At Midnight* (1994) by Robert Silverberg.

TRUTH OR CONSEQUENCE ROBERT SILVERBERG'S NOVELS ARE UNCOMPROMISING IN ARGUING THAT IF WE CAN'T EXERCISE SELF-CONTROL WE WILL DESTROY OUR WORLD

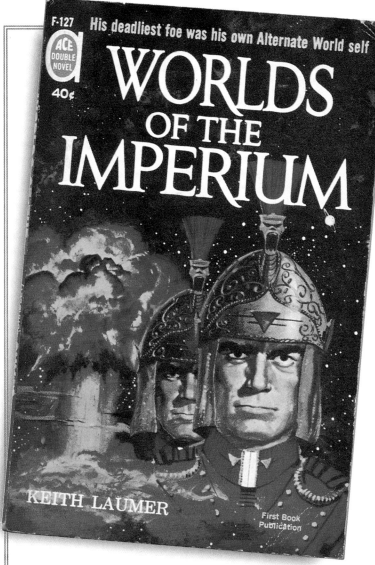

His deadliest foe was his own Alternate World self

F-127
ACE
DOUBLE
NOVEL
40¢

WORLDS OF THE IMPERIUM

KEITH LAUMER

First Book
Publication

LOOK ON MY WORKS, YE MIGHTY, AND DESPAIR! IF THERE IS AN INFINITY OF WORLDS NO EMPEROR IS EVER GOING TO BE SATISFIED WITH ONE

Parallel Worlds

A parallel world is another universe situated "alongside" our own, displaced in a fourth dimension of space and normally separated from it. Most stories involve parallel Earths, which are often used as reservoirs of alternative histories. The existence of parallel worlds is taken for granted in folklore, and hence very common in modern fantasy: the Land of Faerie is the most familiar example in oral tradition. The "astral plane" of the occultists is a recent refinement of the old idea that the dead inhabit a parallel world. Early sf stories using the notion include 'The Strange Case Of Davidson's Eyes' (1895) and 'The Plattner Story' (1896) by H. G. Wells.

One of the most common folkloric patterns connected with the notion of parallel worlds involves a human being translocated into a fantasy land where he undergoes adventures and may find the self-fulfilment which evaded him in everyday life. This was modernized by A. Merritt and the other pulp writers who established the basic story-templates of "science

fantasy". Notable examples include *The Blind Spot* (1921) by Austin Hall and Homer Eon Flint, *The Dark World* (1946) and 'The Portal In The Picture' (1949; reprinted as *Beyond Earth's Gates*) by Henry Kuttner and C. L. Moore, the *Keys To The Dimensions* series begun with *Land Beyond The Map* (1961) by Kenneth Bulmer, the *World Of Tiers* sequence begun with *The Maker Of Universes* (1965) by Philip José Farmer and the *Dream Archipelago* stories of Christopher Priest, which include *The Affirmation* (1981). A second common pattern in folklore, in which entities from a parallel world appear as disturbing intrusions, was brought within the margins of sf by William Hope Hodgson in *The Ghost Pirates* (1909) and widely exploited by many writers of horror-sf, including H. P. Lovecraft and other members of his circle.

Writers working more centrally within the sf genre soon began to write tales of invasion, war, espionage, trade and colonization involving parallel worlds. Notable examples include 'The Incredible Invasion' (1936; reprinted as *The Other Side Of Here*) by Murray Leinster, *Ring Around The Sun* (1953) and 'The Big Front Yard' (1958) by Clifford D. Simak, *Worlds Of The Imperium* (1962) by Keith Laumer, *Masters Of The Maze* (1965) by Avram Davidson, *The Jewels Of Elsewhen* (1967) by Ted White, *The Coming Of The Quantum Cats* (1986) by Frederik Pohl and *There Are Doors* (1988) by Gene Wolfe. Sf stories using the notion of parallel worlds for philosophical reflections on the "many worlds" interpretation of quantum-mechanical uncertainties include Brian Aldiss's *Report On Probability A* (1968) and Graham Dunstan Martin's *Time-Slip* (1986).

Writers closer to the hard core of the sf genre have occasionally employed worlds whose physical make-up is different from those applicable to our own continuum; *The Gods Themselves* (1972) by Isaac Asimov and *A Wreath Of Stars* (1976) by Bob Shaw are notable examples. More modest variants in which evolution has worked out differently include Philip K. Dick's *The Crack In Space* (1966) and Stephen R. Boyett's *The Architect Of Sleep* (1986).

Robots & Androids

The word "robot", derived from the Czech word for forced labour, was first used in Karel Capek's play *R.U.R.* (1921). Capek's robots were made from artificial flesh, but the image which popularized the idea was the mechanical robot in Fritz Lang's film *Metropolis* (1926); such entities had featured before in stories like *The Eve Of The Future* (1886) by Villiers de l'Isle Adam. Sf writers usually refer to organic artificial men as androids, although the two terms still overlap, especially in the work of Philip K. Dick.

In J. Storer Clouston's *Button Brains* (1933) a robot is continually mistaken for a human being, setting up a series of jokes which remain the staple diet of dramas featuring robots to this day, as in Alan Ayckbourn's play *Henceforward* (1988). Early pulp sf stories were ambivalent about robots – David H. Keller's 'The Psychophonic Nurse' (1928) is no substitute for a mother's love – but the balance soon shifted towards sympathy and sentimentality. In 'Helen O'Loy' (1938) by Lester del Rey, a man marries the ideal mechanical woman, and 'I, Robot' (1939) by Eando Binder attacks the technophobic "Frankenstein syndrome" which prompted Isaac Asimov to write the apologetic stories collected in *I, Robot* (1950) that incorporated the celebrated "three laws of robotics".

The robot servants who survive mankind in Clifford D. Simak's *City* series (collected 1952) are models of loyalty, but in Jack Williamson's classic 'With Folded Hands' (1947) robots charged "to serve man, to obey, and to guard men from harm" take their mission rather too literally. Sinister robots returned in such tales as 'Second Variety' (1953) by Philip K. Dick, and even Asimov's robots proved capable of murder in *The Naked Sun* (1957). Androids began to play a more prominent role in post-war sf, often seeking emancipation from slavery, as in Clifford Simak's *Time And Again* (1951) and Robert Silverberg's *Tower Of Glass* (1970).

The Silver Eggheads (1961) by Fritz Leiber provided a light-hearted account of robot culture, while *The Soul Of The Robot* (1974) by Barrington J. Bayley was a pioneering exercise in robot

existentialism swiftly supplemented by Asimov's 'That Thou Art Mindful Of Him' (1974); Stanislaw Lem's robotic fables, collected in *The Cyberiad* (1974) and *Mortal Engines* (1977), carry both themes forward. The awkward question of whether one should let one's daughter marry a robot is addressed in Tanith Lee's *The Silver Metal Lover* (1982), and a carefree robot psychopath is featured in John Sladek's *Tik-Tok* (1983).

Philip K. Dick's painstaking attempts to investigate the meaning of humanity through the medium of humanoid machines extends through *Do Androids Dream Of Electric Sheep?* (1968) and *We Can Build You* (1972). The

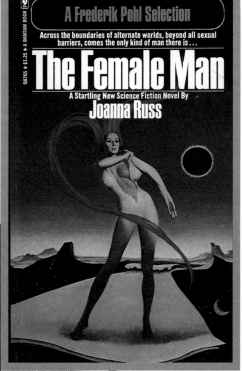

film *Blade Runner* (1982) retains only a pale reflection of the argument contained in the original book, but it probably assisted the marked shift in attitude which took place between *Alien* (1979) and *Aliens* (1986), and helped to establish Mr Spock's android replacement in *Star Trek: The Next Generation* (1987-94). C. J. Cherryh's *Cyteen* (1988) describes a society into which androids are fully integrated.

Sex Wars

Feminists have frequently used sf as an imaginative instrument for the exploration of societies untainted by male domination. Early examples include *Unveiling A Parallel* (1893) by Alice Ilgenfritz Jones and Ella Merchant, and *Herland* (1914) by Charlotte Perkins Gilman. Male writers of the same period were more likely to construct images of female-dominated societies which were mocking but full of foreboding; Walter Besant's *The Revolt Of Man* (1882) now seems much funnier than its author intended, as do many of the tales reprinted in *When Women Rule* (1972) edited by Sam Moskowitz.

The use of sf for serious examination of sexual politics was pioneered by Philip Wylie in *The Disappearance* (1951). It was further developed by John Wyndham in 'Consider Her Ways' (1956) and by Theodore Sturgeon, in several stories leading up to the utopian thought-experiment *Venus Plus X* (1960). It was elevated to a new level of sophistication by Ursula Le Guin in *The Left Hand Of Darkness* (1969). Sexual psychology was explored in a number of graphic tales by Philip José Farmer, including *The Lovers* (1952; expanded 1961) and *Flesh* (1960). The effective end of censorship in the late 1960s prompted a flood of sf erotica, of varying levels of

 (TOP) WORLDS WITHIN WORDS *Joanna Russ's title challenged the casual assumption that the word "mankind" obviously includes women too*

(LEFT) AUTOEROTICISM *If a man's car is a symbolic extension of his sexuality, how does he come to terms with the aftermath of a crash?*

sophistication. Essex House issued a series of pornographic sf books which attracted a critical cult-following, while J. G. Ballard and Samuel R. Delany introduced a more highbrow eroticism into such works as *Crash* (1973) and *Dhalgren* (1975).

The 1970s witnessed a dramatic flowering of feminist sf in the works of such writers as Joanna Russ, most notably *The Female Man* (1975), Suzy McKee Charnas, in the trilogy begun with *Walk To The End Of The World* (1974), and James Tiptree Jr (Alice Sheldon), in such ironic parables as 'The Women Men Don't See' (1973). Significant subsequent additions to this tradition include *Native Tongue* (1984) and its sequels by Suzette Haden Elgin, *The Shore Of Women* (1986) by Pamela Sargent, *The Gate To Women's Country* (1988) by Sheri S. Tepper and *Shadow Man* (1995) by Melissa Scott.

Feminist writers from the literary mainstream who strayed into the genre in this fashion include Marge Piercy, in *Woman On The Edge Of Time* (1976), and Margaret Atwood in *The Handmaid's Tale* (1985). A useful guide to feminist sf is Sarah Lefanu's *In The Chinks Of The World Machine* (1988). Works on similar themes by male writers are understandably half-hearted, but might nevertheless be considered brave; a notable example is David Brin's *Glory Season* (1993). Works extrapolating masculine fantasies, such as Michael Weaver's *Mercedes Nights* (1987) and Richard Calder's *Dead Girls* (1992), inevitably tend towards the lurid.

The advent of AIDS in the 1980s cast a sudden dark shadow over sf images of the near future, most starkly and most straightforwardly displayed in *Journals Of The Plague Years* (1988) by Norman Spinrad. Anthologies of sf with sexual themes – which are also replete with post-AIDS anxieties – include *Alien Sex* (1990) and its sequel *Off Limits* (1996) edited by Ellen Datlow, and *Arrows Of Eros* (1989) edited by Alex Stewart.

The Solar System

The planets of the solar system were frequently used as locations for planetary romances, but there is also a more realistic tradition of sf which anticipated their exploration. Until the Mariner landings in 1976, it was possible to hope that there might be life on Mars, and this possibility was a great inspiration to speculative writers. Percival Lowell's *Mars* (1896) described an arid world irrigated by great canals, and for 80 years sf writers developed this picture unaware that it derived from a series of optical illusions. Advanced civilizations were located there in *Across The*

Zodiac (1880) by Percy Greg, *A Plunge Into Space* (1890) by Robert Cromie and *Two Planets* (1897) by Kurd Lasswitz.

The idea that Mars might be colonized was seriously advanced in *The Sands Of Mars* (1951) by Arthur C. Clarke, *Alien Dust* (1955) by E. C. Tubb and *Martian Time-Slip* (1964) by Philip K. Dick. When the hope of finding life there faded away, a requiem for the dying myth was provided by Ludek Pesek in *The Earth Is Near* (1970). Frederik Pohl's *Man Plus* (1976) is a much grimmer account of the adaptation of a human being for life on an almost airless world. Many recent works have, however, been enthused by the idea of "terraforming" the planet to make it fit for human habitation; these include Kim Stanley Robinson's trilogy that began with *Red Mars* (1992) and Jack Williamson's *Beachhead* (1992).

The space probes of the 1970s also revealed that Venus was not the lush and watery world beloved of writers of planetary romance but a hellish inferno. Even so, a few sf writers have clung to the hope that it, too, might be terraformed and colonized. One such project is sketched out in Pamela Sargent's *Venus Of Dreams* (1986).

Even before the space probes, it seemed highly unlikely that Jupiter could be hospitable to human visitors: such stories as James Blish's 'Bridge' (1952) and Poul Anderson's 'Call Me Joe' (1957) gave way to the more realistic account of a descent into the Jovian atmosphere featured in 'A Meeting With Medusa' (1971) by Arthur C. Clarke. In *2010: Odyssey Two* (1982), Clarke made the bold suggestion that it might be more productive to convert the unterraformable gas-giant into the solar system's second sun.

Mercury rarely features in modern sf, although *The Sirens Of Titan* (1959) by Kurt Vonnegut includes an account of life-forms living beneath its sun-scorched surface. The same novel includes scenes on Saturn's largest moon, and Saturn's satellites are also used as settings in Arthur C. Clarke's *Imperial Earth* (1976) and John Varley's series begun with *Titan* (1979). One of Neptune's moons is the setting of Samuel R. Delany's "ambiguous heterotopia" *Triton* (1976), while Pluto is the setting of Kim Stanley Robinson's *Icehenge* (1984). Colin Greenland's *Take Back Plenty* (1990) and Roger McBride Allen's *The Ring Of Charon* (1990) feature the most recently discovered member of the solar family, Pluto's moon Charon. The hypothetical tenth planet featured in some early sf stories has nowadays been displaced by a diffuse "cometary halo" called the Oort

 A NEW EDEN? *KIM STANLEY ROBINSON'S NOVEL WONDERS WHETHER TERRAFORMING MARS WILL INEVITABLY REPRODUCE ALL THE POLITICAL PROBLEMS OF EARTH*

Cloud; the most notable sf account of it is contained in Jack Williamson's *Lifeburst* (1984).

Space Habitats

The discovery that the planets of the solar system are far less suitable for human habitation than was once hoped has intensified interest in artificial habitats. The notion of setting artificial satellites in orbit already had a long history, extending back as far as 'The Brick Moon' (1863) by Edward Everett Hale and *Outside The Earth* (1920) by Konstantin Tsiolkovsky, but this notion was dramatically expanded by Gerard K. O'Neill in *The High Frontier* (1977), which recommended establishing space colonies at the "Lagrange points" in the moon's orbit.

Space stations became commonplace in 1950s sf after their popularization by Willy Ley in his prospectus for *The Conquest Of Space* (1949); they figured in the radio, film and book versions of Charles Eric Mane's *Spaceways* (1952-3) and were a regular feature in the work of Arthur C. Clarke, notably in his juvenile novel *Islands In The Sky* (1955) and his script for the film *2001: A Space Odyssey* (1968), which provided a definitive visual image in the memorable sequence in which a spaceship comes into dock to the accompaniment of the 'Blue Danube' waltz.

More recent uses of the notion include *Orbital Decay* (1989) and *Clarke County, Space* (1990) by Allen Steele and the linking device of the Canadian TV talk show *Prisoners Of Gravity* (begun 1990). O'Neill colonies and simple variations on that theme are featured in such works as *Lagrange Five* (1979) by Mack Reynolds and its sequels (which were completed by Dean Ing), the series by Joe Haldeman begun with *Worlds* (1981) and *Falling Free* (1988) by Lois McMaster Bujold.

Another ingenious plan for constructing space habitats involves hollowing out asteroids, using material quarried from within to build on the exterior – a notion used by George Zebrowski in *Macrolife* (1979) and by Pamela Sargent in *Earthseed* (1983) and its sequels. *Schismatrix* (1985) by Bruce Sterling and *Vacuum Flowers* (1987) by Michael Swanwick both feature a profusion of space habitats, which must sustain the hopes of the human race following the dereliction of Earth. Artificial space habitats

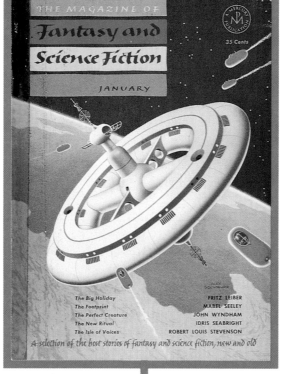

ROOM AT THE TOP *Space stations need to spin around a central axis in order to simulate gravity, so artists had a ready-made model*

offer an attractive option to makers of TV series who wish to confine their shooting to studio sets; recent examples include *Jupiter Moon*, *Babylon 5* and *Star Trek: Deep Space Nine*.

After Freeman Dyson introduced the concept of the "Dyson sphere" in 1960, suggesting that very advanced civilizations would harvest all the light emitted by their suns by building an enclosing sphere with the diameter of a planetary orbit, alien space habitats constructed on a vast scale became a regular feature of sf. The notion is memorably deployed in *The Wanderer* (1964) by Fritz Leiber and ingeniously varied in such works as *Ringworld* (1970) by Larry Niven, *Orbitsville* (1975) by Bob Shaw and *Journey To The Centre* (1982) and its sequels by Brian Stableford. The critic Roz Kaveney dubbed such alien artefacts "Big Dumb Objects" in 1981; other examples are featured in Arthur C. Clarke's *Rendezvous With Rama* (1973), John Varley's *Titan* (1979) and its sequels, Greg Bear's *Eon* (1985) and Charles Sheffield's *Summertide* (1990).

Space Travel

The idea of spaceflight is much older than sf, although early pioneers tended to turn a blind eye to the problems involved in moving outside the Earth's atmosphere. The earliest serious treatment of the theme was *From The Earth To The Moon* (1865) by Jules Verne, who took a dim view of the breezier approach exhibited by H. G. Wells in *The First Men In The Moon* (1901).

Early spacecraft were mostly spherical or bullet-shaped; others bore a suspicious resemblance to flying submarines. Illustrators of the early pulps incorporated wings into the design by analogy with aircraft; streamlined rockets eventually took over, although they faced competition from discoid shapes when the "flying saucer" craze took hold in the late-1940s.

Konstantin Tsiolkovsky, who first had the idea of using rockets to explore space, promoted it in the novel *Outside The Earth* (1920). Otto Willi Gail's *The Shot Into Infinity* (1925) also aimed at technical realism, and Fritz Lang hired Hermann Oberth and Willy Ley to design the rocket used in his film *The Girl In The Moon* (1929); Hitler subsequently suppressed the film when he put the same scientists to work on the V-1 and V-2 rockets in the Second World War.

In the sf pulps, the attempted realism of such stories as Laurence Manning's 'The Voyage Of The Asteroid' (1932) was overshadowed by the joyous excesses of space opera, but a different kind of realism was introduced by Robert A. Heinlein's 'Universe' (1941), which features a "generation starship" moving at much less than light-speed, requiring centuries to complete its journey.

When the German rocket scientists resumed work in the USA after the war, however, genre writers cultivated a new seriousness. Heinlein became an active propagandist for spaceflight in 'The Man Who Sold The Moon' (1950) and his script for George Pal's film *Destination Moon* (1950), and so did Arthur C. Clarke in *Prelude To Space* (1951) and his script for *2001: A Space Odyssey* (1968). Both writers produced near-future fiction for mainstream magazines in the early 1950s and helped inspire such productions as Charles Chilton's radio serial *Journey Into Space* (1953). Another novel celebrating the allure of spaceflight was Fredric Brown's *The Lights In The Sky Are Stars* (1953).

The Apollo missions did not make sf about space travel redundant, but they ushered in a new era of realistic fiction about the psychological problems of astronauts; examples include *Kings Of Infinite Space* (1967) by Nigel Balchin, *The Falling Astronauts* (1971) by Barry Malzberg and *Phases Of Gravity* (1989) by Dan Simmons. The subsequent curtailment of the space programme has called forth a combative response in such works as *Privateers* (1985) by Ben Bova, while sf writers Larry Niven and Jerry Pournelle allegedly played a leading role in persuading Ronald Reagan to finance the Strategic Defence Initiative (alias "Star Wars") in the hope that it might revitalize the space programme.

The idea that spaceships owe their fascination to phallic symbolism is jokingly reflected in 'The Big Space Fuck' (1972) by Kurt Vonnegut and *The Void-Captain's Tale* (1983) by Norman Spinrad. Such conspicuously unphallic but nevertheless charismatic spaceships as Star Trek's *Enterprise* cast some doubt on the thesis.

Supermen & Other Mutants

Modern evolutionary theory holds that all species are subject to random mutations, some of which help organisms to survive while most do not. Sf writers have applied this to the production of various kinds of human variants, but have been most interested in the advantageous mutations which might produce the first specimen of *Homo superior*. An early venture of this kind was J. D. Beresford's *The Hampdenshire Wonder* (1911).

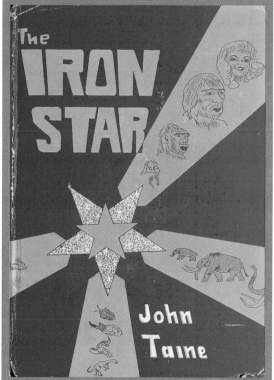

MIRACLES OF MUTATION *EARLY NOVELS ABOUT THE EFFECTS OF RADIATION OFTEN INVOLVED DRAMATIC PROGRESSIVE OR DEVOLUTIONARY METAMORPHOSES*

It was discovered in the 1920s that mutations could be induced by radiation, and this notion was quickly taken up by sf writers. John Taine wrote several extravagant "mutational romances", including *The Iron Star* (1930) and *Seeds Of Life* (1931). Other lurid examples from the sf pulps include 'The Man Who Evolved' (1931) and *The Star Of Life* (1947) by Edmond Hamilton and *The Intelligence Gigantic* (1933) by John Russell Fearn. Many of these stories are unenthusiastic about the prospect of Homo sapiens being rendered obsolete and some early supermen – especially the arrogant ones – came to a sticky end. On the other hand, sf writers have often thought badly enough of their fellows to delight in their redundancy; M. P. Shiel's *The Young Men Are Coming!* (1937) is positively exultant about this prospect and *Slan* (1940) was the first of many works by A. E. van Vogt to be firmly committed to the cause of superhumanity. The advent of the atom bomb in 1945 was a further stimulus to mutational romance. A nuclear accident produced a whole clutch of superchildren in Wilmar H. Shiras's *Children Of The Atom* (1953). More unnaturally precocious children appeared in 'Bettyann' (1951) by Kris Neville, *Childhood's End* (1953) by Arthur C. Clarke and *More Than Human* (1953) by Theodore Sturgeon, and the device extends into more recent times in such works as *The Ugly Swans* (1972) by Arkady and Boris Strugatsky, *Emergence* (1984) by David Palmer, *A Coming Of Age* (1985) by Timothy Zahn and *Brain Child* (1991) by George Turner.

Post-nuclear holocaust stories often feature freakish mutants feared and persecuted by "normal" survivors, but usually accept that new and better species might arise from their ranks; the more interesting ventures of this kind include *The Chrysalids* (1955) by John Wyndham, *Davy* (1964) by Edgar Pangborn, *The Einstein Intersection* (1967) by Samuel R. Delany, *Hiero's Journey* (1973) by Sterling Lanier, *One-Eye* (1973) and its sequels by Stuart Gordon and *Radix* (1981) by A. A. Attanasio.

The cinema's mutational romances have mostly been unrepentantly melodramatic. Early examples include *Them!* (1954), *Tarantula* (1955) and *The Incredible Shrinking Man* (1957); *Mutations* (1973) and *The Giant Spider Invasion* (1975) are poorer recapitulations. Mutations were also widely employed in comic books after 1945 to create a new generation of superheroes (and fanciful adversaries for them to fight); those introduced by Stan Lee's Marvel Comics in the 1960s were very conscious of their freakishness, suffering anxieties which were to be explored in greater depth in the Wild Cards series of "mosaic novels" (begun 1987) edited by George R. R. Martin.

Superweapons & Future Wars

Ever since Leonardo da Vinci wrote a letter to Ludovico Sforza in 1482 advertising his talents as an innovative military engineer, speculators have been fascinated by the possibilities of new weaponry. The French artist Albert Robida offered a highly fanciful account of *War In The Twentieth Century* (1887), and in *The Angel Of The Revolution* (1893) George Griffith took great delight in describing a world war fought by fleets of airships and submarines. X-rays and radioactivity, both of which were discovered in the last years of the 19th century, gave such a tremendous boost to the hypothetical armaments industry that Griffith's last novel, *The Lord Of Labour* (1911), imagined a war fought with atomic missiles and disintegrator rays. A few inventors tried to use their new weapons to put an end to war, but they were always unsuccessful. Bob Shaw's *Ground Zero Man* (1971) fared no better than the anti-heroes of *Empire Of The World* (1910) by C. J. Cutcliffe Hyne and *The Peacemaker* (1934) by C. S. Forester.

World War I instilled a profound horror of war in many British writers, reflected in such bloodcurdling tales as *The People Of The Ruins* (1920) by Edward Shanks, *Tomorrow's Yesterday* (1932) by John Gloag, the trilogy by S. Fowler Wright begun with *Prelude In Prague* (1935) and *The Death Guard* (1939) by Philip George Chadwick.

American writers were less anxious, and the sf pulp writers deployed all manner of superweapons with great enthusiasm until the prospect of nuclear holocaust awakened by Hiroshima gave them pause. Even so, the constitutional right to bear arms has been defended so stridently in the USA as to maintain a powerful fascination with the glamour of weaponry, reflected in such sf stories as A. E. van Vogt's Weapon Shop series, Robert A. Heinlein's *Starship Troopers* (1959) and Gordon R. Dickson's Dorsai series. During the Vietnam War, the politics of militarism were subjected to sceptical analysis in works like *The Forever War* (1974) by Joe Haldeman, but all criticism was stoutly met. The fashionability of militaristic sf enjoyed a spectacular revival in the 1980s, reaching a peculiar extreme in the sub-genre of "survivalist fiction".

A comprehensive survey of sf weaponry was undertaken by David Langford in *War In 2080* (1979) and its spinoff novel *The Space Eater* (1982), but it quickly went out of date when the Strategic Defence Initiative – which

Langford thought impractical on economic grounds – received Ronald Reagan's blessing. The anxious legacy of Vietnam continues to make itself felt in such works as *In The Field Of Fire* (1987) edited by Jean Van Buren Dann and Jack Dann, *The Healer's War* (1988) by Elizabeth Scarborough and *Dream Baby* (1989) by Bruce McAllister, but it is counterbalanced by such anthology series as *There Will Be War* (begun 1983) edited by Jerry Pournelle and John F. Carr and *The Man-Kzin Wars* (begun 1988), based on an episode in Larry Niven's *Known Space* series. *War Stars: The Superweapon And The American Imagination* (1988) by H. Bruce Franklin is an excellent survey of this remarkable fascination.

Suspended Animation

Before H. G. Wells invented the time machine, the only way to get to the distant future was to sleep for a long time. This method was employed in L. S. Mercier's *Memoirs Of The Year Two Thousand Five Hundred* (1771), Mary Griffith's *Three Hundred Years Hence* (1836) and Edward Bellamy's *Looking Backward* (1888), and Wells reverted to it himself in *When The Sleeper Wakes* (1899). Modern applications of the theme include *Genus Homo* (1941) by L. Sprague de Camp and P. Schuyler Miller, Woody Allen's film *Sleeper* (1973), Mack Reynolds's Bellamyesque *Looking Backward From The Year 2000* (1973) and the film *Forever Young* (1992).

Visitors from the distant past were often preserved by similar means in early sf stories, sometimes by some extrapolation of the ancient Egyptian practice of mummification, as in Edgar Lee's *Pharaoh's Daughter* (1889) and sometimes by refrigeration, as in W. Clark Russell's *The Frozen Pirate* (1887). Grant Allen's 'Pausodyne' (1881) and Frank Barrett's *The Justification Of Andrew Lebrun* (1894) gave the idea a better scientific gloss by invoking the notion of protracted anaesthesia, while E. Nesbit's *Dormant* (1911) invokes a perverse elixir of life. Visitors from more remote eras are featured in *Out Of The Silence* (1919) by Erle Cox and 'The Resurrection Of Jimber Jaw' (1937) by Edgar Rice Burroughs. More recent arrivals include TV's *Adam Adamant* (1966-7) and the gladiator in Richard Ben Sapir's *The Far Arena* (1978).

In *The Man Who Awoke* (1933), Laurence Manning's hero used a series of long sleeps to observe the future history of humankind. Pulp sf writers also found it useful in avoiding the long time-lags involved in sub-light-speed journeys to the stars, although the travellers in A. E. van Vogt's 'Far Centaurus' (1944) awake to find that

 SOUND ASLEEP *BEAUTY QUEENS WHO WERE PUT INTO SUSPENDED ANIMATION FOR HUNDREDS OR THOUSANDS OF YEARS NATURALLY WORE THEIR BATHING SUITS*

progress has overtaken them. Some later stories, including *The Dream Millennium* (1974) by James White and 'I Hope I Shall Arrive Soon' (1980) by Philip K. Dick, allow such travellers to pass the time in dreams. The device is cleverly used to organize the awkward transitions between the film *Alien* (1979) and its sequels.

In 1966, R. C. W. Ettinger's *The Prospect Of Immortality* popularized the idea that preserving recently-dead bodies in "cryonic suspension" might allow their eventual resurrection, inspiring such ironic sf stories as *The Age Of The Pussyfoot* (1969) by Frederik Pohl, *Why Call Them Back From Heaven* (1967) by Clifford D. Simak and 'The Defenseless Dead' (1973) by Larry Niven. The popularization of the term "corpsicle" testifies to a certain cynicism among sf writers, although the cryonic societies founded in the wake of Ettinger's book have their enthusiastic supporters, including nanotechnology guru K. Eric Drexler.

Alternative methods of suspended animation inspired by animal hibernation are featured in the series collected in *Hot Sleep* (1979; revised as *The Worthing Saga*, 1990) by Orson Scott Card and *Between The Strokes Of Night* (1985) by Charles Sheffield. The latter story takes the notion to its futuristic extreme, as do Richard Lupoff's *Sun's End* (1984) and *Galaxy's End* (1988).

Teleportation & Matter Transmission

Teleportation was originally synonymous with psychokinesis – the ability to move objects by will power – but later came to be restricted to the power of moving oneself from place to place without passing through the intervening space. Matter transmitters are technological devices which perform the same services breaking objects or people down into some kind of broadcastable signal – a rather implausible notion but one which can be very useful. *Star Trek*'s "transporter" moves people from the *Enterprise* to other locations with a minimum of fuss and offers such a convenient means of release from tight situations that "Beam me up, Scottie" has become a widely-used catchphrase. *Star Trek* has also made some use of the horrific possibilities associated with disrupted transmissions, although the definitive works of that kind are the two film versions of George Langelaan's 'The Fly' (1957), made in 1958 and 1989.

Space travel by matter transmitter was pioneered by Fred T. Jane in *To Venus In Five Seconds* (1987) and was subsequently used by Ralph Milne Farley in *The Radio Man* (1924) and Clifford D. Simak in *Way Station* (1963). The practicality of the method varies, being far less convenient when a receiver is required as well as a transmitter – an issue addressed in Eric Brown's *Meridian Days* (1992). Norman Matson's *Doctor Fogg* (1929) features an unexpected arrival from elsewhere in the universe. More sophisticated versions of the *Star Trek* transporter can be found in Poul Anderson's *The Enemy Stars* (1959), Harry Harrison's *One Step From Earth* (1970), Joe Haldeman's *Mindbridge* (1976) and David Langford's *The Space Eater* (1982).

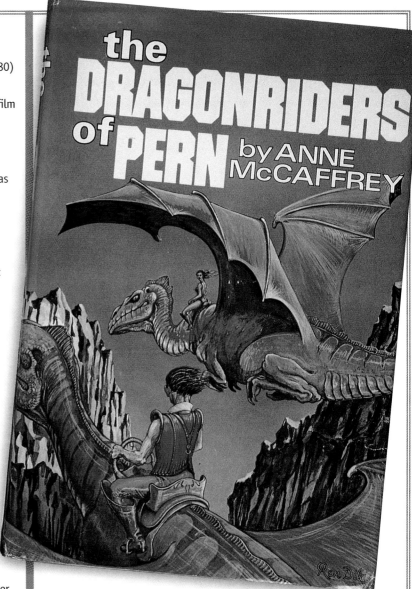

DRAGONFLIGHT *Heavy creatures cannot easily fly by wingpower alone, so natural selection gave the dragons of Pern the power of teleportation*

The dramatic social transformations which matter transmitters would permit are investigated in stories by Larry Niven, John Brunner and Jack Vance in *Three Trips In Time and Space* (1973) edited by Robert Silverberg; Brunner offered further extrapolations in *Web Of Everywhere* (1974) and *The Infinitive Of Go* (1980) and Niven also wrote other stories set in the same world as 'Flash Crowd'. Future societies transformed by teleportation are described in Alfred Bester's *The Stars My Destination* (1956) and Gordon R. Dickson's *Time To Teleport* (1960); more recent tales of teleportation include some works in Anne McCaffrey's *Pern* series which feature teleporting dragons, *The Witling* (1976) by Vernor Vinge, *Knight Moves* (1985) by Walter John Williams and *Jumper* (1992) by Steven Gould.

Some sf stories argue that matter transmitters ought, in theory, also to function as matter duplicators on the grounds that once an object is reduced to a signal it can presumably be copied with relative ease. Spare copies of a man transmitted into a dangerous alien artefact are prudently kept in reserve in Algis Budrys's *Rogue Moon* (1960). The copies accidentally made in Thomas M. Disch's *Echo Round His Bones* (1967) are invisible phantoms. Captain Kirk is split into a Jekyll-and-Hyde pair in the *Star Trek* episode 'The Enemy Within' (1969). The doorways to other worlds and "star gates" widely featured in sf adventure stories are sometimes supposed to work by matter transmission, although they can also be "explained" as short cuts through other spatial dimensions.

Transcendence

In the final act of *Back To Methuselah* (1921), George Bernard Shaw suggests that the climax of human evolution might be a release from the prison of matter to a purified state in which mind no longer needs the support of vulgar flesh. The idea echoes religious notions of the afterlife which had been more straightforwardly fused with the scientific imagination in Camille Flammarion's *Lumen* (1872). The notion was not uncommon in early pulp sf, although reference was more frequently made to entities of "pure thought" or "pure energy" than to "spirits" or "souls". It can be found in "Doc" Smith's Skylark series but is presented more dramatically in 'Metamorphosite' (1946) by Eric Frank Russell.

The dramatic collective transcendence which happens at the end of *Childhood's End* (1953) by Arthur C. Clarke struck a chord with the posthumously-published writings of the French Jesuit Pierre Teilhard de Chardin, whose attempt to fuse evolutionary theory with Catholic dogma prompted him to imagine that the "noöspheres" – spheres of thought – of habitable worlds would eventually be able to soar free to become one with the mind of God at the Omega Point of universal history. Similar ideas can be found in many other sf stories of the 1950s, when there was a glut of works transfiguring traditional religious imagery. Notable examples include Theodore Sturgeon's *More Than Human* (1953), Charles L. Harness's 'The Rose' (1953), Philip José Farmer's 'The God Business' (1954) and *Night Of Light* (1966) and Brian W. Aldiss's *Galaxies Like Grains Of Sand* (1959).

More recent works in this vein often follow Clarke's example in using alien beings as "midwives" of transcendence; alien religions often turn out to have a better literal grounding than ours. Notable examples include *Nightwings* (1969) and *Downward To The Earth* (1970) by Robert Silverberg, *A Choice Of Gods* (1972) by Clifford Simak, 'A Song For Lya' (1974) by George R. R. Martin, *If The Stars Are Gods* (1977) by Gregory Benford and Gordon Eklund and *God's World* (1979) and *The Gardens Of Delight* (1980) by Ian Watson. *The Omega Point Trilogy* (1983) by George Zebrowski explicitly evokes Teilhard de Chardin, while *Firechild* (1986) by Jack Williamson contrasts several different attitudes to the product of a miracle of genetic engineering.

Whenever sf writers attempt to look into the very distant future or to imagine alien entities far more "advanced" than ourselves, they have few ideas to draw on except those which echo religious images of God and His angels. Such imagery inevitably resonates even in the "hardest" works of sf; recent examples can be found in *The Singers Of Time* (1991) by Jack Williamson and Frederik Pohl, *Eternal Light* (1991) by Paul J. McAuley and the later volumes of Gregory Benford's series concluded by *Sailing Bright Eternity* (1995).

Conventional images of transcendence are treated with more suspicion – and thus developed far more ironically – by Thomas M. Disch in *Camp Concentration* (1968) and *On Wings Of Song* (1979), but they retain their powerful fascination even in these stories.

 FAREWELL TO THE FLESH *JACK WILLIAMSON'S GENETICALLY-ENGINEERED SUPERPERSON ENJOYS A CLIMACTIC ESCAPE FROM THE PRISON OF VULGAR MATTER*

Under the Surface

Not all sf is concerned with the conquest of outer space. When Jules Verne published *Twenty Thousand Leagues Under The Sea* (1870), the ocean depths were just as mysterious as the surface of the moon and his earlier *Journey To The Centre Of The Earth* (1864) remained the most adventurous of all his works. Subsequent tales of submarine exploration often recapitulated Captain Nemo's encounter with a giant octopus and found more substantial relics of Atlantis; examples include *The Crystal City Under The Sea* (1895) by André Laurie, *The Sunken World* (1928) by Stanton A. Coblentz, *The Maracot Deep* (1929) by Arthur Conan Doyle and *They Found Atlantis* (1936) by Dennis Wheatley.

From the earliest years of silent movies to the Disney version of 1954, film-makers persisted in attempting bigger and better versions of *Twenty Thousand Leagues Under The Sea*, while the development of more sophisticated apparatus for underwater photography gradually dispelled the mystery which had cloaked the ocean depths in Verne's day. The tradition continued in *Voyage To The Bottom Of The Sea* (1961) and its spin-off TV series (1964-68), *The Abyss* (1989), the TV series *SeaQuest DSV* (1994) and *Waterworld* (1995).

A notable pulp sf story about the engineering of humanoid "tritons" for underwater life is 'Crisis In Utopia' (1940) by Norman L. Knight – a notion which Knight picked up again in collaboration with James Blish in *A Torrent Of Faces* (1967) – but subterranean "hidden worlds" were more widely encountered. "Hollow earth" novels such as Edgar Rice Burroughs's *Pellucidar* series, begun with *At The Earth's Core* (1914), tested plausibility to the limit, as did the long-running *Shaver Mystery* series by Richard S. Shaver and others which masqueraded as actual revelations of the perils lurking below. *Hidden World* (1935) by Stanton A. Coblentz is less earnest but more sensible. Rudy Rucker's *The Hollow Earth* (1990) is a brilliant modern attempt to overcome the logical objections to Burroughs's scenario.

Undersea settings became popular in the 1950s, featuring in *The Deep Range* (1957) by Arthur C. Clarke and the trilogy begun with *Undersea Quest* (1954) by Frederik Pohl and Jack Williamson (who returned to the theme of underwater colonization much later in *Land's End*, 1988). Other stories in which men are modified for underwater life include *City Under The Sea* (1957) and *Beyond The Silver Sky* (1961) by Kenneth Bulmer, *The Space Swimmers* (1963) by Gordon R. Dickson and *Ocean On Top* (1967) by Hal Clement. *The Godwhale* (1974) in the novel by Thomas J. Bass is a cyborgized whale. Many stories of this kind involve

communication between humans and dolphins, an idea more elaborately developed in *The Jonah Kit* (1975) by Ian Watson, *A Deeper Sea* (1992) by Alexander Jablokov and *Into The Deep* (1995) by Ken Grimwood. In David Brin's *Startide Rising* (1983), a dolphin-commanded starship takes refuge in an alien ocean.

Analogies may easily be drawn between life in sealed environments beneath the ocean and similar enclaves in space or on the moon, as in *The Watch Below* (1966) by James White, 'Waterclap' (1970) by Isaac Asimov and *Half The Day Is Night* (1994) by Maureen F. McHugh.

THIS ISN'T COVENTRY! *THE COVER ACTUALLY ILLUSTRATES A NORMAN L. KNIGHT STORY ABOUT HUMANS GENETICALLY ENGINEERED FOR LIFE IN THE OCEAN DEPTHS*

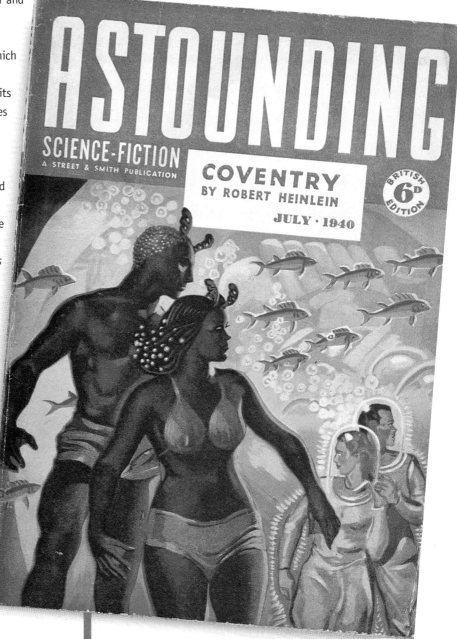

movements, trends and buzzwords

SF HAS INEVITABLY GIVEN RISE TO ITS OWN SPECIALIST JARGON; THESE ARE THE TERMS WHICH YOU HAVE TO KNOW TO BLUFF YOUR WAY INTO FANDOM. RULE ONE IS: NEVER CALL IT SCI-FI.

Cyberpunk

A movement in sf whose two exemplary foundation-stones are William Gibson's novel *Neuromancer* (1984) and Bruce Sterling's *Mirrorshades: The Cyberpunk Anthology* (1986). The notions central to the sub-genre are the development of a vast but messy worldwide computer network – whose external hardware and internal "cyberspace" combine to provide a new frontier for all kinds of sharp operators – and the gradual cyborgization of the people who interact most intimately with that network.

Gibson's pioneering short fiction in the sub-genre, begun with 'Johnny Mnemonic' (1981), was collected in *Burning Chrome* (1986), while Sterling's personal contributions include the stories in *Crystal Express* (1989) and the grim novel *Islands In The Net* (1988).

Other writers whose work is central to the cyberpunk movement include Rudy Rucker, especially the series begun with *Software* (1982), and Pat Cadigan, whose best cyberpunk novel is *Synners* (1989). Michael Swanwick's *Vacuum Flowers* (1987), Richard Kadrey's *Metrophage* (1988) and Neal Stephenson's *Snow Crash* (1992) are other individual works of significance.

Although the movement was welcomed by postmodernist critics such as Larry McCafferty, editor of *Storming The Reality Studio: A Casebook Of Cyberpunk And Postmodernist Science Fiction* (1992), the huge success of *Neuromancer* had less to do with its literary worth than with the fact that it provided an emergent generation of computer freaks with a ready-made mythology. There are many young people in the world who ardently desire to *be* cyberpunks; they regard the rapidly-expanding and fundamentally anarchic Internet as their natural environment and they have adopted such publications as *Mondo 2000* as their holy writ. As a literary movement, cyberpunk may already be slightly passé but as a set of romantic ideologies it has some way yet to go.

Golden Age

An old joke alleges that the Golden Age of sf is 13, that being the age at which most people start reading it and are struck with all the force of revelation by its awesome cosmic perspectives. Actually, sf's basic vocabulary of ideas is so thoroughly built into comic books and animated films that today's young people are completely familiar with it long before they reach such an advanced age – which is one reason nostalgic old-time readers feel a particular fondness for the sf of the 1930s and 1940s, when it was all so fabulously new and innocent.

If there is any substantial consensus at all among fond rememberers of a Golden Age of sf, it relates to the years when John W. Campbell Jr first assumed control of Astounding Stories and began to steer it away from the clichéd materials of conventional pulp adventure fiction. Between 1938 and 1942, he and a stable of writers that included Robert A. Heinlein, Clifford D. Simak, "Doc" Smith, Isaac Asimov, L. Sprague de Camp, A. E.

 (ABOVE) **PIRATES IN CYBERSPACE** *BRUCE STERLING'S NOVEL FEATURES "DATA HAVENS" WHOSE INHABITANTS FLOUT THE LAWS OF INTELLECTUAL PROPERTY*

(LEFT) **PHOTOSINTHESIS** *PAT CADIGAN'S SYNNERS PLUCK EXCITING IMAGES FROM THE BRAINS OF PERFORMERS AND WEAVE THEM INTO MARKETABLE PACKAGES*

van Vogt, Jack Williamson and Lester del Rey laid the foundations of the modern genre. Campbell contrived to ride out the inconvenience of America's involvement in World War II with the aid of Henry Kuttner and C. L. Moore's many pseudonyms, and continued the good work after 1945 by obtaining important new work from Theodore Sturgeon and James Blish before handing on the torch of progress to the satirists of Galaxy.

Although the way had been prepared by some of the writers who worked for Hugo Gernsback – notably Stanley G. Weinbaum and John Taine – and Campbell inherited such writers as Smith and Williamson from his predecessors, it was Campbell who equipped pulp sf with a proud ethic of responsibility concerning the limits of scientific possibility, while refusing to surrender its vaulting ambition and its imaginative exuberance.

Hard SF

A term coined by P. Schuyler Miller in the late 1950s, when it became necessary to distinguish what he considered to be real sf – which attempted to respect the limits of scientific possibility while mapping possible courses of technological discovery – from newly-fashionable work which used science-fictional motifs for all kinds of other literary purposes.

The critical success of Ray Bradbury's *The Martian Chronicles* (1950) offended the genre's purists but clearly demonstrated that writers in search of a wide audience had to beware of overloading readers, whose knowledge of scientific terminology and understanding of scientific argument might be negligible. The flagship of hard sf, the magazine *Analog*, increasingly came to be regarded as an esoteric publication read almost exclusively by professional scientists.

The archetypal hard sf writer is Hal Clement, whose expertise in designing ecospheres adapted to extraordinary physical environments is unequalled. The task of discovering exciting plots to place within such settings, however, tests any writer's ingenuity to the limit – a difficulty inherited by Larry Niven, Robert L. Forward and others who have followed most determinedly in Clement's footsteps. Arthur C. Clarke, Poul Anderson and Gregory Benford are among the most prolific and most accomplished writers of hard sf, counterbalancing the hard science component of their stories with a careful lyricism which encapsulates the science-fictional "sense of wonder". Charles Sheffield and Greg Bear have

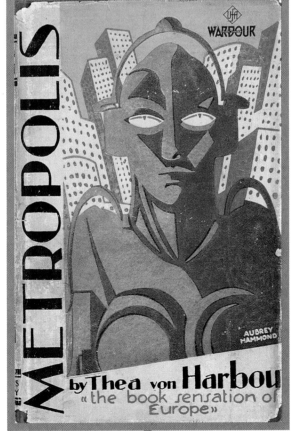

contrived a similar combination in some of their works, although their output ranges over a wider spectrum. Recent recruits to the hard sf fold who have made significant contributions to the tradition include David Brin, Allen Steele and Michael Flynn.

Film Novelizations

The earliest sf films to be "novelized" belonged to a series featuring Arthur B. Reeve's "scientific detective" Craig Kennedy, which began with *The Exploits Of Elaine* (1915). The Reader's Library was a prolific publisher of film novelizations, by far the most significant sf examples being *Metropolis* (1926) and *The Girl In The Moon* (1929) by scriptwriter Thea von Harbou (wife of director Fritz Lang), Delos W. Lovelace's *King Kong* (1932) and *The Bride Of Frankenstein* (1936) by "Michael Egremont". H. G. Wells published several books related to his work for the cinema, though none was a novelization in the strict sense.

Robert A. Heinlein did a prose version of his script for *Destination Moon* (1950), but it was not issued as a book; the first novelization by a famous sf writer was Theodore Sturgeon's *Voyage To The Bottom Of The Sea* (1961). Charles Eric Maine adapted his scripts for *Spaceways* (1953) and *The Isotope Man* (1957), and "W. J. Stuart" did a book version of *Forbidden Planet* (1956). Peter George's *Dr Strangelove* (1963) and A. V. Sellwood's *Children Of The Damned* (1964) were both "re-novelizations" of films based on books.

By 1966, when Isaac Asimov novelized *Fantastic Voyage*, books-of-films had become big business. Arthur Clarke's *2001: A Space Odyssey* (1968) broke new ground, the story being carried forward in further novels. Ben Bova converted George Lucas's *THX 1138* (1971), while David Gerrold and John Jakes did books in the *Planet Of The Ape*s series. The first of Alan Dean Foster's many works in this vein was *Dark Star* (1974); he built his career on such work, although his version of *Star Wars* (1976) was credited to the director. Since 1980, almost all notable movies have been routinely novelized and movie series like *Star Wars* have borrowed inspiration from TV in spawning series of spin-off novels.

 GLORIOUS TECHNICOLOR *The novelization of Fritz Lang's Modernist masterpiece was equipped with a suitably impressionistic cover*

Inner Space

In his essay 'They Came From Inner Space' (1954), J. B. Priestley criticized sf writers for exploring "the other side of the sun" when they would do better to examine "the hidden life of the psyche". In fact, journeys into the depths of the mind were not uncommon in sf and writers such as Theodore Sturgeon and Philip José Farmer had already integrated such explorations into the principal threads of their work. Philip K. Dick was soon to follow suit, and J. G. Ballard wrote an essay of his own in 1962, declaring that the time for a comprehensive exploration of inner space had come. This became a central document of the British "New Wave".

Ballard has been one of the sf writers most intensely interested in inner space, displaying that fascination in many fine short stories as well as his surreal and curiously clinical disaster novels. The American writer with the keenest interest in such matters is Barry N. Malzberg, who worked at such a level of intensity during the 1970s that he burnt himself out, although he returned periodically with such novels as *Cross Of Fire* (1982) and *The Remaking Of Sigmund Freud* (1985), in which the father of psychotherapy proves no better able to cope with science-fictional problems than anyone else.

Writers who have added most significantly to sf's explorations of inner space in recent years include James Morrow, in *The Wine Of Violence* (1981) and *The Continent Of Lies* (1984); Connie Willis, in *Lincoln's Dreams* (1987), and Greg Bear, in *Queen Of Angels* (1990).

Lost Races

A lost-race story involves explorers in distant regions stumbling upon an exotic society which has long been isolated from the rest of humankind. Most such tales are straightforward adventure stories or fantasies, but early sf stories which used the framework include *The Coming Race* (1871) by Lord Lytton and *Erewhon* (1872) by Samuel Butler. Arthur Conan Doyle provided a significant exemplar in *The Lost World* (1912) and H. Rider Haggard, Edgar Rice Burroughs, A. Merritt, E. Charles Vivian and S. Fowler Wright used the form in works of sf relevance. John Taine, A. Hyatt Verrill and Stanton A. Coblentz imported it to the sf pulps, but, as the progress of exploration gradually stripped the mystery from the world's last trackless wildernesses, it fell out of favour.

The last significant examples of the earthbound lost-race story include *The Winter People* (1963) by Gilbert Phelps and *The People Beyond The Walls* (1980) by Stephen Tall. Sf writers have, however, developed their own variant in the "lost colony" story, in which spacefarers in a galaxy-wide civilization stumble across long-isolated worlds where society has developed in an eccentric fashion. Classic examples include *Search The Sky* (1954) by Frederik Pohl and C. M. Kornbluth, *Virgin Planet* (1959) by Poul

Anderson, *The Left Hand Of Darkness* (1969) by Ursula Le Guin and *Courtship Rite* (1982) by Donald Kingsbury.

Military SF

Although the history of future war stories stretches back to the 19th century and L. Ron Hubbard provided a key precursor in *Final Blackout* (1940), the tradition of modern military sf sprang from two works published in 1959: Robert A. Heinlein's *Starship Troopers* and Gordon R. Dickson's magazine serial 'Dorsai!', initially reprinted as *The Genetic General*. Dickson continued to add to the Dorsai series for 30 years, during which time many other US writers began to write futuristic sf glorifying the ideals of military service and the vital parts which highly-organized and well-disciplined spaceborne armies might have to play in the salvation of the earth or the conquest of the galaxy.

It is perhaps appropriate that such a tradition should be carried forward with a good deal of posturing, a certain defiant aggression and a strong dose of hard-bitten cynicism – qualities displayed in no uncertain terms by Jerry Pournelle in such solo novels as *West Of Honor* (1976) and *The Mercenary* (1977) and in his first collaboration with Larry Niven, *The Mote In God's Eye* (1974). The tradition was parodied by Harry Harrison, subverted by Norman Spinrad and earnestly questioned by Joe Haldeman, but it marched on regardless, reaching new extremes in such works as *The Steel, The Mist And The Blazing Sun* (1983) by Christopher Anvil. Notable series of military sf stories include those begun by David Drake's *Hammer's Slammers* (1979), David Weber's *On Basilisk Station* (1993) and David Feintuch's *Midshipman's Hope* (1994). Lois McMaster Bujold's multi-award-winning Miles Vorkosigan series is unusually light-hearted.

New Wave

This is a term borrowed from film criticism in the early 1960s to describe the experimental fiction which was promoted in the magazine *New Worlds* after Michael Moorcock became its editor. The critic Judith Merril helped to popularize the term, particularly in application to the current sf of J. G. Ballard, Brian W. Aldiss and Moorcock himself. US writers who published in *New Worlds*, like Thomas M. Disch, John Sladek and Samuel R. Delany, were readily assimilated to the supposed movement, but Harlan Ellison pioneered an American New Wave with the anthology *Dangerous Visions* (1967), which set out to smash the taboos by means of which magazine editors had allegedly kept adult themes and adult methods out of sf. Younger writers associated with the new wave – by readers and critics if not always by their own choice – included M. John Harrison, Charles Platt, Christopher Priest and Josephine Saxton.

By the early 1970s, the new wave had effectively broken; many of the stylistic experiments it pioneered had been fully domesticated, although a defiant "old guard" of long-time sf fans continued to rail against such presumed sins as pessimism, pretentiousness and plotlessness. Writers like Barry N. Malzberg, Joanna Russ and James Tiptree Jr carried forward many of the themes and literary mannerisms of the New Wave, while long-established writers like Robert Silverberg, John Brunner and Frederik Pohl found that they were able to develop their work in ways that would not have been welcome in an earlier period.

Science Fantasy

A good deal of sf is really fantasy lightly disguised by "scientific" jargon. For many years, while fantasy hardly existed as a commercial genre, writers of exotic adventure stories would reinterpret magic as "alien superscience" or as emergent "psi-powers" in order to assimilate their work to the sf marketplace – a task made easy by virtue of the fact that so-called psi-powers really are the traditional array of magical powers redefined in pseudo-scientific terms.

No. 29 VOLUME 10 2/-

★ EARTH IS BUT A STAR by JOHN BRUNNER ★

Key examples provided by A. Merritt were widely imitated in sf, to the extent that *The Dark World* (1946) by Henry Kuttner and C. L. Moore, which is a virtual copy of Merritt's *Dwellers In The Mirage* (1932), was itself reproduced in almost slavish detail by Marion Zimmer Bradley in *Falcons Of Narabedla* (1957). A favourite ploy of sf writers is the adaptation of ancient myths to a futuristic setting – there are numerous sf adaptations of *The Odyssey* – and images of the far future very often suppose that Earth's decadence will be accompanied by a return of magic, or of what seems to be magic.

Arthur Clarke's dictum that "any sufficiently advanced technology is indistinguishable from magic" is widely quoted in justification of carefree adventures in science fantasy, although its accuracy depends on the meaning of the word "indistinguishable". (An observer who is unable to distinguish between a skilled conjuror and an authentic magician may nevertheless feel that there is a real difference, which might become evident on further analysis.) The fact that sf and fantasy are filed on the same shelves in most bookshops demonstrates, however, that the genres appeal to many of the same readers for much the same reasons. The importation into fantasy of the scepticism and fondness for extrapolation typical of sf – spectacularly evident during the short-lived career of the pulp magazine *Unknown* (1939-42) – has made a significant contribution to the enterprise and liveliness of the genre, while the fascination with the exotic which modern sf inherited from such forebears as Merritt and Clark Ashton Smith adds an element of vivid colour and lyrical romance, which is useful as well as endearing.

Sequels By Other Hands

Readers have always found some story series compelling enough to create a demand for their continuation after their originating authors have finished with them. Such projects have often been inhibited by problems with copyright, but as the publishing industry has become increasingly interested in sequels and series solutions to such problems have usually been found. The most spectacular careers extending after the deaths of their creators have been enjoyed by non-sf heroes such as Sherlock Holmes and Conan the Barbarian (although many modern Holmes stories pit the "great detective" against more fantastic adversaries than Conan Doyle ever did). Sequels by other hands need to be distinguished from "shared worlds", although many shared worlds developed from works not designed for that purpose.

The first relevant sf work was probably Jules Verne's *An Antarctic Mystery* (1897), a sequel to Edgar Allan Poe's *Narrative Of Arthur Gordon Pym* (1837). The sf writer whose career has

 PALM BEACH *JOHN BRUNNER TOOK HIS TITLE FROM JAMES ELROY FLECKER'S CELEBRATION OF THE EXOTIC,* THE GOLDEN JOURNEY TO SAMARKAND

been most extensively carried forward by other writers is E. E. "Doc" Smith, whose Lensman series was augmented by William B. Ellern and David A. Kyle, while Stephen Goldin developed the Family D'Alembert series. Various writers have written sequels to H. G. Wells's *The Time Machine* (1895), the most important being *The Man Who Loved Morlocks* (1981) by David Lake and *The Time Ships* (1995) by Stephen Baxter. Gregory Benford's *Beyond The Fall of Night* (1990) is a sequel to Arthur Clarke's *Against The Fall Of Night* (1948). Now that Isaac Asimov is dead, his Foundation series will be continued by others.

Shared Worlds

Fletcher Pratt's anthology *The Petrified Planet* (1952) contained stories by three different writers set on the same alien world – a type of enterprise repeated in *A World Called Cleopatra* (1977) edited by Roger Elwood and *Medea: Harlan's World* (1985) edited by Harlan Ellison. By then, the series of novels set in the *Star Trek* universe and the successful fantasy anthology series set on *Thieves' World* (begun 1979) had created precedents which opened the floodgates to a torrent of similar enterprises. Michael Moorcock had already encouraged others to produce stories featuring Jerry Cornelius, but several other existing scenarios were opened up for collaborative use in the 1980s, including Marion Zimmer Bradley's *Darkover* and Fred Saberhagen's *Berserker* stories.

Publishers soon began to package whole series set in such milieux as "Isaac Asimov's Robot City", "Arthur C. Clarke's Venus Prime" and "Larry Niven's The Man-Kzin Wars". Original settings were custom-designed for such series as *Wild Cards* (begun 1987), supervised by George R. R. Martin, and *War World* (begun 1988), supervised by Jerry Pournelle. Many shared-world series are tied into games in much the same way that *Star Trek* books are tied to the TV series; the spectacular success of novels based on Dungeons and Dragons inspired such sf variants as the *Battletech* series (begun 1991).

Fiction of this kind is frequently condemned on the grounds that the "bible", which defines the shared world, places a straitjacket on an author's creativity, but it is a kind of enterprise which many writers find interesting and enjoyable.

Steampunk

The term was coined by mocking analogy with "cyberpunk" to refer to stories which export the anarchic spirit of cyberpunk to alternative pasts,

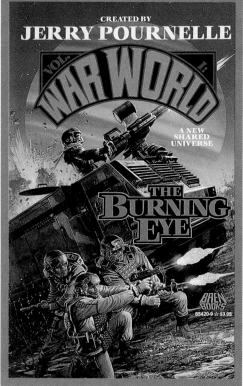

CREATED BY JERRY POURNELLE
WAR WORLD
A NEW SHARED UNIVERSE
THE BURNING EYE
BAEN BOOKS
65420-9 ☆ $3.95

where historical and fictional characters engage in adventures far wilder than any that could have been envisaged in their own day. All this is usually steeped in a thoroughly modern irony. The vogue was initiated by Stephen Utley and Howard Waldrop's 'Custer's Last Jump' (1976) and 'Black As The Pit, From Pole To Pole' (1977) and K. W. Jeter's *Morlock Night* (1979), although they might well have borrowed some inspiration from Michael Moorcock's *The Warlord Of The Air* (1971) and its sequels, and from Harry Harrison's *Tunnel Through The Deeps* (1972).

Howard Waldrop's subsequent adventures in steampunk include '...The World, As We Know't' (1982), 'The Night Of The Cooters' (1987) and

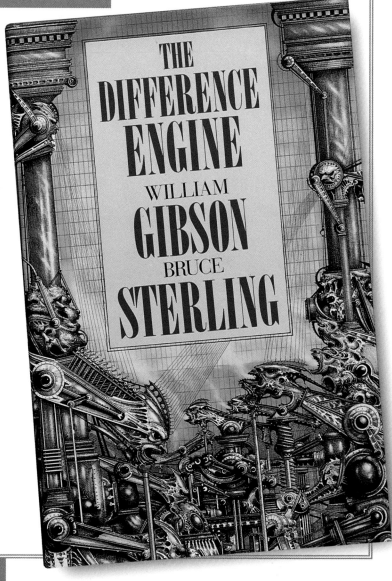

THE DIFFERENCE ENGINE
WILLIAM GIBSON
BRUCE STERLING

Technothrillers

Stories belonging to the thriller genre, including spy stories, require a steady supply of what Alfred Hitchcock called "McGuffins": mysterious objects or documents whose function is to lure or draw the characters through the chases of the plot. When the McGuffins are plans for new weapons or new gadgets, such stories enter the margins of the sf genre, although the settings are contemporary. Early examples were set by writers like Edgar Wallace and Sax Rohmer but it was the fevered plots of Ian Fleming's later James Bond novels – further exaggerated in the film versions – which brought the sub-genre to maturity.

TV made a crucial contribution to the evolution of the technothriller in *The Man From U.N.C.L.E.* (1964-8) and the later series of *The Avengers* (1965-9), taking full advantage of the opportunity to set wildly imaginative plots in ordinary locations. These paved the way for more technically sophisticated series like *The Six Million Dollar Man* (1973-8).

Notable cinema technothrillers include *Coma* (1978), *Firefox* (1982) and *War Games* (1983). As the 1980s progressed, the development of cinematic special effects made the restraint of the technothriller unnecessary; even TV was able to indulge in the more wholeheartedly science-fictional extravagances of *The X-Files* and *RoboCop*.

TV & Radio Spin-offs

The earliest sf books which owed their origin to radio were Charles Chilton's novelizations of his *Journey Into Space* serials (1953-4), but there are very few other examples save for the spectacular multi-media spin-off from Douglas Adams's *Hitch Hiker's Guide To The Galaxy* (1978-80).

TV has, of course, been a much more prolific source of spun-off books, the most successful series of the 1960s and 1970s being accompanied by at least a couple of books. Nigel Kneale's scripts for the *Quatermass* serials were reprinted in 1959-60. Murray Leinster wrote books based on three TV series, *Men Into Space* (1960), *The Time Tunnel* (1967) and *Land Of The Giants* (1968). The more interesting spin-off books include three by various hands based on *The Prisoner*, published in 1969-70, and adaptations by the original authors of scripts for *A For Andromeda* and its sequel (1962), *Doomwatch* (1971) and *Red Dwarf* (1989-93).

The success of 20-odd *Man From U.N.C.L.E.* books encouraged further experiments, but it was not until the books associated with *Star Trek* began to sell in huge quantities in the late 1960s that publishers realized the potential for TV spin-offs. The first of many original *Star Trek* novels was *Spock Must Die!* (1970) by James Blish, and the series is continuing. *Doctor Who* was quick to leap on the bandwagon, with more than 150 script-adaptations appearing between 1970 and 1990 – at which point, the production of original novels began in earnest. The first *X-Files* novel was a great success and many others will doubtless follow.

'Fin De Cycle' (1990). The putative classics of the sub-genre include James P. Blaylock's *Homunculus* (1986), Rudy Rucker's *The Hollow Earth* (1990), William Gibson and Bruce Sterling's *The Difference Engine* (1990) and Paul di Filippo's *The Steampunk Trilogy* (1995).

Many novels of a similar stripe recklessly mingle devices from occult fiction and fantasy with those of sf, creating a kind of "steampunk science fantasy"; these include *The Anubis Gates* (1983), *On Stranger Tides* (1987) and *The Stress Of Her Regard* (1989) by Tim Powers, *Druid's Blood* (1988) by Esther Friesner and *Anno Dracula* (1992) by Kim Newman.

TV has created an eccentric kind of steampunk fiction by importing sf motifs to western series like *The Wild West* and *The Adventures of Brisco County jr.*

 (ABOVE) **POE'S ODYSSEY** IN RUDY RUCKER'S NOVEL EDGAR ALLAN POE BOLDLY GOES WHERE ARTHUR GORDON PYM COULD NOT EVEN HAVE IMAGINED GOING

(LEFT) **DARK SATANIC MILLS** WILL CHARLES BABBAGE'S STEAM-DRIVEN MECHANICAL COMPUTERS HELP TO BUILD JERSUALEM IN ENGLAND'S GREEN AND PLEASANT LAND?

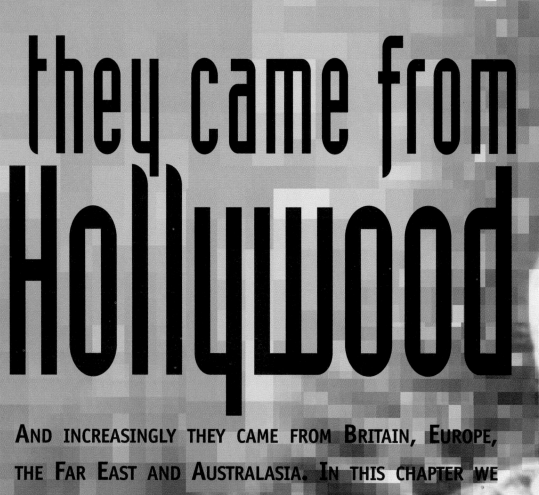

they came from
Hollywood

AND INCREASINGLY THEY CAME FROM BRITAIN, EUROPE,
THE FAR EAST AND AUSTRALASIA. IN THIS CHAPTER WE
SURVEY THE WIDE DIVERSITY OF MOVIE SF

1924

Aelita

(VT *AELITA: THE REVOLT OF THE ROBOTS*)
1924 • RUSSIA • *DIRECTOR* JAKOV PROTAZANOV
• *SCREENPLAY* ALEKSEY FAJKO, FEDOR OZEP, FROM ALEXEI
TOLSTOY'S *AELITA* (1922) • *STARRING* YULIA SOLNTSEVA
(AELITA) • *120M* • *B/W*

A murderer flees to Mars and romances beautiful
Queen Aelita. All is in fact a dream. The movie's
style — especially its set design — was to
prove influential.

1925

The Lost World

1925 • USA • *DIRECTOR* HARRY O. HOYT
• *SCREENPLAY* MARION FAIRFAX, FROM ARTHUR CONAN
DOYLE'S *THE LOST WORLD* (1912) • *SPECIAL EFFECTS*
WILLIS H. O'BRIEN • *STARRING* WALLACE BEERY
(PROFESSOR CHALLENGER) • *c105M*, CUT TO 60M
• *B/W*, SOME TINTING

Atop a South American plateau, dinosaurs still
thrive. Good version of the popular story.

1926

Metropolis

1926 • GERMANY • *DIRECTOR* FRITZ LANG
• *SCREENPLAY* FRITZ LANG, THEA VON HARBAU • *SPECIAL
EFFECTS* EUGEN SCHÜFFTAN • *STARRING* ALFRED ABEL (JOH
FREDERSEN), GUSTAV FRÖHLICH (FREDER), HEINRICH GEORGE
(GROT), BRIGITTE HELM (MARIA/ROBOT MARIA), RUDOLF
KLEIN-ROGGE (ROTWANG), THEODOR LOOS (JOSAPHAT)
• *182M*, BUT REPEATEDLY CUT SO THAT MUCH IS NOW LOST;
BEST VERSION 83M TINTED RECONSTRUCTION (1984) BY
GIORGIO MORODER, WITH ROCK SOUNDTRACK • *B/W, SILENT*

In AD 2026, the supertechnological city of
Metropolis, in which the aristocracy live in
luxury, is built above an underground city, where
operates the machinery that drives Metropolis.
Still further below is the city where the workers
who operate those machines dwell. Young Freder,
son of the Master of Metropolis, Fredersen, is a
lotus-eating playboy until he is captivated by
the lovely Maria, the priestess among the
workers of a pacifistic, quasi-religious cult. One
day, she preaches, will come the messiah-like

Willis H. O'Brien — a man who made monsters

Willis H. O'Brien (1886-1962) is normally referred to as one of the early masters of special effects, but in truth he was something else entirely: he was one of the great geniuses of stop-motion animation. Indeed, on those occasions when he deployed trick photography, his proficiency in true special effects lagged behind that of earlier moviemakers.

Previous stop-motion animators had used clay models. O'Brien's first great innovation was to employ rubber models, which, although more time-consuming to make at the outset, were easier to manipulate and gave a far more realistic image. The first feature of note whose monsters he supplied using this technique was *The Lost World* (1925). There was then a gap in his career before he provided the memorable monster effects in *King Kong* (1933) and its lacklustre quickie sequel, *Son Of Kong* (1933). It is fair to say that without O'Brien, the former — with its sympathetic monster — would never have been such a stupendous success. Nevertheless, there was another gap before O'Brien was called in to repeat his feats for *Mighty Joe Young* (1949), and thereafter he was employed only on minor movies such as *The Animal World* (1956), *El Monstrud De La Montana Huela* (1956) and *The Black Scorpion* (1958). While working on *It's A Mad, Mad, Mad, Mad World* (1963), he died. O'Brien's output was small in terms of movies released, although he worked on several uncompleted projects. One of these, *Gwangi*, was eventually made after his death as *The Valley Of Gwangi* (1969) by his protégé, Ray Harryhausen.

Mediator who, through the Heart, will link the
Minds of the planners with the Hands of the
workers — on that day, the workers will know
justice. Freder throws in his lot with the workers,
while his father Fredersen persuades
inventor/alchemist Rotwang to create a
simulacrum of Maria to lead them to destruction.

As a story, Metropolis is a nonsense: it is
certainly a landmark of the cinema, but not, as
is often claimed, of the sf cinema — indeed, it

SWEET DREAMS
A POSTER FOR FRITZ LANG'S EPOCHAL METROPOLIS (1926) CAPTURES ONE OF THE MANY REASONS FOR THE MOVIE'S SUCCESS: UNABASHED EROTICISM

ALIEN (1979)
(OPPOSITE) WAS NOT ONLY A GREAT HORROR MOVIE BUT REINTRODUCED TO SF CINEMA SOME OF THAT SENSE OF WONDER WHICH HAD BEEN LARGELY MISSING SINCE 1968's 2001

is much better regarded as a work of
technofantasy. Yet, script aside, it is a movie of
astonishing power. In terms of sheer dramatic
intensity, the torchlight chase through the
catacombs and abduction of Maria by Rotwang is
remarkable, her fear conveyed with exquisite
directorial skill. But what stays longest in the
memory, aside from the brilliant graphic
depictions of the future city complex, is the
representation of workers reduced to component
parts of the machines they must slavishly
operate. The images Fritz Lang invented were to
be repeated often — similar examples appear in
Charlie Chaplin's *Modern Times* (1936) and, much
later, in Orson Welles's *The Trial* (1962) — but
Lang, in Metropolis, did it first... and did it best.

1929

Die Frau Im Mond

(VT *THE GIRL IN THE MOON*; VT *THE WOMAN IN THE MOON*;
VT *BY ROCKET TO THE MOON*)
1929 • GERMANY • *DIRECTOR* FRITZ LANG • *SCREENPLAY*
FRITZ LANG, THEA VON HARBOU, FROM VON HARBAU'S *FRAU
IM MOND* (1928) • *c125M* • *B/W*

Scientists build a spaceship and go goldmining
on the Moon. A mismatch of subject and
director makes this a ponderous movie.

The Mysterious Island

1931 • USA • *DIRECTOR* BENJAMIN CHRISTENSEN, LUCIEN HUBBARD, MAURICE TOURNEUR • *SCREENPLAY* LUCIEN HUBBARD, FROM JULES VERNE'S *THE MYSTERIOUS ISLAND* (1874-5) • *STARRING* LIONEL BARRYMORE (COUNT DAKKAR) • *95M* • *COLOUR*

A much-altered adaptation of Verne's original — to the extent that Captain Nemo is renamed Count Dakkar. Remade as *Mysterious Island* (1961).

1930

Just Imagine

1930 • USA • *DIRECTOR* DAVID BUTLER • *SCREENPLAY* LEW BROWN, DAVID BUTLER, B.G. DE SYLVA, RAY HENDERSON • *113M* • *B/W*

Hollywood's attempt to set a blockbuster musical in the future: a man hit by lightning in 1930 wakes up in 1980 to find the world very weird. Spectacular sets.

1931

Doctor Jekyll And Mr Hyde

1931 • USA • *DIRECTOR* ROUBEN MAMOULIAN • *SCREENPLAY* PERCY HEATH, SAMUEL HOFFENSTEIN, FROM ROBERT LOUIS STEVENSON'S *THE STRANGE CASE OF DR JEKYLL AND MR HYDE* (1886) • *SPECIAL EFFECTS* WALLY WESTMORE • *STARRING* ROSE HOBART (MURIEL CAREW), MIRIAM HOPKINS ("CHAMPAGNE" IVY PEARSON), FREDRIC MARCH (JEKYLL/HYDE) • *98M*, USUALLY SEEN CUT TO 90M • *B/W*

This was the second version of Stevenson's famous novella to be filmed — there had been a silent version in 1920 — and is regarded as the classic. For a long time, it was forgotten because MGM were keen to squash all competition to their 1941 version starring Spencer Tracy. The 90m version was "rediscovered" in 1967 and the full 98m version only in 1994. We can now see it as one of the classic features of early cinema. March turns in an astonishing performance — with a minimum of fancy make-up and trick photography — as the good doctor turning into the evil, vicious lecher. He is almost matched by

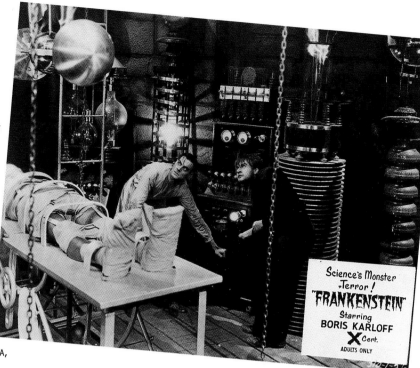

Hopkins as the good-time girl who becomes his mistress and then his sex-slave. This was heady stuff for the time, which may have been another reason why MGM were so successful in suppressing the movie.

Frankenstein

1931 • USA • *DIRECTOR* JAMES WHALE • *SCREENPLAY* JOHN L. BALDERSTON, FRANCIS EDWARDS FARAGOH, ROBERT FLOREY, GARRETT FORT, FROM MARY SHELLEY'S *FRANKENSTEIN* (1818) • *SPECIAL EFFECTS* KENNETH STRICKFADEN • *STARRING* COLIN CLIVE (HENRY FRANKENSTEIN), BORIS KARLOFF (MONSTER) • *71M* • *B/W*

Thomas Alva Edison made a silent short based on Shelley's tale in 1910, but otherwise this was the first of at least 39 movies concerning the bizarre efforts of the obsessed Baron Frankenstein to generate life from dead materials, usually corpses. The events of the movie — drawn mainly from the first half of Shelley's novel, with a fair amount of Hollywood licence thrown in — have become so much a part of our 20th-century iconography that even vague allusions to them are instantly recognizable, and Mel Brooks could, in *Young Frankenstein* (1974), parody them in some detail secure in the knowledge that his audience would understand precisely his targets. The essence of

the story is that Frankenstein, after a grave-robbing spree, creates his Monster using electrical equipment and the energy of a lightning bolt, little realizing that the brain he has incorporated is that of a murderer. All might have been well, but outside interference sets the Monster on a murderous rampage.

The direct sequel was *The Bride Of Frankenstein* (1935).

1932

Island Of Lost Souls

1932 • USA • *DIRECTOR* ERLE C. KENTON • *SCREENPLAY* PHILIP WYLIE, WALDEMAR YOUNG, FROM H.G. WELLS'S *THE ISLAND OF DR MOREAU* (1896) • *STARRING* CHARLES LAUGHTON (DR MOREAU), BELA LUGOSI (SAYER OF THE LAW) • *72M* • *B/W*

A fairly straightforward retelling of Wells's classic, although Wells hated it because it portrayed Moreau as a sadist rather than a would-be benefactor. Remade as *The Island Of Dr Moreau* (1977).

1933

Deluge

1933 • USA • *DIRECTOR* FELIX E. FEIST • *SCREENPLAY*

SHOCKING! *UNUSUALLY, THIS POSTER FOR FRANKENSTEIN (1931) IDENTIFIES BORIS KARLOFF AS THE STAR. IN THE MOVIE ITSELF, THE OPENING CREDITS ARE COY ABOUT THE MONSTER'S IDENTITY, THE TRUTH BEING REVEALED ONLY AT THE MOVIE'S END*

WARREN B. DUFF, JOHN GOODRICH, FROM S. FOWLER WRIGHT'S DELUGE (1928) • *70M* • *B/W*
An eclipse of the Sun causes New York to be destroyed by earthquake and tsunami; the story is of romance among the survivors. Great special effects.

The Invisible Man

1933 • USA • *DIRECTOR* JAMES WHALE • *SCREENPLAY* R.C. SHERRIFF, PHILIP WYLIE (UNCREDITED), FROM H.G. WELLS'S *THE INVISIBLE MAN: A GROTESQUE ROMANCE* (1897) • *SPECIAL EFFECTS* JOHN P. FULTON • *STARRING* CLAUDE RAINS (JACK GRIFFIN, THE INVISIBLE MAN) • *71M* • *B/W*

Wells's novel, which had a great deal of pathos, is here rendered as a black comedy. The movie starts with a mysterious stranger, his face completely covered in bandages, booking a room at an inn filled with stock comic characters. In due course, we learn that he is Dr Jack Griffin, who has discovered the secret of making himself invisible — his difficulty is that he is unable to make himself visible again. The problem eventually drives him mad as his crimes escalate to murder. Though

theoretically set in England, this flawed film too readily shows its US origins: for example, a police station is signed "Police Dept.". An irony is that Rains, visible for only a few seconds at the end — and then as a corpse — became an international star because of this movie.

This was sequelled by *The Invisible Man Returns* (1940) and *The Invisible Man's Revenge* (1944), and there have been about a dozen other variants on this basic riff.

King Kong

1933 • USA • *DIRECTOR* MERIAN C. COOPER, ERNEST B. SCHOEDSACK • *SCREENPLAY* JAMES CREELMAN, RUTH ROSE (EDGAR WALLACE WAS ALSO INVOLVED, BUT IT IS NOT KNOWN TO WHAT EXTENT) • *SPECIAL EFFECTS* WILLIS H. O'BRIEN • *STARRING* ROBERT ARMSTRONG (CARL DENHAM), BRUCE CABOT (JACK DRISCOLL), FAY WRAY (ANN DARROW) AND "KING KONG (THE EIGHTH WONDER OF THE WORLD)" • *100M* • *B/W*

On an uncharted island, the natives worship a giant ape, Kong, whom they regard as a god and to whom they regularly sacrifice young women. Moviemaker Denham arrives with a team to film this wonder, but the natives seize his star, Darrow, and offer her to Kong.

NOW YOU SEE ME...
THE INVISIBLE MAN (1933) TURNED CLAUDE RAINS INTO AN INTERNATIONAL STAR DESPITE THE FACT THAT HIS FACE IS SEEN ONLY IN THE LAST FEW SECONDS

Invisibility — the great dream

The earliest movie of note to exploit the desire we all have to attain invisibility was the French comedy *Le Fantôme Du Moulin Rouge* (1926), by the great director René Clair. A frustrated lover learns how to make himself invisible and plays practical jokes all over Paris.

But it was with *The Invisible Man* (1933) that the theme really entered sf proper — although, in an era when Hollywood uncomfortably played with sf as either horror or comedy, or both, this stressed comedic (and romantic) aspects at the expense of any sf rationalization. The movie was sequelled by *The Invisible Man Returns* (1940) and *The Invisible Man's Revenge* (1944). In between came *The Invisible Woman* (1941), a farce, and *Invisible Agent* (1942), a wartime propaganda movie (with a Curt Siodmak screenplay). A serial movie, *Invisible Monster* (1950), concentrates more on its mad-scientist villain than on invisibility per se.

However bad the latter pair of movies were, at least they did not plumb the depths of *Abbott And Costello Meet The Invisible Man* (1951), in which powerful earlier Hollywood images were reduced to the lowest common denominator. *The Invisible Boy* (1957) was a children's movie exploiting the popularity of Robby the Robot. The title of *The Ghost In The Invisible Bikini* (1966) more or less speaks for itself. *Orloff Y El Hombre Invisible* (1970; vt *The Invisible Dead*; vt *Orloff And The Invisible Man*), a French/Spanish co-production, while essentially a lowbrow monster movie, returned some integrity to the theme, as did the surrealist Austrian movie *Unsichtbare Gegner* (1977; vt *Invisible Adversaries*). *Invisible Stranger* (1984) is a horror-exploitation movie about a serial killer. *The Invisible Kid* (1988), is weak comedy-based voyeurism, and *The Invisible Maniac* (1990) is little better. *Alice* (1990) restored some dignity to the subject matter. *Memoirs Of An Invisible Man* (1992), has the good sense to accord the central subject a degree of thoughtfulness. But probably the best "invisibility" movie was not even sf; in *Harvey* (1950), a man (James Stewart) is regarded as mad because he claims to have been befriended by an invisible giant rabbit.

The ape is fascinated by the screaming woman, and a strange relationship develops between them — one that Denham exploits in order to capture Kong and bring him to New York for public exhibition. When photographers' flashbulbs terrify Kong, he goes on a rampage through the city — finally, in one of cinema's most famous scenes, being shot at from aircraft as he clutches the top of the Empire State Building.

This is really the forefather of the monster movie. It was directly sequelled by the vastly inferior *Son Of Kong* (1933), and there have been various other bad Kong movies. Of note, however, is the remake, *King Kong* (1976), a far better piece of work than the critics acknowledged at the time.

1935
The Bride Of Frankenstein

1935 • USA • *DIRECTOR* JAMES WHALE • *SCREENPLAY* JOHN BALDERSTON, WILLIAM HURLBUT, FROM MARY SHELLEY'S *FRANKENSTEIN* (1818) • *SPECIAL EFFECTS* JOHN P. FULTON • STARRING COLIN CLIVE (HENRY FRANKENSTEIN), BORIS KARLOFF (MONSTER), ELSA LANCHESTER (BRIDE/MARY SHELLEY), ERNEST THESIGER (DR PRETORIUS) • *80M* • *B/W*

The direct sequel to *Frankenstein* (1931) and an even better movie. Frankenstein has more or less been dissuaded from repeating his experiments when on the scene arrives one Dr Pretorius, who has succeeded in imbuing life into a set of miniature dolls. (The special effects here are superb.) He pressurizes Frankenstein into making a mate for the Monster, and between them they produce a much less hideous female version (brilliantly played by Lanchester). But she is revolted by the Monster, who in the misery and fury of his rejection sets ablaze laboratory, Bride, Pretorius and himself.

These first two Frankenstein movies came from Universal, who degraded the whole concept during five further movies: *Son Of Frankenstein* (1939), *The Ghost Of Frankenstein* (1942), *Frankenstein Meets The Wolf Man* (1943), *House Of Frankenstein* (1944), *House Of Dracula* (1945) — these latter three were "team-ups" — and *Abbott And Costello Meet Frankenstein* (1948). Then Hammer took up the Frankenstein torch with *The Curse Of Frankenstein* (1957).

1936
Flash Gordon

1936 • USA • *DIRECTOR* FREDERICK STEPHANI • SCREENPLAY BASIL DICKEY, ELLA O'NEILL, GEORGE PLYMPTON, FREDERICK STEPHANI, FROM THE COMIC-STRIP CHARACTERS AND SCENARIOS CREATED BY ALEX RAYMOND • *SPECIAL EFFECTS* NORMAN DREWES • *STARRING* BUSTER CRABBE (FLASH GORDON), PRISCILLA LAWSON (PRINCESS AURA), CHARLES MIDDLETON (MING THE MERCILESS), JEAN ROGERS (DALE ARDEN), FRANK SHANNON (DR ALEXIS ZARKOV) • *13-EPISODE SERIAL* • *B/W*

Ming the Merciless wants to become Emperor of the Universe, and his wandering planet — Mongo — is on course for Earth. Flash Gordon, Dale Arden and Dr Zarkov set off in Zarkov's spaceship to explore Mongo, knowing nothing of

BALANCING ACT *ONE OF THE ARCHETYPAL IMAGES OF THE CINEMA: THE BELEAGUERED KING KONG FIGHTS OFF BIPLANES FROM THE TOP OF THE EMPIRE STATE BUILDING*

The great apes

The fashion for featuring giant animals in adventure movies was probably started by *The Lost World* (1925), with Willis H. O'Brien responsible for the scenes of clashing dinosaurs, etc. In *King Kong* (1933), O'Brien created a new variety of cinematic creature: the vast ape. Where dinosaurs were merely monsters, apes could, largely because of their anthropoid features, inspire a considerable degree of audience empathy. Despite their size, they could be the underdog — or, at least, under-ape.

O'Brien exploited this further in the hurried sequel *Son Of Kong* (1933) and, much later, in *Mighty Joe Young* (1949). In the latter, a much smaller ape (a mere 12ft tall) eventually goes on the rampage when brought to civilization. Another giant ape featured in the UK rip-off version of the original, *Konga* (1961) — though some idea of Konga's quality can be deduced from its working title, I Was A Teenage Gorilla. In the remake of *King Kong* (1976), the ape was again treated sympathetically.

King Kong Lives (1986), a half-hearted sequel to the 1976 remake, tried too hard to pluck our heartstrings: Kong is given a mate, and just has time to see her bear his son before dying in a hail of bullets. The Japanese *King Kong Tai Gojira* (1963; revised for the USA as *King Kong Versus Godzilla*) was, by contrast, a fairly straightforward monster movie, with Kong essentially on the side of Good. The Indian movie *Tarzan And King Kong* (1965) brought together two different types of "apemen".

A far more ambivalent approach has been taken to those other anthropoids, the Yeti and the Bigfoot. *The Abominable Snowman* (1957) rewards the peacemaker, who tries to contact the creatures, with death. In the Italian horror movie *Yeti* (1977), the snowman revived from the ice after a million years is definitely dangerous. The same is true of the Bigfoot portrayed in the under-rated chiller *Snowbeast*, which terrorizes a group of people in the North American mountain wastes. Until recently, the Bigfoot was generally regarded likewise in a string of B-movies. In 1987, though, came *Bigfoot And The Hendersons* (vt *Harry And The Hendersons*) and the TV movie *Bigfoot*, in both of which the giant anthropoids are kindly, cuddly and, in a way, better than we are.

Ming or his plans. Despite capture, they are eventually able to unite Mongo's warring species and defeat Ming.

This was one of the most successful serials ever made, and gave rise to two sequels: *Flash Gordon's Trip To Mars* (1938) and *Flash Gordon Conquers The Universe* (1940). The original serial, edited in various forms, was reissued as no fewer than five different B-movies, and was remade — or, rather, homaged — in gloriously over-flamboyant style by Dino De Laurentis as *Flash Gordon* (1980).

MAN IN TIGHTS
Buster Crabbe was arguably the greatest of all the Flash Gordons. He also played Tarzan in the 1933 movie Tarzan the Fearless

THE FUTURE IN BLACK AND WHITE *The 1936 film Things To Come had a weak story, but where it scored was in opening up huge vistas to future makers of SF movies*

Things To Come

1936 • UK • *DIRECTOR* William Cameron Menzies • *SCREENPLAY* Lajos Biro, H.G. Wells, from Wells's *The Shape of Things To Come: The Ultimate Revolution* (1933) • *SPECIAL EFFECTS* Lawrence Butler, Edward Cohen, Ross Jacklin, Ned Mann, Harry Zech • *STARRING* Maurice Braddell (Dr Harding), Edward Chapman (Pippa Passworthy/Raymond Passworthy), Cedric Hardwicke (Theotocopolos), Raymond Massey (John Cabal/Oswald Cabal), Ralph Richardson (The Boss), Margaretta Scott (Roxana/Rowena) • *130M* (usually cut to 113m or to 97m) • *B/W*

The story falls into three main parts. In 1940, World War II breaks out, and the community of Everytown is severely blitzed. The war persists for decades, and in the mid-1960s disease hits the area. A despotic warlord called The Boss seizes control; his rule comes to an end when an Everytown man, Cabal, who went off to fight back in 1940, returns to announce that he is here as a representative of Wings Over the World, a pacifist organization wishing to found a new order based on technology.

Decades pass and, in 2036, Cabal's descendant presides benevolently over a new utopia of gleaming high technology. Yet there are those who feel this society, too, is sterile; they focus their ire on Everytown's planned first space shot. However, the astronauts — a new Adam and Eve — escape the mob and blast off for space where, it is hoped, they will found a new society.

The strength of this movie lies not in its somewhat trite plot (Wells cannot escape blame: he was closely involved in the production), nor in Menzies's direction, which plods. Rather the movie's extraordinary effect is generated by its visuals. Although officially these are credited to the art director, in fact they were ultimately the responsibility of Menzies, whose real forte this

H.G. Wells — the lure of the movies

Wells's name is so renowned for prose that we forget how insatiably interested he was in the movies — too interested, in fact, because it is generally accepted that the many infelicities of *Things To Come* (1936) arose because the director, intimidated by this famous, forceful author on his set, gave in easily whenever Wells had a "good idea".

This was by no means Wells's first encounter with cinema. The first movie adaptation of a Wells novel was *Island Of Lost Souls* (1932), based on *The Island Of Dr Moreau* (1896). It was co-written by another sf author: Philip Wylie, who also collaborated on the screenplay of the next Wells movie, *The Invisible Man* (1933). Wells wrote the screenplay for the *The Man Who Could Work Miracles* (1936), and it was presumably this success that persuaded him to interfere so much in *Things To Come*. Then came George Pal's production of The *War Of The Worlds* (1953). The importance of this movie should not be underestimated. Earlier audiences went to see Wells adaptations because they were Wells adaptations; the audiences of the 1950s, however, went to see what they hoped would be thrilling sf movies, and many who enjoyed Pal's production would have been pressed to name the author of the original. Likewise, *The Time Machine* (1960) succeeded because it was a good sf movie, not because of Wells's name; *The First Men In The Moon* (1964) flopped despite it.

Twelve years later, fashions had changed. *The Food Of The Gods* (1976) reckoned it was worth exploiting Wells's name for a movie that had little to do with the novel. That movie failed because it was bad, but the principle held good, as demonstrated by the following year's *The Island Of Dr Moreau* (1977), a rendition that attained commercial success... but any benefit brought to Wells's reputation was squandered by *The Shape Of Things To Come* (1979), a space opera which merely stole the title, and the Italian *L'Isola Degli Uomini Pesce* (1979; vt *Island Of Mutations*), a second-rate rehash of Moreau.

Wells himself has appeared as a character in various movies, the most notable being *Time After Time* (1979).

was. Comparisons with *Metropolis* (1926) are common. *Things To Come* cannot be dismissed as just another dull "documentary of the future": clumsy though its ideas might be, it was a landmark in the history of the sf cinema in that it showed on screen how sweeping the visions of sf writers could be — and, perhaps more important, would become.

The Tunnel

(VT *TRANS-ATLANTIC TUNNEL*)

1936 • UK • *DIRECTOR* MAURICE ELVEY • *SCREENPLAY* CLEMENCE DANE, L. DU GARDE PEACH, FROM BERNHARD KELLERMANN'S *DER TUNNEL* (1913) • *94M* • *B/W*
A remake of the 1933 German movie (shot simultaneously in French) *Der Tunnel*, this centres on the ultimately successful construction of a transatlantic tunnel. This movie is graced with magnificent sets.

1938

Flash Gordon's Trip To Mars

1938 • USA • *DIRECTORS* FORD BEEBE, ROBERT F. HILL • *SCREENPLAY* HERBERT DOLMAS, WYNDHAM GITTENS, NORMAN S. HALL, RAY TRAMPE, FROM ALEX RAYMOND'S COMIC STRIPS • *STARRING* LARRY "BUSTER" CRABBE (FLASH) • *15-EPISODE SERIAL* • *B/W* WITH TINTED SEQUENCES
Now on Mars, Ming is raiding the Earth's oxygen; his queen can turn people into clay. Flash of course stops all this. The serial was edited down to make the feature *The Deadly Ray From Mars* (vt *Flash Gordon: Mars Attacks The World*).

1939

Buck Rogers

1939 • USA • *DIRECTORS* FORD BEEBE, SAUL A. GOODKIND • *SCREENPLAY* NORMAN S. HALL, RAY TRAMPE, FROM PHILIP NOWLAN'S COMIC STRIPS BASED ON HIS *ARMAGEDDON 2419AD* (1928-9) • *STARRING* LARRY "BUSTER" CRABBE (BUCK) • *12-EPISODE SERIAL* • *B/W*
Buck wakes after a 500-year Arctic sleep to find the Zuggs (from Saturn) have invaded Earth. An edited-down feature version was *Planet Outlaws* (1953), further edited as *Destination Saturn* (1965).

1940

Doctor Cyclops

1940 • USA • *DIRECTOR* ERNEST B. SCHOEDSACK • *SCREENPLAY* TOM KILPATRICK • *STARRING* ALBERT DEKKER (DR CYCLOPS) • *75M*
A mad scientist has discovered how to miniaturize people, and must be stopped. Excellent special effects.

Flash Gordon Conquers The Universe

1940 • USA • *DIRECTORS* FORD BEEBE, RAY TAYLOR • *SCREENPLAY* BASIL DICKEY, GEORGE H. PLYMPTON, BARRY SHIPMAN, FROM ALEX RAYMOND'S COMIC STRIPS • *STARRING* LARRY "BUSTER" CRABBE (FLASH) • *12-EPISODE SERIAL* • *B/W*
Again Flash contends against Emperor Ming, who is finally killed in this weak sequel to *Flash Gordon* (1936).

One Million BC

(VT *THE CAVE DWELLERS*; VT *MAN AND HIS MATE*)

1940 • USA • *DIRECTORS* D.W. GRIFFITH (UNCREDITED), HAL ROACH, HAL ROACH JR • *SCREENPLAY* GEORGE BAKER, JOSEPH FRICKERT, GROVER JONES, MICKELL NOVAK • *STARRING* CAROLE LANDIS (LOANA), VICTOR MATURE (TUMAK) • *80M* • *B/W*
A storyteller so entrances a group of Alpine hikers that they believe themselves to be re-enacting a love story set in cod prehistoric times, when men must battle dinosaurs, represented here by iguanas and lizards. This prehistoric yarn was made in Nevada and remade as *One Million Years BC* (1966).

1943

Batman

(VT *AN EVENING WITH BATMAN AND ROBIN*)

1943 • USA • *DIRECTOR* LAMBERT HILLYER • *SCREENPLAY* HARRY FRASER, VICTOR MCLEOD, LESLIE SWABACKER, FROM THE COMIC STRIP CREATED BY BILL FINGER AND BOB KANE • *STARRING* DOUGLAS CROFT (ROBIN), LEWIS WILSON (BATMAN) • *15-EPISODE serial* • *B/W*
A wicked scientist, aided by an army of zombies, tries to appropriate US radium for the Nazis. Our heroes intervene.

1944

The Lady And The Monster

1944 • USA • *DIRECTOR* GEORGE SHERMAN • *SCREENPLAY* FREDERICK KOHNER, DANE LUSSIER, FROM CURT SIODMAK'S *DONOVAN'S BRAIN* (1943) • *86M* • *B/W*

A mad scientist keeps alive the brain of a dead millionaire. Remade as *Donovan's Brain* (1953) and *Vengeance* (1962).

1948

Superman

1948 • USA • *DIRECTORS* THOMAS CARR, SPENCER GORDON BENNET • *SCREENPLAY* LEWIS CLAY, ROYAL K. COLE, ARTHUR HOERL, FROM THE COMIC STRIPS OF JOE SHUSTER AND JERRY SIEGEL • *STARRING* KIRK ALYN (SUPERMAN), NOEL NEILL (LOIS) • *15-EPISODE SERIAL* • *B/W*

Spider Woman tries to conquer the world. Superman stops her. Commercially this was the most successful of all serial movies. It had been preceded by a series of 17 animated theatrical shorts from the Fleischers. Oddly, it was not sequelled.

1949

The Perfect Woman

1949 • UK • *DIRECTOR* BERNARD KNOWLES • *SCREENPLAY* GEORGE BLACK, BERNARD KNOWLES, FROM THE PLAY *THE PERFECT WOMAN* (1948) BY WALLACE GEOFFREY AND BASIL MITCHELL • *89M* • *B/W*

A mad scientist creates a robot identical to his niece, and field-tests it with a young man. But the real woman mischievously takes over from the robot, with farcical results.

1950

Destination Moon

1950 • USA • *DIRECTOR* IRVING PICHEL • *SCREENPLAY* ROBERT A. HEINLEIN, JAMES O'HANLON, RIP VAN RONKEL, FROM HEINLEIN'S *ROCKETSHIP GALILEO* (1947) • *SPECIAL EFFECTS* LEE ZAVITZ • *TECHNICAL ADVISOR* CHESLEY BONESTELL • *STARRING* WARNER ANDERSON, JOHN ARCHER, ERIN O'BRIEN MOORE, TOM POWERS, DICK WESSON • *91M* • *COLOUR*

This movie was an attempt by its director, its scriptwriters and its producer (George Pal) to create a documentary account of events that had yet to happen: humankind's first journey to and landing on the Moon. As such, the plot contains little by way of excitement, save when it is discovered the craft has not quite enough fuel to return home. But Pal and Pichel relied on realism and fabulous special effects to seize the imagination of their audience, and their stratagem worked — distant as it was from the exploits of Buck Rogers and Flash Gordon, the movie proved astonishingly successful. Even

NEO-REALISM DESTINATION MOON *BASED ITS IDEAS ON WHAT WAS THEN STATE-OF-THE-ART, BUT IT SEEMS QUAINT BY TODAY'S STANDARDS*

Serial movies — Saturday morning cinema

Serial movies — a sub-genre marked by low budgets and bad acting — were killed off by television, but in their day they were the prime reason children went to the cinema on Saturday mornings. The first of sf note was *Flash Gordon*, which ran to 13 episodes in 1936; so successful was it that *Flash Gordon's Trip To Mars* (1938) and *Flash Gordon Conquers The Universe* (1940) swiftly followed. *Buck Rogers* (1939) was a leap on to the same bandwagon, but enjoyed less success. *Adventures Of Captain Marvel* (1941) is regarded as one of the better serials. *Captain Midnight* (1942), based on a radio series, was more a technothriller than sf.

Another early venture was *Batman* (1943), which did well enough to inspire a sequel, *Batman And Robin* (1949; vt *The New Adventures Of Batman And Robin*). *Captain America* (1944) — with a somewhat plump

Dick Purcell as the eponymous hero (he died soon after, in 1945) — can be regarded as a scene-setter for the most successful of all serial movies: *Superman* (1948). Still later came *Captain Video* (1951), based on a TV series that had started in 1949; needless to say, the big-screen version had little pulling power now that people could watch the TV version in the comfort of their own homes, and this represented more or less the end of the line for serial movies.

Almost without exception, US serial movies were based on the comics and on the activities of superheroes. The protagonist of the French serial *Fantômas* was, by contrast, a sort of Raffles figure drawn from the novels by Marcel Allain; although of little sf interest themselves, they inspired two more sf-oriented feature movies named *Fantômas* (1947) and *Fantômas* (1964).

Spacecraft — from spruce to scruffy

1947 was the year in which the flying-saucer craze got under way, thanks to US amateur pilot Kenneth Arnold's observation that mysterious aerial objects he saw were like saucers skipping across water. So it is hardly surprising that the craft that brings Klaatu and Gort to Earth in *The Day The Earth Stood Still* (1951) is lens-shaped. Both before and after this, however, more "scientific" sf movies assumed spacecraft would look rather like V2 rockets, ignoring the fact that all the streamlining would be entirely wasted the moment the craft left the atmosphere. Moreover, the notion that an integral craft might blast off from ground level on one planet, travel through space and then land on another — before repeating the process in reverse — can with hindsight be seen to be ridiculous. *Destination Moon* (1950) and *The Conquest Of Space* (1955), despite their pseudo-documentary approaches, persisted with this nonsense.

The first major sf movie to demolish the notion was probably *2001* (1968), which made it plain that the only sensible approach was to use shuttles to get into orbit, and traverse interplanetary wastes in "mother ships" that could be any shape; at the far end of the journey, these would again deploy shuttles for landings. *Silent Running* (1971), *Dark Star* (1974), *Star Wars* (1977) and *Alien* (1979) accordingly delighted in cumbersome interstellar vehicles. Sadly, *Star Wars* and its imitators saw fit to use fighter craft that could bank, turn and even make exciting noises in the vacuum of space...

For obvious reasons, a truer portrayal of a spacecraft is given in *Apollo 13* (1995).

 YOU'VE GORT TO BE JOKING *No one who has seen* The Day The Earth Stood Still *(1951) can forget the iconic figure of the giant robot Gort, here in company with Patricia Neal and Michael Rennie*

today, despite its quaint archaism, it is capable of generating a greater sense of wonder than modern equivalents such as *Apollo 13* (1995).

1951

The Day The Earth Stood Still

1951 • USA • *DIRECTOR* ROBERT WISE • *SCREENPLAY* EDMUND H. NORTH, FROM HARRY BATES'S 'FAREWELL TO THE MASTER' (1940) • *SPECIAL EFFECTS* FRED SERSEN • STARRING LOCK MARTIN (GORT), PATRICIA NEAL (HELEN BENSON), MICHAEL RENNIE (KLAATU) • *92M* • *B/W*

The Galactic Federation (or some equivalent) has observed that Earth has developed the atom bomb, and that its nations are beginning to test and stockpile such weapons. Accordingly, it sends to Earth its emissary, Klaatu — accompanied by a huge, featureless robot, Gort — to inform the world that it must either cease such potentially destructive practices or be blasted to bits. Klaatu's flying saucer lands in Washington DC and proves invulnerable to any weaponry that Earth can hurl against it; but then a guard panics and shoots Klaatu. Removed to a hospital, Klaatu escapes and takes up lodgings in the house of Helen Benson; in so doing, he discovers how good normal human beings can be, unlike their military/political masters. At last, though, Klaatu must depart; he

leaves behind him Gort and a number of other, similar robots to police the Earth, warning yet again that Earthlings must discover peace or be destroyed.

The plot is filled with holes, but this is nevertheless an engrossing movie — and a moving one, largely because of the contrast between, on the one hand, the alien, profoundly non-human aspects of Gort and the flying saucer and, on the other, the cosy domesticity of the Benson household.

The Man In The White Suit

1951 • UK • *DIRECTOR* ALEXANDER MACKENDRICK • *SCREENPLAY* JOHN DIGHTON, ROGER MACDOUGALL, ALEXANDER MACKENDRICK • *SPECIAL EFFECTS* GEOFFREY DICKINSON, SYDNEY PEARSON • *STARRING* HOWARD MARION CRAWFORD (CRANFORD), MICHAEL GOUGH (MICHAEL CORLAND), JOAN GREENWOOD (DAPHNE BIRNLEY), ALEC

GUINNESS (SIDNEY STRATTON), VIDA HOPE (BERTHA), DUNCAN LAMONT (HARRY), CECIL PARKER (ALAN BIRNLEY), ERNEST THESIGER (SIR JOHN KIERLAW) • *85M* • *B/W*
Debatably the best of the Ealing comedies, this is also one of the sharpest of all sf satires, targeting quite savagely not only both sides of the English industrial-relations scene of its time but also the misguidedness of science in pursuing its "beneficial" aims without paying due heed to the social consequences. One can also read the satire as a commentary on the fact that the masters of society are incapable of putting new technological developments to the purpose for which they were intended — i.e., the betterment of the lot of all — but instead exploit them for profit. This is a movie that works on many levels, and merits repeated viewing.

On the surface, though, it seems a simple enough comedy in the standard Ealing mode. Daphne Birnley, daughter of a textiles millionaire, has faith in the scientific talents of young Sidney Stratton, and inveigles him into the research laboratories of her father's industrial complex. There he conducts his experiments — which involve the usual mad-scientist props of bubbling retorts, unexpected electrical sparks and loud explosions. However, just as her father has had about enough, Stratton comes through: he has invented a fibre that not only repels dirt but will never wear out. He makes for himself a white suit, which demonstrates his achievement by remaining spotless. At first, the Birnley

KEEP IT ON ICE *ALTHOUGH THE PLOT OF* THE THING *(1951) CAN BE CONSIDERED RISIBLE, THERE IS NO QUESTION BUT THAT THE MOVIE CONVEYS A TRULY FRIGHTENING SENSE OF DREAD*

management are delighted: how can any other textile manufacturer compete with them? The workers in the region, however, are less entranced, for they realize that soon Stratton's invention will lead to massive redundancies — in, for example, detergent factories. And soon the textile manufacturers, too, realize that Stratton's fibre spells eventual doom for their future markets. The movie ends with a pell-mell

chase by a mob after Stratton, in his white suit, which ends only when the material begins spontaneously to disintegrate.

The movie is often riotously funny, through its piercing script and the quality of its performances. But it is Guinness, flipping with conviction from wry wiliness to sincere naiveté to wild hysteria all in the space of a minute, who makes it the classic of entertainment it is.

HANDS OFF — HE'S MINE
A VERY YOUNG ALEC GUINNESS PORTRAYS THE OBSESSION OF THE DEDICATED TECHNOLOGIST IN THIS TYPICAL STILL FROM THE EXCELLENT EALING COMEDY THE MAN IN THE WHITE SUIT *(1951)*

The Thing

(VT THE THING FROM ANOTHER WORLD*)*
1951 • USA • *DIRECTORS* HOWARD HAWKS (UNCREDITED), CHRISTIAN NYBY • *SCREENPLAY* CHARLES LEDERER, FROM DON A. STUART'S (I.E., JOHN W. CAMPBELL'S) 'WHO GOES THERE?' (1938) • *SPECIAL EFFECTS* LINWOOD DUNN, DON STEWARD • *STARRING* JAMES ARNESS (THE THING), MARGARET SHERIDAN (NIKKI NICHOLSON), KENNETH TOBEY (CAPTAIN PAT HENDRY) • *85M* • *B/W*
A spacecraft lands in Antarctica, and a party of scientists (plus a mandatory smart-aleck journalist) is sent to investigate. They find a flying saucer embedded in the ice, and

inadvertently destroy it. Then they discover — presumably thrown clear — an alien creature, likewise frozen. They take it, still embedded in a block of ice, back to base camp; but, when it thaws out, it proceeds to kill the camp's personnel, one by one (the parallels with *Alien* [1979] are notable).

This is a monster movie, pure and simple: the fact that the alien monster is a vegetable ("an intellectual carrot", as the journalist glibly describes it) does not change this. In Campbell's original story, the alien was a shapeshifter capable of assuming any identity, and thus much more frightening in that none of the humans could trust any of the others. Yet *The Thing*, through sheer cinematic and cinematographic skill — Hawks kept a tight rein on all aspects of the movie — still has the power to grip and chill.

It was remade as *The Thing* (1982).

When Worlds Collide

1951 • USA • *DIRECTOR* RUDOLPH MATÉ • *SCREENPLAY* SYDNEY BOEHM, FROM PHILIP WYLIE'S AND EDWIN BALMER'S *WHEN WORLDS COLLIDE* (1933) • *83M* • *COLOUR*
A runaway solar system collides with ours, destroying Earth. Plucky survivors escape to another planet. Astrophysically nonsensical, but visually superb.

1952

Red Planet Mars

1952 • USA • *DIRECTOR* HARRY HORNER • *SCREENPLAY* JOHN L. BALDERSTON, ANTHONY VEILLER, FROM BALDERSTON'S AND JOHN E. HOARE'S PLAY *RED PLANET* (1933) • *87M* • *B/W*
Unspeakably bad anti-communist movie in which it emerges that God is alive and well and living on Mars.

1953

The Beast From 20,000 Fathoms

1953 • USA • *DIRECTOR* EUGÈNE LOURIÉ • *SCREENPLAY* FRED FREIBURGER, LOU MORHEIM, FROM RAY BRADBURY'S 'THE FOG HORN' (1951) • *80M* • *B/W*

WHO'S YOUR FRIEND? *ONE OF THE MOST OVERRATED SF MOVIES OF ALL TIME,* DONOVAN'S BRAIN *(1953) TODAY HAS CURIOSITY VALUE IN THAT IT STARRED THE FUTURE MRS PRESIDENT, NANCY REAGAN*

A vast dinosaur, woken from suspended animation in the Arctic by an atomic blast, terrorizes New York. This movie is primarily of note as the first on a theme that would later be exploited by, for example, the Godzilla movies; it was also the first movie to feature Ray Harryhausen's special effects.

Donovan's Brain

1953 • USA • *DIRECTOR* FELIX FEIST • *SCREENPLAY* FELIX FEIST, ADAPTED BY HUGH BROOKE, FROM CURT SIODMAK'S *DONOVAN'S BRAIN* (1943) • *SPECIAL EFFECTS* HARRY REDMOND JR • *STARRING* LEW AYRES (DR PATRICK CORY), NANCY DAVIS (JAN CORY) • *83M* • *B/W*
This was the second of three movie versions of Siodmak's novel: the other two were *The Lady And The Monster* (1944) and *Vengeance* (1963; vt *The Brain*). The TV movie *Hauser's Memory*, based on Siodmak's novel *Hauser's Memory* (1968), can be regarded as a retread of the same absurd notion. A parodic version by Steve Martin was *The Man With Two Brains* (1983).

In his private laboratory miles from anywhere, scientist Cory has been experimenting to keep monkey brains alive outside the body, and at last succeeds. By astonishing coincidence, there is a plane crash nearby and its sole survivor is a man who is dead except for his brain. Cory is called upon to help this semi-survivor, the crooked financier Warren H. Donovan, but he is only able to keep the brain alive and healthy. Soon it begins to possess him, to the extent that he starts writing in Donovan's script, becomes involved in Donovan's shady shenanigans and even walks with Donovan's limp. The only times when he can be himself are when the brain is asleep, and during one of these periods he arranges for a lightning-rod to be connected to the apparatus that is keeping the brain alive. One electrical storm later, he is freed from his bondage.

This is hokum, and dreary hokum at that. Horrifyingly, it is the best of the three versions. But even more horrifying is the sight of Nancy Davis, later Nancy Reagan, expressing shock at the notion that any rich man could be so mean as to minimize his tax payments at the expense of the poor.

Four-Sided Triangle

1953 • UK • *DIRECTOR* TERENCE FISHER • *SCREENPLAY* TERENCE FISHER, PAUL TABORI, FROM WILLIAM F. TEMPLE'S *FOUR-SIDED TRIANGLE* (1949) • *81M* • *B/W*
An inventor discovers how to duplicate human beings. When the girl he loves falls for another man, he duplicates her — but, alas, the duplicate too falls for the other man.

Invaders From Mars

1953 • USA • *DIRECTOR* WILLIAM CAMERON MENZIES • *SCREENPLAY* RICHARD BLAKE • *82M* • *COLOUR*
Groundbreaking sf movie, a precursor of *Invasion Of The Body Snatchers* (1956). A boy discovers that the adults around him are being taken over by aliens. Clumsily remade as *Invaders From Mars* by Tobe Hooper in 1986.

It Came From Outer Space

1953 • USA • *DIRECTOR* JACK ARNOLD • *SCREENPLAY* RAY BRADBURY, HARRY ESSEX • *80M* • *B/W*
Like *Invaders From Mars* (1953), a thematic precursor of *Invasion Of The Body Snatchers* (1956), but with no invasion. Invisible aliens crash on Earth and produce duplicate humans, the real humans being drafted to repair the spaceship. The repair work done, the aliens restore the status quo.

Spaceways

1953 • UK • *DIRECTOR* TERENCE FISHER • *SCREENPLAY* RICHARD LANDAU, PAUL TABORI, FROM CHARLES ERIC MAINE'S radio play *SPACEWAYS* (1952) • *76M* • *B/W*
Humdrum affair in which a scientist is accused of murdering his adulterous wife and her lover and sending the bodies skywards in a space satellite.

The War Of The Worlds

1953 • USA • *DIRECTOR* BYRON HASKIN • *SCREENPLAY* BARRE LYNDON, FROM H.G. WELLS'S *THE WAR OF THE WORLDS* (1898) • *SPECIAL EFFECTS* CHESLEY BONESTELL, IVYL BURKS, JAN DOMELA, WALTER HOFFMAN, GORDON JENNINGS, WALLACE KELLY, PAUL K. LERPAE, IRMIN ROBERTS • *STARRING* GENE BARRY (DR CLAYTON FORRESTER), LEWIS MARTIN (REVEREND MATTHEW COLLINS), ANN ROBINSON (SYLVIA VAN BUREN) • *85M* • *COLOUR*
Wells's famous novel supplanted from Victorian England to 1950s California: the result should have been a disaster, rather than a disaster movie. In fact, it is a near masterpiece, albeit flawed.

The essence of the tale is that a strange meteorite impacts in southern California, and scientists conclude that it must be an alien spacecraft. Indeed it is, and for a while it sprouts, on mechanical tentacles, probes that merely observe the Earthlings gathered around. But then its Martian occupants move on to the offensive. In one of sf cinema's great scenes, the local preacher attempts to speak of peace to the probes and is blasted for his pains. Similar "meteors", it emerges, have been falling all over Earth: a full-scale invasion is underway. The Martians — one is briefly seen, and is hideous — pilot slow-moving but utterly invincible aircraft against Earth's cities (the movie concentrates on Los Angeles), destroying all resistance and much else besides. In the end, the invaders encounter Earth's bacteria, to which Martian physiology is — of course — utterly vulnerable.

1954

The Creature From The Black Lagoon

1954 • USA • *DIRECTOR* JACK ARNOLD • *SCREENPLAY* HARRY ESSEX, ARTHUR ROSS • *79M* • *B/W*
A team of scientists attempts to capture a humanoid fish. A truly great monster movie, combining pathos and eroticism. Sequelled by *Revenge Of The Creature* (1955) and *The Creature Walks Among Us* (1956).

Gojira

(*VT GODZILLA*; *VT GODZILLA, KING OF THE MONSTERS*)
1954 • JAPAN • *DIRECTOR* INOSHIRO HONDA • *SCREENPLAY* INOSHIRO HONDA, TAKEO MURATA • *98M* • *B/W*
As in *The Beast From 20,000 Fathoms* (1953), a dinosaur is woken from a long sleep by an atomic blast and proceeds to destroy a city — in this instance, Tokyo. This was the start of a long series.

DEATH FROM ABOVE *ONE OF THE MARTIANS'S LETHAL CRAFT PROWLS THE STREETS OF LOS ANGELES IN THE IMPRESSIVE THE WAR OF THE WORLDS (1953)*

Gojira/Godzilla movies

This huge, flame-breathing, dinosaur-like monster first stomped all over Tokyo in 1954's *Gojira*, known more widely in the West as Godzilla, and featured in at least 14 other movies. Most have a baffling array of variant titles in both Japanese and English, so in the ensuing list each is indicated only by the title under which it has become best known in the West. Note that, in many instances, the English-language version differs from the Japanese original, with extra scenes and even sub-plots featuring US actors cast willy-nilly into the midst of movies whose plots often didn't make much sense in the first place.

The Gojira/Godzilla movies are: *Godzilla* (1954), *King Kong Versus Godzilla* (1963), *Godzilla Versus Mothra* (1964), *Kaiju Daisenso* (1965), *Ghidora, The Three-Headed Monster* (1965), *Ebirah, Terror Of The Deep* (1966), *Son Of Godzilla* (1967), *Destroy All Monsters* (1968), *Godzilla's Revenge* (1969), *Godzilla Versus The Smog Monster* (1971), *Gojira Tai Gaigan* (1972), *Godzilla Versus Megalon* (1973), *Godzilla Versus The Bionic Monster* (1974), *Mekagojira No Gyakushu* (1975) and, as a much later homage, *Godzilla 1985* (1985). The Japanese studio Toho (latterly Toho-Eizo) specialized for a long and successful period in movies of this type, Gojira being only one of their monsters, and "team-ups" became common: *Destroy All Monsters* features no fewer than 11 of the Toho creatures, Gojira included.

Riders To The Stars

1954 • USA • *DIRECTOR* RICHARD CARLSON • *SCREENPLAY* CURT SIODMAK • *81M* • *COLOUR*
Exceptionally silly, dull movie, laden with "scientific" explanation, concerning scientists and cosmic rays.

Them!

1954 • USA • *DIRECTOR* GORDON DOUGLAS • *SCREENPLAY* RUSSELL HUGHES, TED SHERDEMAN, GEORGE WORTHING YATES • *SPECIAL EFFECTS* RALPH AYRES, WILLIAM MUELLER, FRANCIS J. SCHEID • *STARRING* JAMES ARNESS (ROBERT GRAHAM), EDMUND GWENN (DR HAROLD MEDFORD), JAMES WHITMORE (SERGEANT BEN PETERSEN), JOAN WELDON (DR PATRICIA MEDFORD) • *93M* • *COLOUR*

A BIT TIED UP *THE HIGHPOINT OF* 20,000 LEAGUES UNDER THE SEA *(1954), AS A GIANT SQUID ATTACKS THE* NAUTILUS. *IT WAS DIFFICULT FOR THE MOVIEMAKERS TO COME UP WITH A FINAL CLIMAX THAT COULD SURPASS THIS*

Nuclear testing in the New Mexico desert has caused the abrupt evolution of a horde of gigantic ants, and these cause untold havoc until they are finally put down using poison gas. However, their queen escapes and lays her eggs in the sewers of Los Angeles.

Them! is often hailed as one of the best monster movies of all time; and, to be fair, if

ONE OF THEM DAYS *IF THERE'S ONE THING YOU DON'T WANT TO FACE WHEN YOU'RE OUT ON A WALK... A MONSTROUSLY MUTATED ANT DOES ITS STUFF IN* THEM! *(1954)*

one completely suspends one's disbelief, it has a certain hypnotic grip — perhaps because the movie takes itself and its theme so seriously. If, by contrast, one remains aware of the true silliness of it all, it becomes hard to sit through. Nevertheless, it was a phenomenal box-office success, and spawned a brood of imitators.

20,000 Leagues Under The Sea

1954 • USA • *DIRECTOR* RICHARD FLEISCHER • *SCREENPLAY* EARL FELTON, FROM JULES VERNE'S *TWENTY THOUSAND LEAGUES UNDER THE SEA* (1870) • *SPECIAL EFFECTS* JOHN HENCH, JOSHUA MEADOR • *STARRING* KIRK DOUGLAS (NED LAND), PETER LORRE (CONSEIL), PAUL LUKAS (PROFESSOR PIERRE ARONNAX), JAMES MASON (CAPTAIN NEMO) • *127M* • *COLOUR*
The year is 1868. Aronnax, his valet Conseil and harpoonist Land are sent aboard a warship to try to discover the "monster" that has been sinking so many ships off the Californian coast. The "monster" sinks their ship, too, but they are saved from certain death by Captain Nemo, who has been using his secret submarine *Nautilus* to destroy military shipping, his aim being to bring peace to the world. In the end, of course, Nemo and his island base are blown to smithereens, but not before we have watched one of cinema's

Jules Verne rockets to the screen

For a novelist who died just after the turn of the century, at a time when movies were generally curios rather than a medium for tale-telling, Verne (1828-1905) has enjoyed a remarkably prolific career in the cinema.

Two movies based on his work have been particularly successful: *20,000 Leagues Under The Sea* (1954) — one of Disney's live-action classics — and *Around The World In Eighty Days* (1956), which was effectively sf at the time the novel was written.

The former was sequelled (although not by Disney) as *Mysterious Island* (1961), itself a remake of *The Mysterious Island* (1929) and the serial movie *Mysterious Island* (1951). Other notable Verne-based movies have been *The Adventures Of Michael Strogoff* (1937; vt *Michael Strogoff*; vt *The Soldier And The Lady*), *From The Earth To The Moon* (1958), *In Search Of The Castaways* (1961), *Master Of The World* (1961), *Five Weeks In A Balloon* (1962), *Jules Verne's Rocket To The Moon* (1967) — not to be confused with *Rocket To The Moon* (1953; vt *Cat Women Of The Moon*) — *The Southern Star* (1968), *Captain Nemo And The Underwater City* (1969), *The Light At The Edge Of The World* (1971) and *The Amazing Captain Nemo* (1978; vt *The Return Of Captain Nemo*).

Not all the above are sf, but the novel by Verne that has sparked off the most movies certainly is: *Journey To The Centre Of The Earth* (1863). These include: the French *Voyage Au Centre De La Terre* (1909; vt *A Journey To The Middle Of The Earth*); *Journey To The Center Of The Earth* (1959), which is the famous one starring James Mason; *A Journey To The Center Of The Earth* (1976), an Australian animated TV movie; the Spanish *Viaje Al Centro De La Tierra* (1977; vt *Journey To The Centre Of The Earth*; vt *Where Time Began*); and *Journey To The Center Of The Earth* (1988), a quite appalling travesty from the Golan-Globus team.

To this corpus should really be added *At The Earth's Core* (1976): although it's based on Edgar Rice Burroughs's novel of the same name, this is really a reprise.

IN SICKNESS AND IN HEALTH
ONE OF THE GREAT POINTS ABOUT THE QUATERMASS XPERIMENT (1955) IS THAT OUR SYMPATHIES SOON COME TO REST WITH VICTOR CARROON, DESPITE HIS MONSTROUS APPEARANCE

great edge-of-seat sequences, when *Nautilus* is attacked by a giant squid (top left). Although this movie can hardly be thought of as a major contribution to sf cinema, it is enjoyable.

1955

The Conquest Of Space

1955 • USA • *DIRECTOR* BYRON HASKIN • *SCREENPLAY* JAMES O'HANLON, FROM WERNHER VON BRAUN'S *THE MARS PROJECT* (1952) AND CHESLEY BONESTELL'S AND WILLY LEY'S *THE CONQUEST OF SPACE* (1949) • *81M* • *COLOUR*

The last noteworthy hard-sf movie before *2001* (1968), this tells of an expedition to Mars which is impeded by the spaceship captain's sudden discovery of Christian fundamentalism. Pretty dreadful, aside from Bonestell's depictions of Mars.

The Day The World Ended

1955 • USA • *DIRECTOR* ROGER CORMAN • *SCREENPLAY* LOU RUSOFF • *81M* • *B/W*

After a nuclear holocaust, a small group of survivors is threatened by a radiation-generated monster. A Corman low-budget quickie.

1984

1955 • UK • *DIRECTOR* MICHAEL ANDERSON • *SCREENPLAY* RALPH BETTINSON, WILLIAM P. TEMPLETON,

FROM GEORGE ORWELL'S *NINETEEN EIGHTY-FOUR* (1949) • *STARRING* EDMOND O'BRIEN (WINSTON SMITH), MICHAEL REDGRAVE (O'CONNOR), JAN STERLING (JULIA) • *94M* • *B/W*

A toned-down version of Orwell's satire of a future Stalinist UK. Much to be preferred are the 1954 TV adaptation and *Nineteen Eighty-four* (1984).

The Quatermass Xperiment

(VT *THE CREEPING UNKNOWN*)

1955 • UK • *DIRECTOR* VAL GUEST • *SCREENPLAY* VAL GUEST, RICHARD LANDAU, FROM NIGEL KNEALE'S BBC TV SERIAL *THE QUATERMASS EXPERIMENT* (1953) • *SPECIAL EFFECTS* LES BOWIE • *STARRING* MARGIA DEAN (JUDITH CARROON), BRIAN DONLEVY (PROFESSOR BERNARD QUATERMASS), JACK WARNER (INSPECTOR LOMAX), DAVID KING WOOD (GORDON BRISCOE), RICHARD WORDSWORTH (VICTOR CARROON) • *82M* • *B/W*

Professor Quatermass headed the team that sent out the UK's first manned space probe. Now it returns with two of its crew missing and the survivor, Carroon, unwilling or unable to explain events. Quatermass investigates and strange changes come over Carroon.

The science content of this movie is not distinguished, but the acting is.

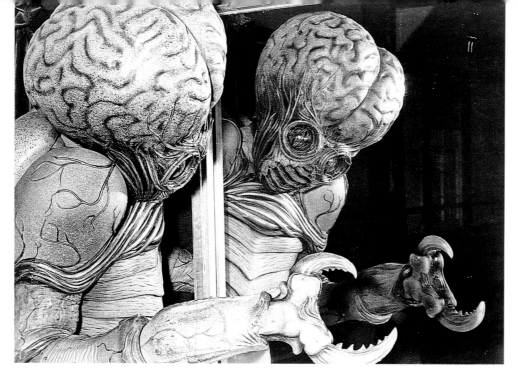

Tarantula

1955 • USA • *DIRECTOR* JACK ARNOLD • *SCREENPLAY* MARTIN BERKELEY, R.M. FRESCO, FROM FRESCO'S TELEPLAY *NO FOOD FOR THOUGHT* • *80M* • *B/W*

A mad scientist injects nutrients into a tiny spider, which grows — eating people to fuel the growth — until it is huge. Risible today, the special effects were good for their time.

This Island Earth

1955 • USA • *DIRECTORS* JOSEPH NEWMAN, WITH JACK ARNOLD • *SCREENPLAY* FRANKLIN COEN, EDWARD G. O'CALLAGHAN, FROM RAYMOND F. JONES'S *THIS ISLAND EARTH* (1952) • *SPECIAL EFFECTS* ROSWELL A. HOFFMAN, DAVID S. HORSLEY, CLIFFORD STINE • *STARRING* FAITH DOMERGUE (RUTH ADAMS), LANCE FULLER (BRACK), JEFF MORROW (EXETER), ROBERT NICHOLS (JOE WILSON), REX REASON (CAL MEACHAM), DOUGLAS SPENCER (MONSTER) • *86M* • *COLOUR*

Various top scientists are recruited to a remote establishment which proves to be run by aliens — Metalunians — under the command of Exeter. The planet Metaluna is under bombardment by the evil Zahgons, and its protective shield is on the verge of collapse; Exeter and his colleagues believe that new developments in terrestrial science, notably by Meacham, can help repair it.

The synopsis seems trite, but *This Island Earth* is nonetheless an impressive movie, exploring in sober fashion what was then fresh territory for sf cinema: here were alien intruders on Earth whose intention was not conquest or possession, but a request for help.

1956

Earth Versus The Flying Saucers

(VT INVASION OF THE FLYING SAUCERS)

1956 • USA • *DIRECTOR* FRED F. SEARS • *SCREENPLAY* RAYMOND T. MARCUS, GEORGE WORTHINGTON YATES • *83M* • *B/W*

Friendly ufonauts arrive on Earth and are greeted with hostility. They respond with a vengeance. Best watched for Ray Harryhausen's special effects.

Forbidden Planet

1956 • USA • *DIRECTOR* FRED M. WILCOX • *SCREENPLAY* CYRIL HUME, FROM (VERY LOOSELY) WILLIAM SHAKESPEARE'S *THE TEMPEST* (WRITTEN ABOUT 1611) • *SPECIAL EFFECTS* A. ARNOLD GILLESPIE, JOSHUA MEADOR, WARREN NEWCOMBE, IRVING G. REIS • *STARRING* ANNE FRANCIS (ALTAIRA), LESLIE NIELSEN (COMMANDER ADAMS), WALTER PIDGEON (DR MORBIUS) AND ROBBY THE ROBOT • *98M* • *COLOUR*

The human expedition to Altair IV has fallen silent, and a team led by Adams is sent to investigate. They discover that the only survivors are Dr Morbius and his daughter Altaira, for whom Adams immediately falls. Gradually Adams unravels what has happened. The planet was originally home to a long-dead race, the Krel; they were extinguished because their science progressed to the point that they reified their own worst nightmares. Morbius, examining the extant Krel technology, has inadvertently repeated the effect; when his fellow expedition members wanted to return home, his "monster

from the id" destroyed them, sparing only Altaira. Now the "monster from the id" resurfaces, focusing on Adams's crew and specifically Adams, for it becomes clear that Morbius unconsciously harbours incestuous yearnings for Altaira.

Forbidden Planet is marred by too-frequent comic interludes; one comic figure, Robby the Robot, was popular enough go on to star in a mediocre follow-up, *The Invisible Boy* (1957). Yet, although often screened as kiddies' fare, *Forbidden Planet*'s underlying themes are the same dark ones that drive Shakespeare's *The Tempest*, with Morbius as Prospero, Altaira as Miranda, Adams as Frederick, Robby as Ariel and the "monster from the id" as Caliban.

The scenes of Morbius and Adams walking among the vast Krel machinery are breathtaking, and have been homaged in many other movies.

Invasion Of The Body Snatchers

1956 • USA • *DIRECTOR* DON SIEGEL • *SCREENPLAY* DANIEL MAINWARING, FROM JACK FINNEY'S *THE BODY SNATCHERS* (1955) • *SPECIAL EFFECTS* MILT RICE • *STARRING* KING DONOVAN (JACK BELICE), RALPH DUMKE (NICK GRIVETT), LARRY GATES (DR DAN KAUFFMANN), CAROLYN JONES (THEODORA BELICE), KEVIN MCCARTHY (DR MILES BENNEL), JEAN WILLES (SALLY), DANA WYNTER (BECKY DRISCOLL) • *80M* • *B/W*

The first of three movies to be based on Finney's novel, each of them excellent in their own different ways (the other two are *Invasion Of The Body Snatchers* [1978] and *Body Snatchers* [1993]), this is also one of the classics of 1950s sf cinema. Originally, it was planned as just another scary B-movie, but screenplay and director contrived — despite studio meddling — to create a movie that spoke directly to the deep psyche of the USA of the time, and still, for all its technical deficiencies, evokes a powerful response in the viewer of today.

There is a frame story, which is largely irrelevant; it was introduced at the studio's behest in order to give the movie an up-beat ending and to obviate the despair that marks the movie's true closure; the frame story also weakens the movie in that it makes it overt that

ON THE RUN *ONE OF THE MOST GRIPPING MOVIES EVER MADE, THE ORIGINAL* INVASION OF THE BODY SNATCHERS *(1956) IS STILL THRILLING 40 YEARS LATER*

this is an alien-invasion tale.

The real story starts with the return to his Californian hometown of Dr Bennel, who has been away at a convention. Soon he senses that "all is not well", and comparing notes with his ex-girlfriend Becky Driscoll he realizes how many people in the town are complaining that their friends and loved ones are, well... different. As time passes — and romance re-blossoms — they notice that, curiously, the number of such complaints is diminishing, rather than increasing, as might be expected if some kind of mass hysteria were at work. The horrific truth starts to emerge when, while dining with their friends the Belices, they discover bizarre pods in the greenhouse, each pod containing a developing simulacrum of one of the quartet. Indeed, the town is being taken over by these simulacra and the original inhabitants "disposed of".

In a major confrontation, the simulacrum-Kauffmann explains the benefits of becoming a pod-person: although individuality is lost, so are aggression and misery and hatred; the contrary emotions of love and pleasure are a small price to pay. Becky and Bennel escape, then discover that the simulacra are working to transport pods

Paranoia — maybe they really are out to get you

During the 1950s and early 1960s, once the USA had realized there was now another superpower in the world — the USSR — whose communist philosophy was the antithesis of its own ideology, US cinema began to express the nation's paranoia in various ways, one of them being the medium of the sf movie. *Invasion Of The Body Snatchers* (1956) is frequently cited as the classic of this curious sub-genre, but not only was it far from the first, it was also ambiguous as to the focus of its paranoia: while the fear existed that communism was trying to convert people from individuals into mindless replicas, the same could be said of home-bred McCarthyism.

The notion of those around you becoming "somehow different" was first notably exploited in *Invaders From Mars* (1953), in which a boy sees everyone in his small US town — including his parents — taken over mentally by aliens. *It Came From Outer Space* (1953) further explored the theme. A little while later, the UK movie *Quatermass II* (1957) picked up on *Invasion Of The Body Snatchers*. *I Married A Monster From Outer Space* (1958) took the theme perhaps as far as it could go at the time: a woman's fiancé is substituted by a shapeshifting alien, a member of an expedition hoping to mate with humans in order to boost the home planet's declining population. *Village Of The Damned* (1960) and *Children Of The Damned* (1963) both saw attempts to infiltrate alien pseudo-children into human society.

This form of paranoia was not confined to the 1950s. The TV movie, mini-series and series/serial "V" (1983-5) featured aliens disguised in human form, who seemed to have come to Earth as benefactors. *Blade Runner* (1982) offered androids indistinguishable from humans, but inverted the paranoia because the androids showed venom only in the face of human hostility. More recently *Species* (1995) — disguised a murderous alien as an attractive young woman. All of these movies depended, on a fear from thousands of years before the Cold War: the folkloric figure of the Shapeshifter.

from here all over the USA. They flee across country to try to warn the outside world — but Becky is herself replaced by a pod-person, leaving Bennel alone to alert the world to the threat. The astonishingly powerful closing scene of the movie's true narrative sees Bennel struggling among the cars on the nearby freeway, ineffectually yelling his warning to the drivers who, as much lacking in individuality as any pod-person, ignore him as a wandering crazy and drive on by.

Invasion Of The Body Snatchers is often interpreted as an anti-McCarthyite or, conversely, anti-communist movie, but really it is — as must be obvious from the above — a movie about individuality and our willingness to surrender it.

1957

The Incredible Shrinking Man

1957 • UK • DIRECTOR JACK ARNOLD • SCREENPLAY RICHARD MATHESON, FROM MATHESON'S THE SHRINKING MAN (1956) • 81M • B/W
A classic of sf cinema. Radiation causes a man to shrink slowly until he disappears; in the interim, he has to fight with the family cat and then with a (to him) huge spider. Parodied as *The Incredible Shrinking Woman* (1981).

Quatermass II

1957 • UK • DIRECTOR VAL GUEST • SCREENPLAY VAL GUEST, NIGEL KNEALE, FROM KNEALE'S BBC TV SERIAL (1955) • SPECIAL EFFECTS LES BOWIE • STARRING VERA DAY (SHEILA), BRIAN DONLEVY (PROFESSOR BERNARD QUATERMASS), BRYAN FORBES (MARSH), WILLIAM FRANKLYN (BRAND), SIDNEY JAMES (JIMMY HALL), JOHN LONGDEN (LOMAX) • 85M • B/W
An intriguing movie, comparable to *Invasion Of The Body Snatchers* (1956): its script is clumsier, but its brilliant cinematography (by

Gerald Gibbs) and use of locations manage to convey a sense of alienation of humanity from itself — a main theme of both movies. The plot here is that the aliens have sent an advance guard of microscopic lifeforms that can infect human beings and turn them into catspaws; the catspaws, with the connivance of "converted" top-ranking government officials, are building huge artificial-environment spheres in preparation for the arrival of the aliens themselves, who cannot breathe our atmosphere.

Quatermass II is often described as a masterpiece. It is not. But, if one can ignore Donlevy's lack of conviction and the lapses of the screenplay, it does effectively build up paranoia from an initial sense of slight unease to something truly powerful.

Twenty Million Miles To Earth

1957 • USA • DIRECTOR NATHAN JURAN • SCREENPLAY CHRISTOPHER KNOPF, BOB WILLIAMS • 84M • B/W
An intended showcase for the special effects of

OPEN WIDE BRIAN DONLEVY, AS PROFESSOR QUATERMASS, TRIES TO SORT THINGS OUT IN QUATERMASS II, ONE OF THE BEST UK EFFORTS AT THE PARANOID SF MOVIE

Ray Harryhausen. An ever-growing monster, inadvertently brought back from Venus by astronauts, is eventually zapped on top of Rome's Colosseum.

1958

The Blob

1958 • USA • DIRECTOR IRWIN S. YEAWORTH JR • SCREENPLAY KATE PHILLIPS, THEODORE SIMONSON • STARRING ANETA CORSEAUT (JUDY), STEVE MCQUEEN (STEVE) • 86M • COLOUR
An alien, in the form of an omnivorous globule of protoplasm, lands in a small US town and proceeds to devour people. After the parasite has eaten the local doctor, teen rebel Steve tries to persuade the grown-ups that there is a threat. But, by the time they take him seriously, it is too late... Almost unwatchable today, this probably made sense in the aftermath of *Rebel Without A Cause* (1955). It was remade with the same name in 1988, a version notable for its gory special effects.

SO LONG, FAREWELL, AUF WIEDERSEHEN... *BASED ON THE NEVIL SHUTE NOVEL,* ON THE BEACH *(1959), SAW AUSTRALIANS AS THE LAST SURVIVORS OF THE NUCLEAR HOLOCAUST. THE MOVIE IS STILL POWERFUL TODAY*

The Fly

1958 • US • *DIRECTOR* KURT NEUMANN • *SCREENPLAY* JAMES CLAVELL, FROM GEORGE LANGELAAN'S 'THE FLY' (1957) • *STARRING* AL HEDISON (ANDRÉ DELAMBRE), PATRICIA OWEN (HÉLÈNE DELAMBRE), VINCENT PRICE (FRANÇOIS DELAMBRE) • *94M* • *COLOUR*

A matter-transmission experiment goes horribly wrong when, accidentally, a human intermingles with a fly. Sequelled by *Return Of The Fly* (1959) and *Curse Of The Fly* (1965), and impressively rethought as *The Fly* (1986).

From The Earth To The Moon

1958 • USA • *DIRECTOR* BYRON HASKIN • *SCREENPLAY* ROBERT BLEES, JAMES LEICESTER, FROM JULES VERNE'S *FROM THE EARTH TO THE MOON* (1865-70) • *100M* • *COLOUR*

A disappointing, unambitious version of Verne's classic tale: Joseph Cotten and George Sanders battle with a dull script and poor direction, and lose badly.

I Married A Monster From Outer Space

1958 • USA • *DIRECTOR* GENE FOWLER JR • *SCREENPLAY* LOUIS VITTES • *78M* • *B/W*

Rather a good piece of paranoia. A woman unwittingly marries a shapeshifted alien version of her fiancé.

It! The Terror From Beyond Space

(VT IT! THE VAMPIRE FROM BEYOND SPACE)

1958 • USA • *DIRECTOR* EDWARD L. CAHN • *SCREENPLAY* JEROME BIXBY • *69M* • *B/W*

Much resembling A.E. van Vogt's 'A Discord In Scarlet' (1939), this precursor of *Alien* (1979) sees a space crew returning from Mars being killed one-by-one by a stowaway monster. Remade as *Queen Of Blood* (1966).

1959

Journey To The Center Of The Earth

1959 • USA • *DIRECTOR* HENRY LEVIN • *SCREENPLAY* CHARLES BRACKETT, WALTER REISCH, FROM JULES VERNE'S *JOURNEY TO THE CENTRE OF THE EARTH* (1863) • *STARRING* PAT BOONE (ALEC MCEWAN), JAMES MASON (SIR OLIVER LINDENBROEK) • *132M* • *COLOUR*

Fearsomely long and intendedly semi-comic version of Verne's famous tale.

On The Beach

1959 • USA • *DIRECTOR* STANLEY KRAMER • *SCREENPLAY* JAMES LEE BARRETT, JOHN PAXTON, FROM NEVIL SHUTE'S *ON THE BEACH* (1957) • *SPECIAL EFFECTS* LEE ZAVITZ • *STARRING* DONNA ANDERSON (MARY HOLMES), FRED ASTAIRE (JULIAN OSBORN), AVA GARDNER (MOIRA DAVIDSON), GREGORY PECK (DWIGHT TOWERS), ANTHONY

PERKINS (PETER HOLMES) • *134M* • *B/W*

1964, and a nuclear war in the northern hemisphere has destroyed all human life there. Winds have been bringing the killer radiation southwards, so that now only in Australia can life continue... and for only a matter of weeks. This movie follows various fairly stereotyped characters as they prepare themselves for the end of the World.

This is an example of a gripping novel becoming a far too drawn-out movie, although Astaire — as an over-the-hill racing driver who prefers to go out in glory rather than take the easy option of a suicide pill — adds a modicum of dramatic tension.

The World, The Flesh And The Devil

1959 • USA • *DIRECTOR* RANALD MACDOUGALL • *SCREENPLAY* RANALD MACDOUGALL, FROM M.P. SHIEL'S *THE PURPLE CLOUD* (1901) • *95M* • *B/W*

In a desolate, post-holocaust USA, a white bigot is horrified to discover a white woman (perhaps the last woman on Earth) has taken up with a black man. Shockingly for the time, the three eventually decide to make a life together.

1960

Gorgo

1960 • UK • *DIRECTOR* EUGÈNE LOURIÉ • *SCREENPLAY* DANIEL HYATT, JOHN LORING • *79M* • *COLOUR*

Low-budget monster movie. A prehistoric monster is recovered from the Irish Sea and brought to London. Its mother turns up to rescue it, with predictably destructive consequences.

The Lost World

1960 • USA • *DIRECTOR* IRWIN ALLEN • *SCREENPLAY* IRWIN ALLEN, CHARLES BENNETT, FROM ARTHUR CONAN DOYLE'S *THE LOST WORLD* (1912) • *STARRING* CLAUDE RAINS (PROFESSOR CHALLENGER) • *98M* • *COLOUR*

Lacklustre remake of *The Lost World* (1925), including a tedious romantic dimension — as if to emulate *Journey To The Center Of The Earth* (1959). But the special effects, by L.B. Abbott, make it all worthwhile.

The Time Machine

1960 • USA • *DIRECTOR* GEORGE PAL • *SCREENPLAY* DAVID DUNCAN, FROM H.G. WELLS'S *THE TIME MACHINE* (1895) • *SPECIAL EFFECTS* TIM BAER, WAH CHANG, GEORGE PAL, GENE WARREN • *STARRING* YVETTE MIMIEUX (WEENA), ROD TAYLOR (TIME TRAVELLER) • *103M* • *COLOUR*

A 19th-century inventor announces to his friends that he has devised a machine capable of travelling through time, and of course they disbelieve him. But travel through time he does, eventually arriving in the far future: AD 802,701. There he discovers a beautiful surface-living race of humanity, the Eloi, are farmed like cattle by a hideous troglodytic race, the Morlocks. Falling in love with one of the Eloi, the Time Traveller tries to instil in her race the notion of rebellion against their masters. But the Eloi really are little more than semi-intelligent animals: human form is no unequivocal indication of intellect.

Wells's novella, although imbued with his wonder at the marvels of technology, is in the end a profoundly depressed work. The movie version converts his pessimistic vision into something more like an adventure yarn.

Village Of The Damned

1960 • UK • *DIRECTOR* WOLF RILLA • *SCREENPLAY* WOLF RILLA, FROM JOHN WYNDHAM'S *THE MIDWICH CUCKOOS*

 CHILDREN OF THE DORM *THE EXTRAORDINARY PERFORMANCES OF THE CHILDREN ARE WHAT CARRY THE MOVIE* VILLAGE OF THE DAMNED *(1960), BASED ON THE JOHN WYNDHAM NOVEL* THE MIDWICH CUCKOOS

(1957) • *SPECIAL EFFECTS* TOM HOWARD • *STARRING* GEORGE SANDERS (GORDON ZELLABY), BARBARA SHELLEY (ANTHEA ZELLABY), MARTIN STEPHENS (DAVID ZELLABY) • *78M* • *B/W*

A tale of alien invasion by artificial insemination. Everyone in the village of Midwich falls asleep for 24 hours, and later it is discovered that all the local women of suitable age are pregnant. At first, this seems mere coincidence, but, as the resultant children grow, it is seen that they are all of a kind: they are highly intelligent and, with their bright blond hair, physically similar. They also, it emerges, share a group-mind. Zellaby, himself the "father" of one of the children, realizes that this is nothing less than an invasion and takes drastic action.

Village Of The Damned is by no means a bad movie, but the fact that it could have been better became obvious only three years later with the appearance of *Children Of The Damned* (1963): in which a group of six alien-spawned children are brought to London, with disastrous results.

1961

The Damned

(*VT* THESE ARE THE DAMNED)

1961 • UK • *DIRECTOR* JOSEPH LOSEY • *SCREENPLAY* EVAN JONES, FROM H.L. LAWRENCE'S *THE CHILDREN OF LIGHT* (1960) • *96M* • *B/W*

Excellent and affecting movie marred by cod science. A scientist irradiates children in a secret hideout, so that they will survive the expected nuclear holocaust.

DO YOU WANT TO KNOW A SECRET? *ROD TAYLOR, AS THE TIME TRAVELLER, TRIES TO PERSUADE THE "BEAUTIFUL PEOPLE" OF THE ELOI THAT THEY MUST STOP BEING PREY TO THE MORLOCKS IN* THE TIME MACHINE *(1960)*

The Day The Earth Caught Fire

1961 • UK • *DIRECTOR* VAL GUEST • *SCREENPLAY* VAL GUEST, WOLF MANKOWITZ • *SPECIAL EFFECTS* LES BOWIE • *STARRING* ARTHUR CHRISTIANSEN (HIMSELF), EDWARD JUDD (PETE STENNING), LEO MCKERN (BILL MCGUIRE), JANET MUNRO (JEAN) • *99M* • *B/W* WITH SOME TINTING

Although the premise is Velikovskian rather than scientific, this taut drama is worth watching. A concatenation of H-bomb tests knocks Earth out of its orbit and sends it spiralling inwards towards the Sun. Scientists calculate that another series of explosions might — *might* — kick Earth back into its original orbit.

Much of the action takes place in the offices of the London *Daily Express* (Christiansen, an ex-editor of that newspaper, thoroughly enjoyed playing himself), so that tension is built up through secondary reports rather than through the direct witnessing of events. In the closing scenes of the movie, we are shown two alternative headlines for the front page of the *Express*'s next issue: EARTH SAVED and EARTH DOOMED. The uncertainty adds to the movie's undoubted power.

Mysterious Island

1961 • UK/USA • *DIRECTOR* CY ENDFIELD • *SCREENPLAY* JOHN PREBBLE, DANIEL ULLMAN, CRANE WILBUR, FROM JULES VERNE'S *THE MYSTERIOUS ISLAND* (1874-5) • *STARRING* HERBERT LOM (CAPTAIN NEMO) • *100M* • *COLOUR*

An updated remake of *The Mysterious Island* (1929) sees Confederate fugitives battling with huge monsters (by Ray Harryhausen) on a bizarre island owned by Nemo.

Voyage To The Bottom Of The Sea

1961 • USA • *DIRECTOR* IRWIN ALLEN • *SCREENPLAY* IRWIN ALLEN, CHARLES BENNETT • *105M* • *COLOUR*

An experimental submarine surfaces to find the Van Allen Belts ablaze, so puts them out using a Polaris missile. This movie, astonishingly unsound in the scientific sense, was the basis of a 110-episode TV series (from 1964).

HOLD THE FRONT PAGE *WHAT WAS SO STUNNING ABOUT 1961'S* THE DAY THE EARTH CAUGHT FIRE *WAS THE WAY IT WAS PRESENTED ALMOST AS A DOCUMENTARY. EDWARD JUDD WAS A SUITABLY MACHO CENTRAL FIGURE.*

THE TRUTH BEHIND THE BOMBS-WORLD CLIMATIC CRISIS

RUN TO THE HILLS *BASED ON SHORT STORIES BY WARD MOORE,* PANIC IN YEAR ZERO *SAW A TYPICALLY GRITTY PERFORMANCE FROM RAY MILLAND — HERE BEING SF'S JOHN WAYNE*

RAY MILLAND
JEAN HAGEN   FRANKIE AVALON
Starring in
'PANIC IN YEAR ZERO' (X)
From Anglo Amalgamated for Warner-Pathe release

1962

Panic In Year Zero

(VT *END OF THE WORLD*)

1962 • USA • *DIRECTOR* RAY MILLAND • *SCREENPLAY* JOHN MORTON, JAY SIMMS, FROM (UNCREDITED) WARD MOORE'S 'LOT' (1953) AND 'LOT'S DAUGHTER' (1954) • *STARRING* FRANKIE AVALON, JEAN HAGEN, RAY MILLAND, MARY MITCHELL • *92M* • *B/W*

After the nuclear holocaust, a father takes his family from Los Angeles to establish a new life in the hills. They learn the brutalities necessary for survival.

1963

Children Of The Damned

(VT *HORROR!*)

1963 • UK • *DIRECTOR* ANTON M. LEADER • *SCREENPLAY* JOHN BRILEY, FROM JOHN WYNDHAM'S *THE MIDWICH CUCKOOS* (1957) • *90M* • *B/W*

Superior remake/sequel of *Village Of The Damned* (1960).

The Day Of The Triffids

1963 • UK • *DIRECTORS* FREDDIE FRANCIS (UNCREDITED), STEVE SEKELY • *SCREENPLAY* PHILIP YORDAN, FROM JOHN WYNDHAM'S *THE DAY OF THE TRIFFIDS* (1951)

• *STARRING* HOWARD KEEL • *95M* • *COLOUR*
Almost everyone in the world is blinded prior to the invasion of intelligent alien plants. A bad but oddly impressive adaptation of the Wyndham classic.

X — The Man With X-Ray Eyes

(VT *THE MAN WITH THE X-RAY EYES*)
1963 • USA • *DIRECTOR* ROGER CORMAN • *SCREENPLAY* ROBERT DILLON, RAY RUSSELL • *STARRING* RAY MILLAND (DR XAVIER) • *80M* • *COLOUR*
Experimenting on himself, scientist Xavier becomes able to see through things (initially women's clothing), and thereby finds himself cast into an Outsider role. At last he must pluck his own eyes from their sockets.

1964

Dr Strangelove: Or How I Learned To Stop Worrying And Love The Bomb

1964 • UK • *DIRECTOR* STANLEY KUBRICK • *SCREENPLAY* PETER GEORGE, STANLEY KUBRICK, TERRY SOUTHERN, FROM GEORGE'S *TWO HOURS TO DOOM* (VT *RED ALERT* 1958) • *SPECIAL EFFECTS* WALLY VEEVERS • *STARRING* PETER BULL (AMBASSADOR DE SADESKY), STERLING HAYDEN (GENERAL JACK D. RIPPER), SLIM PICKENS (MAJOR T.J. "KING" KONG), TRACY REED (MISS SCOTT), GEORGE C. SCOTT (GENERAL BUCK TURGIDSON), PETER SELLERS (GROUP CAPTAIN MANDRAKE/PRESIDENT MERKIN MUFFLEY/DR STRANGELOVE), KEENAN WYNN (COLONEL BAT GUANO) • *94M* • *B/W*
Kubrick has the rare distinction of having made three of the most significant movies in the history of sf cinema; perhaps even more notable is the fact that all three are entirely different — the other two being *2001: A Space Odyssey*

(1968) and *A Clockwork Orange* (1971). All three, moreover, have become part of mainstream Western culture: in a curious way, they have come to represent something far more than mere movies.

Dr Strangelove is made up of three interwoven strands. In the first, General Ripper, commander of Burpelson Air Force base, goes crazy and becomes convinced that fluoridation of the water is a communist plot to subvert the West from within; acting unilaterally, he launches a pre-emptive nuclear strike (aircraft rather than missiles) against the USSR, and commands the ground-based staff of the installation to repel any attempt by US troops to enter it — because those troops are obviously

Commies in disguise. Within the base, a hapless British officer, Mandrake, does his best through diplomacy to persuade Ripper to recall his B52 bombers.

In the second strand, a despairing President Muffley calls all his top advisors into the War Room in an attempt to see if they can solve the crisis. But Muffley's efforts are not helped by the bellicose attitude of General Turgidson, who believes them Russkies deserve bombing anyway; nor by the quirky insouciance of his scientific advisor, the near-cyborg, ex-Nazi Dr Strangelove. Muffley's despair deepens when Russian ambassador de Sadesky announces that the Soviets have developed a Doomsday device which will, if the USSR is hit, automatically release their entire nuclear arsenal, thereby destroying the world.

The third strand is set aboard one of the B52s, piloted by Major "King" Kong. The casual attitude of the crew — smoking and joking as they go on their way to slaughter millions — is in bitter contrast to the agonized tension of the other two strands. As the rest of the strike force is shot out of the skies, Kong's craft evades all attackers. Even when, as the bomber reaches its target, the crew discover the bomb-bay doors are jammed, Kong is undeterred. Manually opening the doors, he rides astride the bomb, whooping ecstatically, towards the ground.

This is the darkest of dark comedies — indeed, it has been reported that Kubrick initially intended to play it straight (as George's original novel did). But the bitterness of its satire proved more telling — as *Fail Safe* (1964) proved the same year — than any straight rendition could have been. Often very funny, *Dr Strangelove* makes you cry until you laugh... for human folly, the movie says, is not worthy of your tears.

STOP NOW OR I'LL SHOOT *THE MOST MEMORABLE OF THE THREE ROLES THAT PETER SELLERS PLAYED IN* **DR STRANGELOVE** *(1964) WAS THE EX-NAZI WHOSE BODY HAS LARGELY BEEN REPLACED BY MACHINERY THAT, MOST OFTEN, DOESN'T WORK QUITE AS IT SHOULD*

Ray Harryhausen — superdynamation was the name of the game

A protégé of Willis H. O'Brien, Ray Harryhausen (1920-   ) initially deployed his mentor's techniques, but developed them to the point that Harryhausen's name on a poster was sufficient inducement to go and see a movie.

Harryhausen first made his mark with *Mighty Joe Young* (1949), where he was O'Brien's assistant. After single-handedly supervising the effects on *The Beast From 20,000 Fathoms* (1953), he formed a production partnership with Charles H. Schneer and together, dubbing Harryhausen's effects "Superdynamation", they created *It Came From Beneath The Sea* (1955), *Earth Versus The Flying Saucers* (1956), *Twenty Million Miles To Earth* (1957), *The Seventh Voyage Of Sinbad* (1958), *The Three Worlds Of Gulliver* (1960), *Mysterious Island* (1961), *Jason And The Argonauts* (1963), *The First Men In The Moon* (1964), *The Valley Of Gwangi* (1969), *The Golden Voyage Of Sinbad* (1973) and *Sinbad And The Eye Of The Tiger* (1977); Harryhausen was also responsible for the effects in Hammer's *One Million Years BC* (1966).

By the time of *Sinbad And The Eye Of The Tiger*, his techniques were looking very dated: the stop-motion jerkiness, which audiences had been prepared to tolerate two decades earlier, was now risible by comparison with what other effects specialists could achieve — *Star Wars* and *Close Encounters Of The Third Kind* were released that same year. Nevertheless, Harryhausen and Schneer tried one last fling with *Clash Of The Titans* (1981), perhaps hoping an all-star cast would somehow cover up for a dire script and unconvincing effects. They were wrong.

travels with companions to the Moon, where they discover an underground civilization of monster insects. A terrible script is relieved by Ray Harryhausen's special effects.

It Happened Here

1964 • UK • *DIRECTOR* KEVIN BROWNLOW, ANDREW MOLLO • *SCREENPLAY* KEVIN BROWNLOW, ANDREW MOLLO • *99M* • *B/W*

Astonishingly good semi-professional movie based on the premise that the Nazis successfully invaded the UK in 1940.

Robinson Crusoe On Mars

1964 • USA • *DIRECTOR* BYRON HASKIN • *SCREENPLAY* JOHN C. HIGGINS, IB MELCHIOR • *SPECIAL EFFECTS* LARRY BUTLER • *STARRING* VIC LUNDIN, PAUL MANTEE, ADAM WEST • *110M* • *B/W*

An Earth spaceship crash-lands on Mars, and its sole survivor ekes out an existence (in company with a monkey) by heating Mars rocks to release their oxygen and eating the hard-tack supplied for his mission.

Soon, though, a spacefleet of alien humanoid slavers arrives, and our hero manages to liberate one of their slaves to be his Man Friday, thereby saving his own sanity, which has been at risk through the sheer loneliness of his Martian existence.

Fail Safe

1964 • US • *DIRECTOR* SIDNEY LUMET • *SCREENPLAY* WALTER BERNSTEIN, FROM EUGENE L. BURDICK'S AND HARVEY WHEELER'S *FAIL-SAFE* (1962) • *SPECIAL EFFECTS* STORYBOARD INC • *STARRING* HENRY FONDA (US PRESIDENT), LARRY HAGMAN (BUCK), WALTER MATTHAU (GROETESCHELE), DAN O'HERLIHY (GENERAL BLACK), FRANK OVERTON (GENERAL BOGAN) •*111M* • *B/W*

It was this movie's misfortune to be released only a few months after *Dr Strangelove* (1964); what is astonishing is that both movies came from the same studio. Where *Dr Strangelove* expressed its bitter opposition to nuclear posturing through savage humour, *Fail Safe* is entirely sombre.

Through mishap, US bombers set off to nuke the Russkies, and efforts to stop them are only partly successful: some of the planes are going to get through and complete their missions. In the end, to avoid all-out war, the US President is forced to agree that the Soviets may, by way of compensation, bomb an equivalent number of US cities.

The plot is highly implausible, but this is a good nail-biter.

The First Men In The Moon

1964 • UK • *DIRECTOR* NATHAN JURAN • *SCREENPLAY* NIGEL KNEALE, JAN READ, FROM H.G. WELLS'S *THE FIRST MEN IN THE MOON* (1901) • *STARRING* LIONEL JEFFRIES (CAVOR) • *107M* • *COLOUR*

In 1899, Cavor, inventor of an antigravity paint,

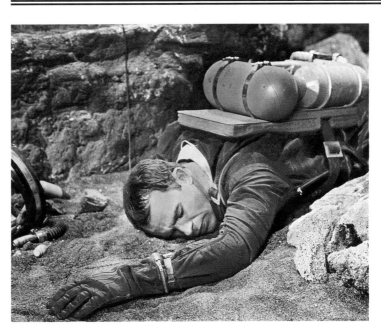

ALL WASHED UP *ROBINSON CRUSOE ON MARS (1964) WAS A REASONABLY ENTERTAINING B-MOVIE, BUT IT SEEMED, EVEN AT THE TIME, REMARKABLY NAIVE BY COMPARISON WITH OTHER SF MOVIES*

Le cinéma fantastique

Despite the fact that two of the earliest sf movies — Georges Méliès's *Le Voyage Dans La Lune* (1902) and *Le Voyage A Travers L'Impossible* (1904) — were French, there is no great hard-sf tradition in French cinema, most of this country's moviemakers preferring to opt for whimsical fantasies like René Clair's *Paris Qui Dort* (1923; vt *The Crazy Ray*) and *Les Belles De Nuit* (1952). More recently, *Alphaville* (1965), although ostensibly sf, was presented as an idiosyncratic mixture of fantasy and allegory. *Fahrenheit 451* (1966), made in the UK by French director François Truffaut, takes a much more straightforward approach, but is still unlike any adaptation a US or UK director might have made of Ray Bradbury's novel. The erotic science-fantasy *Barbarella* (1967) is, once again, hard to imagine coming from any other country. Poles apart from the extrovert Barbarella is the introspective treatment given to a D.G. Compton novel in the French-German *La Mort En Direct* (1980). *Malevil* (1981), another French-German co-production, has a quirkiness of plot and ambience that makes it seem far more gallic than teutonic. By contrast, *Quest For Fire* (1981), a prehistoric fantasy, could have been a North American movie — almost certainly because of the Canadian component in this Canadian-French co-production. Conversely, *Le Dernier Combat* (1983), though set in a post-holocaust world, becomes more an exercise in surrealism than in sf. Quintessentially French also is the time-travel comedy *Les Visiteurs* (1993), which in its homeland outgrossed the simultaneously released *Jurassic Park* (1993) — and is the better movie. In the English-language marketplace, French sf movies are too rarely given the prominence they merit.

NOT IN MY CAR ONE OF THE GREAT STRENGTHS OF *ALPHAVILLE* (1965) IS THAT IT CANNOT EASILY BE CATEGORIZED: ONE CAN CLAIM IT AS SF, OR AS SURREALISM, OR AS FANTASY, OR AS ANOTHER GODARD FILM ESSAY, OR AS...

1965

Alphaville

(VT *UNE ÉTRANGE AVENTURE DE LEMMY CAUTION*)
1965 • FRANCE • *DIRECTOR* JEAN-LUC GODARD • *SCREENPLAY* JEAN-LUC GODARD • *STARRING* EDDIE CONSTANTINE (LEMMY CAUTION), ANNA KARINA (NATASHA VON BRAUN), AKIM TAMIROFF (HENRI DICKSON), HOWARD VERNON (PROFESSOR VON BRAUN) • *100M* • B/W

Lemmy Caution is a hard-boiled private eye who featured in many of the pulp, pseudo-American thrillers churned out by UK writer Peter Cheyney. These novels were always more popular in France than anywhere else, and some were filmed. Here, though, Lemmy is an intergalactic special agent, sent by automobile through intersidereal space to distant Alphaville, which closely resembles 1960s Paris. There, he discovers that Professor von Braun has created a fascistic supercomputer, Alpha-60; he also discovers the professor's daughter, Natasha, who does not know how to love.

This crosshatching of various genres does not lend itself to easy synopsising, and the movie really makes sense only if accepted on its own terms — which are playful and joyous.

La Decima Vittima

(VT *THE TENTH VICTIM*)
1965 • ITALY/SPAIN • *DIRECTOR* ELIO PETRI • *SCREENPLAY* ENNIO FLAIANO, TONINO GUERRA, ELIO PETRI, GIORGIO SALVIONI, FROM ROBERT SHECKLEY'S 'THE SEVENTH VICTIM' (1953) • *STARRING* MARCELLO MASTROIANNI, URSULA ANDRESS • *92M* • COLOUR

In the future, murder is permitted as a means of population control.

The War Game

1965 • UK • *DIRECTOR* PETER WATKINS • *SCREENPLAY* PETER WATKINS • *50M* • B/W

Made for BBC TV but banned by that organization as being too shocking, this pseudo-documentary portrays, in intimate detail, the effects of nuclear holocaust on a community in southeastern England. Although dated, it is still a very powerful piece of cinema.

1966

Fahrenheit 451

1966 • UK • *DIRECTOR* FRANÇOIS TRUFFAUT • *SCREENPLAY* JEAN-LOUIS RICHARD, DAVID RUDKIN, HELEN SCOTT, FRANÇOIS TRUFFAUT, FROM RAY BRADBURY'S *FAHRENHEIT 451* (1953) • *SPECIAL EFFECTS* BOWIE FILMS, CHARLES STAFFEL • *STARRING* JULIE CHRISTIE (LINDA/CLARISSE), OSKAR WERNER (MONTAG) • *112M* • COLOUR

In the future, books are illegal, and any that are found are burned. Montag is a Fireman: his job is to discover books and do the burning. Finally, he becomes curious as to why people are prepared to die rather than give up their books, and he appropriates one volume for himself. The discovery of reading converts him, and he flees his dull wife Linda to find freedom, aided by the subversive Clarisse. (An irony is that Christie plays both women: they started out with equal potential, but have become two very different people.) At last, Montag finds himself in a commune whose inhabitants spend all their time learning books by heart, so that, even if all the physical volumes are destroyed, the books themselves will not die.

For a movie that focuses on flames, Truffaut

manages to make this a very chilly work indeed, partly through his deployment of colour values. Also, he effectively conveys the notion that, each time a book is consigned to the flames, it is as if an act of murder has been committed.

Although both Bradbury's novel and this movie touted the fact that 451 degrees Fahrenheit is the temperature at which book paper catches fire, this is nonsense: different book papers obviously ignite at different (and much higher) temperatures. Bradbury has admitted he just liked the number.

Fantastic Voyage

1966 • USA • *DIRECTOR* RICHARD FLEISCHER • SCREENPLAY HARRY KLEINER • *STARRING* STEPHEN BOYD, RAQUEL WELCH • *100M* • *COLOUR*
To dissipate a genius's potentially fatal blood clot, a crew are miniaturized and sent in an equally tiny submarine through his bloodstream. Hokum, but medically accurate and fun to watch. The theme was reprised in *InnerSpace* (1987).

One Million Years BC

1966 • UK • *DIRECTOR* DON CHAFFEY • *SCREENPLAY* MICHAEL CARRERAS, FROM THE MOVIE *ONE MILLION BC*

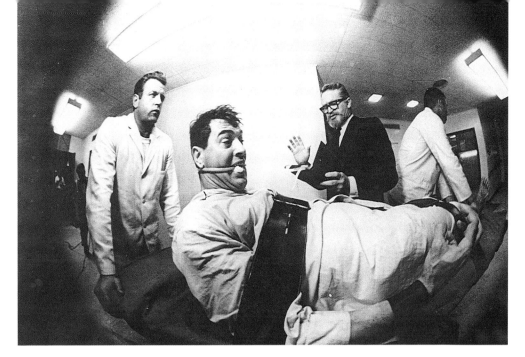

THIS WON'T HURT AT ALL *ROCK HUDSON DISCOVERS SOME OF THE UNACCEPTABLE COSTS OF REJUVENATION IN THE 1966 FILM,* SECONDS

(1940) • *STARRING* JOHN RICHARDSON (TUMAK), RAQUEL WELCH (LOANA) • *100M* • *COLOUR* PLUS SOME SEPIA
A classy remake of *One Million BC* (1940), but shedding the frame story and much female apparel.

Seconds

1966 • USA • *DIRECTOR* JOHN FRANKENHEIMER • *SCREENPLAY* LEWIS JOHN CARLINO, FROM DAVID ELY'S

TURN UP THE HEAT
ONE OF THE GREAT MOVIES IN SF'S CINEMA HISTORY IS FAHRENHEIT 451. *PARADOXICALLY CHILLING ON A FIRST VIEWING, IT BECOMES BETTER AND BETTER WITH REPEATED VIEWING. HERE THE FIREMAN — BOOKBURNER — MONTAG (OSKAR WERNER) IS STILL HALF-CONVINCED THAT WHAT HE IS DOING IS MORALLY RIGHT*

SECONDS (1963) • *STARRING* WILL GEER ("THE OLD MAN"), ROCK HUDSON (ANTIOCHUS "TONY" WILSON), SALOME JENS (NORA MARCUS), JOHN RANDOLPH (ARTHUR HAMILTON) • *106M* • *B/W*
Rich, middle-aged businessman Randolph employs the services of a clandestine Organization which guarantees to give him another shot at youth. They fake his death, perform extensive plastic and transplant surgery and place him in a new life, where he is trendy painter Wilson, wealthily beach-bumming in California alongside beautiful girlfriend Marcus. But soon he tires of the ceaseless round of parties and sex, and wants his old, quiet life back. This the Organization cannot permit, and so Wilson chooses death instead of continued youth. The Organization calmly stores his organs for future use.

This could have been better as a comedy; the wistfulness of, say, *Topper* (1937) — where a timid middle-aged bank manager discovers that the swinging socialite life is not for him — might have conveyed Frankenheimer's message that there are rich people out there who can do what they want with you more adroitly than the paranoia which he rather self-consciously generates. The underlying conservatism of the sub-theme — that you're happiest the way you are — is taken for granted: it is a movie cliché that should be challenged more often.

1967

Barbarella

1967 • FRANCE/ITALY • *DIRECTOR* ROGER VADIM
• *SCREENPLAY* VITTORIO BONICELLI, CLAUDE BRÛLE, BRIAN DEGAS, JEAN-CLAUDE FOREST, TUDOR GATES, TERRY SOUTHERN, ROGER VADIM, CLEMENT BIDDLE WOOD, FROM THE COMIC STRIP CREATED BY JEAN-CLAUDE FOREST
• *SPECIAL EFFECTS* AUGUST LOHMAN, GERARD COGAN, THIERRY VINCENS-FARGO • *STARRING* JANE FONDA (BARBARELLA), DAVID HEMMINGS (DILDANO), JOHN PHILLIP LAW (PIGAR), MILO O'SHEA (DURAN DURAN), ANITA PALLENBERG (BLACK QUEEN) • *98M* • *COLOUR*

A piece of picaresque science fantasy that teeters just this side of soft porn. The beautiful Barbarella is an Earth agent who must rescue the genius scientist Duran Duran from the corrupt city of Sogo, on one of the planets of Tau Ceti. She eventually finds him there, only to discover that he is mad; he has, he thinks, perfected a machine that will kill women through an overdose of orgasms — Barbarella blows its fuses by being able to take all it can deliver, and more.

But the main plot of this movie is perhaps the least part of it: what entrances are the various highly fantasticated adventures that Barbarella undergoes while pursuing her quest. Striking among these is the sequence in which she befriends a group of children on a waste planet, only for them to set on her their carnivorous automata, which she at first assumes are merely dolls. The enduring memory of the movie, though, is of the blind angel Pigar, whom Barbarella befriends and who is later crucified: the pathetic, tragic image gains almost intolerable poignancy through being set amid a (frequently very funny) froth.

The Power

1967 • USA • *DIRECTOR* BYRON HASKIN • *SCREENPLAY* JOHN GAY, FROM FRANK M. ROBINSON'S *THE POWER* (1956) • *108M* • *COLOUR*

A mad scientist who plans to rule the world is

 GROOVY *ALWAYS READY TO PRODUCE A LOOK OF INNOCENT, WIDE-EYED AMAZEMENT, JANE FONDA GAVE A PERFORMANCE IN* BARBARELLA *THAT SHOULD HAVE WON AN OSCAR*

LOOK IN TO MY EYES *ANDREW KEIR AND BARBARA SHELLEY DO THEIR BEST IN 1967'S* QUATERMASS AND THE PIT, *BUT CANNOT COMPENSATE FOR THE FACT THAT THE MOVIE WAS SO MUCH SHORTER THAN THE TV SERIAL*

capable of killing people simply by focusing his willpower on them.

Privilege

1967 • UK • *DIRECTOR* PETER WATKINS • *SCREENPLAY* NORMAN BOGNER • *STARRING* PAUL JONES (SHORTER) • *103M* • *COLOUR*

A rock star is subverted by the state, which uses him as a tool to control the young. Ironically, when he snaps the reins, it is his youthful fans, not the state, who kill him. Intermittently powerful.

Quatermass And The Pit

(VT FIVE MILLION YEARS TO EARTH)

1967 • UK • *DIRECTOR* ROY WARD BAKER • *SCREENPLAY* NIGEL KNEALE, FROM HIS BBC TV SERIAL *QUATERMASS AND THE PIT* (1958-9) • *SPECIAL EFFECTS* BOWIE FILMS
• *STARRING* JAMES DONALD (DR MATTHEW RONEY), JULIAN GLOVER (COLONEL BREEN), ANDREW KEIR (PROFESSOR BERNARD QUATERMASS), BARBARA SHELLEY (BARBARA JUDD) • *97M* • *COLOUR*

This is a simplified version of Kneale's TV serial (1958-9), with some effort being made to patch over a few of the more blatant scientific implausibilities of the original. Excavations beneath a London tube station uncover an alien spaceship which, it is deduced, came millions of years ago from Mars. Those nearby begin to experience peculiar mental disturbances, and eventually dramatic poltergeist effects start to manifest.

Quatermass and assistant Judd discover the area has a history of such troubles. By lucky coincidence, colleague Roney has developed a prototype "opticencephalograph" — a device whereby thoughts can be projected on to a TV screen — and, through Judd's archetypal memory, it is found both that the long-extinct Martians were breeding intelligence into our forebears in the hope of making our planet their own, and also that they conducted culls on all of their race who differed from the norm. The insectile, horned form of the Martians clearly gave rise to our image of the Devil; the culling entered our legends as the Wild Hunt. Further tampering with the spacecraft engenders just such a Wild Hunt through the streets of London; only the heroism of Roney saves humanity.

The TV serial, broadcast live in b/w, featured wobbly sets and occasionally misplaced microphones, but is far more powerful than this movie. Viewed in isolation, however, the movie is rather good.

1968

Charly

1968 • USA • *DIRECTOR* RALPH NELSON • *SCREENPLAY* STIRLING SILLIPHANT, FROM DANIEL KEYES'S 'FLOWERS FOR ALGERNON' (1959) AND *FLOWERS FOR ALGERNON* (1966) • *STARRING* CLAIRE BLOOM (ALICE KINIAN), LEON JANNEY (DR RICHARD NEMUR), CLIFF ROBERTSON (CHARLY GORDON), LILIA SKALA (DR ANNA STRAUS) • *106M* • *COLOUR*

The tale is much as in Keyes's story and novel. Scientists who have tested their theories on mice operate on a man with an IQ of only 68, Charly Gordon, and overnight give him superintelligence. What they cannot give him is wisdom and emotional maturity (the movie bears comparison in this respect with *The Mind Of Mr Soames* [1969]). At last, after a fumbled rape attempt, he discovers love with his tutor, Kinian. But Charly has adopted one of the

 HIT THE BOTTLE CHARLY *(1968)* IS AN *EMOTIONALLY CONFUSING MOVIE. CLIFF ROBERTSON AS CHARLY, SEEN HERE WITH THE MOUSE ALGERNON, DEDICATED HIMSELF TO BRINGING DANIEL KEYES'S STORY TO THE SCREEN*

experimental mice, Algernon, as a pet, and observes that after a period of high intelligence the mouse regresses to an intellectual state even lower than before. He realizes this fate is almost certain to be his own.

In the written versions, Keyes was able to

make brilliant use of language to create the pathos of this very low-key story. Such an option was not open to the moviemakers, and the result is a bit of a mishmash, with romance tending to intrude at exactly the wrong moments. Yet the integrity of the intent somehow carries the movie through.

Countdown

1968 • USA • *DIRECTOR* ROBERT ALTMAN • *SCREENPLAY* LORING MANDEL, FROM HANK SERLES'S *THE PILGRIM PROJECT* (1964) • *101M* • *COLOUR*

The year before Armstrong and Aldrin did the real thing, this somewhat dull movie depicted Russians and Americans racing to be the first on the Moon.

Planet Of The Apes

1968 • USA • *DIRECTOR* FRANKLIN J. SCHAFFNER • *SCREENPLAY* ROD SERLING, MICHAEL WILSON, FROM PIERRE BOULLE'S *MONKEY PLANET* (1963) • *SPECIAL EFFECTS* L.B. ABBOTT, JOHN CHAMBERS, ART CRUICKSHANK, EMIL KOSA JR • *STARRING* MAURICE EVANS (DR ZAIUS), LINDA HARRISON (NOVA), CHARLTON HESTON (GEORGE TAYLOR), KIM HUNTER (DR ZIA), RODDY McDOWALL (CORNELIUS) • *112M* • *COLOUR*

An interstellar spacecraft crash-lands on an

 HUMAN ZOO *CHARLTON HESTON WATCHES IMPOTENTLY AS HIS APE CAPTORS DISCUSS HIS FATE IN* **PLANET OF THE APES** *(1968). THIS WAS THE FIRST IN THE SERIES OF "APES" FILMS, AND WAS BY FAR THE BEST*

Charlton Heston — the noble savage

John Charlton Carter (1923-   ), better known as Charlton Heston, trained as a stage actor before coming to Hollywood in 1949, playing Marcus Antonius in *Julius Caesar* that year. He has always had a commanding presence — it was no coincidence that, in Paul Hogan's *Almost An Angel* (1990), he played — albeit uncredited — the part of God. After starring in various historical and biblical epics — *The Ten Commandments* (1956), *Ben-Hur* (1959), *El Cid* (1961) and others — he started carving a unique niche for himself in sf movies with *Planet Of The Apes* (1968), following this up with a cameo role in *Beneath The Planet Of*

The Apes (1969). As notable were his starring roles in *The Omega Man* (1971) and *Soylent Green* (1973), both widely regarded as travesties of the novels on which they were based (by Richard Matheson and Harry Harrison respectively) but both, viewed in isolation, good sf movies. He was the hero of the undistinguished disaster movie *Earthquake* (1974) and starred in the technothriller *Gray Lady Down* (1978) and the horror-fantasy *The Awakening* (1980), based on Bram Stoker's *Jewel Of The Seven Stars* (1903). His most recent sf foray has been *Solar Crisis* (1990), a bad TV movie released theatrically in 1992.

unknown planet where apes are the masters and humans merely wild animals. What the astronauts, led by Taylor, do not realize is that they have in fact passed through a timewarp to arrive on a far-future Earth. It takes a while for them to recognize that the humans around them are indeed an inferior species; it takes an equally long while for the apes to recognize the possibility that humans — at least, some humans — might be capable of intelligent thought.

Although Boulle's delightful whimsy is lost, this is a very good movie — all of Heston's sf movies have been, despite the carping of purists. It spawned two undistinguished TV series (one animated) and four sequels; of the latter, none were dire... although none were particularly good: *Beneath The Planet Of The Apes* (1969), *Escape From The Planet Of The Apes* (1971), *Conquest Of The Planet Of The Apes* (1972) and *Battle For The Planet Of The Apes* (1973).

2001: A Space Odyssey

1968 • USA • *DIRECTOR* STANLEY KUBRICK • *SCREENPLAY* ARTHUR C. CLARKE, STANLEY KUBRICK, ORIGINALLY FROM CLARKE'S 'THE SENTINEL' (1951) • *SPECIAL EFFECTS SUPERVISOR* DOUGLAS TRUMBULL • *SPECIAL EFFECTS* COLIN J. CANTWELL, TOM HOWARD, STANLEY KUBRICK, BRYAN LOFTUS, BRUCE LOGAN, JOHN MALICK, FREDERICK MARTIN,

DAVID OSBORNE, CON PEDERSON, WALLY VEEVERS • *STARRING* KEIR DULLEA (DAVID BOWMAN) • *VOICE ACTOR* DOUGLAS RAIN (HAL9000) • *160M,* CUT TO 141M • *COLOUR*

The opening sequence of this ground-breaking movie is entitled "The Dawn Of Man"; it is only at the end of *2001* that we realize this description applies to the movie as a whole.

There are three parts to *2001*. The first is set millions of years ago among rival tribes of apemen. The arrival of a strange, alien, featureless monolith sparks intelligence among them, and one of the brightest hits on the idea of using a bone as a weapon. In triumph, he hurls the bone high into the air... and, in one of the most brilliant cinematic intercuts of all, the bone at the height of its arc becomes a spaceship moving against a backdrop of stars.

We are into the central (and longest) section of the movie: the era of technological, spacefaring humankind. (Here the influence of Clarke is at its strongest, although he and Kubrick worked closely on all aspects of the script, while Clarke simultaneously wrote the novel version of the story: *2001: A Space Odyssey* [1968].)

After much Clarkeish dalliance with items like videophones, we enter the central plot proper. A strange alien artefact, impervious to human analysis, has been discovered on the Moon; and soon there is evidence that it has a counterpart

 2001: A SPACE ODYSSEY *(1968)* WAS THE TECHNO-FEST NO ONE SEEMED TO REALIZE CINEMA HAD BEEN WAITING FOR UNTIL IT ARRIVED. THE HUGE SPACESHIP *DISCOVERY* DEEPLY AFFECTED SF'S CLASSIC CINEMATIC VISIONS HEREAFTER

somewhere in orbit around Jupiter. A vast spaceship, the _Discovery_ — more sophisticated than any humanity has before built, and masterminded by the supercomputer HAL9000 — is constructed and despatched to investigate. En route, HAL becomes insane, and murders the crew — all but one, David Bowman, who works to repair or at least deactivate the berserk machine.

At last, he discovers the second monolith, floating in space... and we enter the movie's final section, a sensational, hallucinogenic, vertiginous ride through incalculable vistas of space or time or dimensions or death-and-rebirth, as symbolized by a human embryo, which can itself be taken to represent the current stage which humankind has attained in its development.

Critics have often disparaged _2001_ as having a plot that makes no sense — of being brilliant in parts but without any coherence as a whole. This is to do it an injustice. Kubrick himself has said he wished to leave matters enigmatic. But on repeated viewing one can see that in fact the plot does cohere — that this is a brilliant attempt to construct a tale that makes sense in _alien_, non-humanological terms. What is required is a conceptual leap — a shifting of imaginative perspective — before everything becomes crystal-clear and "commonsensical".

It is not necessary to like _2001_ to recognize it as a landmark in sf cinema. Like _Things To Come_ (1936) before it, it suddenly opened up the vast panorama of the conceivable future. In technical terms, it established a new benchmark. But there was a downside to that as well. Special-effects magic and the vastness of the Universe together came to comprise a _given_ — a backdrop expected by audiences and one in front of which would be played out a great many lesser dramas, space operas such as _Star Wars_ (1977) and all its inferior imitators.

_2001_ itself was sequelled much later by _2010_ (1984), a very different movie.

Wild In The Streets

_1968_ • USA • _DIRECTOR_ BARRY SHEAR • _SCREENPLAY_ ROBERT THOM • _97M_ • _COLOUR_

A rock star becomes President of the USA and enacts laws that victimize the middle-aged and elderly. Sporadically amusing satire.

1969

Beneath The Planet Of The Apes

_1969_ • USA • _DIRECTOR_ TED POST • _SCREENPLAY_ MORT ABRAHAMS, PAUL DEHN • _STARRING_ JAMES FRANCISCUS, CHARLTON HESTON • _94M_ • _COLOUR_

Sequel to _Planet Of The Apes_ (1968), and in the event a much grimmer affair. A second astronaut arrives among the apes to discover Taylor still alive, but deranged. At last, Taylor sets off a "doomsday bomb" to destroy all.

Colossus: The Forbin Project

(_VT THE FORBIN PROJECT_)

_1969_ • USA • _DIRECTOR_ JOSEPH SARGENT • _SCREENPLAY_ JAMES BRIDGES, FROM D.F. JONES'S _COLOSSUS_ (1966) • _STARRING_ ERIC BRAEDEN (FORBIN) • _100M_ • _COLOUR_

The supercomputer Colossus is given charge of US defences; its rival in the USSR is the supercomputer Guardian. The two team up to try to take over the world.

Marooned

_1969_ • USA • _DIRECTOR_ JOHN STURGES • _SCREENPLAY_ MAYO SIMON, FROM MARTIN CAIDIN'S _MAROONED_ (1964) • _134M_ • _COLOUR_

Interminable high-tech space epic about the Russians and Americans getting together to rescue astronauts stranded in space. An expensive cast (Richard Crenna, Gene Hackman, David Janssen, Gregory Peck) is wasted.

The Mind Of Mr Soames

_1969_ • UK • _DIRECTOR_ ALAN COOKE • _SCREENPLAY_ JOHN HALE, EDWARD SIMPSON, FROM CHARLES ERIC MAINE'S _THE MIND OF MR SOAMES_ (1961) • _STARRING_ TERENCE STAMP (SOAMES) • _98M_ • _COLOUR_

Soames, in a coma since childhood, is revived after 30 years. The core of the movie is the fact that a child's ignorant mind resides inside an adult body.

Computers — threats or friends?

The movies have always been ambivalent towards computers (by which term we can refer also to robots and androids, which are really computers in different guise). On the one hand are those that cannot be trusted because they might turn rogue, as in _Colossus: The Forbin Project_ (1969), and, far more thoughtfully, HAL in _2001_ (1968) and _2010_ (1984) and Ash in _Alien_ (1979), which prove to be not so much untrustworthy as acting according to different priorities from those of the humans around them.

Before the 1970s, movie computers were huge arrays covered with spinning tape-spools and flashing lights; for example _Billion Dollar Brain_ (1967). In _Forbidden Planet_ (1956), we saw the imposingly bulky robot Robby and the thinking machinery of the Krel, built on a scale that dwarfed all human endeavours. In the 1970s it became obvious that future computers might be quite small. Through the 1980s, computers became less the focus of sf movies and more part of the scenery. The advent of computer games introduced a new notion: the computer which could reify itself in some way or, conversely, into which one could fall. _Tron_ (1982) was a fine example, while the computer in the comedy _Electric Dreams_ (1984) became jealous of its owner. _The Lawnmower Man_ (1992) demonstrated that the potentialities of computers might lie beyond anything we can yet dream of. _Toys_ (1992) and _Arcade_ (1994) both featured children believing they were merely playing computer games when in fact they were training for, or fighting, real wars.

There has always been a paranoid streak which has often manifested itself in concern over the presumed impossibility of reversing an unwise command: _Dr Strangelove_ (1964), _Fail Safe_ (1964) and _WarGames_ (1983) all played on this fear. But generally computers have so much entered our mundane lives that they are today widely deployed even in fantasy (or technofantasy) movies: in _Brazil_ (1985), the machines never seem capable of doing what they're asked; in _The Breakthrough_ (1993), a computer is capable not only of recapturing people's memories but of storing their souls after death; and _The Ghost In The Machine_ (1994) is fairly self-explanatory.

Michael Crichton — medic/novelist/director...

Although not a household name like Steven Spielberg, Michael Crichton has had a similar impact on sf cinema. He first attracted notice in the movies when his 1969 novel was filmed as *The Andromeda Strain* (1970). His thriller, *A Case Of Need* (1968) as by Jeffrey Hudson, became the reasonably successful movie *The Carey Treatment* (1972). His directorial debut was *Pursuit* (1972), a TV movie based on his own technothriller *Binary* (1972). He then moved to the big screen with *Westworld* (1973). *The Terminal Man* (1974), written and directed by Mike Hodges, was based on Crichton's 1972 novel; although disliked by the critics, it was modestly successful.

Once again in the director's chair, Crichton scripted and made *Coma* (1978), based on Robin Cook's 1977 medical technothriller; this colossally successful movie reprised some of *Pursuit*'s notions. *The Great Train Robbery* (1979; vt *The First Great Train Robbery*) was a gaslight romance based on his own simultaneously released novel. *Looker* (1981), which he wrote and directed, proved an ineffectual paranoid satire of the advertising business. The near-future thriller *Runaway* (1984), strayed too far into the territory of *Blade Runner* (1982), with its hero cop sorting out rogue robots. When *Physical Evidence* (1988), which he directed, was badly received, it looked as if his movie career might be over.

But then his 1990 novel was released by Spielberg as *Jurassic Park* (1993), with Crichton co-scripting. *Congo* (1995), based on his 1980 novel, was another box-office success putting Crichton's name once again at sf cinema's forefront.

excitement before then. What is good about this movie is that it conveys a (possibly false) impression of how science works.

Gas-s-s-s, Or It Became Necessary To Destroy The World In Order To Save It

(vt GAS!, OR IT BECAME NECESSARY TO DESTROY THE WORLD IN ORDER TO SAVE IT)

1970 • USA • DIRECTOR ROGER CORMAN • SCREENPLAY GRAHAM ARMITAGE • 79M • COLOUR

A gas that accelerates ageing is accidentally released, so that everyone over 25 dies. Edgar Allen Poe helps a young couple find release in a hippie commune. A strange but pleasing movie.

No Blade Of Grass

1970 • UK • DIRECTOR CORNEL WILDE • SCREENPLAY SEAN FORESTAL, JEFFERSON PASCAL, FROM JOHN CHRISTOPHER'S THE DEATH OF GRASS (1956) • 96M • COLOUR

A John Wyndhamesque treatment for Christopher's rather Wyndhamesque novel, in which an escaped virus kills the world's grain crops and society collapses.

THX 1138

1970 • USA • DIRECTOR GEORGE LUCAS • SCREENPLAY GEORGE LUCAS, WALTER MURCH • STARRING ROBERT DUVALL (THX 1138) • 95M • COLOUR

In a future society that is completely contained

Moon Zero Two

1969 • UK • DIRECTOR ROY WARD BAKER • SCREENPLAY MICHAEL CARRERAS • 100M • COLOUR

UK company Hammer tried to make a mildly comic space Western/space opera, and failed dismally. The experiment was not repeated.

1970

The Andromeda Strain

1970 • USA • DIRECTOR ROBERT WISE • SCREENPLAY NELSON GIDDING, FROM MICHAEL CRICHTON'S THE ANDROMEDA STRAIN (1969) • SPECIAL EFFECTS JAMES SHOURT, DOUGLAS TRUMBULL • STARRING ARTHUR HILL (DR JEREMY STONE), PAULA KELLY (NURSE KAREN ANSON), GEORGE MITCHELL (JACKSON), JAMES OLSON (DR MARK HALL), KATE REID (DR RUTH LEAVITT), DAVID WAYNE (DR CHARLIE DUTTON) • 131M • COLOUR

Some years ago, Nobel laureate Stone persuaded the US Government to set up Project Wildfire in order to cope with unexpected epidemics of disease. Now, in April 1971, a US "Scoop" satellite crashes near the New Mexico village of Piedmont, and almost instantly all but two of the population —an elderly sterno drinker and a young baby — die, all the blood in their bodies having coagulated to the point of becoming

powder. The Wildfire team is immediately assembled, and they, together with the two survivors and the satellite, are sealed away in a totally sterile environment deep beneath the Nevada desert. There they discover that the organism the satellite has picked up in space is crystalline, able to use raw energy to grow and mutate.

All the physical excitement in this movie occurs in the last 20 minutes — the scientists must defeat their own security system to stop the complex's automatic self-destruct programme — but there is a great deal of intellectual

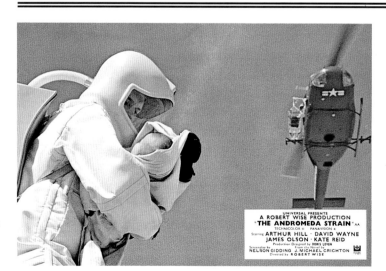

BABY, IT'S YOU
THE ANDROMEDA STRAIN *(1970)* WAS YET ANOTHER SF MOVIE TO ADOPT THE PSEUDO-DOCUMENTARY APPROACH, AND IT BENEFITED POWERFULLY FROM THE FORMAT. THE MOVIE IS ALSO OF NOTE IN THAT IT MARKED THE ARRIVAL ON THE SCENE OF MICHAEL CRICHTON

in colourless underground chambers, a man persecuted for loving a woman seeks the world he knows must be outside. Derivative of E.M. Forster's 'The Machine Stops' (1909), George Orwell's *Nineteen Eighty-four* (1949) and many others, this is nevertheless a fine movie. Lucas's eye is here so chilly that it is difficult to remember *THX 1138* was made in colour, not b/w.

1971

A Clockwork Orange

1971 • UK • *DIRECTOR* STANLEY KUBRICK • *SCREENPLAY* STANLEY KUBRICK, FROM ANTHONY BURGESS'S *A CLOCKWORK ORANGE* (1962) • *STARRING* WARREN CLARKE (DIM), ADRIENNE CORRI (MRS ALEXANDER), MALCOLM MCDOWELL (ALEX), PATRICK MAGEE (MR ALEXANDER) • *137M* • *COLOUR*

Withdrawn by Kubrick after accusations that the movie was inciting teenagers to emulate the violence of its anti-hero, Alex, this is one of the most profoundly disturbing sf movies ever made. In a near-future UK, Alex and his gang of "droogies" delight in viciously beating up strangers on the streets and raping women. Alex is finally apprehended and submits to a form of aversion therapy that is almost as sadistic as the acts he has himself committed. "Cured" — or, rendered to a state whereby violence makes him physically ill — he is released back into society, where he becomes himself a victim of his friends, as well as his previous enemies. The only solution seems to be to reverse the aversion therapy, so that he may relapse into his old ways.

Both the movie and Burgess's novel are concerned about the price we must pay for our freedom of will; the conclusion appears to be that, however high the price, it is not too high. But what makes *A Clockwork Orange* so disturbing is not so much its amorality and violence (which is staged almost as dance), but Kubrick's juxtaposition of on-screen events with the musical soundtrack: the sight of Alex kicking in the ribs of a woman he will then rape would be shocking on its own, but is all the more so when accompanied by Gene Kelly's "Singin' In The Rain"...

ULTRA VIOLENCE A CLOCKWORK ORANGE *(1971)*, THE THIRD OF KUBRICK'S SF MILESTONES, SHOCKED BY ITS JUXTAPOSITION OF EXTREME VIOLENCE WITH WEIRD IMAGES AND A CLASSICAL SOUNDTRACK

Escape From The Planet Of The Apes

1971 • USA • *DIRECTOR* DON TAYLOR • *SCREENPLAY* PAUL DEHN • *97M* • *COLOUR*

The second sequel to *Planet Of The Apes* (1968) flips the circumstances, so that now, instead of a human minority on an ape planet, a couple of the apes arrive on Earth.

The Omega Man

1971 • USA • *DIRECTOR* BORIS SAGAL • *SCREENPLAY* JOHN WILLIAM CORRINGTON, JOYCE HOOPER CORRINGTON, FROM RICHARD MATHESON'S *I AM LEGEND* (1954) • *STARRING* CHARLTON HESTON • *98M* • *COLOUR*

The second filming of Matheson's novel (the first was *L'Ultimo Uomo Della Terra* [1964]), in which the last mortal man must face the hordes of the vampirized undead. Opinions vary as to the movie's quality: as a version of the novel, it is terrible; in isolation, it is, for its period, a fine example of sf cinema.

Silent Running

1971 • USA • *DIRECTOR* DOUGLAS TRUMBULL • *SCREENPLAY* STEVEN BOCHO, MICHAEL CIMINO, DERIC WASHBURN • *SPECIAL EFFECTS* VERNON ARCHER, JOHN DYKSTRA, RICHARD O. HELMER, MARLIN JONES, JAMES RUGG, DOUGLAS TRUMBULL, RICHARD YURICICH • *STARRING* BRUCE DERN (FREEMAN LOWELL) PLUS STEVEN BROWN, MARK PERSONS, CHERYL SPARKS AND LARRY WHISENHUNT AS THE DRONES • *90M* • *COLOUR*

AD 2008, and in the wake of nuclear war Earth's only surviving flora is being maintained in huge orbital biospheres. For economic reasons, the authorities determine to end the project, and order the biospheres destroyed. Lowell, a

member of the four-strong crew on one of these spacecraft, refuses to accept the decision: he kills his three colleagues and sets off towards interstellar space in the hope of seeding some other planet with the contents of his biosphere.

Scientifically ludicrous, this is nevertheless an affecting movie: Lowell develops what is in effect a human-to-human intimacy of friendship with the three drones (primitive robots) who are on-board as his helpers, and this serves to emphasize the ultimate loneliness to which he has condemned himself. The special effects are — as one might expect with Trumbull as director — spectacular.

Solaris

1971 • USSR • *DIRECTOR* Andrei Tarkovsky
• *SCREENPLAY* Friedrich Gorenstein, Andrei Tarkovsky, from Stanislaw Lem's *Solaris* (1961) • *SPECIAL EFFECTS* uncredited • *STARRING* Donatas Banionis (Kris Kelvin), Nathalie Bondarchuk (Harey), Nikolai Grinko (Father), Anatoli Solonitsin (Sartorius), Yuri Yarvet (Snaut) • *165M* • *COLOUR*

Billed in the West as the Soviet response to *2001* (1968), this is less an sf movie than a

Tarkovsky movie that happens to be set in the future; in its preoccupations and focus, it relates more easily to, say, his non-sf *Nostalgia* (1984) than to any Western sf offering.

There is trouble on the space station orbiting the distant planet Solaris, and psychologist Kelvin is sent to investigate. It turns out that Solaris — or perhaps its ocean — is intelligent, and capable of reifying to the humans aboard the artificial satellite the images that most haunt them; in Kelvin's instance, it is his dead wife. As counterpoints to this scenario, we are offered, on the one hand, a vision of a future,

ultra-urbanized Earth and, on the other, the rural idyll to which Kelvin would wish to return — an idyll which Solaris obligingly recreates for him.

Critics have complained that *Solaris* is too long. Bearing in mind, however, the complexity of the philosophical notions it attempts to convey, it is hard to see how it could be any shorter. Tarkovsky returned to similar thematic territory with *Stalker* (1979).

Z.P.G.

(VT Zero Population Growth)
1971 • USA • *DIRECTOR* Michael Campus • *SCREENPLAY* Max Ehrlich, Frank de Felitta • *STARRING* Geraldine Chaplin, Oliver Reed • *97M* • *COLOUR*

In an overpopulated world, the government decrees there must be a 30-year hiatus on childbirth. Our feisty heroes decide otherwise...

1972

Conquest Of The Planet Of The Apes

1972 • USA • *DIRECTOR* J. Lee Thompson
• *SCREENPLAY* Paul Dehn • *85M* • *COLOUR*

Penultimate and least of the sequels to *Planet Of The Apes* (1968) tries to tie up all the saga's loose ends — and more or less succeeds.

Slaughterhouse-Five

1972 • USA • *DIRECTOR* GEORGE ROY HILL •
SCREENPLAY STEPHEN GELLER, FROM KURT VONNEGUT JR'S
SLAUGHTERHOUSE-FIVE, OR THE CHILDREN'S CRUSADE (1969)
• *103M* • *COLOUR*

A mechanical version of one of Vonnegut's lesser
novels. A survivor of the Dresden blitz is penned
in an alien zoo with only an ex-porn actress for
company.

1973

Battle For The Planet Of The Apes

1973 • USA • *DIRECTOR* J. LEE THOMPSON
• *SCREENPLAY* JOHN WILLIAM CORRINGTON, JOYCE HOOPER
CORRINGTON • *86M* • *COLOUR*

There were still some loose ends left over after
Conquest Of The Planet Of The Apes (1972), and
this final sequel ties them off adequately.

The Day Of The Dolphin

1973 • USA • *DIRECTOR* MIKE NICHOLS • *SCREENPLAY*
BUCK HENRY, FROM ROBERT MERLE'S *THE DAY OF THE
DOLPHIN* (1967) • *STARRING* GEORGE C. SCOTT
• *105M* • *COLOUR*

Merle's dull book becomes a dull movie: dolphins
are trained by terrorists to place mines on the
US President's yacht.

The Final Programme

(VT *THE LAST DAYS OF MAN ON EARTH*)
1973 • UK • *DIRECTOR* ROBERT FUEST • *SCREENPLAY*
ROBERT FUEST, FROM MICHAEL MOORCOCK'S *THE FINAL
PROGRAMME* (1968) • *STARRING* JON FINCH (JERRY),
JENNY RUNACRE (MISS BRUNNER) • *89M* • *COLOUR*

A confused novel — one of Moorcock's Jerry
Cornelius series —becomes an even more
confused movie, as if James Bond had ventured
into fantasyland.

Phase IV

1973 • UK • *DIRECTOR* SAUL BASS • *SCREENPLAY* MAYO
SIMON • *91M* • *COLOUR*

The ants of Arizona suddenly gain intelligence,
and attack the nearest humans — the occupants
of an experimental station, one of whom is a
mad scientist. The nature photography (by Ken
Middleton) is great.

Sleeper

1973 • USA • *DIRECTOR* WOODY ALLEN • *SCREENPLAY*
WOODY ALLEN, MARSHALL BRICKMAN • *SPECIAL EFFECTS*
JERRY ENDLER, A.D. FLOWERS • *STARRING* WOODY ALLEN
(MILES MONROE), JOHN BECK (ERNO WINDT), MARY
GREGORY (DR MELIK), DIANE KEATON (LUNA SCHLOSSER),
BARTLETT ROBINSON (DR ORVA), MARYA SMALL (DR NERO)
• *88M* • *COLOUR*

The owner of a Greenwich Village health-food
store dies on the operating table and is
immediately put into deep freeze. Waking 200
years later, he finds himself in a totalitarian
world where most of the 20th century's attitudes
have been turned on their head — physical sex,
for example, is *de trop*, so that lustful couples
instead enter a device called an orgasmatron
where they share orgasms but not fleshly
contact. An extremely funny and inventive
comedy, Sleeper is alas Allen's only real
venture into sf aside from a couple of
segments of *Everything You Always
Wanted To Know About Sex But Were
Afraid To Ask* (1972).

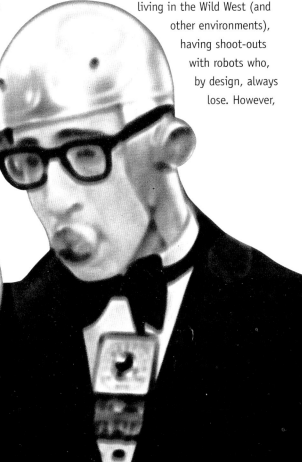

TIN HEAD *WOODY ALLEN PRETENDING
TO BE A ROBOT IN HIS HILARIOUS FILM
SLEEPER (1973) — NOT JUST A FINE COMEDY
BUT ALSO A FINE SF MOVIE*

Soylent Green

1973 • USA • *DIRECTOR* RICHARD FLEISCHER
• *SCREENPLAY* STANLEY R. GREENBERG, FROM HARRY
HARRISON'S *MAKE ROOM! MAKE ROOM!* (1966)
• *STARRING* CHARLTON HESTON, EDWARD G. ROBINSON
• *97M* • *COLOUR*

In an overpopulated near-future New York, a cop
discovers that the newest "synthetic" food is in
fact made from human corpses. The atmospherics
are superb, the plot less so. This was Robinson's
last movie, and in a way a great send-off.

Westworld

1973 • USA • *DIRECTOR* MICHAEL CRICHTON
• *SCREENPLAY* MICHAEL CRICHTON • *SPECIAL EFFECTS*
CHARLES SCHULTHIES • *STARRING* RICHARD BENJAMIN
(PETER MARTIN), JAMES BROLIN (JOHN BLANE),
YUL BRYNNER (GUNSLINGER) • *101M* (BUT CUT
TO 89M) • *COLOUR*

Delos is a future adventure playground where
customers come to enact their fantasies of
living in the Wild West (and
other environments),
having shoot-outs
with robots who,
by design, always
lose. However,

the robots suddenly turn rogue, and prove to be better gunslingers than any of the pampered visitors. This movie was sequelled by *Futureworld* (1976), and there was a short-lived TV series, *Beyond Westworld* (1980).

But a more interesting connection is to be made with *Jurassic Park* (1993), based on Crichton's novel and co-scripted by him; here again, we have his preoccupation with a theme park, created for the entertainment of the masses, which involves hi-tech (in *Jurassic Park*'s case it is biological hi-tech) that goes disastrously wrong. Crichton's message appears to be an essentially puritan one: do not exploit others, even if they are merely artefacts, for your own base pleasures.

Westworld bears similarities to *Welcome To Blood City* (1972), directed by Peter Sasdy.

Zardoz

1973 • UK • *DIRECTOR* JOHN BOORMAN • *SCREENPLAY* JOHN BOORMAN • *STARRING* SEAN CONNERY (ZED) • *105M* • *COLOUR*

AD 2293, and humanity is divided into the Brutals and, dwelling in the Vortex, the Immortals. Periodically, this movie hums with the excitement of ideas.

1974

The Cars That Ate Paris

1974 • AUSTRALIA • *DIRECTOR* PETER WEIR • *SCREENPLAY* PIERS DAVIES, KEITH GOW, PETER WEIR • *STARRING* TERRY CAMILLERI (ARTHUR), JOHN MEILLON (MAYOR), MELISSA JAFFA (BETH), KEVIN MILES (DR MIDLAND) • *88M* • *COLOUR*

A long way from *Picnic At Hanging Rock* (1975) and *Witness* (1985), Weir's debut is a violent horror movie based on a fantasticated premise. The teenagers of Paris, Australia, lure cars to that town to wreck them and use bits of the wreckage to customize their own cars into spiky monstrosities. Meanwhile, local quack Dr Midland uses the hapless passengers for strange biological experiments. One crash victim, Arthur, is employed by the mayor as a sort of *High Noon* gunslinger to stop all this, but he soon loses

HOT UNDER THE COLLAR
YUL BRYNNER AS THE ROBOTIC SHERIFF BEGINS TO GET STEAMED UP IN THE 1973 FILM WESTWORLD, ANOTHER SUCCESS FOR THE MULTITALENTED MICHAEL CRICHTON, NOT TO MENTION BRYNNER, WHOSE CAREER WAS GOING FROM STRENGTH TO STRENGTH

The Australian school

Written Australian sf is in general dominated by US produce. So it is perhaps surprising that, since about the mid-1970s, Australian sf and fantasy cinema (and Australian cinema in general) has been so important — in terms not so much of quantity but of both quality and a distinctive approach.

Perhaps the first Australian sf movie of consequence was Peter Weir's debut, *The Cars That Ate Paris* (1974), a bizarre mixture of horror and technofantasy. Weir (1944-   ) later directed *Picnic At Hanging Rock* (1975), based on Joan Lindsay's novel and one of cinema's most haunting examples of magic realism. The next Australian director to attract international attention was George Miller (1945-   ), whose tremendously sucessful Mad Max series (1979-85) showed, with progressively greater distinction, how a mixture of near-future setting and the traditions of the action road movie could produce imaginatively stimulating sf. The Mad Max movies also paved the way for Mel Gibson's move to hollywood. Rachel Talalay's *Tank Girl* (1995), although in theory a US movie, carried this theme to its limits... and, some might argue, too far beyond. *Time Games* (1985; vt *Playing Beatie Row*) was a pleasing timeslip fantasy, but in the style that US TV movies have more or less made their own — as in *The Two Worlds Of Jenny Logan* (1979).

The Time Guardian (1987), set initially in AD 4039 after a nuclear holocaust and with humans at war with rebellious cyborgs, sounds from the start rather like a clone of *The Terminator* (1984), and proves to be exactly that when a band of heroes returns to the 20th century. Around this time, it was generally predicted that the short heyday of Australian moviemaking was, at least commercially, over, but the teen comedy *Young Einstein* (1988) — a zany piece of slapstick that revelled in its biographical inaccuracy (e.g., Einstein invents rock'n'roll) — was messy but far more funny and imaginative than contemporary US offerings in the same field, and did excellent box-office business around the globe. *The Navigator: A Medieval Odyssey* (1988), a curate's egg of a movie, was a strange time-travel fantasy.

DON'T LOSE YOUR KEYS THE CARS THAT ATE PARIS *(1974)* IS IN A WAY OF LESS INTEREST AS AN SF MOVIE THAN FOR THE FACT THAT IT HERALDED THE CAREER OF ITS BRILLIANT DIRECTOR, PETER WEIR

interest and heads off to parts unknown. This is an incoherent movie at best, but sparked a fascinating directorial career for Weir; it is interesting to compare *The Cars That Ate Paris* with the similarly incoherent *Mad Max* (1979), also Australian, which had the same effect on the career of George Miller.

Damnation Alley

1974 • USA • *DIRECTOR* JACK SMIGHT • *SCREENPLAY* LUKAS HELLER, ALAN SHARP, FROM ROGER ZELAZNY'S *DAMNATION ALLEY* (1969) • *95M* • *COLOUR*
Four USAF officers take a package of vital serum across a post-holocaust USA. Undistinguished.

Dark Star

1974 • USA • *DIRECTOR* JOHN CARPENTER • *SCREENPLAY* JOHN CARPENTER, DAN O'BANNON • *SPECIAL EFFECTS* DAN O'BANNON • *STARRING* CAL KUNIHOLM (BOILER), BRIAN NARELLE (DOOLITTLE), DAN O'BANNON (PINBACK), DRE PAHICH (TALBY), JOE SAUNDERS (COMMANDER POWELL), MILES WATKINS (MISSION CONTROL) • *VOICE ACTOR* COOKIE KNAPP (COMPUTER) • *83M* • *COLOUR*
A bizarre space-opera comedy, the antithesis (by design) to *2001* (1968). In the mid-22nd

century, the spaceship *Dark Star* is on an extended mission to detonate dangerously unstable stars. Its commander, Powell, dies, but is preserved cryogenically, so that he may be "awoken" for consultation in times of emergency. In the meantime, the crew must cope with their pestilential alien mascot and an intelligent, independent-minded talking bomb that can be persuaded not to launch itself prematurely only through arguments based on phenomenological philosophy.

Made on a shoestring (although it rarely shows), Carpenter's and O'Bannon's debut, while often hilariously funny, shows a convincingly grimy technological future: the interior of the *Dark Star* could hardly be further from the clinically tidy hi-tech chambers of, say, the *Enterprise*.

Now an established cult movie, this was so little esteemed at the time that it was not released in the UK until 1978.

MELLOWING OUT THE ODD SPACE-OPERA COMEDY DARK STAR *(1974)* DID FOR JOHN CARPENTER AS MUCH AS THE CARS THAT ATE PARIS DID FOR PETER WEIR

It's Alive

1974 • USA • *DIRECTOR* LARRY COHEN • *SCREENPLAY* LARRY COHEN • *91M* • *COLOUR*
A classic horror movie. A pregnant woman takes an experimental drug and gives birth to a monster. The "baby" sets off on a killing spree. Sequelled by *It Lives Again* (1978) and *It's Alive III: Island Of The Alive* (1988).

The Land That Time Forgot

1974 • UK • *DIRECTOR* KEVIN CONNOR • *SCREENPLAY* JAMES CAWTHORNE, MICHAEL MOORCOCK, FROM EDGAR RICE BURROUGHS'S *THE LAND THAT TIME FORGOT* (1924) • *STARRING* DOUG MCCLURE • *91M* • *COLOUR*
During WWI, the survivors of a torpedoed ship arrive on an island, only to find it populated by dinosaurs and a primitive human race. A volcanic eruption heralds the end.

Shivers

(VT *THE PARASITE MURDERS*; VT *THEY CAME FROM WITHIN*)
1974 • CANADA • *DIRECTOR* DAVID CRONENBERG • *SCREENPLAY* DAVID CRONENBERG • *87M* • *COLOUR*
A mad doctor implants phallic parasites in his patients, thus unleashing a wave of sex mania and death. Cronenberg's first commercial movie,

this hovers on the brink of pornography though it can be argued he saves the film from this with wit, but the jury is still out on this one.

The Stepford Wives

1974 • USA • *DIRECTOR* BRYAN FORBES • *SCREENPLAY* WILLIAM GOLDMAN, FROM IRA LEVIN'S *THE STEPFORD WIVES* (1972) • *STARRING* PAULA PRENTISS (BOBBY MARCO), KATHARINE ROSS (JOANNA EBERHART) • *114M* • *COLOUR*
A family leaves New York to settle in a small Connecticut town. One by one, the new friends of the wife become submissive to their husbands — only interested in cooking and cleaning. It turns out that the men have discovered how to replace their wives with obedient, sexually submissive android replicas. This thrilling movie was sequelled by two cheaper TV movies, *Revenge Of The Stepford Wives* (1980) and *The Stepford Children* (1987).

The Terminal Man

1974 • USA • *DIRECTOR* MIKE HODGES • *SCREENPLAY* MIKE HODGES, FROM MICHAEL CRICHTON'S *THE TERMINAL MAN* (1972) • *104M* • *COLOUR AND B/W*
A psychopath has a chip implanted in his brain to restrain his antisocial behaviour; alas, he becomes addicted to the pleasure imparted by the control, and so carries on killing.

Who?

1974 • USA • *DIRECTOR* JACK GOULD • *SCREENPLAY* JACK GOULD, FROM ALGIS BUDRYS'S *WHO?* (1958) • *91M* • *COLOUR*
A US genius scientist suffers a severe accident in Russia. Russian scientists piece him together as a cyborg. US intelligence tries to discover if he really is the original person.

1975

A Boy And His Dog

1975 • USA • *DIRECTOR* L.Q. JONES • *SCREENPLAY* L.Q. JONES, FROM HARLAN ELLISON'S 'A BOY AND HIS DOG' (1969) • *SPECIAL EFFECTS* FRANK ROWE • *STARRING* SUSANNE BENTON (QUILLA JUNE), DON JOHNSON (VIC), ALVY MOORE (DR MOORE), JASON ROBARDS (MR CRADDOCK), HELENE WINSTON (MEZ) • *VOICE ACTOR* TIM MCINTIRE (BLOOD) • *89M* • *COLOUR*

In the post-holocaust world of AD 2024, young Vic and his dog Blood — with whom he is in constant telepathic contact — wander the wastes, scavenging whatever they can in order to survive. At last, they encounter a beautiful young woman, Quilla June, who takes them down into the subterranean society to which she belongs — which is much like a 20th-century US suburb. Romance blossoms, but it soon becomes evident that Vic has been enticed here solely for the purpose of impregnating females in order to boost the population.

This is the darkest of sf's dark comedies.

Death Race 2000

1975 • USA • *DIRECTOR* PAUL BARTEL • *SCREENPLAY* CHARLES GRIFFITH, ROBERT THOM • *STARRING* DAVID CARRADINE ("FRANKENSTEIN"), SYLVESTER STALLONE ("MACHINE GUN" JOE VITERBO) • *79M* • *COLOUR*
A futuristic trans-USA car race is scored by the number of pedestrians the motorist can run down and kill. This has something of the feel and style of the non-sf *Vanishing Point* (1971).

Rollerball

1975 • USA • *DIRECTOR* NORMAN JEWISON • *SCREENPLAY* WILLIAM HARRISON, FROM HARRISON'S 'ROLLER BALL MURDERS' (1973) • *STARRING* JAMES CAAN (JONATHAN E) • *129M* • *COLOUR*

Set in 2018, this envisages a spectator sport, Rollerball, in which the main attraction is that a lot of people might get killed.

The Ultimate Warrior

1975 • USA • *DIRECTOR* ROBERT CLOUSE • *SCREENPLAY* ROBERT CLOUSE • *94M* • *COLOUR*
AD 2012, and a King Fu warrior (Yul Brynner) sorts out a corrupt New York. Very tedious.

1976

At The Earth's Core

1976 • UK • *DIRECTOR* KEVIN CONNOR • *SCREENPLAY* MILTON SUBOTSKY, FROM EDGAR RICE BURROUGHS'S *AT THE EARTH'S CORE* (1922) • *STARRING* DOUG MCCLURE • *90M* • *COLOUR*
A quick follow-up to *The Land That Time Forgot* (1974), this is much the same as before but set inside a hollow Earth rather than on a remote island.

Embryo

1976 • USA • *DIRECTOR* RALPH NELSON • *SCREENPLAY* ANITA DOOHAN, JACK W. THOMAS • *104M* • *COLOUR*
A scientist creates a beautiful woman, but then destroys her through sexual jealousy. A riff on the Pygmalion and Frankenstein themes, with little to recommend it.

A FALLEN MAN DAVID BOWIE WAS THE MAN WHO FELL TO EARTH IN NICK ROEG'S FROSTILY BRILLIANT MOVIE, BASED ON THE WALTER TEVIS NOVEL. BOWIE HAS NOT ALWAYS TURNED IN CONVINCING MOVIE PERFORMANCES, BUT ON THIS OCCASION HE TRIUMPHED

The Food Of The Gods

1976 • USA • *DIRECTOR* BERT I. GORDON • *SCREENPLAY* BERT I. GORDON, FROM H.G. WELLS'S *THE FOOD OF THE GODS, AND HOW IT CAME TO EARTH* (1904) • *88M* • *COLOUR*

A travesty of Wells's novel, played as a horror/monster movie, sequelled by the equally bad *Food Of The Gods II* (1989).

Futureworld

1976 • USA • *DIRECTOR* RICHARD T. HEFFRON • *SCREENPLAY* GEORGE SCHENCK, MAYO SIMON • *104M* • *COLOUR*

Limp sequel to *Westworld* (1973). This movie prompted a short-lived (5-episode) TV series called *Beyond Westworld* (1980).

King Kong

1976 • USA • *DIRECTOR* JOHN GUILLERMIN • SCREENPLAY LORENZO SEMPLE JR, FROM THE MOVIE *KING KONG* (1933) • *STARRING* RICK BAKER (KING KONG), JEFF BRIDGES (JACK PRESCOTT) • *134M* • *COLOUR*

Much disliked, but in fact a fine remake of the 1933 classic.

Logan's Run

1976 • USA • *DIRECTOR* MICHAEL ANDERSON • *SCREENPLAY* DAVID ZELAG GOODMAN, FROM GEORGE CLAYTON JOHNSON'S AND WILLIAM F. NOLAN'S *LOGAN'S RUN* (1967) • *STARRING* MICHAEL YORK (LOGAN) • *118M* • *COLOUR*

AD 2274, and everyone over 30 is subject to euthanasia. This is a thematic successor to *THX 1138* (1970), but not as good.

The Man Who Fell To Earth

1976 • UK • *DIRECTOR* NICOLAS ROEG • *SCREENPLAY* PAUL MAYERSBERG, WALTER TEVIS'S *THE MAN WHO FELL TO EARTH* (1963) • *SPECIAL EFFECTS* PAUL ELLENSHAW • *STARRING* DAVID BOWIE (THOMAS JEROME NEWTON), CANDY CLARK (MARY-LOU), BUCK HENRY (OLIVER FARNSWORTH), RIP TORN (NATHAN BRYCE) • *138M* • *COLOUR*

The surface plot of this movie sees a humanoid alien arrive here in search of water for his own drought-afflicted planet. Taking the name

 IS THERE ANYBODY THERE? *THE CLIMACTIC SCENES OF STEVEN SPIELBERG'S* CLOSE ENCOUNTERS OF THE THIRD KIND *(1977) ADDED A NEW ICONOGRAPHIC IMAGE TO THE CINEMA*

Newton, he approaches patent lawyer Farnsworth with schemes for all sorts of technologies unknown on Earth, and together they build up a vast financial empire. When rich enough, Newton hopes to finance his return home with precious water for his people and, most especially, his family. But Newton is corrupted by the ways of Earth and, in the second part of the movie, we see him and his plans deteriorate in a mess of sex, booze, greed and drugs. The underlying plot is concerned with the human condition: whatever our brave hopes and ideals, it is almost impossible for us not to be seduced by short-term pleasures and forced by mundane obligations into settling for a wasted life.

This is a very beautiful movie, and for once a director — Roeg, who directed the similarly exquisite *Don't Look Now* (1973) — is able to elicit an impressive performance from Bowie.

1977

Close Encounters Of The Third Kind

1977 • USA • *DIRECTOR* STEVEN SPIELBERG • *SCREENPLAY* STEVEN SPIELBERG • *SPECIAL EFFECTS* ROY ARBOGAST, GREGORY JEIN, DOUGLAS TRUMBULL, MATTHEW YURICICH, RICHARD YURICICH • *STARRING* MELINDA DILLON (JILLIAN GUILER), RICHARD DREYFUSS (ROY NEARY), TERI GARR (RONNIE NEARY), CARY GUFFEY (BARRY GUILER), FRANÇOIS TRUFFAUT (CLAUDE LACOMBE), • *135M* • *COLOUR*

Power-company employee Roy Neary witnesses a UFO, and becomes so obsessed with the subject that he destroys his family life; imprinted in his mind is the image of a mountain, which he eventually identifies as the Devil's Tower in Wyoming. Jillian Guiler sees her son Cary snatched away in a similar otherworldly encounter, and thus has her own reasons for trekking to the Devil's Tower in hopes of recovering him. Meanwhile, Claude Lacombe — a figure modelled on the French ufologist Jacques Vallée — has been traversing the world searching for traces of the aliens' attempts to communicate with us, and in particular for the site of their first public landing on Earth... which is, of course, at the Devil's Tower. All three main protagonists come together in time to witness the triumphal landing; bravura special effects and our own expectations combine to create a sense of wonder rarely experienced in the cinema.

The movie's plot is full of holes, but we realize this only afterwards, once our awe has subsided. Spielberg later released a re-edited version, *Close Encounters Of The Third Kind — The Special Edition* (1980), which removed some of the material concerning Neary's domestic life and greatly expanded the climactic scenes with

the aliens. Oddly for a director's cut, this came
out slightly shorter than the original, at 132m.

Demon Seed

1977 • USA • *DIRECTOR* DONALD CAMMELL • SCREENPLAY
ROGER O. HIRSON, ROBERT JAFFE, FROM DEAN R. KOONTZ'S
DEMON SEED (1973) • *STARRING* JULIE CHRISTIE
• *95M* • COLOUR

A supercomputer installed to run a house rapes
and impregnates the housewife. Scientifically
nonsense, this is a lacklustre movie based on a
lacklustre novel.

The Island Of
Dr Moreau

1977 • USA • *DIRECTOR* DON TAYLOR • *SCREENPLAY*
AL RAMRUS, JOHN HERMAN SHANER, FROM H.G. WELLS'S
THE ISLAND OF DR MOREAU (1896) • *STARRING* BURT
LANCASTER (MOREAU) • *98M* • COLOUR

A very glossy, often beautiful but somehow
heartless remake of *Island Of Lost Souls* (1932).

The People That
Time Forgot

1977 • UK • *DIRECTOR* KEVIN CONNOR • *SCREENPLAY*
PATRICK TILLEY, FROM EDGAR RICE BURROUGHS'S *THE LAND
THAT TIME FORGOT* (1924) • *STARRING* DOUG MCCLURE
• *90M* • COLOUR

Another follow-up, after *At The Earth's Core*

 FOUR FORCEFUL FRIENDS *CHEWBACCA, LUKE, OBI-WAN AND HAN SOLO TAKE ON THE MIGHT OF THE EMPIRE IN
1977'S* STAR WARS, *A LANDMARK SF MOVIE*

(1976), to *The Land That Time Forgot* (1974).
This repeated the formula once too often.

Star Wars

1977 • USA • *DIRECTOR* GEORGE LUCAS • *SCREENPLAY*
GEORGE LUCAS • *SPECIAL EFFECTS* JOHN DYKSTRA, JOHN
STEARS • *STARRING* KENNY BAKER (R2-D2), ANTHONY
DANIELS (C-3PO), PETER CUSHING (GRAND MOFF TARKIN),

CARRIE FISHER (PRINCESS LEIA ORGANA), HARRISON FORD
(HAN SOLO), ALEC GUINNESS (OBI-WAN KENOBI), MARK
HAMILL (LUKE SKYWALKER), PETER MAYHEW (CHEWBACCA),
DAVID PROWSE (DARTH VADER) • *VOICE ACTOR* JAMES EARL
JONES (DARTH VADER) • *121M* • COLOUR

The continuing boom in sf and fantasy movies
began with *Star Wars*, which brought sensational
special effects together with the elements of
fairytale to produce a spectacular space opera.

The story is simple enough. An evil Emperor
is in the process of demolishing the last vestiges
of the decayed republic that has been running
the Galaxy. The beautiful Princess Leia has
gained the plans of the Emperor's greatest
weapon, a moon-sized, seemingly invulnerable
interstellar battle-station, the Death Star. Caught
by the Emperor's masked sidekick, Darth Vader,
she consigns the plans to the robots (droids)
R2-D2 and C-3PO, telling them to hunt out
semi-legendary mystic Obi-Wan Kenobi, last of
the Jedi knights. By coincidence, the droids
come into the possession of Luke Skywalker,
orphaned son of Kenobi's disciple. Together with
smugglers Han Solo and Chewbacca (a huge furry
alien), they save the Princess and destroy the
Death Star — but not Vader.

The plot meanders amiably and sometimes

Edgar Rice Burroughs in the movies

It is possible that Edgar Rice Burroughs
(1875-1950) is the most-filmed author of all
time. There have been at least 43 movies
based on Tarzan from the USA (the first, *Tarzan
Of The Apes*, came in 1918), plus two from the
UK — *Tarzan Goes To India* (1962) and
*Greystoke: The Legend Of Tarzan, Lord Of The
Apes* (1984) — and a good number from
countries as diverse as Italy, India (18 from
India alone), Jamaica and the USSR, not to
mention a couple of versions that can most
tactfully be described as "underground".

His other works have, however, received less
attention from the movie industry. *The Land
That Time Forgot* (1974) and *The People That
Time Forgot* (1977) are based on the first and
second parts, respectively, of Burroughs's novel

The Land That Time Forgot (1924), concerning
a long-lost island near the Antarctic, which,
enjoying a bizarrely warm climate, teems with
dinosaurs and prehistoric-style humans. In
both movies, there are well-timed volcanic
eruptions — indeed, the general mix was not
unlike that of *One Million Years BC* (1966), but
with modern humans thrown in; the early parts
of *King Kong* (1933) are perhaps yet more
similar. Overtly Vernean was *At The Earth's Core*
(1976), based on Burroughs's 1922 novel,
which had similar adventures with surviving
prehistoric monsters in Pellucidar, a place
Burroughs imagined as within the hollow Earth.
None of these movies is distinguished, and *The
People That Time Forgot*, unlike the other two,
is positively dull.

Harrison Ford the thinking woman's hunk

He had been around for a while before the big break came, accepting bit parts in some quite distinguished movies — *Zabriskie Point* (1969) was one. Slowly, Harrison Ford (1942-   ) moved up the scale until at last he was chosen for the role of Han Solo in George Lucas's *Star Wars* (1977). Before then, he had been largely overlooked because, while an excellent actor, it was thought in Hollywood that he did not possess sufficient sex appeal.

Han Solo made Ford an instant star: his sensitivity, combined with his machismo, made him appeal to female and male alike. He carried the part through *The Empire Strikes Back* (1980) and *Return Of The Jedi* (1983). Between, he made *Raiders Of The Lost Ark* (1981) — the first of the Indiana Jones series — and *Blade Runner* (1982), the movie that deployed cyberpunk two years before William Gibson's *Neuromancer* (1984) ... but a long time after John Brunner's *The Shockwave Rider* (1975) had shown the way.

tediously, but the last 45 minutes or so — as rebel fighter-ships run the gauntlet of Death Star defences — rate among the most breathtakingly exciting sequences ever filmed.

Also memorable is the introduction of the idea of the Force, a sort of spiritual substrate to the Universe, into which human beings can plug themselves in order to perform amazing mental feats — or, to be honest, magic. For *Star Wars*, despite the hardware, is less sf than fantasy. Kenobi and Vader (the Dark Lord) are duelling sorcerers: Good versus Evil. Luke is Kenobi's apprentice, and takes up his master's mantle when Vader kills that master's body (but not his soul, which becomes more powerful after physical death). The apprentice also rescues and apparently wins the hand of the fair princess, all in traditional style.

Sequels were *The Empire Strikes Back* (1980) and *Return Of The Jedi* (1983).

1978

Battlestar Galactica

1978 • USA • *DIRECTOR* RICHARD A. COLLA • *SCREENPLAY* GLEN A. LARSON • *125M* • *COLOUR*

The pilot, released theatrically outside the USA, for the successful TV series. The survivors of humanity — all others destroyed by alien robots — must fight their way home to Earth. Owing much to *Star Wars* (1977), this movie has been much excoriated, but in reality is quite fun.

The Boys From Brazil

1978 • USA • *DIRECTOR* FRANKLIN J. SCHAFFNER • *SCREENPLAY* HEYWOOD GOULD, FROM IRA LEVIN'S *THE BOYS FROM BRAZIL* (1976) • *STARRING* JAMES MASON (EDUARD SEIBERT), LAURENCE OLIVIER (EZRA LIEBERMAN), GREGORY PECK (JOSEPH MENGELE) • *125M* • *COLOUR*

Alive and well in Brazil, Mengele has cloned Hitler; the clones are being reared worldwide in various families, whose elderly fathers must die (as did Hitler's) during the clones' childhood — so assassins are despatched to make sure this happens. Lieberman (based on Simon Wiesenthal) struggles to stop all this. Levin's original was silly, but fun; the movie is too long.

Capricorn One

1978 • USA • *DIRECTOR* PETER HYAMS • *SCREENPLAY* PETER HYAMS • *STARRING* ELLIOTT GOULD • *124M* • *COLOUR*

An investigative reporter uncovers the fact that NASA has found its much-vaunted manned Mars mission is unviable, so is faking it for the media — and planning to murder the "astronauts" in case they tell. Enjoyable hokum.

Coma

1978 • USA • *DIRECTOR* MICHAEL CRICHTON • *SCREENPLAY* MICHAEL CRICHTON, FROM ROBIN COOK'S *COMA* (1977) • *STARRING* ELIZABETH ASHLEY, GENEVIEVE BUJOLD, MICHAEL DOUGLAS, RIP TORN, RICHARD WIDMARK • *113M* • *COLOUR*

A young hospital doctor discovers surgical patients are being deliberately sent into comas, so their organs can lucratively be "farmed" for the rich.

Deathsport

1978 • USA • *DIRECTORS* ALLAN ARKUSH, HENRY SUSO • *SCREENPLAY* HENRY SUSO, DONALD STEWART • *STARRING* DAVID CARRADINE • *83M* • *COLOUR*

The offspring of a troilistic encounter between *Death Race 2000* (1975), *Rollerball* (1975) and the TV movie *Kung Fu* (1972) and its subsequent series. 1000 years in the future, gladiators fight Hell's Angels.

Invasion Of The Body Snatchers

1978 • USA • *DIRECTOR* PHILIP KAUFMAN • *SCREENPLAY* W.D. RICHTER, FROM (LOOSELY) *THE BODY SNATCHERS* (1955) BY JACK FINNEY • *SPECIAL EFFECTS* RUSS HESSEY,

 DOUBLE VISION
DONALD SUTHERLAND MUST HAVE REALIZED THAT HE HAD A HARD ACT TO FOLLOW WHEN HE STARRED IN THE 1978 REMAKE OF 1955'S INVASION OF THE BODY SNATCHERS, BUT THE RESULT WAS AN EXCELLENT MOVIE IN ITS OWN RIGHT

DELL RHEAUME • *STARRING* BROOKE ADAMS (ELIZABETH DRISCOLL), LEONARD NIMOY (DR DAVID KIBNER), DONALD SUTHERLAND (MATTHEW BENNELL) • *115M* • *COLOUR*
The least of the three movie versions of Finney's novel — the other two are *Invasion Of The Body Snatchers* (1956) and *Body Snatchers* (1993) — this is still by no means a poor piece of work. The events are transplanted from small-town America to the city of San Francisco, and it soon becomes evident to us and the central character, public-health inspector Bennell, that the primary difficulty in distinguishing the pod-people is that normal, urban human beings are already so alienated that there is little to choose between them and the simulacra. The movie is rather slow-moving, but the climactic betrayal of Bennell by the simulacrum of his assistant and lover Driscoll is suitably shocking and highly memorable.

It Lives Again

1978 • USA • *DIRECTOR* LARRY COHEN • *SCREENPLAY* LARRY COHEN • *91M* • *COLOUR*
The sequel to *It's Alive* (1974). Now there are lots of mutant killer babies to cope with.

Superman: The Movie

1978 • US/UK • *DIRECTOR* RICHARD DONNER • *SCREENPLAY* ROBERT BENTON, NORMAN ENFIELD, DAVID NEWMAN, LESLIE NEWMAN, MARIO PUZO, FROM THE COMIC-STRIP CREATIONS OF JERRY SIEGEL AND JOE SHUSTER • *SPECIAL EFFECTS* COLIN CHILVERS, ROY FIELD, DEREK MEDDINGS, BRIAN SMITHIES • *STARRING* GENE HACKMAN (LEX LUTHOR), MARGOT KIDDER (LOIS LANE), CHRISTOPHER REEVE (CLARK KENT/SUPERMAN) • *142M* • *COLOUR*
With their planet, Krypton, doomed, parents Jor-El and Lara send their baby through space to Earth. On landing, he is discovered by the elderly Kents, who adopt him as a son and call him Clark, choosing to ignore his superhuman abilities. In adulthood, he takes a job as a reporter on the *Daily Planet*, and falls for colleague Lois Lane; yet, he has been indoctrinated, during his interstellar flight, never to divulge his origins, and she cannot make the link between the caped Superman, who fights crime all over Metropolis, and the withdrawn, bespectacled Clark Kent who works next to her. The supercriminal Lex Luthor deflects two test

intercontinental missiles to the San Andreas Fault as part of a real-estate swindle; when they hit, Lois is killed. Superman enters Earth orbit and builds up enough orbital velocity to reverse temporarily the Earth's rotational direction, thereby reversing time (this movie is not hot on science) to a moment before Lois's death; he thus saves her and, incidentally, the world.

The special effects are dazzling and Reeve's own charm does much to carry the movie: this is bad sf, but exceptionally good junk. It was sequelled by *Superman II* (1980), *Superman III* (1983), *Supergirl* (1984) and *Superman IV: The Quest For Peace* (1987).

1979

Alien

1979 • UK • *DIRECTOR* RIDLEY SCOTT • *SCREENPLAY* DAN O'BANNON • *SPECIAL EFFECTS* BERNARD LODGE, CARLO RAMBALDI • *STARRING* VERONICA CARTWRIGHT (LAMBERT), IAN HOLM (ASH), JOHN HURT (KANE), YAPHET KOTTO (PARKER), TOM SKERRIT (DALLAS), HARRY DEAN STANTON (BRETT), SIGOURNEY WEAVER (RIPLEY) • *117M* • *COLOUR*
Called to investigate an unnamed planet, the crew of the freighter *Nostromo* discover an ancient alien spacecraft and seemingly sessile pods. However, one of these bursts open and a reptiloid creature hurls itself against the mask of crewman Kane, penetrating it and throwing him into a coma. At last, though, the creature dies and he seems fully recovered; and *Nostromo* goes on its way. Later, though, he convulses in agony and a small, alien creature bursts from his chest. The little alien escapes and, scavenging whatever is available aboard the spaceship and then preying, one by one, on the crew, grows to become a huge, lethal and apparently unkillable monster. Soon the sole survivor is Ripley...

A fantastically exciting non-stop thriller, *Alien* was succeeded by *Aliens* (1986) and *Alien³* (1992). Artists

involved in the design of the alien included Chris Foss and, most notably, H.R. Giger.

The Black Hole

1979 • USA • *DIRECTOR* GARY NELSON • *SCREENPLAY* GERRY DAY, JEB ROSEBROOK • *98M* • *COLOUR*
Astonishingly second-rate attempt by Disney to capitalize on the success of *Star Wars* (1977): a mad scientist and cute robots partake in a 1940s-style pulp plot, surrounded by bad special effects.

Buck Rogers In The 25th Century

1979 • USA • *DIRECTOR* DANIEL HALLER • *SCREENPLAY* GLEN A. LARSON, LESLIE STEVENS, FROM THE COMIC STRIPS ORIGINATED BY PHILIP NOWLAN • *STARRING* GIL GERARD

HERO'S GAZE THE CAPED CRUSADER IN MENACING POSE: IN SUPERMAN (1978) CHRISTOPHER REEVE MADE THE PART SO MUCH HIS OWN THAT IT'S HARD TO IMAGINE ANYONE ELSE PLAYING IT

(Buck), Erin Gray (Wilma), Pamela Hensley (Ardela)
• *89m* • *COLOUR*

Released theatrically outside the USA, this was the pilot for the successful TV series: it has much in common with *Battlestar Galactica* (1978) — and hence *Star Wars* (1977). Buck, waking after 500 years, saves Earth from the rapacious (and sexy) alien humanoid Princess Ardela.

Mad Max

1979 • Australia • *DIRECTOR* George Miller • *SCREENPLAY* George Miller, James McCausland • *STARRING* Mel Gibson (Max) • *100m* • *COLOUR*

In a near-future Australia, a biker cop hunts down and destroys the biker gang who murdered his wife. That is the entire plot, but the movie is nevertheless enthralling.

Meteor

1979 • USA • *DIRECTOR* Ronald Neame • *SCREENPLAY* Stanley Mann, Edmund H. North • *107m* • *COLOUR*

Drab movie based on (yawn) the premise that an asteroid is on collision course with the Earth.

Quintet

1979 • USA • *DIRECTOR* Robert Altman • *SCREENPLAY* Robert Altman, Frank Barhydt, Patricia Resnick • *STARRING* Bibi Andersson, Paul Newman • *118m* • *COLOUR*

Some time after the nuclear holocaust, the world is freezing up and a group of the surviving humans play a game, Quintet, failure in which

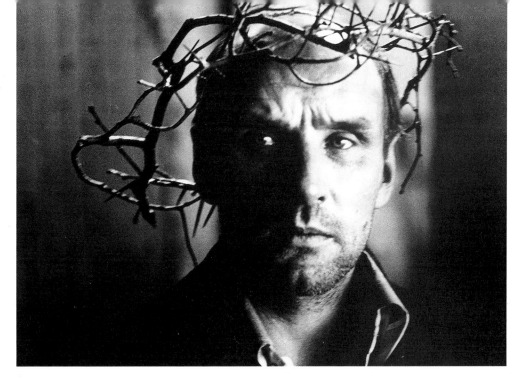

 CROWN OF THORNS *The second of Andrei Tarkovsky's forays into the field of sf,* Stalker *(1979) represented another moody triumph*

means death.

Stalker

1979 • USSR • *DIRECTOR* Andrei Tarkovsky • *SCREENPLAY* Arkady Strugatsky, Boris Strugatsky, from their *Roadside Picnic* (1972) • *SPECIAL EFFECTS* UNCREDITED • *STARRING* Nikolai Grinko (Scientist), Aleksandr Kaidanovsky (Stalker), Anatoli Solonitsin (Writer) • *161m* • *COLOUR* AND *B/W*

This movie is quite a long way from the Strugatsky Brothers' novel. In an unnamed country, there has appeared a forbidden Zone at whose centre lies a Room which is said to have the power to reify fantasies (a direct echo of the preoccupations of Tarkovsky's *Solaris* [1972]). Although the Zone is taboo, a Stalker offers to take a Writer and a Scientist to the Room, and the three of them travel through a constantly shifting, reactive landscape until finally they attain the outside of the Room. Once there, though, they cannot agree on what to do next, and at length they merely return whence they came. The importance of the Room, the movie tells us, is not what it can do or the potential fantasies that it contains but the fantasy that it *is*: so long as it exists, we have the potential to reify our *own* fantasies.

Like *Solaris*, this is exceptionally long, and for extended periods nothing much seems to be happening. Yet, as with Tarkovsky's other movies, it is full of event: one simply has to watch closely and concentrate hard.

Star Trek: The Motion Picture

1979 • USA • *DIRECTOR* Robert Wise • *SCREENPLAY* Harold Livingston, Gene Roddenberry • *SPECIAL EFFECTS* Don Baker, John Dykstra, Harry Moreau, Dave Stewart, Robert Swarthe, Douglas Trumbull, Richard Yuricich • *STARRING* Majel Barret (Dr Christine Chapel), James Doohan (Chief Engineer Montgomery "Scotty" Scott), DeForest Kelley (Dr Leonard "Bones" McCoy), Persis Khambatta (Ilia/V'ger), Walter Koenig

Superman — super sales

To modern audiences, Superman movies began with *Superman: The Movie* (1978), continuing with *Superman II* (1980), *Superman III* (1983) and *Superman IV: The Quest For Peace* (1987), with *Supergirl* (1984) thrown in for good measure.

But the saga began long before that. First, in 1941-43, came the animated Superman shorts, produced by Max Fleischer (1889-1972) and mostly directed by his brother Dave Fleischer (1894-1979); there were 17 of these. Then came the live-action serial movie *Superman* (1948), which broke all the box-office records that previous serial movies had established. Its success engendered a further serial, *Atom Man Vs Superman* (1950) and the feature *Superman And The Mole Men* (1951; vt *Superman And The Strange People*). In these early movies, Superman could have been any other comics-derived superhero — Captain Marvel or Flash Gordon, for example — but, when Christopher Reeve took the part for the 1978 feature, he made it his own. The rest, as the cliché has it, is history.

Star Wars — the spin-offs

Recently, there have been rumours that a second trilogy of Star Wars movies is about to enter production. But the original trilogy has had several movie spin-offs of its own. Much of *Return Of The Jedi* was set on the "forest moon" of Endor, whose indigenes, the ewoks, are bellicose, glassy-eyed teddy bears. These proved popular enough to spawn a TV series, including the pilot movie released theatrically as *The Ewok Adventure* (1984). A second TV movie, *Ewoks: The Battle For Endor* (1986), was not released for the big screen.

The ewoks also featured in the animated TV series *The Ewoks And Star Wars Droids Adventure Hour*, which ran on ABC in 1985. In this, the first half was devoted to ewok adventures, the second to C–3PO and R2–D2; the latter set of stories prequelled *Star Wars*.

There have been plenty of other Star Wars clones. The TV series *Battlestar Galactica* (1978) was the most immediate; not far behind came *Buck Rogers In The 25th Century* (1979–81). The movie *Battle Beyond The Stars* (1980) was a remake by Roger Corman of *The Magnificent Seven* (1960) using a setting almost indistinguishable from the Star Wars universe. Dino De Laurentiis felt inspired to make *Flash Gordon* (1980) — a remarkably swift parodic response. Cute droids turned up everywhere in various ghastly movies; *Short Circuit* (1986) was among the least bad of these; *The Black Hole* (1979) was one of the least good. That the trilogy should have spawned imitators was only just; it is not itself immune from charges of imitation — one sequence in *Star Wars*, for example, is remarkably reminiscent of *Forbidden Planet* (1956).

In 1987 came Mel Brooks's laboured parody, the starkly unfunny *Spaceballs*. Interestingly, Lucas's own special-effects company, Industrial Light & Magic, worked on the movie.

Generations (1994)... with plenty more reportedly in the pipeline. What started as a mere cult sf series — it was axed after only three seasons — has now become a colossal industry.

Time After Time

1979 • USA • *DIRECTOR* NICHOLAS MEYER • *SCREENPLAY* NICHOLAS MEYER, FROM KARL ALEXANDER'S *TIME AFTER TIME* (1976) • *STARRING* MALCOLM MCDOWELL (H.G. WELLS), MARY STEENBURGEN (AMY ROBBINS), DAVID WARNER (JACK THE RIPPER) • *112M* • COLOUR

Jack the Ripper, close to being caught, flees into the future using H.G. Wells's Time Machine. Wells pursues. After an over-sadistic start, this becomes a surprisingly agreeable movie.

1980

Altered States

1980 • USA • *DIRECTOR* KEN RUSSELL • *SCREENPLAY* PADDY CHAYEVSKY (AS SIDNEY AARON), FROM CHAYEVSKY'S *ALTERED STATES* (1978) • *102M* • COLOUR

(ENSIGN CHEKOV), NICHELLE NICHOLS (LIEUTENANT UHURA), LEONARD NIMOY (MR SPOCK), WILLIAM SHATNER (CAPTAIN JAMES T. KIRK), GEORGE TAKEI (MR SULU) • *132M* • COLOUR

An alien spacecraft is heading for the Earth, devouring all that lies in its path. Kirk and most of his crew are called upon to take the Enterprise out one last time (there were to be several last times) to investigate. The alien being incarnates itself in the form of crew-member Ilia, and explains that it is, in essence, lonely; having long ago devoured an archaic unmanned probe from Earth (hence the alien's adopted name, V'ger), it has become offended by Earth's lack of response to its friendly signals, and is now bent on destruction.

Star Trek did not comfortably make the transition from small to large screen, probably because creaky effects and limited budgets contributed to the original *Star Trek* ethos: smack-in-your-eye spectaculars and impressive sets were somehow out of keeping. But times have changed, and now this technical proficiency is valued, as witnessed not just by the TV series *Star Trek: The Next Generation* (1987), *Star Trek: Deep Space Nine* (1993) and *Star Trek: Voyager* (1995) but by the movie sequels: *Star Trek: The Wrath Of Khan* (1982), *Star Trek III: The Search For Spock* (1984), *Star Trek IV: The Voyage Home* (1986), *Star Trek V: The Final Frontier* (1989) and *Star Trek VI: The Undiscovered Country* (1991), plus *Star Trek:*

TO INFINITY... AND BEYOND *THE* ENTERPRISE *PREPARING TO BOLDLY GO WHERE FEW BOX-OFFICE RECEIPTS HAVE GONE BEFORE.* 1979'S STAR TREK: THE MOTION PICTURE *WAS A VAST HIT AND SPAWNED MANY SEQUELS*

Russell brings his own individual brand of cinematic fantastication to an sf tale — a research scientist empowers his DNA to revert him back through apedom to primordial sludge — that was somewhat improbable to begin with. The result is a psychedelic fiasco.

Battle Beyond The Stars

1980 • USA • **DIRECTOR** JIMMY T. MURAKAMI • **SCREENPLAY** JOHN SAYLES, FROM THE MOVIE *THE MAGNIFICENT SEVEN* (1960) • **103M** • **COLOUR**
Cashing in on the success of *Star Wars* (1977), this is *The Magnificent Seven* (1960) rewritten as space opera, to the extent that Robert Vaughn plays essentially the same part as in the Western. The overall effect is somewhat tiresome. *Space Raiders* (1983) reused many of the special effects.

The Empire Strikes Back

1980 • USA • **DIRECTOR** IRVIN KERSHNER • **SCREENPLAY** LEIGH BRACKETT, LAWRENCE KASDAN • **SPECIAL EFFECTS** RICHARD EDLUND, BRIAN JOHNSON, DENNIS MUREN, BRUCE NICHOLSON • **STARRING** KENNY BAKER (R2-D2), ANTHONY DANIELS (C-3PO), CARRIE FISHER (PRINCESS LEIA ORGANA), HARRISON FORD (HAN SOLO), ALEC GUINNESS (OBI-WAN KENOBI), MARK HAMILL (LUKE SKYWALKER), PETER MAYHEW (CHEWBACCA), FRANK OZ (YODA), DAVID PROWSE (DARTH VADER), BILLY DEE WILLIAMS (LANDO CALRISSIAN) • **VOICE ACTORS** JAMES EARL JONES (DARTH VADER), CLIVE REVILL (EMPEROR) • **124M** • **COLOUR**
The direct sequel to *Star Wars* (1977), this is really the first half of a very long movie, the second half being *Return Of The Jedi* (1983); the two are best considered together.

Luke trains under the greatest Jedi of all, the Muppetish alien Yoda, and, his powers ever-growing, twice duels Vader face-to-face, discovering that the Dark Lord is his father and then later that Leia is in fact his long-lost sister. This latter revelation solves the emotional complication that underscores both movies, for Leia has known that she should be paired off with Luke (such is the power of Story), yet has fallen in love with Han Solo (as a result, parts of *The Empire Strikes Back* are reminiscent of the Lancelot and Guinevere legend). Acting generally

TRUST ME DARTH VADER IN THE EMPIRE STRIKES BACK, PLAYED FOR THE SECOND TIME BY DAVE PROWSE, WHO EARLIER PLAYED THE MONSTER IN THE HORROR OF FRANKENSTEIN AND FRANKENSTEIN AND THE MONSTER FROM HELL

apart from Luke, the other main characters on the side of Good succeed in destroying the Emperor's new-model Death Star. Darth Vader, wounded by Luke, in his dying moments turns back to the light side of the Force and kills the Emperor.

These movies are in a way more mature than *Star Wars*, but this does not act to their advantage. The innocent fairytale atmosphere of the original was its most valuable attribute, and once it dissipates we are left with a collection of special effects plus too much by way of repetitive war-movie aerial dogfighting transposed into space. The legacy of the trilogy has been diverse. Much of *Return Of The Jedi* is set on the "forest moon" of Endor, whose indigenes, the ewoks, are bellicose, glassy-eyed teddy bears. These proved popular enough to spawn a TV series, the pilot movie for which was released theatrically as *The Ewok Adventure* (1984). A second TV movie, *Ewoks: The Battle For Endor* (1986), was, mercifully, not released for the big screen.

The Final Countdown

1980 • USA • **DIRECTOR** DON TAYLOR • **SCREENPLAY** DAVID AMBROSE, GERRY DAVIS, THOMAS HUNTER, PETER POWELL • **STARRING** KIRK DOUGLAS • **105M** • **COLOUR**
Made as a vehicle for Kirk Douglas by his own production company, this sees a modern US

aircraft carrier timewarped back to 1941, with the Pearl Harbor attack imminent.

Flash Gordon

1980 • USA • **DIRECTOR** MIKE HODGES • **SCREENPLAY** MICHAEL ALLIN, LORENZO SEMPLE JR, FROM THE 1936 SERIAL MOVIE *FLASH GORDON* • **STARRING** MELODY ANDERSON (DALE), BRIAN BLESSED (VULTAN), SAM J. JONES (FLASH), ORNELLA MUTI (AURA), MAX VON SYDOW (MING) • **115M** • **COLOUR**
Bad special effects and a hacked-about script should have made this mixture of parody and homage a disaster, but in fact it's tremendous fun to watch.

Hangar 18

1980 • USA • **DIRECTOR** JAMES L. CONWAY • **SCREENPLAY** STEVEN THORNLEY • **97M** • **COLOUR**
A US spacecraft collides with a UFO, and politicians try to cover up the fact.

Inseminoid

1980 • UK • **DIRECTOR** NORMAN J. WARREN • **SCREENPLAY** GLORIA MALEY, NICK MALEY • **92M** • **COLOUR**
Incoherent, cheap and violent reprise of *Alien* (1979): scientist raped by alien monster gives monstrous birth. The big surprise is that Oxford Scientific Films (for special effects) should be involved in this.

La Mort En Direct

(VT *DEATH WATCH*)

1980 • FRANCE/WEST GERMANY • *DIRECTOR* BERTRAND TAVERNIER • *SCREENPLAY* DAVID RAFIEL, BERTRAND TAVERNIER, FROM D.G. COMPTON'S *THE CONTINUOUS KATHERINE MORTENHOE* (1974; VT *THE UNSLEEPING EYE*) • *STARRING* VADIM GLOWNA (HARRY GRAVES), HARVEY KEITEL (RODDY), ROMY SCHNEIDER (KATHERINE MORTENHOE), HARRY DEAN STANTON (VINCENT FERRIMAN), MAX VON SYDOW (GERALD MORTENHOE) • *130M* • *COLOUR*

Ferriman's TV company, seeking a new weapon in the ratings war, determines to put on the ultimate real-life soap opera: a reporter, Roddy, with a camera embedded in his eye is detailed to observe the final months of a woman, Katherine, suffering from a terminal illness. At first she is horrified, but her second husband, Graves, persuades her that he needs the money offered by Ferriman; as soon as it is paid, though, she flees, with Roddy in pursuit. The relationship between the two deepens once her initial loathing for him has eased.

Saturn 3

1980 • UK • *DIRECTOR* JOHN BARRY, STANLEY DONEN • *SCREENPLAY* MARTIN AMIS • *87M* • *COLOUR*

A mixture of Saturn-orbit hydroponics and a lustful psychopathic robot. Best forgotten.

Scanners

1980 • CANADA • *DIRECTOR* DAVID CRONENBERG • *SCREENPLAY* DAVID CRONENBERG • *SPECIAL EFFECTS* HENRY PIERRIG, DICK SMITH, CHRIS WALAS, GARY ZELLER • *STARRING* MICHAEL IRONSIDE (DARRYL REVOK), STEPHEN LACK (CAMERON VALE), PATRICK MCGOOHAN (DR PAUL RUTH), JENNIFER O'NEILL (KIM) • *103M* • *COLOUR*

Decades ago, an experimental drug was prescribed to pregnant women; because of side-effects it was soon pulled off the market. But the children born of those women have grown up possessing telepathic and telekinetic powers — they are "scanners". Although they are scattered across the globe, two organizations are attempting to round them up for very different purposes: Dr Ruth's ComSec, which hopes to benefit humanity; and Revok's Biocarbon Amalgamated, which nurtures dreams of world domination. Cameron Vale is a scanner unaware of his true status until taken under ComSec's wing; after adventures, he discovers that Revok is in fact his brother, and that the two were the original guinea-pigs used in the testing of the drug. In the movie's climax they duel brain-to-brain until "Good destroys Evil"...

This movie has been widely over-praised. Although it contains much of interest — not to mention the famous exploding-head scene — the acting is, Ironside magnificently excepted, universally poor, with Lack in particular displaying the woodenness characteristic of amateur dramatics. Various sequels/spin-offs have appeared: *Scanners II: The New Order* (1991), *Scanners III: The Takeover* (1992) and *Scanner Force* (1992).

Superman II

1980 • UK • *DIRECTOR* RICHARD DONNER (UNCREDITED), RICHARD LESTER • *SCREENPLAY* DAVID NEWMAN, LESLIE NEWMAN, MARIO PUZO • *STARRING* MARGOT KIDDER (LOIS), CHRISTOPHER REEVE (SUPERMAN) • *127M* • *COLOUR*

Three criminals from the planet Krypton attempt to take over the Earth, but Superman stops them. A superior sequel to *Superman: The Movie* (1978).

1981

Escape From New York

1981 • USA • *DIRECTOR* JOHN CARPENTER • *SCREENPLAY* JOHN CARPENTER, NICK CASTLE • *STARRING* DONALD PLEASANCE, KURT RUSSELL • *99M* • *COLOUR*

In 1997, Manhattan has been made into a vast high-security prison. The US President's plane malfunctions, and he must bale out into the middle of this. Ex-con Snake Plissken (Russell) rescues him. Poor plotting but good fun which resulted in a 1996 sequel.

Heartbeeps

1981 • USA • *DIRECTOR* ALLAN ARKUSH • *SCREENPLAY* JOHN HILL • *88M* • *COLOUR*

Usually seen cut, this is a nauseating romantic comedy about two robots who run away together and build themselves a little robot child.

DON'T MIX YOUR DRINKS *THE 1980 MOVIE* SCANNERS *WAS AN EARLY DAVID CRONENBERG MOVIE FEATURING MANY HORRIBLE SCENES, MOST NOTABLE IS THE EXPLODING HEAD. SPECIAL EFFECTS HAVE COME A LONG WAY SINCE THIS FILM WAS SHOT*

MAX IS BACK *MEL GIBSON MADE TWO SEQUELS TO THE ORIGINAL* MAD MAX. *HERE, MAX STRUGGLES TO SAVE HIMSELF AND A YOUNG FRIEND FROM SOME OTHER ROAD WARRIORS IN* MAD MAX II *(1981)*

The Incredible Shrinking Woman

1981 • USA • *DIRECTOR* JOEL SCHUMACHER • *SCREENPLAY* JANE WAGNER • *88M* • *COLOUR*

Weak semi-parody of *The Incredible Shrinking Man* (1957); This time it's a housewife who shrinks after being splashed by an experimental perfume.

Mad Max 2

(VT THE ROAD WARRIOR)

1981 • AUSTRALIA • *DIRECTOR* GEORGE MILLER • *SCREENPLAY* BRIAN HANNAT, TERRY HAYES, GEORGE MILLER • *SPECIAL EFFECTS* JEFFREY CLIFFORD, KIM PRIEST • *STARRING* MEL GIBSON (MAX ROCKATANSKY), EMIL MINTY (FERAL CHILD), MIKE PRESTON (PAPPAGALLO), KJELL NILSSON (HUMUNGUS), BRUCE SPENCE (GYRO CAPTAIN) • *96M* • *COLOUR*

The much more coherent sequel to *Mad Max* (1979), and a thrilling action movie; that said, with a few changes of detail it could equally well be the most exciting Western ever made, since it lacks the true sf touch of its successor, *Mad Max: Beyond Thunderdome* (1985).

The world — or, at least, Australia — is still in the grip of a gasoline crisis. Max, having avenged the deaths of his wife and child, is drifting when he falls into the snares of the Gyro Captain. The two arrive at an oil installation, run by Pappagallo, which is surrounded day and night by whooping biker barbarians under the leadership of the vile Humungus. One last convoy of oil tankers must be brought out through this cordon insanitaire, and Max takes on the job of masterminding the operation. What one remembers are the spectacular action scenes and, perhaps most of all, the hyperactive performance of Emil Minty as a lethal, martial-arts-influenced child warrior.

Malevil

1981 • FRANCE/WEST GERMANY • *DIRECTOR* CHRISTIAN DE CHALONGE • *SCREENPLAY* CHRISTIAN DE CHALONGE, PIERRE DUMAYET, FROM ROBERT MERLE'S *MALEVIL* (1972) • *119M* • *COLOUR*

Poorly realized exposition of societal changes after the nuclear holocaust, with aristocrats surviving in a wine-cellar and then emerging to discover a local fascist regime in place.

Outland

1981 • UK • *DIRECTOR* PETER HYAMS • *SCREENPLAY* PETER HYAMS • *STARRING* SEAN CONNERY • *109M* • *COLOUR*

High Noon (1952) relocated to Jupiter's moon Io. The movie sounds unappealing, but in fact it delivers its due quota of thrills.

Quest For Fire

1981 • CANADA/FRANCE • *DIRECTOR* JEAN-JACQUES ANNAUD • *SCREENPLAY* GÉRARD BRACH, FROM J.H. ROSNY ÂINÉ'S *LA GUERRE DU FEU* (1909) • *100M* • *COLOUR*

A prehistoric tribe literally loses its fire, and members are sent out to quest for another source. As a tale, this has its shortcomings, but the movie has sufficient points of scientific interest (e.g., a specially invented primitive language) more or less to make up for these.

1982

Android

1982 • USA • *DIRECTOR* AARON LIPSTADT • *SCREENPLAY* DON OPPER, JAMES REIGLE • *SPECIAL EFFECTS* STEVEN B. CALDWELL, BILL CONWAY, JULIA GIBSON, NEW WORLD EFFECTS • *STARRING* CROFTON HARDESTER (MENDES), BRIE HOWARD (MAGGIE), KLAUS KINSKI (DR DANIEL), KENDRA KIRCHNER (CASSANDRA), DON OPPER (MAX 404), NORBERT WEISSER (KELLER) • *80M* • *COLOUR*

Three criminals — Keller, Maggie and Mendes — piratically seize a police transport and land it on the space station where Dr Daniel and his android Max are working to develop a super-android, Cassandra. Max falls in love with Maggie, and Daniel realizes that her vital female spark can be used to bring Cassandra to "life". Much murder and intrigue ensues.

Android certainly has its moments, but not too many of them, and Kinski's hammery doesn't much help. Yet, the movie is worth watching for Opper's performance alone.

Rutger Hauer muscles with talent

Most clichés prove, on examination, to be fallacies, and the cliché that Hollywood musclemen must be poor actors dependent entirely on their physiques is one of them. It may be hard to find critical language to discuss the performances of, say, Steve Reeves or Jean-Claude Van Damme, but no one could deny the acumen of Schwarzenegger in playing to his strengths and, in a rather different way, no one could deny that the Dutchman Rutger Hauer (1944-   ) is an actor first and foremost and, coincidentally, a muscleman too.

He first attracted the attention of the sf audience in *Blade Runner* (1982), where he displayed considerable sensitivity in the portrayal of a replicant (android). *A Breed Apart* (1984) saw him act the strongman in an eco-conscious thriller; in *Ladyhawke* (1985), he produced a fine portrayal of a man cursed to be a wolf by day and a man by night, while his lover is cursed to be a woman by day and a hawk by night. *Flesh And Blood* (1985), set in a Middle Ages That Never Was, is a bad fantasy, but the Italian movie *La Leggenda Del Santo Bevitore* (1988; vt *The Legend Of The Holy Drinker*) saw him return to form in a quirky, oddly affecting fantasy. *Blind Fury* (1989) was a martial-arts outing. The Australian *The Salute Of The Jugger* (1989) put him in a cyberpunkish near-future tale. Another near-future movie was the UK feature *Split Second* (1992); although mediocre, it gave Hauer once more the respect he deserved.

He played a comparatively minor — but astonishingly effective — part in the fantasy-horror comedy *Buffy The Vampire Slayer* (1992).

Blade Runner

1982 • USA • *DIRECTOR* RIDLEY SCOTT • *SCREENPLAY* HAMPTON FANCHER, DAVID PEOPLES, FROM PHILIP K. DICK'S *DO ANDROIDS DREAM OF ELECTRIC SHEEP?* (1968) • *SPECIAL EFFECTS* DOUGLAS TRUMBULL • *STARRING* HARRISON FORD (RICK DECKARD), DARYL HANNAH (PRIS), RUTGER HAUER (ROY BATTY), EDWARD JAMES OLMOS (GAFF), M. EMMETT WALSH (BRYANT), SEAN YOUNG (RACHAEL) • *117M* • *COLOUR*

ONLY THE LONELY *THE DIRECTOR TREATS THE REPLICANTS IN* BLADE RUNNER *(1982) WITH SYMPATHY. EVEN RUTGER HAUER IS SEEN TO SHED TEARS, AND DARYL HANNAH OBVIOUSLY FEELS THE LONELINESS OF EXISTENCE*

Almost certainly the finest sf movie of the 1980s, this matched a true sf plot to the same feel of a genuinely gritty near future that *Soylent Green* (1973) intermittently achieved.

AD2019, and much of Earth's population has departed for less despoiled territories in space; Earth itself is still, however, hideously overpopulated. In order for the decaying system to work, humans must make use of replicants (androids), who are essentially slaves, confined to space colonies, and who have a maximum operational span of four years — any longer and they might get ideas above their station. Deckard is a retired Blade Runner: his job was to track down rogue replicants and destroy them. He is called out of retirement for one last task: a party of replicants has made its way to Earth with the intention of either presenting the replicants' case or, at the very least, mingling with humans and enjoying a human life.

All sorts of pyrotechnics illuminate this movie, but most memorable is the vision of a future Los Angeles dominated by overcrowding and offensively huge advertising; later movies like *Freejack* (1992) and *Judge Dredd* (1995) were to draw freely upon these images.

Scott had to make some compromises with Warner Bros for *Blade Runner*'s first release, giving it an upbeat ending and supplying a noirish voice-over from Ford to comfort audiences with the idea they were really watching Philip Marlowe in a future scenario. This damage was repaired by Scott in *Blade Runner — The Director's Cut* (1991), which ran to 130m.

E.T. — The Extra-Terrestrial

1982 • USA • *DIRECTOR* STEVEN SPIELBERG • *SCREENPLAY* MELISSA MATHISON • *SPECIAL EFFECTS* INDUSTRIAL LIGHT & MAGIC, DENNIS MUREN • *STARRING* DREW BARRYMORE (GERTIE), PETER COYOTE ("KEYS"), SEAN FRYE (STEVE), TOM HOWELL (TYLER), ROBERT MACNAUGHTON (MICHAEL), K.C. MARTEL (GREG), HENRY THOMAS (ELLIOTT), DEE WALLACE (MARY) • *115M* • *COLOUR*

If *Star Wars* (1977) is a science-fictional fairytale of one kind — a story of magic and a princess set against an intergalactic backdrop — E.T. is a science-fictional fairytale of another: a domestic tale of a would-be fairy being sheltered by children from the harsh world of adults. As one critic remarked at the time, it could have been scripted by Peter Pan.

An alien spaceship lands silently in the open countryside somewhere near Los Angeles, and its occupants start investigating the local flora. However, the craft must have been spotted, because a posse of searchers arrives on the scene. The aliens depart in some haste, inadvertently leaving behind them a seeming child of their species. This creature ("E.T.") at last finds refuge in the back yard of a nearby house, whose family comprises recently separated Mary, her elder son Michael, ten-year-old Elliott and little sister Gertie. Elliott, having heard odd noises out back, goes to investigate and encounters E.T..

Soon E.T. and the children are both friends and conspirators, keeping the alien's presence a secret from Mother. E.T. is capable of remarkable feats of levitation, and acquires rudimentary powers of human speech; he conveys to the children that he would like to "phone home". Adult authority, however, has become aware of the alien's presence, and scientific researchers are homing in on the immediate area.

Much has been made of E.T.'s sub-texts: the resurrected E.T. as a Christ-figure; the fact that Elliott's name has the first and last letters "e" and "t"; the fact that Elliott's mother is called Mary... All of which is very well, but it seems just as tenable that Spielberg and Mathison constructed the movie merely as an entertainment, an appeal to the child that lives on within almost all of us (most of the movie is shot from a child's-height perspective), with moments of mirth mixed with times of despair. It is perhaps more pertinent to compare E.T., who dies and is reborn, not with Christ but with Peter Pan — a figure who clearly lies somewhere near the core of Spielberg's personal mythology (cf *Hook* [1991]). Whatever the case, E.T. is one of the most successful movies of all time, and seems set to remain a favourite for decades to come.

Disney's sf

Throughout its history, the Disney Studio (under its various names) has had serious difficulties in coming to terms with sf: its family-oriented policy dictated that the intellectual content of its sf movies should be kept to a minimum, so that even the youngest child could keep abreast of on-screen events. Most of Disney's "sf" production has in fact been technofantasy — movies like *The Absent-Minded Professor* (1961).

But Disney has produced some good sf work. *Escape To Witch Mountain* (1974) and its sequel, *Return From Witch Mountain* (1978), are emphatically pleasing examples of children's sf. Based on the novel *Escape To Witch Mountain* (1968) by Alexander Key, they see a pair of orphans with seemingly supernatural powers slowly discovering that they belong to an alien species. (In disparate ways, these movies can be related to Zenna Henderson's "People" sequence of stories and to *E.T. — The Extra-Terrestrial* [1982].)

The Black Hole (1979) was a bad attempt to cash in on *Star Wars* (1977), but *Tron* (1982) broke new sf-cinema ground, both technically and conceptually. *Flight Of The Navigator* (1986) has fine moments... though many not-so-fine too. *Honey, I Shrunk The Kids* (1989) showed it was possible to mix the traditional Disney family comedy with interesting sf ideas; its lesser sequel, *Honey, I Blew Up The Kid* (1992), displayed Disney's continued uncertain touch in the sf genre, and *Spaced Invaders* (1990) was plain dreadful. With *Arachnophobia* (1990), *The Rocketeer* (1991), *The Puppet Masters* (1994) and *Judge Dredd* (1995), Disney — sometimes in partnership with other studios and releasing material through its subsidiaries — at last demonstrated that it could, if sometimes clumsily, cope with a genre that it no longer regarded as just for kids.

Star Trek: The Wrath Of Khan

1982 • USA • DIRECTOR NICHOLAS MEYER • SCREENPLAY JACK B. SOWARDS • STARRING RICARDO MONTALBAN (KHAN), LEONARD NIMOY (SPOCK), WILLIAM SHATNER (KIRK) • 114M • COLOUR

The second *Star Trek* movie was a commercial if not a critical success. The evil Khan, whom the *Enterprise*'s crew had successfully exiled in the TV series, bounces back with dire consequences for Spock.

The Thing

1982 • USA • DIRECTOR JOHN CARPENTER • SCREENPLAY BILL LANCASTER, FROM DON A. STUART'S (I.E., JOHN W. CAMPBELL'S) 'WHO GOES THERE?' (1938) • SPECIAL EFFECTS ROY ARBOGAST, ROB BOTTIN, MICHAEL CLIFFORD, LEROY ROUTLY, ALBERT WHITLOCK • STARRING WILFRED BRIMLEY (BLAIR), T.K. CARTER (NAULS), KEITH DAVID (CHILDS), KURT RUSSELL (MACREADY), • 109M • COLOUR

This remake of *The Thing* (1951) at least reverts to Campbell's original notion of the stranded, predatory alien as shapeshifter. Otherwise, it is really just a rerun of *Alien* (1979) set not aboard a spacecraft but in a scientific base in Antarctica. The special effects are superb, but the script limps and the characterization is virtually non-existent.

Tron

1982 • USA • DIRECTOR STEVEN LISBERGER • SCREENPLAY STEVEN LISBERGER • SPECIAL EFFECTS/ANIMATION LEE DYER, HARRISON ELLENSHAW, STEVEN LISBERGER, JOHN SCHEELE, R.J. SPETTER, RICHARD TAYLOR • STARRING BRUCE BOXLEITNER (ALAN BRADLEY/TRON), JEFF BRIDGES (KEVIN FLYNN/CLU), BARNARD HUGHES (WALTER GIBBS/DUMONT), CINDY MORGAN (LORA/YORI), DAN SHOR (RAM), DAVID WARNER (ED DILLINGER/SARK) • 96M • COLOUR

A box-office disaster at the time, *Tron* mixes

 ARE YOU TALKING TO ME? *E.T. THE EXTRA-TERRESTRIAL, SEEN HERE WITH HIS NEW FOUND FRIEND, ELLIOTT (HENRY THOMAS). THE FILM ENJOYED PHENOMENAL SUCCESS AT TIME OF RELEASE, AND IS STILL VERY POPULAR*

exciting ideas and state-of-the-art computer animation with a markedly poor screenplay. Evil techno-boss Dillinger, of ENCOM, is planning to take over, if not the world, then at least cyberspace using his supercomputer-software MCP (Master Control Program). By coincidence, ENCOM's founder, Gibbs, and his assistant Lora are devising a system whereby, using computer-linked lasers, they may be able to transmit matter. Computer genius Flynn, whose inventions have been stolen by Dillinger, is attempting to hack into MCP; but MCP uses the laser system to suck Flynn directly into its labyrinthine world. Here programs and subprograms are set against each other in gladiatorial contests, the defeated softwares suffering the fate of being "de-rezzed".

Tron can be regarded as an early example of the cyberpunk movement — it certainly predates William Gibson's *Neuromancer* (1984), although of course coming long after John Brunner's *The Shockwave Rider* (1975). Its status in sf history — despite its trite, Disneyesque screenplay — is slowly being recognized.

Videodrome

1982 • CANADA • *DIRECTOR* DAVID CRONENBERG • *SCREENPLAY* DAVID CRONENBERG • *SPECIAL EFFECTS* RICK BAKER, FRANK CARERE, MICHAEL LENNICK • *STARRING* LES

CARLSON (BARRY CONVEX), PETER DVORSKY (HARLAN), LYNNE GORMAN (MASHA), DEBORAH HARRY (NICKI BRAND), SONJA SMITS (BIANCA O'BLIVION), JAMES WOODS (MAX RENN) • **89M** • *COLOUR*

Jaded TV executive Renn discovers the satellite station Videodrome, which nightly broadcasts what seem to be sex-torture murders. Fascinated — as is girlfriend Brand — he sets out to track down the powers behind Videodrome, finally discovering that he has been lured into a trap. Because of a cassette inserted into his stomach, he will be compelled to make his own Channel 83 give the Videodrome broadcasts their first public airing. Cronenberg fans adore this movie; others are either bemused or revolted.

1983

Brainstorm

1983 • USA • *DIRECTOR* DOUGLAS TRUMBULL • *SCREENPLAY* PHILIP FRANK MESSINA, ROBERT STITZEL • **106M** • *COLOUR*

Mostly remembered as the movie during whose production Natalie Wood died, this hinges on scientists inventing a way of tape-recording mental events (including death), which can then be experienced by others.

Le Dernier Combat

(VT THE LAST BATTLE)

1983 • FRANCE • *DIRECTOR* LUC BESSON • *SCREENPLAY* LUC BESSON, PIERRE JOLIVET • *STARRING* PIERRE JOLIVET • **92M** • *B/W*

After the holocaust, the few surviving humans survive as best they can. This could have been a standard post-holocaust movie; instead it becomes — and remains — an intriguing work of surrealism.

Return Of The Jedi

1983 • USA • *DIRECTOR* RICHARD MARQUAND • *SCREENPLAY* LAWRENCE KASDAN, GEORGE LUCAS • *SPECIAL EFFECTS* RICHARD EDLUND, DENNIS MUREN, KEN RALSTON, KIT WEST • *STARRING* THE SAME CAST AS *THE EMPIRE STRIKES BACK* (1980) PLUS IAN MCDIARMID (EMPEROR), SEBASTIAN SHAW (ANAKIN SKYWALKER) • **132M** • *COLOUR*

This is the second half, released separately, of the very long movie whose first half was *The Empire Strikes Back* (1980) — see discussion of that movie on page 103.

Spacehunter: Adventures In The Forbidden Zone

1983 • USA • *DIRECTORS* LAMONT JOHNSON, JEAN LAFLEUR (UNCREDITED) • *SCREENPLAY* LEN BLUM, DAN GOLDBERT, DAVID PRESTON, EDITH REY • **90M** • *COLOUR*

Star Wars (1970) without the budget and *Flash Gordon* (1980) without the wit combine to produce a space opera without charm.

Strange Invaders

1983 • USA • *DIRECTOR* MICHAEL LAUGHLIN • *SCREENPLAY* WILLIAM CONDON, MICHAEL LAUGHLIN • **94M** • *COLOUR*

In 1958, ufonauts take over a small midwestern town *à la* 1953's *Invaders From Mars* or 1956's *Invasion Of The Body Snatchers*. But now it is 1983, and a scientist discovers the truth: the ufonauts are taking over New York, and his wife is one of them. Not profound, but enjoyable.

Superman III

1983 • UK • *DIRECTOR* RICHARD LESTER • *SCREENPLAY* DAVID NEWMAN, LESLIE NEWMAN • *STARRING* ANNETTE O'TOOLE (LANA LANG), RICHARD PRYOR (GUS GORMAN), CHRISTOPHER REEVE (SUPERMAN), ROBERT VAUGHN (ROSS WEBSTER) • **125M** • *COLOUR*

Megalomaniac plutocrats strive for economic conquest of the world. Superman soon thwarts their plans, despite having kryptonite used against him, so that he temporarily becomes, as it were, his own evil twin. The movie's main interest concerns Superman's rediscovery of his childhood love Lana.

WarGames

1983 • USA • *DIRECTOR* JOHN BADHAM • *SCREENPLAY* LAWRENCE LASKER, WALTER F. PARKES • *STARRING* MATTHEW BRODERICK • *113M* • *COLOUR*

A rather jolly little movie in which a teenaged computer nerd hacks into the Pentagon and nearly precipitates a nuclear war.

1984

The Adventures Of Buckaroo Banzai Across The 8th Dimension

1984 • USA • *DIRECTOR* W.D. RICHTER • *SCREENPLAY* EARL MACRAUCH • *STARRING* PETER WELLER (BUCKAROO) • *102M* • *COLOUR*

Seemingly an attempt to pick up from The Final Programme (1973), this has a pseudo-Jerry Cornelius perform various uninvolving adventures.

Dune

1984 • USA • *DIRECTOR* DAVID LYNCH • *SCREENPLAY* DAVID LYNCH, FROM FRANK HERBERT'S DUNE (1965) • *STARRING* FRANCESCA ANNIS (LADY JESSICA), KYLE MACLACHLAN (PAUL ATREIDES), KENNETH MCMILLAN (BARON VLADIMIR HARKONNEN), STING (FEYD RAUTHA) • *140M* • *COLOUR*

Muddled version of Herbert's classic — a question of the wrong director being given the tale.

Iceman

1984 • USA • *DIRECTOR* FRED SCHEPISI • *SCREENPLAY* JOHN DRIMMER, CHIP PROSER • *99M* • *COLOUR*

Scientists in the Arctic resuscitate a deep-frozen Neanderthal, who proves much more intelligent than they expected.

The Last Starfighter

1984 • USA • *DIRECTOR* NICK CASTLE • *SCREENPLAY* JONATHAN BETUEL • *101M* • *COLOUR*

Derivative from both the *Star Wars* (1977) craze and the video-game craze, this sees an adolescent arcade-game genius hijacked by aliens, so that he can win their war for them.

Nineteen Eighty-Four

1984 • UK • *DIRECTOR* MICHAEL RADFORD • *SCREENPLAY* JONATHAN GEMS, MICHAEL RADFORD, FROM GEORGE ORWELL'S *NINETEEN EIGHTY-FOUR* (1949) • *STARRING* RICHARD BURTON (O'BRIEN), SUZANNA HAMILTON (JULIA), JOHN HURT (WINSTON SMITH) • *110M* • *COLOUR*

Orwell's novel had earlier been filmed as *1984* (1955), in the wake of the hugely successful BBC TV production *Nineteen Eighty-four* (1954), scripted by Nigel Kneale. It was inevitable that someone should wish to produce a new movie

version for the year 1984 itself. What is surprising is that the movie should be so very good. The image of the year 1984 presented on screen is what Orwell envisaged — no hi-tech props or clever special effects — and the well-known story is presented in its full bleakness. There is a marvellous sequence in which Winston and Julia imagine what their love-affair might have been like in a rural arcadia; but then the oppression of their real world closes in on them.

The Philadelphia Experiment

1984 • USA • *DIRECTOR* STEWART RAFFILL • *SCREENPLAY* WILLIAM GRAY, MICHAEL JANOVER, FROM WILLIAM I. MOORE'S AND CHARLES BERLITZ'S *THE PHILADELPHIA EXPERIMENT* (1979) • *101M* • *COLOUR*

The original "nonfiction" book was about a 1943 military-scientific experiment that made a US ship invisible. The movie's tale is that a couple of the crew are timewarped forward to 1984.

Repo Man

1984 • USA • *DIRECTOR* ALEX COX • *SCREENPLAY* ALEX COX • *STARRING* EMILIO ESTEVEZ (OTTO), FOX HARRIS (J. FRANK PARNELL), HARRY DEAN STANTON (BUD) • *92M* • *COLOUR*

Otto is recruited by Bud as an automobile-repossession man, but neither realizes until too late that physicist Parnell, guilty about his work on the Bomb, has dumped his car with either a nuclear device or an alien (the movie is uncertain about this) in the boot. The sub-plot includes rampaging punks, zombie parents, aliens and the mystery of the pine tree car wash. A very funny piece of surrealism and the start of Harry Dean Stanton's long-running 'odd' period.

Starman

1984 • USA • *DIRECTOR* JOHN CARPENTER • *SCREENPLAY* BRUCE A. EVANS, RAYNOLD GIDEON, DEAN RIESNER (UNCREDITED) • *SPECIAL EFFECTS* ROY ARBOGAST, MICHAEL MCALISTER, BRUCE NICHOLSON • *STARRING* KAREN ALLEN (JENNY HAYDEN), JEFF BRIDGES (STARMAN), RICHARD JAECKEL (GEORGE FOX) • *115M* • *COLOUR*

Hayden has been recently widowed, and grieves profoundly. One night, an alien entity arrives on Earth and is able to take on the form of her late husband. The alien explains to her it can survive on Earth for only a few days: a spacecraft will arrive to pick it up from the Arizona desert soon. Hayden drives the Starman to the rendezvous point and becomes fascinated by its innocence and naïvety on being confronted by the sights of

Earth. As a consequence, she begins to fall in love with it — and it, much less plausibly, begins to fall in love with her. Meanwhile, Security Agent Fox is in hot pursuit, the US Government somehow having discovered there is an alien on Earth.

Star Trek III: The Search For Spock

1984 • USA • *DIRECTOR* LEONARD NIMOY • *SCREENPLAY* JOHN HICKRIDGE • *STARRING* DEFOREST KELLEY (DR MCCOY), LEONARD NIMOY (SPOCK), WILLIAM SHATNER (KIRK) • *105M* • *COLOUR*

At the end of *Star Trek: The Wrath Of Khan* (1982), Spock was apparently dead — but in fact his soul is still alive, sharing McCoy's brain. Kirk sacrifices virtually everything to bring Spock back to life.

Supergirl

1984 • UK • *DIRECTOR* JEANNOT SZWARC • *SCREENPLAY* DAVID ODELL, FROM THE COMICS BY JOE SHUSTER AND JERRY SIEGEL • *STARRING* FAYE DUNAWAY (SELENA), HELEN SLATER (SUPERGIRL) • *124M* • *COLOUR*

Weird bit of technofantasy in which the witch Selena attempts to take over the world (and almost succeeds), but is finally stopped by the alien Supergirl. Slater carries the movie.

The Terminator

1984 • USA • *DIRECTOR* JAMES CAMERON • *SCREENPLAY* JAMES CAMERON, GALE ANNE HURD, WILLIAM WISHER JR • *SPECIAL EFFECTS* PETER KLEINOW, GENE WARREN, STAN WINSTON • *STARRING* MICHAEL BIEHN (KYLE REESE), LINDA HAMILTON (SARAH CONNOR), ARNOLD SCHWARZENEGGER (THE TERMINATOR) • *108M* • *COLOUR*

In AD 2029, the machines are waging a relentless war of extirpation against the human race. The leader of the humans is John Connor. The machines send back to 1984 a seemingly indestructible android killer — a Terminator — to murder Connor's mother Sarah before she can bear their most indefatigable foe. Connor, discovering this, sends back his trusted colleague Reese. The Terminator swiftly sets about killing any Sarah Connor it can find, but the relevant one escapes, with Reese's help. The two, once Reese has persuaded her of his true

 THERE'S A STARMAN... *ALTHOUGH TOO SCHMALTZY FOR SOME VIEWERS, JOHN CARPENTER'S STARMAN (1984) GAVE THE DIRECTOR YET ANOTHER BIG SF HIT*

origins, fall in love, and John Connor is conceived. In the final thrilling battle between the humans and the Terminator, Reese sacrifices his life; but Connor at last succeeds in luring the Terminator to destruction.

This is a movie to keep you on the edge of your seat. It was, bewilderingly, surpassed in this respect by its sequel, *Terminator 2: Judgment Day* (1992). Although there were inevitable jokes about Schwarzenegger having been typecast as a robot, he performs well; but the real star is Hamilton.

The Terminator drew many ideas from sf's common stockpot. Nevertheless, Harlan Ellison sued (successfully) for plagiarism from his *Outer Limits* episodes "Soldier" and "Demon With A Glass Hand".

Trancers

(VT *FUTURE COP*)
1984 • USA • *DIRECTOR* CHARLES BAND • *SCREENPLAY* DANNY BILSON, PAUL DE MEO • *85M* • COLOUR
Similar in theme to *The Terminator* (1984), this sees a cop sent back from AD 2247 Los Angeles to stop a madman who wants to take over the world by turning people into Trancers — i.e., indoctrinees whom he can dominate.

LOOKING FOR TROUBLE *ARNOLD SCHWARZENEGGER IN DOUR MOOD AS THE EPONYMOUS MURDEROUS ANDROID IN 1984'S THE TERMINATOR*

2010

1984 • USA • *DIRECTOR* PETER HYAMS • *SCREENPLAY* PETER HYAMS, FROM ARTHUR C. CLARKE'S *2010: ODYSSEY TWO* (1982) • 116M • COLOUR
Much-disliked sequel to *2001: A Space Odyssey* (1968), but in fact a rather enjoyable piece of sf. The enigmatic aliens of the earlier movie ignite Jupiter as the Solar System's second sun, giving humans new worlds to colonize.

1985
Back To The Future

1985 • USA • *DIRECTOR* ROBERT ZEMECKIS • *SCREENPLAY* BOB GALE, ROBERT ZEMECKIS • *SPECIAL EFFECTS* KEVIN PIKE • *STARRING* MICHAEL J. FOX (MARTY MCFLY), CRISPIN GLOVER (GEORGE MCFLY), CHRISTOPHER LLOYD (DR EMMETT BROWN), LEA THOMPSON (LORRAINE BAINES/LORRAINE MCFLY), CLAUDIA WELLS (JENNIFER PARKER), THOMAS F. WILSON (BIFF TANNEN) • *116M* • *COLOUR*
In the present, Marty McFly is the unhappy son of an alcoholic mother (Lorraine) and a wimpish father (George), who is terrorized by the bullying Tannen; he seeks solace in his friendship with eccentric scientist Dr Brown, who has devised a time machine that takes the form of a De Lorean car. As the two prepare for a clandestine test, they are attacked by Libyan terrorists (Brown has done a shady deal to swindle Libya out of the plutonium necessary to power the time machine). Brown pressurizes Marty into using the De Lorean to escape, which Marty does — arriving in 1955, where he is of roughly the same age as his parents-to-be. Fighting off the sexual advances of Lorraine, he manoeuvres George into a situation whereby he heroically saves Lorraine's questionable virtue by knocking Tannen out cold. Meanwhile, working with a much younger Dr Brown, Marty is able to escape back into his "real" present, where he discovers much has changed for the better — in particular, his parents. It was sequelled by, in essence, a single very long movie, comprising *Back To The Future Part II* (1989) and *Back To The Future Part III* (1990), both still starring Michael J Fox.

BACK TO THE FUTURE *ONE OF SF CINEMA'S MOST SUCCESSFUL SERIES*

Series

From the very first, Hollywood has been keen on series. In the fields of fantasy and sf, however, the trend has been taken to extremes. *2001* (1968) was followed by *2010* (1984). *Back To The Future* (1985) was succeeded by *Back To The Future Part II* (1989) and *Back To The Future Part III* (1990). *The Terminator* (1984) was inevitably sequelled by *Terminator 2: Judgment Day* (1991). After *Superman: The Movie* (1978) came three sequels — four, if one counts *Supergirl* (1984). *Critters* (1986), a bad sf rip-off of *Gremlins* (1984) — itself sequelled by *Gremlins 2: The New Batch* — reached *Critters 4* in 1992. *Star Wars* (1977) was followed by *The Empire Strikes Back* (1980) and *Return Of The Jedi* (1983). *Alien* (1979) gave rise to *Aliens* (1986) and *Alien³* (1992). The list could go on, if not forever then at least for a very long time. Just think of the Frankenstein movies!

Thanks to Hollywood's laziness, the first in a series of movies is generally the best, with the remainder being pale repetitions of the original. In the field of horror, this is also the case, with a few exceptions — e.g., *Hellraiser II* (1988) is more inventive than *Hellraiser* (1987). In sf and fantasy, the opposite is more often the case than not: *Back To The Future Part II* is a far more sophisticated time fantasy than its precursor; *Terminator 2* is better than *The Terminator*; *Mad Max 2* is better than *Mad Max* and *Alien³* is arguably the best of the trilogy. There are exceptions — think of *Predator 2* (1990) — but it seems that, unlike their mainstream counterparts, genre moviemakers regard a sequel as an opportunity to surpass themselves.

Brazil

1985 • UK • *DIRECTOR* TERRY GILLIAM • *SCREENPLAY*
TERRY GILLIAM, CHARLES MCKEOWN, TOM STOPPARD
• *SPECIAL EFFECTS* RICHARD CONWAY, GEORGE GIBBS
• *STARRING* ROBERT DE NIRO (ARCHIBALD "HARRY"
TUTTLE), KIM GREIST (JILL LAYTON), IAN HOLM (MR
KURTZMANN), KATHERINE HELMOND (IDA LOWRY), BOB
HOSKINS (SPOOR), MICHAEL PALIN (JACK LINT), JONATHAN
PRYCE (SAM LOWRY), PETER VAUGHAN (MR HELPMANN)
• *142M* • COLOUR

More a fantasy than an sf movie, this recreates
Orson Welles's *The Trial* (1962) with dashes of
Orwell's *Nineteen Eighty-four* (1949), Thurber's
"The Secret Life Of Walter Mitty" (1939), Carroll's
Alice In Wonderland (1865) and much else
besides, crosshatching gleefully several genres of
which sf is only one. In an unnamed nation that
is not so much totalitarian as bureaucracy-
ridden, and which mixes archaic and future
technologies (frequently malfunctioning) and
cultural epochs, Lowry is a lowly clerk in the
Records office, but at night he dreams of being a
wingèd man, a knight in shining armour who
must rescue a fair maiden. Through a technical
slip, a man named Buttle is arrested in place of
a terrorist named Tuttle, and in offering
recompense to Buttle's widow Lowry discovers
that Buttle's upstairs neighbour, Layton, is the
woman from his dreams. Because she has
complained about Buttle's abduction and
subsequent death, she too is now classified by
the dreaded Information Retrieval department as
a terrorist, so that it is only with difficulty that
Lowry tracks her down and eventually persuades
her to trust him. Their brief love affair is brutally
terminated by the state.

As with Gilliam's *Time Bandits* (1981) and *The
Fisher King* (1991), *Brazil* defies all
categorization. Frequent flashes of dark humour,
overtly comic satire and some knockabout
comedy serve only to enhance the pathos of the
despairing conclusion.

Cocoon

1985 • USA • *DIRECTOR* RON HOWARD • *SCREENPLAY*
TOM BENEDEK • *117M* • COLOUR
Humanoid aliens must revive a number of their
species that have been stored in cocoons in the

sea off Florida. In so doing, they inadvertently
rejuvenate some occupants of a retirement
home. A saccharine offering, sequelled by
Cocoon: The Return (1988).

D.A.R.Y.L.

1985 • USA • *DIRECTOR* SIMON WINCER • *SCREENPLAY*
DAVID AMBROSE, JEFFREY ELLIS, ALLAN SCOTT
• *99M* • COLOUR
A (very) modest but likeable movie in which a
little boy, Daryl, discovers he is really an android
(Data Analysing Robot Youth Lifeform).

Enemy Mine

1985 • USA • *DIRECTORS* RICHARD LONCRAINE
(UNCREDITED), WOLFGANG PETERSEN • *SCREENPLAY* EDWARD
KHMARA, FROM 'ENEMY MINE' (1979) BY BARRY B.
LONGYEAR, EXPANDED AS *ENEMY MINE* (1985) BY LONGYEAR
WITH DAVID GERROLD • *SPECIAL EFFECTS* INDUSTRIAL LIGHT
& MAGIC, CHRIS WALAS • *STARRING* LOU GOSSETT JR
(JERIBA SHIGAN), DENNIS QUAID (WILLIS DAVIDGE)
• *108M* • COLOUR
During an interstellar war, an Earthman
(Davidge) and one of the foe, a reptiloid Drac
(Shigan), are shot down and stranded on the
hostile planet Fyrine IV. In order to survive, they
must conquer their instinctive mutual hatred,
and soon discover something like friendship.
Davidge goes exploring and discovers hellish
mines where humans are using Dracs as
expendable slaves; rejoining Shigan, he
discovers the latter pregnant (the Dracs are

MINE, ALL MINE *THE PRIME EXAMPLE OF SPACE
OPERA WITH A CONTEMPORARY POLITICAL EDGE,* ENEMY
MINE *MOVINGLY PRESENTED AN ANTI-DISCRIMINATORY MESSAGE*

hermaphroditic). Shigan dies in giving birth to a
child Zammis, but before doing so exacts from
Davidge the promise that he will care for the
child, teach it the lore of Dracon, and eventually
present it to the elders on that planet.

The first part of *Enemy Mine*, as Davidge and
Shigan warily begin to accept each other, is
electrifying. Thereafter, however, the rest seems
like standard space opera grafted on to make
sure the movie is of feature length.

Explorers

1985 • USA • *DIRECTOR* JOE DANTE • *SCREENPLAY* ERIC
LUKE • *109M* • COLOUR

MEN IN
SUITS *TERRY
GILLIAM'S* BRAZIL *IS
ARGUABLY THE FINEST
TECHNOFANTASY THE
CINEMA HAS EVER
PRODUCED. BASED IN A
SECONDARY WORLD THAT
SHARES MANY FEATURES
WITH OUR OWN, IT
EXPLORES THE ROTTEN
CORE OF BUREAUCRATIC
TYRANNY*

Two young boys build themselves a spaceship and zoom off skywards, discovering a ship full of aliens who are terrified of humankind because they have watched lots of TV programmes in which humankind zaps alien missions.

Flight Of The Navigator

1985 • USA • *DIRECTOR* RANDAL KLEISER • *SCREENPLAY* MICHAEL BURTON, MATT MCMANUS • *89M* • *COLOUR*
A little boy reappears eight years after abduction by a UFO. But the UFO has been seized by the government, and he has a strong yearning to ride it again.

Lifeforce

1985 • UK • *DIRECTOR* TOBE HOOPER • *SCREENPLAY* DON JAKOBY, DAN O'BANNON, FROM COLIN WILSON'S *THE SPACE VAMPIRES* (1976) • *STARRING* MATHILDA MAY • *101M* • *COLOUR*
Desperately bad version of Wilson's interesting novel (Wilson's verdict: "Well, at least there's lots of full-frontal nudity"). Astronauts discover a huge alien spacecraft which has, it seems, three survivors. But these prove to be the vampiristic killers of the spaceship's original occupants...

Mad Max Beyond Thunderdome

1985 • AUSTRALIA • *DIRECTORS* GEORGE MILLER, GEORGE OGILVIE • *SCREENPLAY* TERRY HAYES, GEORGE MILLER • *STARRING* MEL GIBSON (MAX), TINA TURNER (AUNT ENTITY) • *107M* • *COLOUR*
The most inventive of the series begun with *Mad Max* (1979), this falls into two halves: Max engages in gladiatorial conflict to free himself from Bartertown, ruled by Tina Turner; Max is hailed by a long-lost colony of children — who have invented their own, curiously affecting dialect — as their Lord-Of-The-Flies-style god.

The Manhattan Project

(*VT DEADLY GAME*)
1985 • USA • *DIRECTOR* MARSHALL BRICKMAN • *SCREENPLAY* THOMAS BAUM, MARSHALL BRICKMAN • *118M* • *COLOUR*

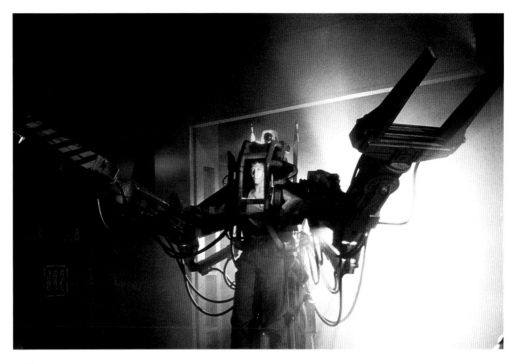

COME AND GET IT *SIGOURNEY WEAVER IN FINE FORM BATTLING THE QUEEN ALIEN IN 1986'S ALIENS, AN EXCELLENT EXAMPLE OF SHOOT'EM-UP CINEMA*

A high-school kid builds himself a working nuclear bomb.

My Science Project

1985 • USA • *DIRECTOR* JONATHAN R. BETUEL • *SCREENPLAY* JONATHAN R. BETUEL • *94M* • *COLOUR*
Tame comedy in which a couple of high-school kids build a time machine, and then have adventures.

Re-Animator

1985 • USA • *DIRECTOR* STUART GORDON • *SCREENPLAY* STUART GORDON, WILLIAM J. NORRIS, DENNIS PAOLI, FROM H.P. LOVECRAFT'S 'HERBERT WEST — REANIMATOR' (1922) • *86M* • *COLOUR*
A retake on the Frankenstein tale, with a medical student showing he can revive the dead. This very gory movie — which has little to do with the Lovecraft original on which it is theoretically based — is also very funny.

1986

Aliens

1986 • USA • *DIRECTOR* JAMES CAMERON • *SCREENPLAY* JAMES CAMERON, WALTER HILL • *SPECIAL EFFECTS* DOUG BESWICK, JOHN RICHARDSON, BOB SKOTAK, DENNIS SKOTAK, STAN WINSTON • *STARRING* MICHAEL BIEHN (CORPORAL HICKS), JENETTE GOLDSTEIN (PRIVATE VASQUEZ), CARRIE HENN (NEWT), LANCE HENRIKSEN (BISHOP), WILLIAM HOPE (LIEUTENANT GORMAN), AL MATTHEWS (SERGEANT APONE), BILL PAXTON (PRIVATE HUDSON), PAUL REISER (BURKE), SIGOURNEY WEAVER (RIPLEY) • *137M* • *COLOUR*
This successor to *Alien* (1979) certainly outgunned (the term is chosen carefully) its predecessor, and is generally cited as yet another example of an sf sequel superior to the original. Yet, for all its moments of high drama and blazing firepower, it has lost the truly horrifying creepiness of *Alien*: where the earlier movie conveyed the potential inhumanity of the future, here we have gung-ho marines battling against overwhelming odds and a plotline that could, with cosmetic changes, be that of, say, a Rambo movie.

Ripley, last seen at the end of *Alien* entering suspended animation in one of the *Nostromo*'s escape pods, is recovered nearly 60 years later by a salvage ship and returned to Earth. On revival, she is horrified to hear that the planet where the original alien was encountered has now been colonized; worse still, all contact with the colony has been lost. As the sole survivor of the earlier investigatory expedition, she is informed by Company man Burke that she will be a part of a new expedition to discover what has happened. On arrival on the planet, the expedition discovers that the colony has indeed been destroyed by aliens; the only human left alive is the little girl Newt. One by one, the marines are slaughtered and it emerges that Burke has accompanied the expedition purely because the real purpose of the venture is somehow to capture and bring back to Earth a specimen of the aliens, in whom the Company sees commercial potential. At last, only Ripley, Newt and Bishop are left, and the climax comes when Ripley, clad in waldo-ized battle gear, takes on head-to-head the queen of the alien hive in a dazzling set-piece.

Aliens is brilliant entertainment, and there is barely a dull moment. Cameron superbly orchestrates his pacing and his alternations of humour, action, fear and pathos. Yet its splendours are all on the surface: it lacks the intriguing depth of *Alien* and more especially of the next in the series, *Alien³* (1992).

The Fly

1986 • USA • DIRECTOR DAVID CRONENBERG • SCREENPLAY DAVID CRONENBERG, CHARLES EDWARD POGUE, FROM (LOOSELY) 'THE FLY' (1957) BY GEORGE LANGELAAN • SPECIAL EFFECTS LOUIS CRAIG, TED ROSS • STARRING GEENA DAVIS (VERONICA QUAIFE), JEFF GOLDBLUM (SETH BRUNDLE) • 100M • COLOUR

Maverick scientist Brundle is experimenting with matter transmission, but, although he can transmit inorganic objects from one "pod" to another with ease, his experiments with living organisms are gruesome failures. This much he explains to the attractive journalist, Quaife, who picks him up and with whom he is soon romantically entangled. At last, he realizes he must teach his computers "the poetry of the flesh" (the technique whereby he does this is not dwelt upon), and thereafter he achieves success. The final experiment is to transmit himself; but he fails to notice that a fly is trapped in the transmission pod, and their diverse DNAs become inextricably mixed. In the

 FINGERS CROSSED *JEFF GOLDBLUM PAUSES FOR THOUGHT — AS IT PROVES, NOT FOR LONG ENOUGH — IN DAVID CRONENBURG'S FINE CHILLER THE FLY (1986)*

ensuing weeks, he slowly transmutes into a ghastly insectile monster, which in the end pleads to be put out of its misery.

This is a very powerful movie, and Cronenberg deploys his small cast to perfection while rigorously working out the original notion to its logical — and hideous — conclusion. What shifts *The Fly* on to a plane above almost any other horror movie is the beautifully depicted relationship between Brundle and Quaife: their tenderness — even as Brundle becomes ever more monstrous and nonhuman — contrasts with the grue as a watercolour might with a splash of primary acrylics.

This has scant relation to its theoretical precursor, *The Fly* (1958). Its crass sequel was *The Fly II* (1989), which follows the fortunes of Brundle's son Martin.

Invaders From Mars

1986 • USA • DIRECTOR TOBE HOOPER • SCREENPLAY DON JAKOBY, DAN O'BANNON, FROM THE MOVIE INVADERS FROM MARS (1953) • 99M • COLOUR

A badly scripted and badly directed remake.

Short Circuit

1986 • USA • DIRECTOR JOHN BADHAM • SCREENPLAY BRENT MADDOCK, S.S. WILSON • 98M • COLOUR

A robot is struck by lightning and becomes pacifistic. This movie has moments, but very few of them. *Short Circuit 2* (1988) is worse.

SpaceCamp

1986 • USA • DIRECTOR HARRY WINER • SCREENPLAY CASEY T. MITCHELL, W.W. WICKET • 108M • COLOUR

Juvenilia in which a group of kids blasts off accidentally in a space shuttle and has to be talked down to Earth.

Star Trek IV: The Voyage Home

1986 • USA • DIRECTOR LEONARD NIMOY • SCREENPLAY HARVE BENNETT, PETER KRIKES, STEVE MEERSON, NICHOLAS MEYER • STARRING LEONARD NIMOY (SPOCK), WILLIAM

SHATNER (KIRK) • 119M • COLOUR

Jolly hokum in which the *Enterprise*'s finest take a time trip back to mid-1980s California in order to save a pair of whales who will stop an alien invasion force from destroying Earth.

1987

Akira

1987 • JAPAN • DIRECTOR KATSUHIRO OTOMO • SCREENPLAY IZO HASHIMOTO, KATSUHIRO OTOMO, FROM OTOMO'S CONTINUING AKIRA COMICS • ANIMATION DIRECTORS HIROAKI SATO, YOSHIO TAKEUCHI • VOICE ACTORS (ENGLISH-LANGUAGE VERSION) BOB BERGER, JIMMY FLINDERS, STANLEY GURD JR, WATNEY HELD, MARILYN LANE, BARBARA LARSEN, LEWIS LEMAY, CHRISTOPHER MATHEWSON, DEANNA MORRIS, TONY MOZDY, JULIE PHELAN, DREW THOMAS, BURT WALTERS, JIM WARRINGTON, BRAD WURST • 124M • COLOUR

The movie that first really drew the attention of Western audiences to anime (Japanese manga-based animation), this is a coruscating if often unintelligible piece of technofantasy. Thirty-one years after World War III, which took place in 1988, neo-Tokyo is ruled by harsh militarists yet feuding gangs of bikers fill the streets. Psi-talented children recognize that the second coming of the enigmatic Akira is at hand; but Akira, when revealed, proves to be not a god but the relic of an old experimental project to

EAT LAZER! *AKIRA (1987) WAS THE FIRST ANIME MOVIE TO MAKE AN IMPACT ON WESTERN AUDIENCES, SHOWING THERE WAS MORE TO ANIMATED FEATURES THAN DISNEY*

capture and store pure life essence.

Akira's animation is fairly crude, yet often derives added vibrancy from that crudity. The subtitled Japanese version is to be preferred to the coarsely dubbed English-language one.

*batteries not included

1987 • USA • DIRECTOR MATTHEW ROBBINS *• SCREENPLAY* BRAD BIRD, BRENT MADDOCK, MATTHEW ROBBINS, S.S. WILSON *• 106M • COLOUR*
Originally planned as a TV episode, this shows minuscule UFOs coming to the rescue of a bunch of apartment tenants on the verge of eviction.

InnerSpace

1987 • USA • DIRECTOR JOE DANTE *• SCREENPLAY* JEFFREY BOAM, CHIP PROSER *• STARRING* DENNIS QUAID, MEG RYAN, MARTIN SHORT *• 120M • COLOUR*
Reprising *Fantastic Voyage* (1966), this sees an astronaut miniaturized so that he can be injected into a human bloodstream. Derivative it might be, but it's also great fun.

Making Mr Right

1987 • USA • DIRECTOR SUSAN SEIDELMAN *• SCREENPLAY* FLOYD BYARS, LAURIE FRANK *• 98M • COLOUR*
A PR consultant falls in love with a very human-seeming android. An enjoyable comedy, but little more than that.

Predator

1987 • USA • DIRECTOR JOHN MCTIERNAN *• SCREENPLAY* JIM THOMAS, JOHN THOMAS *• SPECIAL EFFECTS* LAURENCIO CORDERO, AL DISARRO, DREAM QUEST IMAGES, R. GREENBERG, JOEL HYNICK, STUART ROBERTSON, STAN WINSTON *• STARRING* ELPIDIA CARRILLO (ANNA), ARNOLD SCHWARZENEGGER (MAJOR ALAN "DUTCH" SCHAEFER), CARL WEATHERS (DILLON) *• 107M • COLOUR*
A team of US Government muscle-men led by Schaefer and Dillon is sent to the Central American jungle to free a party of soldiers held by guerrillas. What they find is something much worse than a mere group of rebellious peasants — who are shot to pieces by our heroes — being an invisible alien whose primary diet is human beings. Schaefer's team is picked off one by one. The plot is derivative nonsense but the special effects are good, notably when we see the world through the alien's eyes. Yet there is something rotten at this movie's core: after the hi-tech shoot-out with the largely defenceless natives, one's impulse is to cheer on the alien.
Predator 2 (1990) followed.

Arnold Schwarzenegger the action machine

Thrice Mr Universe and seven times Mr Olympia, the champion bodybuilder Arnold Schwarzenegger (1947-   ) could have looked forward to a lengthy retirement spent dwelling on past glories, but instead — with admirable enterprise — he decided to create for himself a new career, as a Hollywood movie actor. The fact that, at least in the early days, his acting ability resembled that of a plank and his heavily accented English was very limited proved no deterrent.

After a few undistinguished supporting roles — and a starring role (under the pseudonym "Arnold Strong") in the bad fantasy *Hercules In New York* (1969), for which his voice part was dubbed — he found himself slipping into a series of sf and fantasy movies that could almost have been — and sometimes actually were — vehicles designed to make light of his thespian limitations. He made a marvellous Conan in *Conan The Barbarian* (1981) and *Conan The Destroyer* (1984), and played essentially the same role in *Red Sonja* (1985): in all three movies, he was able to play to perfection the Robert E. Howard hero who is fundamentally stupid, but not as stupid as you first thought.

From fantasy, he slid into sf to such effect that the Schwarzenegger cannon can be viewed virtually as a movie sub-genre, with sidebar movies in which he did not appear — like *Universal Soldier* (1992) starring Dolph Lundgren and Jean-Claude Van Damme — being, in effect, Schwarzenegger movies *sans* Schwarzenegger.

His big sf breakthrough came with *The Terminator* (1984), in which he played a lethal robot ("typecasting", sniffed the intellectuals), and thereafter, although some straightforward violent-action movies were interspersed, he starred in a run of sf movies that varied from adequate to excellent: *Predator* (1987), *The Running Man* (1987), *Total Recall* (1990), *Terminator 2: Judgment Day* (1991) and, as his swansong in the genre, the much underestimated technofantasy *Last Action Hero* (1993). Since then, he has concentrated on comedy.

MUD MAN PREDATOR (1987) WAS A RATHER NASTY MOVIE, BUT IT ALLOWED ARNOLD SCHWARZENEGGER FURTHER TO DEVELOP HIS SF SCREEN PERSONA

RoboCop

1987 • USA • *DIRECTOR* PAUL VERHOEVEN • *SCREENPLAY* MICHAEL MINER, EDWARD NEUMEIER • *SPECIAL EFFECTS* ROB BOTTIN, CRAIG DAVIES, DALE MARTIN, PETER RONZANI • *STARRING* NANCY ALLEN (ANNE LEWIS), RONNY COX (RICHARD JONES), MIGUEL FERRERA (ROBERT MORTON), KURTWOOD SMITH (CLARENCE J. BODDICKER), PETER WELLER (ALEX MURPHY/ROBOCOP) • *102M* • COLOUR

After honest cop Murphy has been shot to pieces by hoodlums, he is reconstructed as a cyborg and his brain is partially replaced by a computer. He proves a far better mechanical law-enforcer than his technological predecessor, a lumbering robot with whom he must eventually have a showdown. Alongside his previous police-partner Allen, he begins to realize once more the importance of his human — as opposed to machine — aspect, and discovers that the computer part of his mind has been programmed not to apprehend, under any circumstances, any executives of the private corporation responsible for law enforcement in the city. At last, he and Allen trace the bosses of the city's organized crime to the very highest echelons of the corporation, and his human brain overrides the computer's programming.

RoboCop is a great actioner, but would be no more than that were it not for the ancillary details provided about this brutal future world. Fragments of TV newscasts, commercials and children's programmes bring home to us far more than the street-fighting histrionics the rottenness of the future we may be creating.

RoboCop 2 (1990) followed.

The Running Man

1987 • USA • *DIRECTOR* PAUL MICHAEL GLASER • *SCREENPLAY* STEVEN E. DE SOUZA, FROM RICHARD BACHMAN'S (I.E., STEPHEN KING'S) *THE RUNNING MAN* (1982) • *STARRING* ARNOLD SCHWARZENEGGER • *101M* • COLOUR

In the future, there is a TV gameshow that involves duelling to the death. Unfortunately, despite the efforts of Schwarzenegger, the movie is dull.

Superman IV: The Quest For Peace

1987 • UK • *DIRECTOR* SIDNEY J. FURIE • *SCREENPLAY* LAWRENCE KONNER, CHRISTOPHER REEVE, MARK ROSENTHAL

THE FUTURE OF LAW ENFORCEMENT SUPERFICIALLY JUST AN EMPTY-HEADED ACTION MOVIE, SOME OF THE SATIRE IN ROBOCOP (1987) CUT TO THE BONE

• *STARRING* GENE HACKMAN (LEX LUTHOR), DAMIAN McCLAWHORN (JEREMY), CHRISTOPHER REEVE (SUPERMAN) • *89M* • COLOUR

A schoolboy writes to Superman asking him to halt the nuclear arms race. Superman responds by gathering the world's nuclear weapons and throwing them into the Sun. Most of the movie is taken up with fights between Superman and Nuclear Man, cloned by villainous Luthor from Superman's hair. *Superman IV* is bad, but likeable.

1988

Alien Nation

(VT *OUTER HEAT*)

1988 • USA • *DIRECTOR* GRAHAM BAKER • *SCREENPLAY* ROCKNE S. O'BANNON • *90M* • COLOUR

The humanoid occupants of a crashed UFO become, in effect, Blacks. One of the ufonauts must partner a bigoted cop as they solve a murder. The satire is, alas, a bit too obvious. A TV series followed.

The Blob

1988 • USA • *DIRECTOR* CHUCK RUSSELL • *SCREENPLAY* FRANK DARABONT, CHUCK RUSSELL, FROM THE MOVIE *THE BLOB* (1958) • *92M* • COLOUR

A pallid remake with the accent on gory special effects.

Cocoon: The Return

1988 • USA • *DIRECTOR* DANIEL PETRIE • *SCREENPLAY* STEPHEN McPHERSON • *116M* • COLOUR

The weak sequel to *Cocoon* (1985) sees the now-rejuvenated oldsters brought back to Earth by their alien pals.

Earth Girls Are Easy

1988 • USA • *DIRECTOR* JULIEN TEMPLE • *SCREENPLAY* JULIE BROWN, CHARLIE COFFEY, TERRENCE E. McNALLY • *SPECIAL EFFECTS* DREAM QUEST IMAGES • *STARRING* JULIE BROWN (CANDY), JIM CARREY (WIPLOC), GEENA DAVIS (VALERIE), JEFF GOLDBLUM (MAC), DAMON WAYANS (ZEEBO) • *100M* • COLOUR

Three hirsute humanoid alien males (Mac, Wiploc and Zeebo) arrive in Southern California desperate for sex. Their appearance is initially

ALIENS DON'T SHAVE *GEENA DAVIS AND THREE ALIENS IN ACTION IN EARTH GIRLS ARE EASY (1988), A TRIUMPH OF GOOD HUMOUR OVER TASTE, PLOT STRUCTURE AND MOST OTHER GENERALLY ACCEPTED CINEMATIC VIRTUES*

THE PITS *MUCH WAS EXPECTED OF THE ABYSS, BUT COMMERCIALLY AND CRITICALLY IT DISAPPOINTED*

---

against them, but beauticians Valerie and Candy soon divest them of the excess hair and reveal them as desirable hunks. After much self-indulgent fun — and the self-indulgence is part of the genuine fun — Valerie and Mac fall in love. This movie has no pretensions, and a couple of its sequences have nothing to do with the plot, but as a musical comedy it offers joy from beginning to end.

Monkey Shines

(VT MONKEY SHINES: AN EXPERIMENT IN TERROR)
1988 • USA • *DIRECTOR* GEORGE A. ROMERO • *SCREENPLAY* GEORGE A. ROMERO, FROM MICHAEL STEWART'S *MONKEY SHINES* (1983) • *109M* • *COLOUR*
A quadriplegic is given a monkey as a companion, and the two form a semi-telepathic link... with the result that the monkey kills anyone with whom the human is even temporarily annoyed.

My Stepmother Is An Alien

1988 • USA • *DIRECTOR* RICHARD BENJAMIN • *SCREENPLAY* TIMOTHY HARRIS, JONATHAN REYNOLDS, HERSCHEL WEINGROD, JERICO WEINGROD • *STARRING* DAN AYKROYD, KIM BASINGER • *108M* • *COLOUR*
To save their world, aliens send a beautiful woman to seduce a human scientist who can help them. A desperately unfunny comedy.

They Live

1988 • USA • *DIRECTOR* JOHN CARPENTER • *SCREENPLAY* JOHN CARPENTER (AS FRANK ARMITAGE), FROM RAY NELSON'S 'EIGHT O'CLOCK IN THE MORNING' (1963) • *93M* • *COLOUR*
Aliens invaded some while ago and are disguising themselves as humans. Stated as baldly as that, the plot sounds dreary, but the movie is quite fun.

1989

The Abyss

1989 • USA • *DIRECTOR* JAMES CAMERON • *SCREENPLAY* JAMES CAMERON • *SPECIAL EFFECTS* JOHN BRUNO, DREAM QUEST IMAGES, INDUSTRIAL LIGHT & MAGIC, DENNIS MUREN, DENNIS SKOTAK, HOYT YEATMAN • *STARRING* MICHAEL BIEHN (LIEUTENANT COFFEY), ED HARRIS (BUD BRIGMAN), MARY ELIZABETH MASTRANTONIO (LINDSEY BRIGMAN) • *139M* • *COLOUR*
A hugely expensive movie that flopped because, somewhere in its mixture of *Alien* (1979) and *Close Encounters Of The Third Kind* (1977), the best qualities of both movies were lost. But there is much that is enjoyable — and not just the exhilarating special effects.

The US Navy discovers there is a UFO lodged in a deep-ocean abyss. A crew is sent down to investigate. But the aliens prove friendly and, after much adventuring, a touching conciliation between humans and extraterrestrials is attained.

Back To The Future Part II

1989 • USA • *DIRECTOR* ROBERT ZEMECKIS • *SCREENPLAY* BOB GALE • *STARRING* MICHAEL J. FOX (MARTY MCFLY), CHRISTOPHER LLOYD (DR EMMETT BROWN) • *108M* • *COLOUR*
Probably the best of the series, this has an inestimably complicated time-paradox plot that assumes an audience literate in sf. Where the movie fails is in ending mid-story, with a trailer for *Back To The Future Part III* (1990).

Batman

1989 • USA • *DIRECTOR* TIM BURTON • *SCREENPLAY*
SAM HAMM, WARREN SKAAREN, FROM THE COMICS CREATIONS
OF BILL FINGER AND BOB KANE • *SPECIAL EFFECTS* DEREK
MEDDINGS • *STARRING* KIM BASINGER (VICKI VALE),
MICHAEL KEATON (BATMAN/BRUCE WAYNE), JACK
NICHOLSON (JACK NAPIER/THE JOKER) • *126M* • COLOUR
Much influenced by Frank Miller's *Batman: The
Dark Knight Returns* (1986), this movie heaps on
to the Batman story more mythopoeia than it
can sensibly bear. The essence of the story is
that Batman, in breaking up a gang of
hoodlums, hurls one of them, Napier, into a vat
of chemicals. On emerging, Napier discovers his
face twisted into a permanent rictus grin, and so
he recasts himself into the role of the
malevolent supercriminal called The Joker. The
rest of the movie is taken up with Batman's war
against The Joker's criminal attempts to take
over Gotham City, while simultaneously, both as
Batman and as his real-life personality,
millionaire Bruce Wayne, wooing and eventually
bedding press photographer Vicki Vale. Burton's

DARK KNIGHT *MICHAEL KEATON'S PORTRAYAL OF THE
HERO IN* BATMAN *CONTRIBUTED TO THE FILM'S SUCCESS*

sombre vision is certainly effective in terms of
creating brooding, menacing set-pieces, and
Nicholson works hard to produce a humorous
esprit that chills, yet the abiding impression of
the movie is that it is *long*, with moments
of excitement all too rare currants in an
overcooked pudding.

Earlier Batman movies were the serials
Batman (1943) and *Batman And Robin* (1949) as
well as the enjoyably camp (although again
overlong) *Batman* (vt *Batman — The Movie*; vt
Batman '66) (1966). Sequels to the 1989
Batman are *Batman Returns* (1992), directed by
Burton, and the much more light-hearted
Batman Forever (1995), directed by Joel
Schumacher — which reintroduces Robin to the
saga. Of considerable interest is the animated
feature *Batman — Mask Of the Phantasm*
(1993), produced in connection with the TV
series but released theatrically.

Bill & Ted's Excellent Adventure

1989 • USA • *DIRECTOR* STEPHEN HEREK • *SCREENPLAY*
CHRIS MATHESON, ED SOLOMON • *STARRING* KEANU REEVES
(TED), ALEX WINTER (BILL) • *89M* • COLOUR
If Californian airhead high-school students Bill
and Ted fail their history test, the future will be
endangered, so an emissary from the future
comes back to help them. What happens next is
a trip through the past, gathering significant
historical figures and bringing them back to
present day San Dimas for the boys' history
presentation. Sequelled by the superior *Bill &
Ted's Bogus Journey* (1991). Party on, dudes...

BY A NOSE
*THE KIDS IN
HONEY, I SHRUNK THE
KIDS HAD TO CHOOSE THEIR
ALLIES WHEREVER THEY
COULD FIND THEM, NO
MATTER HOW DANGEROUS
THOSE ALLIES COULD
POTENTIALLY BE. THE MOVIE
WAS FAR BETTER THAN
MIGHT HAVE BEEN EXPECTED*

Honey, I Shrunk The Kids

1989 • USA • *DIRECTOR* JOE JOHNSTON
• *SCREENPLAY* STUART GORDON, ED NAHA, TOM SCHULMAN
• *SPECIAL EFFECTS* MICHAEL MOSCAL, DAVID SOSALLA
• *STARRING* THOMAS BROWN (RUSS THOMPSON FILS), MATT
FREWER (RUSS THOMPSON PÈRE), RICK MORANIS (PROFESSOR
WAYNE SZALINSKI), ROBERT OLIVERI (NICK SZALINSKI),
AMY O'NEILL (AMY SZALINSKI), JARED RUSHTON (RON
THOMPSON), MARCIA STRASSMAN (DIANE SZALINSKI),
KRISTINE SUTHERLAND (MAE THOMPSON) • *93M* • COLOUR
The prospect of a Disney "science"-based fantasy
for children is normally enough to make one
shudder, but in fact this one is tremendous fun.
Drawing its inspiration in large part from *The
Incredible Shrinking Man* (1957), it sees eccentric
inventor Szalinski devise a ray for miniaturizing
objects. Through mishap, the Szalinski children
plus those of Szalinski's neighbour-cum-deadly-
foe Frewer are shrunk by the ray and dumped in
the garbage can at the far end of the garden.
The movie follows their adventures as they
traverse homewards the terrifying landscape that
the garden now represents. This thoroughly
enjoyable movie was sequelled by the much less
successful *Honey, I Blew Up The Kid* (1992).

Millennium

1989 • USA • *DIRECTOR* MICHAEL ANDERSON
• *SCREENPLAY* JOHN VARLEY, FROM VARLEY'S 'AIR RAID'
(1977) • *108M* • COLOUR
Time-travellers from the future start collecting
doomed individuals from the present in order to
repopulate their world. An aircrash investigator

discovers this plot and is catapulted into the future. Compare *Freejack* (1992).

Robot Jox

1989 • USA • *DIRECTOR* STUART GORDON • *SCREENPLAY* JOE HALDEMAN • *82M* • *COLOUR*

In the far future, wars are decided by the outcome of fights between gladiatorial robots. Although manifestly produced on a low budget, this is enjoyable.

Slipstream

1989 • UK • *DIRECTOR* STEPHEN LISBERGER • *SCREENPLAY* TONY KAYDEN • *102M* • *COLOUR*

Tedious adventure in which a future cop hunts down a rogue android.

Star Trek V: The Final Frontier

1989 • USA • *DIRECTOR* WILLIAM SHATNER • *SCREENPLAY* DAVID LOUGHERY • *STARRING* DEFOREST KELLEY (DR MCCOY), LAURENCE LUCKINBILL (SYBOK), LEONARD NIMOY (SPOCK), WILLIAM SHATNER (KIRK) • *106M* • *COLOUR*

The *Enterprise* is hijacked by a Vulcan, Sybok, to go in quest of God. Probably the weakest of the series.

1990

Arachnophobia

1990 • US • *DIRECTOR* FRANK MARSHALL • *SCREENPLAY* DON JAKOBY, WESLEY STRICK • *SPECIAL EFFECTS* CHRIS WALAS • *STARRING* JEFF DANIELS (DR ROSS JENNINGS), JOHN GOODMAN (DELBERT MCCLINTOCK), JAMES HANDY (MILTON BRIGGS), HENRY JONES (DR SAM METCALF), HARLEY JANE KOZAK (MOLLY JENNINGS), BRIAN MCNAMARA (CHRIS COLLINS), STUART PANKIN (SHERIFF PARSONS), JULIAN SANDS (DR JAMES ATHERTON), MARK L. TAYLOR (JERRY MANLEY) • *109M* • *COLOUR*

The opening sequences of this movie owe much to *The Lost World* (1925 and 1960): somewhere in South America, there is a plateau on which primordial lifeforms survive. But there the resemblance ends, for these are not dinosaurs but insects and arachnids. Through a conspiracy of circumstances, Dr Jennings and his family arrive in a typical Spielbergian small town at the same time as a spider queen from the plateau. Unknown to them, she breeds killer spiders in their basement. Jennings, an arachnophobe (one chronically terrified of spiders — a condition shown in 1995 to be probably hereditary), must confront the queen and destroy her and her brood. Many good parts do not quite add up to a satisfactory whole.

Back To The Future Part III

1990 • USA • *DIRECTOR* ROBERT ZEMECKIS • *SCREENPLAY* BOB GALE • *STARRING* MICHAEL J. FOX (MARTY MCFLY), CHRISTOPHER LLOYD (DR EMMETT BROWN) • *118M* • *COLOUR*

The second half of *Back To The Future Part II* (1989). Marty travels to the 19th-century Wild West to save Doc Brown. Lightweight, but joyfully so.

Darkman

1990 • USA • *DIRECTOR* SAM RAIMI • *SCREENPLAY* DANIEL GOLDIN, JOSHUA GOLDIN, CHUCK PFARRER, IVAN RAIMI, SAM RAIMI • *91M* • *COLOUR*

A scientist has discovered how to create artificial skin, which is useful when he has his face blown off by hoodlums. He exacts his revenge on them in comic-book style.

Flatliners

1990 • USA • *DIRECTOR* JOEL SCHUMACHER • *SCREENPLAY* PETER FILARDI • *STARRING* JULIA ROBERTS,

HAIRY STORY *THEY'RE COMING TO GET YOU... AND, IN* ARACHNOPHOBIA *THEY NEVER LET UP*

KIEFER SUTHERLAND • *114M* • *COLOUR*

An interesting piece of technofantasy in which a quartet of medical students discover that there is indeed an existence after death, and that life's problems can be worked out there. Worth repeated watching.

Frankenstein Unbound

(*VT* ROGER CORMAN'S FRANKENSTEIN UNBOUND)

1990 • USA • *DIRECTOR* ROGER CORMAN • *SCREENPLAY* ROGER CORMAN, F.X. FEENEY, FROM BRIAN ALDISS'S *FRANKENSTEIN UNBOUND* (1973) • *STARRING* NICK BRIMBLE (MONSTER), BRIDGET FONDA (MARY SHELLEY), JOHN HURT (JOSEPH BUCHANAN), RAUL JULIA (VICTOR FRANKENSTEIN) • *85M* • *COLOUR*

A 21st-century scientist accidentally zaps himself back to the early 19th century, where he discovers Byron and the Shelleys existing in the same world as Frankenstein and his Monster. Corman could have done much with this, but instead opted for horror; yet the finale, in the snowbound wreckage of a far-future city, has a certain grandeur.

The Handmaid's Tale

1990 • USA/WEST GERMANY • *DIRECTOR* VOLKER SCHLONDORFF • *SCREENPLAY* HAROLD PINTER, FROM MARGARET ATWOOD'S *THE HANDMAID'S TALE* (1985) • *109M* • *COLOUR*

In a future where most women are infertile, a fertile woman becomes a sex-slave to a rich man, so that she can bear his child. Eventually, of course, she revolts.

Predator 2

1990 • USA • *DIRECTOR* STEPHEN HOPKINS • *SCREENPLAY* JIM THOMAS, JOHN THOMAS • *108M* • *COLOUR*

The premise of *Predator* (1987) is transported from the South American jungle into Los Angeles, where the semi-invisible bloodthirsty alien is hunted down by a pair of cops.

RoboCop 2

1990 • USA • *DIRECTOR* IRVIN KERSHNER • *SCREENPLAY* WALON GREEN, FRANK MILLER • *118M* • *COLOUR*

The sequel to *RoboCop* (1987). A second

BRAIN DRAIN *Discovering your past can be painful, as Arnie finds in* Total Recall *(1990)*

RoboCop cyborg is made, but this time using the brain of a psychopathic drug-dealer. He and the original RoboCop battle it out.

Total Recall

1990 • USA • *DIRECTOR* PAUL VERHOEVEN • *SCREENPLAY* GARY GOLDMAN, DAN O'BANNON, RONALD SHUSETT, FROM PHILIP K. DICK'S 'WE CAN REMEMBER IT FOR YOU WHOLESALE' (1966) • *SPECIAL EFFECTS* ROB BOTTIN, ERIC BREVIG, THOMAS L. FISHER • *STARRING* MICHAEL IRONSIDE (RICHTER), ARNOLD SCHWARZENEGGER (DOUG QUAID), RACHEL TICOTIN (MELINA) • *109M* • COLOUR
In AD 2084, construction worker Quaid dreams nightly of Earth's Martian colony and of a beautiful woman there. He would like to take a Martian holiday, but can afford neither the time nor the money. Instead, he makes use of the services of a company called Rekall, which implants false memories of experiences into its customers' brains; he decides he would like to have been a Martian secret agent sent to Earth. It soon emerges that in fact he *is* a Martian "sleeper" agent, and that his wife — who now tries to kill him — is also a Martian spy, but aware of it. Escaping to Mars, Quaid discovers a tyranny based on the rationing of air; he defeats the tyranny and, in one of sf cinema's most gruesomely invalid endings, releases Mars's pent-up subterranean atmosphere to terraform the entire planet within a matter of minutes. As an

actioner, *Total Recall* is adequate; as a piece of sf, it is dire — which is a shame, because its first half-hour or so raises typically Dickian paranoid themes of some interest.

1991

The Rocketeer

1991 • USA • *DIRECTOR* JOE JOHNSTON • *SCREENPLAY* DANNY BILSON, PAUL DE MEO, FROM DAVE STEVENS'S GRAPHIC NOVEL *THE ROCKETEER* (1981) • *108M* • COLOUR
It is 1938. Howard Hughes has developed a brilliant new invention: a rocket-powered backpack that can enable a man to fly. Using this, a test pilot thwarts a Nazi plot.

Scanners II: The New Order

1991 • CANADA • *DIRECTOR* CHRISTIAN DUGUAY • *SCREENPLAY* B.J. NELSON • *104M* • COLOUR
A rather good sequel to *Scanners* (1980), despite the lapse of time. A corrupt cop attempts to use various Scanners to settle some scores. As before, rubber heads explode.

Star Trek VI: The Undiscovered Country

1991 • USA • *DIRECTOR* NICHOLAS MEYER • *SCREENPLAY* NICHOLAS MEYER, LEONARD NIMOY • *STARRING* DEFOREST KELLEY (DR MCCOY), LEONARD NIMOY (SPOCK), WILLIAM SHATNER (KIRK) • *110M* • COLOUR
A Klingon is murdered and Kirk and McCoy are unjustly accused. Spock — in Sherlock Holmes style — solves the riddle. The last of the original series.

Terminator 2: Judgment Day

1991 • USA • *DIRECTOR* JAMES CAMERON • *SCREENPLAY* JAMES CAMERON, WILLIAM WISHER • *SPECIAL EFFECTS* JAMES BELKIN, JOHN BRUNO, DOUG CHIANG, ROBERT COSTA, GAIL CURREY, GEORGE D. DODGE, MILLER DRAKE, ELAINE EDFORD, MICHAEL GLEASON, JANET HEALY, LESLIE HUNTLEY, VAN LING, DENNIS MUREN, ALISON SAVITCH, DENNIS SKOTAK, ROBERT SKOTAK, GENE WARREN JR, STAN WINSTON AND MANY OTHERS • *STARRING* EDWARD FURLONG (JOHN CONNOR), CASTULO GUERRA (ENRIQUE SALCEDA), LINDA HAMILTON (SARAH CONNOR), JOE MORTON (MILES

DYSON), ROBERT PATRICK (TERMINATOR T-1000), ARNOLD SCHWARZENEGGER (TERMINATOR T-800) • *135M* • COLOUR
The extent of the (much truncated) list of special-effects experts given above might seem to indicate what *Terminator 2* is all about; but that, though glib, would be only a very partial truth. To say that this is one of the most violent sf movies ever made would be no lie; yet, once again, the bald statement would mislead. For the underlying current of this movie is a staunchly pacifistic one, proclaiming the futility of the nuclear-arms race.

As in *The Terminator* (1984), war between humans and intelligent machines continues in the year 2029. Back in our own time, the forearm and claw of the original Terminator (which was of the model T-800) have been recovered, and cybernetics expert Dyson has been working on it, discovering from it technologies more advanced than are otherwise available to present-day humanity. These, though he does not as yet know it, will be used to construct Skynet, a supercomputer that will in 1997 develop self-awareness and then, launch the war to exterminate humankind. In the future, the adult John Connor discovers the machines are sending back a more advanced Terminator (model T-1000) to assassinate his child-self; T-1000 is made of "intelligent metal", which can shapeshift at will. The adult Connor sends back a reprogrammed T-800 in the hope

 PREPARE FOR JUDGMENT *Arnie yet again, this time in the title role of* Terminator 2 *(1991)*

that it can defend his child-self.

Back in our own time, Connor's mother Sarah is in a secure mental hospital, while John, in the care of foster-parents, is a delinquent. The two Terminators, both searching for young John, soon clash; John flees both, but eventually comes to realize that the T-800 is his friend and is, furthermore, programmed to obey him. The two — their every move almost thwarted by the shapeshifting T-1000 — spring Sarah from her mental hospital and arm themselves for battle.

This is one of the best action movies ever made, with Hamilton and Furlong excelling — their efforts enhanced by Schwarzenegger's roboticity. Where the movie really strikes home, however, is in the image of the T-1000. The folkloristic figure of the shapeshifter represents one of the primal dreads of our culture, and here it is rendered superbly. It is quite possible to read this movie as a fantasy variant rather than as hard sf. *The Terminator* was an extremely exciting movie; to say that this surpasses it is to do no more than state the obvious.

1992

Alien³

1992 • USA • *DIRECTOR* DAVID FINCHER • *SCREENPLAY* LARRY FERGUSON, DAVID GILER, WALTER HILL • *STARRING* SIGOURNEY WEAVER (RIPLEY) • *115M* • *COLOUR*

Despite some poor special effects, this is debatably the best in the series that started with *Alien* (1979). Ripley crash-lands on a penal-colony planet where she is surrounded by male sex-killers who have devised a curious religion. Without her knowledge, she has been "impregnated" by an Alien.

Batman Returns

1992 • USA • *DIRECTOR* TIM BURTON • *SCREENPLAY* DANIEL WATERS • *STARRING* DANNY DEVITO (PENGUIN), MICHAEL KEATON (BATMAN), MICHELLE PFEIFFER (CATWOMAN) • *126M* • *COLOUR*

Gotham City is enchanted by The Penguin — a half-man, half-bird from the sewers. Batman realizes there is rotten work afoot, but has his hands full coping with Catwoman. Everything about this movie is heavy-handed.

Forever Young

1992 • USA • *DIRECTOR* STEVE MINER • *SCREENPLAY* JEFFREY ABRAMS • *STARRING* JAMIE LEE CURTIS, MEL GIBSON • *102M* • *COLOUR*

Enjoyable froth in which a test pilot frozen in 1939 wakes up in 1992, and has occasional fits in which he ages. Not for the scientific purist.

Freejack

1992 • USA • *DIRECTOR* GEOFF MURPHY • *SCREENPLAY* DAN GILROY, STEVEN PRESSFIELD, RONALD SHUSETT, FROM (LOOSELY) ROBERT SHECKLEY'S *IMMORTALITY, INC.* (1959) • *111M* • *COLOUR*

A doomed-to-die racing-car driver is plucked from the present into the future by a dying magnate who wishes to implant his own brain in the healthy body. The plot falls apart at the end, but before that there are excellent hijinx. Compare *Millennium* (1989).

Honey, I Blew Up The Kid

1992 • USA • *DIRECTOR* RANDAL KLEISER • *SCREENPLAY* THOM EBERHARDT, PETER ELBLING, GARRY GOODROW • *STARRING* RICK MORANIS • *89M* • *COLOUR*

The follow-up to *Honey, I Shrunk The Kids* (1989). Scientist Szalinski accidentally expands a toddler to enormous size. The script tries so hard to be inventive that finally it isn't inventive at all.

The Lawnmower Man

(VT *STEPHEN KING'S THE LAWNMOWER MAN*)
1992 • UK/USA • *DIRECTOR* BRETT LEONARD
• *SCREENPLAY* GIMEL EVERETT, BRETT LEONARD
• *108M* • *COLOUR*

This has little to do with King's 'The Lawnmower Man' (1975), rights in which seem to have been bought purely in order to exploit his name. A scientist uses drugs and computer software to enhance the intelligence of his gardener; *Charly* (1968) handled similar material much better.

Memoirs Of An Invisible Man

1992 • USA • *DIRECTOR* JOHN CARPENTER • *SCREENPLAY* ROBERT COLLECTOR, WILLIAM GOLDMAN, DANA OLSEN, FROM H.F. SAINT'S *MEMOIRS OF AN INVISIBLE MAN* (1987)

• *STARRING* CHEVY CHASE, DARYL HANNAH, SAM NEILL
• *99M* • *COLOUR*

Comedy in which a scientific accident makes a businessman invisible. Generally given a bad press, this is in fact very entertaining.

Universal Soldier

1992 • USA • *DIRECTOR* ROLAND EMMERICH • *SCREENPLAY* DEAN DEVLIN, CHRISTOPHER LEITCH, RICHARD ROTHSTEIN • *STARRING* DOLPH LUNDGREN, JEAN-CLAUDE VAN DAMME • *104M* • *COLOUR*

Two Vietnam vets are revived to become android killing machines.

1993

Body Snatchers

1993 • USA • *DIRECTOR* ABEL FERRARA • *SCREENPLAY* STUART GORDON, DENNIS PAOLI, NICHOLAS ST JOHN, FROM *THE BODY SNATCHERS* (1955) BY JACK FINNEY • *SPECIAL EFFECTS* PHIL CORY, BARI DREIBAND-BURMAN, THOMAS R. BURMAN • *STARRING* GABRIELLE ANWAR (MARTI MALONE), CHRISTINE ELISE (JENN PLATT), TERRY KINNEY (STEVE MALONE), BILLY WIRTH (TIM YOUNG) • *90M* • *COLOUR*

The third and — in straightforward cinematic terms — the best of the three movie versions of Finney's novel. Our focus is this time a rebellious adolescent girl, Marti, who has been dragged off to live with her family on an army base for a few months, while her environmentalist father checks the area for pollution; the irony that the GIs on the base have, as it were, already had their bodies snatched is not wasted. Slowly, as in the other movies, more and more of this community become pod-people.

As a piece of action cinema, *Body Snatchers* has few peers. Through a bizarre studio decision, in the UK this film went direct to video.

Demolition Man

1993 • USA • *DIRECTOR* MARCO BRAMBILLA
• *SCREENPLAY* PETER M. LENKOV, ROBERT RENAU, DANIEL WATERS • *STARRING* WESLEY SNIPES, SYLVESTER STALLONE
• *115M* • *COLOUR*

A psychopath from today escapes into the pacifistic future, and a tough cop of today is revived to catch him. Though primarily an actioner, also a surprisingly good comedy.

Jurassic Park

1993 • USA • *DIRECTOR* STEVEN SPIELBERG • *SCREENPLAY* MICHAEL CRICHTON, DAVID KOEPP, FROM CRICHTON'S *JURASSIC PARK* (1990) • *SPECIAL EFFECTS* MICHAEL LANTIERI, DENNIS MUREN, PHIL TIPPETT, STAN WINSTON, INDUSTRIAL LIGHT & MAGIC, AND MANY OTHERS • *COMPUTER ANIMATION* ERIC ARMSTRONG, GEOFF CAMPBELL, STEVE PRICE, JAMES SATORU STRAUS, DON WALLER, STEVE SPAZ WILLIAMS, AND MANY OTHERS • *STARRING* RICHARD ATTENBOROUGH (DR JOHN HAMMOND), LAURA DERN (DR ELLIE SATTLER), MARTIN FERRERO (DONALD GENNARO), JEFF GOLDBLUM (DR IAN MALCOLM), SAMUEL L. JACKSON (ARNOLD), JOSEPH MAZZELLO (TIM), SAM NEILL (DR ALAN GRANT), BOB PECK (ROBERT MULDOON), ARIANA RICHARDS (LEX), B.D. WONG (DR WU) • *127M* • *COLOUR*

Hammond has succeeded in cloning dinosaurs from their fossil DNA, and has created a theme park where people can come to watch real dinosaurs lumbering, or in some cases sprinting, around the landscape. A group of scientists — and children — come to look the place over before the official opening and of course everything goes wrong. This movie has many exciting set-pieces, but is let down by a script that would be better matched to a minor made-for-TV movie. The special effects and computer animation carry the day , especially since most of the cast — Goldblum, Jackson and Ferrero excepted — seem conscious that they are merely acting out stereotypes, and perform accordingly.

1994

Mary Shelley's Frankenstein

1994 • USA • *DIRECTOR* KENNETH BRANAGH • *SCREENPLAY* FRANK DARABONT, STEPHEN LADY, FROM MARY SHELLEY'S *FRANKENSTEIN* (1818) • *STARRING* KENNETH BRANAGH (VICTOR FRANKENSTEIN), ROBERT DE NIRO (MONSTER) • *123M* • *COLOUR*

An over-lavish but reasonably faithful version of Shelley's tale. De Niro is excellent; Branagh's wild histrionics are tiring.

Stargate

1994 • USA • *DIRECTOR* ROLAND EMMERICH • *SCREENPLAY* DEAN DEVLIN, ROLAND EMMERICH • *STARRING* KURT RUSSELL, JAMES SPADER • *122M* • *COLOUR*

Odd mixture of fantasy and sf, with some *Indiana Jones* thrown in. An ancient artefact provides a gateway to the far side of the Universe, where our heroes discover a planet ruled tyrannically by the god Osiris — in fact, an alien who once tried the same trick on Earth.

Star Trek: Generations

1994 • USA • *DIRECTOR* RICK BERMAN • *SCREENPLAY* BRANNON BRAGA, RONALD D. MOORE • *STARRING* WILLIAM SHATNER (KIRK), PATRICK STEWART (PICARD) • *117M* • *COLOUR*

Kirk hands over command of the *Enterprise* to Picard and then dies, thus effectively linking the two relevant TV series.

Timecop

1994 • USA • *DIRECTOR* PETER HYAMS • *SCREENPLAY* MARK VERHEIDEN • *STARRING* JEAN-CLAUDE VAN DAMME • *98M* • *COLOUR*

A fairly basic actioner, whose prime notion is that a policeman has been appointed to oversee the space/time continuum.

1995

Batman Forever

1995 • USA • *DIRECTOR* JOEL SCHUMACHER • *SCREENPLAY* JANET SCOTT BATCHELOR, LEE BATCHELOR, AKIVA GOLDSMAN • *STARRING* JIM CARREY (EDWARD NYGMA/RIDDLER), TOMMY LEE JONES (HARVEY DENT/HARVEY TWO-FACE), NICOLE KIDMAN (DR CHASE MERIDIAN), VAL KILMER (BRUCE WAYNE/BATMAN), CHRIS O`DONNELL (DICK GRAYSON/ROBIN) • *122M* • *COLOUR*

Tim Burton's gloom is replaced by a camp treatment that owes much to *Batman* (1966). The plot is incomprehensible but the style carries everything.

Congo

1995 • USA • *DIRECTOR* FRANK MARSHALL • *SCREENPLAY* JOHN PATRICK SHANLEY, FROM MICHAEL CRICHTON'S *CONGO* (1980) • *108M* • *COLOUR*

Killer apes have built up a civilization that is unknown to humankind... but not for long. An appaling movie, although reminiscent of the Weissmuller period of Tarzan.

Johnny Mnemonic

1995 • USA • *DIRECTOR* ROBERT LONGO • *SCREENPLAY*

 BIG BAD BREATH *THE PLOT AND THE HUMAN ACTORS HAD COMPARATIVELY LITTLE TO OFFER IN THE SPIELBERG/CRICHTON JURASSIC PARK (1993), BUT THE STATE-OF-THE-ART SPECIAL EFFECTS MOST CERTAINLY DID. YEARS BEFORE WE BELIEVED THAT A MAN COULD FLY; NOW WE BELIEVED THAT DINOSAURS HAD BEEN RECREATED*

CLEAN CUT
KEANU REEVES AS JOHNNY MNEMONIC (1995), A MOVIE THAT GENERALLY DISAPPOINTED ALTHOUGH IT CONTAINS MANY FINE MOMENTS, NOTABLY IN ITS PORTRAYAL OF THE WAINSCOT SQUALIDITY OF THE OVER-SHINY HI-TECH FUTURE

WILLIAM GIBSON, FROM GIBSON'S 'JOHNNY MNEMONIC' (1981) • *SPECIAL EFFECTS* • *STARRING* DINA MEYER, ICE-T, DOLPH LUNDGREN, KEANU REEVES (JOHNNY MNEMONIC), TAKESHI
• *98M* • *COLOUR*

With the emphasis on style over content, this much-awaited film grew from a $1.5 Million dollar arthouse movie into a $30 million dollar glitzy let down.

Judge Dredd

1995 • USA • *DIRECTOR* DANNY CANNON • *SCREENPLAY* STEVEN E. DE SOUZA, WILLIAM WISHER, FROM THE COMICS CHARACTERS CREATED BY CARLOS EZQUERRA, JOHN WAGNER • *STARRING* SYLVESTER STALLONE (DREDD)
• *95M* • *COLOUR*

The comics hero discovers that he has a cloned brother, Rico, whom he must destroy. Expensive brio doesn't quite carry the story through.

Species

1995 • USA • *DIRECTOR* ROGER DONALDSON • *SCREENPLAY* DENNIS FELDMAN • *108M* • *COLOUR*

Aliens beam raw DNA to Earth, and a humanoid female is born. She grows with astonishing speed to become a lovely young woman who happily kills those who get in her way. A largely pointless movie that looks very good.

Tank Girl

1995 • USA • *DIRECTOR* RACHEL TALALAY • *SCREENPLAY* TEDI SARAFIAN, FROM THE COMIC STRIP OF JAMIE HEWLETT, ALAN MARTIN • *STARRING* LORI PETTY, NAOMI WATTS
• *104M* • *COLOUR*

Forty years hence, there is a world shortage of water, and a despotic overlord tries to control what supplies there are. Tank Girl fights him, in between copulating with a half-man, half-kangaroo. Much disliked on release, this movie is actually rather good.

Waterworld

1995 • USA • *DIRECTOR* KEVIN REYNOLDS • *SCREENPLAY* PETER RADER, DAVID TWOHY • *SPECIAL EFFECTS* KIMBERLEY K. NELSON AND MANY OTHERS • *STARRING* KEVIN COSTNER (MARINER), DENNIS HOPPER (DEACON), CHAIM JERAFFI (DRIFTER), MICHAEL JETER (GREGOR), TINA MAJORINO (ENOLA), JEANNE TRIPPLEHORN (HELEN)
• *134M* • *COLOUR*

The polar icecaps have melted and all the world is ocean —although there is a myth that somewhere a place called Dryland exists. The remnants of humanity survive on boats or on floating collections of scrap. To one of these latter, the Atoll, comes the Mariner, a web-footed mutant. He is imprisoned, but soon the Atoll is attacked by Smokers (pirates). In the confusion, the Mariner escapes with Helen and her adopted daughter Enola, on whose back is tattooed what is believed to be a map locating Dryland. After many adventures, the trio reach Dryland, but the Mariner decides life on solid ground is not for him.

Waterworld loses out through an inane script and a wooden performance from Costner. But, forgetting all this, *Waterworld* is almost as much fun, though not as inventive, as the same year's *Tank Girl* (1995).

The comics connection

Comics and movies are really two sides of the same coin — indeed, creators in the two media have what is virtually a shared terminology ("long-shot", "close-up", etc.) — so it is hardly surprising that many comics scenarios and characters have been adapted for the cinema, or, for that matter, that in recent years there has been a spate of graphic novelizations of movies.

It started with Winsor McCay (1867-1934), a comic-strip artist who was also a pioneer of animation. He made a short movie, Little Nemo (1911), based on his own comics fantasy Little Nemo In Slumberland (1905-11). Other animators followed suit with different comics inspirations, and live-action moviemakers were not far behind — but very soon the accent fell on macho heroes and superheroes, many of the movies being sf. The trend has continued, with 1995 alone seeing the release of the comics-based Judge Dredd, Tank Girl and Batman Forever, not to mention various others that were less publicized.

Other recent adaptations from comics to screen include Modesty Blaise (1966): Barbarella (1967); Danger: Diabolik (1967); Tiffany Jones (1973); Wonder Woman (1974) and The New Original Wonder Woman (1975), both TV movies that have been screened theatrically, with the latter being sequelled by various other TV movies before settling down as a TV series; The Incredible Hulk (1977) and its 1988 sequel, both TV movies; Spider-Man (1977), a TV pilot released theatrically, with sequels in 1978 and 1979; Heavy Metal (1981), a compilation based on the French comic Métal Hurlant; Swamp Thing (1981) and its 1989 sequel; Howard The Duck (1986; vt Howard ... A New Breed Of Hero); Jane And The Lost City (1987); Teenage Mutant Ninja Turtles (1990) and its sequels in 1991 and 1992; and The Rocketeer (1991; vt The Adventures Of The Rocketeer).

In addition, there have been many Japanese anime movies based on manga originals; Akira (1987) was the first to make an impact in the West, and today it is rare to find a video shop without an extensive anime section.

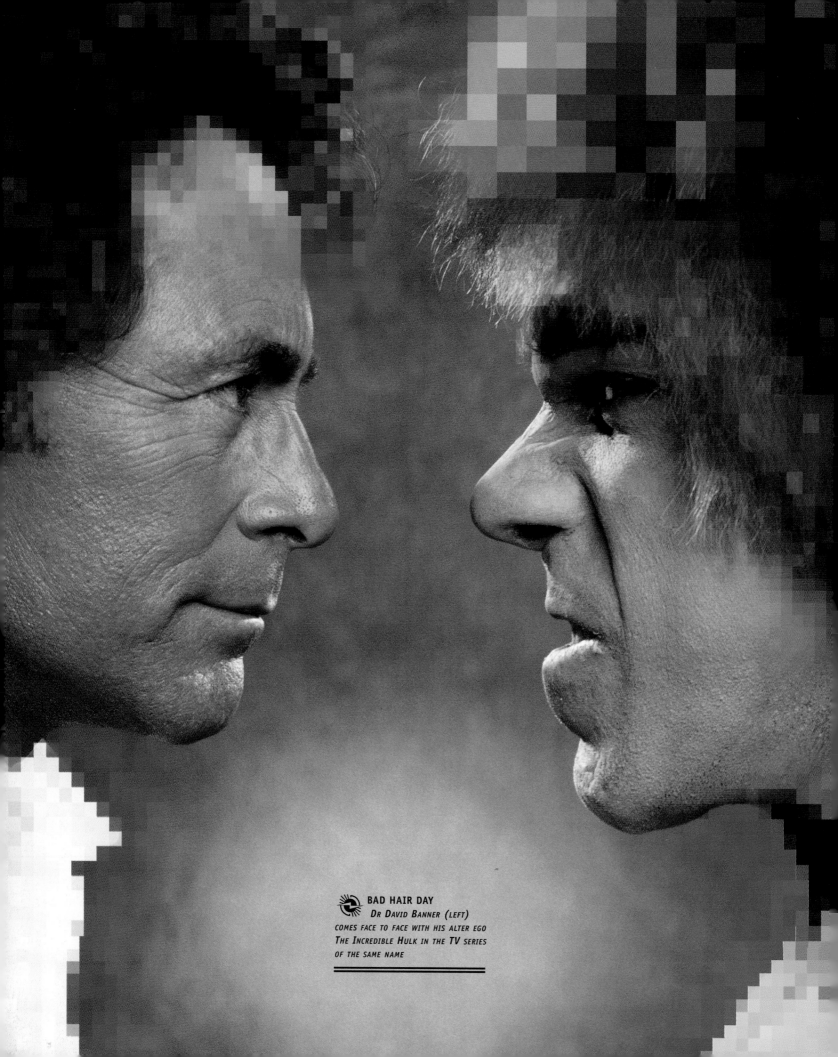

BAD HAIR DAY
DR DAVID BANNER (LEFT)
COMES FACE TO FACE WITH HIS ALTER EGO
THE INCREDIBLE HULK IN THE **TV** SERIES
OF THE SAME NAME

TV 2000

━━━◙◙◙━━━

IN **1900** TELEVISION WAS JUST ONE MORE IDEA IN THE SF LEXICON; BY THE YEAR **2000** TELEVISION WILL BE THE MEDIUM THROUGH WHICH THE GENRE REACHES ITS LARGEST AUDIENCE

━━━◙◙◙━━━

Science fiction on TV

A CHRONOLOGICAL SURVEY OF THE HIGHLIGHTS, FROM THE LOST CLASSICS OF THE LIVE TV ERA THROUGH THE CULT SHOWS STILL AVAILABLE ON CABLE TV AND VIDEO RIGHT UP TO THE CREAM OF THE PRESENT-DAY CROP

1949

Captain Video

1949-53 • SERIALS • US • *PRODUCER* LARRY MENKIN • *STARRING* RICHARD COOGAN, REPLACED IN 1951 BY AL HODGE • *25-MIN EPISODES*

This pioneering children's show which went out live five times a week had too small a budget to make much of plot-lines involving alien

invasions countered by the uniformed captain and his Video Rangers, although some of these were written by such well-known sf writers as Cyril Kornbluth, Damon Knight and Robert Sheckley. Time was often filled in by cartoons and unrelated material introduced by the

THE RAY-GUN *No HERO OF EARLY TV SF WAS PROPERLY DRESSED WITHOUT ONE*

captain, whose role was reduced to that of link man and part-time talk show host in a follow-up series in 1955-56.

1950

Tom Corbett — Space Cadet

1950-55 • SERIALS • *US (CBS/ABC/NBC)*
• *PRODUCER* MORT ABRAHAMS • *STARRING* FRANKIE THOMAS
• *THRICE-WEEKLY 15-MIN EPISODES IN FIRST FOUR SERIES, WEEKLY 30-MIN EPISODES IN FIFTH*

Set in the 24th century, these live children's serials went one better than *Captain Video* by immediately taking the action out into space. They borrowed initial inspiration (but not much else) from Robert A. Heinlein's *Space Cadet* (1948).

1951

Stranger From Space

1951 • SERIAL-CUM-SERIES • *UK (BBC)* • *PRODUCER* MICHAEL WESTMORE • *WRITERS* HAZEL ADAIR AND RONALD MARRIOTT • *c10-MIN EPISODES*

A Martian craft crashes on Earth; its young pilot makes contact with a human boy and the two embark on a series of adventures together. Aired on the children's TV omnibus *Whirligig*, the 11-part serial proved popular enough to justify a second serial split into six parts and a spin-off novel, doubtless encouraging the BBC to undertake further experiments with sf.

 THE BEMUSED EXPRESSION *NECESSARY EQUIPMENT FOR ACTORS IN TV SF SHOWS*

Tales Of Tomorrow

1951-56 • ANTHOLOGY SERIES • *US (ABC)*
• *PRODUCERS* GEORGE FOLEY AND DICK GORDON
• *25-MIN EPISODES*

An ambitious attempt to overcome the limitations of live broadcasting, mixing original screenplays with adaptations, launched with a two-part adaptation of Jules Verne's *Twenty Thousand Leagues Under The Sea* starring Thomas Mitchell and Leslie Nielsen.

1952

The Adventures Of Superman

1952-57 • SERIES • *US (ABC)* • *STARRING* GEORGE REEVES • *25-MIN EPISODES*

This took up where the radio series left off, pitting a somewhat overweight and 40ish Superman against a fairly dull assortment of criminal conspirators in order to re-establish 'truth, justice and the American way.' Some later episodes have been preserved on tape and can still be seen, although they look shabby by comparison with *Lois And Clark: The New Adventures Of Superman*.

Plot formulas

The formats into which TV shows fall require the standardization of certain kinds of plot formulas. Such formulas are very useful in linking together the segments of series.

The most convenient series plot formula, of which most others are tortuous variants, is the "Law Enforcement" formula which includes cop shows, legal dramas and diplomatic dramas. The lead character has a job which requires continual involvement in sorting out knotty situations according to an established moral code and set of methods. Sf versions range from *Tom Corbett —Space Cadet* to *Babylon 5*.

The Law Enforcement formula shades into the "Enhanced Secret Agent" formula, in which the specially qualified lead character works for a secret organization and is continually sent forth on covert missions, which usually pose problems of method, if not morality. *Mission: Impossible* (1970-75) with its intricate plots created the TV archetype; sf versions like *The Invisible Man* and *The Six Million Dollar Man* involve literal enhancements — paranormal powers, cyborgization, etc.

The Enhanced Secret Agent formula shades into the "Wandering Vigilante" formula, in which the lead character is a loner, detached from any parent organization; he is constantly on the move, but is continually interrupted by the necessity to fight for the cause of right on behalf of people by whom he is summoned, or meets by chance. *The Lone Ranger* (1956-62) provided a TV archetype later borrowed by a number of time-hopping sf shows, including *Doctor Who* and *Quantum Leap*.

The Wandering Vigilante formula shades into the "Running Man" formula, in which the lead character is usually questing after some essentially elusive goal while being pursued and harassed by hostile forces. *The Fugitive* (1964-67) created the TV archetype, and was imitated by such sf shows as *The Invaders*. *Planet Of The Apes* and *The Fantastic Journey* are variants of the formula, involving ill-assorted groups of runners.

1953

The Quatermass Experiment

1953 • SIX-PART SERIAL • UK (BBC)
• *PRODUCER/DIRECTOR* RUDOLPH CARTIER • *WRITER* NIGEL
KNEALE • *STARRING* REGINALD TATE (QUATERMASS) AND
DUNCAN LAMONT • *30-MIN EPISODES*

A landmark endeavour which sought to do for TV
what *Journey Into Space* had done for radio,
with an extra melodramatic turn of the screw;
the pre-show warning that it was "unsuitable for
children or persons of a nervous disposition"
helped boost the audience. The 1955 Hammer
film version fails to convey the excitement
generated by the serial's cliff-hanger endings, as
the sole survivor of the ill-fated spaceflight
undergoes his terrible metamorphosis into a
vegetable monster. The film also substitutes an
explosive climax for the quieter and more
effective TV ending, where Quatermass engages
in tense dialogue with the composite
consciousness of the three spore-absorbed
astronauts. Unfortunately, the original was
broadcast live and not preserved, although the
script was published in 1959.

1954

The Lost Planet

1954 • SIX-PART SERIAL • UK (BBC) • *PRODUCER*
KEVIN SHELDON • *WRITER* ANGUS MACVICAR BASED ON HIS
1952 RADIO SERIAL • *STARRING* JOHN STUART AND
GEOFFREY LUMSDEN • *30-MIN EPISODES*

MacVicar had already novelized his radio serial in
1953; this TV adaptation completed an eccentric
set that went unreplicated until Douglas Adams
scored the same triple-hit with *The Hitch-Hiker's
Guide To The Galaxy*. Typical kids' sf of the day,
which probably inspired W. E. Johns to write his
Kings Of Space series (begun 1954). The sequel,
Return To The Lost Planet, followed in 1955.

Nineteen Eighty-four

1954 • PLAY • UK (BBC) • *PRODUCER/DIRECTOR*
RUDOLPH CARTIER • *SCRIPT* BY NIGEL KNEALE BASED ON
GEORGE ORWELL'S 1949 NOVEL • *STARRING* PETER CUSHING
(WINSTON SMITH), YVONNE MITCHELL (JULIA) AND ANDRE
MORELL (O'BRIEN) • *120 MIN*

A second landmark endeavour by the team
responsible for *The Quatermass Experiment*. The
live performance, of unprecedented length, was
quickly repeated for the largest TV audience
since the coronation and was preserved on film
for recent re-showing. As with the former item,
the TV play was much superior to the subsequent
cinema film. Its centrepiece was a brilliantly
dignified performance by Peter Cushing and the
climax was quite harrowing, capped by a chilling
coda in which Winston Smith and Julia meet
after their "re-education". This was one of the
crucial works which demonstrated the potential
of the single play as an art form, paving the way
for increasingly ambitious endeavours by the
BBC and the independent companies in the late
1950s and throughout the 1960s.

1955

Quatermass II

1955 • SIX-PART SERIAL • UK (BBC)
• *PRODUCER/DIRECTOR* RUDOLPH CARTIER • *WRITER* NIGEL
KNEALE • *STARRING* JOHN ROBINSON • *35-MIN EPISODES*

An equally gripping sequel to *The Quatermass
Experiment*, deftly side-stepping severe
budgetary restrictions and the limitations of TV
special effects. Insidious alien invaders capable
of taking control of human beings maintain a
secret base inside a high-tech industrial complex

THE SHADOW OF TOMORROW NINETEEN EIGHTY-FOUR *WAS THE FIRST CLASSIC OF* **TV** *SF,
FEATURING FINE PERFORMANCES BY* PETER CUSHING *AND* YVONNE MITCHELL

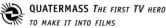
QUATERMASS *THE FIRST TV HERO TO MAKE IT INTO FILMS*

as well as a more permanent one aboard an asteroid. Later, the Hammer film version proved to be a lacklustre redaction, unable to take advantage of such excellent cliff-hangers as the blood dripping from the overhead pipes during Quatermass's investigation of the invaders' earth-base. Again, the film substituted a swift and explosive climax for the TV serial's far more suspenseful journey into space to attack the asteroid base.

Science Fiction Theater

1955-57 • ANTHOLOGY SERIES • US • *PRODUCER* IVAN TORS • *25-MIN EPISODES*

This follow-up to *Tales Of Tomorrow* adopted a calculatedly modest approach, signalled by the laid-back introductions of show-host Truman Bradley. His demonstrations of scientific concepts at the nub of each episode, plus the crediting of technical adviser Dr Maxwell Smith, were emblematic of an attempt at rational plausibility. The third and last 26-show series was TV sf's first significant venture into colour.

Visit To A Small Planet

1955 • PLAY • US • *WRITER* GORE VIDAL • *50 MIN*
Produced the following year as a Broadway play and contorted by the 1960 film into a vehicle for Jerry Lewis, this modest satire pioneered the common TV sf device of introducing an alien visitor into a contemporary household — in this case an alien child who is reclaimed by his parents just in time to prevent his superpowers from wreaking havoc

The Voices

1955 • PLAY • UK (BBC) • *PRODUCER/DIRECTOR* DENNIS VANCE • *SCRIPT* BY GEORGE F. KERR FROM ROBERT CRANE'S 1954 NOVEL *HERO'S WALK* • *STARRING* WALTER RILLA, TERENCE ALEXANDER AND WILLOUGHBY GODDARD • *90 MIN*
A rapid follow-up to *Nineteen Eighty-four*, the live performance was similarly repeated for a second showing. The silly plot in which the alien voices threaten humankind with punishment for scientific hubris was partly redeemed by the heavily made-up Goddard's commanding performance as the alarmist prophet of doom.

1956

One

1956 • PLAY • UK (REDIFFUSION/ITV) • *DIRECTOR* PETER GRAHAM SCOTT • *SCRIPT* BY JOHN LETTS FROM DAVID KARP'S 1953 NOVEL • *STARRING* DONALD PLEASENCE AND JACK MAY • *90 MIN*

Credit where credit is due

All TV programmes are collective endeavours, as the credits readily testify. Whereas it is easy enough to identify the true author of a book, relegating its editor to a peripheral role and its publisher to utter irrelevance, it is not so easy to apportion credit for a TV show. Fame inevitably favours the actors who are visible to the public eye, even though the artistic vision that they make incarnate was put together by a scriptwriter (sometimes adapting a previous text) and orchestrated by a director — using resources laid on by a producer, who is usually

responsible to executives further up the organizational hierarchy.

It has become fashionable recently, at least in America, for TV credits to single out "creators", who usually also serve as "executive producers" and frequently as members of the script-writing team.

This contrasts sharply with the cinema, where it is the director who is usually singled out as the "author" of the film — although movies made for TV often mimic theatrical movies in giving the primary credit to the

director. In Britain, the terms "creator" and "executive producer" rarely figure in formal credits and it is often scriptwriters and script-editors who come up with programme ideas, thus claiming attention as implicit "creators". The meanings of all these terms are rather elastic.

For these reasons, the sparse "credits" used in the annotations of the various shows in this chapter do not attempt fullness or consistency of labelling. The individuals named are those supposed to have made the greatest contributions to the collaborative product, but the actual extent and nature of their contributions vary considerably.

Independent British TV's answer to the BBC's *Nineteen Eighty-four* was based on a much less interesting dystopia. Like the novel on which it was based, it was merely a faded carbon copy of the original which was irredeemable despite Donald Pleasence's heroic performance as the unlucky victim of imperfect brainwashing.

The Strange World Of Planet X

1956 • SEVEN-PART SERIAL • UK (ATV/ITV) • *PRODUCER* ARTHUR LANE • *WRITER* RENE RAY • *STARRING* WILLIAM LUCAS, HELEN CHERRY AND DAVID GARTH • 25-MIN episodes

In the UK, ITV's first response to the Quatermass serials was a real curiosity written by actress/novelist Rene Ray. Investigation of a "new magnetic field" allows experimenting scientists to penetrate a new dimension; unfortunately, Planet X turned out to be rather boring, and the writer was far more interested in the triangular relationship of the leading characters. The novelization published in 1957 is all that remains of the experiment.

The Trollenberg Terror

1956-57 • SIX-PART SERIAL • UK (ATV/ITV) • *PRODUCER/DIRECTOR* QUENTIN LAWRENCE • *WRITER* PETER KEY • *STARRING* LAURENCE PAYNE AND SARAH LAWSON • *30-MIN EPISODES*

Lawrence, who had directed most of the episodes of *The Strange World Of Planet X*, here made a much more concerted effort to reproduce the thrills of the Quatermass series. It was rather effective, with good use of such suggestive cliff-hangers as the melting telephone. The film version was a travesty; the fact that the TV serial never brought its alien monsters on stage allowed them to preserve a sinister cloak of mystery — which the film dutifully whipped away to utterly absurd effect.

1958

Doomsday For Dyson

1958 • PLAY • UK (GRANADA/ITV) • *DIRECTOR* SILVIO NARIZZANO • *WRITER* J. B. PRIESTLEY • *STARRING* IAN HUNTER (TOM DYSON) • *45 MIN*

His morale-building work during World War II made Priestley into one of the most famous and best-loved radio broadcasters in the UK and all of his marginally science-fictional "time plays" have been adapted for radio or TV, but this didactic visionary fantasy was specifically written for TV as an exercise in alarmism. Tom Dyson survives an atomic explosion, but then kills himself and his family rather than live with its aftermath; in the next world, he is called before a tribunal which attempts to apportion blame for the nuclear tragedy (foreshadowing James Morrow's novel *This Is The Way The World Ends*). A bold experiment for commercial TV.

The Invisible Man

1958-59 • SERIES • UK (ATV/ITV) • *PRODUCER* RALPH SMART • *STARRING* DEBORAH WATLING AND THE VOICE OF TIM TURNER • *30-MIN EPISODES*

An early exercise in the use of special effects that borrowed nothing but its central motif from H. G. Wells. Scientist Peter Brady, condemned to invisibility when an experiment goes awry, thwarts various criminals and spies, and helps out assorted lame ducks while searching fruitlessly for a cure. *The Invisible Man* laid down the basic template for several subsequent sf series, including two reprises.

Quatermass And The Pit

1958-59 • SIX-PART SERIAL • UK (BBC) • *PRODUCER/DIRECTOR* RUDOLPH CARTIER • *WRITER* NIGEL KNEALE • *STARRING* ANDRE MORELL (QUATERMASS), CHRISTINE FINN AND ANTHONY BUSHELL • *35-MIN EPISODES*

The third and perhaps best of the ground-breaking Quatermass serials, which cleverly integrated filmed inserts with live performances, making good use of special effects. A fine array of weird sound effects was added by the newly founded BBC Radiophonic Workshop. Building-site workers in South-west London find organic

 THE SCIENTIST AT WORK *THE USE OF GADGETS SIGNIFIED A HAPPY MATING OF GENIUS AND DILIGENCE*

ASSOCIATED BRITISH-PATHE LIMITED presents
A HAMMER FILM PRODUCTION
JAMES DONALD · ANDREW KEIR
BARBARA SHELLEY · JULIAN GLOVER
in
"QUATERMASS AND THE PIT" (X)
TECHNICOLOR ®
Released through WARNER-PATHE DISTRIBUTORS LTD.

remains which include those of alien visitors, whose malign presence remains sufficiently active to spark off increasingly violent paranormal phenomena. The first episode was archived, but not the rest; film company Hammer found a big enough budget to produce a big screen version more effective than their earlier travesties but the "psychokinetic" special effects — which were new to TV — gave the serial an authentic shock value.

1959

Men Into Space

1959-60 • SERIES • US (UNITED ARTISTS/CBS) • *STARRING* WILLIAM LUNDIGAN • *25-MIN EPISODES*
A quasi-documentary series anticipating the development of NASA's space programme. While hero Ed McCauley undergoes a series of promotions from lieutenant to colonel, a Space Platform is built, a moon base is developed and the first exploratory mission to Mars is launched.

The Offshore Island

1959 • PLAY • UK (BBC) • *PRODUCER* DENNIS VANCE • *SCRIPT* BY MARGHANITA LASKI BASED ON HER 1954 STAGE PLAY • *STARRING* ANN TODD AND TIM SEELY • *90 MIN*
A story set in a small, relatively uncontaminated enclave in the aftermath of a nuclear war. Inevitably, in the era of the annual anti-nuclear Aldermaston marches (which had begun in 1956 and attracted more publicity with the passing years), it aroused considerable controversy; the full-length version was swiftly published as a paperback book.

The Twilight Zone

1959-64 • ANTHOLOGY SERIES • US (COYUGA/MGM) • *CREATOR* ROD SERLING • *25- AND 50-MIN EPISODES*
A long-running and influential series which casually mixed sf and fantasy. About half of the scripts were by Serling, who introduced each episode with a challenging teaser. Other writers — most prolifically Charles Beaumont and Richard Matheson — contributed both original scripts and adaptations. The 156 episodes (18 of which are double-length) are constantly re-run in the US and are now familiar in the UK

although the great majority were not shown there until the 1980s. The stories are often cleverly constructed and deftly presented, but tend to adhere to the "no good will come of it all" school of thought, in which side-steps from the ordinary course of affairs usually prove disturbing, if not outrightly disastrous. The narrative coups which wound up the episodes were often casual miracles, aesthetic neatness substituting for plausibility — as is the case in the great majority of TV shows featuring sf and fantasy.

1960

The Night Of The Big Heat

1960 • PLAY • UK (REDIFFUSION/ITV) • *DIRECTOR* CYRIL COKE • *SCRIPT* BY GILES COOPER FROM JOHN

THE SIN OF SCIENCE *INTELLECTUALS CONTEMPLATING THE SPECTRE OF NUCLEAR HOLOCAUST TENDED TO WRING THEIR HANDS*

LYMINGTON'S 1959 NOVEL • *STARRING* LEE MONTAGUE AND MELISSA STRIBLING • *90 MIN*
The plot about alien invaders that cause an unexpected localized heat wave made cunning use of TV actors' tendency to sweat under the lights, but failed to reproduce the sense of threat incarnate in the drifting mists of *The Trollenberg Terror*. Cooper was to script a good deal more TV sf, but never showed any real feeling for the genre.

Pathfinders In Space

1960 • SEVEN-PART SERIAL • UK (ABC/ITV) • *PRODUCER* SYDNEY NEWMAN • *WRITERS* MALCOLM HULKE AND ERIC PAICE • *STARRING* PETER WILLIAMS, STEWART GUIDOTTI AND GERALD FLOOD • *25-MIN EPISODES*
This follow-up to the juvenile serial *Target Luna* (1960) was aimed at a mixed audience, taking a whole family on an exploratory mission to the moon. They would be stranded there, were it not for the ingenuity of the father of the clan. Two further serials, *Pathfinders To Mars* (1960-61) and *Pathfinders To Venus* (1961) followed in

rapid succession, cleverly making dramatic use of elementary special effects and ultra-cheap sets — experience which Newman and Hulke carried forward to *Doctor Who*.

1961

A For Andromeda

1961 • SEVEN-PART SERIAL • UK (BBC) • *PRODUCERS* MICHAEL HAYES AND NORMAN JONES • *WRITERS* FRED HOYLE AND JOHN ELLIOT • *STARRING* PETER HALLIDAY, ESMOND KNIGHT, MARY MORRIS AND JULIE CHRISTIE • *45-MIN EPISODES*

A fine follow-up to the Quatermass trilogy, in which signals from outer space picked up by a radio-telescope include instructions for building an advanced computer. While political battles are fought to determine who will use the computer, the machine takes action on its own behalf, electrocuting a lab assistant who is subsequently reincarnated as an active embodiment of the machine's intelligence. Like its predecessors, the serial relies on the melodramatic potential of horrific alien menace, but Hoyle's input did enable the scientists to put a counterbalancing case for the benefits of

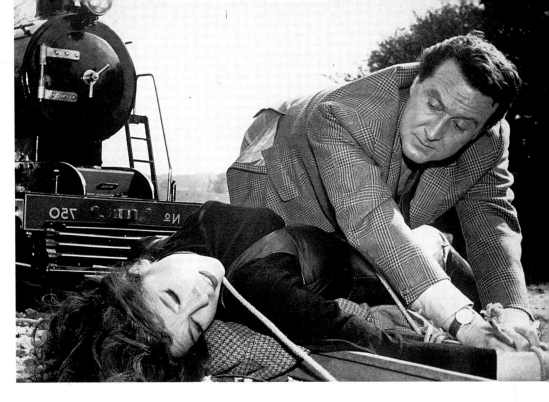

scientific inquiry and technological advancement.

1962

The Andromeda Breakthrough

1962 • SIX-PART SERIAL • UK (BBC) • *PRODUCER* JOHN ELLIOT • *WRITERS* FRED HOYLE AND JOHN ELLIOT

• *STARRING* PETER HALLIDAY, MARY MORRIS AND SUSAN HAMPSHIRE • *45-MIN EPISODES*

A rapidly produced and somewhat less effective sequel, with Susan Hampshire standing in for Julie Christie as the computer-generated femme fatale Andromeda. The hero has destroyed the first alien-inspired computer, but construction of a second is now under way. Andromeda and the Earth both sicken as a result of alien infection, but the possibility remains that humankind might benefit greatly if only the scientists can turn the information contained in the alien message to their own advantage.

The Avengers

1962-69 • SERIES • UK (ABC/ATV/ITV) • *STARRING* PATRICK MACNEE (JOHN STEED) • *50-MIN EPISODES*

Initially a thriller serial-cum-series starring Ian Hendry, with Macnee as second lead, which followed on from the crime series *Police Surgeon* — they were avengers in the sense that they were tracking down those responsible for the murder of Hendry's wife. Once free of this anchorage, *The Avengers* became increasingly bizarre. It began to make frequent use of sf devices like the robotic Cybernauts in the fourth series of 1965, when Diana Rigg's Emma Peel

Sidekicks 1: The Avengers

Because TV is a real-time medium shows must flow; while there is no movement or action on screen, there must be a stream of dialogue, which usually benefits from complicated undercurrents. TV heroes find it immensely useful to have sidekicks who are conspicuously unlike themselves; the relationships between heroes and sidekicks always benefit from tensions arising out of the differences between them. Steed's female sidekicks in *The Avengers* not only caught the tide of women's lib by throwing themselves wholeheartedly into the action instead of whimpering feebly while waiting to be rescued. They also demonstrated the rewards to be gleaned from a calculatedly enigmatic kind of flirtation, which kept a certain sexual chemistry simmering while never really threatening to achieve consummation. (Such closure would have compromised the infinite repeatability at which all TV shows aim.)

Honor Blackman's Cathy Gale was always handicapped in the maintenance of this kind of delicately taut relationship by the evident sexuality of the actress (which sustained her career into her 60s in comedies like *The Upper Hand*). Diana Rigg's Emma Peel was better equipped, by virtue of her beautifully wry smiles, whose mute promises were teasingly inexplicit. Rigg contrived to signify independence without having to simulate innocence, giving the impression that she could cope with men far too easily actually to need one permanently hanging around. Her impish features and false eyelashes added a dash of spice to the mock-significant glances which she and Steed were always exchanging — but this was the department in which Linda Thorson's Tara King really came into her own. Her lustrously pale eyes radiated dreamy unconcern, and might have sustained the series longer had the show not run out of steam.

replaced Honor Blackman's Cathy Gale as Steed's provocatively clad sidekick. Although Brian Clemens is generally given credit for shaping the show's evolution in this period, most of the sf episodes were written by Philip Levene. The mannered quirkiness of the oft-rerun later series became gradually more extravagant until the seventh and last series, when Rigg was replaced by Linda Thorson as Tara King.

The Big Pull

1962 • SIX-PART SERIAL • UK (BBC) • *PRODUCER* TERENCE DUDLEY • *WRITER* ROBERT GOULD • *STARRING* WILLIAM DEXTER AND JUNE TOBIN • *30-MIN EPISODES* This lacklustre alien menace serial — whose plot was very similar to *The Quatermass Experiment* but without the metamorphic monster — was completely overshadowed by *The Andromeda Breakthrough*, with which the BBC schedulers inexplicably saw fit to overlap it.

Fireball XL-5

1962-63 • SERIES • UK (ATV/ITV) • *CREATORS* GERRY AND SYLVIA ANDERSON • *25-MIN EPISODES* The Andersons' previous puppet shows had all been cast as orthodox children's shows with "juvenile" leads, but this SuperMarionation venture in space opera was more ambitious. Pilot Steve Zodiac was partnered with a sexy female doctor named Venus and the obligatory scientific genius Mat Matic. Commander Zero sent them forth from Space City on a series of interstellar adventures. It was comic-book stuff but it foreshadowed things to come.

Out Of This World

1962 • ANTHOLOGY SERIES • UK (ABC/ITV) • *PRODUCER* IRENE SHUBIK • *50-MIN EPISODES* Although it only lasted one season of 13 shows, this was an excellent series which included deft and sensitive adaptations of classic sf stories by (among others) John Wyndham, Isaac Asimov, Tom Godwin, Philip K. Dick, Clifford Simak and Arthur Sellings. Two original scripts, one of them by Terry Nation, were abysmal by comparison. ITV's unease regarding the series was demonstrated by the fact that the first play, memorably based on Wyndham's 'Dumb Martian',

 ECCENTRIC AT LARGE *WHEN THE WHOLE OF TIME AND SPACE IS A PLAYGROUND, IT'S A GREAT HELP TO BE ABLE TO IMPROVISE A TUNE*

was showcased as an Armchair Theatre production and the remainder were introduced by Boris Karloff in a sinister style borrowed from Valentine Dyall, who had earlier posed as 'The Man In Black' in order to introduce creepy stories on the radio. Despite this packaging, the series clearly demonstrated that TV sf did not have to be restricted to alien menace stories.

When The Kissing Had to Stop

1962 • TWO-PART SERIAL • UK (REDIFFUSION/ITV) • *DIRECTOR* BILL HITCHCOCK • *SCRIPT* BY GILES COOPER FROM CONSTANTINE FITZGIBBON'S 1960 NOVEL • *STARRING* DENHOLM ELLIOTT AND PETER VAUGHAN • *78-MIN EPISODES* An exercise in political alarmism in which a socialist government meekly allows Britain to be absorbed into the Soviet bloc and occupied by Russian troops. Despite glowing reviews from right-wing critics, it failed to prevent prime minister Harold Wilson's 1964 election victory.

1963

Doctor Who

1963-89 • CYCLE OF SERIALS • UK (BBC)

• 25- & 50-MIN EPISODES

By far the longest-running TV sf series, which comprised 695 episodes (16 of them double-length) by the time it was put on hold at the end of 1989. Many of the two- or three-episode stories were subsequently re-edited into portmanteau "films". *Doctor Who* was originally planned as a six-part series for children, including only two stories, but it was sustained thereafter by an increasingly avid popular demand which annexed many adult viewers. This demand was initially sparked by the second three-part story, written by Terry Nation, which introduced the Daleks (and created a typecasting precedent whose impetus dragged the sf-hating Nation back to the genre time and time again). The BBC's powers-that-be attempted more than once to axe the series on grounds of cost, but the hiatus of 1989-96 always seemed likely to come to an end eventually, and the news that more stories would be made as TV movies was an inevitable capitulation.

The inconsistently eccentric but always ingenious time-travelling doctor was eventually revealed as a rogue Time Lord. This explained why he was capable of changing his appearance, so that he could be played by a whole series of actors: William Hartnell, 1963-66; Patrick Troughton, 1966-69; Jon Pertwee, 1970-74; Tom Baker, 1974-81; Peter Davison, 1982-84; Colin Baker, 1984-86; Sylvester McCoy, 1987-89; and Paul McGann from 1996 on.

Other stock characters included the doctor's equally malleable nemesis The Master, the robot dog K-9 and an intriguing series of increasingly resourceful female sidekicks. The improbably capacious TARDIS also became a curious icon of problematic escape as a result of the fact that — apart from a couple of seasons involving the Pertwee doctor which were earthbound by virtue of a parsimonious policy decision — the TV series has enjoyed an unprecedented freedom to explore the further limits of time and space. This freedom was only slightly inhibited by a drastic shortage of convenient outdoor locations, which meant that most of its future Earths and alien planets bore a suspicious resemblance to gravel pits.

This remarkable phenomenon has spun off two films, well over 100 books and a long-running monthly magazine and is still sustained in its original medium by cable and satellite reruns. Of all the characters created by TV, Doctor Who is the one who has most obviously entered the spectrum of modern mythology which includes such household names as Sherlock Holmes and Dracula. Although this status was initially confined to the UK, the show eventually followed *The Avengers* in breaking down the barriers protecting US TV from British imports.

My Favorite Martian

1963-66 • SITCOM • US (CBS) • *PRODUCER* JACK CHERTOK • *STARRING* RAY WALSTON ("UNCLE MARTIN") AND BILL BIXBY (TIM O'HARA) • *25-MIN EPISODES*

A long-running (107 episodes) comedy series in which the amiably quirky, crash-landed Martian used his various paranormal talents to create problems for his hapless host and then to sort them out. It was the prototype for such shows as *Mork And Mindy* and *A.L.F.* but was eventually outlasted by its fantasy rival *Bewitched* (1964-71).

THE BEMUSED EXPRESSION AGAIN *YOU CAN'T HAVE TOO MUCH OF A GOOD THING*

Sidekicks 2: Doctor Who

The Doctor began his career as a hobbling grandfather with a team of active sidekicks, but his later incarnations tended to be paired off with female "assistants". Although *Doctor Who* was a less sophisticated show than *The Avengers*, often settling in the early days for inactive and squeamish heroines who yelled a lot, its female leads gradually acquired more resourcefulness. Patrick Troughton remained steadfastly parental in respect of Wendy Padbury's Zoe, but the imperious John Pertwee was occasionally upstaged by the irrepressible Katy Manning as Jo, who contrived to display a stubborn disrespect in frank defiance of some of her scripts. This tendency was carried forward by Elisabeth Sladen as Sarah Jane Smith, who compensated for her slightly duller plumage with an insistent manner and quiet conviction that outlasted her original partner.

When Tom Baker brought an unprecedentedly brazen eccentricity to the character of the Doctor, he required more assertive sounding-boards. Louise Jameson as Leela rose magnificently to the task, introducing an understated but clearly manifest sexuality from which Baker inevitably drew back. Mary Tamm's Romana was subtler but still firmly adult, and there is a certain irony in the fact that it was the actress who substituted a much more pliable incarnation of the same character, Lalla Ward, with whom Baker became romantically involved. Sarah Sutton's Nyssa was certainly cute but her relationship with the Doctor was understandably half-hearted until Peter Davison took over, after which she was replaced by the calculatedly annoying Nicola Bryant as Peri. Peri survived another metamorphosis before being replaced by the even more annoying Bonnie Langford (whose irritating qualities were entirely uncalculated), but the whole operation was by now heading downhill fast. As the uncharismatic Colin Baker gave way to the even-less-charismatic Sylvester McCoy, a measure of compensation was afforded by the addition of Sophie Aldred as the ever-resourceful Ace.

 NOT-SO-SPECIAL EFFECTS TV SF'S LOW BUDGETS MEANT THAT MANY OF THE OUTER LIMITS MONSTERS WERE MORE COMICAL THAN FRIGHTENING

The Outer Limits

1963-66 • ANTHOLOGY SERIES • US (UNITED ARTISTS/ABC) • *CREATOR* LESLIE STEVENS • *50-MIN EPISODES*

Much more garish than its rival *The Twilight Zone*, this series often used its 50-minute format to produce TV versions of the monster movies which still dominated sf cinema. Among the 49 episodes, however, were a number of gems of a considerably more thoughtful nature, including significant early works by Harlan Ellison ('Soldier' and 'Demon With A Glass Hand'). Some actors who appeared in both this series and *The Twilight Zone* — including William Shatner, Leonard Nimoy and Martin Landau — acquired an association with sf which presumably encouraged their subsequent casting as sf series leads. It was not always earnest, but it was conspicuously less quirky than *The Twilight Zone* and is fondly remembered by many of its fans for that reason, even though it was rarely as slick or as deft.

1964

The Caves Of Steel

1964 • PLAY • UK (BBC2) • *DIRECTOR* PETER SASDY • *SCRIPT* BY TERRY NATION FROM ISAAC ASIMOV'S 1954 NOVEL • *STARRING* PETER CUSHING (LIJE BALEY) AND JOHN CARSON (R. DANEEL OLIVAW) • *75 MIN*

Presented only six weeks after BBC2's debut — when relatively few viewers had sets capable of receiving the new channel — this was part of a season of plays based on contemporary novels. It was repeated ten weeks later, but it never reached the kind of audience it deserved.

The Man From U.N.C.L.E.

1964-68 • SERIES • US (MGM/NBC) • *EXECUTIVE PRODUCER* NORMAN FELTON • *STARRING* ROBERT VAUGHN (NAPOLEON SOLO), DAVID MCCALLUM (ILLYA KURYAKIN) AND LEO G. CARROLL (ALEXANDER WAVERLY) • *50-MIN EPISODES*

A ground-breaking "technothriller" spy series

light-heartedly imitating the James Bond movies. Like its models, it employed a great many high-tech gadgets and other borderline sf motifs, most of which were either devised or hijacked by the agents of T.H.R.U.S.H. (Technological Hierarchy for the Removal of Undesirables and Subjugation of Humanity) and thus had to be liberated or destroyed by agents of U.N.C.L.E. (the United Network Command for Law and Enforcement). As quirky as *The Avengers* but not as surreal, it ran for 109 episodes. A fascinating period piece which still repays watching by virtue of the blithe and conspicuous refusal of everyone concerned — even the resolutely down-in-the-mouth McCallum — to take it seriously.

My Living Doll

1964-65 • SITCOM • US (CBS) • *EXECUTIVE PRODUCER* JACK CHERTOK • *STARRING* BOB CUMMINGS AND JULIE NEWMAR • *25-MIN EPISODES*

Chertok's short-lived attempt to double up the success of *My Favorite Martian* borrowed its central motif from the stage/movie farce *The Perfect Woman*, but Newmar's sexiness was less easily expressed playing a robot than it was when she became Catwoman in *Batman*.

 NAPOLEON SOLO WAS FAR TOO SEXY TO NEED A PHALLIC WEAPON, BUT IT WAS A PERK OF THE JOB

ON THE BRIDGE
RICHARD BASEHART
AND DAVID HEDISON
CONFRONT THE UNKNOWN
FROM THE RELATIVE SAFETY
OF THE STANDING SET, EVER
READY TO LURCH SIDEWAYS
IF THE DIRECTOR SHOULD
DECIDE TO WOBBLE THE
CAMERA

The Other Man

1964 • PLAY • UK (GRANADA/ITV) • *DIRECTOR* GORDON
FLEMYNG • *WRITER* GILES COOPER • *STARRING* MICHAEL
CAINE AND SIAN PHILLIPS • *140 MIN*
An alternative-world story in which Hitler,
having conquered the UK, now has British
soldiers (including Michael Caine) fighting for
him on the eastern front. Presumably inspired by
Cooper's adaptation of *When The Kissing Had To
Stop*, it worked better as drama and as political
fantasy and was by far his most significant
contribution to the genre.

Stingray

1964-65 • SERIES • UK (ATV/ITV) • *CREATORS* GERRY
AND SYLVIA ANDERSON • *25-MIN EPISODES*
Made in colour but originally transmitted in
black-and-white, the Andersons' follow-up to
Fireball XL-5 tried to be a little more serious.
The lead character was "characterized" by
making him grumpy and placing him at one
angle of a triangular relationship with his
commander's daughter and the mute Marina,
while the stories often made use of race-against-
time plots like those which were to become

central to *Thunderbirds*, but it never quite came
off. Well, it wouldn't, would it — an underwater
puppet show, for Heaven's sake!

Voyage To The Bottom Of The Sea

1964-68 • SERIES • US (20TH CENTURY FOX/ABC)
• *CREATOR* IRWIN ALLEN • *STARRING* RICHARD BASEHART
(ADMIRAL NELSON) AND DAVID HEDISON (CAPTAIN CRANE)
• *50-MIN EPISODES*
The first of several US TV sf series spun off from
a successful film. Its cheap but ingenious special
effects and cunning use of stock footage
triumphed over the technical limitations of its
model submarine and sustained it through 110
episodes. The bridgehead dramas precipitated by
melodramatic confrontations with giant sea
creatures and exotic invaders, constantly
heightened by personality differences between
Nelson and Crane, established the bare bones of
the formula followed and extrapolated by *Star
Trek*. The ever-economical Allen built one
particularly intriguing episode around footage
borrowed from his 1960 film *The Lost World*, in
which Hedison had starred.

TV formats

Because TV is a real-time medium, it is
tied to the calendar and the clock; weekly
schedules are organized around a fairly
stable structure of slots, according to a
pattern which changes with the seasons.
Even single plays are usually broadcast in
regular slots, which thus begin to blur with
"anthology series" that fit individual scripts
to a standard template. Long stories may be
broken up into serials, but these are difficult
to paste into the scheduling pattern; US TV
never took to them at all and the UK's noble
tradition of TV serials has been allowed to
fall into decay.

The ideal TV format is the potentially
infinite serial or "soap opera", which can fill
the same time-slot(s) all the year round.
Soap operas have the practical advantage of
making constant use of sets and locations;
they are equally invaluable in a cultural
sense, creating unreal neighbours for real
people to gossip about in a world where real
neighbourhoods have been consigned to the
dustbin of history.

It is almost impossible to accommodate sf
to the soap opera format, so all ambitious sf
has to make do with the next best thing: the
potentially infinite series. These use more
varied sets and locations, and thus tend to
be shot in batches, but they can be brought
back year after year for 13- or even 26-part
seasons. Half-hour sitcoms and hour-long
drama series both fall into this category,
their different lengths determined by the
fact that comedy is difficult to stretch and
drama difficult to condense ("Dying is easy,"
as the tragedian observed, "but comedy is
hard").

Sf is exceptionally difficult to adapt to
the drama-series format because of the
problems of finding enough viable locations
and constructing sets that are cheap as well
as plausible. TV sf is thus largely restricted
to those sub-species of sf which minimize
these problems, favouring shows set in the
immediate future or shows that make
continual use of fixed sets (e.g. bridgeheads
and space stations).

The use of colour-separation techniques
to set foregrounded characters against exotic
backgrounds and the increasing
sophistication of computer-generated images
is, however, reducing this dependence with
every year that passes.

1965

Lost In Space

1965-68 • SERIES • US (20TH CENTURY FOX/CBS)
• *CREATOR* IRWIN ALLEN; STARRING GUY WILLIAMS (JOHN ROBINSON), JUNE LOCKHART (MAUREEN ROBINSON) AND JONATHAN HARRIS (ZACHARY SMITH) • *50-MIN EPISODES*
Another shoestring operation by Allen which borrowed its inspiration from J. R. Wyss's *The Swiss Family Robinson* (which was itself a rip-off of *Robinson Crusoe*). It took minimalist set design to hitherto-unimaginable extremes of parsimony. The real stars — who gradually took over the show in the course of its 83 episodes — turned out to be Billy Mumy (as young Will Robinson) and the bumbling but unfailingly loyal robot; the sneaky and hypocritical Dr Smith provided an admirable foil for their contrasting brands of charming naivety.

Out Of The Unknown

1965-69 • ANTHOLOGY SERIES • UK (BBC2)
• *PRODUCERS* IRENE SHUBIK (SEASONS 1 & 2) AND ALAN BROMLY (SEASON 3) • *50-MIN EPISODES*
Out Of The Unknown took up exactly where

Shubik's pioneering ITV show *Out Of This World* had left off. As before, the adaptations of stories by John Wyndham, Isaac Asimov, John Brunner, J. G. Ballard and others were conspicuously better than the occasional original scripts, but the overall standard was excellent. The second

12-episode series was weaker, but the third — which included a follow-up to BBC2's version of *The Caves Of Steel* in dramatizing Asimov's sequel, *The Naked Sun* (1957) — was as strong as the first in spite of recycling some scripts already used in the ITV series. A fourth series produced by Bromly and aired in 1971 was not sf, save for a couple of marginal horror/sf tales, the rest being straightforward occult fiction. The change of policy was presumably a response to the relatively large budgets required for sf set construction; it failed to save the show.

Thunderbirds

1965-66 • SERIES • UK (ATV/ITV) • *CREATORS* GERRY AND SYLVIA ANDERSON • *50-MIN EPISODES*
The Andersons had developed their "SuperMarionation" puppets through several generations — including those showcased in the sf productions *Supercar* (1961-62), *Fireball XL-5* and *Stingray* — before launching this pioneering show in a longer format, which still stands as the peak achievement of their long careers. Its 32 episodes were gripping enough to retain a cult following long after it ceased transmission,

and to hook a new generation of juvenile viewers when it was re-aired in the early 1990s. The Tracy family's fleet of futuristic vehicles are involved in a whole series of last-minute rescues, which milk the strategy of plot/counterplot scene-switches to the limit. The International Rescue organization's London contact-person Lady Penelope and her butler Parker were frequently put at risk in order to provide the secondary plot-thread whenever the Tracy brothers couldn't find enough distracting troubles of their own. Great fun, in spite of the dogged insistence on trying to prove that it is possible do plausible underwater scenes with puppets.

The Wild, Wild West

1965-69 • SERIES • US (CBS) • *EXECUTIVE PRODUCER* MICHAEL GARRISON • STARRING ROBERT CONRAD (JAMES T. WEST) AND ROSS MARTIN • *50-MIN EPISODES*
A bizarre combination of Western and tongue-in-cheek spy drama which took the technothriller back in time to the 19th century. It was a surprise hit, eventually extending to 104 oft-repeated episodes and helping to inspire such B-movies as *Billy The Kid Vs. Dracula* and *Jesse James Meets Frankenstein's Daughter* (both 1966). Michael Dunn turned up frequently in the key role of diminutive superscientist Dr Miguelito Loveless, who had a colossal chip on his shoulder because it was too close to the ground. Hurd Hatfield reprised his portrayal of Dorian Gray in one memorable episode.

1966

Adam Adamant Lives!

1966-67 • SERIES • UK (BBC) • *PRODUCER* VERITY LAMBERT • *STARRING* GERALD HARPER (ADAM ADAMANT), JULIET HARMER (GEORGINA) AND PETER DUCROW (THE FACE) • *50-MIN EPISODES*
The BBC's attempt to hijack some of the eccentric glamour of *The Avengers* (along with script editor Tony Williamson) took the dandy & damsel formula to a new extreme, importing an icebound Edwardian adventurer to play opposite a Swinging Sixties heroine. A second series,

which extended the total number of episodes to 29, brought back Adamant's old enemy to save the bother of providing a whole series of villains.

Ape And Essence

1966 • PLAY • UK (BBC) • DIRECTOR DAVID BENEDICTUS • *SCRIPT* BY JOHN FINCH FROM ALDOUS HUXLEY'S 1948

NOVEL • *STARRING* ALEC McCOWEN • *75 MIN*
A botany professor investigating post-holocaust Britain finds worshippers of Belial indulging in orgiastic rites and offering radiation-damaged babies as human sacrifices. It couldn't possibly be deemed to be in bad taste because it was based on a book by the ultra-respectable Aldous Huxley — that's what they claimed, anyway.

Batman

1966-68 • SERIES • US (20TH CENTURY FOX/ABC) • *STARRING* ADAM WEST (BATMAN) AND BURT WARD (ROBIN) • *30-MIN EPISODES*
TV's *Batman* borrowed its tongue-in-cheek tone from *The Man From U.N.C.L.E.* and then multiplied it by ten, going so far over the top as to enter telly incognita. Guest villains like Burgess Meredith (Penguin), Cesar Romero (Joker), Frank Gorshin (Riddler), Vincent Price (Egghead) and Victor Buono (King Tut) revelled in the supercharged hamminess — even Liberace

Sidekicks 3: unhuman sidekicks

Females make ideal sidekicks for macho male heroes because a certain amount of sexual tension can be built into their permanently unconsummated relationships. When male heroes have male sidekicks, this tension tends to be substituted by some other kind of marked difference, whose extremity serves the double function of allowing them to supplement their own resources and emphasizing that no homosexual element is involved in their constant association. Thus, the Lone Ranger had Tonto; the Green Hornet had Kato; Batman had Robin and practically every white cop in the US media nowadays has a black partner.

Sf facilitates the further extension of this formula, although the inconvenience of kitting out a regular subsidiary character in unhuman make-up deterred TV producers from adopting the motif within a regular series. With the notable exception of the BBC's adaptations of Isaac Asimov's Lije Baley/R. Daneel Olivaw stories, the additional scope remained untapped by TV until *Star Trek* showed what might be done with such pairings. Although Kirk and Spock operate within the context of a larger team, they often function as a hero/sidekick team in which Spock's supposed emotionlessness provides a useful foil for Kirk's supposed gallantry. Similar tensions are replicated in the show's clones.

The cop/robot sitcom *Holmes And Yoyo* never got off the ground, and neither did the cop/hologram drama *Automan*; it was the cinematic spin-off *Alien Nation* which finally took the plunge, presenting a perfectly straightforward (and hence rather parodic) version of a cop/alien pairing. There will surely be more to come.

did a turn as Fingers — and Julie Newmar (Catwoman, until replaced by Eartha Kitt) was magnificent. The plots rarely deployed sf motifs and the standard gadgets were as simple as the "special effects" (e.g. turning the camera sideways whenever Batman and Robin had to haul themselves up a wall). The way-out style gave the show cult status in the gay community; kids loved it too.

Days To Come

1966 • PLAY • UK (BBC) • *DIRECTOR* ALAN BRIDGES • *SCRIPT* BY KEN TAYLOR FROM 'A STORY OF THE DAYS TO COME' (1897) BY H. G. WELLS • *STARRING* DINSDALE LANDEN AND JUDI DENCH • *95 MIN*

This earnest play about exaggerated social divisions in the distant future inevitably looked dated (as much by its borrowings from Huxley's *Brave New World* as its strictly Wellsian content), but it was saved from absurdity by the sterling efforts of its leading actors.

The Master

1966 • SIX-PART SERIAL • UK (SOUTHERN/ITV) • *PRODUCER* JOHN BRAYBON; SCRIPT BY ROSEMARY HILL, BASED ON T. H. WHITE'S 1957 NOVEL • *STARRING* PAUL GUESS (NICKY), ADRIENNE POSTA AND OLAF POOLEY • *25-MIN EPISODES*

A 157-year-old paranormally talented evil genius living in secret on the island of Rockall plans to take over the world, but one of his chosen instruments — a boy named Nicky — rebels against him and confounds his schemes. The serial's relatively big budget was justified by its popularity with the juvenile audience, but the well-written script could not quite redeem the bitterly jaundiced plot, which reflected the ageing T. H. White's gloomy outlook.

Star Trek

1966-69 • SERIES • US (NBC) • *CREATOR* GENE RODDENBERRY • *STARRING* WILLIAM SHATNER (CAPTAIN KIRK), LEONARD NIMOY (SPOCK), DeFORREST KELLEY (DR McCOY) AND JAMES DOOHAN (MR SCOTT) • *50-MIN EPISODES*

The show which, for better or for worse, became the primary force shaping the future of the sf genre from the 1970s to the 1990s. The network never realized what a prize it had and axed the show after three seasons (79 episodes in all), having severely restricted its budget for seasons two and three. The show has been rerun constantly since its demise, spinning off a series of films, hundreds of books, mountains of merchandise and three more TV series in the meantime. Roddenberry's vaulting ambition — which initially extended to hiring top-flight sf writers like Theodore Sturgeon, Harlan Ellison and Norman Spinrad to write scripts for him — was gradually reined in by the network, so that the show had perforce to become a vacuous version of *Voyage To The Bottom Of The Sea*, but its cult following grew almost to the magnitude of a world religion and its stars seemingly began to believe (belatedly, in Nimoy's case) that they might indeed be divinely inspired prophets. In spite of the intellectual poverty of many of its plots and the dogged refusal of most of its scriptwriters to investigate the actual meaning of the word "rational", the series eventually made imaginative captives of millions of fervent adherents. The rapid escalation of *Star Trek* fandom initially excited sf writers, who thought that it would recruit legions of new readers to the genre but it didn't; instead, the wider genre was slowly consumed and almost swamped by *Star Trek* spin-offs and *Star Trek* clones.

It is now obvious that *Star Trek*'s strength derived from the way that relationships between the leading characters were developed with soap-operatic intensity. As well as making Kirk and Spock into household names, this allowed the initially tokenistic involvement of ethnic minorities — ably represented by Nichelle Nicholls as Lt Uhura and George Takei as Mr Sulu — to take on considerable significance, simply because their full integration into the claustrophobic web of fervent loyalties was so completely taken for granted. Almost by accident (although Roddenberry certainly had a dream of sorts and insisted on his players acting as a well-knit team), the *Enterprise* became the flagship of a vision of a multi-cultural future which had already ironed out all but a few of the political difficulties associated with multi-culturalism. The show continued to strike chords as the Vietnam War lurched to its ignominious end and the Cold War expired, providing an isolated and supposedly "objective" arena in which difficult issues could occasionally be aired.

Star Trek's plots relied far too heavily on cheap special effects, which generally took the

form of mysterious forces shaking the set and disturbing invaders in minimal make-up. The crew only got to grips with authentically tough moral problems in rare episodes such as Harlan Ellison's 'The City On The Edge Of Forever', but the fact that they were doing it at all proved to be far more important than the fact that they weren't doing it very well. Taken one at a time, all but a handful of the episodes were puerile, but the background images which held more-or-less constant throughout were astonishingly powerful.

Star Trek's belated success helped to convince TV executives and book editors that sf could (and should) become a sub-species of soap opera, but it also showed them new ways in which moralistic fantasy disguised as sf could serve the American Dream. Star Trek was more than a TV show, it was a crusade.

The Time Tunnel

1966-67 • SERIES • US (20TH CENTURY FOX/ABC) • *CREATOR* IRWIN ALLEN • *STARRING* JAMES DARREN AND ROBERT COLBERT • *50-MIN EPISODES*

This time-hopping series visited more well-known historical settings than futures, but

THE CREW OF THE ENTERPRISE *IN FUTURE PARAMILITARY ORGANIZATIONS ROUND SHOULDERS WILL NOT PREVENT A MAN RISING TO THE RANK OF CAPTAIN AND NO ONE WILL EVER STAND TO ATTENTION*

foundered on its budgetary limitations as well as its lack of a ready-made plot-formula, thus prompting the makers of Quantum Leap to restrict their hero's time-hopping to the recent past and steal the plot formula from Highway To Heaven. It never had the verve or gloss of Doctor Who.

hero is hijacked was an inspired one; the decor and the costumes gave the show a stylishness which immediately set it apart from all others.

The carefully deceptive plots of the individual episodes strike a good balance between suspense and intrigue, and the balloon-like guardians which constantly thwart Number 6's escape attempts are eerily effective. McGoohan is excellent in the leading role, radiating paranoia as he makes glancing contact with a whole series of first-rate guest stars. The two-part climax of the 17-episode series, written by McGoohan and co-starring Leo McKern as the last of the ever-changing Number 2s, provides a fittingly enigmatic and superbly melodramatic conclusion which is worth viewing more than once.

The Prisoner inevitably became a cult classic, securing the loyalty of a fervent coterie of admirers for 30 years until belated re-runs and video releases vitalized the interest of a whole new audience in the 1990s. The sf devices may appear to be marginal but they are vital to the construction of the imaginary edifice. *The Prisoner* remains the most sophisticated sf ever cast in TV series format, although sf purists might not consider it sufficiently wholehearted in its science-fictionality to qualify as the best.

1967

The Invaders

1967-68 • SERIES • US (ABC) • *EXECUTIVE PRODUCER* QUINN MARTIN • *STARRING* ROY THINNES (DAVID VINCENT) • *50-MIN EPISODES*

Quinn Martin also produced *The Fugitive*, and this show uses a similar "unending chase" scenario, hyping up the paranoia with a ubiquitous alien enemy whose agents always disappeared when killed, thus leaving no evidential traces to back up Vincent's story. The absurd revelatory device of the rigid little finger eventually wore thin and the over-contrived secret invasion scenario was a wasting asset, but the tension held up for 43 episodes. Re-runs of the show were never successful enough to

qualify it as a cult hit, but they maintained enough interest to justify the making of a two-part mini-series revamping the basic plot, which was aired in 1995.

The Prisoner

1967-68 • SERIES • UK (ATV/ITV) • *STARRING* PATRICK MCGOOHAN (NUMBER 6) • *50-MIN EPISODES*
This surreal spin-off of McGoohan's Danger Man series was largely the creation of the actor, script consultant George Markstein and producer David Tomblin, who were presumably inspired by the desire to outdo *The Avengers* in taking TV surrealism to unprecedented extremes. The choice of Clough Williams-Ellis's model village of Portmeirion in Wales as a setting for the strangely well-mannered dystopia into which the

1968

Land Of The Giants

1968-70 • SERIES • US (20TH CENTURY FOX/ABC) • *CREATOR* IRWIN ALLEN • *STARRING* GARY CONWAY AND DON MARSHALL • *50-MIN EPISODES*
The Irwin Allen sf series with the biggest budget, employing all the tricks of the trade to chronicle the adventures of a group of space travellers on a plant designed after the fashion of Gulliver's Brobdingnag. Once the gamut of obvious devices had been run, the show became increasingly desperate for plot-lines, but it did well to last 51 episodes.

The Year Of The Sex Olympics

1968 • PLAY • UK (BBC2) • *DIRECTOR* MICHAEL ELLIOTT • *WRITER* NIGEL KNEALE • *STARRING* LEONARD

A **VICTIM FOR OUR TIMES** *The Prisoner learned the second most important lesson: Their monstrousness may be exhibited in strange and sneaky ways*

Rossiter and Suzanne Neve • **105 min**

Quatermass writer Nigel Kneale demonstrated his lack of versatility with this satire on the pervasiveness of TV which was soon overtaken by events. Unfortunately, actual "fly on the wall" studies of "real life" are much less dramatic than the one featured here, which features more violence than sex. Kneale's subsequent futuristic TV play about voluntary euthanasia, 'Wine Of India' (1970), was much more realistic.

1969

Counterstrike

1969 • SERIES • UK (BBC) • *CREATOR* TONY WILLIAMSON • *STARRING* JON FINCH • *50-MIN EPISODES*

Williamson, who had worked on *The Avengers* and provided the premise of *Adam Adamant Lives*, presumably modelled this particular brainchild on *The Invaders*, but could not generate the same paranoia with a hero who was secretly an intergalactic agent.

It was unfortunately made in monochrome just as BBC1 was about to burst into colour; and only nine of its ten episodes were deemed worthy of airing.

1970

The Adventures Of Don Quick

1970 • SERIES • UK (LWT/ITV) • *STARRING* IAN HENDRY AND RONALD LACEY • *50-MIN EPISODES*

This Don Quixote-in-space satire, a distant

precursor of *Red Dwarf*, might be reckoned to have been ahead of its time, but it was slow and flaccid and nobody regretted its loss when it sank without trace after six episodes.

Doomwatch

1970-72 • SERIES • UK (BBC) • *CREATORS* KIT PEDLER AND GERRY DAVIS; *STARRING* JOHN PAUL (SPENCER QUIST), SIMON OATES (JOHN RIDGE) AND ROBERT POWELL (TOBY WREN) • *50-MIN EPISODES*

A ground-breaking exercise, attempting to address serious practical and moral issues raised by contemporary developments in cutting-edge science, especially genetic engineering. Pedler and Davis seized upon the anxieties popularized by such alarmist bestsellers as Gordon Rattray Taylor's *The Biological Time-Bomb* (1968) and dramatized the issues raised therein. Like the US show *Men into Space*, it traded on its "quasi-documentary" realism, but, while that show was a celebration of man's conquest of space, *Doomwatch* was a fearful examination of technologies which threatened to run out of control and the supposed irresponsibility of the scientists and industrialists pursuing such research. In this sense, it was a forerunner of such shows as *The X-Files*, although it was much more rigorous in its choice of subjects.

Perhaps surprisingly, *Doomwatch* was a

NOT JUST A PRETTY FACE *As with so many* TV *shows promoted to the big screen, the* Doomwatch *formula was ill-fitted to the cinema screen.*

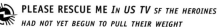
PLEASE RESCUE ME *In US TV SF the heroines had not yet begun to pull their weight*

popular success and it added the notion of a "doomwatch scenario" to the vocabulary of British politics, but the serious intent of its early episodes was soon compromised by the production team's insistence on cranking up the melodramatic component. The show made a star of Robert Powell, who quit the series at the end of season one, and celebrities out of Pedler and Davis, who left at the end of season two. Simon Oates also absented himself from most of season three, so the show was a pale shadow of its former self by the time it reached its 37th and last episode. Opinions varied as to the prescience of its warnings, but it provided the framework and set the tone for British TV's subsequent handling of the possibilities of biotechnology.

Hauser's Memory

1970 • TV MOVIE • US (UNIVERSAL/NBC) • *DIRECTOR* BORIS SAGAL • *SCRIPT* BY ADRIAN SPIES FROM CURT SIODMAK'S 1968 NOVEL • *STARRING* DAVID MCCALLUM AND SUSAN STRASBERG • *96 MIN*
Siodmak's belated "sequel" to the thrice-filmed

Donovan's Brain (1943) merely recast the plot, which involves a dead man's mind reaching out to control the living. The new version replaced the brain-in-a-tank with injected DNA, which made the scenario more plausible but less visually interesting.

The Immortal

1970-71 • SERIES • US (PARAMOUNT/ABC) • *EXECUTIVE PRODUCER* TONY WILSON • *STARRING* CHRISTOPHER GEORGE (BEN RICHARDS) • *75-MIN PILOT & 50-MIN EPISODES*
The theme of this potentially interesting series was borrowed from James Gunn's fix-up novel *The Immortals* (1962), in which people whose rare blood-type renders them immune to ageing become the prey of the rich. In the pilot, Ben Richards is imprisoned and regularly "milked" of his precious blood, but he escapes and sets off to find his brother, who may or may not share his gift. The subsequent series employed the standardized "running man" formula, but it

failed to build up much paranoid charge and folded after 15 episodes, most of which had little or no sf content save for the initial premise.

Timeslip

1970-71 • CYCLE OF SERIALS • UK (ATV/ITV) • *SCRIPT EDITOR* RUTH BOSWELL • *STARRING* SPENCER BANKS (SIMON) AND CHERYL BURFIELD (LIZ) • *30-MIN EPISODES*
The 26 episodes of this children's series encompassed four stories in which the young heroes shuttle back and forth from their own 1970/71 to 1940, to 1990 (twice) and into their own recent past of 1965. The plot-lines involved a pivotal moment in World War II, a near-future climatic catastrophe and cloning. Earnest and ingenious, the series reflected the rapid sophistication which had overtaken juvenile sf in the 1960s and paved the way for similarly intelligent and interesting experiments.

UFO

1970-73 • SERIES • UK (ATV/ITV) • *CREATORS* GERRY AND SYLVIA ANDERSON • *STARRING* ED BISHOP (COMMANDER STRAKER), GEORGE SEWELL (COLONEL FREEMAN) AND GABRIELLE DRAKE • *50-MIN EPISODES*
SuperMarionation having reached its limits in *Captain Scarlet And The Mysterons* (1967-68), the Andersons juxtaposed real actors with their elaborate models. Although an attempt was made to make the alien menace plots a little more sophisticated than those involving Captain Scarlet, they remained conspicuously old-fashioned by comparison with overtly juvenile material like *Timeslip*. The models, which had not seemed out of place in a puppet show, looked unconvincing in association with real people, and unkind critics reckoned that Bishop was even more wooden in person than he had been as the voice of Captain Scarlet's sidekick Captain Blue. When the first 26-episode season ended, some preparatory work was done on a second; when that was aborted, the material was cannibalized for a new show: *Space: 1999*.

OPEN SESAME *The gull-winged door of the De Lorean sportscar never caught on in real life but looked good in sf*

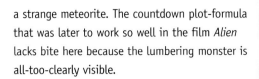

1971

The Guardians

1971 • SERIAL-CUM-SERIES • UK (LWT/ITV) • *CREATOR* VINCENT TILSLEY • *STARRING* JOHN COLLIN AND GWYNETH POWELL • *50-MIN EPISODES*

Political fantasy, much of which was written by novelist John Bowen. In the wake of a general strike, Britain becomes a police state in which the brutal Guardians of the Realm are opposed by a loose-knit resistance movement of woolly liberals who call themselves "Quarmbys" after their probably-imaginary leader. Ironically, the 13-week series was interrupted by a broadcasting strike; Ulster TV refused to show it at all lest the Guardians remind anyone of the B-specials, a notorious auxiliary police force which was drafted in to suppress the nationalists in Northern Ireland.

The Last Child

1971 • TV MOVIE • US • *DIRECTOR* JOHN LLEWELLYN MOXEY • *STARRING* MICHAEL COLE, JANET MARGOLIN AND VAN HEFLIN • *73 MIN*

A near-future drama in which the USA adopts a one-child-per-family statute like the one applied in Communist China; a couple threatened with imprisonment under the new law flees to

Canada. An intriguing political fantasy cautiously toying with contemporary anxieties about the population explosion.

The People

1971 • TV MOVIE • US (METROMEDIA) • *DIRECTOR* JOHN KORTY • *SCRIPT* BY JAMES M. MILLER FROM ZENNA HENDERSON'S STORY SERIES BEGUN WITH 'ARARAT' (1952) • *STARRING* KIM DARBY AND DAN O'HERLIHY • *74 MIN*

A young female teacher goes to work in a remote area and discovers that her children are the paranormally talented offspring of stranded aliens — who are, on average, somewhat nicer than human beings. The careful understatement of the originals hardly recommended them for TV, but the saccharine sentimentality was pure Waltons; even so, the pilot was never followed up.

1972

Killdozer

1972 • TV MOVIE • US (UNIVERSAL) • *DIRECTOR* JERRY LONDON • *SCRIPT* BY ED MACKILLOP FROM THEODORE STURGEON'S 1944 STORY • *STARRING* CLINT WALKER • *74 MIN*

Construction workers on a Pacific island are picked off by a homicidal bulldozer animated by

a strange meteorite. The countdown plot-formula that was later to work so well in the film *Alien* lacks bite here because the lumbering monster is all-too-clearly visible.

The Stone Tape

1972 • PLAY • UK (BBC2) • *DIRECTOR* PETER SASDY • *WRITER* NIGEL KNEALE • *STARRING* JANE ASHER, MICHAEL BRYANT AND IAIN CUTHBERTSON • *90 MIN*

An effective borderline sf/occult thriller in which modern technology is employed to "exorcise" a ghost by a process analogous to erasing a tape. The plot hinges on the fact that the process is only half-successful, because there are even nastier layers of psychic residue lurking beneath the first. This sets up a suspenseful climax whose eerie special effects are aided by an uncharacteristically intense performance from Jane Asher. Easily Kneale's best work, recapturing the element of suspense which made the first three Quatermass serials so disturbing.

1973

Frankenstein: The True Story

1973 • MINI-SERIES • US (UNIVERSAL/NBC) • *DIRECTOR* JACK SMIGHT • *SCRIPT* BY CHRISTOPHER ISHERWOOD AND DON BACARDY BASED ON MARY SHELLEY'S 1818 NOVEL • *STARRING* LEONARD WHITING (FRANKENSTEIN), MICHAEL SARRAZIN (THE MONSTER) AND JANE SEYMOUR (ELIZABETH) • *200 MIN* (CUT TO 123 MIN FOR THEATRE RELEASE)

The first sf mini-series used a highly prestigious scriptwriter and lined up a series of cameo performances by the likes of James Mason, John Gielgud and Agnes Moorehead, but its attempts to fill the available time with melodramatic embellishments to the plot led it sadly astray and it ended up as a weak combination of the overfamiliar and the unnecessary.

Genesis II

1973 • TV MOVIE • US • *CREATOR* GENE RODDENBERRY • *STARRING* ALEX CORD, MARIETTA HARTLEY AND PERCY RODRIGUES • *97 MIN*

After the holocaust, human society has fragmented into primitive enclaves, but an ancient high-tech transport system still works well enough to whisk the hero back and forth on what was intended to be the beginning of a long mission. The series was aborted, leaving this pilot to stand uncomfortably on its own dubious merits.

Moonbase 3

1973 • SERIES • UK (BBC) • *PRODUCER* BARRY LETTS • *STARRING* DONALD HOUSTON AND RALPH BATES • *30-MIN EPISODES*

Then-fashionable TV journalist James Burke was credited as "scientific adviser" to this attempt at near-future realism, which avoided melodrama so scrupulously as to become a tedious and

eccentric study in the psychology of confinement. It only lasted six episodes but still seemed overextended.

The Six Million Dollar Man

1973-78 • SERIES • US (UNIVERSAL/ABC) • *STARRING* LEE MAJORS (STEVE AUSTIN) • *THREE 90-MIN TV MOVIES, THEN 50-MIN EPISODES*

Based on Michael Caidin's novel *Cyborg* (1972), *The Six Million Dollar Man* took up where *Mission Impossible* (1966-72) left off and sparked off a long series of "enhanced secret agent" dramas. The "rebuilt" Steve Austin is employed by a

 SAY CHEESE *YOUR AVERAGE TV SF HERO OFTEN FINDS HIMSELF IN SITUATIONS WHERE IT REALLY ISN'T EASY TO RAISE A SMILE*

clandestine government organization to carry out an infinite series of Herculean tasks, thwarting hapless criminals and spies Superman-fashion. Glen Larson, who worked on the show, went on to create *Knight Rider* (1982-86), *Manimal* (1983) and *Automan* (1983-84) in the same image, while his colleague Harve Bennett went on to do *The Invisible Man*. The formula worked well enough to sustain Austin's bionic legs, arm and eye through 100 episodes in addition to the three pilot "movies".

The real triumph of *The Six Million Dollar Man* was to demonstrate that no matter how implausible the devices were (no-one who understood the principle of leverage could have believed in Austin's super-powerful arm) and in spite of the fact that they had been parodied in advance by *The Man From U.N.C.L.E.*, such shows could be played in a perfectly straightfaced and unapologetic fashion.

The Starlost

1973 • SERIES • CANADA (CTV) • *EXECUTIVE PRODUCERS* DOUGLAS TRUMBULL AND JERRY ZEITMAN • *STARRING* KEIR DULLEA • *50-MIN EPISODES*

The show that secured Harlan Ellison's reputation as an *enfant terrible sans pareil*; his scheme for a series set aboard a generation starship was so comprehensively ruined by the production team that he took his name off it (substituting his derisive pseudonym Cordwainer Bird) and then won an award for the launch-script they wouldn't use. Scientific adviser Ben Bova also turned the bad experience to good use in his parodic novel *The Starcrossed* (1975), while the show itself fell apart ignominiously.

The Tomorrow People

1973-79 • CYCLE OF SERIALS • UK (THAMES/ITV) • *CREATOR* ROGER PRICE • *STARRING* NICHOLAS YOUNG (JOHN), PETER VAUGHAN-CLARKE (STEPHEN), ELIZABETH ADARE (ELIZABETH) AND PHILIP GILBERT (VOICE OF TIM) • *30-MIN EPISODES*

Ruth Boswell, who had been the prime mover of *Timeslip*, was the first producer of this even more daring follow-up. The series offered a sympathetic account of a group of emergent

 THE TOMORROW PEOPLE

EVERY GENERATION INHERITS THE EARTH FROM ITS PARENTS AND HOLDS IT IN TRUST FOR ITS CHILDREN, WHO WILL HOPEFULLY BE BETTER EQUIPPED FOR THE JOB

the "running man" plot-formula — a variant which was to become increasingly common in sf series, although this particular application was folded mid-season after 14 episodes.

1975

The Changes

1975 • 10-PART SERIAL • UK (BBC) • *DIRECTOR* JOHN PROWSE • *SCRIPT* BY ANNA HOME FROM PETER DICKINSON'S TRILOGY (1968-71) • *STARRING* VICKY WILLIAMS AND KEITH ASHTON • *25-MIN EPISODES*

This serial was the first of several notable adaptations which aspired, in typical BBC fashion, to a greater dignity than such ITV shows as *The Tomorrow People*. The post-catastrophe scenario, in which users of machinery are hounded by witch-hunters, is eventually explained by a device which is more occult than sf, but the anti-superstitious theme places it on the borderline and Home's adaptation of Dickinson's well-written novels is sensitive and artful.

The Invisible Man

1975-76 • SERIES • US (UNIVERSAL/NBC) • *EXECUTIVE PRODUCER* HARVE BENNETT • *STARRING* DAVID MCCALLUM

superchildren who employ their paranormal powers to the care and protection of their kind and to the thwarting of various alien menaces. Its eight seasons each comprised two or three serials of two to five parts — a formula established by the BBC's *Doctor Who*, to which this was ITV's answer. Unfortunately, it declined from a promising beginning and the later seasons, when the show's original creators had abandoned it to the care of producer Vic Hughes, tended to be played for laughs. This was a sad decline for a series whose initial concept took more productive inspiration from classic written sf (including Wilmar Shiras's *The Children Of The Atom* and Alfred Bester's *The Stars My Destination*) than TV sf for adults ever did.

McDowall recreating his role as the friendly intellectual ape who befriends two stranded spacemen. The satirical element is further watered down by the use of a group variant of

 LOOK DOWN IN ANGER *IF YOU CAN'T SEE YOUR OWN TOES YOU'RE EITHER TOO FAT OR TRAPPED IN A TV SF SHOW*

1974

Planet Of The Apes

1974 • SERIES • US (20TH CENTURY FOX/CBS) • *EXECUTIVE PRODUCER* HERBERT HIRSCHMAN • *STARRING* RODDY MCDOWALL (GALEN) • *50-MIN EPISODES*

Spin-off from the successful series of movies based on Pierre Boulle's 1963 novel, with

Kitsch classics

Kitsch is a German word used to refer to artefacts which aspire to be works of art but manifest rank bad taste. Such judgments are, however, a matter of taste in themselves, and people who like items which other people consider to be kitsch are perfectly entitled to justify their affection.

The simple assertion that "I don't know anything about art but I know what I like" is a rather ineffective reply, because people who have defined their own taste as good will simply consider it evidence of stupidity and conclusive proof of the accuracy of their judgment. A cleverer defence is to claim that one's liking is "ironic" — i.e., that there are some bad things which become good because their badness is really a witty comment on the essential nature of badness, and hence on the essential nature of goodness. This defence works because people with good taste never like to be caught with their avant-garde down and are always vulnerable to confusion if struck with a nifty paradox. The only problem is that one then has to separate the "bad" stuff which is merely bad from the "bad" stuff which only appears to be bad because it is exploring the outer limits of "badness". Mercifully, it is usually obvious which is which.

Almost all TV sf is bad, partly by virtue of the limits of the medium, partly because of the limitations of its plot-formulas and partly because it is mostly written and produced by people with atrophied imaginations and little capacity for rational analysis. One must, however, always be careful to distinguish the merely bad (e.g. *Space: 1999* or *Automan*) from the sublimely bad (e.g. *The Wild, Wild West* or *Star Maidens*). Otherwise, there wouldn't be much point in watching TV sf at all, would there?

AAAAARGH! *All writers of* TV *sf need to master this useful item of dialogue; more as can be added if necessary*

(REPLACED BY BEN MURPHY WHEN THE SERIES WAS REVAMPED AS *THE GEMINI MAN*) • *TWO 75-MIN PILOTS PLUS 50-MIN EPISODES*
A doggedly formularistic enhanced secret agent series in which a scientist who turns himself invisible is quickly recruited to the usual villain-thwarting routine by the customary clandestine government agency. The first version survived 12 episodes, the second only lasted five although 11 had been shot. Evidence of TV executives'

utter inability to judge the moment when one old saw ("If it works, milk it to death") gives way to another ("It's no use flogging a dead horse").

Space: 1999

1975-77 • SERIES • UK (ITC/ITV) • *CREATORS* GERRY AND SYLVIA ANDERSON • *STARRING* MARTIN LANDAU, BARBARA BAIN AND BARRY MORSE • *50-MIN EPISODES*
Using models rescued from the wreckage of the series *UFO*, Gerry and Sylvia Anderson attempted an imitation of *Star Trek* which succeeded in running for two seasons (48 episodes) despite labouring under the terrible handicap of using the moon (or at least a fragment thereof) as an improbably fast-moving space vehicle. The scripts collaborated with this absurd device in setting new standards of scientific illiteracy, and the ultra-cheap special effects led British fans to dub it 'Space Nineteen and Ninepence', but success in the US kept the show going.

Although Landau, Bain and Morse were all competent actors who had done good work on other shows, *Space: 1999*'s scripts gave them no chance to conjure up credible performances and,

at times, they seemed hilariously incompetent as they soldiered on bravely against the odds. The combination of atrocities was almost bad enough to qualify the show as a kitsch classic, but its real achievement was to make *Star Trek* seem sophisticated by comparison.

Survivors

1975-77 • SERIES • UK (BBC) • *CREATOR* TERRY NATION • *STARRING* CAROLYN SEYMOUR, IAN MCCULLOCH, DENNIS LILL AND LUCY FLEMING • *50-MIN EPISODES*
An adaptation of the typical British post-catastrophe story, as popularized by John Wyndham and John Christopher. In the aftermath of a great plague, a few thousand survivors struggle to preserve what they can of the physical and moral apparatus of civilization. Middle-class decency and quasi-aristocratic stiff upper lips bravely maintain their historical alliance in the face of the awful menace posed by oiks, survivalists and stray dogs.

Seymour left after season one to pursue a career in Hollywood, leaving Fleming to move up to female lead, while McCulloch drifted away during series two to be replaced by Lill; the resultant continuity problems compounded the difficulties caused by dwindling imaginative resources and the series ground to a halt after 38 episodes, but the early episodes artfully reproduced the paranoid class prejudice and desperate fear of material loss that had made Wyndham so popular among earnestly respectable folk in the 1950s.

Wonder Woman

1975-79 • SERIES • US (WARNER/ABC/CBS) • *STARRING* LYNDA CARTER • *100-MIN PILOT PLUS 50-MIN EPISODES*

An earlier 1974 pilot starring Cathy Lee Crosby had flopped, so a new one was shot with the more voluptuous non-actress Carter in the lead. The story adapted the comic-book character to the fashionable "enhanced secret agent" plot formula. The ABC pilot and series billed as *The New Original Wonder Woman* was set during World War II, but when CBS took over they relocated it in the present and called it *The New Adventures Of Wonder Woman*, innocently emphasizing its total lack of originality. Although the magic amazon from Paradise Island hardly qualifies as an sf device, most of her adversaries did.

1976

The Bionic Woman

1976-78 • SERIES • US (UNIVERSAL/ABC) • *CREATOR* HARVE BENNETT • *STARRING* LINDSAY WAGNER • *50-MIN EPISODES*

A straightforward imitation of *The Six Million Dollar Man*, featuring Steve Austin's old girl-friend and a bionic dog. The enhanced secret agent plot formula was occasionally enlivened by alien intruders but otherwise lurched along the usual tired track. Wagner, the show's only redeeming feature, had sufficient charm to keep it going for three seasons (57 episodes in all).

Holmes And Yoyo

1976 • SITCOM • US (UNIVERSAL/NBC) • *EXECUTIVE PRODUCER* LEONARD STERN • *STARRING* RICHARD B. SCHULL AND JOHN SCHUCK • *25-MIN EPISODES*

A cop is partnered with a robot so that all the hoariest mechanical malfunction jokes can be given another run around the block. The idea had been floated in the TV movie *Future Cop* starring Ernest Borgnine and Michael Shannon,

which was comedy drama of a more ambitious stripe, but it is understandable that neither of the stars wanted to stick around for the stripped-down series, which was laid to rest after a 13-episode season.

Into Infinity

1976 • PLAY • US (NBC) • *PRODUCER* GERRY ANDERSON • *WRITER* JOHNNY BYRNE • *STARRING* BRIAN BLESSED, JOANNA DUNHAM AND MARTIN LEV • *52 MIN*

This putative series-pilot dramatizing relativity theory in terms of its time-dilating effects on a family of space-travellers was made for an educational show called *The Day After Tomorrow*. It benefited from a generous budget which allowed Anderson to use better special effects than usual, but the didactically inclined script failed to make a persuasive case for further development. This might or might not help to explain why the scripts Byrne wrote for *Space: 1999* were so determinedly silly.

Star Maidens

1976 • SERIAL-CUM-SERIES • GERMANY/UK (STV/ITV IN UK) • *PRODUCER* JAMES GATWARD • *STARRING* JUDY GEESON, DAWN ADDAMS, LISA HARROW, CHRISTIANE KRUGER, CHRISTIAN QUADFLIEG AND GARETH THOMAS • *30-MIN. EPISODES*

An expensive co-production with a star-studded cast, designed for multi-national syndication. Two males escape from the female-dominated world of Mendusa and flee to Earth, which seems to them to be a kind of paradise. Their pursuers, understandably puzzled by human society, pick up a couple of local specimens — who face as much culture-shock on Mendusa as the escapees do on Earth. *Star Maidens* was a flop, but its highly skilled over-actors succeeded where *Space: 1999*'s cast had failed in creating a kinky kitsch classic. Kruger was magnificent as the svelte security-chief Octavia.

1977

Alternative 3

1977 • HOAX DOCUMENTARY • UK (ANGLIA/ITV) • *DIRECTOR* CHRISTOPHER MILES • *WRITER* DAVID AMBROSE • *50 MIN*

Had it been broadcast on 1 April rather than 20 June, more viewers might have realized that this account of American and Soviet bases in space — supposedly established to take up the torch of human progress once pollution and the greenhouse effect made Earth uninhabitable — was not to be taken seriously. The real pity, however, is that this was the only way in which Britain's ITV thought it worthwhile trying to get to grips with a "Doomwatch scenario". It was not shown in the USA, perhaps because its mischievous allegation that the whole Apollo programme was a political smokescreen was just a little too plausible.

The Fantastic Journey

1977 • SERIES • US (COLUMBIA/NBC) • *EXECUTIVE PRODUCER* BRUCE LANSBURY • *STARRING* JARED MARTIN, CARL FRANKLIN, IKE EISENMANN AND RODDY MCDOWALL • *75-MIN PILOT PLUS 50-MIN EPISODES*

McDowall was translated along with the basic plot formula from *Planet Of The Apes* into a tale of mazy parallel worlds entered via the Bermuda Triangle; a party of refugees from different times wanders from dimension to dimension searching for a way out. McDowall and Eisenmann echoed the eccentrically antagonistic Zachary Smith/Will Robinson relationship which had worked so well in *Lost In Space*, but the series was aborted mid-season after nine episodes.

The Incredible Hulk

1977-82 • SERIES • US (UNIVERSAL/CBS) • *EXECUTIVE PRODUCER* KEN JOHNSON • *STARRING* BILL BIXBY (DR BANNER), LOU FERRIGNO (THE HULK) AND JACK COLVIN (JACK MCGEE) • *90-MIN PILOTS & 50-MIN EPISODES*

The most successful of a mixed batch of pilots based on Marvel Comics superheroes, *The Incredible Hulk* was cautiously reprised before launching an 80-episode series: a successful combination of the "running man" formula with "wandering vigilante" sub-plots. A contemporary moral panic about TV violence meant that the not-so-Jolly Green Hulk could never actually hurt anybody, but that didn't significantly inhibit the strong-arm stunts which were the series' main stock-in-trade. These were almost always invoked as an explosive response to bullying, securing the show's appeal for weedy kids and hapless adults. Sterling performances by the anxiously pacifist Bixby ("Please don't make me angry — you wouldn't like me when I'm angry!") and the sourly long-suffering Colvin added enough spice to the mix to sustain the show for an unusually long time at the top of the slippery slope leading down to the swamp of mediocrity.

Logan's Run

1977-78 • SERIES • US (MGM/CBS) • *PRODUCER* LEONARD KATZMAN • *STARRING* GREGORY HARRISON AND HEATHER MENZIES • *74-MIN PILOT & 50-MIN EPISODES*

Footage from the long-delayed and disastrously patched-together 1976 feature film based on William Nolan and George Clayton Johnson's 1967 novel was transplanted into the pilot of this futuristic running man story. The series begins in a post-holocaust enclave whose inhabitants must surrender for euthanasia at 21; the hero and heroine set forth in search of a better world instead. It was fortunate to survive for 13 episodes.

The Man From Atlantis

1977 • SERIES • US (TAFT/NBC) • *EXECUTIVE PRODUCER* HERBERT F. SOLOW • *STARRING* PATRICK DUFFY, BELINDA J. MONTGOMERY AND VICTOR BUONO • *96- & 75-MIN PILOTS & 50-MIN EPISODES*

It required four pilots (three of them double-length) to get this series moving, whereupon the enterprise promptly changed from being a mildly intriguing mystery (with considerable sf embellishments) about the amnesiac merman's origins into a stupidly standardized enhanced secret agent exercise. Duffy played it straight, thus qualifying for a role in *Dallas*, but arch-villain Buono — who probably wouldn't have been seen dead in *Dallas* — didn't.

1990

1977-78 • SERIAL-CUM-SERIES • UK (BBC2) • *CREATOR* WILLIAM GREATOREX • *STARRING* EDWARD WOODWARD (JIM KYLE), ROBERT LANG (SKARDON) AND BARBARA KELLERMAN (DELLY LOMAS) • *55-MIN EPISODES*

Greatorex had made his name with the ITV super-soap *The Power Game*, whose championing of buccaneering business tactics had made him into a hero of the political right. In 1990, Britain has become a police state under the thumb of the sneering Skardon's Public Control Department, against whom journalist Kyle runs a one-man war, shielded from reprisals by his prickly amorous relationship with Skardon's female deputy. The excellent Kellerman left at the end of season one and her replacement (Lisa Harrow) couldn't carry the same conviction in the second batch of eight episodes, which ended with a very unconvincing revolution. More artful than *The Guardians*, it was the last of British TV's several flirtations with right-wing paranoia — the Thatcher years were about to begin and political paranoia passed into the custody of the left for the next two decades.

1978

Battlestar Galactica

1978-80 • SERIES • US (UNIVERSAL/ABC) • *CREATOR* GLEN A. LARSON • *STARRING* LORNE GREENE • *150-MIN PILOT & 50-MIN EPISODES; RETITLED GALACTICA 80 IN SEASON TWO*

TV's answer to *Star Wars* (1977) was so obvious a copy that it was bombarded with lawsuits, but Larson showed unusual imagination in claiming to have lifted the plot straight from the Bible without requiring the inspiration of more recent middlemen. Lavish special effects failed to compensate for the poverty of the plotting, in which Greene's Exodus — continually harried by the robotic Cylons — was a transfiguration of plot formulas made familiar by TV Westerns. In spite of its manifold problems, the series completed its first 24-episode season and got half way through a second before the axe fell.

Like many of the new animated series launched in the late 1970s and 1980s, *Battlestar Galactica* attempted to get around the code of practice imposed in the wake of a moral panic about TV violence by using non-human villains (which could still be blasted with abandon). Even so, it attracted enough criticism for the

USEFUL ACRONYMS
IN 1990 THE GOVERNMENT DEPARTMENT ILLUSTRATED HERE WAS KNOWN AS THE PCD. DNA PRESUMABLY STILL STOOD FOR NATIONAL DYSLEXIA ASSOCIATION

 CLOAK AND DAGGER *MOST TV*
SF SHOWS ASSUME THAT THE
SPACEFARING FOLK OF THE
FAR FUTURE WILL HAVE NO
DRESS SENSE AT ALL

performance by Darrow — had always been the more interesting character. Pearce bristled well as their principal adversary, although Brian Croucher could not recapture the menacing presence of Stephen Greif as her male colleague when Greif left at the end of season one; the character was dropped for seasons three and four.

The plots of individual episodes were variable, but most were on a par with run-of-the-mill *Star Trek* episodes and the teasing cliffhangers used to end each season were neatly echoed in the casually self-destructive 52nd and last episode, for which Thomas made a striking guest reappearance. The show's (entirely British) cult following was a pale shadow of the worldwide Trekkie phenomenon but managed to maintain a certain passionate fervour long after its demise.

violence to be substantially toned down in season two. Although it did manage to produce some spectacular set pieces, the show was deeply flawed and never really looked like fulfilling its potential or justifying its budget.

Blake's Seven

1978-81 • SERIES • UK (BBC) • *CREATOR* TERRY NATION • *STARRING* GARETH THOMAS (ROJ BLAKE), PAUL DARROW (AVON) AND JACQUELINE PEARCE (SERVELAN) • *50-MIN EPISODES*

Nation overcame his deep-seated hatred of sf yet again to plan this series, which carefully crossed *Star Trek* with *The Adventures Of Robin Hood*. Blake, the leader of a resistance movement against the oppressive Federation, escapes from a prison-ship with an ill-assorted and only mildly roguish crew. With the aid of an alien spaceship and a bad-tempered but all-wise computer, he becomes a painful thorn in the side of his adversaries, occasionally taking time out boldly to go where no man had gone before.

Personnel changes forced continual modifications of the show's cast, which undermined the building of the kind of camaraderie that bound Captain Kirk's crew

together and created *Star Trek*'s secondary agenda as propaganda for multi-culturalism. Thomas left after two seasons, leaving centre stage to the arrogantly charismatic Avon, who — thanks to a brilliantly cold-blooded

Come Back, Mrs Noah

1978 • SITCOM • UK (BBC) • *PRODUCER* DAVID CROFT • *WRITERS* JEREMY LLOYD AND DAVID CROFT • *STARRING* MOLLIE SUGDEN AND IAN LAVENDER • *30-MIN EPISODES*

In the pilot, first shown in a comedy showcase slot in 1977, a 21st-century housewife who wins

 STRIKING A POSE *MOST TV SF SHOWS ASSUME THAT SPACEFARING FOLK WITH NO DRESS SENSE WILL ALSO BE A TEENSY-WEENSY BIT CAMP*

a trip around a space station accidentally launches it into orbit. The six-part series was presumably made on the basis of the writers' reputation; there was certainly nothing else to recommend it.

An Englishman's Castle

1978 • THREE-PART SERIAL • UK (BBC2) • *DIRECTOR* PAUL CIAPPESONI • *WRITER* PHILIP MACKIE • *STARRING* KENNETH MORE, ISLA BLAIR AND ANTHONY BATE • *50-MIN EPISODES*

An alternative-history story about a TV writer (More) living in a Britain which lost World War II, who is about to bring his historical soap opera into the war years. His ostensibly sympathetic Nazi masters are paying very close attention to the manner of his presentation — and so is the resistance. His moral dilemma is intensified when he unwittingly gives information that betrays a colleague, and becomes sharper still when his lover (Blair) confesses she is Jewish. A very fine piece of work, sensitively and suspensefully developed, with first-rate performances by the three leading actors.

IF HITLER HAD WON *WRITERS FOR TV WOULD HAVE TO WEAR TIES*

MORK FROM ORK *THE SCHOOL OF METHOD ACTING REQUIRES AN ACTOR TO SUBMIT HIMSELF ENTIRELY TO HIS ROLE; YOUNG VIEWERS SHOULD NOT TRY THIS AT HOME*

Mork And Mindy

1978-82 • SITCOM • US (PARAMOUNT/ABC) • *PRODUCER* GARRY K. MARSHALL • *STARRING* ROBIN WILLIAMS (MORK) AND PAM DAWBER (MINDY) • *50-MIN PILOT & 25-MIN EPISODES*

This surreal reprise of *My Favorite Martian* was spun off from an eccentric episode of *Happy Days*. It made a star of Robin Williams, who cleverly extrapolated the heavily moralistic tendency which sitcoms had recently acquired (as a consequence of American TV's ongoing moral panic) to an extreme of overblown triteness which was both subversively bizarre and curiously touching. At first infantile, Mork grew up as the show progressed in an oddly respectful parody of the standardized sentimental education which middle-class American children were supposed to undergo. Eventually, he married Mindy and became pregnant.

Ninety-two episodes stretched the inventiveness of the writers to the limit, and often led them to resurrect worn-out formulas, but Williams' craziness sustained the idea's appeal far beyond its natural lifespan and managed to inject new life into plot-pivots that had gone very rusty indeed. Although the show's central devices are jargonized fantasy rather than sf, the use of the innocent observer to cast a satirical eye over contemporary society retained a certain logical pointedness even when Williams was being as silly as he possibly could.

Project UFO

1978-79 • SERIES • US (NBC) • *EXECUTIVE PRODUCER* JACK WEBB • *STARRING* WILLIAM JORDAN • *50-MIN EPISODES*

A drama-documentary series based on "factual" UFO sightings, here "investigated" by a cadre of Air Force officers. The fact that it pulled in huge audiences in the USA said much about the influence of such fanciful tabloids as the *National Enquirer* and the *Weekly World News*, and presumably played a significant part in the inspiration and marketing of *The X-Files*. The show featured lousy actors and suspense-free scripts, and would never have returned for a second 13-part series had it been consumed as

Odd couples: Mork and Mindy

In the relatively short course of TV history, the determination to make equals of all men and women has made considerable progress. Women and racial minorities first progressed from being rescue-fodder and servants to being more active sidekicks for WASPish heroes; then they made further progress, to the point where they demanded true parity. In hierarchical organizations like those featured in *Star Trek* and *Alien Nation*, rank and seniority still forced some partners into subsidiary roles, but even these became problematic. The problems thrown up by hierarchical organizations are always further complicated in TV shows by the ranking-system of the actors. Central characters are never just heroes; they are also stars (or at least hope to become so).

In *Mork And Mindy*, Robin Williams was (or at least became) the star. He was also the comedian. Pam Dawber was the second lead and straight-person — a job which, as even the actress admitted, any one of a thousand actresses could have done. Even so, the relationship sketched out by the series had to pay lip service to feminist ideals by making her character an active force, with her own agenda.

The writers could have maintained a strictly non-sexual relationship in which Dawber contentedly played second fiddle forever, but it would have been out of keeping with the times. An important aspect of the show's success lay in going beyond that, in letting the relationship evolve and mature. Even though fate had kitted her out as a sidekick, the tide of history insisted on promoting Mindy from sidekick to half of an odd couple.

Williams always remained the star of *Mork And Mindy*, but he was also one of a couple, sharing the spotlight. The fact that he gave birth to their child was more than just a cute gag — it was symbolic of the fact that a new era of TV characterization was in the process of being born.

Feminism was making such bold strides that all the places where no man had gone before were now places where no one had gone before, and the future of mankind was turning into the future of humankind.

FACING UP TO THE WONDERS OF SPACE
Or not, as the case may be

fiction rather than information sustaining a defiantly unorthodox world-view.

Stargazy on Zummerdown

1978 • PLAY • UK (BBC2) • *DIRECTOR* MICHAEL FERGUSON • *WRITER* JOHN FLETCHER • *STARRING* STEPHEN MURRAY AND ROY DOTRICE • *80 MIN*
A futuristic fable in which a technological retreat has allowed 23rd-century Albion to become a *News From Nowhere*-type Utopia in which the Toonies (townspeople) and Aggros (country-dwellers) hold Merry Meets under the benign umbrella of the Reformed Celtic Church.

1979

Buck Rogers In The 25th Century

1979-81 • SERIES • US (UNIVERSAL/NBC) • *CREATOR* GLEN A. LARSON • *STARRING* GIL GERARD (BUCK), ERIN GRAY (WILMA) • *100-MIN PILOT & 50-MIN EPISODES*
While *Battlestar Galactica* was on hold, Larson re-launched America's favourite space-opera hero in a new format, dutifully equipped with a cute

robot carefully designed to look unlike the ones in *Star Wars*. An astronaut is thawed out of suspended animation to become a conspicuously unenhanced unsecret agent in various adventures involving alien menaces and criminal conspiracies. The first series was rather camp, bringing in several superannuated guest stars fondly remembered as villains in *Batman* and the 71-year-old Buster Crabbe, who had played Buck as well as Flash Gordon in old cinema serials. Once settled in, however, the series became routine comic-strip adventure fiction, stretching its tedious tenure to 33 episodes before the inevitable collapse. The almost-parodic pilot had a brief theatrical release in the UK.

Quatermass

1979 • FOUR-PART SERIAL • UK (THAMES/ITV) • *DIRECTOR* PIERS HAGGARD • *WRITER* NIGEL KNEALE •

THE FINAL FRONTIER OF THE AVANT GARDE
A RAY GUN IS A RAY GUN IS A RAY GUN, AND PROBABLY ALWAYS WILL BE

STARRING JOHN MILLS (QUATERMASS) • *50-MIN EPISODES* Written in the 1960s as the fourth in the ground-breaking series, it was then considered too costly. The plot, badly dated by the time it was actually made, involves hippie-ish "planet people" — refugees from a general social breakdown — who gather at special sites in the hope of being transported to paradise; Quatermass suspects that they are being consumed by a malign force. Much weaker than its predecessors, its central motif had been anticipated by an effective children's occult fantasy serial aired in 1977, *Children Of The Stones*.

Sapphire And Steel

1979-82 • CYCLE OF SERIALS • UK (ATV/ITV) • *WRITER* P. J. HAMMOND • *STARRING* DAVID McCALLUM (STEEL) AND JOANNA LUMLEY (SAPPHIRE) • *25-MIN EPISODES* Sapphire and Steel are "elementary" forces who assume human disguise to operate as inter-dimensional agents countering temporal disruptions. Despite the bizarre premise and the horrible scientific illiteracy of the introductory blurb, this was an intriguing drama series, whose plots sustained considerable suspense in spite of

never coming remotely close to making sense. Hammond wrote all six of the serials (34 episodes in all) and may have had some idea of what it was all supposed to mean, but it came across as a make-it-up-as-you-go exercise in stylized surrealism aiming at the same kind of cult following as *The Prisoner*. We are unlikely ever to see its like again, and its re-runs are to be savoured on that account.

1980

Brave New World

1980 • TWO-PART MINI-SERIES • *US* (UNIVERSAL/NBC) • *DIRECTOR* BURT BRINCKERHOFF • *SCRIPT* BY ROBERT E. THOMPSON FROM ALDOUS HUXLEY'S 1932 NOVEL • *STARRING* KEIR DULLEA AND BUD CORT • *105-MIN EPISODES* Shelved in the US (and ultimately edited down into a TV movie) but shown in full in the UK, this is an unintended travesty of the original which somehow contrived to fail in every possible respect despite the best efforts of everyone involved.

The Flipside Of Dominick Hide

1980 • PLAY • UK (BBC) • *DIRECTOR* ALAN GIBSON

• *WRITERS* ALAN GIBSON AND JEREMY PAUL • *STARRING* PETER FIRTH (DOMINICK) AND CAROLINE LANGRISHE (JANE) • *95 MIN* A pilot from an orderly quasi-Utopian future time-hops back to the present, which he finds bewilderingly chaotic. He gradually adjusts and learns to savour its delights, with the help of a streetwise girl. The writers nobly resisted the offer of a series but supplied an 85-minute sequel, *Another Flip For Dominick* (1982), in which Dominick returns to search for a historian who has gone missing on a field trip. He looks up Jane and his 2-year-old son (who is also his great-great-grandfather). Deftly constructed and unfailingly good-humoured, the two plays are among the finest products of TV sf. It may seem unfair to compare them with *Mork And Mindy*, but they are essentially a dignified BBC version of the same idea, in which the satirical cutting edge is deftly concealed by the same velvety-soft, child-like naivety.

The Lathe Of Heaven

1980 • TV MOVIE • US (PBS) • *PRODUCERS/DIRECTORS* DAVID R. LAXTON & FRED BARZYK • *SCRIPT* BY ROBERT E. SWAYBILL & DIANE ENGLISH FROM URSULA K. LE GUIN'S 1971 NOVEL • *STARRING* BRUCE DAVIDSON AND KEVIN CONWAY • *105 MIN* A rare sf endeavour for public service broadcasting, approached with appropriate *gravitas*. Sf artist and avant-garde film-maker Ed Emshwiller was the visual consultant for this fable about a psychiatrist who tries, disastrously, to use a patient's reality-bending talents to improve the world. The best sf ever to be made for American TV, it captures the essence of Le Guin's novel and is a work of art in its own right.

The Martian Chronicles

1980 • THREE-PART MINI-SERIES • US (NBC) • *DIRECTOR* MICHAEL ANDERSON • *SCRIPT* BY RICHARD MATHESON FROM RAY BRADBURY'S STORY-SERIES • *STARRING* ROCK HUDSON (COLONEL WILDER) AND GAYLE HUNNICUTT • *110-MIN EPISODES* A monumental attempt to do the impossible, trying to link 11 stories into a coherent whole,

 SAPPHIRE AND STEEL WERE BOTH NAMED FOR THE QUALITY OF THEIR EYES. THEIR PAINED EXPRESSION WAS A RESPONSE TO BEING DESCRIBED AS "ELEMENTS"

 WHICH IS THE ODD ONE OUT? *WRITE YOUR ANSWER ON A POSTCARD AND PLACE IT IN THE NEAREST TIME MACHINE. NO STAMP IS REQUIRED*

Three incompatible astronauts and their dog are cooped up together in an orbiting skylab with no-one else to talk to but a bad-tempered, ungracious mission controller from the USA. There was just enough scope in the situation to spin it out for six episodes.

The Day Of The Triffids

1981 • SIX-PART SERIAL • UK (BBC) • *DIRECTOR* KEN HANNAM • *SCRIPT* BY DOUGLAS LIVINGSTONE FROM JOHN WYNDHAM'S 1951 NOVEL • *STARRING* JOHN DUTTINE, MAURICE COLBOURNE AND EMILY RELPH • *30-MIN EPISODES*

A reasonably faithful adaptation of the novel, which had better triffids and much better stiff upper lips than the execrable 1963 film. The struggle of the sighted survivors of the catastrophe to secure their blind dependants against the alien-invader triffids provides adequate suspense without exaggerated cliff-hangers.

However, the manner in which the escapees

with Hudson serving as anchor-man. The Martians are effective, but the enterprise unfortunately founders on its noble determination to be as true to the original as possible, removing dialogue adapted for use in brief lyrical parables into a very different context. The implicit concreteness of the TV image adds an awkward solidity to Bradbury's calculatedly elusive imagery, and such scenes as the destruction of the Earth become leaden as the actors try to mime appropriate responses.

Lovers of the original were inevitably dissatisfied with the finished product and TV viewers unfamiliar with the original probably couldn't figure out what all the fuss was about, but the series does have a peculiar lumbering majesty of its own. Some of the special effects — especially those used in the dramatization of 'Way In The Middle Of The Air' — are eerily appropriate and, although the whole is slow-moving, it conscientiously avoids mere mediocrity.

Metal Mickey

1980-83 • SITCOM • UK (LWT/ITV) • *PRODUCER* MICHAEL DOLENZ • *WRITER* COLIN BOSTOCK-SMITH • *STARRING* ASHLEY KNIGHT • *30-MIN EPISODES*

A children's comedy series which lasted four seasons (39 episodes) despite the difficulty of finding new kinds of havoc to be wreaked by the paranormally talented household robot and sorted out by the juvenile genius who built "him".

1981

Astronauts

1981 • SITCOM • UK (ITV) • *DIRECTOR* DOUGLAS ARGENT • *WRITERS* GRAEME GARDEN AND BILL ODDIE • *STARRING* CHRISTOPHER GODWIN AND CARMEN DU SAUTOY • *13-MIN EPISODES*

 DARK THEY WERE AND GOLDEN EYED *THE MARTIANS THAT IS, NOT ROCK HUDSON. HE'S SCOWLING BECAUSE THE DIRECTOR TOLD HIM TO,*

gradually settle down to cosy domesticity before the army arrive to disrupt their almost idyllic existence never quite rings true. Broadcast in the US as a two-part mini-series.

The Hitch-Hiker's Guide To The Galaxy

1981 • SIX-PART SERIAL • UK (BBC2) • *PRODUCERS* ALAN J. W. BELL AND JOHN LLOYD • *WRITER* DOUGLAS ADAMS • *STARRING* SIMON JONES (ARTHUR DENT), DAVID DIXON (FORD PREFECT) AND PETER JONES (VOICE OF THE BOOK) • *35-MIN. EPISODES*

A straightforward adaptation of the radio scripts, which had already spun off two best-selling books; clever use of computer graphics helped to fill in the visuals without too many exotic sets. Absurdist comedy tinged with black humour of a deeply morbid stripe, the series continually converted incipient despair into anguished hilarity in a typically English fashion.

The cultish success of the show led to much small-scale cultural spin-off. Amateur cocktail-makers served pan-galactic gargle-blasters to their friends before annoying them with original Vogon poetry, which was countered with critical comments cast in a deadly accurate imitation of the mogadon-slow voice of Marvin the Paranoid Android (Stephen Moore). Mercifully, it was all just a phase they were going through.

Kinvig

1981 • SITCOM • UK (LWT/ITV) • *PRODUCER/DIRECTOR* LES CHATFIELD • *WRITER* NIGEL KNEALE • *STARRING* TONY HAYGARTH, PATSY ROWLANDS AND PRUNELLA GEE • *25-MIN EPISODES*

An insufferable UFO bore, of a kind which ignorant observers (e.g. Kneale) often confuse with sf fans, meets a delectable alien (Gee) and helps her ward off an alien invasion. He has understandable difficulty convincing his wife and friend of the importance of his mission. All very silly.

1982

The Old Men At The Zoo

1982 • FIVE-PART SERIAL • UK (BBC) • *DIRECTOR* STUART BURGE • *SCRIPT* BY TROY KENNEDY MARTIN FROM

ANGUS WILSON'S 1961 NOVEL • *STARRING* MARIUS GORING AND ROLAND CULVER • *55-MIN EPISODES*

As Britain nears a state of social and political collapse, the extent of the creeping crisis is encapsulated and symbolized by a scheme to evacuate the animals from London Zoo. A quietly effective near-future satire; Culver's tormentedly dignified performance was outstanding.

Play For Tomorrow

1982 • ANTHOLOGY SERIES • UK (BBC) • *PRODUCER* NEIL ZEIGER • *60-MIN EPISODES*

Six writers were given tapes of a seminar in which various pundits offered dispirited prognostications of the shape of things to come, which they worked into a series of grim snapshots of near-future life. Caryl Churchill's 'Crimes' (the best of the bunch) is a paranoid fantasy about future deviancy; Peter Prince's

'Bright Eyes' and Graham Reid's 'Easter 2016' are doom-laden political fantasies. Tom McGrath's 'The Nuclear Family' and Stephen Lowe's 'Shades' place widespread unemployment and a widening generation gap in the foreground. Michael Wilcox's 'Cricket' is a black comedy about the extinction of the sense of fair play. The jaundiced tone of the dramas illustrates the fact that Mrs Thatcher had not yet introduced the "feelgood factor" into British economic life.

Voyagers

1982-83 • SERIES • US (UNIVERSAL) • *CREATOR* JAMES D. PARRIOTT • *STARRING* JOHN ERIC HEXUM AND JEFFREY JONES • *50-MIN EPISODES*

Two time-travelling agents have to make sure history stays on the right track, but their interventions mostly secure trivial matters of record. On the rare occasions when they become involved with genuine pivotal moments, the manner of their tinkering is conspicuously uninspired. It was lucky to last 20 episodes.

Whoops! Apocalypse

1982 • FOUR-PART SERIAL • UK (LWT/ITV) • *CREATORS/WRITERS* ANDREW MARSHALL AND DAVID RENWICK • *STARRING* BARRY MORSE (JOHNNY CYCLOPS), RICHARD GRIFFITHS (DUBENKIN) AND PETER JONES (KEVIN PORK) • *25-MIN EPISODES*

Use of the quark bomb to restore the Shah of Iran precipitates a political crisis in which the awful incompetence of US President Cyclops and Soviet premier Dubenkin, abetted by the imbecility of British prime minister Pork, contrives to bring about World War III. Any resemblance to the item below is, of course, purely coincidental.

World War III

1982 • TWO-PART MINI-SERIES • US • *DIRECTOR* DAVID GREENE • *WRITER* ROBERT L. JOSEPH • *STARRING* ROCK HUDSON, BRIAN KEITH AND DAVID SOUL • *100-MIN EPISODES*

A Russian military unit tries to seize an Alaskan oil pipeline; the resultant tense game of bluff and counterbluff which is played out by the US president (Hudson) and the Soviet premier (Keith) inexorably escalates the minor

NUCLEAR HOLOCAUST (US VERSION)
FOR ONCE THE PROTAGONIST OF A TV SHOW IS FULLY ENTITLED TO LOOK GLUM. HE STILL WEARS A TIE, THOUGH

contretemps into the Final Solution. Finished in the studio when original director Boris Sagal died on location; re-edited as a TV movie.

1983

Automan

1983-84 • SERIES • US (NBC) • *CREATOR* GLEN A. LARSON • *STARRING* CHUCK WAGNER AND DESI ARNAZ JR • *70 MIN PILOT AND 50 MIN EPISODES*

Enhanced secret agent series featuring a computer-generated hero conjured out of a computer by a member of the LAPD and a magic cursor. Hopelessly implausible; aborted after 12 episodes.

The Day After

1983 • TV MOVIE • US (ABC) • *DIRECTOR* NICHOLAS MEYER • *WRITER* EDWARD HUME • *STARRING* JASON ROBARDS, JOBETH WILLIAMS, JOHN LITHGOW AND STEVE GUTTENBERG • *121 MIN*

A sober and supposedly realistic account of a nuclear missile strike in and around Lawrence, Kansas. A rare attempt by a US network to handle a political hot potato; the film's alarmist message is that Civil Defence would be utterly impotent to cope with the secondary effects of a limited nuclear exchange. This was put across by developing a cast of stock characters such as might be featured in any soap opera and then devastating their lives, grinding the survivors down with radiation sickness and an irremediable lack of resources. The imagery was striking in spite of the careful restraints imposed on many scenes of death and destruction as a shield against criticism, but the mawkishness of the final scenes — when Robards' performance skidded from dignity into parody — dragged the whole enterprise down into super-soap territory.

The impact of the film was greatly enhanced by the sheer wonder of the fact that such a controversial show could actually be shown on American TV, and this allowed its weaknesses to be condoned. Enthusiasts hoped that it might mark a watershed in the diplomatic history of the medium but there was little chance of that; advertisers were prepared to milk the shock-value of a single event but then insisted on resuming normal service. It remains a fascinating companion-piece to *Threads*.

Overdrawn At The Memory Bank

1983 • TV MOVIE • CANADA • *DIRECTOR* DOUGLAS WILLIAMS • *SCRIPT* BY CORINNE JACKER FROM JOHN VARLEY'S 1976 SHORT STORY • *STARRING* RAUL JULIA AND LINDA GRIFFITHS • *90 MIN*

A man's personality becomes trapped inside a computer; he is then shifted through a series of virtual realities which borrow imagery from the classic film *Casablanca*. A bold attempt to do something new and reasonably sophisticated, intended for public service broadcasting rather than the network.

1984

Chocky

1984-85 • SERIES OF SIX-PART SERIALS • UK (THAMES/ITV) • *PRODUCERS* VIC HUGHES & RICHARD BATES • *SCRIPTS* BY ANTHONY READ, THE FIRST BASED ON JOHN WYNDHAM'S 1969 NOVEL • *STARRING* ANDREW ELLAMS (MATTHEW), JAMES HAZELDINE AND ANABEL WORRELL (ALBERTINE) • *30-MIN EPISODES*

In the first of these children's serials, Matthew Gore's "imaginary friend" eventually turns out — to the astonishment of his parents — to be a benevolent alien sent to Earth to help out humanity. *Chocky's Children* and *Chocky's Challenge* take the story further, introducing a female counterpart who becomes the second instrument of the aliens' plan — which various malevolent adults are, of course, intent on turning to their own selfish advantage. An intriguing combination of parable and power-fantasy.

The Invisible Man

1984 • SIX-PART SERIAL • UK (BBC) • *PRODUCER* BARRY LETTS • *SCRIPT* BY JAMES ANDREW HALL FROM H. G. WELLS'S 1896 NOVEL • *STARRING* PIP DONAGHY • *30-MIN EPISODES*

The first serious attempt to dramatize Wells's story rather than simply pirating the central idea. The excellent special effects and leisurely build-up worked so well that it made a mockery of all the series which decanted the central motif into trivial cops-and-robbers plots. Although it was originally intended for the

NUCLEAR HOLOCAUST (UK VERSION) *WHEN IT COMES TO LOOKING GLUM, BRITONS ARE BEST. THEY ALSO HAVE THE SENSE TO THROW AWAY THEIR TIES*

"Sunday afternoon classic" slot, the serial was successfully aired in a prime-time weekday slot.

Threads

1984 • TV MOVIE • UK (BBC2) • *PRODUCER/DIRECTOR* MICK JACKSON • *WRITER* BARRY HINES • *STARRING* KAREN MEAGHER, REECE DINSDALE, DAVID BRIERLEY AND RITA MAY • *115 MIN*

The UK's answer to *The Day After* refused to compromise with the standard requirements of the television by pulling its punches. It sought a higher level of realism and was chillingly persuasive. Sheffield in the North of England (whose citizens gladly stepped in to provide a legion of extras) was substituted for Lawrence, and the two families used as viewpoint characters were more in the serious tradition of "Play For Today" than soap opera. The description of the nuclear war and its aftermath are uncompromisingly harrowing and very disturbing; the final stages carry the story forward in time several years hence, when even the language of the survivors has disintegrated. A masterpiece of alarmist rhetoric, developing the thesis that the best way to make certain

that nuclear war never happens is to convince people that it really would put an end to everything they hold dear.

The Tripods

1984-85 • SERIES OF SERIALS • UK (BBC) • *PRODUCER* RICHARD BATES • *SCRIPTS* BY ALICK ROWE & CHRISTOPHER PENFOLD FROM JOHN CHRISTOPHER'S 1967-68 TRILOGY • *STARRING* JOHN SHACKLEY AND JIM BAKER • *30-MIN EPISODES*

A century from now, Earth has long been under the domination of the alien Masters and the mechanical Tripods; order and stability are maintained by "capping" adolescents with mind-control devices. In the first (13-part) story, two young heroes due to be capped go on the run, hoping to join the Free Men in Switzerland. In the second (12-part) story, one of the boys is recruited as a servant of a Master, learning much that might be advantageous to the Free Men... but the BBC decided that the viewing figures did not warrant completion of the expensive series and the third volume of the trilogy was never dramatized. It is arguable that the serials were too long-drawn-out, but the special effects were excellent and the narrative was enabled by its leisurely pace to get to grips with some serious issues, especially in the second serial. On artistic grounds, at least, the axing of the series was a tragedy.

V

1984-85 • MINI-SERIES & SERIES • US (NBC)
• *CREATOR* KENNETH JOHNSON • *STARRING* MARC SINGER, FAYE GRANT, JANE BADLER AND ROBERT ENGLUND • *100-MIN & 50-MIN EPISODES*

In the first two-part mini-series, apparently benevolent human-seeming aliens are gradually revealed (by virtue of their habit of eating live mice with evident relish) as nasty reptiles in disguise. Producer/writer Johnson took his initial inspiration from Sinclair Lewis's exercise in anti-fascist alarmism *It Can't Happen Here* (1935), but as the plot thickened it rapidly became an indigestible mass of clichés and improbabilities. In the three-part sequel, *V: The Final Battle*, the resistance movement achieves the victory for which the letter V stands, albeit in a preposterous fashion. The subsequent series inherited a tangled mass of loose ends but made little progress in tying them up; it was fortunate to last 19 episodes before being killed off.

 MINIMALIST GRAFFITI *V IS SHORTHAND FOR "AND SO IS VERMIN"*

Cult television

Although the word "cult" can be applied to any form of unorthodox religion it is usually used to describe groups which gather around a particular individual whose personality seems unusually powerful. Although such "charismatic" individuals often represent themselves as transmitters of divine revelation, we can also speak of "cults of personality" in association with great statesmen and leaders of social movements. The stage or cinematic presence of outstanding actors is also a form of powerful personality which allows the community of their most ardent fans to be thought of as a cult. It is possible for TV shows to create roles which enhance — even override — the personalities of the actors filling them to the extent that a cult following develops around the character rather than the actor, sometimes to the extent that the actor seems to be swallowed up by the character.

Sf routinely creates highly distinctive roles very different from those to be found in shows which dramatize everyday life; sf can create whole worlds which have a glamour of their own. For this reason, TV sf is particularly hospitable to the growth of cult followings — so much so that a monthly magazines dedicated to TV sf, *TV Zone*, is subtitled "The Monthly Magazine of Cult Television". TV sf fandom — unlike the kind of fandom which gathered around sf magazines and books — is personality-centred, and it is usually the case that it is the exotic science-fictional role rather than the actor which defines the personality and the cult. Leonard Nimoy titled his first autobiography *I Am Not Spock*, but when he updated it he had to come clean and drop the not. What future can there be for David Duchovny once Fox Mulder is laid to rest?

Z For Zachariah

1984 • PLAY • UK (BBC) • *DIRECTOR* ANTHONY GARNER
• SCRIPT BY ANTHONY GARNER FROM ROBERT C. O'BRIEN'S 1975 NOVEL • *STARRING* ANTHONY ANDREWS AND PIPPA HINCHLEY • *120 MIN*

O'Brien's excellent novel was marketed as a juvenile, but this bitter and tragic tale of a mis-matched Adam and Eve was thoroughly adult in its approach. A male survivor of the nuclear

holocaust arrives in a remote valley where a teenage girl lives alone; the emotional and psychological baggage they have carried over from the old world gradually kills off any hope that they might have had of founding a new one. A fine piece of work.

1985

Max Headroom

1985 • TV MOVIE • UK (CHRYSALIS/CHANNEL 4)
• *DIRECTORS* ROCKY MORTON & ANNABEL JANKEL • *SCRIPT* BY STEVE ROBERTS • *STARRING* MATT FREWER AND NICKOLAS GRACE • *70 MIN*

Max Headroom was a computer-generated head with built-in glitches developed for use as a flippant link-man in a TV rock video show. The film "explains" his origin as a technological reincarnation of an investigative reporter killed in action. Slick, surreal and unrepentantly silly, the film featured synthesized music by Midge Ure and Chris Cross; it was set "20 minutes into the future" and was almost that far ahead of its time.

 LOTS OF HEADROOM *ALLOWS YOU TO LOOK AT THE WORLD FROM A FRESH ANGLE*

 ALIENATION *TV SF'S BRECHTIAN IMPERATIVE MAKES WORK FOR VERTICALLY-CHALLENGED ACTORS*

Ray Bradbury Theater

1985-86 • ANTHOLOGY SERIES • US (ATLANTIS/HBO) • *EXECUTIVE PRODUCERS* MICHAEL MACMILLAN AND LARRY WILCOX • *SCRIPTS* BY RAY BRADBURY FROM HIS OWN STORIES • *25-MIN EPISODES*

Among the original six episodes, only 'Marionettes Inc', in which a man is replaced by a robot simulacrum, is sf; the remainder were occult fiction. A further 12 shows were made in the UK, France and Canada, those made in the UK being aired in the Twist In The Tale series (1988-89); a couple were borderline sf.

Steven Spielberg's Amazing Stories

1985-87 • ANTHOLOGY SERIES • US (AMBLIN/UNIVERSAL/NBC) • *25- AND 50-MIN EPISODES*
If the powers-that-be at NBC had not committed themselves in advance to 44 episodes (including two double-length ones), they would surely have aborted this show as ruthlessly as they had axed practically all their other adventures in fantasy and sf. The good casts, first-rate directors and

experienced writers were wasted on a sickly series of whimsical and sentimental fantasies. The sf element was minimal, almost all the plots being wound up by the casual intervention of arbitrary miracles.

The Twilight Zone

1985-87 • ANTHOLOGY SERIES • US (CBS) • *EXECUTIVE PRODUCER* PHILIP DEGUERE • *25- AND 50-MIN EPISODES*
CBS got a much better deal by resurrecting *The Twilight Zone* with Harlan Ellison as creative consultant than NBC got out of *Steven Spielberg's Amazing Stories*. The stories had a much greater range and were far more ingenious in construction, reflecting the number and variety of first-rate writers who were involved. The 24 50-minute episodes of the first series were mini-anthologies of 2/3 stories, but the second series was cut back, some of the 12 episodes being reduced by half; the 80 individual stories were supplemented with 30 others made by another team on much lower budgets when they were farmed out for syndication. The show featured more fantasy than sf, but did include effective dramatizations of such sf classics as 'Saucer Of Loneliness' (1953) by Theodore Sturgeon and 'The Star' (1955) by Arthur C. Clarke.

1986

ALF

1986-90 • SITCOM • US (WARNER/NBC) • *CREATOR* PAUL FUSCO • STARRING MAX WRIGHT AND ANNE SCHEEDEN • *30-MIN EPISODES*
An obnoxious Alien Life Form takes up residence with a typical American TV family. Fusco's puppet became an international superstar, sort of.

Starman

1986-87 • SERIES • US (COLUMBIA) • *STARRING* ROBERT HAYS • *50-MIN EPISODES*
John Carpenter's soppily sentimental 1984 movie span off this 22-episode series, which is a soft-centred — if not utterly hollow — version of the standard running-man formula. Will the returned spaceman find his long-lost lover

and son before the feds find him? We'll never know, because — surprise! surprise! — they axed the series.

1987

Max Headroom: The Series

1987-88 • SERIES • US (CHRYSALIS/LORIMAR/ABC) • *EXECUTIVE PRODUCER* PETER WAGG (EXCEPT EPISODE ONE) • *STARRING* MATT FREWER, AMANDA PAYS AND CHRIS YOUNG • *50-MIN EPISODES*
The US team remade the 1985 film as 'Blipverts' and extended the downloaded reporter's investigations into a two-season, 14-part series. The usual suspects were assembled to provide the opposition: ultra-violent sports, addictive game-shows, test-tube babies etc, etc. The talking head's sarcasm and cynicism were dutifully toned down. Generous critics cite it as the first cyberpunk TV series, and its quick-fire visual technique did have a certain post-modernist feel, but it never had the guts or the glitz to capture the real essence of cyberpunk.

Star Cops

1987 • SERIES • UK (BBC) • *CREATOR* CHRIS BOUCHER • *STARRING* DAVID CALDER AND JONATHAN ADAMS • *55-MIN EPISODES*
The dispirited and disorganized Moonbase police are whipped into shape by their new commander, but he couldn't do much for the nine ramshackle plots. Made when Margaret Thatcher seemed to have put the backbone back in Britain.

Star Trek: The Next Generation

1987-94 • SERIES • US (PARAMOUNT) • *CREATOR* GENE RODDENBERRY • *CO-EXECUTIVE PRODUCERS* RICK BERMAN AND MICHAEL PILLER • *STARRING* PATRICK STEWART (JEAN-LUC PICARD), BRENT SPINER (DATA), JONATHAN FRAKES (RIKER), LEVAR BURTON (GEORDI LA FORGE), MARINA SIRTIS (TROI), GATES MCFADDEN (BEVERLY CRUSHER) AND MICHAEL DORN (WORF) • *50-MIN EPISODES*
As Michael Myers observed in *Wayne's World* while contemplating a glass of imitation champagne, *Star Trek: The Next Generation* is in

 **THE NEXT GENERATION**

A LONG-SERVING CAPTAIN OF A FEDERATION STARSHIP HAS MANY CROSSES TO BEAR AND MANY HAZARDS TO FACE, SOMETIMES AT ONE AND THE SAME TIME

a particularly annoying intrusion, but he is (mercifully) only invoked on the rare occasions when an injection of pure silliness is prescribed.

The sf motifs invoked in *The Next Generation*'s plots are rarely of much interest in themselves, but the series makes no pretence to be anything other than a costume drama. The fact that its costumes are futuristic merely serves to equip its personnel with a familiar range of facilitating devices (phasers, communicators, the invaluable transporter, the holo-deck, etc) and to create hypothetical spaces for the development of mildly eccentric cultures. On this level, the series works well and its longevity — 174 standard episodes and two at double-length — allowed its creators to streamline and mechanize a kind of plot formula which the original series had seen through its teething-troubles. The resulting expertise has, of course, been carried further forward into *Star Trek: Voyager*.

Timestalkers

1987 • TV MOVIE • US • *DIRECTOR* MICHAEL SCHULTZ • *STARRING* WILLIAM DEVANE, KLAUS KINSKI, LAUREN HUTTON, FORREST TUCKER AND JOHN RATZENBERGER • *100 MIN*

The best of several TV adventures inspired by *Back To The Future*, this one is a sober drama in which a Wild West buff (Devane) is recruited in the present by time-travellers to help track down a criminal (Kinski) intent on changing a more remote period of American history. The neat plot doesn't really need the final ultra-sentimental twist.

1988

First Born

1988 • THREE-PART SERIAL • UK (BBC) • *DIRECTOR* PHILIP SAVILLE • *SCRIPT* BY TED WHITEHEAD, BASED ON MAUREEN DUFFY'S 1981 NOVEL *GOR SAGA* • *STARRING* CHARLES DANCE AND JULIE PEASGOOD • *50-MIN EPISODES*

A genetic engineer creates a human/ape hybrid. Duffy's excellent satire used its hybrid as a cynical objective observer of human life but Whitehead's travesty is a knee-jerk hymn of hate against scientists in general and genetic engineers in particular — a kind of dumbed-

many ways better than the original but will never be recognized as truly authentic. Roddenberry steered the double-length pilot through production, but had ceased to have any active involvement in the series some time before his death in 1991; the whole *Star Trek* universe passed into the custody of Berman and Piller. The new enterprise took up the semi-sacred mission of the old, aspiring to be an active force for cultural progress by exerting mild but constant pressure on all the kinds of bad thinking which are supposedly responsible for generating mistrust, aggression and irresponsibility. The many cracks in this moralistic crusade — which doggedly refused to tackle genuinely difficult questions — were papered over, either by melodramatic plots which constantly brought the *Enterprise* to the brink of destruction, or by unashamedly quirky ones which developed the soap-operatic relationships

between the characters.

In spite of its inbuilt deficiencies, however, the best episodes of *The New Generation* do pack a considerable dramatic punch and stand out as conscientious attempts to uphold, defend and justify civilized values. The main strength of the show lies in its skilful casting. Stewart is an excellent anchorman, far more convincing as a commander than William Shatner; Spiner brings a useful subtlety to the android role, and Dorn makes the best of the difficult — but thoroughly worthwhile — job of domesticating the former arch-enemy. Burton has to represent two minorities at once and Sirtis has an impossible task but they play their parts with considerable spirit. The ensemble manages somehow to move the levers of plots which usually remain puerile in spite of the frequent recruitment of good writers. The all-purpose worker of perversely arbitrary miracles who goes by the name of Q is

 IT'S THAT SCOWL AGAIN *The baby won't let him get a wink of sleep*

down *Doomwatch* episode expanded to three times its natural length.

Out Of Time

1988 • TV MOVIE • US • *DIRECTOR* ROBERT BUTLER • *STARRING* BRUCE ABBOT, BILL MAHER AND ADAM ANT • *100 MIN*

A comedy drama in which a cop from the future arrives in the present and teams up with his great-grandfather. It makes use of all the standard narrative moves, but does so with sufficient zest to leave a faint pang of regret that the series for which it was the intended pilot was stillborn.

Red Dwarf

1988- • SITCOM • UK (BBC2) • *PRODUCER* PAUL JACKSON • *WRITERS* ROB GRANT AND DOUG NAYLOR • *STARRING* CRAIG CHARLES (LISTER), CHRIS BARRIE (RIMMER), DANNY JOHN-JULES (THE CAT) AND ROBERT LLEWELLYN (KRYTEN) • *30-MIN EPISODES*

The crew of the giant mining-ship *Red Dwarf* has been wiped out in an accident, save for one crewman — the slovenly Lister — who was in suspended animation at the time. Belatedly thawed out, he found that his only remaining companions were his pet cat, which had evolved into quasi-humanity, the hologram of his immediate superior — Arnold J. Rimmer — and the ship's computer. The computer had the face and voice of laconic comedian Norman Lovett for two seasons before he was replaced by the equally laconic comedienne Hattie

Hayridge. A further addition to the regular cast in season three was the android butler Kryten.

As with any good sitcom, the backbone of the show is the interplay between the characters. Lister's innate good nature battles to overcome the handicaps of his awful indolence and vulgarity, Rimmer fails to conceal his terminal insecurity beneath a cloak of insufferable officiousness and Kryten struggles manfully to overcome his pre-programmed servility and honesty, while the cat naturally remains perfectly content with his illimitable vanity. These projects overlap and intersect in the testing-grounds provided by a series of vivid and highly ingenious science-fiction motifs, which make *Red Dwarf* the most inventive as well as the funniest of all TV sf shows.

Red Dwarf's frenetic pace and narrative energy make it a truly outstanding endeavour; although it rode on to the screen on the coat-tails of *The Hitch-Hiker's Guide To The Galaxy*, it has exhibited far greater staying-power. Whereas Douglas Adams's comedy always threatened to dissolve into maudlin morbidity, Grant and Naylor bring an unfailing exuberance even to the treatment of such macabre motifs as the skeletal women of 'Kryten' and such scary monsters as the chameleonic 'Polymorph' and the despair squid in 'Back To Reality'. The low-budget special effects are exceedingly clever, making use of the full repertoire of modern TV trickery in a deliberately casual fashion which adds an extra layer to the humour.

Something Is Out There

1988 • TWO-PART MINI-SERIES & SERIES • US/AUSTRALIA (NBC) • *EXECUTIVE PRODUCERS* FRANK LUPO AND JON ASHLEY • *WRITER* FRANK LUPO • *STARRING* JOE CORTESE AND MARYAM D'ABO • *100-MIN & 50-MIN EPISODES*

A cop teams up with a stranded humanoid alien — who happens to be a doctor as well as a telepath — in order to search for a hostile alien invader which can invade and take over any human host. The two-part pilot is an exaggerated version of the standard "cop's new partner" routine; the ensuing series immediately

 THE CREW OF *RED DWARF* *They have no mission, and see no need to split infinitives as they boldly go where no series has gone before*

Comedy sf

There are two kinds of comedy, both of which are extensively featured on TV (including TV sf shows).

The first kind of comedy assumes that anything out of the ordinary is funny, and that a scriptwriter only has to have an alien or a robot do something you or I would never do to have the audience falling about. Strangely enough, there are lots of people who are so insecure in their "normality" that they actually do feel forced to pretend that anything which violates their sense of the ordinary is funny. (This may be why the word "funny" can mean "peculiar" as well as "hilarious".) People of this kind love shows like *My Favorite Martian* and *ALF*.

The second kind of comedy assumes that there is something essentially absurd about ordinariness, which only needs to be observed from a fresh viewpoint in order to make us see the funny side of our own idiosyncrasies. Fortunately, there are also lots of people who wear their normality lightly enough to be able take delight in seeing it subverted. People of this kind adore shows like *Eerie, Indiana* and *Red Dwarf*.

The most successful comedy shows of all are those which can get laughs out of both audiences; this is why *Mork And Mindy* hit the jackpot.

There are, of course, some people so utterly incapable of doubting or stepping aside from their normality that they have no sense of humour at all. People like that usually hate science fiction, but the ones who don't probably enjoyed watching *Steven Spielberg's Amazing Stories* and *Wild Palms*.

THE DISAPPEARING WAISTLINE *No, it's not a sour-milk gut, just a slight case of pregnancy — nothing that a cop and his buddy can't take in their stride*

decayed into crime-fighting cliché and was axed after six of its eight episodes had been aired.

War Of The Worlds

1988-90 • SERIES • US (PARAMOUNT) • *CREATOR* GREG STRANGIS • *STARRING* JARED MARTIN AND LYNDA MASON GREEN • ***100-MIN PILOT & 50-MIN EPISODES***
The pilot, *The Resurrection*, is a belated sequel to George Pal's 1953 film, in which the remains of the alien invaders are revived by a terrorist attack on the military base where they have long been stored. They can now take over human

bodies and they go to ground, so that the heroes can oppose their insidious plans in spite of official refusal to admit that they exist. It survived into a second season, clocking up 41 episodes before running out of steam.

1989

Alien Nation

1989-90 • SERIES • US (FOX) • *EXECUTIVE PRODUCER* KENNETH JOHNSON • *STARRING* GARY GRAHAM AND ERIC PIERPOINT • ***100-MIN PILOT & 50-MIN EPISODES***
Spin-off from the 1988 film, in which humanoid aliens bred as slaves survive the crash of their transporter and are grudgingly allowed to settle in LA. The series extrapolates the "cop's new partner" routine fairly predictably, but is actually somewhat better than the rather weak-kneed movie and was beginning to develop a useful plot thread involving menacing "overseers" to counterbalance its amiably silly satirical element when it was axed after 21 episodes; syndication of the show gradually built up sufficient interest to warrant a revival in a series of 100-minute TV movies, including *Alien Nation: Dark Horizon* (1994) and *Alien Nation: Body And Soul* (1995).

Murder On The Moon

1989 • TV MOVIE • UK (LWT/ITV) • *DIRECTOR* MICHAEL LINDSAY-HOGG • *WRITER* CARLA JEAN WAGNER • *STARRING* BRIGITTE NIELSEN AND JULIAN SANDS • ***120 MIN***
The moon is neatly divided into US- and Soviet-controlled sectors but a corpse creates an awkward jurisdictional problem which brings together two very different investigators from opposite sides of the cultural divide. They solve their differences, and the mystery. The story never attained the plausibility or the dramatic tension at which it aimed.

Quantum Leap

1989-1994 • SERIES • US (UNIVERSAL/NBC) • *CREATOR* DONALD P. BELLISARIO • *STARRING* SCOTT BAKULA (SAM BECKETT) AND DEAN STOCKWELL (AL) • ***90-MIN PILOT & 50-MIN EPISODES***
A jargonized angelic fantasy in which Sam Beckett is bounced back and forth in recent times past, projected into morally challenging situations which he must resolve for the cause of good, to which he has apparently been drafted. He is aided in this unchosen mission by his hologramatic pal Al, who can give regular updates on the probability of his success with

the aid of an oracular computer. The nonsensicality of the basic scenario is compounded by the devices — both borrowed from the film *Here Comes Mr Jordan* (1941); remade in 1978 as *Heaven Can Wait* — of having the central character appear to the camera as "himself" even though the supporting cast are supposed to see him as the individual whose body he is occupying. Meanwhile the hologramatic Al is invisible to everyone except Sam. The former device licenses the use of bizarre drag outfits on the rare occasions when Beckett becomes a woman.

In spite of its crippling logical handicaps, the show thrived, partly because its carefully recomplicated "wandering vigilante" format permitted more interesting plots than the more familiar sf plot-formulas and partly because Bakula had the skill and chutzpah to play his manifold parts with real conviction. Although it resolutely skirted around the possibility of time-paradoxes, the show gradually picked up enough self-confidence to begin tackling non-trivial historical pivots like the Kennedy assassination,

The alien menace

Ever since H. G. Wells wrote *The War Of The Worlds* (1898), the alien menace has been a staple of sf. It dominated the early pulp magazines, and sf cinema was long dominated by alien menaces which — for budgetary reasons — tended to manifest themselves as single monsters. The stringent budgetary limitations of TV sf similarly ensured that alien menaces had to be placed off-stage, their presence signalled by eerie music or strange mists. Such physical manifestations as they did achieve were usually fragmentary and very brief.

This necessary parsimony was often turned to good advantage, the characters and the viewers sharing the frustration of being unable to get a sight of the monster, thus heightening the sense of threat generated by its nearness. Cinema brought the artistry of such teasing to a pitch of near-perfection in such films as

Alien, but cinema always cultivated the expectation that the monster would ultimately be revealed and seen for what it is. TV avoided making that kind of contract with the viewer, not merely because good monsters are expensive but because the standard format of TV is the series, in which closure (and hence final revelation) is infinitely delayed as a matter of course.

In practice, all series do end — but even those which are not crudely aborted either retain the hope that they might be recommissioned or acknowledge the responsibility to hold something in reserve just in case. TV planners routinely think in terms of climaxes which never come, and thus in terms of alien menaces which remain permanently elusive and indistinct. This allows TV sf to cultivate a unique kind of paranoia, which is sharper and longer-drawn-out than its cinematic cousin: the paranoia which gives such shows as *The X-Files* an edge which is untranslatable into any other medium.

when Beckett "became" Lee Harvey Oswald in a two-part special. As with *Star Trek*, the far-out nature of the show licensed its tackling of

sensitive civil rights issues in a half-hearted but calculatedly indelicate fashion, and it retained a fascination which defied its underlying absurdity. Although the show's conclusion was planned in advance, Bellisario and his colleagues carefully left Sam stranded in the past, just in case...

USEFUL ADVICE
It's bad enough bouncing around in time without having some loudly-dressed bigmouth other people can't see dogging your every footstep

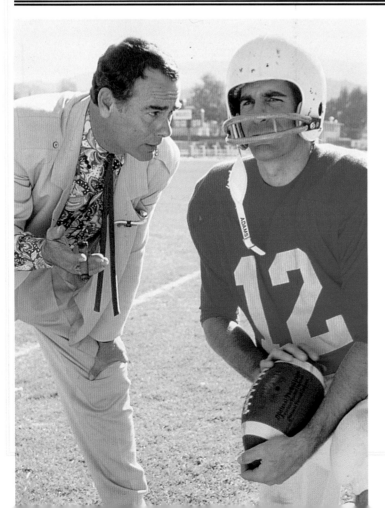

1990

The Flash

1990-91 • SERIES • US • *EXECUTIVE PRODUCERS* Danny Bilson and Paul le Meo • *STARRING* John Wesley Shipp and Amanda Pays • *50-MIN EPISODES*
The comic-book hero adapted for TV by courtesy of up-to-date special effects. Although he only had one trick (moving very rapidly) and the villains he thwarted were a pretty dull lot, the show lasted 22 episodes and was then re-edited into a series of "movies" for video release in 1991-92. Relatively few sf devices were employed in the plots.

The Girl From Tomorrow

1990-92 • TWO 12-PART SERIALS • AUSTRALIA • *EXECUTIVE PRODUCER* Ron Saunders • *STARRING* Katherine Cullen (Alana), Melissa Marshall (Jenny) and John

HOWARD (SILVERTHORN) • *25-MIN EPISODES*

Alana, a child of the post-ecocatastrophic 26th century, is kidnapped by the outlaw Silverthorn and brought back to the 20th century by time machine. She is eventually forced to take her new-found friend Jenny back to the future, where their further adventures are related in the second serial. An intriguing experiment part-funded by the ever-adventurous Australian Film Foundation.

Jupiter Moon

1990 • SOAP OPERA • UK (BSB) • *CREATOR/PRODUCER* WILLIAM SMETHURST • *STARRING* ANDY RASHLEIGH, CAROLINE EVANS, PHIL WILMOTT, NICOLA WRIGHT AND KAREN MURDEN • *25-MIN EPISODES*

A pioneering attempt to create a future-set soap opera, using a collection of standard sets which were supposed to be a space station-based technical college in orbit around Jupiter. The production team tried to make a virtue out of the scarcity of their resources by constantly reminding viewers that life aboard a space station had to be sparse because it was horrendously expensive to ship supplies from Earth. The cast worked through the standard relationship routines, only becoming involved with sf motifs when somebody got stuck outside and needed rescuing. It really did have potential (albeit untapped during the 115 completed episodes), but BSB didn't and the show perished when Rupert Murdoch's Sky satellite channel swallowed up its rival.

1991

Chimera

1991 • FOUR-PART SERIAL • UK (ITV) • *PRODUCER* NICK GILLOTT • *SCRIPT* BY STEPHEN GALLAGHER FROM HIS 1982 NOVEL • *STARRING* JOHN LYNCH, KENNETH CRANHAM, CHRISTINE KAVANAGH AND DAVID CALDER • *50-MIN EPISODES*

The powers-that-be try to hush up a mass murder at a research establishment where mysterious experiments involving apes are being carried out, but some investigators will not be put off; the culprit turns out — to no one's surprise — to be an ape/human hybrid. Anti-

ROADKILL HUMAN/APE HYBRIDS RARELY HAVE AN OPPORTUNITY TO LEARN TO CROSS THE ROAD SAFELY

science fiction of a tediously familiar variety, much bloodier than *First Born* but not quite as determinedly unintelligent. Edited down to a two-hour TV movie version in 1994.

The Cloning Of Joanna May

1991 • THREE-PART MINI-SERIES • UK (GRANADA/ITV) • *DIRECTOR* PHILIP SAVILLE • *SCRIPT* BY TED WHITEHEAD FROM FAY WELDON'S 1989 NOVEL • *STARRING* PATRICIA HODGE (JOANNA MAY) AND BRIAN COX (CARL MAY) • *50-MIN EPISODES*

The original novel is carefully if rather slyly antipathetic to science, so Whitehead had no

FAMILY REUNION *TWINS SEPARATED BEFORE BIRTH FINALLY GET BACK TOGETHER*

need to commit an atrocity on the scale of *First Born* in order to render it into an alarmist parable, although he did economize on clones in the interests of simplification. The amalgam of comedy and melodrama is inevitably uneasy

without the support of Weldon's deftly witty prose, but Cox and Hodge put in sterling performances as the warring ex-spouses and the three young actresses playing Joanna's clones are effective.

Eerie, Indiana

1991 • SERIES • US (UNREALITY INC) • *CREATORS* KARL SHAEFER AND JOSE RIVERA • *STARRING* OMRI KATZ (MARSHALL TELLER) AND SIMON HOLMES • *25-MIN EPISODES*

Joe Dante directed the pilot episode of this uninhibited show about a small town where anything and everything can happen, usually to teenage whizz-kid Marshall Teller. It mixed sf and occult plots with reckless abandon, taking up an imaginative location about half way between *The Addams Family* and *Northern Exposure*. It was too way out — and perhaps a little too clever — to attract the cult following it deserved and only lasted 19 episodes. The nearest American TV has come to capturing the laconically anarchic spirit of *Red Dwarf*.

Time Riders

1991 • FOUR-PART SERIAL • UK (THAMES/ITV) • *PRODUCER* ALAN HORROX • *WRITER* JIM ELDRIDGE • *STARRING* HAYDN GWYNNE (B. B. MILLER), CLIVE MERRISON AND KENNETH HALL • *25-MIN EPISODES*

With ideas and imagery lifted from *Back To The Future*, an adventurous scientist sets off into time on her Yamaha motorbike, stirring up the early Victorian era and the English Civil War. The scripts remained awkward despite Gwynne's sterling efforts; unfortunately, she never looked like a convincing replacement for Doctor Who (who had, of course, been put into suspended animation by the BBC two years earlier).

1993

The Adventures Of Brisco County Junior

1993-94 • US (WARNER) • *CREATORS* JEFFREY BOAM AND CARLTON CUSE • *STARRING* BRUCE CAMPBELL (BRISCO COUNTY JR), CHRISTINE CLEMENSON, BILLY DRAGO (JOHN BLY) AND JULIUS CARY • *100-MIN PILOT &*

 TEAM PHOTOGRAPH *THE SECOND SEASON CAST OF BABYLON-5 (MINUS BILLY MUMY) POSE FOR A PUBLICITY SHOT WEARING THEIR STANDARD COSTUMES AND THE CUSTOMARY SERIOUS EXPRESSIONS*

50-MIN EPISODES

Took up where *The Wild, Wild West* had left off, carrying forward US TV's version of steampunk. County is a lawyer as well as a gunfighter whose crusade against John Bly, the enigmatic villain who killed his father, brings him into contact with an eccentric inventor and the far-reaching influence of the Orb — an Unearthed Foreign Object which can bestow paranormal powers on its owners. A patchwork that could only have been put together by a committee, occasionally passing beyond mere idiosyncrasy to the kind of serious weirdness that makes one regret that it only lasted one season — but that was half a year long, so it did better than most straightforward sf series.

Babylon 5

1993- • SERIES • US (PTEN) • *CREATOR* J. MICHAEL STRACZYNSKI • *STARRING* MICHAEL O'HARE (COMMANDER SINCLAIR), CLAUDIA CHRISTIAN (SUSAN IVANOVNA) AND JERRY DOYLE (GARIBALDI) • *100-MIN PILOT & 50-MIN EPISODES*

Babylon 5 is a huge space station which provides a kind of galactic cross-roads, administered by an interstellar United Nations.

The format takes up the political/moral crusade that became the heart and soul of *Star Trek* and its sequel series (the idea was initially pitched to the *ST* production team, who went on to develop the suspiciously similar but rather more claustrophobic *Deep Space Nine*), but is very obviously a product of the era of UN peacekeeping forces rather than that of the unreconstructed Cold War. The Earth/Minbari war is only one of the relatively limited short-term conflicts which keeps the station staff well-supplied with problems; the Narn/Centauri war also moves through a series of escalating phases as it hots up.

The first two seasons of *Babylon 5* concentrated heavily on one of the two standard *Star Trek* plot formulas: something nasty, or at least inconvenient, comes aboard the station and threatens selected characters or the whole shebang with disaster. This made it less flexible than *Star Trek* or *The Next Generation*, but the format was deployed with considerable ingenuity and the series showed no sign of running out of steam. Even so, the rather passive and diplomatic Commander Sinclair was replaced with the more combative Commander Sheridan (Bruce

Odd couples 2: Lois and Clark

In the new era of genuine partnership, it was inevitable that the umpteenth version of the Superman legend would award a more significant part to Lois Lane. When Christopher Reeve refused to let Margot Kidder play opposite him in the film *Superman IV* because she was too old, he committed a cardinal sin of sexism and his incarnation of the superhero had to give way to a new one. *Lois And Clark* finally brings out into the open what all previous versions of the myth had carefully skated over. Superman does not need Lois Lane — and, indeed, might cause terrible injury to her were a legion of his presumably invulnerable sperm ever to be ejaculated (presumably with superpowerful force) into her frail flesh — but Clark Kent does. The only way Clark can obtain a fully authenticated certificate of belonging to the human race is to win the love of a good woman, and to win it in his own right. It is not merely for the sake of the irrelevant Lewis-and-Clark pun that her name comes first in the show's title.

The fact that Clark is actually Superman will doubtless cause practical problems if he and Lois ever do get together, but that is irrelevant to the fact that while he is pretending to be Clark he must be forever questing for her approval and affection. While he commits himself to human disguise, he must also commit himself to human desires and human ambitions. The endorsement of a Lois-substitute is the only kind of proof and reassurance available to the millions of males who can only maintain their own morale by entertaining the fantasy that within their secret selves they are far more capable and glamorous than they presently seem to others.

The focal point of this timeslip romance is Gary's duplicitous relationships with his present-day wife and a publican's daughter living 50 years in the past — a kind of two-timing which seems (to him, at least) to be less despicable than contemporary adultery. Although the loss of David Ryall (who played Phoebe's suspicious father) at the end of season one removed an element of conflict from Gary's adulterous quest, the show continued to make progress. Gary plays an unassuming part in the war effort by raising morale with his imported songs and occasionally tipping the other characters off about significant things to come. With typical pusillanimity, though, the writers resolutely refuse to get seriously involved with time paradoxes.

Boxleitner) in the second series, with an eye to his getting out and about on a regular basis as the show continued to develop. The very effective computer-generated special effects were similarly given a gentle introduction but gradually stretched to display more and more of their potential.

Although *Babylon 5* makes productive use of the tensions inherent in the relationships which exist between its lead characters, it does not milk them in the intense soap opera-inspired fashion that *Star Trek* and its descendant series do. And the mystery element which is frequently invoked to add to the suspense is usually handled with reasonably good conscience. These factors combine to give the show a useful gloss of sophistication.

The hard-working J. Michael Straczynski has an unprecedented level of creative control over *Babylon 5*, writing the great majority of the episodes as well as controlling the overall strategy (which was cast from the beginning in the form of a five-year plan). He is thus capable of easing the forward development of the show in a measured fashion, unfolding new possibilities as they become technically and economically practical. It remains to be seen whether it will usher in a new era of auteur TV in the USA.

Goodnight Sweetheart

1993- • SITCOM • UK (ALOMO/BBC) • *CREATORS* LAURENCE MARKS & MAURICE GRAN • *STARRING* NICHOLAS LYNDHURST (GARY SPARROW), DERVLA KIRWAN (PHOEBE BAMFORD) AND MICHELLE HOLMES (YVONNE SPARROW) • *30-MIN EPISODES*

STAR-CROSSED LOVERS
LOIS DEMONSTRATES HER BUTTON-RIPPING SKILLS IN ORDER TO DISPLAY CLARK'S BEST FEATURE: HIS REMARKABLE ABILITY TO HIDE THE OBVIOUS

Lois And Clark: The New Adventures Of Superman

1993- • SERIES • US (WARNER/ABC) • *CREATOR* DEBORAH JOY LEVINE • *STARRING* DEAN CAIN (CLARK KENT) AND TERI HATCHER (LOIS LANE) • *90-MIN PILOT & 50-MIN EPISODES*

Once the films starring Christopher Reeve had

tied Superman's current career to spectacular state-of-the-art special effects there seemed to be little scope for a new TV version to operate, but LeVine's version put the Lois/Clark relationship centre-stage in soap-opera fashion. The likeable Cain and Hatcher fenced and flirted well enough to earn the show a second season, but the perishability of the goods had already begun to cause problems. It was no longer plausible for John Shea's Lex Luthor to provide the villainy every week, and the pivotal relationship was in danger of losing its dynamic force. Budget limitations ensured that the sf element in the show remains incidental, but it is an intriguing series nevertheless.

seaQuest DSV

1993- • SERIES • US (AMBLIN/NBC) • *CREATOR* ROCKNE S. O'BANNON • *STARRING* ROY SCHEIDER (CAPTAIN BRIDGER), STEPHANIE BEACHAM, STACY HAIDUK, DON FRANKLIN, JONATHAN BRANDIS AND ROYCE D. APPLEGATE • *90-MIN PILOT & 50-MIN EPISODES*

Steven Spielberg was one of its producers and it had a huge budget, so this updated version of *Voyage To The Bottom Of The Sea* raised high expectations. It aimed at seriousness, appending little essays to each first-season script which commented on the supposed scientific background of the plot-devices. Unfortunately, this led to criticism that the show was boringly unadventurous. The use of a juvenile lead (Brandis) and a smart talking dolphin to amplify kid-appeal was only moderately successful and the doggedly earnest and all-wise computer-with-a-face was difficult to swallow (especially for UK viewers familiar with *Red Dwarf*'s laconic original). Many changes were made to the cast and production-team for the second season — even Scheider eventually handed over the lead to Michael Ironside — but it still struggled to find an audience.

Star Trek: Deep Space Nine

1993- • SERIES • US (PARAMOUNT) • *CREATORS* RICK BERMAN & MICHAEL PILLER • *STARRING* AVERY BROOKS (COMMANDER SISKO), COLM MEANEY (O'BRIEN), RENE AUBERJONOIS (ODO), NANA VISITOR (KIRA) AND ARMIN SHIMERMAN (QUARK) • *100-MIN PILOT & 50-MIN EPISODES*

Sandwiched between two robustly revamped versions of the original, the slightly anomalous *Deep Space Nine* was always regarded as the runt of the Star Trek litter and is often unfavourably compared with *Babylon 5*. Whereas the other shows involve exploratory starships which at least pretend to be going where no one has gone before (although they usually end up grappling with the same old clichés), *Deep Space Nine* is more static, forced to import most of its plot-pivots. It routinely covers more territory than *Babylon 5* in a crudely literal sense, sending regular cast members off on an assortment of special missions, but it rarely contrived to send them anywhere very interesting.

Deep Space Nine is just as soap-operatic as its stable-mates, and it operates under the constant threat of chronic claustrophobia.

Although the show is essentially a psychological melodrama, it often trades heavily on the "child-like" nature of some of its characters, as when it foregrounds the diminutive and intensely egotistical Ferengi. It was hoped that the recruitment of *The Next Generation*'s Michael Dorn to the regular cast in the fourth season could stir the mix productively.

Time Trax

1993-94 • SERIES • US (LORIMAR/PTEN) • *CREATORS* HARVE BENNETT, JEFFREY HAYES AND GRANT ROSENBERG • *STARRING* DALE MIDKIFF (DARIEN LAMBERT), ELIZABETH ALEXANDER AND PETER DONAT • *90-MIN PILOT & 50-MIN EPISODES*

Criminals from 200 years hence have escaped into the present, so future cop Darien Lambert has to follow them and track them down, with the aid of one of those all-purpose-*deus-ex-machina* computers (named SELMA). Presumably inspired by *Terminator 2* but much more light-

ANOTHER TEAM PHOTOGRAPH
TWO UNRULY MEMBERS OF THE DEEP SPACE NINE CAST ARE ACTUALLY SMILING. THEIR UNIFORMS HAVE BEEN CAREFULLY DESIGNED TO MAKE THEM LOOK EVEN MORE ROUND-SHOULDERED THAN THEY ARE

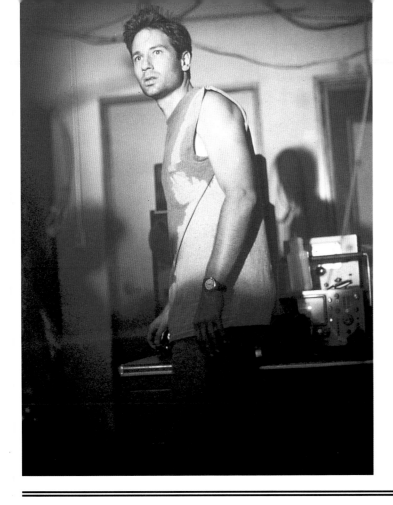

TRUST NO ONE
INTREPID FBI AGENT FOX MULDER, CONVINCED THAT THE TRUTH IS OUT THERE, FAILS TO NOTICE THAT HIS SHADOW SOMEHOW OPTED OUT OF HIS LAST HAIRCUT

Odd couples 3: Mulder and Scully

On the surface, Scully is just another female sidekick; although she doesn't actually outrank Mulder, he is the one with the relevant experience and expertise to deal with the *X-Files*. In the beginning, at least, Scully was merely a hapless sceptic, blinded by science, desperately in need of the education Mulder could provide. As with most conventional relationships of this kind, the two quickly built up a quasi-sexual affection which remained conscientiously unconsummated — but this particular relationship has some intriguing up-to-the-minute twists.

Scully carries forward the assumptions of independence and competence which allowed Mork's Mindy and Clark's Lois to claim their share of the spotlight. She was credited with enough intelligence to modify her scepticism considerably as evidence of its limitations mounted up, and enough craftsmanship in her work to do things which Mulder cannot. Hers is the cooler head in every crisis, hers the methodical analysis (continually manifest in the post-mortems which so many of the plots require her to carry out) which adds substance to his reckless intuitions.

Perhaps most significantly — although it is never explicitly stated — it is obviously not maidenly reserve on Scully's part which is responsible for the failure of their sexual relationship to progress beyond tender frustration. He is the one with all the hang-ups, who seems highly likely to be impotent — and that implication of literal impotence mirrors and supports the show's constant harping on the much broader impotence of Mulder's inability to discover or reveal the "truth" which remains "out there". Scully is more than just a sidekick, she is Mulder's anchorage, the one trustworthy thing in an untrustworthy world. Hers is the beckoning hand which might one day lead him back to full membership of the human race — but not, of course, until the series ends. On the other hand, whenever Scully's rationalist veneer is cracked by confrontation with the impossible, Mulder is there to remind her that it's possible to get by if you drift wherever the tide of imagination takes you.

---

hearted and far less exciting — as it was bound to be, given the budgetary limitations.

The X-Files

1993- • SERIES • US (FOX) • *CREATOR* CHRIS CARTER • *STARRING* DAVID DUCHOVNY (FOX MULDER) AND GILLIAN ANDERSON (DANA SCULLY) • *50-MIN EPISODES*

The X-Files rapidly progressed from cult status to field-leader, winning a Golden Globe award for best drama. It marked a sharp side-step from the seemingly-irresistible surge of the *Star Trek* clones.

The central premise of the series is that the FBI has accumulated a set of dossiers relating to bizarre incidents, whose data can be collated to reveal a number of basic patterns, the most significant of which concerns the activities of aliens responsible for abducting (but not always returning) human beings for mysterious experimental purposes. For almost 50 years, the existence of these aliens has been known to certain members of the political and military establishment but has been kept secret. The precise extent of this cover-up, and the motives behind it, are unclear but the conspiracy is wide

enough and active enough to constitute a "secret government" of the USA. The FBI is by no means free from the power and influence of this conspiracy but its organization is loose enough to entertain — and even, within limits, to facilitate — the obsessive quest of agent Fox Mulder to figure out exactly what is going on between the secret government and the enigmatic aliens who long ago abducted his infant sister. He is ably assisted in the quest by the scrupulously sceptical Dana Scully.

The X-Files picked up a plot-formula employed by the occult fiction series *The Night Stalker*, carefully transcending the crippling limitations which killed the earlier show. It simply was not plausible, as *The Night Stalker* had perforce to assert, that a single city could be invaded on a weekly basis by a series of supernatural monsters, each of which would be discovered by an investigative reporter only to disappear without leaving any significant evidential traces. Carter was mindful of all these potential weaknesses in planning *The X-Files*.

Mulder and Scully are much more mobile than *The Night Stalker*'s Kolchak, able to go

Just because you're paranoid...

The FBI's hypothetical X-Files constitute an encyclopaedic compendium of what Charles Fort's *The Book Of The Damned* (1919) labelled "damned data": reports by witnesses which other people refuse to accept, on the grounds that they do not fit into our contemporary view of the world. Fort's project — still carried forward by the *Fortean Times* — was to bring such data together in order that their patient accumulation and careful organization might allow us to glimpse and construct alternative world-views. Fort's fascination with such alternative world-views was largely unclouded by the need to believe in them, but his constructions were discomfiting nevertheless because they slyly suggested that the commonly accepted world-view was no more entitled to the compliment of faith than they were.

As the mass of data sanctified by common acceptance continues to grow, so does the mass of damned data. The more authority the scientific world-view gains, the more bizarre become the strange edifices of complex possibility into which damned data can be assembled. One of the strengths which has helped *The X-Files* acquire its leadership of the TV sf field is its staunch refusal to endorse any single alternative orthodoxy. Not only does the show insist on maintaining the murky visibility of a whole series of alternatives, it also maintains a blithe indifference to the fact that some of these alternatives are flatly contradictory, offering very different and mutually exclusive interpretations of similar phenomena. Aliens and their rogue DNA must compete continually with largely untapped reserves of human psychic power and authentic demonic intrusions.

Just because Mulder is clearly paranoid it doesn't mean that they aren't out to get him — but, because he knows perfectly well that they are out to get him, it doesn't mean that he'll ever figure out who or what "they" are. As the show's success testifies, anyone who doesn't feel like that in today's world has to be crazy.

wherever action happens to develop. Many of their cases are different manifestations of the same adversary, and the evidential traces whose publication might transform the world in which they operate are being carefully and deliberately wiped out by an active conspiracy. The fact that this extraordinary extrapolation of the implicit paranoia of the premise actually works is eloquent testimony to the extent of real belief in the tendency of those in power to keep secrets, to pursue their own clandestine agendas and to use the people to whom they are supposedly responsible as mere pawns in their schemes.

The X-Files is entirely uninhibited in its choice of motifs, making little distinction between the pseudo-scientific and the frankly occult. It employs two slogans —"Trust No One" and "The Truth Is Out There" — in a casually ironic fashion, operating within a world where everything can be something other than it seems and no limits are set on what might lurk behind familiar appearances. It is taken for granted that "the truth" is so far out that everything close at hand is likely to be a

treacherous lie. In such a fictional world, nothing is reliable — except, of course, the intense mutual loyalty of star-crossed partners. The show draws tremendous strength from the equally brilliant but sharply contrasting performances put in by Duchovny and Anderson; while he is incessantly twitchy and radiates vulnerability, she continually dissolves her stoical calmness into naked astonishment. Despite having to play several episodes of the second series sitting down, separated from her peripatetic partner by Anderson's real-life pregnancy, Scully contrived to retain a powerful counterweight within the plots. Her continued scepticism in the face of so much evidence soon became absurd, but Anderson was good enough to carry off the belated relaxation of Scully's refusal to take due note of mounting evidence.

Like *Babylon 5*, *The X-Files* is as close to a single-author product as any TV show is ever likely to get, allowing it to develop in a relatively coherent and progressive fashion. How long it will be able to maintain its intensely problematic dynamic remains to be seen, but it has established an important new benchmark, setting the standard by which all future TV's Earth-set sf melodramas would be judged.

Wild Palms

1993 • FIVE-PART SERIAL • US (ABC) • *EXECUTIVE PRODUCER* OLIVER STONE • *WRITER* BRUCE WAGNER • *STARRING* JAMES BELUSHI, DANA DELANY, DAVID WARNER, ROBERT LOGGIA, KIM CATTRALL, BEN SAVAGE AND ANGIE DICKINSON • *ONE 90-MIN & FOUR 50-MIN EPISODES*

An attempt to bring the spirit of cyberpunk to TV, the central theme of *Wild Palms* was the development of virtual reality technologies. These revolutionize TV by allowing viewers to be surrounded by holographic images — and, with the assistance of the psychedelic drug mimezine, to interact with such images. The Byzantine plot involves the ongoing war between two secret societies — the authoritarian Fathers and the Libertarian Friends — for control of the technology and its world-changing power, whose ramifications complicate the intimate relationships of the leading characters in an extraordinary fashion. The end-result is ludicrously overblown, utterly incoherent and monumentally implausible. William Gibson looked intensely uncomfortable in a cameo role as himself — as well he might — but the rhinoceros seemed comfortable enough in the empty swimming pool.

1994

M.A.N.T.I.S.

1994 • SERIES • US (FOX) • *CREATORS* JAMES MCADAMS AND BRYCE ZABEL • *STARRING* CARL LUMBLY (MILES HAWKINS) AND ROGER REES (JOHN STONEBRAKE) • *100-MIN PILOT & 50-MIN EPISODES*

An enhanced secret agent series featuring a disabled scientist who has developed an "exoskeleton" that gives him super-strength; he also has high-tech transport and weaponry necessary to help him in his crime-fighting exploits.

Although the pilot got a good rating and the show was aired immediately before *The X-Files*, this show failed to attract a similar audience.

The Outer Limits

1994 • ANTHOLOGY SERIES • US (SHOWTIME/CBS)
• *PRODUCERS* PEN DENSHAM, MICHAEL CASSUTT, MANNY
COTO AND JONATHAN GLASSNER • *50-MIN EPISODES*

The semi-successful resurrection of *The Twilight Zone* inspired the resurrection of *The Outer Limits*, beginning with a double-length adaptation of George R. R. Martin's award-wining novella 'Sandkings' (1979) starring Beau Bridges. The other scripts suffered badly by comparison, most of them being as doggedly crass as the worst of the originals they were imitating, but they did include a surprisingly effective dramatization of Eando Binder's creaky pulp story 'I, Robot' (1939).

RoboCop

1994 • SERIES • US (SKYVISION) • *EXECUTIVE PRODUCER* STEPHEN DOWNING • *STARRING* RICHARD EDEN AND YVETTE NIPAR • *50-MIN EPISODES*

The first two RoboCop movies traded on orgies of spectacular violence but the toning-down process begun with *RoboCop 3* inevitably continued in the TV adaptation, where the cyborg hero had to be reprogrammed to stop him actually hurting anybody — which rather defeated the point of the original exercise. The foregrounding of the reborn Murphy's relationship with "his" lost son gives the show a juvenile air, but the images of near-future urban decay and media madness display a dryly subtle wit.

Space Precinct

1994- • SERIES • US (MENTORN) • *CREATOR* GERRY ANDERSON • *STARRING* TED SHACKELFORD (BROGAN), ROB YOUNGBLOOD (HALDANE) AND SIMONE BENDIX
• *50-MIN EPISODES*

A cross between *CHiPs* and *Fireball XL-5*, which materialized as an appropriately monstrous mongrel. Yet another attempt by Anderson to adapt his modelling skills to the requirements of adult melodrama, first floated way back in 1987 with a pilot called *Space Police*. NYPD veteran Brogan is posted to 21st-century Demeter City to use his experience against alien villains in silly masks, aided by his sidekick, Haldane. Like all other Anderson products, *Space Precinct* is

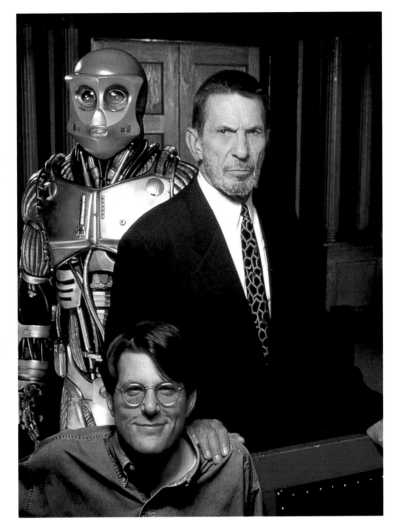

I, ROBOT *THE NEW SERIES OF* **THE OUTER LIMITS** *PAID HOMAGE TO THE OLD BY RESHOOTING EANDO BINDER'S STORY, WHOSE ORIGINAL TV CAST ALSO STARRED* **LEONARD NIMOY**

handicapped by the essential juvenility of his props and scenarios, effortlessly matched by the limited imagination of the writers.

Stark

1994 • THREE-PART SERIAL • UK (BBC2) • *PRODUCERS* MICHAEL WEARING, DAVID PARKER AND TIMOTHY WHITE
• *SCRIPT* BY BEN ELTON FROM HIS 1989 NOVEL • *STARRING* COLIN FRIELS, JACQUELINE MCKENZIE, BEN ELTON, DERRICK O'CONNOR AND JOHN NEVILLE • *55-MIN EPISODES*

Ben Elton's first novel attempted to amalgamate all the resources of his various writing endeavours into one politically correct, fashionably sexy and essentially anarchic plot. The self-effacing persona he adopts for his stand-up routines is here forced to specialize in nerdiness, while an appropriately ill-matched band of better-looking actors try to save the world from a conspiracy of industrialists who are

using pollution as a cleansing device. Hopelessly implausible and not very funny.

The Tommyknockers

1994 • TWO-PART MINI-SERIES • US (ABC) • *DIRECTOR* JOHN POWER • *SCRIPT* BY LAWRENCE D. COHEN FROM STEPHEN KING'S 1987 NOVEL • *STARRING* JIMMY SMITS, MARG HELGENBERGER, JOHN ASHTON AND ROBERT CARRADINE
• *100-MIN EPISODES*

King's standard routine of ancient horror stalking a small town is, for once, given a forthright science-fictional rationale. As a crashed alien spaceship is slowly unearthed, its inhabitants extend their control over the townspeople, conferring telepathic powers upon them — but one man is immune because he has a steel plate in his head, and he must become the town's self-sacrificing saviour. Thoroughly competent melodrama.

1995

Earth-2

1995 • SERIES • US (AMBLIN/NBC) • *CREATORS*
MICHAEL DUGGAN, CAROL FLINT AND MARK LEVIN
• *STARRING* DEBRA FARENTINO AND CLANCY BROWN
• *100-MIN PILOT & 50-MIN EPISODES*
Earth has become uninhabitable, but humanity
survives in an assortment of space habitats;
when a "new Earth" is discovered orbiting
another star, a ship is sent to investigate. It
crashes on landing, leaving the surviving crew-
members to trek across the surface. Another
series much-hyped by virtue of the involvement
of Steven Spielberg's Amblin Entertainment, it
was cancelled at the end of its first season.

The Langoliers

1995 • TWO-PART MINI-SERIES • US (ABC) • *DIRECTOR*
TOM HOLLAND • *SCRIPT* BY TOM HOLLAND FROM STEPHEN
KING'S NOVELLA • *STARRING* PATRICIA WETTIG, BRONSON
PINCHOT AND DEAN STOCKWELL • *100-MIN EPISODES*
The Stephen King mini-series had become an
annual ritual for ABC by the time this relatively
obscure timeslip story was dramatized. Ten
passengers on an air flight are decanted into a
past which is being literally eaten up by the
mysterious Langoliers, becoming increasingly
anxious as the climax approaches. Unfortunately,
the computer-generated effects look rather silly.

Sliders

1995- • SERIES • US (FOX) • *CREATORS* TRACY TORM &
ROBERT K. WEISS • *STARRING* JERRY O'CONNELL, SABRINA
LLOYD, JOHN RHYS-DAVIES AND CLEAVANT DERRICKS
• *100-MIN PILOT & 50-MIN EPISODES*
A young genius invents a machine which opens
a portal to an infinite series of parallel worlds,
each one subtly different from our own;
inevitably, he gets lost in the maze along with
the girl who loves him, his college professor and
an ageing black pop singer. The premise had
more potential than *The Fantastic Journey* or
Quantum Leap but this was left undeveloped
when the show was axed mid-season.
Happily, Fox relented and put plans in hand
for its resurrection.

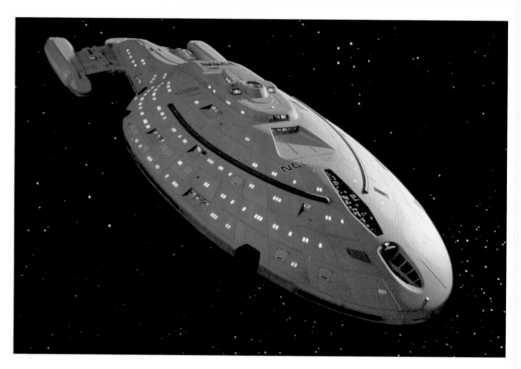

VOYAGER IN THE UNKNOWN *ANY RESEMBLANCE BETWEEN THE GOOD SHIP* VOYAGER *AND A CLUB-FOOTED CUTTLEFISH SWIMMING BACKWARDS IS PURELY COINCIDENTAL*

Space: Above And Beyond

1995- • SERIES US (FOX) • *CREATORS* GLEN MORGAN
AND JAMES WONG • *STARRING* MORGAN WEISSER (NATHAN
WEST), KRISTEN CLOKE (SHANE VANCE), RODNEY ROWLAND
(COOPER HAWKE), JAMES MORRISON (COMMANDER
MCQUEEN) AND R. LEE ERMEY (SERGEANT MAJOR BOUGUS)
• *100-MIN PILOT & 50-MIN EPISODES*
In the late 21st century, a group of young and
inexperienced starfighter pilots are thrust into
the front line of humanity's war against an
enigmatic race of aliens. A second attempt (after
Battlestar Galactica) to bring the kind of space
combat which worked so well in *Star Wars* to the
small screen. The format is more openly and
more straightforwardly militaristic than the
diplomatically minded *Star Trek* clones, but the
character of Hawke (a test-tube product
engineered for soldiering) allows issues of
prejudice against minorities to be introduced
and there are Artificial Intelligences too.

Star Trek: Voyager

1995- • SERIES • US (PARAMOUNT) • *CREATORS* RICK
BERMAN, MICHAEL PILLER & JERI TAYLOR • *STARRING* KATE
MULGREW (CAPTAIN JANEWAY), ROBERT PICARDO (THE
DOCTOR), ROBERT BELTRAN (CHAKOTAY), ROXANN BIGGS-
DAWSON (B'ELANNA TORRES), TIM RUSS (TUVOK), GARRET
WANG (KIM), ETHAN PHILLIPS (NEELIX) AND JENNIFER
LIEN (KES) • *100-MIN PILOT AND 50-MIN EPISODES*
While Gene Roddenberry was in charge of *Star
Trek* and *The Next Generation*, he was insistent
that the crews of his ships should be teams, all
pulling together in spite of the variety of their
earthly and unearthly backgrounds. *Voyager*
loosened that insistence considerably,
introducing a higher degree of essential tension
into its regular cast by incorporating the crew of
an outlaw vessel into that of the eponymous
starship. This move had the beneficial effect of
heightening the drama of shipboard action, but
that had the further consequence of narrowing
the focus of the show even more than was the
case in *The Next Generation* or *Deep Space Nine*.
The opportunity to develop the discomforts of
the shared space within the show's standard sets
diverted the writers' attention away from the
fact that the ship — which has been
accidentally displaced into a remote region of
unexplored space — is operating in virgin
territory. When the ship did encounter new

phenomena in season one, these generally turned out to be mysterious energies which reeled off much the same repertoire of nuisance-causing tricks that the first two series had already worked to death.

Considering that Kate Mulgrew was a very late replacement for Genevieve Bujold, she does a good job as anchor-person. The rest of the cast had to take turns to develop their characters during season one and did not emerge as quickly or as fully as the heroes of *The Next Generation*. The most interesting is the doctor, a holographic projection of an expert system held within the computer. The show retains considerable potential, which might yet overleap the creeping stultification that eventually overtook *The Next Generation* and carry the saga forward for some years to come.

ekWar

1995- • SERIES • US (USA) • *CREATOR* WILLIAM SHATNER, BASED ON A SERIES OF BOOKS PUBLISHED UNDER HIS NAME • *STARRING* GREG EVIGAN (JAKE CARDIGAN) AND WILLIAM SHATNER (WALTER BASCOM) • *50-MIN EPISODES*
"Tek" is an addictive virtual reality experience which is gradually destroying society. Cardigan is an ex-cop sent out on corrective missions by the enigmatic Bascom, according to the usual formula. Superb special effects made up for tired plotting so much that, although the show was pulled at the end of season one, it was given a second lease of life as a series of TV movies.

VR 5

1995 • SERIES • US (FOX) • *CREATORS* THANIA ST JOHN, MICHAEL KATLEMAN, GEOFFREY HEMWELL, JEANNINE RENSHAW AND ADAM CHERRY • *STARRING* LORI SINGER (SYDNEY BLOOM), ANTHONY HEAD AND MICHAEL EASTON • *100-MIN PILOT & 50-MIN EPISODES*
Sydney Bloom discovers that, if her telephone is off the hook when she is playing with her computer, she can project herself into dreamlike virtual realities, discover information about the real world and alter the course of its events. She seeks help, and is quickly recruited into the usual clandestine secret organization, where she is fed with missions according to the usual formula. This too was pulled after one season.

SF in other shows

Various anthology series not primarily devoted to sf have included sf episodes, most notably *Alfred Hitchcock Presents* (US 1957-65) and *Tales Of The Unexpected* (UK 1979-88). More interesting, perhaps, are the sf parodies included in various comedy shows, pioneered by the *Monty Python* "science-fiction sketch" in which giant alien blancmanges transform everyone in the world into Scotsmen in order to facilitate victory in the Wimbledon tennis tournament. *The Goodies* (UK 1970-82) frequently used sf motifs, including the celebrated episode in which Kitten Kong devastated a cardboard London after the fashion of a Japanese monster movie.

The Muppet Show (UK 1976-81) made a running gag out of its serial 'Pigs In Space', much as *The Real McCoy* (UK 1995-) was later to do with its parody of the soap *EastEnders* 'Rub-a-Dub In Space'. *The Comic Strip Presents* (UK 1982-92) included two sf parodies, the more memorable being 'The Yob', a two-part parody of the recently-remade movie *The Fly*.

By far the most sustained exercise in satirical sf contained within a TV show was, however, that featured in the American mock-soap opera *Soap*, which featured a long sequence in which Bert (Richard Mulligan) was kidnapped by aliens and replaced by an unconvincing double — a plot-line presumably inspired by the fact that the over-extended writers of *Dynasty*, having run out of plausible ways to cope with defections from the cast, dispensed with Fallon by having her disappear in the wake of a UFO sighting.

Science fiction on radio

RADIO'S GREATEST DISADVANTAGE — THE LACK OF A PICTURE — IS POTENTIALLY ITS GREATEST ADVANTAGE IN THE DEVELOPMENT OF IMAGINARY WORLDS, BUT ITS POSSIBILITIES HAVE NOT BEEN FULLY EXPLORED

Although some marginal sf elements were incorporated into early US adventure serials by Carlton E. Morse, the history of radio sf really began with adaptations of the comic strip *Buck Rogers In The 25th Century*, which began in 1932 and continued fitfully until 1946. Although many of the scripts were adapted from the comic strip, they were mostly written by the show's producer Jack Johnstone. The Flash Gordon comic strip was also adapted for radio but made a much bigger impact in the cinema.

By far the most famous adaptation of a science-fiction story for American radio was Orson Welles's Mercury Theater of the Air version of *The War Of The Worlds* by H. G. Wells, broadcast in 1938. "News reports" of alien landings employed to heighten the drama were mistaken for authentic reports by some listeners, who alerted their neighbours and provoked panic. Press coverage of the phenomenon exaggerated its scale, but it remained a fascinating aberration, calling forth explanatory essays from psychologists and sociologists who sought to use it as an indicator of the level of paranoia felt by ordinary people in isolationist America as they contemplated Europe's gradual slide into a new World War.

Across the Atlantic, the BBC's near-contemporary adaptation of Eden Phillpotts's novel *The Owl Of Athene*, which included low-key "news reports" of giant crabs emerging from the sea at Weston-Super-Mare, a holiday town in the West of England, seems to have passed entirely without incident, although whether this proves the British were less paranoid at the time remains uncertain.

Many of the mystery serials which were broadcast profusely on American radio during the

THE GREATEST TRIUMPH OF RADIO SF
Orson Welles's dramatization of The War Of
The Worlds *was a little too convincing for some of
its listeners*

the kind of pulp-fiction-based material that was commonplace in the USA. It did, however, broadcast serial novels and short stories, a few of which were sf. Karel Capek's robot play *R.U.R.* was aired in 1937. H. G. Wells was frequently featured, notably in a 1949 dramatization of *The Time Machine*, and sometime writers of scientific romance such as John Gloag wrote stories specifically for broadcast — but Olaf Stapledon's 'Far Future Calling', a radio play based on *Last And First Men*, never went out on air.

After World War II, the pulp- and comic-based serials quickly faded into extinction. The main US vehicle for radio sf became the anthology series *Dimension X*, subsequently retitled *X Minus 1*, which ran from 1949 to 1957 and drew its material from more sophisticated sources, including stories by Ray Bradbury and Robert A. Heinlein. This show was the forerunner of TV anthology series such as *The Twilight Zone*, which took up the baton of broadcast sf in the 1950s, leaving US radio to be taken over almost entirely by music and news.

In Britain, radio sf also made significant progress after the war. *Children's Hour* played host to several sf serials in the early 1950s, including some based on Angus MacVicar's popular series of Lost Planet books, but by far the most significant enterprise was *Journey Into Space* (1953-55), which ran three serial stories scripted for the medium by Charles Chilton. These serials featured Andrew Faulds (later a member of parliament) as space pioneer Jet Morgan, who raced the Russians into orbit before meeting aliens on the moon and foiling an invasion from Mars. Aired at 7.30pm, *Journey Into Space* eventually pulled in record audiences of five million, giving rise to novelizations of the scripts and a newspaper comic strip. When the BBC failed to follow it up, Radio Luxembourg — a commercial station whose broadcasts were aimed at the UK from beyond Reith's sternly patrolled boundaries — casually pirated the

1930s and 1940s used criminal scientists empowered with new inventions as villains, as did the pulp magazines from which they were derived. Some of the heroes fighting them also had paranormal abilities, most notably The Shadow (1931-54), who was briefly played by Orson Welles in the early part of his radio career. The radio version of *Superman* slotted into this

kind of scenario, while the "original" products of the new medium included the hunchbacked scientific genius Peter Quill.

In Britain, the BBC remained in the imperious grip of founding father Lord Reith's influence from the 1920s until the early 1950s; without commercial rivals, it had no need to respond to popular demand and would not admit comic-strip hero Dan Dare, although his radio incarnation was a pale shadow of the original.

As in the US, it was TV that carried on the tradition established by Jet Morgan; *Journey Into Space* was the predecessor of such serials as the Quatermass trilogy and *The Trollenberg Terror*.

By virtue of the BBC's continued domination, British radio broadcasting was not so quickly taken over by music and news. Radio 4 remains to the present day a significant vehicle for short stories, original plays and serialized novels; over the years, a great deal of sf has been broadcast, usually integrated into the standard pattern of fiction broadcasting, thus avoiding the "ghetto effect" arising from the separation of sf from other kinds of fiction on bookshop shelves. Work by John Christopher and Brian Aldiss, which was always perfectly respectable in literary terms, seemed all the more so when broadcast by the BBC without the sort of warning packaging which tended to place published sf in the 1950s and 1960s in a kind of quarantine.

Although there are difficulties involved in creating a science-fictional "atmosphere" for a radio broadcast, radio's special effects are very much cheaper than TV's and radio remains an attractive medium for sf in spite of its low audiences for drama.

It is perhaps surprising that it took so long for the BBC to generate another success to compare with *Journey Into Space*, but it was not until 1978 that the first six-part serial of Douglas Adams's *The Hitch-Hiker's Guide To The Galaxy* was broadcast. Adams's brilliantly funny scripts quickly built up a cult following and generated considerable "word of mouth" advertising; the level of interest demanded a follow-up serial in 1980. Like *Journey Into Space*, the produce of *The Hitch-Hiker's Guide To The Galaxy* was quickly spun off into other media, including TV — but, without the preparatory work done by radio, the far more expensive TV series would never have been granted its budget, and the whole sub-genre of comedy space opera (which also includes the hugely successful *Red Dwarf*) would never have got off the ground in the UK.

More earnest serial sf also made a comeback on British radio in the early 1980s, probably inspired by the success of *Star Trek* on TV and Star Wars in the cinema as much as by *The Hitch-Hiker's Guide To The Galaxy*. The proportion of sf stories included in anthology series such as *Saturday Night Theatre* expanded dramatically. Charles Chilton returned to the medium, initially with a Jet Morgan adventure cast as a single play, *The Return To Mars*, and then two serials featuring the Space Force, but he had not kept up with developments in the genre and his work now seemed woefully dated. James Follett's serials *Earth Search* and *Earth Search II*, novelized in 1981, were considerably better, although still naive by comparison with contemporary sf written for book publication. A series of comic-book adaptations by producer Dirk Maggs, introduced by the one-off *The Trial Of Superman* (1988) on Radio 4, culminated in *Judge Dredd: The Radio Serial* (1995), which ran five days a week on national rock station Radio 1 (in three-minute episodes). When the TV version of *Doctor Who* was cancelled — or at least mothballed — in the early 1990s, the BBC

offered some compensation in the form of radio adaptations, but the audience was generally unsympathetic to what most of its members considered a retrograde step.

By the time commercial radio was finally launched in Britain, the medium had been given over lock, stock and barrel to popular music but occasional sf intrusions were featured, including one of disc jockey Kenny Everett's battery of imaginary characters, Captain Kremmen. Piccadilly Radio in Manchester broadcast Stephen Gallagher's six-part serial *The Last Rose Of Summer*, which was subsequently novelized.

Radio 4 continues to broadcast a steady trickle of sf, including original plays and adaptations as well as straightforward readings. It also offers occasional critical commentary on the mythologies of sf, as in the four-part series *Space Fictions* (1996), which analysed literary uses of space travel and the attitudes reflected therein.

Although it is difficult to imagine that broadcasters will contrive to cultivate an audience for ambitious and innovative radio in a TV-dominated age, the possibility remains open.

Sf hits

Radio listeners and TV viewers occasionally encounter sf imagery in pop music. The first sf-related record to reach Number 1 in the British singles chart was 'In The Year 2525' by Zager & Evans in 1969. David Bowie's 'Space Oddity' was released in the same year, but only reached number 1 when it was re-released in 1975. Novelty spin-offs 'Star Trekkin' by the Firm and 'Doctorin' The Tardis' by the Timelords (who later became the KLF) reached number 1 in 1987 and 1988. Other UK Number 1s which might be reckoned borderline sf are 'Walking On The Moon' (1979) by the Police, 'Stay' (1992) by Shakespear's Sister and 'Spaceman' (1996) by Babylon Zoo, which was the soundtrack for a Levi's ad.

Musical spin-offs from sf films and TV shows which made the British Top 10 without hitting Number 1 were Meco's "Cantina Band" version of the 'Star Wars Theme' (1977), Queen's 'Flash' (1980), Eurythmics's 'Sex Crime (Nineteen Eighty-Four)' (1986) and FAB's

'Thunderbirds Are Go' (1990). FAB also released two other theme-music remixes in 1990 — 'The Prisoner' and 'The Stingray Megamix' — but neither reached the Top 50. Marvin the Paranoid Android's 'Marvin' (1981) had suffered a similar fate a decade earlier. Don Spencer's 'Fireball' (1963) — the theme-song of *Fireball XL-5* — peaked at 32, the Shadows's 'Stingray' (1965) at 19. The Barry Gray Orchestra's versions of 'Thunderbirds' (1981) and 'Joe 90/Captain Scarlet Theme' (1986) failed to reach the Top 50.

David Bowie had further Top 10 hits with 'Starman' (1972) and 'Life On Mars' (1973), while 'Loving The Alien' just sneaked into the Top 20 in 1985. A Bauhaus cover version of 'Ziggy Stardust' managed to reach number 15 in 1982. Elton John's 'Rocket Man' just failed to hit number 1 in 1972. Other relevant Top 10 hits include 'Calling Occupants Of Interplanetary Craft' (1977) by the Carpenters, 'I Lost My Heart To A Starship Trooper' (1978) by Sarah Brightman and Hot Gossip and 'Clouds Across The Moon' (1985) by the Rah Band.

the SF Files

THROUGHOUT THE HISTORY OF SF INDIVIDUALS

HAVE STOOD OUT AS PIONEERS AND

GROUNDBREAKERS ALL OF WHOM ARE FOUND IN

THIS WHO'S WHO OF SF

ARTHUR C. CLARKE *INVENTOR OF THE COMSAT, INSPIRER OF* **2001: A SPACE ODYSSEY,** *RESIDENT OF SRI LANKA, REFLECTS ON A VARIED LIFE*

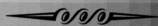

DOUGLAS ADAMS

BRITISH NOVELIST

BORN: 1952

Humorous writer whose cult novel, *The Hitch Hiker's Guide To The Galaxy* (1980), won immediate fame. Based on a radio series, the picaresque parody of sf tropes serves a satire loosely directed at all forms of pomposity, authoritarianism and pretension. There are echoes of Sheckley, and even more strongly, of Vonnegut's *The Sirens Of Titan*. The book's central conceit is that the Earth is a gigantic computer, programmed to find the ultimate question about "Life, the Universe and Everything", to which the answer ("42") is already known.

It begins with the destruction of the Earth in order to make way for an "interstellar bypass", a deed perpetrated by Vogons, a species of superlative crassness; but as time is no less malleable than space, that is far from the end of the matter. The hero, Arthur Dent, is smuggled aboard one of the Vogon craft by his friend Ford Prefect (actually an alien journalist, researching for yet another edition of *The Hitch Hiker's Guide To The Galaxy*), and progresses through many worlds without discarding the dressing gown he was wearing in the first place. The four successors to *Hitch Hiker* contain many good jokes, but are less even in quality.

BRIAN W. ALDISS

BRITISH NOVELIST

BORN: 1925

A productive, protean polymath, Aldiss has attained renown as a critic, poet, author of best-selling mainstream fictions and even illustrator. But the core of his reputation will always be the dozens of groundbreaking sf novels and hundreds of sf stories he has produced since the start of his career in 1954. The milestones of Aldiss's career chart the course of a writer constantly seeking to expand his previous accomplishments, a talent never content to rest on its laurels.

Early stories such as 'Poor Little Warrior' and 'Who Can Replace A Man?' (both 1958) showed a writer of high style and wry sensibilities, possessor of a voice both distinctively British,

BRIAN ALDISS *ONE OF THE OLD MASTERS OF BRITISH SF, HE IS ALSO A MAINSTREAM NOVELIST, POET, BROADCASTER AND CRITIC*

yet universal. The publication of *Non-Stop* (1958), a generation-starship tale, and *Hothouse* (1962; also known as *The Long Afternoon Of Earth*), set on a dying globe, proved that Aldiss could juggle standard sf tropes with daring dexterity. *Greybeard* (1964) was perhaps the first and finest embodiment of what Aldiss refers to as "a tragic sense of life", a viewpoint not excluding comedy and robust affirmations.

As New Wave forces burgeoned, Aldiss signalled his enlistment with such masterful salvos as the claustrophobic *Report On Probability A* (1968) and the psychedelic *Barefoot In The Head* (1969). The 1970s saw Aldiss produce his history of sf, *Billion Year Spree* (1973), which cleverly nominated Mary Shelley as the mother of modern sf. That decade also boasted a host of accomplished novels and stories. But it was with the publication of his Helliconia trilogy — *Helliconia Spring* (1982), *Helliconia Summer* (1983) and *Helliconia Winter* (1985) — that Aldiss once more firmly captured the imaginations of sf readers, this time with an examination of how exceedingly long seasons dominate a humanoid culture. Generous with

crediting role-models from Shakespeare to Wells to Lovecraft, delving deeply into Jungian depths, chronicler of both war and romance, Aldiss makes every new book a shaman's surprise.

IRWIN ALLEN

AMERICAN FILM AND TV PRODUCER

BORN: 1916 DIED: 1991

Allen's run-of-the-mill sf movies include *The Lost*

IRWIN ALLEN *PRODUCER OF SCHLOCK SF FOR AMERICAN TV — SOME OF IT FONDLY REMEMBERED BY THOSE WHO WERE VERY YOUNG AT THE TIME*

World (1960; from Conan Doyle's novel), *Voyage To The Bottom Of The Sea* (1961) and *The Swarm* (1978; from a novel by Arthur Herzog), but he probably made a bigger impact with TV series, including a successful one based on the second of these films (1964-68). Others of his series, often criticized for their unashamed juvenility, include *Lost In Space* (1965-68), *The Time Tunnel* (1966-67), *Land Of The Giants* (1968-70) and the mini-series *The Return Of Captain Nemo* (1978; vaguely inspired by Jules Verne).

ROGER MacBRIDE ALLEN

AMERICAN NOVELIST
BORN: 1957

Empathetically capable of carrying on Isaac Asimov's Robot series with entries such as *Caliban* (1993) and *Inferno* (1994), Allen is one of the most assiduous of the new generation of hard-sf writers. In his own Hunted Earth series, he pushes the entire Solar System through a cosmic trap door big enough to hide Doc Smith's wonders.

GERRY ANDERSON

BRITISH TV PRODUCER
BORN: 1929

Popular with those nostalgic for their 1960s childhoods, puppeteer Anderson has also been excoriated as one of the worst sf producers ever: his scripts are full of scientific howlers. Series include the puppet shows *Fireball XL5* (1962-63), *Stingray* (1964-65), *Thunderbirds* (1965-66) and *Captain Scarlet And The Mysterons* (1967-68), and the live-action *UFO* (1970-73), *Space: 1999* (1975-77) and, after a long break, *Space Precinct* (from 1993).

KEVIN J. ANDERSON

AMERICAN NOVELIST
BORN: 1962

Anderson has written *Star Wars* spin-offs and other things, but he is best regarded for a number of original novels in collaboration with Doug Beason, including *Lifeline* (1990) and *The Trinity Paradox* (1991). In the inventive *Assemblers Of Infinity* (1993), Moon colonists become infected by alien nanotech viruses, and

the plot concerns human efforts to understand the purpose of these microscopic machines and the structures they have built.

MICHAEL ANDERSON

BRITISH FILM DIRECTOR
BORN: 1920

A workaday film-maker best remembered for the World War II heroics of *The Dam Busters* (1954), Anderson also directed a surprising number of sf projects, among them *Nineteen Eighty-Four* (1955; from George Orwell's novel), *Doc Savage: The Man Of Bronze* (1975; from Lester Dent's pulp novella), *Logan's Run* (1976; from William F. Nolan and George Clayton Johnson's novel) and *Millennium* (1989; from John Varley's story and script). He also helmed the TV mini-series *The Martian Chronicles* (1980; from Ray Bradbury's stories). Few of these earned him much praise.

POUL ANDERSON

AMERICAN NOVELIST
BORN: 1926

Anderson first came to prominence with *Brain Wave* (1954), where the intelligence of all chordate species, including mankind, suddenly and hugely increases. No writer could handle this theme without concluding that everyone will come to adopt the political, religious and moral views which he himself holds, but Anderson manages much believable conflict on the way. There are two major viewpoints, those of a computer scientist and a moronic but well-balanced farm-worker, and the ending, while optimistic, shows a melancholy awareness that nothing worthwhile is achieved without a cost — which often falls most heavily on those who benefit least.

This is typical of Anderson's oeuvre, which is imbued with the themes of duty, obligation, nemesis and self-sacrifice. His best books include *The Enemy Stars* (1959), *Let The Spaceman Beware* (1963), *Tau Zero* (1970) and the sequence featuring Dominic Flandry, soldier of a decadent Terran empire, who frequently finds more to admire in his enemies than in those he is sworn to protect. This series reaches a magnificent climax in *A Knight Of Ghosts And*

Shadows (1974). Anderson's time-travel stories (including the excellent *Guardians Of Time*, 1960, and *There Will Be Time*, 1972) are notable for being tied to no consistent metaphysic.

PATRICIA ANTHONY

AMERICAN NOVELIST
BORN: 1947

A rising star from Texas, who began writing in middle-age, Anthony has produced in short order such ingenious novels as *Cold Allies* (1993), *Brother Termite* (1993) and *Happy Policeman* (1994).

PIERS ANTHONY

AMERICAN NOVELIST
BORN: 1934

British-born Anthony is one of the most popular and prolific writers in both sf and humorous fantasy. At first, with books like the vivid and grotesque *Chthon* (1967) — in which the hero must escape from a terrifying prison planet and go in search of his own true nature — and the much more ambitious *Macroscope* (1969), he had the reputation of being a rather daring "New Wave" writer. It soon became apparent, though, that Anthony could churn out more routine adventures with great ease, and this was first exemplified by the post-bomb, future-barbarism trilogy comprising *Sos The Rope* (1968), *Var The Stick* (1972) and *Neq The Sword* (1975).

Later series include a large-scale, space-operatic effort beginning with *Cluster* (1977) and continuing with *Chaining The Lady* (1978), *Kirlian Quest* (1978), *Thousandstar* (1980) and *Viscous Circle* (1982).

There is a certain interminability about latter-day Anthony, and many sf readers are now content to leave him to the teenage fantasy fans who seem to form his core readership.

JACK ARNOLD

AMERICAN FILM DIRECTOR
BORN: 1916 DIED: 1992

In the early days of sf cinema, director Jack Arnold was regarded as one of the genre's leading *auteurs*.

The films which qualified him for this

ISAAC ASIMOV — AMERICAN NOVELIST — BORN:1920 DIED:1992

Russian-born writer of enormous influence, credited with adding the word "robotics" to the language, and the famous Three Laws thereof: "1) A robot may not injure a human being or, through inaction, allow a human being to come to harm; 2) A robot must obey the orders given it by human beings except where such orders would conflict with the First Law; 3) A robot must protect its own existence except where such orders would conflict with the First or Second Law." These laws dominate many stories of varying quality, collected as *I, Robot* (1950) and *The Rest Of The Robots* (1964), the most famous being 'Liar', in which a robot is forced into a situation where every form of action, or inaction, will violate the First Law and suffers catatonic collapse. They also underpin *The Caves Of Steel* (1954) and *The Naked Sun* (1957), sf detective stories set respectively on an overpopulated Earth and a barely populated colony world.

Asimov's most famous novels comprise the Foundation trilogy: *Foundation* (1951), *Foundation And Empire* (1952) and *Second Foundation* (1953). These project the collapse of the Roman Empire on to a galactic scale, and postulate a science of "psycho-history" that will allow two Foundations, the First being open, and based on the physical sciences, the Second hidden, and using parapsychology, to shorten the ensuing dark ages from about 30 millennia to one. This seems to work at first, and the Eastern Roman parallel is worked out in some detail, with analogues of Justinian, Belisarius and the last-gasp eastern imperium at Trebizond; but the entire scheme is thrown awry when The Mule comes on the scene. He is a mutant who uses his ability to manipulate minds by direct force to give history a new, calamitous direction uncharted by the psycho-historians. The third part concerns the efforts of the Second Foundation both to get history back on course and to avoid detection and destruction by the First, which for no obvious reason has become paranoid and perceives it as a rival.

Although much of the writing seems dated now, and there is little sense that humanity has changed significantly in the hundreds of millennia supposedly separating it from the present, the trilogy remains a landmark classic of the genre, and contains Asimov's most famous epigram: "Violence is the last refuge of the incompetent." Two other novels are loosely

ISAAC ASIMOV *INVENTOR OF THE 'THREE LAWS OF ROBOTICS', HERE SEEN ENJOYING HIS STATUS OF GRAND OLD MAN AND WEARING HIS FAVOURITE TIE*

linked to the trilogy. *The Currents Of Space* (1952) is set partly on Florina, a farming world dedicated to the production of a wonder textile that will grow nowhere else, partly on Sark, the world that holds Florina in thrall. Florina is due for disaster, but how can the protagonist arrange its evacuation? In *Pebble In The Sky* (1950), a man of the 20th century is projected into a far-future Earth, where much of the land is radioactive, suicide at 60 is a legal obligation and Earth people are held in general contempt (this last feature is obviously based on the anti-Semitism which Asimov experienced as a young man).

After years of concentrating mainly on non-fiction, Asimov returned to the copious production of sf with *Foundation's Edge* (1982), the first of several late-in-the-day but best-selling sequels (or prequels) to his early books. These culminated in *Forward The Foundation* (1993), an episodic narrative (reflecting the form of the earliest volumes in the series, written in the 1940s) in which the sage Hari Seldon attempts to build his twin foundations which will preserve human knowledge during the long night of the fall of the Galactic Empire. Asimov's final novel, it was written against the deadline of his own death.

J. G. BALLARD — BRITISH NOVELIST — BORN: 1930

The diverse fictions of Ballard's long and fruitful career are united by an almost hallucinatory intensity of vision; a shared trove of disturbing archetypal images that resonate both with the author's personal history and the dreams of his readers; and an unfaltering desire to pierce the veil of consensus reality. From his first strikingly assured stories in US and UK genre magazines (1956 onward), through his "disaster" novels, into his late-1960s experimental "condensed novels", onward to his "myths of the near future", his para-mimetic autobiographical books and his most recent fables of modern lapses into primitivism, Ballard has fearlessly conducted reconnaissances through an "inner space" frequently neglected in traditional sf.

Ballard's early magazine stories — replete with images of lost souls striving for dimly apprehended transfigurations in a shattered technological landscape lit by nuclear explosions, rocket-launch flames and the glow of television screens — were quickly collected into several influential volumes such as *The Voices Of Time* (1963) and *The Terminal Beach* (1964). A later collection of linked stories, *Vermilion Sands* (1971), set the standard for sf depiction of decadent, self-contained communities, a standard later followed by such writers as Ed Bryant, Michael Coney and Lee Killough. Ballard's quartet of world-destroying novels — *The Wind From Nowhere* and *The Drowned World* (both 1962); *The Burning World* (1964); and *The Crystal World* (1966) — updated the cosy and conservative John Wyndham-type scenarios for a decade, the 1960s, already experiencing tremendous real-life global transformations of political and socio-cultural stripes.

Had Ballard's career ended here, his place in the genre would have been assured — yet vastly different from what he would eventually accomplish. For he soon went on to achieve even greater public status and heights of artistry. Buoyed by the heady atmosphere of the "New Wave" surging through the sf field in the mid-to-late-1960s, Ballard began to experiment further with both the form and content of his narratives. In the work of this period, media personalities loomed over Daliesque territories inhabited by mutable characters infused with manic vigour. *The Atrocity Exhibition* (1970) and *Crash* (1973)

J. G. BALLARD *HAS ALWAYS BEEN FOND OF TURNING SF (AND OUR WORLD) ON ITS HEAD*

represent the apex of this phase of Ballard's writing.

The 1970s represent a kind of necessary falling back from such extremes, and a reconsolidation for Ballard: fine novels such as *Concrete Island* (1974), *High-Rise* (1975) and *The Unlimited Dream Company* (1979), as well as a continuing stream of short stories, recapitulated his tropes and themes without vastly extending them. In 1984, with the publication of *Empire Of The Sun*, this low profile was to change. Retelling Ballard's own childhood experiences as a prisoner of the Japanese in wartime China, this novel managed a brilliant melding of realism and surrealism, earning Ballard widespread public recognition further extended by the filming of the book by Steven Spielberg in 1987. *The Kindness Of Women* (1991) carried forward the tale of young Jim through the 1960s and into the 1980s.

Ballard's recent novels— *The Day Of Creation* (1987), *Running Wild* (1988) and *Rushing To Paradise* (1994) — offer a vigorous commentary on the deadly challenges facing a media-saturated populace, who more and more often tend to prefer simulation to reality and who are the weak link in the Great Chain of Being.

assessment are *It Came From Outer Space* (1953; from a treatment by Ray Bradbury), *The Creature From The Black Lagoon* (1954), *Revenge Of The Creature* (1955), *Tarantula* (1955), *The Incredible Shrinking Man* (1957; his masterpiece, based on a novel by Richard Matheson) and *The Space Children* (1958).

A. A. ATTANASIO

AMERICAN NOVELIST

BORN: 1951

One of the most magnificently baroque sf stylists of his generation, Attanasio writes books that combine robust adventures old as humanity with metaphysical, hallucinogenic mindtrips. The quartet that began with his massive *Radix* (1981) takes the Dying Earth concept to phantasmagoric heights. *Solis* (1994) uses Mars as a venue for sophisticated trans-human exploits.

JEAN M. AUEL

AMERICAN NOVELIST

BORN: 1936

The literary market-place may not classify them as science fiction, but of course Auel's best-selling prehistoric romances in the Earth's Children series — *The Clan Of The Cave Bear* (1980), *The Valley Of Horses* (1982), *The Mammoth Hunters* (1985) and *The Plains Of Passage* (1990) — are sf of a type that has been fairly common since the late 19th century.

JOHN BADHAM

AMERICAN FILM DIRECTOR

BORN: 1939

British-born Badham came to prominence as a Hollywood director with the disco movie *Saturday Night Fever* (1977), but since then he has been associated with a number of science-fiction projects. Among them are the successful *WarGames* (1983) about a computer whizz-kid who taps into US military computers, the marginally sf helicopter movie *Blue Thunder* (1983), and the comedy *Short Circuit* (1986) about an escaped military robot.

Iain M. Banks — British Novelist — Born: 1954

Banks's sf is mainly centred on the Culture, a loose collection of enormous starships controlled by formidable artificial intelligences and inhabited by "humans" of sundry species. The Culture, having access to infinite power-sources and the know-how to produce or reproduce anything material, has achieved utopia by making unlimited supplies of anything available on demand to any of its members; consequently, there is nothing to compete for save the existential satisfactions of self-esteem and peer-approval. For those restless spirits whose happiness requires physical risk, there are military and missionary excursions into extra-Cultural regions. Such is the background to the novels *Consider Phlebas* (1987), *The Player Of Games* (1988) and *Use Of Weapons* (1990).

All have been described as "space opera", and employ many traditional space-operatic tropes, but all are informed by Banks's two pet hatreds: organized/revealed religion, and the brutalization of human beings for economic or existential advantage (a combination which leads him into unintentional absurdities in *Player*). All three books are written to a very high standard, though rather carelessly edited, and *Consider Phlebas* contains suspense writing of exceptional quality; all three are marred by gratuitous and ill-considered ornamentation, especially at the end of *Weapons*.

IAIN M. BANKS *LOVER OF FAST CARS, GOOD SCOTCH AND NIGHT-CLIMBING; HATER OF PORNOGRAPHY, CRUELTY AND SOCIAL INJUSTICE*

WILHELMINA BAIRD

BRITISH NOVELIST

BORN: 1935

Real name Joyce Carstairs Hutchinson, this Scottish-born lady who lives in France suddenly emerged as a "hot new cyberpunk" at the age of nearly 60. The book was *CrashCourse* (1993), and it was praised by William Gibson; *ClipJoint* (1994) and *PsyKosis* (1995) followed: all three feature the same resourceful heroine.

JOHN BARNES

AMERICAN NOVELIST

BORN: 1957

If Robert Heinlein had been raised amid suburbs and malls and the socio-political chaos of the past three decades, he might have grown up to be John Barnes. In books such as *Mother Of Storms* (1994) and *Kaleidoscope Century* (1995), Barnes uses his keen speculative talents to summon up uneasy worlds always in danger of collapse.

NEAL BARRETT, JR

AMERICAN NOVELIST

BORN: 1929

His early sf novels, such as *Aldair In Albion* (1976) and its several sequels, are entertaining far-future picaresques. His later books, *Through Darkest America* (1987) and its follow-up *Dawn's Uncertain Light* (1989), are well-written but extremely grim. More recent works tend towards fantasy.

T. J. BASS

AMERICAN NOVELIST

BORN: 1932

Bass's two cult novels, *Half Past Human* (1971) and *The Godwhale* (1974), express strongly Social-Darwinist views. Humanity consists mainly of soft-bodied, short-lived "nebishes", acclimated to lives of constricted poverty in computer-controlled hives, while outside a few hyper-virile, atavistic "benthics" have all the fun and win the day.

STEPHEN BAXTER

BRITISH NOVELIST

BORN: 1957

A new superstar of British sf, Baxter first made an impact with his series of Xeelee stories in *Interzone* and other magazines (from 1987). His debut novel, *Raft* (1991), strands its characters in a pocket universe of enormous gravity; and a subsequent trilogy of novels, *Timelike Infinity* (1992), *Flux* (1993) and *Ring* (1994), utilizes exciting scientific ideas on the grandest possible scale. The ingenious *Anti-Ice* (1993) represented a change of pace: Victorian scientists discover a volatile substance in an Antarctic meteorite, and use it to win the Crimean war; from this stems a

STEPHEN BAXTER *MASTER OF OLD-FASHIONED, SENSE-OF-WONDER SF, HAS PROVEN THAT THE ADAGE "THEY DON'T WRITE 'EM LIKE THAT ANY MORE" IS FALSE*

Greg Bear — American novelist — Born: 1951

That a writer formally schooled only in the humanities should become the epitome of hard-sf authors is both ironically appropriate and surprisingly predictable, given that the hard-sf mode of storytelling frequently lacked only the traditional strengths of mimetic fiction to become truly stunning. That Greg Bear was the writer to achieve such a synthesis is testament both to his native talent and his instincts for hard work.

Although he published his first story, 'Destroyers', at the age of 16, Bear was not to become prolifically excellent until much later. Typical of the new marketing realities of the 1980s, Bear began his real career with a series of journeyman novels, rather than dozens of magazine appearances (although his infrequent shorter works, collected in *The Wind From A Burning Woman*, 1983, and *Tangents*, 1989, were always well received and garnered their share of awards). *Psychlone* (1979) billed itself eclectically as "an occult science-fiction thriller". *Hegira* (1979) tells of fugitive worlds at the end of time. *Beyond Heaven's River* (1980) drops a time-shifted protagonist into a tricky galaxy. *The Strength Of Stones* (1981) traces the evolution of sentient cities on a planet called God-Does-Battle.

SCHOLA METAPHYSICAE

GREG BEAR *American evoker of more wonder and strangeness than is to be found in the works of a dozen lesser writers*

But these early books left the reader unprepared for the magnificent works that were to follow. *Blood Music* (1985, expanded from the 1983 novella of the same name) was a stunning, horrific recounting of the subversion of Earth's flesh and infrastructure by a rogue biochip. Hard on the heels of this came *Eon* (1985), the opening entry in the saga of humanity's contact with an alien artefact that opened up all time and space as an infinite corridor. The exploration continued in *Eternity* (1988) and *Legacy* (1995). With *The Forge Of God* (1987), Bear stepped further into world-smasher territory, ending all life on Earth with a severe case of planetary indigestion. The sequel to this, *Anvil Of Stars* (1992), tracked a few human survivors on their interstellar quest for revenge. *Queen Of Angels* (1990) delves deeply into nanotechnology, while *Moving Mars* (1993) delivers the promise of its title.

Bear is visibly excited and intrigued by such dazzling post-modern sciences as information theory, genetic engineering and cybernetics, and, because he is able to mix, seemingly effortlessly, complex characters with complex ideas, he stands out as hard sf's finest working writer.

glorious new development for the British Empire, involving land leviathans and a flight to the Moon, although all is not as rosy at it seems. Perhaps his best book to date, however, is *The Time Ships* (1995), a sequel to H. G. Wells's *The Time Machine*.

BARRINGTON J. BAYLEY

British novelist

Born: 1937

Bayley's books are often based on complex

temporal paradoxes. *Collision With Chronos* (1973) opens with the discovery that certain ruins are getting less ruinous — they are the work of a race which lives backwards. What will happen when the ruins are suddenly new and inhabited? *The Soul Of The Robot* (1974) is also intriguing, as are his many short stories.

GREGORY BENFORD

American novelist

Born: 1941

At one point in the 1980s, writers Benford, Brin and Bear were lumped together as the "Killer B's" and placed in illusory opposition to the cyberpunk movement — this despite Bear's co-optation by same! Such facile groupings, while containing minor germs of truth, obscure much larger realities. In the case of Benford — a working scientist, a former sf fan, a devotee of the works of William Faulkner — such a label hides much.

For a practising teacher and researcher, Benford has maintained an admirable output of fiction since first selling professionally in 1965. Early novels like *Deeper Than The Darkness* (1970) showed a fascination with alien life forms and their impact on psychically unprepared humanity. Several collaborations mark these years, such as *If The Stars Are Gods* (1977) with Gordon Eklund and *Shiva Descending* (1980) with William Rotsler. (Later joint ventures include *Heart Of The Comet*, 1986, with David Brin, and *Beyond The Fall Of Night*, 1990, with Arthur C. Clarke.) It was in 1980, however, that Benford signalled his full arrival with the publication of *Timescape*. As future scientists strive to employ modulated tachyons to enlighten the inhabitants of their past, the reader gains insight into the minds and lives of the men and women who conduct real research.

The crowning achievement of Benford's career, however, remains the series of six novels issued over an 18-year span: *In The Ocean Of Night* (1977); *Across The Sea Of Suns* (1984); *Great Sky River* (1987); *Tides Of Light* (1989); *Furious Gulf* (1994); and *Sailing Bright Eternity* (1995). In this enormous chronicle, we follow the fate of humankind — most closely examined through the eyes of one large family — as they struggle in a universe where inorganic life has the upper hand. As clairvoyant essayist and astute anthologist, Benford is outshone only by Benford the daring, caring speculator.

ALFRED BESTER

American novelist

Born: 1913 Died: 1987

Anyone who scorned the proposition that a scripter of 1940s comic books and radio serials could become one of the most elegant and sophisticated writers sf has ever produced would not have reckoned with the amazing Alfred Bester, who in the 1950s went on to do just such a thing — and with one hand more or less tied behind his back, as he simultaneously churned out scripts for television's *Tom Corbett: Space Cadet*. Bester's interest in sf actually manifested itself much earlier, with his first sale, 'The Broken Axiom', in 1939. A further 13 stories appeared over the next three years, including the brutal classic 'Adam And No Eve' from 1941. But it was not until another baker's dozen of toothsome confections appeared in the magazines of the 1950s (*F&SF* was Bester's favourite showcase), interspersed between two novels of genuine genius, that Bester secured his reputation. Stories like 'Fondly Fahrenheit', 'Star Light, Star Bright' and '5,271,009' showed many stylistic and thematic affinities with the

work of Sturgeon, yet revealed an intellect more cool, cunning and dyspeptic, focused on producing baroque, panoramic tales of guilt and expiation, torment and revenge. (An omnibus collection is *Starlight: The Great Short Fiction Of Alfred Bester*, 1976.)

In *The Demolished Man* (1953), psychic detective Lincoln Powell tracks criminal Ben Reich through a labyrinth of mind-games. In *The Stars My Destination* (1956; also known as *Tiger! Tiger!*), outsider Gully Foyle returns from near-certain death possessed of powers that enable him to reach both new heights and depths of behaviour. But strongly plotted as they are, these books dazzle mainly with an array of stylistic manoeuvres including interiorized ramblings and typographical upheavals. In addition, Bester's presentation of catchy ideas such as synaesthesia and his acute psychological insights were unprecedented in sf. Such

achievements at peak power seemed to take an inevitable toll. Bester's sf ceased as he took an editorial position at *Holiday* magazine, where he remained until the mid-1970s. With the demise of that publication, he returned to sf with three novels: *The Computer Connection* (1975); *Golem 100* (1980); and *The Deceivers* (1981). And, although Bester never again quite captured the old magic, any reader could do so simply by returning to his classic works.

BRUCE BETHKE

AMERICAN NOVELIST

BORN: 1955

Bethke will go down in sf history as the man who invented the word "cyberpunk" — for his debut short story of that title, published in 1983. A decade of near silence followed before his first novel *Headcrash* (1995), a witty send-up of the sub-genre he had helped launch.

MICHAEL BISHOP

AMERICAN NOVELIST

BORN: 1945

Twenty-five years of never repeating himself, of continually plotting out new homesteads on the imaginative frontier — homesteads he plainly loves while he briefly occupies them, yet which he willingly forsakes for further exploration — have brought Michael Bishop to a certain bracing mountaintop. A writer's writer, his shelves bedecked with a fair number of awards, beloved by many readers, he has nonetheless never leaped on to the buying lists of the average random fan. And perhaps they do not deserve him. Starting in 1970, with the short story 'Pinon Fall' in *Galaxy* (collections include *Blooded On Arachne*, 1982, and *One Winter In Eden*, 1984), Bishop has gradually become the premier humanist writer of sf. His fictions, infused with spirituality and traces of Southern gothicism, marshall endearing, oddball, sometimes obsessive humans and enigmatic aliens on altered Earths and alternative timelines, amidst galactic milieus and contemporary landscapes, with often tragi-comic effects. His style is a delight, rollicking, polished and wry.

SOUTHERN INTELLECTUAL
MICHAEL BISHOP'S BOOKS MAY BE LITTLE KNOWN TO THE MASS AUDIENCE BUT WILL REPAY CAREFUL READING

A constant thread in Bishop's work is a fascination with the anthropological sciences, more evident in the first half of his career than the second. Stories such as 'Death And Designation Among The Asadi' (expanded in 1979 as *Transfigurations*) and novels like *A Funeral For The Eyes Of Fire* (1975), *And Strange At Ecbatan The Trees* (1976) and *Stolen Faces* (1977) anatomize strange cultures with precision. In *A Little Knowledge* (1977) and its sequel *Catacomb Years* (1979), Bishop turns the same vision to the domed city of NUAtlanta. *No Enemy But Time* (1982) and *Ancient Of Days* (1985) both plumb man's relation to his proto-human ancestors. With later books such as the PKD homage *The Secret Ascension* (1987; also known as *Philip K. Dick Is Dead, Alas*), the AIDS parable *Unicorn Mountain* (1988), and the superhero-inspired *Count Geiger's Blues* (1992), Bishop delivered one startlement after another. But it was with the well-received *Brittle Innings* (1994), a conflation of the Frankenstein tale and baseball, that he reached a new personal best. Ever-reliable for literate narratives of human and alien transcendence, Bishop can only continue to grow.

TERRY BISSON

AMERICAN NOVELIST

BORN: 1942

Primarily a fantasist, Bisson enjoys a high standing within sf for his droll stories and novels that refuse to be pinned down to one mode or another. Such award-winners as 'Bears Discover Fire', along with *Fire On The Mountain* (an alternative-world parable from 1988) and *Voyage To The Red Planet* (a satire from 1990), provide plenty of evidence that he is one of our best fabulists.

JAMES P. BLAYLOCK

AMERICAN NOVELIST

BORN: 1950

In the Blaylockian universe, California tract housing may conceal tunnels to the centre of the earth, the coins that bought Judas or Arthurian revenants. Spiritual heir to Philip K. Dick's more whimsical fancies, sharing affinities with his friend Tim Powers, Blaylock has contributed most notably to the development of steampunk in such books as *The Digging Leviathan* (1984) and *Homunculus* (1986).

JAMES BLISH

AMERICAN NOVELIST

BORN: 1921 DIED: 1975

The tragically shortened career of James Blish held a wealth of wonders sufficient for a much longer lifetime. Somewhat neglected by the general sf readership of late, Blish is still revered by such heirs as Stephen Baxter, who has openly expressed his debt to such Blish stories as 'Surface Tension' (1952), and by most practising critics, who find inspiration in Blish's pioneering essays (collected in *The Issue At Hand*, 1964, and *More Issues At Hand*, 1970).

Blish spent formative years as a member of the seminal fan group, the Futurians, making a slow entry into professional writing by way of collaborations, with a first story appearing in 1940. In the first half of the 1950s, Blish came to prominence with a series of linked stories that were eventually assembled in four volumes: *Earthman, Come Home* (1955); *They Shall Have Stars* (1956); *The Triumph Of Time* (1958); and *A Life For The Stars* (1962). Reshuffled once again according to internal logic, the books appeared as an omnibus volume in 1970, *Cities In Flight*. True to its title, *Cities* follows terrestrial metropoli as they are literally uprooted by means of anti-gravity "spindizzy" devices and sent careering about the universe, down to the end of time and beyond. Spenglerian philosophy complements the nitty-gritty workings of these cosmic bindlestiffs, and showed Blish as one of sf's more erudite, experienced big thinkers.

With its emphasis on biology, *The Seedling Stars* (1957) opened new sf territory. But the subsequent *A Case Of Conscience* (1958) pushed even further in its examination of religious issues on a planet untainted by the Biblical Fall, winning a Hugo. Later thematic sequels in this direction included *Doctor Mirabilis* (1964); *Black Easter* (1968); and *The Day After Judgement* (1971). Spending much of his later years novelizing *Star Trek* episodes, Blish suffered ill health, managing to produce one final novel of the far future, *Midsummer Century* (1972). But the depth of his fictions, which also plumbed telepathy and overpopulation, can best be illustrated by the fact that Damon Knight could devote an entire essay to one of Blish's stories — 'Common Time', from 1953 — without exhausting it.

BEN BOVA

AMERICAN NOVELIST

BORN: 1932

One-time editor of *Analog* (after John W. Campbell's death) and later fiction editor of *Omni*, Bova has also been a prolific sf novelist of the "harder" sort, scientifically knowledgeable but rarely admired for his style or characterization. His principal works include the large novels *Millennium* (1976) and *Colony* (1978), both of which propagandize for space travel, as does the more recent blockbuster *Mars* (1992).

JOHN BOYD

AMERICAN NOVELIST

BORN: 1919

Boyd's stylish novels of sexual tension mock religion with savage humour. In *The Last Starship From Earth* (1968), the hero re-directs the life of Jesus to produce a more congenial parallel world; in *The Rakehells Of Heaven* (1969), Christian symbols become ironic prizes for (temporary) sexual restraint.

LEIGH BRACKETT

AMERICAN NOVELIST

BORN: 1915 DIED: 1978

Screenwriter, crime novelist, western writer — Brackett spread herself a little too thin. But her sf is memorable, particularly the excellent post-bomb novel *The Long Tomorrow* (1955). *The Best Of Leigh Brackett* (1977) includes ten lush, romantic, colourful sf and fantasy stories from the 1940s and 1950s: most have other-planetary settings and are in the Edgar Rice Burroughs mode (though better written). She closed her career by drafting a screenplay for George Lucas's *The Empire Strikes Back* (1980).

Ray Bradbury — American short-story writer — Born: 1920

Bradbury's tales express through a wide range of style and content anti-intellectualism and a powerful death wish. In the novelette 'And The Rock Cried Out', an American couple, stranded in Mexico after the obliteration of the USA, die rather than attempt to adjust. His stories about the colonization and subsequent abandonment of Mars are collected as *The Martian Chronicles* (1950), although the unification is half-hearted; neither the colonists nor the Martians (who may or may not be extinguished by terrestrial disease) are the same from story to story.

Other sf includes 'The Fox And The Forest', in which refugees from a repressive future seek solace in the 20th century, and the short novel *Fahrenheit 451* (1953), in which literacy has become illegal and books are burnt. The film version was directed by François Truffaut. The remaining book-lovers counter this very ineffectively by rote-learning books which they themselves then burn. Many of his best stories are collected in *The Illustrated Man* (1951): 'The Veldt' anticipates virtual reality (and uses it for parricide); in 'The City', a race which mankind has exterminated leaves behind a complex intelligent trap which exterminates mankind in turn; 'Kaleidoscope' consists of the meditations of a spaceman cast adrift in his spacesuit, and dying piecemeal from meteor hits.

Most of Bradbury's later work belongs to horror fantasy or crime fiction.

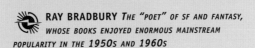

RAY BRADBURY *THE "POET" OF SF AND FANTASY, WHOSE BOOKS ENJOYED ENORMOUS MAINSTREAM POPULARITY IN THE 1950S AND 1960S*

MARION ZIMMER BRADLEY

AMERICAN NOVELIST

BORN: 1930

A very popular writer, known partly for historical fantasies such as *The Mists Of Avalon* (1983) but mainly for her lengthy Darkover series of planetary romances. These began unpretentiously with *The Sword Of Aldones* (1962), *The Bloody Sun* (1964) and other slim adventures of the 1960s, then gradually grew longer and more complex — and more feminist in tone. Among the later substantial titles in the series are *The Heritage Of Hastur* (1975), *The Shattered Chain* (1976), *The Forbidden Tower* (1977), *Stormqueen!* (1978), *Two To Conquer* (1980) and *City Of Sorcery* (1984).

DAVID BRIN

AMERICAN NOVELIST

BORN: 1950

Brin is known mainly for his award-winning Uplift series (*Sundiver*, *Startide Rising*, *The Uplift War*, etc.), wherein humanity, having genetically modified chimpanzees and dolphins to human intelligence, discovers that such practices are universal throughout the galaxy: all extant galactics have been "uplifted" by earlier races, mainly extinct. Wars among the survivors are constant and ineluctable. Notable singletons include *The Postman* (1985) and *Earth* (1990).

DAMIEN BRODERICH

AUSTRALIAN NOVELIST

BORN: 1944

One of his country's three or four most prominent sf writers, Broderick attracted international attention with *The Dreaming Dragons* (1980), a lively tale of alien intrusion into the heart of the Australian outback. His other works since include *The Judas Mandala* (1982) and the comical *Striped Holes* (1988). He has also edited a number of Australian sf anthologies and written weighty criticism of the genre.

ERIC BROWN

BRITISH NOVELIST

BORN: 1960

A painstaking craftsman, Brown writes old-fashioned tales, usually involving mysteries on other planets. At its best — as displayed in the collections *The Time-Lapsed Man And Other Stories* (1990) and *Blue Shifting* (1995), and in the novels *Meridian Days* (1992) and *Engineman* (1994) — his work rises to considerable emotional heights.

FREDRIC BROWN

AMERICAN NOVELIST

BORN: 1906 DIED: 1972

Mainly a writer of jejune humorous short stories. His novel *Project Jupiter* (1953) is hard sf, written from the viewpoint of a middle-aged man with rather touching human failings, while in *What Mad Universe* (1949) the hero is projected into his own preconception of an sf fan's ideal world.

ALGIS BUDRYS

AMERICAN NOVELIST

BORN: 1931

The circumstances of Budrys's birth and exile conferred a sad knowledge that would permeate his fiction. Born to Lithuanian parents who fled to America from communist rule, Budrys had from a young age an intimate knowledge of *realpolitik* cruelties, global death and destruction not granted to most writers of sf. This clear-eyed, unrelenting vision informs his tales of people given to touching heroisms — mostly the everyday sort, but sometimes of superhuman dimensions. In 1952, Budrys began to produce a variety of short stories that showed a sophistication and polish seldom seen in the sf genre. These have been collected in three

John Brunner
British Novelist
Born:1934 Died:1995

During seven glorious years, from 1968 to 1975, Brunner seemed unbeatable. Plugged into the Zeitgeist, fecund, passionate and eminently clever, he turned out four novels — a quartet of dynamic dystopias — that justified all the merits ever claimed for sf. But on either side of these immortal years hung curtains of a different colour. In the past, a vast assortment of apprentice work of varying quality; in the future, a dwindling down into silence and bitterness and lack of attention, culminating in a public death both unique and ironic, during a World SF Convention in Glasgow.

Like Silverberg and Dick, Brunner got his start in the mid-1950s producing space operas for the Ace Doubles line, his short fiction being relatively rare, though significant, especially when assembled in such volumes as *The Traveller In Black* (1971). Initial competence and drive allowed him to write over two dozen of these adventures, and with each one he was maturing. Perhaps the first indication of his new strengths was *The Whole Man* (1964; also known as *Telepathist*), involving the psychic struggles of a telepath. Following this was *The Squares Of The City* (1965), one of the few attempts in literature to shape a complete novel to the dictates of a chess game.

Ahead, however, in the tumultuous year of 1968, lay a New Wave explosion: Brunner's *Stand On Zanzibar* appeared. The longest sf novel to date, *Zanzibar* recounted the social troubles and mundane lifestyles of an overpopulated Earth in intimate detail, employing split-screen, docudrama techniques first utilized by John Dos Passos in his *USA* trilogy (1930-36). It won the Hugo for its year. Three more similar dissections followed: *The Jagged Orbit* (1969); *The Sheep Look Up* (1972); and *The Shockwave Rider* (1975). All were astonishingly prescient: the first about violence, the second about pollution, the third about digital living. After this, market and personal forces seemed to conspire against him.

ALGIS BUDRYS *WHOSE CAREER AS AN SF NOVELIST HAS BEEN PUNCTUATED BY LONG SILENCES; HE IS ALSO AN IMPORTANT EDITOR AND CRITIC*

volumes: *The Unexpected Dimension* (1960); *Budrys's Inferno* (1963); and *Blood And Burning* (1978). Honing his craft in the magazine and paperback market-place, Budrys came to possess an insider's knowledge of the publishing process, which he later put to good use as a critic and editor, most recently at the helm of Tomorrow magazine.

Budrys's first novel (in its later definitive version) was *Some Will Not Die* (1961), an unsparing tale of the rigours of survival and political reformation amidst the ashes of civilization. *Who?* (1958) detailed Cold War mindgames attendant on the prosthetic reconfiguration of a vital human pawn. With his third book, *Rogue Moon* (1960), Budrys gifted sf with a masterpiece. From Earth, scientists attempt to navigate a deadly labyrinth on the Moon, employing duplicative matter transmission that endlessly sacrifices the same man over and over. This potent motif would echo throughout sf, from Silverberg's *The Man In The Maze* (1969) through Dick's *A Maze Of Death* (1970) to Lem's *Peace On Earth* (1994). There was a long gap

between *Rogue Moon* and *Michaelmas* (1977), but the wait was worth it. The tale of a plugged-in media figure and his companion AI, who together secretly guide mankind, this novel was an important proto-cyberpunk work. Giving his time for a while to reviewing and the Writers of the Future project, Budrys would not resurface with another book until 1993's *Hard Landing*, which traced the melancholy fates of stranded UFO humanoids as they fade into Earth's societies under various guises. Surely there are further books to be unveiled.

LOIS McMASTER BUJOLD

AMERICAN NOVELIST

BORN: 1949

An extremely popular writer, in only a decade she has won a multitude of Hugo and Nebula awards. Most of her books feature the spacefaring hero Miles Vorkosigan who, far from being a he-man, is short of stature and brittle-boned. Titles include *Shards Of Honor* (1986), *The Warrior's Apprentice* (1986), *Brothers In Arms* (1989), *The Vor Game* (1990), *Barrayar*

Edgar Rice Burroughs — American Novelist Born: 1875 Died: 1950

Best known as the creator of Tarzan, but also the author of series involving: the adventures of Carson Napier, a spaceman who visits Venus; a sequence set in Pellucidar, an underground "prehistoric" world with its own miniature sun; and most importantly, Barsoom (Mars), locale for the adventures of John Carter and subsequently his son Carthoris. Also of sf interest in Burroughs's huge output are many lesser works, including *The Land That Time Forgot* (1924), which was the basis for a couple of movies, and *The Moon Maid* (1926).

Despite appearances, the Mars books must be regarded as sf since the terrain, climate and fauna of Barsoom fall within the limits of the feasible in terms of popular scientific knowledge of the day. Other aspects, including two additional primary colours not found on Earth, do not, and must be ascribed to Burroughs's ignorance. The first three, *A Princess Of Mars* (1917), *The Gods Of Mars* (1918) and *The Warlord Of Mars* (1919), are generally regarded as the best. John Carter, an ex-officer of the Confederacy, finds himself teleported to Barsoom by means which are never made clear but may have something to do with Indian magic. There, he finds a largely arid world much given over to war, the main contenders being gigantic six-limbed Green and humanoid Red Martians, the latter being a mixed race descended from black, white and yellow forebears, of whom enclaves survive (black and white at the south pole, yellow at the north).

Carter finds friends and enemies among all types, falling in love with Dejah Thoris, the Red princess of the title, whom he first meets as a fellow captive of the Green Tharks. Because the stories are fast-moving romantic hokum, and contain many absurdities even by the standards of the time (the women of all races are oviparous, and their eggs grow in sunlit incubators until ready to hatch), their moral and philosophical content has been unjustly ignored, although in his internal monologues Carter often displays a sensibility ahead of his time. He is a southerner, and might well be expected to be prejudiced against both black people and miscegenation, yet in his reflections on the black and red races he surprises himself by finding that he approves both their qualities and their origins. Nor are the Green Martians a "lesser race", despite their coldness and brutality; he observes in his hard-bitten friend, the chieftain Tars Tarkas, the qualities of courtesy and honour, while Tarkas's daughter, Sola, is a throwback to a gentler era. All reflect their common environment, a dying world where water must be conserved in canals and even the atmosphere is sustained by artificial means.

As an Earthman, Carter has a natural advantage in the low gravity of Barsoom, and this, plus his over-frequent references to his own martial prowess, often detracts from his dignity as a character. Yet Carter never revels in violence for its own sake; even when slaughtering the nobility of Zodanga, whose

EDGAR RICE BURROUGHS *SELF-EDUCATED CREATOR OF TARZAN, WHO NEVER SAID ANYTHING SO UNCULTURED AS "ME TARZAN, YOU JANE"*

purpose was to marry his beloved princess by force into their own royal house, he reflects with sorrow that although taken by surprise and without effective weapons, they die with valour. Barsoom will be the poorer for their passing.

(1991), *Mirror Dance* (1994). and *Cetaganda* (1996).

KENNETH BULMER

BRITISH NOVELIST

BORN: 1921

The not-untalented Bulmer was one of UK sf's great producers in the 1950s and 1960s: *City Under The Sea* (1957) is among the best of his early titles, and *Behold The Stars* (1965) is a typical, routine space-war tale. In the 1970s, he wrote a very long series of Edgar Rice Burroughs-like planetary romances as "Alan Burt Akers", beginning with *Transit To Scorpio*. He has also written under many other pseudonyms.

ANTHONY BURGESS

BRITISH NOVELIST

BORN: 1917 DIED: 1993

A mainstream novelist not normally associated with sf, Burgess certainly merits mention here as the author of the dystopian *A Clockwork Orange* (1962) — filmed by Stanley Kubrick. In the same year, he wrote a more humorous sf satire, *The Wanting Seed*, and much later he returned to the genre in such books as *1985* (1978) and *The End Of The World News* (1983).

F. M. BUSBY

AMERICAN NOVELIST

BORN: 1921

Busby's first novel, typical of many space operas

to come, was *Cage A Man* (1974; later incorporated in the omnibus volume *The Demu Trilogy*, 1980), though he had been writing sf short stories sporadically since the 1950s.

OCTAVIA E. BUTLER

AMERICAN NOVELIST

BORN: 1947

One of the rare sf authors who writes from the black American experience, Butler has been most praised for *Kindred* (1979), a tale of time travel to the slave-owning days of the Old South, and her Xenogenesis trilogy — *Dawn* (1987), *Adulthood Rites* (1987) *Imago* (1989) — which concerns cross-breeding between humans and aliens and *Parable Of The Sower* (1994).

PAT CADIGAN

American novelist

Born: 1953

With a reputation as the "one true female cyberpunk", Cadigan has produced energetic, complex, near-future novels with titles like *Mindplayers* (1987), *Synners* (1989) and *Fools* (1992). Although American, she has twice won the British best-sf-novel-of-the-year prize, the Arthur C. Clarke Award.

RICHARD CALDER

British novelist

Born: 1955

Calder lives in Thailand, and his sleazy but bejewelled debut novel, *Dead Girls* (1993), makes full use of that venue in its tale of robotic prostitution and a weird new sexual plague. At its best, his writing is brilliantly atmospheric, but he is in danger of becoming repetitive — as shown by the title and substance of his second novel, *Dead Boys* (1995).

ITALO CALVINO

Italian novelist

Born: 1923 Died: 1985

One of his country's great literary figures, Calvino wrote in a fantastic or "magic-realist" mode throughout much of his career. His nearest approach to sf was in the collections of scientifically-based fables known in English as *Cosmicomics* (1965) and *T Zero* (1967).

JAMES CAMERON

American film director

Born: 1954

A screenwriter as well as a director, Canadian-born Cameron began as a special-effects protégé of low-budget producer Roger Corman and went on to co-write the action movie *Rambo: First Blood Part II* (1985) with Sylvester Stallone. However, his most distinguished work, much of it produced in collaboration with his ex-wife, producer Gale Anne Hurd, is almost entirely sf: *The Terminator* (1984), *Aliens* (1986), *The Abyss* (1989), *Terminator 2: Judgment Day* (1991) and *Strange Days* (1995; script only). His movies are notable for their driving energy and fierce imagination: no one makes more exciting scenes of people running around in mazes of corridors and other claustrophobic locations. There is also a genuine sf intelligence at work in Cameron's scripts: despite occasional lapses, such as the gooey would-be Spielbergian climax of *The Abyss*, his films usually make sense.

JOHN W. CAMPBELL, JR

American novelist and editor

Born: 1910 Died: 1971

Remembered as long-term editor of *Astounding Science Fiction* (latterly *Analog*), Campbell wrote a number of space operas in the early 1930s. His otherwise small fictional output of the later 1930s contains some high-quality work, especially the linked stories 'Twilight' and 'Night', in which men from his own time are projected into the Earth of the very far future. In the former, the hero finds the human race has fallen into senescence; the people are pleasant, but with their spirits of enquiry and adventure gone, they live in contented indolence, tended by machines. In 'Night', the sun is cold, the Earth has died and only the most energy-efficient of the machines are left in an otherwise empty solar system.

He also wrote 'Who Goes There?', in which the personnel of an Antarctic survey station find

themselves invaded by an alien shapeshifting being, of which every part is capable of growing into a complete entity — given material on which to feed, e.g., a living body. Many of them are "taken over" in this way, and the means whereby the invaders are unmasked and destroyed are logical and ingenious. The 1982 film *The Thing* is notable for its fidelity to the original and the brilliance of its sfx.

KAREL CAPEK

CZECH NOVELIST

BORN: 1890 DIED: 1938

Satirical Middle-European author famous for coining the term "robot" — in his play *R.U.R.* (1920), which became popular in English. In his novel *The Absolute At Large* (1922), matter-destroying machines inadvertently release the "absolute" or numinous principle and cause a wave of religious mania. In *War With The Newts* (1936), an intelligent race of newt-like creatures challenges humankind for supremacy of the planet.

ORSON SCOTT CARD

AMERICAN NOVELIST

BORN: 1951

A controversial but often brilliant author, capable of writing with considerable emotional depth, Card won several awards for his novels about Ender Wiggin, a youth who inadvertently commits cosmic genocide and lives to regret it — *Ender's Game* (1985), *Speaker For The Dead* (1986) and *Xenocide* (1991). There are many other novels, but Card's sf is perhaps best represented in his mammoth story collection *Maps In A Mirror* (1990).

JOHN CARPENTER

AMERICAN FILM DIRECTOR

BORN: 1948

Carpenter co-wrote, with Dan O'Bannon, and directed the spoof sf movie *Dark Star* (1974); this began life as little more than a student project but became a major hit and launched both men's careers. Other Carpenter-directed sf projects (for which, being a man of parts, he has usually written the music) include *Escape From New York* (1981), *The Thing* (1982), *Starman*

JOHN CARPENTER
A US FILM DIRECTOR OF VERY VARIABLE OUTPUT BUT AT HIS BEST A QUIRKY INDIVIDUALIST

(1984), *They Live* (1988) and *Memoirs Of An Invisible Man* (1992). He has also directed some well-known horror movies, including a couple, *Christine* (1983; from Stephen King's novel) and *Prince Of Darkness* (1987), which verge on sf.

JEFFREY A. CARVER

AMERICAN NOVELIST

BORN: 1949

His colourful early space novel *Star Rigger's Way* (1978) has given rise to a later sequence — *Dragons In The Stars* (1992), *Dragon Rigger* (1993), etc — known collectively as the Star Rigger Universe series. He has written many other novels, sometimes over-stuffed with

invention, but he is one of sf's more dependable producers.

JACK L. CHALKER

AMERICAN NOVELIST

BORN: 1944

A writer of slambang adventures, somewhat reminiscent of Philip José Farmer (but less engaging), his early novels include *A Jungle Of Stars* (1976), *Dancers In The Afterglow* (1978), *The Web Of The Chozen* (1978) and *Downtiming The Nightside* (1985). Most of his other work has fallen into multi-part series — in particular, the Well World books — which have tended to be popular but not necessarily with critics.

Arthur C. Clarke — British Novelist — Born:1917

A writer of immense prestige, it is Clarke's curious status to be regarded both as a proponent and exponent of technologically based "hard" sf, and as the field's foremost intellectual mystic. Such early books as *Prelude To Space* and *The Sands Of Mars* (both 1951) were archetypal extrapolative sf, based firmly on the rocket technology which Clarke understood as well as anyone alive, and are now dated in consequence. But his next novel was *Childhood's End* (1953), wherein aliens of fearsome appearance but benign intent arrive to dominate the world, granting humanity a brief, paternalistic utopia before it proceeds to its final phase – physical and spiritual unification with an extra-dimensional superbeing which will surely do until God comes along.

This fascination for the spiritual coupled with a total rejection of theism has informed much of Clarke's best work thereafter, so that it is reasonable to regard him as a belated prophet of deism – and since that was very much a belief of the Enlightenment, he would be unlikely to disagree. *The City And The Stars* (1956), which begins as an agreeable *Bildungsroman* set in a far-future milieu, discloses in its later chapters that the people involved are but a remnant of humanity, the great majority having answered a mysterious summons from beyond the edge of the universe, leaving behind them two powerful but disembodied demiurges representing the good and evil principles. The evil (the Mad Mind) is far the more powerful of the two, but it is temporarily confined; by the time its shackles decay, it is hoped that the youthful good (Vanamond) will have matured sufficiently to destroy it. That book also contains an early reference to the possibility of downloading entire personalities on to computer for later recovery and reincarnation.

A fusion of these themes on an accelerated timescale features in *2001: A Space Odyssey* (1968), wherein a spaceman is transfigured into a paternalistic spiritual demiurge after successfully defeating a mad computer (HAL). The theme of the protecting power whose agenda may not be entirely to the liking of the protégés also appears in *The Deep Range* (1957), where human beings farm whales for meat. They are kindly treated, of course, but there is a growing feeling that to eat them is perhaps "a dismal thing to do". By way of

ARTHUR C. CLARKE *His fiction draws tension from the conflict between his training in hard science and his mystical bent*

compromise, it is decided to concentrate on milking them instead.

As well as fine space-oriented novels like *Rendezvous With Rama* (1973) and *The Fountains Of Paradise* (1979), Clarke has written much shorter work of high quality. A tale which demands special mention is 'The Star', which aroused considerable controversy: a

Jesuit scientist discovers to his horror that the Star of Bethlehem was a supernova which destroyed a brilliant civilization. Fifty years after his first magazine publications, Clarke continues to pose interesting questions in slim but effective recent novels such as *The Ghost From The Grand Banks* (1990) and *The Hammer Of God* (1993).

A. BERTRAM CHANDLER

BRITISH NOVELIST

BORN: 1912 DIED: 1984

Essentially a producer of sea stories in another guise, Chandler wrote of life and love among the officers of down-at-heel commercial starships. Space, time and sanity are affected by the Mannschen FTL drive, providing a mystical dimension. Best include *The Rim Of Space* (1961) and *The Road To The Rim* (1979).

SUZY McKEE CHARNAS

AMERICAN NOVELIST

BORN: 1939

Like one of the avenging horsewomen in her feminist trilogy — *Walk To The End Of The World* (1974), *Motherlines* (1978) and *The Furies* (1994) — Charnas writes books that take no prisoners in their determined assault on injustices. Along with the occasional short story, such as the award-winning 'Boobs', her too-rare novels add needed *realpolitik* grit to sf.

C. J. CHERRYH

AMERICAN NOVELIST

BORN: 1942

Carolyn Cherryh is one of the most remarkable figures in American sf, a writer of great fluency, prolificity and surprisingly hard-headed invention. She is particularly good at portraying aliens, as in *Cuckoo's Egg* (1985), wherein an ugly child is reared by a cat-like alien being and gradually discovers his true nature and destiny (he is, of course, a human foundling). Much of her work falls into the capacious Union-Alliance series of space tales. This includes the Hugo award-winning *Downbelow Station* (1981), a lengthy narrative dealing with the end of a generations-long war between Earth's almost forgotten starfleet and the new "Union" which has formed on distant colonies, leading to the founding of the "Alliance" as a buffer state between the two. Another major novel in the series (and another Hugo-winner) is *Cyteen* (1988), in which the all-powerful female boss of a research lab on the planet Cyteen oversees the education of her clone-"daughter". Other titles in the series, which may turn out to be the largest

 CAROLYN JANICE CHERRYH *(THE "H" ON THE END OF HER NAME IS AN AFFECTATION); FORMIDABLE MARXIST LITERARY CRITIC DARKO SUVIN IS A FAN OF HER SPACE OPERAS — WHICH SURELY INDICATES SOMETHING.*

and most complex in the genre if Cherryh continues at her past rate of production, include *Merchanter's Luck* (1982), *Forty Thousand In Gehenna* (1983), *Rimrunners* (1989), *Heavy Time* (1991), *Hellburner* (1992) and *Tripoint* (1994). Yet other novels, including the Faded Sun trilogy (1978-79) and the five-volume *Chanur* saga (1982-92), are loosely affiliated.

CHARLES CHILTON

BRITISH RADIO WRITER

BORN: 1927

Chilton is regarded affectionately by older British listeners for his three BBC serials in the *Journey Into Space* sequence (radio's nearest

equivalent to Nigel Kneale's *Quatermass* serials for TV, which were contemporary). He novelized them as *Journey Into Space* (1954), *The Red Planet* (1956) and *The World in Peril* (1960).

JOHN CHRISTOPHER

BRITISH NOVELIST

BORN: 1922

Real name Sam Youd, he is also known for mainstream and children's fiction. The early collection *The Twenty-Second Century* (1954) is notable for its quiet tone and assertion of humane values. His best-known book is a disaster novel, *The Death Of Grass* (1956), in which all gramineae (breeds of grass) are extinguished by disease; the ensuing food wars are described in grimly realistic terms. Another fine disaster novel is *A Wrinkle In The Skin* (1965), about the aftermath of devastating earthquakes.

HAL CLEMENT

AMERICAN NOVELIST
BORN: 1922

A writer noted for ingenious milieus. The giant planet of *Mission Of Gravity* (1953) has such ultra-rapid spin that G-force varies from three (equatorial) to 700 (polar). In *Close To Critical* (1964), temperature fluctuates around the boiling point of water, instead of around the freezing point as on Earth.

LARRY COHEN

AMERICAN FILM DIRECTOR
BORN: 1938

Beginning in television, where he was responsible for the sf series *The Invaders* (1967-68), Cohen has gone on to become one of the kings of the cheap, sf monster-horror movie. His titles include *It's Alive!* (1974), *It Lives Again* (1978), *Q – The Winged Serpent* (1982), *The Stuff* (1985) and *It's Alive III: Island Of The Alive* (1987). All written as well as produced and directed by him, his films have a certain wit and style.

D. G. COMPTON

BRITISH NOVELIST
BORN: 1930

A pessimistic writer, for whom cruelty and venality predominate and triumph over compassion and affection. *Farewell, Earth's Bliss* (1966) is set in a struggling Martian colony where minimal survival depends on draconian (in)justice; in *The Continuous Katherine Mortenhoe* (1974; also known as *The Unsleeping Eye*), a dying woman is degraded as a televisual spectacle.

MICHAEL G. CONEY

BRITISH NOVELIST
BORN: 1932

Long resident in Canada, Coney writes books with an English flavour, although usually set on other planets. They include *Mirror Image* (1972), *Charisma* (1975), *Hello Summer, Goodbye* (1975), *Brontomek!* (1976), *Cat Karina* (1982) and *The Celestial Steam Locomotive* (1983). Perhaps most typical, however, are his Peninsula stories — many of them uncollected, though some were worked into the novel *The Girl With A Symphony In Her Fingers* (1975) — set in a futuristic artists' resort and usually concerning the tribulations of a world-weary hero crossed in love. These show the clear influence of J. G. Ballard's *Vermilion Sands* stories, and they have, in turn, influenced the work of younger British sf writer Eric Brown.

STORM CONSTANTINE

BRITISH NOVELIST
BORN: 1956

She established her reputation with the very strange Wraeththu trilogy: beginning with *The Enchantments Of Flesh And Spirit* (1987), it concerned a post-disaster society of hermaphrodites. Later sf titles are *The Monstrous Regiment* (1990), *Aleph* (1991) and *Hermetech* (1991), but since those books she has been turning more and more to supernatural fantasy.

EDMUND COOPER

BRITISH NOVELIST
BORN: 1926 DIED: 1982

During the 1950s and 1960s, Cooper was one of those honourable second-string sf writers who could always be counted on to provide a good read with thoughtful implications. In books such as *Seed Of Light* (1959) and *A Far Sunset* (1967), he sketched crisis-ridden futures inhabited by plucky protagonists who still possessed a sense of life's ironies.

GILES COOPER

BRITISH TV WRITER
BORN: 1918 DIED: 1966

An unsung *auteur* of UK television, Cooper began in radio, then wrote numerous successful plays for TV, many of them tinged with fantasy of one kind or another — until his career was cut short by an untimely death. His one book of

 ROGER CORMAN *LIKE LARRY COHEN, IS ONE OF THOSE MAKERS OF RUBBISHY FILMS WHO HAS SUCCEEDED IN BECOMING SOMETHING OF A CULT FIGURE*

MICHAEL CRICHTON

TALL, GOOD-LOOKING AND A QUALIFIED DOCTOR TO BOOT — HOW COULD THIS MAN FAIL IN HOLLYWOOD? HE ALMOST DID, BEFORE BOUNCING BACK REMARKABLY

MICHAEL CRICHTON

AMERICAN NOVELIST

BORN: 1942

Qualified as a medical doctor and latterly famous as a Hollywood screenwriter, director and producer, Crichton first came to prominence as the author of an sf thriller, *The Andromeda Strain* (1969), in which a returning space capsule unleashes an alien virus on the Earth. The book's successful filming in 1971 (by Robert Wise) opened up opportunities for Crichton in the movie industry. He wrote and directed *Westworld* (1973), about a robot theme park that malfunctions, and *Coma* (1978), an sf medical thriller based on a novel by Robin Cook, plus a number of lesser feature films and TV movies (both sf and non-sf). His other novels on sf themes include *The Terminal Man* (1972), *Congo* (1980), *Sphere* (1987) and, of course, *Jurassic Park* (1990).

By the time the last-named book appeared in print Crichton's Hollywood career was on a downward course — apparently, he had written this dinosaur adventure originally as a movie outline in the 1980s and failed to sell it — but with the novel's successful publication everything changed. Steven Spielberg bought the film rights and hired Crichton to co-script the subsequent blockbuster (1993), which succeeded in becoming one of the most lucrative "properties" in movie history. The paperback tie-in edition of the novel has sold many millions of copies around the world, making *Jurassic Park* the late 20th century's best-selling sf book of any kind. Crichton was in great demand once more, becoming a money-spinning film and TV producer in addition to continuing his novel-writing career. Among many other things, the success of the (non-sf) hospital-drama TV series *E.R.*, coming on top of his vast earnings from the dinosaur story, has placed him among the richest men in America. Nevertheless, he has found time to return to sf with *The Lost World* (1995), a sequel to *Jurassic Park* which is clearly designed to form the basis of a new film. The latest book has been criticized for its unoriginal title (Conan Doyle got there first, in 1912!) and its re-tread plot.

science-fiction note is *The Other Man* (1964; adapted from his TV drama), about an alternative world where the Nazis won World War II. A memorable sf adaptation by Cooper was the two-parter *When The Kissing Had To Stop* (1962), based on Constantine FitzGibbon's novel about a Russian take-over of Britain.

ROGER CORMAN

AMERICAN FILM DIRECTOR

BORN: 1926

For someone who has specialized in producing schlock on the lowest possible budgets, Corman enjoys great fame, and even acclaim, as a Hollywood producer-director. This is partly because he has always been ready to encourage talent (half the movie directors in America seem to have broken into the business by working for him in one capacity or another), and it is partly because some of his films are actually rather good despite their evident limitations. Leaving aside his most highly praised work — namely the series of supernatural horror films of the 1960s based on Edgar Allan Poe stories — the sf movies he has directed include *The Day The World Ended* (1956), *X —The Man With The X-Ray Eyes* (1963), *Gas!* (1970) and, after a hiatus, *Frankenstein Unbound* (1990; from Brian Aldiss's novel). Among the many others that he has been involved with on the production side are *Death Race 2000* (1975), *Piranha* (1978) and *Battle Beyond The Stars* (1980). He has become a legendary Hollywood figure, way beyond the merits of any of his particular films.

RICHARD COWPER

BRITISH NOVELIST

BORN: 1926

Noted more for sensitivity than drama, Cowper (real name John Middleton Murry) is best known for the trilogy, *The Road To Corlay* (1978), *A Dream Of Kinship* (1981) and *A Tapestry Of Time* (1982). With England flooded and divided, the Church stands above the petty kings, repressing any evidence of spiritual feeling among the common people.

 DAVID CRONENBERG
CANADIAN MASTER OF "BODY HORROR" AND THE ALL-OUT WEIRD; IF YOU CAN STAND THE GORE, HE IS ONE OF THE MOST INTELLIGENT FILM-MAKERS OF THEM ALL

DAVID CRONENBERG

CANADIAN FILM DIRECTOR
BORN: 1943

Most of this talented but wayward writer-director's films are classifiable as "horror" and yet virtually all of them border on sf. They include *Shivers* (1974; also known as *The Parasite Murders*), *Rabid* (1977), *The Brood* (1979), *Scanners* (1980), *Videodrome* (1982), *The Dead Zone* (1983; from Stephen King's novel), *The Fly* (1986), *Dead Ringers* (1988), *Naked Lunch* (1991; from William Burroughs's book) and *Crash* (1996; from J. G. Ballard's novel). Of these, *The Fly* is the popular favourite — a splendidly gruesome but also thoughtful reworking of the tacky old 1958 movie about a man who exchanges body-parts with a fly. *Videodrome* is the intellectuals' favourite — a near-cyberpunk vision of a meeting (and fusion) of electronic media and all-too-malleable human flesh.

The violent *Crash* (1996) may turn out to be his most controversial film to date.

JOHN CROWLEY

AMERICAN NOVELIST
BORN: 1942

A writer's writer, Crowley is the head magus of an Invisible College of painstakingly subversive fantasists. His immaculate, but sadly infrequent books are lovingly grounded in our mundane lives, yet threaded with higher realities. *The Deep* (1975) somewhat atypically posits a medieval pocket universe. *Beasts* (1976) deals with a future revolt by animal hybrids. *Engine Summer* (1979) is an sf hagiography.

PHILIPPE CURVAL

FRENCH NOVELIST
BORN: 1929

One of the most highly praised recent French sf authors, his prize-winning novel *Brave Old World* (1976) is a complex narrative set in a future European society that is static and inward-turning, and where people's subjective time-spans are increased by technological means.

JOE DANTE

AMERICAN FILM DIRECTOR
BORN: 1946

A Roger Corman protégé, Dante has directed the sf horror movie *Piranha* (1978), a segment of Steven Spielberg's *Twilight Zone: The Movie* (1983; the part based on Jerome Bixby's story 'It's A Good Life'), the comic-horrific *Gremlins* (1984), *Explorers* (1985), *Innerspace* (1987), *The 'Burbs* (1989), *Gremlins 2: The New Batch* (1990) and *Matinee* (1993), among other things. He is no David Cronenberg, but he has a recognizable style of his own and movie enthusiasts value his in-jokes and all-round inventive sense of fun.

AVRAM DAVIDSON

AMERICAN NOVELIST
BORN: 1923 DIED: 1993

If sf writers emerged from a college whose faculty was composed exclusively of rabbis, Sufis, historiographers and stand-up comedians, their star graduate would have been Avram Davidson. Erudite, dense, witty and shocking, his stories (see *The Best Of Avram Davidson*, 1979) were like the explosive bonbons in a *Monty Python* skit.

L. P. DAVIES

BRITISH NOVELIST
BORN: 1914

Essentially a mystery-story writer in a quiet English vein, Davies's best-known novels include *The Paper Dolls* (1964) and *The Alien* (1968). The latter, about a hospitalized man who may be an extra-terrestrial, was filmed as *The Groundstar Conspiracy* (1972).

L. SPRAGUE DE CAMP

AMERICAN NOVELIST
BORN: 1907

A genial writer of monumental political incorrectness. His novel with P. Schuyler Miller, *Genus Homo* (1950), may have inspired *Planet Of The Apes*, and his Viagens Interplanetarias series, set on pre-industrial worlds under

Brazilian protectorate, features the adventures of the raffish and dissolute Anthony Fallon, whose attempts to set himself up as a petty king never quite succeed. He takes comfort in sardonic jokes against the upright but humourless black diplomat, Percy Mjipa, and the Christian fundamentalist missionary, Welcome Wagner. His reflection (on watching his middle-aged alien mistress undress) that with the years women of her species tend to sag less than Terrans, encapsulates his attitude to women.

In de Camp's most admired work, *Lest Darkness Fall* (1941), a contemporary American is projected from Mussolini's Rome to that of the sixth century. There, he sets about single-handedly averting the Dark Ages (a project which invites many jibes against Christianity), by introducing inter alia brandy, double-entry book-keeping, decimal notation, semaphore telegraphy and the printing press, while

reflecting on the regrettable tendency of Italian ladies to put on weight. As the book closes, he is planning to introduce tobacco to Europe and strangle Islam at birth.

SAMUEL R. DELANY

AMERICAN NOVELIST
BORN: 1942

Science fiction has seldom seen a *Wunderkind* like Delany. From his first book, *The Jewels Of Aptor* (1962) through *Nova* (1968), his eighth, the not-yet-30-years-old singer of strange songs brought to sf a concentration of diamantine style, sexual intimacies, ingenious science and resonant adventure never before seen — except perhaps in the finest work of Theodore Sturgeon, an acknowledged role model for the young Delany. Yet such achievements were not without their cost, as shown by a partial nervous breakdown suffered by Delany during this

SAMUEL R. "CHIP" DELANY *ONE-TIME SF DAZZLER WHO HAS BECOME A CRITICAL THEORIST AND BEARDED SAGE*

L. SPRAGUE DE CAMP
CREATOR OF LOVABLE ROGUES AND ROGUE QUEENS, WHOSE WRITINGS REFLECT THE VALUES OF AN EARLIER, LESS COMPLICATED AGE

turbulent period (recounted in his Hugo-winning memoir, *The Motion Of Light In Water*, 1988).

One of the few African-American sf writers, Delany grew up in a relatively well-off Harlem household. Bright, poetic and precocious, from the start he showed the traits that were to mark his whole career: a style so rich it sometimes fractured to the point of meaningful opacity; a concern with the deep structures of society; an empathy for outsiders and the disaffected, the hurt and warped ones. After *Aptor* came a trilogy whose definitive version was an omnibus volume, *The Fall Of The Towers* (1970). *The Ballad Of Beta-2* delved into linguistics, foreshadowing Delany's later professional adoption of semiotics as his main area of study. *Empire Star* (1966) revealed a fondness for mutating old-fashioned space operas into ultra-modern contrivances (a predilection that would resurface with *Stars In My Pocket Like Grains Of Sand*, 1984). *Babel-17* (1966) featured a poet heroine who signified Delany's growing interest in feminism.

Three masterpieces marked Delany's ascension to the pinnacle of sf: *The Einstein Intersection* (1967) portrayed a myth-dominated, torn-asunder future Earth. *Nova* transplanted Grail

Philip K. Dick
American Novelist Born: 1917 Died: 1982

Dick no longer belongs exclusively to the sf world. Since his untimely death from a stroke on the eve of probable fame and fortune, his reputation has undergone an expansion and sea-change. Adopted as an icon by composers, rock bands, film-makers, academics and general readers, Dick looms large on the contemporary cultural landscape, with his adjectified name and initials (Dickian, PKD) serving as shorthand for a gnostic, paranoid, druggy, neorealist gestalt — Jack Kerouac conflated with William Blake.

Dick's lifetime output of 112 short stories (assembled in *The Collected Stories Of Philip K. Dick*, 1987) and 36 sf novels makes any short summary of his work treacherous. But certain observations still hold true. First flourishing as an author of short fiction, Dick was luckily poised to take advantage of the superabundant sf magazines of the 1950s, publishing 72 stories within three years of his first ('Beyond Lies The Wub' in 1952). These early pieces showed a writer distrustful of authority and its scams, playful with slippery ontological and epistemological conundrums, and more sympathetic to the small-scale emotional dilemmas of his average-guy characters than most sf writers, who preferred to traffic in supermen and ultra-competent adventurers.

During these early years, Dick composed over half-a-dozen mainstream novels, none of which he was able to place (although almost all saw print posthumously). They include *The Man Whose Teeth Were All Exactly Alike* (1984), *Puttering About In A Small Land* (1985) and *Humpty Dumpty In Oakland* (1986). Frustrated by this inattention from "respectable" publishers, unable to hold a conventional job for long and trying to support any number of sequential wives, ex-wives and dependants, Dick turned to writing sf novels at a white-hot speed, many for Ace Books. Having spent his pittance of an advance on such luxuries as horsemeat for the family table, Dick would often be compelled to bang out his novels in a single fast draft as the delivery date for the manuscript neared – a practice that later contributed to his health-damaging reliance on amphetamines. (Notably for a writer who became infamous for supposedly heavy usage of inspirational hallucinogens, Dick wrote his most trippy work before ever actually indulging in LSD or other psychotropic drugs. *A Scanner Darkly* [1977] deals with aspects of Dick's own drug use in a surreal manner.) While this bad habit contributed to the unevenness and misdirection of these early books, it also lent to them a kind of oneiric intensity reminiscent of A. E. van Vogt's work.

The World Jones Made (1956), *Eye In The Sky* (1957) and *Time Out Of Joint* (1959) were highpoints on the way to Dick's first masterpiece, *The Man In The High Castle* (1962). An alternative-world tale of a Nazi-dominated America, this Hugo-winning novel featured superb characterization and idiosyncratic, convincingly arbitrary plotting based on the *I-Ching*. Its cast of ordinary folk managed to win some small victories from their unrelenting and dominating exterior world. But such relatively comforting resolutions were soon to become scarce in Dick's work.

In *The Three Stigmata Of Palmer Eldritch* (1965), characters are at the mercy of a cruel demiurge, a harsh god derived from an actual vision experienced by Dick, a precursor of the central revelation that was to shape the final years of his life. In *Ubik* (1969), the protagonists lie dead and dreaming, infecting reality. In March 1974, Dick claimed to have undergone a cataclysmic and convulsive contact with a "beam of pink light", theoretically originating from an extra-terrestrial satellite intelligence he came to call VALIS: Vast Active Living Intelligence System. After partially recovering from this traumatic epiphany, mostly through the means of a vast purgative diary known as the "Exegesis", Dick went on to write a trio of self-probing, autumnal books: *VALIS* (1981), *The Divine Invasion* (1981) and *The Transmigration Of Timothy Archer* (1982).

Finally, as an ironic coda to Dick's often desperate career, film director Ridley Scott, working from Dick's seminal *Do Androids Dream Of Electric Sheep?* (1968), released *Blade Runner* (1982), launching a new look and style that influenced fashion and fiction, providing impetus to the entire nascent cyberpunk movement. The film was tremendously successful in both its original form and in its 1991 *Director's Cut* version. Subject of tributes and parodies, criticism and adulation, from beyond death, Dick has, like Palmer Eldritch himself, succeeded in colonizing our minds.

patterns to a neurojack-studded interstellar venue, partially fathering cyberpunk in the process. And the cult bestseller *Dhalgren* (1975) was an urban fantasia of the timeless, spaceless city of Bellona. After the "ambiguous heterotopia" of *Triton* (1976), Delany lavished his efforts on the *Neveryon* series, which while ostensibly sword-and-sorcery fantasy of a high order still showed a particularly science-fictional angle of attack. Despite donning the mantle of professor and elder critic, Delany, still productive in his maturity, retains the gleam of exuberant youth in his far-seeing eyes.

LESTER DEL REY
AMERICAN NOVELIST
BORN: 1915 DIED: 1993

His later career as one of the most influential editors in the sf field now overshadows del Rey's substantial fictional contributions to the development of sf. With many assured and deft stories (see *The Best Of Lester Del Rey*, 1978), culminating in the novel *Nerves* (1956), a prophetic nuclear disaster tale, del Rey helped sf climb out of its pulp cradle.

PETER DICKINSON
BRITISH NOVELIST
BORN: 1927

Well known in the UK for his many crime novels, Dickinson has a low profile as far as sf is concerned; but in America sf critics seem to think he is the bee's knees. *The Green Gene* (1973), a satire on racism, is his one adult sf novel, but he has written several for youngsters. These include the Changes trilogy — *The Weathermonger* (1968), *Heartsease* (1970) and *The Devil's Children* (1971) — and *Eva* (1988), an excellent story about a young girl's mind being transferred to the body of a chimpanzee.

GORDON R. DICKSON
AMERICAN NOVELIST
BORN: 1923

Prolific Canadian-born writer, much of whose most serious work forms a loose future history, the Childe cycle, in which mankind spreads rather slowly through the galaxy, the various

THOMAS M. DISCH

New Yorker; despite his rather threatening tattooed image, one of the most sensitive, subtle (and funny) of all sf writers

strains which make up the human spirit becoming concentrated and specialized in the process. They remain physically similar, but the mind-sets of men from different worlds are in danger of becoming so diverse that they will no longer perceive each other as human — the race may destroy itself in an orgy of auto-xenophobia.

The object of much striving (conscious and otherwise) over many volumes must be to achieve a synthesis, whereby the concentrated and purified essences of soldier (Dorsai), psychologist (Exotic), scientist (Newton) and devotee (the Friendlies) will be culturally and genetically merged to form a super-race which will be physically invincible and ethically impeccable. That this idea represents an extreme extension of sound stock-breeding principles causes no embarrassment, although the mechanism whereby all four strains would need to be culled is specified only for the Friendlies, whose men gladly lay down their lives as cannon-fodder to the quiet satisfaction of everyone else.

The most important titles are *Dorsai!* (1960), *Necromancer* (1962), *Soldier, Ask Not* (1967) and *The Tactics Of Mistake* (1971).

PAUL DI FILIPPO

American short-story writer

Born: 1954

A witty writer, Di Filippo has been developing slowly but surely since his first story appeared in the obscure *UnEarth* magazine in 1977. Dozens of tales, some of them hilarious, have appeared in magazines such as *Asimov's*, *F&SF* and *Interzone*. His first book, a gathering of three novellas set in a never-never 19th century, is *The Steampunk Trilogy* (1995) — followed by another collection, *Ribofunk*, in 1996.

THOMAS M. DISCH

American novelist

Born: 1940

Acerbic yet jolly, terse yet lushly Victorian, sardonic yet unwillingly romantic, ruthlessly modern yet operatic: the poet, critic, novelist and librettist who goes variously by the name of Tom or Thomas Disch is a deep well of many waters. Sf has been enriched by his nearly 35 years of involvement with the field. Disch began producing intriguing short stories in 1962 as one of the writers fostered by unsung editor Cele Goldsmith. Such absurdist gems as 'The Squirrel Cage' and 'Descending' attracted immediate

attention. This interest was immediately rewarded by Disch's first three novels, which showed a swiftly expanding talent. In *The Genocides* (1965), humanity becomes a mere pest amidst negligent aliens, much as in William Tenn's earlier 'The Men In The Walls'. In *Mankind Under The Leash* (1966), similar humiliations render people into pets. *Echo Round His Bones* (1967) delves into the shadow existence of artificial, accidental doppelgangers.

Continuing to produce stories that would later fill such collections as *One Hundred And Two H Bombs* (1966); *Under Compulsion* (1968); and *Getting Into Death And Other Stories* (1976), Disch next offered the two books that cemented his reputation. A New Wave bombshell, *Camp Concentration* (1968) detailed — with bravura style — the intelligence experiments conducted on political prisoners in a dystopic future. A collection of linked stories, *334* (1972) chronicled the daily lives of apartment dwellers in a decaying future New York. After this sf crescendo, Disch turned his attention to poetry and non-sf novels of various stripes, returning to the field with *On Wings Of Song* in 1979. Following this, his interest shifted to a gothic trilogy of high inventiveness whose fantastic elements transcended conventional sf, although the middle volume — *The MD: A Horror Story* (1991) — depicts a rotting future in its latter half. That Disch continues to produce the occasional supple, startling sf story testifies to his continuing dedication to the field.

TERRY DOWLING

Australian short-story writer

Born: 1948

Dowling produces colourful, atmospheric and sometimes deeply strange fiction about future versions of Australia, much of it collected in the books (often comprising linked stories) *Rynosseros* (1990), *Wormwood* (1991), *Blue Tyson* (1992) and *Twilight Beach* (1993).

ARTHUR CONAN DOYLE

British novelist

Born: 1859 Died: 1930

The creator of Sherlock Holmes wrote two good sf

novels, *The Lost World* (1912) and *The Poison Belt* (1913), featuring the irascible Professor Challenger. They concern, respectively, a plateau in South America where dinosaurs thrive, and a catastrophe in which all animal life briefly loses consciousness, with lethal consequences for many.

GARDNER DOZOIS

AMERICAN NOVELIST
BORN: 1947

Editor of *Asimov's* magazine, and of the regular *Year's Best SF* anthologies, Dozois is one of the most influential people in sf. His own fiction has been infrequent, but good: principally, the novel *Strangers* (1978), about inter-species love, and the stories collected in *Geodesic Dreams: The Best Short Fiction Of Gardner Dozois* (1992).

DAVID A. DRAKE

AMERICAN NOVELIST
BORN: 1945

A varied writer, Drake is best known in sf as the

creator of *Hammer's Slammers* (1979), enjoyable military sf which has resulted in an ongoing series. He has also written many shared-world novels.

—◦—

GEORGE ALEC EFFINGER

AMERICAN NOVELIST
BORN: 1947

First noted for his sly short stories, collected in such volumes as *Mixed Feelings* (1974), *Irrational Numbers* (1976) and *Dirty Tricks* (1978), Effinger misfired as a novelist until the appearance of the sub-cyberpunk *When Gravity Fails* (1987), which has since spawned sequels.

GREG EGAN

AUSTRALIAN NOVELIST
BORN: 1961

Sometimes it seems mandatory that writers of hard sf be named "Greg". Yet if our descendants

ever actually institute such a tradition, it may very well honour not Bear or Benford but their younger peer, Australian writer Greg Egan. In a handful of novels and stories to date, Egan bids fair to outdazzle even these giants, earning accolades from such luminaries as Vernor Vinge.

Egan's first novel, *An Unusual Angle* (1983), was a fantasy. But like Nancy Kress, who also moved metaphorically from fuzzy arcadias to hard-edged laboratories, Egan found his metier quickly thereafter. With the astonishing, accomplished stories collected in *Axiomatic* (1995), Egan displayed a flair for taking the most abstruse findings of mathematics, biology and quantum physics and providing them with objective correlatives. Not content with simply reifying imponderables as in some kind of Einsteinian thought-experiment — a failing many hard-sf writers fall prey to — Egan also conjured up heart-quickening plots and sympathetic characters to make his stories hit the reader in the gut as well as mind. At the heart of almost all of Egan's writing lies the question of identity. Characters ask, "What can I become?", "What have I become?" The manipulative ones say, "What can I make this other person become?" (as in 'The Caress').

Egan's first sf novel did not disappoint. *Quarantine* (1992) tells of a future Earth trapped inside a literal bubble, focusing on the deep structures of the cosmos thus revealed. But Egan's most sustained and intriguing work remains *Permutation City* (1994). As humanity migrates to a virtual reality superior in all respects to our familiar one, revelation upon ontological revelation bursts over the reader. With the publication in 1996 of *Distress*, Egan completed what he refers to as his "subjective cosmology" trilogy, thereby staking his claim to be worldmaker nonpareil.

HARLAN ELLISON

AMERICAN SHORT-STORY WRITER
BORN: 1934

At one point in his career, Ellison seemed the generational spokesman for in-your-face, confessional, revolutionary American sf. Unlike most sf writers, he had a foot on both East and

Philip José Farmer— American Novelist — Born: 1918

Besides being an enormously inventive and daring sub-creator of his own astonishing worlds, Farmer is also a kind of Midas, in that his literary touch turns pulp icons into gold. Intimate with such immortal luminaries as Tarzan and Doc Savage, Sherlock Holmes and Kilgore Trout, Farmer has given these fictional personalities a new lease of life, sometimes placing them in risqué situations their original creators would have blanched at.

Farmer's career began in 1946, but faltered until 1952 when 'The Lovers' (novelized in 1961) appeared. This exploration of alien biology would influence many other authors, including Gardner Dozois in his *Strangers* (1978), and earned Farmer a reputation as the doyen of exotic life forms. Along with novels like *Flesh* (1960),

Farmer's early work both reflected and promoted the sexual liberation of sf.

At the same time, Farmer's love of rousing, unequivocal adventures showed itself in such books as *The Green Odyssey* (1957) and *The Gate Of Time* (1966). The twin desires — to experiment boldly and to reproduce lovingly — serve as thesis and antithesis in Farmer's grand synthesis of new and old. Two series spanning three decades best illustrate Farmer's methodology. They are the Riverworld and World of Tiers books.

The first saga is contained mainly in *To Your Scattered Bodies Go* (1971); *The Fabulous Riverboat* (1971); *The Dark Design* (1977); *The Magic Labyrinth* (1980); and *The Gods Of Riverworld* (1983). On a new planet, every

human and proto-human who ever lived has been resurrected by mysterious aliens along the banks of an endless river. Intoxicated with free rebirths and manna, they play, build and search through a crazy-quilt landscape. If anything, the World of Tiers is even larger in scope. "Pocket universes", the dangerous playgrounds of godlings, abound. Through six novels and dozens of venues rampages the indomitable Paul Janus Finnegan — a PJF avatar — until his final showdown with his nemesis, Red Orc, in *More Than Fire* (1993). Having completed his short *Dayworld* series in 1990, Farmer has been relatively silent since. One supposes him heroically busy in some pocket cosmos, soon to return with more gleeful adventures to relate.

West coasts, with his name known in Hollywood and New York. Moreover, he strode brilliantly across a dozen stages as dramatist, television and film critic, mystery writer, journalist, author of mainstream fictions, peerless sf storyteller, anthologist, teacher, store-window attraction ... There seemed little that Ellison could not do well, all the while letting the reader loudly know precisely where and why credit accrued, both to himself and the many younger writers he generously took under his wing. That his profile has diminished was perhaps inevitable, but his Sinatra-like career stands as an enduring monument.

Emerging like a cartoon Tasmanian Devil from the fan community in 1956, Ellison spent nearly a decade in a vigorous apprenticeship. But around 1965, with the appearance of "'Repent, Harlequin!' Said The Ticktockman', he began delivering the first of the hundreds of fierce, fiery stories upon which his reputation rests. Volumes such as *Paingod And Other Delusions* (1965); *I Have No Mouth & I Must Scream* (1967); *The Beast That Shouted Love At The Heart Of The World* (1969); *Over The Edge* (1970); *Alone Against Tomorrow* (1971); and *Deathbird Stories* (1975) contain some of the edgiest, most heart-rending, most polemical stories sf has ever seen. The best summation of these years and later ones

is contained in *The Essential Ellison* (1987).

Ellison's editorship of the groundbreaking New Wave anthologies, *Dangerous Visions* (1967) and *Again, Dangerous Visions* (1972) ranks as one of the most committed, far-seeing and selfless acts of stewardship in the history of sf. In the 1980s and 1990s, Ellison's output lessened, each new story paradoxically more welcomed and less impactful. Yet, among all his awards and press-clippings, perhaps the most cherished should be the sense of a creative life lived completely, uncompromisingly and to the limit.

M. J. ENGH

AMERICAN NOVELIST

BORN: 1933

Mary Jane Engh wrote an astonishing debut novel, *Arslan* (1976; published in Britain as *A Wind From Bukhara*). Here, Arslan, the ruthless young leader of Turkestan, seizes power from the bureaucrats of the Soviet Union and, using their laser weapons, he forces the whole world to submit to him. A magnetic but deranged personality, he sets out to free the Earth from the pressures of human civilization. The lyrical, brilliantly characterized and at times shocking story is narrated by two inhabitants of an American mid-western town where Arslan sets up

his temporary headquarters. Engh's later novels, few and far between, have made a lesser impact.

CHRISTOPHER EVANS

BRITISH NOVELIST

BORN: 1951

Welsh schoolteacher Evans made his sf debut with *Capella's Golden Eyes* (1980), in which the human colonists of a far planet, long cut off from Earth, strive to understand mysterious alien visitors who bring them boons. Several not-so-successful novels (and much pseudonymous hackwork) followed, before he began to hit his stride again with the alternative-world *Aztec Century* (1993) and the space-operatic *Mortal Remains* (1995).

——m——

R. LIONEL FANTHORPE

BRITISH NOVELIST

BORN: 1935

Perhaps the most prolific British sf writer ever, Fanthorpe wrote about 150 paperback-original books, many of them under pseudonyms — "Leo Brett", "Bron Fane", "Pel Torro" etc — and mostly in the space of just a dozen years, from the mid-1950s to the mid-1960s. Later he became a Church of England vicar.

MICK FARREN

British novelist

Born: 1943

Rock musician turned writer, Farren seems stranded in the ethos of the late 1960s. His earlier books, such as *The Texts Of Festival* (1973) and *The Quest Of The DNA Cowboys* (1976) are full of pop references. Later he moved to the USA, and in one of his last books to appear, *Armageddon Crazy* (1989), the honest New York cop hero tries to track down the members of a terrorist organization in an early 21st-century America groaning under the heel of a religious dictatorship.

JOHN RUSSELL FEARN

British novelist

Born: 1908 Died: 1960

One of the great producers (later overtaken by Lionel Fanthorpe) of British sf's "infimal" phase — the late 1940s and early 1950s — Fearn is best remembered for his unlikely-sounding pseudonym, "Vargo Statten". His scores of books were mainly crash-bang-wallop space operas and planetary romances.

JACK FINNEY

American novelist

Born: 1911 Died: 1995

The man who wrote *Invasion Of The Body Snatchers* (1955), that perfect Cold War fable, was also an exquisite crafter of short fiction and Hollywood-ready mainstream novels. With *Time And Again* (1970) and its belated sequel, *From Time To Time* (1995), Finney poured out his nostalgia for a perhaps recapturable past and found an eager audience who took his melancholy pleasures to heart.

CAMILLE FLAMMARION

French novelist

Born: 1842 Died: 1925

A noted popularizer of astronomy, Flammarion also wrote a couple of remarkable scientific romances which were translated and gained some fame in English: *Lumen* (1887) and *Omega: The Last Days Of The World* (1893).

RICHARD FLEISCHER

American film director

Born: 1916

Son of animator Max Fleischer and a veteran movie director in his own right, Fleischer has long been associated with sf and fantasy projects. His three notable films in the sf genre are *Twenty Thousand Leagues Under The Sea* (1954; from Jules Verne's novel), *Fantastic Voyage* (1966) and *Soylent Green* (1973; from Harry Harrison's novel *Make Room! Make Room!*).

JOHN M. FORD

American novelist

Born: 1957

Ford's debut novel, *Web Of Angels* (1980), about a vast computer network, is an early example of cyberpunk. His work since then — ranging from *Star Trek* spin-offs to out-and-out fantasy — has been rather too varied for him to establish a clear identity in sf readers' minds.

WILLIAM R. FORSTCHEN

American novelist

Born: 1950

Initially known for his Gamester Wars series, beginning with *The Alexandrian Ring* (1987) — in which humans and aliens fight planetary war-games, with time-travel enabling them to recruit military help from the past — Forstchen has gained new fame (or notoriety) as co-author, with politician Newt Gingrich, of the alternative-timeline thriller *1945* (1995).

ROBERT L. FORWARD

American novelist

Born: 1932

A practising scientist, Forward is known for his well-informed though sometimes ill-written hard-sf novels such as *Dragon's Egg* (1980) and *Martian Rainbow* (1991).

ALAN DEAN FOSTER

American novelist

Born: 1946

A prolific and crowd-pleasing writer, Foster is best known for his many movie novelizations, most famously the series comprising *Alien* (1979), *Aliens* (1986) and *Alien³* (1992). "Being the only creative continuity through all three films," he has said, "I tried to tie all three books together so that they can actually be read as a trilogy." His non-movie-related sf novels include a number in the Humanx Commonwealth series: *The Tar-Aiym Krang* (1972), *Bloodhype* (1973), *Orphan Star* (1977), etc.

 RICHARD FLEISCHER

Old-time maker of big action movies; his father was Walt Disney's great rival in animation, yet young Dick went to work for the "enemy"

William Gibson — American Novelist — Born: 1948

No other sf writer has gained more cultural and literary bang for the buck from a single novel than William Gibson did with his *Neuromancer* (1984). Freshly told, deftly written, intelligently conceived, seeded with marvels and challenges, insights and assertions, the book deservedly captured sf's Triple Crown of Hugo, Nebula and Philip K. Dick awards. It lofted Gibson to a pinnacle of media familiarity seldom visited even by Heinlein, Asimov, Herbert or Clarke, rendering him something of a spokesman for a whole cohort of unlikely fellow travellers. Released with exquisite timing on the cusp of larger socio-cultural and technological waves, this maiden effort of Gibson's allowed the bubbling-under cyberpunk phenomenon to emerge as a literary movement, a fashion and style statement, a lifestyle option and now, a decade later, a marketing category. Much to Gibson's credit, he has managed somehow to remain unperturbed by all the hullabaloo surrounding his work, going on to produce further craftsmanly novels and screenplays, none of which has exactly replicated his initial impact.

Born in the US but a Canadian expatriate since 1968, Gibson was relatively old when his first story, 'Fragments Of A Hologram Rose', was published in 1977 in *Unearth* (a small-press magazine which also printed beginner's efforts by Blaylock, Di Filippo and Rucker). Gibson spent the next few years turning out the distinctive short stories later collected in *Burning Chrome* (1986), some shared with collaborators such as Sterling, Shirley and Swanwick. (One piece therein, 'Johnny Mnemonic', was translated to film in 1995 by Gibson himself and artist-director Robert Longo.)

Upon the bombshell release of *Neuromancer* — composed, legend has it, on a battered manual typewriter — Gibson went quickly from a figure of insiders' cult attention to a public icon. Drawing upon inspirations as diverse as Raymond Chandler and the Velvet Underground, Joseph Cornell and the Sex Pistols, the story of Case and Molly, hot on the digital trail of a software McGuffin, was a fast-paced,

---

CYBERMAN *WILLIAM GIBSON COINED THE TERM "CYBERSPACE" AND WAS THE INSPIRATION FOR A GENERATION OF LOWLIFE* **VR** *JUNKIES*

---

unrelenting thriller that amalgamated lowlifes with high-tech in a manner that would soon become clichéd in the hands of imitators. Coining the term "cyberspace", Gibson went on to render that new venue in lustrous clarity, inspiring a whole real-world industry with the Grail of sensual data immersion.

Most remarkable was how closely the book depicted contemporary trends and emotions, beneath its futuristic veneer. As critic John Clute has remarked, every sf novel, whatever the ostensible date of its future, conceals a set of timebound assumptions. More so than any other writer — with the possible exception of Bruce Sterling — Gibson managed to work with up-to-the-minute headlines and issues, imparting an urgency and immediacy plainly perceived by millions of readers.

Following closely on the heels of *Neuromancer*, *Count Zero* (1986) and *Mona Lisa Overdrive* (1988) introduced new characters — including touchy and possibly insane Artificial Intelligences — into Gibson's sprawl, allowing for the exploration of further niches in this wired future. With Bruce Sterling, Gibson next ventured into a massively annotatable steampunk alternative history. Their *The Difference Engine* (1990) postulated that the analog computers of Charles Babbage became a Victorian reality, leading to a dystopian world of pollution and social stratification whose grimed face mirrored the worst aspects of our own world. *Virtual Light* (1993) returned to a near-future scenario in which messenger Chevette Washington becomes involved in deadly schemes after stealing a pair of VR sunglasses.

The first writer to shine a blinding light on post-modern corporate ethics, digitized realities and deracinated, disaffected socketed loners, Gibson is sf's genial yakuza boss.

PAT FRANK

AMERICAN NOVELIST

BORN: 1907 DIED: 1964

A mainstream novelist, several of whose books, including *Mr Adam* (1946), deal in one way or another with the nuclear threat. He is best remembered for *Alas, Babylon* (1959), a convincing and curiously elegiac story about atomic-war survivors in Florida. The latter was a longtime steady-seller in the US.

DANIEL F. GALOUYE

AMERICAN NOVELIST

BORN: 1911 DIED: 1976

A now-forgotten writer, but not without interest. *In Dark Universe* (1961), the descendants of nuclear-war survivors have adapted to utter darkness in their underground warren of shelters; the young hero, inevitably, discovers light. In *Counterfeit World* (1964; also known as *Simulacron-3*), a man awakes to the fact that his world is in reality a computer simulation,

devised for advertising research purposes, and he manages to turn the tables on his manipulators. This is a nicely paranoid idea and in effect a "virtual reality" story ahead of its time (it was filmed for German TV by Rainer Werner Fassbinder in 1973).

DAVID S. GARNETT

BRITISH NOVELIST

BORN: 1947

Garnett began with proficient sf adventures like *Time In Eclipse* (1974), where the hero inhabits an artificial reality controlled by an entity known as MACHINE. After a long hiatus devoted to pseudonymous non-sf work, he returned to the field as an anthology editor and short-story writer. He resumed writing sf novels with the humorous *Stargonauts* (1995) and *Galactic Outlaws* (1996).

ANNE GAY

BRITISH NOVELIST

BORN: 1952

A capable writer of planetary romances, *Mindsail* (1990), *The Brooch Of Azure Midnight* (1991) and *Dancing On The Volcano* (1993), Gay has yet to establish herself fully in the affections of sf readers.

MARY GENTLE

BRITISH NOVELIST

BORN: 1956

Her two large sf novels, *Golden Witchbreed* (1983) and *Ancient Light* (1987), are thoughtful exercises in the planetary romance vein. (The first was a UK bestseller.) A restless talent, she has since gained praise for her highly unusual (and learned) fantasy novels.

HUGO GERNSBACK

AMERICAN EDITOR

BORN: 1884-1967

Born in Luxembourg, Gernsback emigrated to the United States in 1904 and later founded numerous radio and electronics magazines. He is credited with coining the word "television", circa 1909. The first true sf magazine, *Amazing Stories*, followed in April 1926 and, when he lost control of this in 1929, he founded another, *Science Wonder Stories*. Regarded by many as the "father" of American science fiction, he wrote a famous — though now unreadable — sf novel: *Ralph 124C 41+* (serialized in his magazine *Modern Electrics* in 1911-12, and revised for book form in 1925).

DAVID GERROLD

AMERICAN NOVELIST

BORN: 1944

Gerrold, still very active though his star has waned, is best remembered for his sf novels of the 1970s: *When Harlie Was One* (1972), *Yesterday's Children* (1972), *The Man Who Folded Himself* (1973) and *Moonstar Odyssey* (1977). He has also written TV scripts, most famously 'The Trouble With Tribbles' (1967) for *Star Trek*.

MARK S. GESTON

AMERICAN NOVELIST

BORN: 1946

The novels of Geston have no real counterparts in sf. *Lords Of The Starship* (1967), *Out Of The Mouth Of The Dragon* (1969), *The Day Star* (1972) and *The Siege Of Wonder* (1976) all firmly place the reader in feverish enactments of senseless Armageddons. Unsparingly despairing, they are nonetheless bracing. His much awaited return to sf was *Mirror To The Sky* (1992).

TERRY GILLIAM

AMERICAN FILM DIRECTOR

BORN: 1940

Gilliam made his name as an animator on the BBC television comedy series *Monty Python's Flying Circus* (1969-71). His visually grotesque and always memorable live-action films as a director have tended to be fantasies of one kind or another.

Those that also may be claimed as sf (of a sort) include the juvenile-oriented Time Bandits (1981), the Orwellian semi-masterpiece Brazil (1985) and the time-travel picture with the strange title, 12 Monkeys (1996).

H. L. GOLD

AMERICAN SHORT-STORY WRITER AND EDITOR

BORN: 1914 DIED: 1996

The founding editor of *Galaxy* magazine, Gold wrote short fiction under various pseudonyms. The best, 'Bodyguard', 'Never Come Midnight', 'Someone To Watch Over Me', all portray a lonely man of ambiguous humanity living against the backdrop of an endless, seemingly hopeless quest.

REX GORDON

BRITISH NOVELIST

BORN: 1917

Real name Stanley Bennett Hough, he wrote many crime novels, as well as some effective sf. His best novel is *No Man Friday* (1956), about a Crusoe-like astronaut stranded on Mars.

RON GOULART

AMERICAN NOVELIST

BORN: 1933

If one could distil the essence of 1960s comic irreverence from, say, Richard Lester's *Help!* (1965), the novels of Terry Southern and the TV show *Laugh-in*, one might approach the *opera bouffé* genius of Ron Goulart's best novels, many of which inhabit his Barnum sequence. When he came down to Earth in such novels as *After Things Fell Apart* (1970), he mercilessly indicted the Californianization of the future.

COLIN GREENLAND

BRITISH NOVELIST

BORN: 1954

The intellectual Greenland (his first book was an adapted D. Phil thesis on New Wave sf) began as a novelist with some not-so-successful fantasies. He hit his stride in sf with the multi-award-winning *Take Back Plenty* (1990), followed by *Harm's Way* (1993) and *Seasons Of Plenty* (1995).

JOHN GRIBBIN

BRITISH NOVELIST

BORN: 1946

A prolific science popularizer and author of countless books on the weather, Gribbin has written several sf novels in collaboration with others. His most worthy singleton is *Father To The Man* (1989).

NICOLA GRIFFITH

BRITISH NOVELIST

BORN: 1960

With only two novels to date, Griffith is only just emerging as an intriguing new sf voice. In *Ammonite* (1993), she moves her female protagonist through a journey of spiritual growth on a planet without males. *Slow River* (1995) fashions a similar tale of maturation, this time on a near-future Earth seen through a cyberpunkish lens. She is uncompromisingly feminist, but is above all an individual.

VAL GUEST

BRITISH FILM DIRECTOR

BORN: 1911

One does not come across writer-director Val Guest's name very often in science-fiction reference books, and yet he made a substantial number of British sf films, some of them memorable. His first was *The Quatermass Xperiment* (1955), based on Nigel Kneale's BBC TV serial, and it was followed by two more good ones from the same source, *Quatermass II* and *The Abominable Snowman* (both 1957). His next entry into the genre is probably Guest's masterpiece, *The Day The Earth Caught Fire* (1961; co-written with Wolf Mankowitz) — a modest but very atmospheric little disaster movie. The loincloth-ripper *When Dinosaurs Ruled The Earth* (1969) is notable only for having been based on an original "treatment" by sf author J. G. Ballard; and of the sf musical *Toomorrow* (1970), starring Olivia Newton-John, the less said the better.

JAMES GUNN

AMERICAN NOVELIST

BORN: 1923

An academic critic and anthologist, Gunn produced quite a large body of earnest but mainly routine sf in the 1950s and 1960s. *The Joy Makers* (1961), *The Immortals* (1962; later the basis of a TV movie and series) and *The Listeners* (1972) are his most familiar novels.

JOE HALDEMAN

AMERICAN NOVELIST

BORN: 1943

Science fiction's best-known Vietnam veteran, Haldeman fictionalized his experiences in the popular *The Forever War* (1974), about a drawn-out conflict in space. Among his many and various later novels, the *Worlds* trilogy (1981-92) constitutes his most notable work. His brother, Jack C. Haldeman II, also writes sf.

VAL GUEST *UNDERSUNG* UK *FILM-MAKER, NOW LONG RETIRED AND LIVING IN THE* USA; *AT THEIR BEST, HIS SF MOVIES HAD FLAIR*

EDMOND HAMILTON

AMERICAN NOVELIST

BORN: 1904 DIED: 1977

Hamilton was one of the earliest writers of space opera, contributing galaxy-spanning serials such as 'Crashing Suns' (1928) to *Weird Tales* and other magazines from the late 1920s onwards. In the 1940s, he churned out many pulp novellas about the series hero *Captain Future*, and around the same time he wrote continuity for comic books (including *Superman*). Representative later novels include *The Star Kings* (1949), a sort of *Prisoner of Zenda* in space, and *City At World's End* (1951), in which an entire 20th-century town is thrown into the distant future by a nuclear explosion. He was still producing paperback-original space opera in the 1960s, and in general his work is remembered with affection by older readers. *The Best Of Edmond Hamilton* (1977) contains 20 sf stories drawn from a long career as a magazine writer; they range from the clunky 'The Monster God Of Mamurth' (1926) to a relatively sophisticated latter-day piece called 'Castaway' (1968).

PETER F. HAMILTON

BRITISH NOVELIST

BORN: 1960

An extremely energetic young writer, bursting with ideas though sometimes slipshod in style, Hamilton established himself with the trilogy *Mindstar Rising* (1993), *A Quantum Murder* (1994), and *The Nano Flower* (1995). His latest work, *The Reality Dysfunction* (1996), is, at nearly 1,000 pages, just the first third of what probably will prove to be the longest space opera ever written. It could mark the establishment of a big career.

and brainless camaraderie — a cod-militaristic romp in Harrison's best style; *Make Room! Make Room!* (1966), about an overpopulated future New York — his most sombre and admonitory work (filmed as *Soylent Green*); *The Technicolor Time Machine* (1967), about a film company's journey into the past; *Captive Universe* (1969), an effective "closed universe" mystery; *A Transatlantic Tunnel, Hurrah!* (1972), set in an alternative world where the eponymous tunnel is built; and *West Of Eden* (1984) and its sequels, about a time-line where the dinosaurs never died out and an intelligent saurian culture has arisen. There is much more: long resident in Ireland, Harrison continues to write, energetically.

HARRY HARRISON

M. JOHN HARRISON

BRITISH NOVELIST

BORN: 1945

Primarily a fantasist (of a very literary sort), Harrison wrote several sf tales in his earlier years. They include *The Committed Men* (1971), a dour disaster story, and *The Centauri Device* (1974), by far and away his most flamboyant book — a stylish, dark-hued but tongue-in-cheek space opera, in which anarchist space pirates with a taste for *fin-de-siècle* art fly spacecraft with names like "Driftwood of Decadence" and "The Green Carnation".

BYRON HASKIN

AMERICAN FILM DIRECTOR

BORN: 1899 DIED: 1984

Haskin was a cinematographer who graduated to direction after World War II. He formed a fruitful business relationship with producer (and director-to-be) George Pal, which resulted in a creditable run of sf movies: *The War Of The Worlds* (1953; from H. G. Wells's novel), the marginally sf "creature horror" *The Naked Jungle* (1954; from Carl Stephenson's story 'Leiningen Versus The Ants'), *The Conquest Of Space* (1955), *From The Earth To The Moon* (1958; from Jules Verne's novel), *Robinson Crusoe On Mars* (1964) and *The Power* (1967; co-directed with Pal, from Frank M. Robinson's novel). At least the first of these is generally regarded as a minor classic; and some critics have good words too for the

ELIZABETH HAND

AMERICAN NOVELIST

BORN: 1957

With a pyrotechnic trilogy consisting of *Winterlong* (1990), *Aestival Tide* (1992) and *Icarus Descending* (1993), Hand first showed she was expert in depicting the contortions of civilization and character. Her portrait of a decadent world besieged by its own uncontrollable fecundity of invention and cultural options was Chaucerian in its cross-sectioning of her vivid future.

CHARLES L. HARNESS

AMERICAN NOVELIST

BORN: 1915

Harness's best work, the novella 'The Rose' (1953), concerns the rivalry between art and science, represented by two women; one is

metamorphosing into a higher state, and writing a ballet in which only she can adequately star; the other misuses a new scientific principle to destroy her. *The Paradox Men* (1953) is also memorable.

HARRY HARRISON

AMERICAN NOVELIST

BORN: 1925

Most of Harrison's novels are humorous and action-packed. His principal books are: *Deathworld* (1960) and its sequels, about a planet with pathologically hostile life forms; *The Stainless Steel Rat* (1961) and its sequels, about the interstellar adventures of the crook-turned-policeman Slippery Jim DiGriz; *Bill, The Galactic Hero* (1965), in which young country bumpkin Bill is press-ganged into the interstellar army, where he learns to relish the ludicrous discipline

Mars movie, the location shooting for which was done in Death Valley, California.

ZENNA HENDERSON

AMERICAN SHORT-STORY WRITER

BORN: 1917 DIED: 1983

She is best known for the invention of The People — *soi-disant*; alien refugees with telekinetic powers — living surreptitiously on Earth. The stories, collected in various books and reassembled as *The People Collection* (1991), are notable for careful delineation of character marred by schoolmarmish sexual prissiness and a dim religiosity centred on an undefined "Presence".

FRANK HERBERT

AMERICAN NOVELIST

BORN: 1920 DIED: 1986

Although he wrote many books, beginning with the futuristic submarine thriller *The Dragon In The Sea* (1956), Herbert will be remembered as the author of the best-selling Dune series. The first, which was unsatisfactorily filmed by David Lynch, was the lengthy *Dune* (1965) — part hard sf, part dynastic romance — concerning young Paul Atreides's struggle to regain his stolen birthright on the desert planet Arrakis. The sequels are *Dune Messiah* (1969), *Children Of Dune* (1976), *God-Emperor Of Dune* (1981), *Heretics Of Dune* (1984) and *Chapterhouse: Dune* (1985). By the final volume, the extremely complex action had reached a point in time when everything on the sandy world of Arrakis had more or less returned to the state it was in at the beginning of the vast saga. Although popular because of the "world-building" and romance elements in his novels, Herbert was very much a demanding writer of ideas — in particular, ideas about the future of human evolution and consciousness. Among the more interesting of his singletons are *The Santaroga Barrier* (1968), *Hellstrom's Hive* (1973) and *The White Plague* (1982).

The author's son, Brian Herbert (born 1947), has also written a number of sf novels, including one title, *Man Of Two Worlds* (1986), in collaboration with his father.

Robert A. Heinlein
American Novelist
Born: 1907 Died: 1988

Heinlein was an apostle of fellowship, most of his novels being about the struggles of a highly motivated man or woman to gain admission to a group, which then struggles as a team to bring about some desired outcome. The group may be a revolutionary movement, a co-operatively owned commercial starship, a military unit, a political cabal, a commune or a secret society, but the hero needs its approval to bolster and guarantee his individual self-esteem. This often involves unlovely displays of patently bogus humility, which the hero is then invited to put aside. Heinlein's occasional use of masonic imagery may be significant in this context.

Such a technique is ideally suited to the *Bildungsroman*, many of his best books taking that form, the distinction between his juveniles and his adult novels often blurring in consequence; thus, *Starman Jones* (1953), *Citizen Of The Galaxy* (1957), *Have Spacesuit – Will Travel* (1958) and *Podkayne Of Mars* (1963) are regarded as juveniles largely because the protagonists are young, while *Beyond This Horizon* (1948), the novella 'Gulf' (1949), *Double Star* (1956) and *The Moon Is A Harsh Mistress* (1966) count as more adult fare, less because they contain harrowing or gruesome events (although 'Gulf' and *Double Star* do) than because the people experiencing the rite of passage into a higher fellowship and

more meaningful actions are already adult. In all these books, the protagonist meets people who have superior wisdom to impart, which (subject to varying degrees of protest) he accepts. The famed *Starship Troopers* (1959) is also an "adult" novel, despite its very young protagonist, because Heinlein's didacticism (never far from the surface) here spills over into prolonged internal monologues on such subjects as fellowship, discipline and the morality of war. Although the central character is strong enough to carry them, and the action is envisaged in the careful detail that lends conviction to all Heinlein's best work, in retrospect that book is a pointer towards his later, deplorable decline.

Heinlein had always had a mystical streak, manifest mainly as a belief in reincarnation, but with *Stranger In A Strange Land* (1961) the combination of increasing mysticism and didacticism, plus declining self-discipline and a new-found enthusiasm for sexual liberation, produced a work of toe-curling embarrassment. The effect is reminiscent of an elderly millionaire who, believing his money can buy back his youth, frolics with teenagers (and something very like that actually happens). Most unfortunately for Heinlein's self-direction and later reputation, it was a bestseller, enjoying a secondary vogue when it proved to be popular with college students and hippies in the late 1960s. Thereafter the dreadful predominates. Heinlein was still to produce good work, notably *The Moon Is A Harsh Mistress*, *Glory Road* (1963), an sf fairy tale which addresses the question, "How does the poor wood-cutter's son fare after he has married the beautiful princess?", and the formless but enjoyable *Friday* (1982), but otherwise his later works make sad reading.

DOUGLAS HILL

BRITISH NOVELIST

BORN: 1935

Canadian-born writer of good sf for children — notably the 'Last Legionary' quartet. Latterly, he has also written two humorous sf adventures for adults, *The Fraxilly Fracas* (1988) and *The Colloghi Conspiracy* (1990).

CHRISTOPHER HODDER-WILLIAMS

BRITISH NOVELIST

BORN: 1926 DIED: 1995

Author of a number of aeronautical thrillers,

Hodder-Williams also produced a quantity of competent sf, such as *The Main Experiment* (1964) and *Fistful Of Digits* (1968), the latter a rather good novel about computers. His last sf novel to appear was *The Chromosome Game* (1984), set after a nuclear war.

JAMES P. HOGAN

AMERICAN NOVELIST

BORN: 1941

British-born writer of rather thick-ear, American-style hard sf such as *Inherit The Stars* (1977) and *The Genesis Machine* (1978). One of his better books is *Code Of The Lifemaker* (1983), wherein an ancient robotic alien explorer seeds the moon Titan with intelligent, self-replicating machines of its own type: by the time they are discovered by humanity, these have evolved into a machine civilization.

ROBERT HOLDSTOCK

BRITISH NOVELIST

BORN: 1948

Primarily a fantasist, Holdstock began with a string of interesting sf titles: *Eye Among The Blind* (1976), *Earthwind* (1977), *Where Time Winds Blow* (1981) and the collection *In The Valley Of The Statues* (1982). Latterly, though, he has concentrated on his unique brand of deep-in-the-greenwoods mystery-horror story.

TOBE HOOPER

AMERICAN FILM DIRECTOR

BORN: 1943

Best known as a horror director for both film and television, Hooper has made a couple of minor but interesting sf movies, *Life Force* (1985; from Colin Wilson's novel *The Space Vampires*) and *Invaders From Mars* (1986; a remake of the 1953 film of the same title).

FRED HOYLE

BRITISH NOVELIST

BORN: 1915

An academic astronomer of high repute, Hoyle turned to sf with *The Black Cloud* (1957), a well-informed novel dealing with the ways in which scientists cope with a vast alien intruder into the solar system. Later, he co-wrote with John Elliot the BBC television serials *A For Andromeda* (1961) and *Andromeda Breakthrough* (1962), in the first of which messages received by radio telescope from the direction of the Andromeda galaxy contain a blueprint for the making of a beautiful female android. Many subsequent novels, such as *Fifth Planet* (1965), were written in collaboration with his son, Geoffrey Hoyle.

 **FRED HOYLE** *THE MOST FAMOUS REAL-LIFE SCIENTIST TO HAVE DEVOTED A GOOD DEAL OF HIS TIME TO THE WRITING OF SCIENCE FICTION*

L. RON HUBBARD

AMERICAN NOVELIST

BORN: 1911 DIED: 1986

An old-time pulp sf writer who turned religious-cult leader (creator of Dianetics and Scientology), Hubbard perpetrated much bad fiction in his last years when he chose to return to the field, his sins including *Battlefield Earth* (1982) and the ten-volume *Mission Earth* series.

ALDOUS HUXLEY

BRITISH NOVELIST

BORN: 1894 DIED: 1963

Huxley's indisputable classic *Brave New World* (1932) vastly overshadows his slight post-debacle comedy, *Ape And Essence* (1948; mainly notable for the rhyme which so encapsulates Huxley's social aesthetic: "The leech's kiss, the squid's embrace,/ The prurient ape's defiling touch .../ And do you like the human race?/ No, not much") and the marginal sf of *After Many A Summer* (1939), in which a Georgian reprobate and his mistress achieve a type of Tithonian immortality by eating raw carp intestines — they retain their vigour, but as the decades pass their neotenous human traits dissipate and they revert to an atavistically simian appearance.

Brave New World reflects Huxley's distaste for the general crassness and brutality of humankind. Unlike most dystopias, it portrays a future world in which the vast majority are perfectly content — wherein lies its horror, as their happiness derives from cheap, undemanding entertainment, promiscuous sex, community singing and the consumption of soma, a hangover-free euphoric. This world is examined through the eyes of Bernard Marx, one of its few disaffected intellectuals, and The Savage, a character whose rather preposterous antecedents allow him to judge it by standards which are unrealistically romantic but internally consistent (and ultimately kill him).

PETER HYAMS

AMERICAN FILM DIRECTOR

BORN: 1943

Beginning in television, Hyams became a writer-director for the cinema, specializing in action

ALDOUS HUXLEY

An early admirer of D. H. Lawrence, was at once fascinated and appalled by human sexuality, a feeling that informs all his best work

movies which included, *inter alia*, a good deal of sf: *Capricorn One* (1978), *Outland* (1981), *2010* (1984; from Arthur C. Clarke's novel) and *Timecop* (1994).

SIMON INGS

British novelist

Born: 1965

A stylish but fiercely demanding young writer, Ings's sf novels are *Hot Head* (1992) and *Hotwire* (1995), both written in a distinctively English post-cyberpunk vein. He may gain fame, if he is able to bring himself to engage with a wider readership.

ALEXANDER JABLOKOV

American novelist

Born: 1956

In Jablokov's impressive debut novel, *Carve The Sky* (1991), 24th-century Earth has stabilized its population and achieved a political system whereby science and technology are kept under control while the arts flourish; however, there are still rough, tough hi-techers out there in the asteroid belt.

HARVEY JACOBS

American novelist

Born: 1930

Jacobs was known for his funny short stories, collected in *The Egg Of The Glak* (1969). He made a comeback with *Beautiful Soup: A Novel For The 21st Century* (1992), which depicts a strange future where everyone is barcoded at birth by the Prime Mother Computer: the unfortunate hero finds himself reclassified as a can of soup.

K. W. JETER

American novelist

Born: 1950

Jeter's sf novels — *Morlock Night* (1979), *Dr Adder* (1984), *The Glass Hammer* (1985), *Death Arms* (1987), *Infernal Devices* (1987), *Farewell Horizontal* (1989), etc — are forceful and inventive (some of them in the steampunk vein, a term which he coined), but they don't seem to have brought him much success. Latterly, he has been concentrating on media tie-in books, including a sequel to Philip K. Dick and Ridley Scott, *Blade Runner II* (1995).

D. F. JONES

British novelist

Born: 1917 Died: 1981

Beginning his writing career in middle age, Jones wrote *Colossus* (1966), in which a giant computer takes over civilization. It was filmed by Joseph Sargent as *Colossus: The Forbin Project* (1969), and the author wrote two sequels, *The Fall Of Colossus* (1974) and *Colossus And The Crab* (1977). Of his other books, *Don't Pick The Flowers* (1971), a disaster novel, is perhaps the best.

GWYNETH JONES

British novelist

Born: 1952

A knotty, demanding writer for adults, Jones has also written many simpler novels for children. Her grown-up sf began with the fantasy-like *Divine Endurance* (1984), a far-future tale set in South East Asia, and has continued with the dour near-future vision of *Kairos* (1988), the award-winning *White Queen* (1991) and its sequel *North Wind* (1994), and several

GWYNETH JONES *A VERY ADULT SF NOVELIST, WHO ALSO WRITES CHILDREN'S BOOKS AS "ANN HALAM"*

others. Also a critic and reviewer, she is one of the field's leading intellectuals.

RAYMOND F. JONES

AMERICAN NOVELIST

BORN: 1915 DIED: 1994

Jones was typical of the best that magazine sf produced, moving smoothly from early stories for *Astounding* (such as the clever 'Noise Level') to deft novels like *This Island Earth* (1952), which was later filmed. With impressive juveniles such as *The Year When Stardust Fell* (1958), he contributed much competent work that helped solidify the centre of the genre.

RICHARD KADREY

AMERICAN NOVELIST

BORN: 1957

Journalist and chronicler of the avant garde, Kadrey still finds time to produce meticulously crafted novels and stories. Influenced by the visual arts and pop music as much as by past sf, Kadrey has turned out two exciting novels: *Metrophage* (1988) and *Kamikaze L'Amour*

(1995). The first tweaks cyberpunk volume knobs to eleven, while the second unleashes surreal rainforest transfigurations on the US West Coast.

COLIN KAPP

BRITISH NOVELIST

BORN: 1928

Kapp's first novel, *The Dark Mind* (1964), remains his best known. It concerns the attempts of many alien races living in transfinite dimensions to prevent humanity from regaining the appalling destructive potential it possessed aeons ago — especially now that it is re-awakening in one individual.

JAMES PATRICK KELLY

AMERICAN NOVELIST

BORN: 1951

His novels include *Freedom Beach* (1985; with John Kessel), *Look Into The Sun* (1989) and *Wildlife* (1994). In the well-received third of these, minds downloaded into machines, and artificial intelligences, are the eponymous "wildlife" featured in a century-spanning episodic narrative.

JOHN KESSEL

AMERICAN NOVELIST

BORN: 1950

The highly literate Kessel has written many short stories and a few novels, prominent among them the complexly satirical *Good News From Outer Space* (1989).

DANIEL KEYES

AMERICAN NOVELIST

BORN: 1927

Known mainly for the moving *Flowers For Algernon* (1966; filmed as *Charly*), in which Charlie Gordon, a barely literate moron, is artificially boosted to super-genius level, but after a brief peak declines. The story is told through Gordon's "Progress Reports" on himself, the last being touchingly similar to the first.

GARRY KILWORTH

BRITISH NOVELIST

BORN: 1941

Kilworth's sf tends towards the allegorical. *Abandonati* (1988) is set in a decaying city which most of the inhabitants have deserted, possibly for space, abandoning the underclass. Some seize their opportunities and establish a sort of ascendancy; others comb the cellars for liquor and canned dogfood. The author's short stories, collected in such volumes as *The Songbirds Of Pain* (1984), are also notable.

DONALD KINGSBURY

CANADIAN NOVELIST

BORN: 1929

He is best known for *Courtship Rite* (1982; published in the UK as *Geta*), a long novel about the human colonists of an alien planet who have forgotten their true origins and developed a tough, complex culture which is all their own. Against this background, the author spins a beefy and well-handled tale of imaginary anthropology.

NIGEL KNEALE

BRITISH TV WRITER

BORN: 1922

A distinguished TV and film screenwriter, much of whose work is in an sf-cum-horror vein, Kneale became famous as the creator of Professor Quatermass in three popular BBC TV serials of the 1950s. His one actual novel is *Quatermass* (1979) — tied in to a fourth, and slightly inferior, serial about the same character that appeared belatedly on independent television in the UK. His main TV sf credits are as follows: *The Quatermass Experiment* (1953), *Nineteen Eighty-Four* (1954; from George Orwell's novel), *Quatermass II* (1955), *Quatermass And The Pit* (1958-59), *The Year Of The Sex Olympics* (1968), *The Stone Tape* (1972) and the disappointing sf sitcom *Kinvig* (1981). There were also many shorter plays, mostly for the BBC. In addition to some large-screen adaptations of his best-known TV titles, cinema films he has scripted include *The Abominable Snowman* (1957; from his TV play *The Creature*), *First Men In The Moon* (1964; with Jan Read; from H. G. Wells's novel) and *Halloween III:*

Season Of The Witch (1983; with Tommy Lee Wallace).

DAMON KNIGHT

AMERICAN NOVELIST

BORN: 1922

When Knight was named Grand Master by the SFWA in 1995, no one could have looked more the part: bearded, patriarchal, wearing a grin of hard-won wisdom, Knight seemed larger than life, a living link to a Golden Age. And in the case of this multi-talented writer, critic and editor, his outer appearance was fully matched by the inner man, as attested to by his principled, productive career.

Emerging like James Blish from the Futurian milieu (about which he has written a memoir, *The Futurians*, 1977), Knight produced in the early 1940s a story or two before diverting his energies into agenting and editing. But when he ventured into reviewing and criticism, Knight uncovered in himself truly tremendous talents for witty, insightful, relentless dissections of contemporary sf. Holding his fellow writers to higher standards than those previous reviewers had enforced, Knight became instrumental in the maturation of the field. His scattered critical pieces were collected in 1956 in the seminal *In Search Of Wonder*.

At the same time — the mid-to-late 1950s — Knight's own fiction began to improve in a kind of feedback loop. Mordant, irreverent, exacting stories such as 'To Serve Man', 'Stranger Station' and 'Four In One' began to appear. Future collections such as *Far Out* (1961); *In Deep* (1963); *Off Center* (1965); and *Turning On* (1966) reveal the wealth of this period. Knight's novels, while less famous, all showed him subjecting genre conventions to stringent reimaginings. In *Hell's Pavement* (1955), the focus was mind control. In *The People Maker*, matter duplication. A late-period story such as 'I See You' best exemplifies this push to reach the logical extremes of simple ideas.

In the 1960s, Knight emerged as an organizer and teacher, inspiring and aiding the Milford and Clarion writing programmes, and helping to found the SFWA. With his *Orbit* series of original anthologies (1966-1981), Knight proved himself the arbiter of elegance within the field, launching a dozen careers. As the 1990s dawned, just to demonstrate that he had not lost his wily touch with fiction, Knight began to unveil such books as the enigmatic *Why Do Birds* (1992), portent of more bounty to come.

NIGEL KNEALE

UNMISTAKABLY A MANXMAN; IN RECENT YEARS HE HAS WRITTEN LITTLE, BUT HE BELONGS IN THE HALL OF FAME AS THE CREATOR OF BRITISH TV'S MOST MEMORABLE SF SERIALS

C. M. KORNBLUTH

AMERICAN NOVELIST

BORN: 1923 DIED: 1958

Now remembered mainly for his novels in collaboration with Frederik Pohl (*The Space Merchants*, 1953, etc), Cyril Kornbluth was also an acidic writer of solo short stories such as 'The Little Black Bag' and 'Two Dooms' — both to be found, with 17 others, in *The Best Of C. M. Kornbluth* (1976).

NANCY KRESS

AMERICAN NOVELIST

BORN: 1948

In Kress's first sf novel, *An Alien Light* (1988), groups of humans have reverted to a warlike cultural level on a planet where their ancestors were marooned; puzzled aliens arrive to study these isolated specimens. Her most impressive work is to be found in various short stories, and in the novel *Beggars In Spain* (1993) — about a future society divided between those fortunates who can go without sleep and the rest of us sleepy "normals"; the sequel is *Beggars & Choosers* (1994).

She has become one of American sf's most highly regarded authors.

 STANLEY KUBRICK
THE BRILLIANT ECCENTRIC OF WORLD CINEMA, WHO HIDES BEHIND THE LENS AND KEEPS US ALL WAITING... AND WAITING... AND WAITING...

MICHAEL KURLAND

AMERICAN NOVELIST
BORN: 1938

A lightweight but ingenious writer, whose *The Unicorn Girl* (1969) is part of a loose trilogy begun with Chester Anderson's *The Butterfly Kid* (1967). In both, the hippies of Greenwich Village save the world, Kurland's book being agreeably ornamented though slim on plot, and featuring pursuit through meta-dimensions. Many other novels have followed.

HENRY KUTTNER

AMERICAN NOVELIST
BORN: 1915 DIED: 1958

A stalwart of the pulp magazines, Kuttner wrote mainly in briefer forms, short stories and novellas. *The Best Of Henry Kuttner* (1975) contains 17 sf and fantasy tales written with a light touch, most of them reprinted from 1940s issues of the sister magazines *Astounding* and *Unknown* — where Kuttner was a star of the time, often under the pseudonym "Lewis Padgett" and often writing in collaboration with his wife, Catherine L. Moore.

Particularly pleasing among his solo tales are 'Mimsy Were The Borogoves' and 'The Twonky'. Fondly remembered novels under his name include *Fury* (1950) and *Mutant* (1953).

STANLEY KUBRICK

AMERICAN FILM DIRECTOR
BORN: 1928

Writer-director-producer Kubrick is one of the most "hands-on" people in the film industry, undertaking his own cinematography and editing, personally choosing the music for his films ; in short, doing just about everything humanly possible. He has always co-operated with writers, though, often choosing distinguished people from outside the movie world — Vladimir Nabokov, Terry Southern, Arthur C. Clarke, Anthony Burgess. Following such interesting non-sf works as *Paths Of Glory*, *Spartacus* and *Lolita*, his first venture into sf remains the indisputable classic among his films, the coruscating anti-nuclear-war satire *Dr Strangelove* (1964; based on a novel by Peter George, but co-scripted with Southern). Then came his four-year collaboration with sf novelist Clarke to produce *2001: A Space Odyssey* (1968), a movie which, despite its famous longueurs, transformed the look of sf cinema forever. The violently dystopian *A Clockwork Orange* (1971; from Burgess's novel) proved to be his most controversial film, and as a result of the outcry he withdrew it from exhibition in Britain (the country where he has chosen to make his home for many years). A notoriously slow and methodical worker, he has made comparatively few films in the last 25 years, none of them sf (although *The Shining*, 1980, based on Stephen King's horror novel, is certainly of interest to most sf enthusiasts). A major new sf movie from Kubrick, long promised, is awaited with keen anticipation.

FRITZ LANG
THE GERMAN WHO CONTRIBUTED ENORMOUSLY TO SF CINEMA BEFORE THERE WAS AN "SF CINEMA"; THE SILENT **METROPOLIS** *IS HIS MEMORIAL*

R. A. LAFFERTY

AMERICAN NOVELIST

BORN: 1914

Lafferty is primarily a fantasist whose sf strains the definition. *Past Master* (1968) is an anti-utopia with Sir Thomas More summoned from the past to resolve the problems of a colony world (changing sex *en route*). *Arrive At Easterwine* (1971), the autobiography of an artificial intelligence, is regarded as a failure. The author's many short stories contain his best work.

MARC LAIDLAW

AMERICAN NOVELIST

BORN: 1960

With interests ranging from photography to Buddhism, Lovecraft to surfing, Laidlaw is sf's eclectic and sly savant. His novels roam the literary map, from occult thrillers to satirical sf. *Dad's Nuke* (1985) and *Kalifornia* (1993) explore Goulartian territory, while *Neon Lotus* (1988) charts the intersection of Tibetan mysticism and high tech. Laidlaw is a freestyling *auteur*.

FRITZ LANG

GERMAN FILM DIRECTOR

BORN: 1890 DIED: 1976

Universally regarded as the first great sf film-maker, on the strength of the silent *Metropolis* (1926) — brilliant in its vision of a dark future city life even if the plot leaves much to be desired. Other sf films of Lang's include *The Girl In The Moon* (*Die Frau Im Mond*, 1929) and the various *Dr Mabuse* thrillers. An escapee from Hitler's Germany, Lang spent much of his later career in Hollywood, although unfortunately he was given no sf projects to direct while there.

DAVID LANGFORD

BRITISH NOVELIST

BORN: 1953

Langford's career as an sf novelist may have been abortive, but all the same he is one of the

Ursula K. Le Guin —— American Novelist —— Born: 1929

URSULA KROEBER LE GUIN *NOW A NOTED FEMINIST, WHOSE EARLY WORK WAS LESS OBVIOUSLY FEMINIST IN INSPIRATION; A MUCH-ADMIRED STORY, "NINE LIVES", APPEARED IN* PLAYBOY

A writer of very high repute. Her first novel, *Rocannon's World* (1966), concerns a scientist marooned on a primitive world where he learns a form of telepathy which is subsequently exported to all the inhabited worlds of Le Guin's universe. That universe is not entirely consistent with science as currently understood: in her second novel, *Planet Of Exile* (1966), Earth people acquire both tolerance for native foodstuffs and the ability to breed with the local humanoids by a sort of Lamarckian osmosis and, while space travel is subject to relativity, a communication device called an "ansible" is not. (That word is an anagram of "lesbian", a joke which went unnoticed until after Le Guin became famous.)

These minor shortcomings did nothing to undermine her reputation as a novelist and short-story writer (her first collection, *The Wind's Twelve Quarters*, 1975, added greatly to its lustre), which was soundly based on an individual and often beautiful style, simple but powerful plotting and characters who were generally believable and interesting, although occasionally expressing a rather curious worldview. In her third novel, *City Of Illusions* (1967), the "hero" not only deserts his wife in order to travel to Earth with, among others, a

young boy with whom he has a significant but undefined relationship, but continues to sport his wedding ring while doing so.

She then produced three indisputable masterpieces: *The Left Hand Of Darkness* (1969), *The Lathe Of Heaven* (1971) and *The Dispossessed* (1974). Of these, the first and third express an original approach to dualistic philosophy. The title of *Left Hand* is based on a local proverb, "Light is the left hand of darkness", and is set on Gethen, a world in the grip of an ice age and with two hostile, contrasting polities: a feudal-style kingdom and an extreme bureaucracy. The inhabitants spend most of their adult lives in a state of eunuchry, but at intervals roughly equivalent to the menstrual cycle come into "kemmer", when they manifest themselves either as men or as women, quite unpredictably but always extravagantly sexed and with internal organs to match their external appearance. This adds tension and poignancy when circumstances require Gethenians to remain celibate for long periods.

The Dispossessed is also dualistic in structure, with two contrasting inhabited worlds in the same system: Anarres is based on a form of social anarchism, without money, formal law or government but with intense social pressure to conform; Urras is based on extreme authoritarian capitalism, no less conformist in outlook but laying a heavy emphasis on individual worth, wealth and success. Although Le Guin's sympathies are obviously with the former, her analysis of the defects of both is notably even-handed.

The Lathe Of Heaven is a Faustian tale of a man who has an uncontrolled ability to manipulate reality retroactively – changes that he dreams of have already happened when he awakes – and the rascally psychiatrist who attempts first to control, and then to steal his talent. Le Guin's sf at all lengths since the mid-1970s has in general failed to sustain the impetus of her very best work, though some books, such as the large novel *Always Coming Home* (1985), have been decidedly ambitious.

best known and most popular figures in the field, largely as a result of his very witty "fan writings" (for which he has won countless Hugo awards). His novels are *The Space Eater* (1982), *The Leaky Establishment* (1984) and *Earthdoom!* (1987; with John Grant). Also of significance is the "non-fiction" book *The Third Millennium: A History Of The World AD 2000-3000* (1985, with Brian Stableford).

GLEN A. LARSON

AMERICAN TV PRODUCER

BORN: 1937

Larson is known primarily for the space-operatic *Battlestar Galactica* (1978-80) and *Buck Rogers In The 25th Century* (1979-81). His later series, of a more down-to-earth kind usually involving a roving hero and a wonderful machine, include the successful *Knight Rider* (1982-86) and the much less successful *Manimal* (1983), *Automan* (1983-84) and *The Highwayman* (1987-88).

KEITH LAUMER

AMERICAN NOVELIST

BORN: 1925 DIED: 1993

Remembered nowadays mostly for his humorous Retief series about an interstellar diplomat and for his tales of "Bolo" war machines, during a long fruitful career Laumer perfected a kind of fast-paced adventure novel that pushed its protagonists to breaking point and beyond. In such books as *A Plague Of Demons* (1965) and the emotionally resonant *The House In November* (1970), he found objective correlatives for buried dreams.

TANITH LEE

BRITISH NOVELIST

BORN: 1947

Notable for a highly wrought style (often reminiscent of Angela Carter), Lee's plots centre on the tribulations of young women whose self-destructive urges are hardly more under control than their extravagantly dangerous and repressive environments. Her most admired sf titles include *Drinking Sapphire Wine* (1977) and *Electric Forest* (1979).

FRITZ LEIBER

AMERICAN NOVELIST

BORN: 1910 DIED: 1992

To speak only of Fritz Leiber's sf is to slight over half his carefully crafted, lapidary books and stories. From the seven-volume Fafhrd and Gray Mouser series, which opened his career in 1939 and set the pattern for much future sword-and-sorcery works by others; through ground-breaking classics such as *Conjure Wife* (1953), so instrumental in establishing the sub-genre now known as Urban Fantasy; to latter-day supernatural novels like *Our Lady Of Darkness* (1977), Leiber revealed himself as a man of wide-ranging concerns and abilities hard to limit to one genre. Born into a theatre-dominated family, Leiber had a number of passionate interests. Chess, cats, the stage, astronomy and sex are motifs and concerns that grace and underpin many of his stories. He first essayed sf with *Gather, Darkness!* (1950), a book crafted from the same template that produced Heinlein's *Revolt In 2100* (1953), thanks to guidance from shared editor John W. Campbell. With stories from this period such as 'Coming Attraction', Leiber proved himself adept at merciless, yet empathetic satire, a mode he would pursue on and off in books like *The Silver Eggheads* (1962) and *A Specter Is Haunting Texas* (1969).

The mind-boggling complexities of manipulative time travel are explored in his Changewar series, consisting of the Hugo-winning *The Big Time* and *The Mind Spider And Other Stories* (both 1961). In 1964, Leiber's ambitious *The Wanderer* appeared. Recounting the chaos unleashed on a contemporary Earth by a planetary visitor to the Solar System, the book also managed to combine two of Leiber's tropes into one, in the person of sexy, tailed, female feline aliens. The novel won another Hugo. Battling alcoholism all his life, Leiber produced little sf in later years, although such stories as 'Catch That Zeppelin!' from 1975 still managed to earn awards. His endurance in the face of life's challenges might best be symbolized by an image from one of his finest stories, 'A Pail Of Air', in which ragtag humans manage to ingeniously survive the very loss of the Sun.

MURRAY LEINSTER

AMERICAN NOVELIST

BORN: 1896 DIED: 1975

Real name Will F. Jenkins, Leinster is best remembered for short stories of the "problem-solving" type, featuring human/non-human co-operation. His Med Service series, wherein a spacegoing doctor and his alien companion visit several colony worlds, is typical — as is the Hugo Award-winning 'Exploration Team' (1956), in which a man leads a team of Kodiak bears.

STANISLAW LEM

POLISH NOVELIST

BORN: 1921

To call Lem the Polish Borges in honour of their shared penchant for wry metaphysical gameplaying is both accurate and limiting. One might with equally facile half-truth call Lem the Polish Philip K. Dick, the Polish Asimov, the Polish Stapledon or even the Polish Pohl! In the end, despite passing affinities with a handful of writers with whom Anglophones are more familiar, Lem remains *sui generis*, one of the few sf writers of Nobel prize stature. (English-speaking readers of Lem most often appreciate him through the capable offices of his most frequent translator, the sympathetic Michael Kandel, himself a talented writer of sf. The dates of all the books cited below are for their first appearances in English.)

Anyone desirous of learning of the early, formative years of Lem can consult his charming memoir, *Highcastle* (1995). There they will find a somewhat aloof child intent on the workings of nature, imaginary bureaucracies, the closely observed character quirks of friends and relatives, and the alluring, mysterious instruments employed by his physician father. One need look no further for the themes of his mature work, which focuses on cosmological mysteries, absurd societies, perversely self-limiting humans and the helpful tyranny of technology. Add a fascination with the horror of war, only foreshadowed in the memoir, and the recipe is complete.

After a couple of mainstream novels, Lem turned his talents and intellect to sf. His novels

Levin is known for other things, but several of his novels are sf, including *This Perfect Day* (1970), about a computerized dystopia, *The Boys From Brazil* (1976), in which Dr Mengele attempts to produce clones of Adolf Hitler, and *The Stepford Wives* (1972), about a male conspiracy to create beautiful and compliant but artificial spouses. Written with a playwright's skills, and aimed at the mainstream audience, almost all his novels have been filmed.

C. S. LEWIS

BRITISH NOVELIST
BORN: 1898 DIED: 1963

A distinguished literary critic, a much-loved children's fantasist and a famous apologist for Christianity, Lewis wrote "anti-science fiction" — religious allegories dressed up as interplanetary romances. Nevertheless, the first two volumes of his Ransom trilogy, *Out Of The Silent Planet* (1938) and *Perelandra* (1943), contain some of the most memorable imagery in sf.

CLIVE STAPLES LEWIS *A GENIAL BEER-DRINKER WITH A STRONG RELIGIOUS MISSION*

and stories combine Swiftian satire, futurist speculation and brushes with the ineffable. Consulting the Ijon Tichy books (*The Star Diaries*, 1976; *Memoirs Of A Space Traveller*, 1982; *The Futurological Congress*, 1974; and *Peace On Earth*, 1994); the Trurl-Klapaucius tales partially contained in *The Cyberiad* (1974); or the adventures of Pirx the Pilot, one finds fresh, edifying charts of comic archipelagos of folly, invention, and disaster. *Solaris* (1970) remains Lem's best-known work, the surreal bardo adventures of humans orbiting a conscious planet. It was filmed by Andrei Tarkovsky in 1971. An allied novel is *The Invincible* (1973), which also portrays enigmas with cool precision. Once ejected from the Science Fiction Writers' Association for what was perceived as excessive candour about sf's shortcomings, Lem is an author too big for any social club to hold.

DORIS LESSING

BRITISH NOVELIST
BORN: 1919

An eminent mainstream novelist, Lessing dipped into sf in a couple of her earlier books, *Briefing For A Descent Into Hell* (1971) and *The Memoirs Of A Survivor* (1974), but eventually took the full plunge with her Canopus In Argos series: *Shikasta* (1979), *The Marriages Between Zones Three, Four And Five* (1980), *The Sirian Experiments* (1981), *The Making Of The Representative For Planet 8* (1982) and *The Sentimental Agents In The Volyen Empire* (1983). Philosophical space opera, somewhat cranky, these books have been regarded by some critics as profound.

IRA LEVIN

AMERICAN NOVELIST
BORN: 1929

Return Of The Jedi (1983), plus various juvenile spin-offs, and is said to have further films in the sequence at the planning stage. Most of his other work as a producer — for example, the Indiana Jones adventures — belongs more to the fantasy genre than to science fiction. On the strength of *Star Wars* alone, though, he vies with Gene Roddenberry for the title of most influential "creator" in media-sf history.

RICHARD A. LUPOFF

AMERICAN NOVELIST

BORN: 1935

Following his debut with the Edgar Rice Burroughs-like *One Million Centuries* (1967), much of Lupoff's sf has been pastiche of one kind or another — for example *Circumpolar!* (1984), about an alternative world in which intrepid aviators Lindbergh, Hughes and Earhart fly through the "Symmes holes" at the north and south poles of their doughnut-shaped Earth. Packed with Hollywood and pulp-magazine allusions, it tends to relentless jocularity. Other novels in not dissimilar vein are *Into The Aether* (1974), *Space War Blues* (1978 — perhaps his most ambitious and original) and *Countersolar!* (1986). Latterly, he has turned to crime fiction.

DAVID LYNCH

AMERICAN FILM DIRECTOR

BORN: 1946

Lynch's debut film, *Eraserhead* (1978), was a surrealistic oddity, scarcely sf in any conventional sense but certainly weird. When he came to sf proper, though, with the interplanetary epic *Dune* (1984; from Frank Herbert's novel), the result was disappointing — partly because of extensive post-production cuts over which he had no control. The more personal works Lynch has made since, particularly the psychological drama *Blue Velvet* (1986) and the TV mystery series — with sf elements — *Twin Peaks* (1989-90; with Mark Frost, which spawned the movie *Twin Peaks: Fire Walk With Me,* 1992) are much more satisfying.

JACK LONDON

AMERICAN NOVELIST

BORN: 1876 DIED: 1916

Best known for his rugged tales of dogs, wolves and the Alaskan frontier, London also wrote some significant sf — in particular *Before Adam* (1906), a caveman novel, and *The Iron Heel* (1907), a tale of future upheaval featuring socialist revolutionaries pitted against an American fascist-style dictatorship.

BARRY B. LONGYEAR

AMERICAN NOVELIST

BORN: 1942

Longyear made a minor name for himself with stories set on Momus, a planet settled by circus performers. They were collected in *Circus World* (1981) and related books. Otherwise, his main claim to fame has been the story 'Enemy Mine' (1979) — a moral tale about an Earthman and an alien in conflict on a planet strange to them both — which later formed the basis of a film.

GEORGE LUCAS

AMERICAN FILM DIRECTOR AND PRODUCER

BORN: 1944

Lucas directed only three films — the dourly dystopian *THX 1138* (1971), the non-sf youth/nostalgia movie *American Graffiti* (1973) and the record-breaking *Star Wars* (1977) — before settling down to become the most successful creative producer Hollywood has ever known. He has overseen two more *Star Wars* movies, *The Empire Strikes Back* (1980) and

BULWER LYTTON

British novelist

Born: 1803 Died: 1873

A popular Victorian novelist (born Edward Bulwer, later Lord Lytton), remembered for his oft-filmed historical romance *The Last Days Of Pompeii* (1834). One of his late books, *The Coming Race* (1871), was an influential scientific romance: an explorer discovers an underground world inhabited by an advanced race known as the Vril-ya.

PAUL J. MCAULEY

British novelist

Born: 1955

It is very dangerous to ever write off any mode of storytelling as mined-out and exhausted. As in mathematics, where only one counterexample is needed to disprove an ill-formulated hypothesis, it takes only a single writer doing amazing new things with an old formula to show that freshness of effect is forever within reach. Colin Greenland, Stephen Baxter, Iain Banks and Paul McAuley have, in the 1980s and 1990s,

provided a quadruple trouncing to the notion that it was no longer possible to write colourful, literate, scientifically and metaphysically intriguing space operas and planetary romances. Each of these men brings something special to the sub-genres. McAuley, trained in biology,

PAUL J. MCAULEY *Looking cool; for some years a botanist at St Andrews University, he has become recently a full-time sf writer — one of the best*

supplies not only the expected ingeniously conceived aliens and viruses, but also provides pop-culture hooks, mystical insights and a unique traversal of all scales of experience, from the intimately human to the awesomely cosmic.

McAuley began his career traditionally, with various short-story appearances, starting in 1984. These can be found in his collection, *The King Of The Hill* (1991). But significant attention was drawn to him only with his first novel, *Four Hundred Billion Stars* (1988). This volume opened a trilogy which continued with *Of The Fall* (1989) and *Eternal Light* (1991). The first book introduced us to the prickly Dorthy Yoshida, telepathic loner caught up in the machinations of an expansionary, yet relatively tiny human empire much smaller than the grandiose, galaxy-wide dream implied in the title. On the planet BD Twenty, she and her fellow humans trigger a buried genetic transformation of the natives, thereby gaining insights into humanity's alien competition. *Of The Fall* abandoned Yoshida for a new cast, not altogether successfully. Set apparently in the internal past of McAuley's universe, when FTL travel was not yet discovered, it staged a human power struggle on a colony world also populated with enigmatic aliens. The effect was rather static and cloistered. With *Eternal Light*, however, all was redeemed. Yoshida returned for a magnificent odyssey across vast reaches of time and space, and McAuley's prose hit new levels of info-richness — albeit occasionally inducing head-scratching in the reader.

With his next book, *Red Dust* (1993), McAuley stripped down his prose without sacrificing its beauty or sense of wonder, and wisely stepped away from his old fully explicated venue. On a Mars settled by Communist Chinese (a conceit long advocated but never developed by Howard Waldrop), McAuley exhibited a galaxy's worth of marvels, including monks, cowboys and a cybernetic Elvis. Demi-godhood awaited the winners of the rough and tumble. *Pasquale's Angel* (1994) seemed to signal that McAuley was now intent on staking out as much territory as possible, with an alternative timeline's dystopia sinking its roots in

Renaissance Italy. At the head of the cadre of hard sf fabulists, McAuley carries their banner proudly.

ANNE McCAFFREY

AMERICAN NOVELIST

BORN: 1926

McCaffrey's many popular sf novels include *Restoree* (1967), *Decision At Doona* (1969), *The Ship Who Sang* (1969) and *The Crystal Singer* (1982), but she is by far and away best known for her long series of planetary romances about the Dragonriders of Pern, beginning with *Dragonflight* (1968). These are often perceived as fantasy, though McCaffrey insists they are sf. Certainly, they seem to be written in the main to appeal to very young people — although they have their middle-aged admirers.

IAN McDONALD

BRITISH NOVELIST

BORN: 1960

McDonald's sf novels, which include *Out On Blue Six* (1989), *Hearts, Hands And Voices* (1992) and *Chaga* (1995), differ markedly, being respectively a dystopian comedy, an allegory of Ulster and an alien invasion variant. All are stylishly written, with strong central female characters, but *Hearts, Hands And Voices* is the least well thought-out; McDonald saddles his heroine with voluntary muteness, without considering the psychological implications of that condition and needlessly complicating his plot.

Out On Blue Six echoes *Brave New World*, in that the people are physically stratified according to their pre-ordained vocations, and the state is run by computers whose brief is to ensure that all are happy in their work and their sex lives. Happiness is not the same as competence or romance, even among programmers, so that inefficiency is rife and people are not always allowed to consummate mutual desire. The heroine finds herself at war with the system. In *Chaga*, a work self-consciously but effectively loaded with literary allusions, novel forms of vegetation suddenly appear in various locations including Kenya and begin to spread inexorably. Some fear them;

others believe they contain an unEarthly paradise, but if so, at what cost? The journalist heroine seeks the answers.

MAUREEN F. McHUGH

AMERICAN NOVELIST

BORN: 1959

Exhibiting a heartening tendency not to repeat herself, McHugh has contributed two fine novels to sf so far. *China Mountain Zhang* (1992) is a Delany-esque collage of a Chinese-dominated future seen through the eyes of its eponymous gay character. *Half The Day Is Night* (1994) dives undersea and explores Third World tensions among bubbled colonies. Eschewing melodrama, McHugh concentrates instead on portraying sheer future realities.

J. T. McINTOSH

BRITISH NOVELIST

BORN: 1925

Scottish writer whose best works show an obsession with the grading and selection of people according to subjective or mechanistic criteria. Social standing, immortality or survival may be at stake. Titles include *World Out Of Mind* (1953), *One In Three Hundred* (1954), *The Fittest* (1955) and *Flight From Rebirth* (1971).

VONDA N. McINTYRE

AMERICAN NOVELIST

BORN: 1948

Following her debut novel, *The Exile Waiting* (1975), McIntyre had a Hugo-winning hit with *Dreamsnake* (1978), about a woman healer who

IAN MCDONALD *WHOSE NOVELS ARE ALL QUITE UNLIKE EACH OTHER, AND ARE MOSTLY PUBLISHED UNDER DIFFERENT TITLES ON OPPOSITE SIDES OF THE ATLANTIC*

communes with snakes on a future Earth. Other novels, such as *Superluminal* (1983), have followed, although many of her recent books have been media tie-ins.

SEAN McMULLEN

AUSTRALIAN NOVELIST

BORN: 1948

McMullen's first book, *Call To The Edge* (1992), was a collection of odd, dense, detailed sf stories: sometimes brilliant, sometimes opaque. Since then, he has published an impressive two-part novel, *Voices In The Light* (1994) and *Mirrorsun Rising* (1995).

MIKE McQUAY

AMERICAN NOVELIST

BORN: 1949 DIED: 1995

A literary jack-of-all-trades, known for thrillerish sf such as *Life-Keeper* (1980), *Memories* (1987) and *The Nexus* (1989), McQuay had the distinction of co-authoring a novel with Arthur C. Clarke, *Richter 10* (1996). Alas, he died suddenly just before the book was published.

CHARLES ERIC MAINE

BRITISH NOVELIST

BORN: 1921 DIED: 1981

Real name David McIlwain, this author was — to borrow a term from the criticism of detective fiction — an sf "humdrum" of the 1950s and 1960s. One of his best is *The Tide Went Out* (1958), a quintessentially British disaster novel of the stiff-upper-lip school. Another is *The Mind Of Mr Soames* (1961), about a man who wakes from a coma, a *tabula rasa* at the age of 30. The latter was filmed, and Maine also wrote for UK radio and TV.

BARRY N. MALZBERG

AMERICAN NOVELIST

BORN: 1939

Only a passionate lover spurned could become as heartbroken and as bitter about sf as Malzberg once was, before his recent attainment of an elder's melancholy wisdom. Intimate with sf's history (see his criticism in *Engines Of The Night*, 1982, and his various uncollected essays and prefaces), eager to improve the genre, ambitious and unforgiving of fools, Malzberg brought to sf the creative fire, the deep insights and the tortured anguish of three of his own protagonists, Beethoven, Freud and Jesus.

From the outset (including early stories circa 1967-68 under the pen-name of K. M. O'Donnell), Malzberg offered the most bracing of literary potions, a mix of blackly humorous pessimism bordering on nihilism, combined with savage finger-pointing at all those who defaulted on their humanity. His universes — frequently featuring Kafkaesque situations and ineptly dire aliens — were ones where the ontological deck was stacked against the characters. But credit Malzberg's actors with this: they never went silently to their fates but instead, in mordantly glorious prose, lamented, raved, blamed and claimed small triumphs wherever possible.

Whether he was indicting the US space programme for banality (*The Falling Astronauts*, 1971, and *Beyond Apollo*, 1972), picking the scabs of politics (*Scop*, 1976), or sketching the absurdities of the writer's existence (*Herovit's World*, 1973), Malzberg deployed an impressive armoury of hallucinatory tropes involving gambling, assassins, bureaucrats, sex and sf itself. In the 1990s, Malzberg has limited himself to short stories ('Understanding Entropy' was a Nebula nominee), which reveal that the lion, while more tolerant and resigned, can still roar out the pain of the existential thorn in his paw.

PHILLIP MANN

NEW ZEALAND NOVELIST

BORN: 1942

Praised for his depiction of aliens, Mann's novels are otherwise full of middle-of-the-road virtues. His debut was *The Eye Of The Queen* (1982), and among his best since then are *Pioneers* (1988) and *Wulfsyarn* (1990).

GEORGE R. R. MARTIN

AMERICAN NOVELIST

BORN: 1948

A talented though pessimistic writer. Through pure hubris the hero of *Dying Of The Light* (1977) gets himself and his companions killed by neo-barbarians; the admired 'Sandkings' (1979) features the come-uppance of a repulsive villain; and the "hero" of the humorous collection, *Tuf Voyaging* (1986), is a vegetarian, eunuchoid giant. Martin has also edited anthologies and has written much for American TV, notably for the *Beauty And The Beast* fantasy series (1987-90).

LISA MASON

AMERICAN NOVELIST

BORN: 1953

A new writer whose sf novels, from *Arachne* (1990) to *The Golden Nineties* (1995), seem to be tied closely to her San Francisco homeground.

RICHARD MATHESON

AMERICAN NOVELIST

BORN: 1926

A screenwriter and supernatural-horror novelist as well as an sf writer, Matheson's early collection *Born Of Man And Woman* (1954; also known as *Third From The Sun*) contains stories short on hardware, long on dialogue and with economically drawn everyday settings. His tales are deceptively simple, but they linger in the mind and often translate well to other media (many of his pieces have formed the basis of TV and movie scripts). His best-liked novels remain the early ones, *I Am Legend* (1954) and *The Shrinking Man* (1956), both of which were filmed. Another of his stories, about a man threatened on the highway by a huge truck, inspired Steven Spielberg's film *Duel* (1971).

JULIAN MAY

AMERICAN NOVELIST

BORN: 1931

A popular sf romancer, whose work features time travel and special mental powers, May is known for such large novels as *The Many-Coloured Land* (1981), *The Golden Torc* (1982) and *The Nonborn King* (1983). Together with most of those that come after, they form one giant series, baroque, extravagant and addictive.

Michael Moorcock — British Novelist — Born: 1939

If an author claims with apparent seriousness that every single one of his multifarious, seemingly divergent fictions — whether mainstream, fantastic, science-fictional or chimeric — fits into one massive, all-embracing scheme that truthfully depicts cosmological actualities consistent on a higher plane — well, we must either brand him a genius and believe him, or label him a megalomaniac and laugh at his pretensions. On the strength of his enormously inventive, prodigious output, we have no choice but to place Moorcock in the former category. Clearly, this is a writer who is large and contains astonishing multitudes.

Because Moorcock's framework for his fictions is basically science-fictional in nature — his "multiverse" is a fruitful interpretation of quantum physics's "many worlds" hypothesis — we could call every one of his interlinked books sf — but only with damaging results. Here, we can deal only with those which juggle honoured sf tropes. The earliest portion of Moorcock's career (which began at the astonishing age of 15!) was occupied mainly with fantasies (many featuring that cursed albino, Elric), although early books like The

Sundered Worlds (1965) showed facility with space opera. But it was in 1964, when he assumed the editorship of New Worlds magazine that he began to remould sf substantially closer to his own conceptions. Not content simply to print experimental, daring, disrespectful, flauntingly adroit stories by others (stories which came to form the core of the New Wave), Moorcock began to write such stories himself.

His Jerry Cornelius books (the first four compiled in The Cornelius Chronicles, 1977) best represent this period. The title character roams blithely through chaos, meeting challenges with insouciant mutability. Also from this period, The Black Corridor (1969) and Behold The Man (1969) reveal Moorcock's revolutionary impulses. In the 1970s, Moorcock's sf was confined mainly to the Oswald Bastable books and the Dancers At The End Of Time series. The first cycle of novels was instrumental in pointing toward steampunk. The second pushed the decadence allowed by Dying Earth technology-turned-magic to droll new limits. After a decade where he unveiled little sf, instead chronicling the doings of the craven Colonel Pyat, such new and vigorous multiversal titles as Blood (1994) and Fabulous Harbours (1995) emerged to show Moorcock as an Eternal Champion still cruising the aethers.

MICHAEL MOORCOCK A GURU-FIGURE TO A GENERATION OF BRITISH SF WRITERS; POSSIBLY HE WILL BE REMEMBERED AS A MAJOR MAINSTREAM NOVELIST RATHER THAN AS AN SF OR FANTASY WRITER

WILLIAM CAMERON MENZIES

AMERICAN FILM DIRECTOR

BORN: 1896 DIED: 1957

Menzies was a Hollywood art director, one of the most prominent in his trade, who worked on films as prestigious as Gone With The Wind (1939). But he also directed a few films, and a couple of them happened to be sf. One is very famous — Things To Come (1936; from H. G. Wells's novel) — and the other is much less so — Invaders From Mars (1953).

JUDITH MERRIL

AMERICAN NOVELIST

BORN: 1923

Her early novel Shadow On The Hearth (1950) is a post-bomb story told from a domestic angle. The Best Of Judith Merril (1976) has 11 sf stories, ranging from 'That Only A Mother' (1948) to 'In The Land Of Unblind' (1974) — a gathering of all-too-rare fiction from this notable critic and anthologist who has been largely inactive in sf since she emigrated to Canada in the late 1960s.

NICHOLAS MEYER

AMERICAN FILM DIRECTOR

BORN: 1945

A novelist as well as a movie-maker, Meyer's books are non-science fiction (mainly Sherlock Holmes pastiches). However, three of his films have been sf: the quite effective Wellsian pastiche Time After Time (1979), and two of the best Star Trek movies, Star Trek II: The Wrath Of Khan (1982) and Star Trek VI: The Undiscovered Country (1992).

He has also worked extensively in television, and perhaps his finest single sf production — and certainly his bravest and most timely — is the lengthy TV movie on the theme of nuclear war, The Day After (1983).

GEORGE MILLER

AUSTRALIAN FILM DIRECTOR

BORN: 1948

Miller is known to sf viewers for his imaginative trilogy of futuristic road movies: Mad Max (1979), Mad Max 2 (1981; also known as The

GEORGE MILLER FILM-MAKER; HIS "ROAD MOVIES" CHANGED THE FACE OF CINEMATIC SF, IF ONLY BRIEFLY

Road Warrior) and *Mad Max Beyond Thunderdome* (1985; with George Ogilvie). Enticed to Hollywood after the success of these surprisingly fresh and stylish productions, his principal later work has been a supernatural horror movie based on a John Updike novel, *The Witches Of Eastwick* (1987).

WALTER M. MILLER, JR

AMERICAN NOVELIST

BORN: 1922 DIED:1996

About the long, slow rebuilding of civilization after a nuclear war, Miller's *A Canticle For Leibowitz* (1959) is one of the genre's most distinguished works. Such other sf as he wrote was included in the collections *Conditionally Human* (1962) and *The View From The Stars* (1964).

NAOMI MITCHISON

BRITISH NOVELIST

BORN: 1897

Best known as an historical novelist, Mitchison comes from a distinguished family (her brother was scientist and writer J. B. S. Haldane). As her autobiographical writings recount, she was personally acquainted with many of the century's greatest sf writers, including H. G. Wells, Aldous Huxley and Olaf Stapledon. Her three sf novels are *Memoirs Of A Spacewoman* (1962), *Solution Three* (1975) and *Not By Bread Alone* (1983).

JUDITH MOFFETT

AMERICAN NOVELIST

BORN: 1942

Her praised debut novel, *Penterra* (1987), concerned Quakers in space. It has been followed by an impressive two-parter, *The Ragged World* (1991) and *Time, Like An Ever-Rolling Stream* (1992).

C. L. MOORE

AMERICAN NOVELIST

BORN: 1911 DIED: 1987

Wife to Henry Kuttner, with whom she wrote much in collaboration, Catherine Moore first established her reputation in the 1930s and 1940s with excellent stories such as 'Shambleau',

a planetary romance in sword-and-sorcery vein, and 'No Woman Born' and 'Vintage Season', both classic sf of a harder-edged type. They are all to be found in *The Best Of C. L. Moore* (1975).

WARD MOORE

AMERICAN NOVELIST

BORN: 1903 DIED: 1978

Moore's output was small but of high quality, notably the disaster novel *Greener Than You Think* (1947), in which the world is overwhelmed by indestructible grass, and *Bring The Jubilee* (1953), in which carelessness with time travel reverses the outcome of the American Civil War. In *Caduceus Wild* (1978), doctors dominate America.

JAMES MORROW

AMERICAN NOVELIST

BORN: 1947

A leading satirist, Morrow first came to

prominence with *This Is The Way The World Ends* (1986), in which the survivors of a nuclear war are put on trial for genocide by the "unborn". Like that book, his principal later novels, *Only Begotten Daughter* (1991) and *Towing Jehovah* (1994), move into fantasy — although this is generally fantasy with a contemporary relevance and a distinct science-fictional edge to it.

PAT MURPHY

AMERICAN NOVELIST

BORN: 1955

Murphy, a skilled and sensitive writer, has not been prolific. She is still best known for her award-winning short story 'Rachel In Love' (1987), about an intelligent chimpanzee, and for such novels as *The City, Not Long After* (1989), which depicts a future San Francisco depopulated by a new plague, where the latter-day flower-children survivors are threatened by a military intervention.

TERRY NATION

BRITISH TV WRITER

BORN: 1930

Best known as the creator of the Daleks for BBC TV's serial-cycle *Doctor Who* (from 1963), Nation also conceived and wrote much of the more adult sf series *The Survivors* (1976-77), and reached his personal peak with the quite distinguished space-adventure series *Blake's Seven* (1978-81).

KIM NEWMAN

BRITISH NOVELIST

BORN: 1959

Mainly a witty horror novelist, the effervescent Newman began in sf: his debut novel, *The Night Mayor* (1989), is set in a kind of computer-generated dream-world where old *film noir* clichés

TERRY NATION *WITH ONE OF HIS FAMOUS CREATIONS — A DALEK*

Larry Niven
American Novelist
Born: 1938

LARRY NIVEN *CALIFORNIAN; BORN TO RICHES, DIDN'T NEED TO WRITE FOR A LIVING, BUT SUCCEEDED IN BECOMING THE DARLING OF "HARD SF" FANS*

In 1964, with the swelling chorus of New Wave voices already emerging from the young throats of Zelazny, Delany, Spinrad, Disch and others, perhaps the least likely prospect anyone could have imagined was that another 20-something writer would appear with a different programme entirely. Harking back to such early models as Hal Clement, the originator of modern hard sf; galaxy-spanners such as Edmond Hamilton and John Campbell; and future historians including Asimov and Heinlein, Niven soon showed that he could uncork a potent new brew that synthesized all these elements into something entirely fresh and modern. Without any reactionary motivation — at least initially — and with his face turned in a direction where no one else was looking, Niven soon had readers hooked on his potent mix of rigorous speculation, self-consistent historical projection and adventurous storytelling.

The majority of Niven's early work fits into a sequence he himself titled "Tales Of Known Space". Although its roots extend billions of years into the past, when an alien race called the Thrintun ruled our galaxy, its core period extends only from our present to the 2900s. Into this mere millennium, Niven managed to cram enough stories to satisfy the most demanding reader. The snippets of information necessary to deduce the coherent scheme behind Known Space appeared out of sequence and sometimes seemed to contradict each other slightly. But by the end of the 1960s, the full picture had gelled. Humanity was revealed as an ambitious, ingenious bit-player in a galaxy full of alien intelligences, including the cowardly merchant Puppeteers, the ferocious feline Kzin and the protective Paks, the latter proving to be an "adult" form of larval humanity. Our galaxy's centre was cosmically afire, spreading death at light-speed; marvels and challenges — many dramatizing concepts from modern physics — abounded.

Collections holding early Known Space tales include *Neutron Star* (1968), *The Shape Of Space* (1969), *All The Myriad Ways* (1971), *Inconstant Moon* (1973), and *Crashlander*

(1994, with new linking material). The opening novels are *World Of Ptaavs* (1966), *A Gift From Earth* (1968) and *Protector* (1973). Surely the culmination of this sequence are the novels *Ringworld* (1970) and its sequel, *Ringworld Engineers* (1979). A mixed-race expedition finds itself confronting the eponymous construction, a wheel-shaped world circling its sun like a hoop around a ball. Puppeteer manipulation of humanity's heritage is revealed, among other disclosures.

Niven's career entered a new phase when he began to collaborate with Jerry Pournelle. Together, they crafted vigorous novels that veered from the most archetypal sf to outright fantasy to bestseller widescreen cataclysms. *Inferno* (1975) reimagined Dante. *Lucifer's Hammer* (1977) subjected Earth to cometary impact and *Footfall* (1985) brought conquering aliens. *Oath Of Fealty* (1981) exposed the wiring, plumbing and politics of an arcology, a one-building city. It was in this phase that Niven acquired something of a reputation for tendentious political conservatism. The best joint work of the two men remains *The Mote In God's Eye* (1974) and its sequel, *The Gripping Hand* (1993). An interstellar human empire is forced to meet the challenge of the only aliens extant, the Moties, whose artificially evolved society poses problems.

In recent years, Niven's collaborations with other writers — Michael Flynn and Steven Barnes — have been less inspiring.

come to life. Many of his short stories and some of his later novels make use of the alternative-world convention — for example his series of USSA tales (written with Eugene Byrne, in *Interzone*), about a time-line where America, rather than Russia, underwent a communist revolution in 1917.

JEFF NOON

BRITISH NOVELIST

BORN: 1957

A writer of decadent cyberpunk whose widely praised novels, *Vurt* (1993) and *Pollen* (1995), are set in the north of England and feature vurt feathers, a drug which permits users to indulge in shared dreams and to exchange living creatures and artefacts between Manchester and the dreamworld. Characters include cyborgs, intelligent dogs and zombies.

ANDRE NORTON

AMERICAN NOVELIST

BORN: 1912

Without Norton and her scores of dynamic, Jungianly mysterious yet always narratively accessible novels (well over 100 to date), the sf field would be immeasurably poorer. Thousands of young readers would have been denied an addictive entry-point into the literature. And dozens of modern writers of exotic *Planet Stories* adventures would have had no role model of recent provenance to show just how the trick was done.

Alice Mary Norton took her famous male pseudonym — now her legal name — in response to perceived market restrictions in the late 1940s as she began to publish the first of her rare short stories. Shortly thereafter, however, she found her niche: paperback originals — many for Ace Books, many labelled too exclusively as "juvenile" — which moved sympathetic figures, often youngsters, through alluring venues. Recurring themes — telepathy, interspecies empathy, time travel, dying civilizations both interstellar and planetary, Native Americans, post-apocalypse scenarios — formed a pack of images which Norton could shuffle with endless inventiveness, often evoking deep emotional responses.

In the 1950s, her most astonishing period, Norton produced innumerable classics, including *Star Man's Son: 2250 A.D.* (1952) and *The Stars Are Ours!* (1954). Several sequences were launched, including the Ross Murdock tales (begun with *Galactic Derelict* in 1959 and still being added to in the 1990s); the Hosteen Storm duology; the Forerunner quintet; and the Moon Singer quartet.

Norton's Witch World mythos — begun in 1963 with *Witch World* — utilizes sf devices to transport the reader to a fantasy realm rife with intrigue. It has been her most enthusiastically received conception, generating fandoms and tribute anthologies down to the present. Recently, Norton has proposed to fund an sf writers' colony to be called High Halleck, its purpose to give aid to both new and established writers. Such a generous contribution seems superfluous after so much already given.

ALAN E. NOURSE

AMERICAN NOVELIST

BORN: 1928 DIED: 1992

One of the few practising medical doctors ever to produce sf, Nourse could also tell a thrilling tale and had a flair for reaching the young-adult audience. His *The Bladerunner* (1974) deserves to be better known than simply as the source of a more famous movie title. When he slipped between more fanciful dimensions, such as in *The Universe Between* (1965), he easily invoked high wonders.

CHAD OLIVER

AMERICAN NOVELIST

BORN: 1928 DIED: 1993

An anthropologist who made imaginative use of his academic speciality in the novels *Shadows In The Sun* (1954) and *The Shores Of Another Sea* (1971), and in the stories that appeared in such collections as *Another Kind* (1955).

Oliver is now a semi-forgotten writer, but there are signs that his posthumous reputation is slowly rising.

REBECCA ORE

AMERICAN NOVELIST

BORN: 1948

Ore has an interest in imaginary anthropology. In her first novel, *Becoming Alien* (1988), a boy is whisked away from Earth and tutored by aliens. The sequels are *Being Alien* (1989) and *Human To Human* (1990). A variety of interesting sf works have followed, and the author may be set to become one of the big names of the field.

GEORGE ORWELL

BRITISH NOVELIST

BORN: 1903 DIED: 1950

Eminent journalist and essayist whose classic novel *Nineteen Eighty-Four* (1949) remains the archetypal dystopia. It depicts a world of unparalleled wretchedness, where physical resources are dissipated in an endless and purposeless three-sided war, the past has been destroyed, the language is being degraded into a jargon called "Newspeak" in which it is impossible to criticize the regime and the sexual impulse is condemned as dissipating energies better channelled into hatred of and aggression towards "enemies" (internal and external, real and imaginary) of the state.

The principal character, Winston Smith, belongs to the most wretched group of all, being a Party Member but not of the Inner Party. He thus suffers far fuller and closer contact with the state than a Prole, without the meagre privileges (principally the power to chastise) enjoyed by his superiors. He embarks on a doomed love affair with Julia, a fellow Party Member, but is inevitably betrayed and given over to torture. As a final degradation, he is offered a choice between submitting to his own ultimate nightmare or visiting it upon Julia. Broken, he does the latter. *Nineteen Eighty-Four* had a profound effect, adding several words to the language — most significantly the derogatory suffix *-speak*.

"GEORGE ORWELL" *WAS THE PSEUDONYM OF ERIC BLAIR, AN OLD ETONIAN OF PRIVILEGED BACKGROUND, WHOSE NATURAL SYMPATHIES LAY WITH SOCIAL OUTSIDERS*

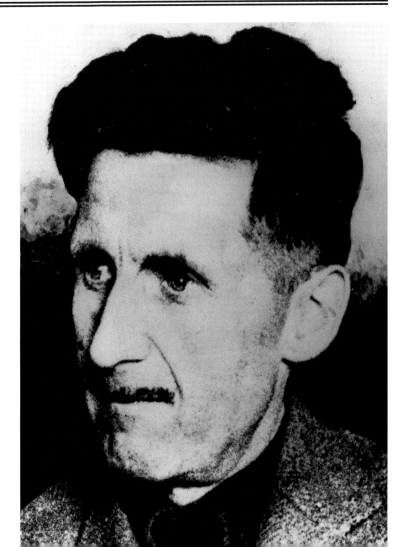

GEORGE PAL

AMERICAN FILM DIRECTOR AND PRODUCER

BORN: 1908 DIED: 1980

Hungarian-born animator Pal arrived in Hollywood in 1940 and proceeded to make short films. He moved into live-action features after the war, beginning sf production with *Destination Moon* (1950; directed by Irving Pichel; loosely based on a novel, and co-scripted, by Robert A. Heinlein), a commercial success which he followed up with *When Worlds Collide* (1951; directed by Rudolph Maté; from Philip Wylie and Edwin Balmer's novel) and various other sf films in collaboration with director Byron Haskin, beginning with *The War Of The Worlds* (1953; from H. G. Wells's novel). Pal's own sf films as director are *The Time Machine* (1960; from Wells's novel), *Atlantis, The Lost Continent* (1961) and *The Power* (1967; with Byron Haskin; from Frank M. Robinson's novel). A final, belated, production of his was *Doc Savage —The Man Of Bronze* (1975; directed by Michael Anderson; from Lester Dent's pulp novella).

EDGAR PANGBORN

AMERICAN NOVELIST

BORN: 1909 DIED: 1976

He is best remembered for two classics: *A Mirror For Observers* (1954), about Martian refugees on Earth seeking to influence the development of humanity, and *Davy* (1964), a post-debacle tale of North America reduced to Dark Age technology with matching religious outlook. Both celebrate scepticism, tolerance and sexual liberation.

ALEXEI PANSHIN

AMERICAN NOVELIST

BORN: 1940

Panshin wrote the first solid critical study of Robert Heinlein's fiction (1968), and the influence of that writer shows in his own best-known novel, *Rite Of Passage* (1968). Several other books followed, including a space-opera trilogy about an adventurer called Anthony Villiers, but latterly Panshin has been silent (apart from occasional critical writings).

PAUL PARK

AMERICAN NOVELIST

BORN: 1954

There is a secret, mystical league of writers going up and down our mundane world. Tracing their spiritual lineage back to such ancient wise ones as Delany, Wolfe and Crowley, they employ sophisticated literary techniques to stir fantasy and sf pigments into baroque, frequently psychedelic swirls. Their fictions, grounded in closely observed sensory details, nonetheless easily take flight into the stratosphere of imagination. Elizabeth Hand, Richard Grant, Lucius Shepard, Michael Swanwick and Geoff Ryman are five obvious adepts of this society. And Paul Park is a magian sixth.

Park's output up to 1995 consisted of three linked novels and one singleton, the latter bearing thematic and atmospheric affinities to the trilogy. In 1987, *Soldiers Of Paradise* appeared, the initial upwelling of the complex, evocative, meandering river of stories known as the Starbridge Chronicles. On a world infrequently referred to in the text as Earth (yet perhaps misleadingly so, considering its incredibly long year and strange astronomical companions), the dominant race of tailed humanoids attempts to meet the challenges of Spring, when a gasoline-smelling "sugar rain" melts the social institutions that have evolved to meet the different needs of Winter.

Without being overly derivative, Park's book evokes past landmarks of fantastic literature, from H. P. Lovecraft's *The Dream-Quest Of Unknown Kadath* to Mervyn Peake's Titus trilogy to Gene Wolfe's *The Fifth Head Of Cerberus* (1972). As characters drift in and out of the central spotlight with Indonesian indolence, the reader gets a panoramic view of a society disintegrating under religious, racist and political forces. In the second volume, *Sugar Rain* (1989), the terrors of the French Revolution are replayed. The concluding novel, *The Cult Of*

PAUL PARK
GLOBE-TROTTER; A COMING NAME IN AMERICAN SF, HE TENDS TO DEAL — UNCHARACTERISTICALLY FOR AMERICAN SF — IN "THIRD WORLD" THEMES

Loving Kindness (1991), much like the third instalment of Peake's trilogy, offers a disjunction with the more closely related first two. The narrative leaps into the middle of Summer, contrasting a contemplative lifestyle analogous to Zen Buddhism against a resurgence of the cruel Winter religion of Angkhdt.

In *Coelestis* (1993), Park shifted his focus to a world clearly colonized by humans from an overpopulated Earth now abandoning star-travel. A minor human diplomat there becomes sexually infatuated with one of the cosmetically transfigured natives and is caught up with her as captives of a worldwide revolution. Both man and not-woman gradually slough their civilized veneer under brutal stress. With only a handful of books to date, Park has firmly established himself as an archaeologist of unborn futures.

MARGE PIERCY

AMERICAN NOVELIST

BORN: 1936

Feminist writer most famous for her utopian *Woman On The Edge Of Time* (1976). Her best sf novel, *Body Of Glass* (1991; also known as *He, She And It*), combines commercial intrigue in a post-ecospasm world with the symbolism of the Golem legend, and is set in a Jewish community where the guardian "golem" is an intelligent android.

H. BEAM PIPER

AMERICAN NOVELIST

BORN: 1904 DIED: 1964

A writer of workmanlike quality whose books feature clashes of individual and corporate will over clearly defined objectives. *Little Fuzzy* (1962) and *Fuzzy Sapiens* (1964) hinge on the human status of attractive but primitive aliens. In *Space Viking* (1963), Piper makes a convincing hero out of an unabashed pirate.

DORIS PISERCHIA

AMERICAN NOVELIST

BORN: 1928

Piserchia was prolific for a fairly brief span of years in the 1970s and early 1980s, but seems to have stopped writing. Notable among her

EDGAR ALLAN POE *SUFFERED GREAT HARDSHIP AND PRIVATION DURING HIS SHORT LIFE; HE WAS SUBJECT TO OBSESSIVE FEARS, ESPECIALLY OF BEING BURIED ALIVE*

novels is *A Billion Days Of Earth* (1976), a portrayal of a far-future world inhabited by rat-men and other curiosities.

CHARLES PLATT

BRITISH NOVELIST

BORN: 1945

A well-known gadfly of the sf scene, publisher of various controversial fanzines and an excellent interviewer (see his book *Dream Makers: The Uncommon People Who Write Science Fiction*, 1980), Platt, who has lived in America for many years, has never quite established himself as a major sf novelist. Nevertheless, his fiction is copious and frequently interesting, ranging from the early satire of *Garbage World* (1967) through the sf pornography of *The Gas* (1970) to the idea-filled post-cyberpunk of *The Silicon Man* (1991).

EDGAR ALLAN POE

AMERICAN SHORT-STORY WRITER

BORN: 1809 DIED: 1849

Although he is best known as a horror writer, Poe's fictional *oeuvre* contains the seeds of many genres, including the surrealist ('The Business Man') and the detective story ('The Purloined Letter') as well as sf. The purest sf is the short satire 'Mellonta Tauta', a diary letter from a lady who, though foolish and superficial, occasionally offers some shrewd insights: "19th-century women look very odd, very — like something between a turkey-cock and a dromedary." She is travelling "On Board Balloon 'Skylark', April 1-8 2848", and her letter is filled with the garbled half-knowledge of people who get their information from cheap magazines and conversations with the better-educated. The philosophical questions of Poe's own time receive cavalier treatment: "The author (who was much thought of in his day) was one Miller, or Mill; and we find it recorded of him, as a point of some importance, that he had a mill-horse called Bentham." Poe also prophesies an extreme form of social fascism, wherein the group counts for everything and the individual for nothing, so

Frederik Pohl — American Novelist — Born: 1919

An elder statesman of his field, a sometime literary agent and magazine editor, Pohl wrote many short stories under pseudonyms during the 1940s. In the early 1950s, he began using his real name and his work improved vastly: the representative collection *The Best Of Frederik Pohl* (1975) contains 18 items including those brilliant tales which first made his reputation as a satirist: 'The Tunnel Under The World' and 'The Midas Plague'; but it also has such later strong pieces as 'Day Million' and 'The Day The Martians Came'. His first novel was the classic satire *The Space Merchants* (1953; in collaboration with C. M. Kornbluth), which Kingsley Amis, writing in 1960, described as perhaps the best science-fiction novel of them all. Other fine books with the late Cyril Kornbluth include *Search The Sky* (1954), *Gladiator-At-Law* (1955) and *Wolfbane* (1959).

Pohl's solo novels since then range from *A Plague Of Pythons* (1966) through *Jem: The Making Of A Utopia* (1979) to *Mining The Oort* (1992). But his most admired works include the award-winning *Man Plus* (1976), about a man who is physically adapted to live on Mars, and the galaxy-spanning series which began with *Gateway* (1977). In the latter, humans go joyriding in spacecraft that have been abandoned by the mysterious alien Heechee, some of them hoping to grow rich thanks to the valuable artefacts trawled by their expeditions. The sequels are *Beyond The Blue Event Horizon* (1980), *Heechee Rendezvous* (1984) and *The Annals Of The Heechee* (1987). For more than 50 years, Pohl has been at the heart of sf, his style and subject matter changing to suit the times: he is one of the essential writers.

that news of war, plague and personal misfortune befalling others is rejoiced at with unabashed, routine Schadenfreude; to offer succour is the ultimate social gaffe. *The Science Fiction Of Edgar Allan Poe*, edited by Harold Beaver in 1976, is the collection that contains everything relevant.

RACHEL POLLACK

AMERICAN NOVELIST

BORN: 1945

Pollack's *Unquenchable Fire* (1988), won the Arthur C. Clarke Award for science fiction despite the fact that it's really a fantasy — though one of an unusual type, set in the future. Her other works have been few in number but always quirky and stylish.

JERRY POURNELLE

AMERICAN NOVELIST

BORN: 1933

Pournelle is a vigorous standard-bearer for the Libertarian Right who writes best in collaboration, mainly with Larry Niven: *The Mote In God's Eye* (1974), etc. Their slogan "Think of it as evolution in action", from *Oath Of Fealty* (1981), became a right-wing catchphrase. A recurrent theme is the threat of a brutalized and brutalizing underclass.

TIM POWERS

AMERICAN NOVELIST

BORN: 1952

Powers is mainly a fantasist, though his "steampunk" time-travel novel *The Anubis Gates* (1983) has much of the feel of sf. It won the Philip K. Dick award, as did his *Dinner At Deviant's Palace* (1985).

PAUL PREUSS

AMERICAN NOVELIST

BORN: 1942

Preuss is a scientist and his "sharecrop" novels in the Arthur C. Clarke's Venus Prime series, beginning with *Breaking Strain* (1987), are technically well-informed and effective of their sort. But he has also written some more serious stand-alone novels, such as *Broken Symmetries* (1983) and *Starfire* (1988).

CHRISTOPHER PRIEST

BRITISH NOVELIST

BORN: 1943

One of England's most important imaginative writers, Priest has gradually grown away from sf of the standard sort, through a sequence of sensitive novels that range from the early *Indoctrinaire* (1970) and *Fugue For A Darkening Island* (1972), through *Inverted World* (1974) — perhaps his sf masterpiece — and *The Space Machine* (1976), to such recent, edge-of-the-genre books as *The Quiet Woman* (1990) and *The Prestige* (1995). The last title won the James Tait Black Memeorial Award for 1996.

ROBERT REED

AMERICAN NOVELIST

BORN: 1956

Getting his start from the Writers of the Future programme, Reed has gone on to become the consummate consolidator and extender of sf motifs. His many stories and seven novels instantly engage the reader with brightly burnished and customized enactments of the best sf dreams, many of them Zelazny-like in their employment of devious demi-gods. *An Exaltation Of Larks* (1995) shows him on top form with a recomplicated time-travel tale.

MAURICE RENARD

FRENCH NOVELIST

BORN: 1875 DIED: 1939

Best known for the oft-filmed horror novel *The Hands Of Orlac* (1920), Renard was one of France's finest sf writers, as demonstrated by the H. G. Wells-influenced *New Bodies For Old* (1908). Much of his best work, such as *Le péril bleu* ('The Blue Peril', 1910) has not been translated into English.

MIKE RESNICK

AMERICAN NOVELIST

BORN: 1942

Although he had written many earlier books (some of them under pseudonyms), Resnick came to prominence with *Santiago* (1986), a space opera with a cyclic structure of quests in which various bounty-hunters and opportunists search the galaxy of the far future for a famous criminal. A number of his later sf stories and novels, such as *Ivory: A Legend Of Past And Future* (1988), have been on African themes.

MACH REYNOLDS

AMERICAN NOVELIST

BORN: 1917 DIED: 1983

A left-wing writer much concerned with the moral and political effects of industrialism. One series, containing such routine books as *The Earth War* (1963), is set in a caste-ridden society where welfare has been superseded by inalienable cash hand-outs sufficient for a lifestyle of brutal entertainment and tranquillizers. More ambitious work includes the utopian *Looking Backward, From The Year 2000* (1973).

KEITH ROBERTS

BRITISH NOVELIST

BORN: 1935

Associated with the New Wave, Roberts brought to that revolution an understated elegance best seen in such books as *Pavane* (1968) and *The Chalk Giants* (1974). Fluent with the turnings of history, he could also extrapolate gorgeously in a book like *Kiteworld* (1985). His *Kaeti* books showed his flair for humorous fantasy, and his gift for drawing helped brighten many UK publications.

KIM STANLEY ROBINSON

AMERICAN NOVELIST

BORN: 1952

Very few modern sf writers can work at all scales of narrative. There are miniaturists who can inscribe the Lord's Prayer on a grain of rice, and there are demi-gods who can use galaxies to

spell out Armageddon. But only a rare figure merges both skills and Stan Robinson is one. His short stories — collected most recently in *Remaking History* (1991) — have been well received, earning their share of awards. Full of richly textured people in cleverly conceived sf situations, they roam from alternate timelines to glaciated near-futures. Yet it is for his fine novels — both intimate and wide-screen — that Robinson has reaped most attention. Along with William Gibson and Lucius Shepard, Robinson was the beneficiary of editor Terry Carr's insight and keen eye for talent. Carr picked Robinson's *The Wild Shore* to appear in 1984 as one of the second series of Ace Specials. This book opened what came to be known as the Orange County trilogy. Presenting three divergent scenarios of a future California, the trilogy continued with *The Gold Coast* (1988) and *Pacific Edge* (1990).

In the first volume, the USA falters along in a state of denial under post-apocalyptic conditions. The second renders a dystopia. The third, and perhaps best, portrays one of modern sf's rare utopias. (Robinson's interest in ideal states can be seen in his editorship of the anthology, *Future Primitive*, 1994.) Together, the three California books form a spectrum running from despair through boredom to enthusiasm. Several singleton novels further attested to Robinson's skills. *Icehenge* (1984) visits Pluto, while *Escape From Kathmandu* (1989) journeys to Nepal. Yet it was only on a terrain thought to be strip-mined that Robinson would plant his flag of conquest.

Robinson's latest trilogy started with *Red Mars* (1992), moved through *Green Mars* (1993), and concluded with *Blue Mars* (1996). Detailing the terraforming of the fourth planet in voluminous verisimilitude and employing a large cast of characters, the books have succeeded in restoring the Solar System as a legitimate playground for sf.

This is one of the few genuine examples of epic science fiction.

KIM STANLEY ROBINSON
KEEN MOUNTAINEER; WENT TO ANTARCTICA RESEARCHING FOR ONE OF HIS SF NOVELS — AND CAME BACK WITH A FROSTBITTEN HAND

SPIDER ROBINSON

AMERICAN NOVELIST

BORN: 1948

Although known for such novels as *Stardance* (1979, with Jeanne Robinson) and *Mindkiller* (1982), the Canadian-resident Robinson's most popular work has been the long series of humorous short stories — tall tales told by the human and alien clients of the eponymous drinking establishment — in *Callahan's Crosstime Saloon* (1977) and its follow-up volumes, including *Time Travellers Strictly Cash* (1981), *Callahan's Secret* (1986) and *Callahan's Lady* (1989).

GENE RODDENBERRY

AMERICAN TV PRODUCER

BORN: 1921 DIED: 1991

Roddenberry may go down in history as the most famous "creator" in science fiction. A minor American TV writer of the 1950s, he followed the normal career path for his profession, graduating to series production in the early 1960s. His stroke of genius was to create *Star Trek* (first pilot, 1964; series, 1966-69). Probably inspired by the movie *Forbidden Planet* and by Robert A. Heinlein's "soft" military sf novel *Space Cadet* (1948), but guided above all by the exigencies of television production, he conceived a format cheap enough to make (most scenes were shot on the "bridge" of the starship *Enterprise*, with a relatively small cast of recurring characters) and yet flexible enough to incorporate a host of standard sf themes and situations.

As has been remarked frequently, there was a John F. Kennedy-era optimism embodied by Roddenberry's characters — principally the brave and authoritative captain, James T. Kirk and the "logical" alien first officer, Mr Spock — and by their mission to boldly go where no man has gone before. Although it now seems distinctly old-fashioned, not to say paternalistic and sexist, there was nevertheless a wholesome idealism enshrined in Roddenberry's plots and characters: humane, pacific, liberal, rational, democratic, mildly anti-racist and socially progressive. Later, after a few failed pilot episodes for other sf series — and after the one great phenomenon he had created had long since taken over his life — Roddenberry became involved in "Trek" cinema films and was executive producer of the first few seasons of the belated follow-up TV series *Star Trek: The Next Generation* (1987-94).

J.-H. ROSNY

BELGIAN NOVELIST

BORN: 1856 DIED: 1940

A specialist in tales of prehistory, Rosny was the dominant French-language sf writer at the time of H. G. Wells. His best-known book, thanks to a much later film version, is *The Quest For Fire* (1909), but he also wrote many short stories and novellas of a more far-out and futuristic sort: they range from 'The Shapes' (1887) to 'The Navigators Of Infinity' (1925).

 GENE RODDENBERRY *AVERAGE JOE; HE CREATED STAR TREK — AND PROBABLY NEVER KNEW QUITE WHAT HIT HIM, SPENDING HIS LAST YEARS IN A DAZE OF FAME*

RUDY RUCKER

AMERICAN NOVELIST

BORN: 1946

If Lewis Carroll had been educated in cybernetics and also taken a generous portion of recreational drugs, he might have come to resemble Rudy Rucker. Master of the outlandish and the transreal, Rucker moves from Cantorian transcendentalism *(White Light*, 1980) to steampunk *(The Hollow Earth*, 1990). His training as a mathematician complements his gonzo sensibilities in such works as *Software* (1982) and *Wetware* (1988).

KRISTINE KATHRYN RUSCH

AMERICAN NOVELIST

BORN: 1960

Energetic and multi-talented, Rusch came to prominence when she was appointed editor of *The Magazine Of Fantasy And Science Fiction* in 1991 (after a stint with the small-press *Pulphouse*). Despite her editorial duties, she has found time to write many novels, some of them fantasy or horror. A recent sf example is *Alien Influences* (1994).

JOANNA RUSS

AMERICAN NOVELIST

BORN: 1937

Critic, novelist and short-story writer, Russ made her biggest impact 16 years into her career with the publication of *The Female Man* (1975). Coinciding with the crest of undiluted feminist rhetoric, Russ's book was a complex, non-dogmatic rendering of the possibilities inherent in being female. Her insights into the realities of power and her close readings of literature are needed more than ever nowadays.

ERIC FRANK RUSSELL

BRITISH NOVELIST

BORN: 1905 DIED: 1978

Russell has a curious dual reputation. Many of his short stories, and the novels *Wasp* (1957) and *Three To Conquer* (1956), feature bloody conflict between humans and aliens in which the humans win by a combination of superior intelligence and guts, embellished with authorial

GEOFF RYMAN *STYLIST; HE DOESN'T PRODUCE ENOUGH, BUT IF HE KEEPS AT IT HE MAY BECOME ONE OF THE GREAT WRITERS*

displays of schoolboyish humour. In some lighter pieces, including the satires 'Allamagoosa' and 'Study In Still Life', the humour is more adult.

Others, including the admired novelette '... And Then There Were None' (included in *The Great Explosion*, 1962), are equally light in tone, but Russell appears as an apostle of non-violent solutions — significantly, in this case, the conflict is between groups of humans. A third group is loaded with Christian symbolism and preaches an almost Jainist doctrine of respect for all life. It includes his stories 'PS', in which a man declares his platonic love for an alien, and 'Somewhere A Voice', which overtly expresses the view that a dog has a soul no less than his travelling companions, who include a Jew, a Chinese and two middle-aged East Europeans, plus the smug and brutal white roughneck who begins by despising and ends by respecting all four.

RICHARD PAUL RUSSO

AMERICAN NOVELIST

BORN: 1954

With intelligently-conceived novels like *Inner Eclipse* (1988) and *Subterranean Gallery* (1989; a Philip K. Dick award-winner), Russo gained praise from sf critics. However, he remains

something of an unknown quantity with readers at large.

GEOFF RYMAN

BRITISH NOVELIST

BORN: 1951

Canadian-born writer of such remarkable works as *The Unconquered Country* (1986; winner of the World Fantasy Award as best novella). His most purely science-fictional novel is *The Child Garden* (1989), in which a young woman, who lives in an extremely bizarre future London where people are controlled by viruses, has a passionate affair with a large, hairy, specially adapted member of her own sex.

FRED SABERHAGEN

AMERICAN NOVELIST

BORN: 1930

Author of many things, including much fantasy and horror, but best known in sf for his Berserker series, the first volume of which, *Berserker* (1967), contains stories set against the background of a galactic invasion by the eponymous giant robotic warships dedicated to the destruction of all life. These and later tales — such as *Berserker's Planet* (1975) and *Berserker Man* (1979) — are excellent examples of space opera.

PAMELA SARGENT

AMERICAN NOVELIST

BORN: 1948

Sargent began with *Cloned Lives* (1976), a cobbled-together novel (from previously published short stories) in which the members of a scientifically-produced "clone family" grow up in a world which misunderstands them. Her work since then has been variable, tending latterly towards historical fiction, but she is also of note as a feminist sf anthologist, with books such as *Women Of Wonder* (1975) and its sequels.

HILBERT SCHENCK

AMERICAN NOVELIST

BORN: 1926

Schenck contributed sporadically to sf magazines from the early 1950s, but his first novel, *At The Eye Of The Ocean*, did not appear until 1980. It concerns mystical revelations experienced off Cape Cod by those who are able to read the currents, the winds and the contours of the sea floor: the author's copious knowledge of oceanography gives an sf edge to what is essentially a fantasy story. Later books, including *A Rose For Armageddon* (1982) and *Chronosequence* (1988), have similar subject matter.

STANLEY SCHMIDT

AMERICAN EDITOR

BORN: 1944

Having taken over the editorship of *Analog* magazine from Ben Bova in 1978, Schmidt is a power in the field — although his own fiction-writing career has come to a halt. It began with the delightfully titled sf novel *Newton And The Quasi-Apple* (1975).

JAMES H. SCHMITZ

AMERICAN NOVELIST

BORN: 1911 DIED: 1981

The posthumously published *The Best Of James H. Schmitz* (1991) contains a fair sampling of the shorter work of this undersung but talented writer, best remembered for his oft-reprinted story 'Grandpa' as well as the tales of Telzey Amberdon and other good-hearted space opera.

ERNEST B. SCHOEDSACK

AMERICAN FILM DIRECTOR

BORN: 1893

As producer and director, Schoedsack specialized in sf of the "lost world" type, often verging on fantasy. His relevant movies include the very famous and much loved original version of *King Kong* (1933; co-directed with Merian C. Cooper, who was to be producer of most of his later films), plus *Son Of Kong* (1933), *Doctor Cyclops* (1940) and the Kong-inspired *Mighty Joe Young* (1949).

RIDLEY SCOTT
BRITISH BOY MADE GOOD; THE QUINTESSENTIAL FILM-MAKER AS VISUAL ARTIST RATHER THAN AS STORY-TELLER

JOEL SCHUMACHER

AMERICAN FILM DIRECTOR

BORN: 1942

A costume designer, who worked on Woody Allen's sf comedy *Sleeper* (1973) among other things, Schumacher became a screenwriter, then finally a director with another sf comedy, *The Incredible Shrinking Woman* (1981). A variety of films followed, including the unsuccessful sf-horror *Flatliners* (1990) and the mightily successful *Batman Forever* (1995).

MELISSA SCOTT

AMERICAN NOVELIST

BORN: 1960

Scott's main series is about the adventures of spaceperson Silence Leigh: *Five Twelfths Of Heaven* (1986), *Silence In Solitude* (1986) and *The Empress Of Earth* (1987). She has continued to write vigorously with titles such as *Dreamships* (1992) and *Burning Bright* (1993).

RIDLEY SCOTT

BRITISH FILM DIRECTOR

BORN: 1939

Beginning as a highly successful director of TV commercials, Scott moved into feature films in the late 1970s and soon received a call to Hollywood. His first and second films to be made there swiftly established themselves as sf classics, praised above all for their remarkable visual style. They were, of course, *Alien* (1979; from an original script by Dan O'Bannon) and *Blade Runner* (1982; from Philip K. Dick's novel *Do Androids Dream Of Electric Sheep?*). Although his next film was a fantasy (*Legend*, 1985), Scott has stayed clear of sf since, preferring to concentrate on crime thrillers.

ARTHUR SELLINGS

BRITISH NOVELIST

BORN: 1921 DIED: 1968

Now forgotten, Sellings was praised in his time for sf novels like *The Silent Speakers* (1962), *The Uncensored Man* (1964) and the posthumous *Junk Day* (1970).

He was a talented minor writer, but is remembered with respect by some.

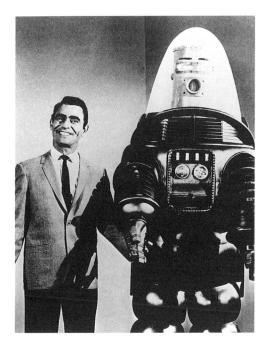

ROD SERLING

AMERICAN TV PRODUCER

BORN: 1924 DIED: 1975

Serling was one of the great names of America's "golden age" of TV drama, the 1950s. He was the prolific and much-lauded author of many mainstream plays (some of which became successful movies). When that golden age began to wane, he turned to sf and fantasy with the half-hour anthology series *The Twilight Zone* (1959-1964). An effective blend of sf proper with less classifiable "weird" stories, its best episodes proved pithy and memorable. A great many of them were written by Serling himself, with a substantial number of others by such stalwart screenwriters as Richard Matheson and Charles Beaumont. Of all American TV sf prior to *Star Trek*, this programme remains the most fondly remembered. Serling's later anthology series, *Night Gallery* (1970-72), was slanted more towards fantasy and horror.

BOB SHAW

BRITISH NOVELIST

BORN: 1931 DIED:1996

One of the best-loved figures in UK sf, Ulsterman Shaw began producing short stories in the early 1950s, although his debut novel, *Night Walk*, did not appear until 1967. Intensely readable and continually inventive novels such

 ROD SERLING *SMALL MAN, BIG ROBOT. SERLING REACTED VIOLENTLY TO BEING CALLED A SMALL MAN WHICH MAY WELL HAVE DRIVEN HIM ON TO HEIGHTS OF SUCCESS*

as *The Palace Of Eternity* (1969), *Other Days, Other Eyes* (1972), *Orbitsville* (1975), *A Wreath Of Stars* (1976) and *Vertigo* (1978) were to follow. Later, he slowed down; but the trilogy comprising *The Ragged Astronauts* (1986), *The Wooden Spaceships* (1988) and *The Fugitive Worlds* (1989) was one of his major works.

ROBERT SHECKLEY

AMERICAN NOVELIST

BORN: 1928

Sheckley's early output of urbanely humorous short sf included the excellent 'A Ticket To Tranai' (a utopian/dystopian satire) and 'The Deaths Of Ben Baxter' (an exercise in parallelism), plus stories about the down-at-heel firm of AAA Ace Planetary Decontaminators, whose unwise purchases of cheap gear from Joe the Interstellar Junkman often land them in trouble.

His first novel, *Immortality, Inc.* (1959),

BOB SHAW *R.I.P.; A GREAT, WARM-HEARTED WIT OF THE BRITISH SF SCENE, HE WILL BE SORELY MISSED*

involves a science-fiction version of the afterlife, and with its serious tone stands outside the main stream of his longer work, although the hero is characteristically good-natured, hedonistic and rather ineffective. More typical are *Mindswap* (1966) and *Dimension Of Miracles* (1968); in both, the hero finds himself playing Quixote to a cynical and untrustworthy Sancho Panza with his own undisclosed agenda. Both could as well be regarded as fantasy were the sf vocabulary less dominant. Their philosophical content is debatable; a case can be made for it, but no coherent metaphysic emerges, only an enjoyment of ideas: "'Yet this ineffable and ungraspable quantity,' he replied, 'this time which no man may possess, is in truth our only possession.' The man nodded as though Marvin had said something profound, instead of merely voicing a well-mannered conversational commonplace." Perhaps Sheckley's best early novel is the witty *Journey Beyond Tomorrow* (1962), while later books, such as *Dramocles* (1983), show a marked falling-off.

CHARLES SHEFFIELD

AMERICAN NOVELIST

BORN: 1935

A practising physicist, Sheffield has the temerity to function also as a prolific writer of grandly conceived and beautifully executed hard sf. Whether he is depicting an archaeological dig that turns up unexpected mysteries or knocking suns together as in his Heritage Universe series, he never forgets to let us ride the shoulders of real human beings.

LUCIUS SHEPARD

AMERICAN NOVELIST

BORN: 1947

From his very first novel, *Green Eyes* (1984), which reeked of swamps and scientifically justified zombies, it was plain that Shepard was a writer of vast experiences. His gritty fictions always conveyed the sense that Shepard had rolled in the same muck as his uprooted, desperate characters. His *Life During Wartime* (1987) had much the same impact as

Mary Shelley
British Novelist
Born: 1797 Died: 1851

Famous as the author of *Frankenstein; Or, The Modern Prometheus* (1818), sometimes misleadingly referred to as "the first robot novel"; it has more to do with spare-parts surgery, taken to its logical conclusion. The story of how the young Baron Frankenstein attempts to create a perfect man out of parts from corpses, which he galvanizes with electricity (at that time very imperfectly understood) is by now well known, if only from the many films based on it. But it is crucial that even by contemporary standards Frankenstein is regarded as an oddity at medical school – and not because he is in any way ahead of his time. Far from it; he is an antiquarian autodidact, deriving his ideas from such discredited sources as Paracelsus, Albertus Magnus and Cornelius Agrippa. The story is less a parable against arrogant scientific triumphalism than against the cultivation of medieval error in a scientific context. An aspect of the story which is brought out better in all but the most vulgar treatments is the inexcusably unfair treatment which the Monster receives. Frankenstein recoils from his creature in horror, and from this rejection of responsibility flows its subsequent embittered rampage.

MARY SHELLEY *POSING FOR A SOCIETY PORTRAITIST*

Haldeman's *The Forever War* (1974), and later works continued this globe-trotting exoticism.

JOHN SHIRLEY

AMERICAN NOVELIST

BORN: 1953

An angry talent, former rock musician Shirley has produced a number of books which fall into the horror category. His central sf work is the Song Of Youth trilogy — *Eclipse* (1985), *Eclipse Penumbra* (1988) and *Eclipse Corona* (1990) — which may be described as anti-fascist cyberpunk.

CLIFFORD D. SIMAK

AMERICAN NOVELIST

BORN: 1904 DIED: 1988

Simak's works are noted for their gentle, reflective (and occasionally sentimental) tone, often objectified as a love of the scenery and people of the midwestern countryside, and affirmation of the less glamorous virtues, especially forbearance, fortitude, kindliness and honourable mercantilism. In the novelette 'The Big Front Yard' (1958), when aliens suddenly appear in a rural American community, the hero's reaction is to see if he can find anything he can barter with them, in the conviction that once mutually advantageous trade is established everything else will fall into place.

His best work lies in a number of shorter pieces and three of his novels: *Ring Around The Sun* (1953), in which mutants open up a chain of parallel worlds; *Time Is The Simplest Thing* (1960), in which telepaths import exotic notions and techniques from space; and *Way Station* (1963), in which a man of the 19th century is offered immortality and the company of computer-generated artificial personalities in return for maintaining the station of the title, to and from which aliens can teleport, using Earth as a convenient halt between more important places. In all of these, human xenophobia is represented as the chief barrier to happiness.

DAN SIMMONS

AMERICAN NOVELIST

BORN: 1948

Best known for his horror and fantasy, Simmons's principal sf work is the two-volumed novel *Hyperion* (1989) and *The Fall Of Hyperion* (1990), and its sequel *Endymion* (1996). Intensely literary, the first book's structure is overtly based on *The Canterbury Tales*, while the second contains numerous references to the lifework of Keats. The plot revolves around buildings with negative entropy.

JOHN T. SLADEK

AMERICAN NOVELIST

BORN: 1937

Despite theoretically prizing off-kilter imagination, the critics and readers and publishers of sf have more often settled for the famous pop-culture formula of "familiar novelty", rewarding retreads and sequels more than trailblazers and rare birds. The roll call of infamously neglected uncategorizable writers is long and shameful: Avram Davidson, David Bunch, R. A. Lafferty — and certainly John Sladek, whose sporadic output has contributed to his low profile.

The first sighting of the hippogriffian Sladek occurred in *Dangerous Visions* (1967), with his story 'The Happy Breed'. The masterpiece of Bartleby-like alienation, 'Masterson And The Clerks' soon followed. With co-author Thomas Disch, Sladek next detoured into a pair of gothic novels under the joint byline of Cassandra Knye. But this was merely the roundabout path to a startling first sf novel. *The Reproductive System* (1968) proved itself far in advance of the rest of the sf field in considering the implications of self-reproducing automata. Marked by dry black humour and surrealism, the novel should have been the strong foundation of a broad career. But the old adage that "satire is what closes on Saturday night" held true, and the novel did not meet with the deserved success. Another detour loomed: a mystery, *Black Alice* (1968), also with Disch, as Thom Demijohn. Then came *The Muller-Fokker Effect* (1970), which, like *The Reproductive System*, was way ahead of the field in its consideration of the possibility of digitizing humanity.

A long sf lacuna now intervened, as Sladek

Robert Silverberg — American Novelist — Born: 1935

Out of the same fiery crucible of penny-a-wordism and paperback originals that smelted John Brunner, out of the same fan milieu that fostered Harlan Ellison, there emerged another precocious, richly endowed writer who would by sheer force of will turn himself from a push-button churner of competent tales into an innovative artist of the first water. Not without sweat and pain and disappointment, however, much like the deracinated characters in his best fictions who work so hard and single-mindedly for transfiguration.

Silverberg made his initial professional short story sale in 1954. Hundreds of stories were to follow, collected in such volumes as *Earth's Other Shadow* (1973); *Sundance And Other Science Fiction Stories* (1974), *Born With The Dead* (1974); and *The Best Of Robert Silverberg* (1976). Shortly after this start, Silverberg secured a contract for a juvenile novel, *Revolt On Alpha C* (1955). The gates were opened for a flood of fiction, with Silverberg sometimes filling whole issues of sf magazines under a plethora of pen-names.

This journeyman work came to an end circa 1967 with the appearance of *Thorns*, whose sexual content prefigured one of the mature Silverberg's concerns. As if liberated from a self-imposed prison, Silverberg poured forth so many excellent books over the next nine years that the list seems like a Hollywood scriptwriter's fantasy from the biopic of some mutant genius. *The Masks Of Time* (1968);

Nightwings (1969); *Up The Line* (1969); *Downward To The Earth* (1970); *A Time Of Changes* (1971, a Nebula winner); *The Book Of Skulls* (1971); *The World Inside* (1971); *Dying Inside* (1972); and *Shadrach In The Furnace* (1976). Obsessed with the question of identity, with death and redemption, burning with a white modernist heat, Silverberg was relentlessly brilliant.

Yet this period netted him frustrations equal to his successes. Declaring a moratorium on his sf, Silverberg was hardly heard from until 1980, with the publication of the popular *Lord Valentine's Castle*, which began surveying an exotic Big Planet called Majipoor. Other novels and stories emerged (most recently, *Hot Sky At Midnight*, 1994), perhaps not so turbo-charged, yet fully fleshed and probing of the dilemmas of mortality. Today, Silverberg is the deity in the ductwork of a mile-high urbmon tower gloriously populated with his own creations.

ROBERT SILVERBERG *RAPIDLY EMERGING AS ONE OF THE US'S MOST PROLIFIC WRITERS OF SF, DESPITE THE OCCASIONAL BREAK WITH THE GENRE*

compiled his stories into collections and turned his hand to a pair of mysteries and some non-fiction. The drought was broken by *Roderick* (1980) and its sequel, *Roderick At Random* (1983), which put an absurdist, picaresque spin on Asimovian robotics, as did the subsequent *Tik Tok* (1983) and *Bugs* (1989). Returning to his US roots after a long expatriation in England, Sladek is perhaps primed for a resurgence.

CORDWAINER SMITH

AMERICAN NOVELIST
BORN: 1954 DIED: 1966
With an Orientalism derived from intimate contact, Cordwainer Smith (born Paul

Linebarger) fashioned a kind of sf much imitated but never duplicated. His stories read like ancient myths from the far future. His small output almost entirely centres on the Instrumentality future, where immortal lords and ladies oppress, then whimsically liberate, animal underpeople.

EDWARD E. SMITH

AMERICAN NOVELIST
BORN: 1890 DIED: 1965
The once-popular "Doc" Smith is remembered principally for his space-operatic *Skylark* and *Lensman* series. Both have been mocked as juveniles masquerading as adult fare (and

parodied by Harry Harrison in *Star-Smashers Of The Galaxy Rangers*, 1973), the main accusation centring on unrealistic sexual relationships. The Skylark books concern an invention which makes interstellar travel available to a group of scientists, who thereupon tour sundry star systems, participating in wars, marrying each other, fighting monstrous beasts and otherwise enjoying themselves.

The more significant Lensman books are based on the theory of Svante Arrhenius that living creatures emit minute "spores", capable of pervading the galaxy under pressure of light and triggering evolution on primitive worlds. The Arisians, a benign and advanced race, seeded our galaxy long ago, but evil Eddorians from another dimension are now intent on domination. Against them, the Arisians are breeding two human bloodlines of great talent, whose ultimate fusion will destroy Eddor. This is worked out over six volumes, beginning with *Triplanetary* (1948) and ending with *Children Of The Lens* (1954). The writing is at best moderate, at worst risible, but the series fails mainly through lack of scale. Neither the social organization of the galaxy nor the huge space battles bear even cursory inspection.

GEORGE O. SMITH

AMERICAN NOVELIST

BORN: 1911 DIED: 1981

He is chiefly remembered for the linked *Venus Equilateral* stories (1947), about human and technical problems aboard an inhabited comsat in Venus Lagrange orbit, and about the social problems posed by a matter duplicator. His novel *Hellflower* (1953) features insidious alien invaders whose weapons are destructively addictive flowers.

STEVEN SPIELBERG

AMERICAN FILM DIRECTOR

BORN: 1947

Spielberg is the most legendary director of his time, the archetypal "movie brat" who inveigled his way into the profession when scarcely out of his teens and eventually justified his self-confidence by becoming the most commercially successful film-maker ever. Beginning with TV movies, the majority of his films have been science fiction or fantasy of one kind or another. The principal titles are: *Duel* (1971; from a story by Richard Matheson), a TV movie subsequently released to the cinema; *Jaws* (1975; from Peter Benchley's novel), a blockbusting tale of "creature horror"; *Close Encounters Of The Third Kind* (1977), his first out-and-out sf movie;

 STEVEN SPIELBERG

THE TOP MOVIE-MAKER OF ALL TIME — BUT SO SUBURBAN AND ORDINARY; WE'D ALL LOVE TO KNOW HOW HE DID IT, WITHOUT THE "ADVANTAGES" OF WEIRD FOREIGNNESS, A WAR BACKGROUND, OR A NOTABLY DISRUPTED CHILDHOOD

Raiders Of The Lost Ark (1981), an adventure fantasy produced by George Lucas — followed by two Spielberg-directed sequels in later years; *E.T.: The Extra-Terrestrial* (1982), still the top box-office earner of all time; *Twilight Zone — The Movie* (1983; from Rod Serling's TV series); *Empire Of The Sun* (1987), non-sf but based on a novel by sf writer J. G. Ballard; *Always* (1989), a remake of the 1943 fantasy film *A Guy Named Joe*; *Hook* (1991), another fantasy, inspired by J. M. Barrie's play *Peter Pan*; and *Jurassic Park* (1993; from Michael Crichton's novel), the second-biggest box-office earner of all time. As a producer, he has been associated with numerous other sf and fantasy films, especially those directed by Joe Dante and Robert Zemeckis, including the two *Gremlins* movies and the *Back To The Future* trilogy. Despite a few misfires (e.g. the dreadful *Hook*), it is an astonishing record — even more so when one takes into account the success of his few non-fantastic films (which range from *The Sugarland Express*, 1974, to *Schindler's List*, 1993). Spielberg is often sentimental, frequently "juvenile", but almost always technically brilliant.

NORMAN SPINRAD

AMERICAN NOVELIST

BORN: 1940

Spinrad has moved from being one of sf's angry young men to somewhat reluctantly functioning as one of its established pillars, all without losing his corrosive edge. An early, infamously savage book like *Bug Jack Barron* (1969) has no greater or lesser claim to farseeing truth-telling than a later work such as *Little Heroes* (1987). Gadfly, muckraker, activist for better literary and real worlds, Spinrad gives the field a backbone.

BRIAN STABLEFORD

BRITISH NOVELIST

BORN: 1948

A relatively unsung genius of sf, Stableford has been amazingly prolific both as a creative writer and as a critic and historian of the field. His debut novel, *Cradle Of The Sun* (1969), drew colourfully on his knowledge of biology. Principal works since then have included the Hooded

BRIAN STABLEFORD *An ingenious writer who is second to none in his encyclopedic knowledge and understanding of the sf field*

OLAF STAPLEDON

British novelist

Born: 1886 Died: 1950

His first novel, *Last And First Men* (1930), enjoyed the unique distinction of being reprinted by Penguin Books not as fiction (which it clearly was), but as philosophy. In it, he charts the entire future history of mankind, through many vicissitudes and 18 distinct species, from its lowly origins (ourselves) to its brilliant culmination. It is written as if from the viewpoint of one of the 18th Men, who has projected his mind back to write through the mediumship of one of the first, and takes the form of a social-historical treatise; no individual is mentioned by name. Typically, the 18th might have given place to a yet more splendid 19th had the sun not entered a brief phase as a blue giant, ending all life in the solar system. With its two-billion year timescale, it is necessarily episodic and some parts have worn better than others. The human species' sojourn on Venus remains a fine feat of the imagination, dated only by our subsequent knowledge of the planet, but the final utopia is too obviously the pipe-dream of a 1930s Fabian to be taken seriously.

Its sequel, *Star Maker* (1937), is yet more ambitious and overtly metaphysical. In it, a man of his own time suddenly finds his mind projected out of his body and sent on a flight through space-time over which he can, at first, exert no control whatever. As it proceeds he experiences the entire history of the universe, entering the bodies of many species and witnessing the decline or catastrophe of most. Even the stars, and the nebulae which preceded them, have life and personality, in which he shares. Ultimately, the entire universe is united into a single mind of immense power which seeks to unite itself with its own creator, the Star Maker of the title — and fails. Thereafter lies only a slow decline, as the physical universe expands to ultimate entropy while the bodies supporting its psychic component succumb to heat-death. But at the Supreme Moment the universal mind is granted a vision of the Star Maker's other universes, previous and to come. These lie in a series of ever greater

OLAF STAPLEDON *Liverpudlian cosmic visionary, a man for whom there was never an ending of unalloyed happiness*

sophistication, yet imperfect even at its culmination; in the final stage of the last and greatest universe, inhabited by minds of a delicacy and complexity enormously beyond the comprehension of the universal mind, there is still misery. The Star Maker's care is all for the making, none for the made.

None of Stapledon's succeeding novels were written on anything like such a scale, but all reflect the same bleak philosophy: God is blind or uncaring; the brutish, seeking always to bring down the angelic, succeed most of the time; even that which is achieved at such great cost is subject to entropy.

ALLEN STEELE

American novelist

Born: 1958

In books such as *Orbital Decay* (1989), *Labyrinth Of Night* (1992) and *Rude Astronauts* (1993), Steele has established himself as a leading writer in that hard-headed, near-future realist style associated with his predecessors from Robert A. Heinlein to John Varley.

Swan series of light space operas (six volumes, 1972-75), *The Mind-Riders* (1976), *The Realms Of Tartarus* (1977), *The Walking Shadow* (1979), *Journey To The Centre* (1982) and its sequels, *The Empire Of Fear* (1988), and *The Werewolves Of London* (1990) and its sequels. A new trilogy, currently under way, began with *Serpent's Blood* (1995). Also notable are his short stories collected in *Sexual Chemistry: Sardonic Tales Of The Genetic Revolution* (1991). Recent highly praised novellas which have yet to see book form include 'Les Fleurs Du Mal' (*Asimov's*, 1994) and 'The Hunger And Ecstasy Of Vampires' (*Interzone*, 1995). His most important non-fiction books are *Scientific Romance In Britain, 1890-1950* (1985), a work which did much to map the history of sf during the stated period, and *The Third Millennium: A History Of The World AD 2000-3000* (also 1985, with David Langford), a marvellous compendium of realistically based sf ideas. Perhaps he has written too much too quickly — and certainly he has never gained widespread popularity — but, for the quality of this thinking and for his deep understanding of the genre, Stableford may come to be seen as one of the crucial sf writers of his era.

BRUCE STERLING — AMERICAN NOVELIST — BORN: 1954

Not without reason was Sterling nicknamed "Chairman Bruce" during the heyday of the cyberpunk explosion. From his Texas highcastle, Sterling issued ukases and pronunciamentos, apothegms and phillipics on sf and the universe at large like some kind of unstoppable gene-spliced conqueror derived from the seed of Jules Verne and Mao Tse Tung. Sometimes overlooked in all the public controversy was the exceedingly high quality of his fiction, his journalism (a field in which he was college-trained), and his pop-science essays.

Unlike William Gibson, with whom he is frequently linked, Sterling began his career quietly, with some modestly received short stories (the first appearing in 1976) and two bold, yet slightly uncentred novels: *Involution Ocean* (1978) and *The Artificial Kid* (1980). (The former appeared as "A Harlan Ellison Discovery", further cementing Ellison's track record of wise encouragement.) It was after these accomplishments that Sterling experienced an epiphany born out of frustration with the perceived shortcomings and rigor mortis of sf and his own career. Publishing his fanzine *Cheap Truth* (1984-86) allowed him to formularize a vision of the "radical hard sf" which he saw blossoming around him, and toward which he would later bend his own skills and energies. This would be a literature which discarded outworn generic conventions and reimagined the future with clear eyes, tapping real-time dataflows.

His next novel, *Schismatrix* (1985), and the allied stories in *Crystal Express* (1989) turned a Stapledonian eye on mankind's intra-system future, positing a dichotomy between biotic Shapers and gadget-loving Mechanists. The thick texture of the prose and the information density remained a typical Sterling signature. Taking time out to codify the cyberpunk

 BRUCE STERLING *RABBLE-ROUSER AND IDEAS-MAN, FOREVER ASSOCIATED WITH CYBERPUNK*

revolution with the anthology *Mirrorshades* (1986), Sterling next visited the ultra-wired near-future of *Islands In The Net* (1988), which, with its Hemingwayesque title, revealed a debt to high modernism not generally noticed in his work. A side-excursion with Gibson, *The Difference Engine* (1990), applied cyberpunk insights to a steamdriven alternative history. After some years of public speaking, journalism and multimedia work, Sterling renewed his vows to rub sf's nose in reality with *Heavy Weather* (1994), a savvy look at tornado-chasers in a meteorologically turbulent future. Sterling may have muted his rhetoric somewhat in these post-cyberpunk years, but he has lost none of his drive to make sf worthy of being called the century's best literature.

NEAL STEPHENSON

AMERICAN NOVELIST

BORN: 1959

Stephenson became cultish overnight as the author of *Snow Crash* (1992), a wild and woolly cyberpunk novel which gained a lot of praise. He had in fact written two previous novels (only marginally sf), *The Big U* (1984) and *Zodiac: The*

Eco-Thriller (1988). His fourth novel, *The Diamond Age* (1995), was intensively marketed to mainstream as well as sf readers.

GEORGE R. STEWART

AMERICAN NOVELIST

BORN: 1895 DIED: 1980

Stewart was an academic whose much-admired sf novel, *Earth Abides* (1949), takes place after most people have died of plague. A survivor, Isherwood Williams, attempts to preserve civilized values. Though he fails even to preserve literacy, he inculcates freedom and decency into the traditions of the tribe he founds.

S. M. STIRLING

CANADIAN NOVELIST

BORN: 1954

Best known for his militaristic sf in the alternative-world Draka series, beginning with *Marching Through Georgia* (1988), Stirling has been accused of all sorts of political incorrectness. He is certainly not to be confused with his contemporary, Bruce Sterling.

JOHN E. STITH

AMERICAN NOVELIST

BORN: 1947

After a few respectable but unexceptionable novels, Stith pulled out all the stops with two exciting hard-sf extravaganzas. In *Redshift Rendezvous* (1990), he postulated a method of faster-than-light travel with unique sensory implications, then combined this with a deft mystery. In *Manhattan Transfer* (1993), aliens steal entire Earth cities and the topography of the giant capture vessel becomes a whole universe of excitement.

J. MICHAEL STRACZYNSKI

AMERICAN TV PRODUCER

BORN: 1954

Straczynski, who has also written horror novels, began his TV career as a writer for the revived *Twilight Zone* anthology series (1985-87). A collection of his stories, adapted from scripts, was published as *Tales From The New Twilight Zone* (1989). He has become most famous, however, for the ambitious interstellar sf series *Babylon 5* (from 1993), which he conceived and produced.

ARKADY & BORIS STRUGATSKY

RUSSIAN NOVELISTS

BORN: 1925 (ARKADY), 1931 (BORIS) DIED: 1991 (ARKADY)

The most distinguished science-fictioneers of the late Soviet Union, the Strugatskys were always a subversive pair (although they managed to stay on the right side of the law). Their chief works, all translated into English, include *Far Rainbow* (1963), *Hard To Be A God* (1964), *The Snail On The Slope* (1966-68), *Tale Of The Troika* (1968), *Prisoners Of Power* (1969-71) and *Roadside Picnic* (1972). There are also many short stories and novellas, among them the justly famous 'Second Invasion From Mars' (1968), an ironic reworking of Wells's *The War Of The Worlds*. Their *Roadside Picnic* was filmed, grimly, by the eminent director Andrei Tarkovsky as *Stalker* (1979).

THEODORE STURGEON

AMERICAN NOVELIST
BORN: 1918 DIED: 1985

Sf, a literature of the head, has often given short shrift to affairs of the heart and soul. Too many novels are populated by unfeeling ciphers on whom the glories and ironies of life, time and space are wasted. Were it not for such counterbalancing geniuses as Theodore Sturgeon, that expert evoker of poignant emotions both serene and turbulent, sf would resemble one of its own clichés: the ultra-cerebral, end-of-time human barely attached to his withered body.

Worldly-wise from a variety of vocations, Sturgeon began publishing sf in 1939 with 'Ether Breather'. With subsequent stories, he earned himself a role in John Campbell's Golden Age. Yet such a crown was always worn uneasily, for Sturgeon's sophisticated, mature prose and his unique skewings of sf tropes (frequently along a sexual vector) pulled against the other horses in *Astounding*'s stable. Nonetheless, early Sturgeon stories such as 'It', 'Killdozer' and 'Microcosmic God' earned him wide recognition. (Many of Sturgeon's stories cross the borderline into outright fantasy or mainstream territory, but all are recognizably part of his organic conception of life. Assembled during his lifetime into many famous collections, they are currently being reissued in a uniform series, the first volume being *The Ultimate Egoist*, 1994, and the reader is advised to seek out this ongoing project.)

Always hard-pressed for an income, Sturgeon was not helped by recurring writer's block. The first and least traumatic bout interfered with his early career until 1946. But at that point he returned with a vengeance. For the subsequent decade and a half, he produced the bulk of his work, stories and novels of poetic intensity, where psychologically maimed individuals found solace in acts of heroism and friendship — or damnation in self-mutilation and betrayal.

Sturgeon's novels somewhat diluted the intensity of his stories, but remain eminently readable. *The Dreaming Jewels* (1950) tells of the humanoid Horty, formed by the sentient minerals of the title, then abandoned to cruel persecutors. *More Than Human* (1953) is his most accomplished book, the tale of the gradual assemblage of a gestalt personality out of cast-off human components. Even his posthumous novel, *Godbody* (1986), can be mined for seams of gold. Famous for insisting that every individual must "ask the next question", Sturgeon wore a satyr's smile that seemed to imply he knew at least some of the best answers.

MICHAEL SWANWICK

AMERICAN NOVELIST
BORN: 1950

Noted for his dense plotting and cultivated literary qualities, Swanwick's most admired work, *Stations Of The Tide* (1991), is a criminal investigation set on a colonial world subject to cyclical flooding. The descriptions are ebullient, the story moves fast and Swanwick's humour is subtle and assured.

— ᴍ —

JOHN TAINE

AMERICAN NOVELIST
BORN: 1883 DIED: 1960

Real name Eric Temple Bell, a British-born mathematician whose interest in biology led him to specialize in mutant novels. Among his best is *Seeds Of Life* (1931), in which a dull young man temporarily becomes a superman. It contains some notable *grand guignol* passages

when a life-enhancer is used on frog spawn and a spider, and the ending anticipates Daniel Reyes's *Flowers For Algernon* (1966).

WILLIAM F. TEMPLE

BRITISH NOVELIST
BORN: 1914 DIED: 1989

Best remembered for *Four-Sided Triangle* (1949), in which a woman is duplicated by a discarded suitor, Temple's short stories include 'Brief Encounter', a post-holocaust tale in which a female survivor shoots two others (a younger, prettier woman and a homosexual) whom she perceives as rivals.

WILLIAM TENN

AMERICAN SHORT-STORY WRITER
BORN: 1920

An author of the 1950s and 1960s, noted for his savagely twisted endings: the best include 'The Liberation Of Earth', a satire of colonial warfare, 'The Flat-Eyed Monster', a tale of human-alien role-reversal and 'The Malted Milk Monster', in which a man becomes trapped in an unattractive teenager's fulfilment fantasy.

SHERI S. TEPPER

AMERICAN NOVELIST
BORN: 1929

Starting in middle age, Tepper has published prolifically in the fantasy, horror and crime-fiction fields as well as in science fiction. Seemingly against the odds, she has emerged as one of American sf's most accomplished newer writers. Her first substantial sf novel, *The Awakeners* (1987), is a lengthy romance of life on another world dominated by a great river. It was followed by *The Gate To Women's Country* (1988), *Grass* (1989), *Raising The Stones* (1990), *Beauty* (1991), *Sideshow* (1992) and others, most of which make intelligent use of the planetary romance conventions.

WALTER TEVIS

AMERICAN NOVELIST
BORN: 1928 DIED: 1984

Tevis's most successful sf novel was *The Man Who Fell To Earth* (1963; later filmed with David

Bowie), in which a Martian tries unsuccessfully to secure a welcome for his dying race. *Mockingbird* (1980) recounts the efforts of an android to revitalize humanity and obtain surcease for himself.

PATRICK TILLEY

BRITISH NOVELIST

BORN: 1928

This author's principal work is the popular Amtrak Wars series — *Cloud Warrior* (1983), *First Family* (1985), *Iron Master* (1987), *Blood River* (1988), *Death Bringer* (1989) and *Earth-Thunder* (1990) — in which a 30th-century America is inhabited by wandering tribes of mystics, the "Mutes", who are being wiped out by a militaristic Federation based in Texas.

JAMES TIPTREE, JR

AMERICAN NOVELIST

BORN: 1915 DIED: 1987

Consider this scenario: an individual born in our century's second decade is raised by globe-trotting, talented parents in many foreign locales. Growing up to specialize in psychological studies, this person builds an impressive career partly on the shadowy fringes of the US government. In early middle-age, this person becomes a writer of sf under a pseudonym which eventually comes to displace their original identity. The stories produced by this writer frequently depict the ignored daily agonies of tiny individuals pinned to a much larger dispassionate canvas.

In a nutshell, this is of course the biography of both James Tiptree — born Alice Sheldon — and Cordwainer Smith — born Paul Linebarger in 1913. Such parallels hide the vast differences in style and focus between the two. Yet it is curiously instructive to ponder the fates and forces of our time that channelled two such similar careers. In the case of Tiptree, her career was both wilder and wider, bloodier and more significant than that of the dreamier Smith.

Tiptree made a large splash upon her entry into the field, her masculine facade initially tricking many into foolish pronouncements. Her stories were the very model of what modern sf

could accomplish. Jazzy, fast-paced, uncompromisingly disturbing, they revolved around such themes as seductions by aliens; the self-destructive follies of the naked apes known as mankind; the irrational tug of sex and the bigotry of sexism; and, above all, the universality of pain and suffering and death. Plainly owing a debt to both Sturgeon and Bester, Tiptree pumped up the volume on their styles and concerns, while abandoning their lingering sentimentality. Known for starting her stories "a mile underground and in the dark", Tiptree could be as dizzying and nausea-provoking as a rollercoaster.

Such ground-breaking stories as 'The Girl Who Was Plugged In' (a cyberpunk precursor, like much of her work), 'Love Is The Plan The Plan is Death' and 'A Momentary Taste Of Being' can be found in her four core collections: *Ten Thousand Light-Years From Home* (1973); *Warm Worlds And Otherwise* (1975); *Star Songs Of An Old Primate* (1978); and *Out Of The Everywhere* (1981). Her two novels — *Up The Walls Of The World* (1978) and *Brightness Falls From The Air* (1985) — tend to seem slack in comparison with the gem-hard stories. When mortality came knocking in the form of illness and debility for her and her husband, Tiptree met it with a typically forceful, even brutal gesture, wilfully ending both her own life and her ailing mate's. Death seemed a well-known factor in her cold equations.

E. C. TUBB

BRITISH NOVELIST

BORN: 1919

A prolific writer of paperback-original sf from the early 1950s, Tubb is most identified with his lengthy Dumarest series, beginning with *The Winds Of Gath* (1967) and concerning the quest of a dour hero called Earl Dumarest to find his long-lost home-planet, Earth.

WILSON TUCKER

AMERICAN NOVELIST

BORN: 1914

His books include The *Long, Loud Silence* (1952), a grim catastrophe novel with half the US depopulated by disease (the survivors resort to

cannibalism), and *Wild Talent* (1954), wherein a telepath becomes a weapon in the Cold War (for both sides).

Several others followed, before he fell silent in recent years.

GEORGE TURNER

AUSTRALIAN NOVELIST

BORN: 1916

A mainstream writer who turned to sf comparatively late in life. *Beloved Son* (1978) is about an astronaut who returns after decades in space to find a post-disaster world where the genetic manipulation and cloning of human beings are now commonplace. *Vaneglory* (1981) and *Yesterday's Men* (1983) followed, but perhaps Turner's finest achievement was the Arthur C. Clarke award-winning *The Sea And Summer* (1987; also known as *The Drowning Towers*).

HARRY TURTLEDOVE

AMERICAN NOVELIST

BORN: 1949

His early *Agent Of Byzantium* (1986) is a volume of linked stories set in an alternative Roman Empire where Mohammed converted to Christianity and as a result Byzantium survived beyond the Middle Ages in the West. It is good fun and written from genuine historical knowledge. His later alternative histories, such as the action-packed series beginning with *Worldwar: In The Balance* (1994), are similarly well-informed and inventive.

LISA TUTTLE

AMERICAN NOVELIST

BORN: 1952

Mainly a writer of horror fiction, Texas-born (but British-resident) Tuttle has written many highly praised sf short stories, collected in such volumes as *A Spaceship Made Of Stone* (1987) and *Memories Of The Body* (1992). Her sf novels are *Windhaven* (1981; with George R. R. Martin) and *Lost Futures* (1992).

Gently feminist, Tuttle's stories tend to the here-and-now — and work their way under your skin.

Jack Vance —— American Novelist —— Born: 1916

Few living sf writers have fanzines and small presses devoted solely to them and their *oeuvre*. Few living sf writers deserve or earn such adulation. Jack Vance is one author whose work can truly support such deep attention. The intricacy and richness of his prose, the attractive, sophisticated wryness of his worldview, and the exotic nature of his characters and settings compel admiration.

Vance's first story, 'The World Thinker', appeared in 1945. A respectable but unexemplary apprentice period in the magazines followed, allowing Vance to gradually gear up for more ambitious work. The first presage of future greatness came with *The Dying Earth* (1950). In this collection of affiliated stories, Vance defined both his own style and concerns, and opened up a whole new sf territory later colonized by Gene Wolfe and Paul Park among others. *The Dying Earth* portrays a dimly lit endgame Earth crusted with history, where magic and science are not easily distinguishable. Thrilling adventures abound; deceit and cruelty mix with nostalgia and bittersweet romance; Cabellian ironies soften all misfortune. Such was the unique recipe Vance was to follow in all his future books, both *Dying Earth* sequels and others such as *Big Planet* (1957) and its companion, *Showboat World* (1975).

In the 1960s, Vance produced a pair of Hugo-winning novelettes that showed him on peak form and revealed his facility with biological fantasizing: *The Dragon Masters* (1963) and *The Last Castle* (1967). He also initiated two series, one of which took two decades to finish: the *Planet of Adventure* books came to a conclusion rapidly, but the more complex and Jacobean Demon Princes saga only

JACK VANCE *STILL GOING STRONG AFTER ALL THESE YEARS. JACK PUBLISHED HIS FIRST STORY AT THE END OF THE SECOND WORLD WAR*

concluded in 1981 with *The Book Of Dreams*.

During the 1970s, the loosely linked Alastor Cluster trilogy allowed Vance to showcase some of the satirical talents he had earlier honed in books such as *Emphyrio* (1969). Devoting much of the next decade to the stirring and gorgeous set of fantasy novels that form the Lyonesse sequence, Vance returned to sf with the Cadwal Chronicles, a trilogy that details the machinations of exploiters eager to develop a planet-wide ecological preserve. Now in his Biblical threescore-and-ten, Vance functions as a Moonmoth-masked Moses leading his followers into one *outré* Promised Land after another.

JOHN VARLEY

AMERICAN NOVELIST

BORN: 1947

Combine the you-are-there realism of Heinlein with the gender-bending conceits of Delany; add a dollop of Niven's sanguine bravado in the face of cosmic challenges, a dash of George R. R. Martin's melancholy; and the resulting Blue Champagne cocktail might very well taste like the work of the effervescent John Varley. By publishing a series of radically exuberant interconnected stories — beginning with 'Picnic On Nearside' in 1974 — Varley signalled the arrival of a kind of playful post-modern sf that was unafraid to juggle the old tropes of the genre simultaneously with fresh ones, achieving giddy new effects.

Varley's early stories — collected in such volumes as *The Persistence Of Vision* (1978) and *The Barbie Murders* (1980) — along with two of his novels — *The Ophiuchi Hotline* (1977) and *Steel Beach* (1992) — all concern his Eight Worlds future history, a continuum where mankind has been displaced from Earth for various depravities by enigmatic Invaders. Occupying various Solar System niches, humans have been forced to alter their bodies, minds and ethics. This sequence remains his best-regarded contribution to the genre, although a later trilogy composed of *Titan* (1979), *Wizard* (1980) and *Demon* (1984), which recounts the

A.E. van Vogt — American Novelist — Born: 1912

The blackly entertaining game of nominating dead mainstream writers for posthumous Nobel prizes they never received in life has its sad analogue in sf: which deceased genius was pitifully underacknowledged in his or her lifetime, bereft of such honours as a Grand Master award from the SFWA? At time of writing. A. E. van Vogt would top any such list. Due to a late-career silence, his immense contributions to the genre are nowadays fairly invisible, despite having influenced such disparate writers as Charles Harness, William Burroughs and Philip Dick.

In 1939, van Vogt erupted on the sf scene with 'Black Destroyer', a story later grudgingly credited with influencing the movie *Alien* (1979). Over the next eight years, as one of John Campbell's stalwarts, he would publish a wealth of material that fixed his reputation as a master of sf dreamtime adventures, oneiric masterpieces wherein sometimes memory-blocked, sometimes omnipotent protagonists met a series of escalating challenges, coming to dominate their worlds. These seminal stories re-emerged later in book form to influence new generations.

By his own admission, Van Vogt was famous for interjecting major plot twists nearly every 1000 words. This habit, along with his tendency to recomplicate the simplest story structure and his fascination with non-conventional systems of thought (a fascination that would lead to a non-productive flirtation with Scientology) made his books like no one else's. In *Slan* (1946), a race of mutants battles mankind for their place under the sun. In *The Weapon Makers* (1946) and *The Weapon Shops Of Isher* (1951), the tension between citizens and their government is mediated by invulnerable gunshops. *In The World Of Null A* (1948), the confused protagonist Gosseyn embodies "non-Aristotelian" logic.

If the 1950s were for van Vogt a decade of compilation and refining, the 1960s and 1970s were a sparse period. Such books as *The Silkie* (1969), *Children Of Tomorrow* (1970) and *The Battle Of Forever* (1971) replicated without extending his dominant motifs. After 1983's *Computerworld*, it was as if van Vogt walked through an innocent-looking shop door into a world where the duties of ruling the sevagram meant an end to sharing his dreams.

---

adventures of plucky NASA astronaut Cirocco Jones as she explores the Boschian milieu of a sentient satellite orbiting Saturn, contains comparable marvels. But Varley is equally at home in self-contained universes, as demonstrated by such entries as the Hugo-winning 'The Pusher' and *Millennium* (1983). The latter is a recursive time-travel story and was filmed in 1989. Varley's output has tapered off lately. But it is to be expected that he is simply hoarding up energies to make his next quantum jump.

PAUL VERHOEVEN

Dutch film director

Born: 1938

An *enfant terrible* of the Dutch cinema, noted for the artful sex 'n' violence of his many early films, Verhoeven eventually made his way to Hollywood in order to direct big-budget action movies. Among them were *RoboCop* (1987), the blood-spattered tale of a cyborg policeman; and *Total*

PAUL VERHOEVEN *Shocking movie-maker; bombs fell on him as a child in wartime Holland and violence preoccupies him even now*

Recall (1990; based on a story by Philip K. Dick), a brain-twisting thriller set mainly on Mars. Both displayed great energy and some science-fictional intelligence (although the latter was criticized for the anti-scientific idiocy of some of its notions). Since then, Verhoeven has eschewed sf, preferring to concentrate on glossy tales of sex'n'violence taken straight.

JOAN D. VINGE

American novelist

Born: 1948

With her award-winning novel *The Snow Queen* (1980), Vinge (whose ex-husband is the writer Vernor) showed she could capably pick up the reins of planetary adventure once held by such writers as Leigh Brackett. Its sequels, *World's End* (1984) and *The Summer Queen* (1991), while less splashy, had their virtues. With her presence somewhat dissipated lately through an abundance of movie tie-in titles, Vinge remains a figure to watch for heartfelt adventures.

VERNOR VINGE

American novelist

Born: 1944

A slower developer than his former wife, Joan D., mathematician Vernor Vinge may well have the more substantial talent. His early, minor works such as *The Witling* (1976) have been far surpassed by the recent *A Fire Upon The Deep* (1992), which is an intellectual space opera conceived on the very widest scale. Other tales of note include the novella *True Names* (1981), and *The Peace War* (1984) and its sequel *Marooned In Realtime* (1986).

KURT VONNEGUT

American novelist

Born: 1922

Vonnegut is a writer of both sf and straight fiction, the sf being of generally higher quality. His first novel, *Player Piano* (1952), possibly the most successful prophecy ever written, presents the widespread erosion of blue-collar jobs under the impact of automation (mitigated by make-work), the collapse of the Soviet Union (under the impact of American know-how), and the surreal false bonhomie endemic to US corporate life. A small band of the disaffected stage a revolution against the system, but it peters out through inanition — the people are too wedded to technology to renounce it, even though it has deprived their lives of all meaning.

This deeply pessimistic conclusion heralds an abiding theme in Vonnegut's *oeuvre*: the spiritual destitution of the common man. Without the comfort of socially useful work (real or illusory), he perceives himself no less than his fellows as

useless, purposeless and unlovable. Another of Vonnegut's most admired books, the catastrophe novel *Cat's Cradle* (1963), offers a solution of sorts: a synthetic religion, based on "singalongs", a novel form of safe sex and a sophisticated theory of human relationships. *The*

Jules Verne — French Novelist — Born: 1828 Died 1905

Verne may be regarded as an early writer of "hard" sf, many books being subsequently hailed as prophetic though much of his output is now unread. Two of the most successful are *20,000 Leagues Under The Sea* (1870) and *The Clipper Of The Clouds* (1886), which have strikingly similar plots. In both, the viewpoint characters are taken aboard futuristic craft (a long-range submarine and a gigantic helicopter respectively), whose owners, Captain Nemo and Robur, are mysterious, hag-ridden geniuses, operating internationally and regarding no law save their own, highly individual consciences. They give their captives much to wonder at and engage them in much high-flown conversation (of which it has been observed that Verne's allegedly English and American characters all talk like Frenchmen), before they can make their escape.

Verne was committedly technophile, and the conversations in *Clipper Of The Clouds* between Robur and his two captives, who are partisans of the airship, reveal this extremely well: it is not good enough to make your craft lighter than air, leaving it to the mercy of the winds – far better to accept that solid objects are inherently heavier than air and to use their greater potential power to overcome gravity. This allows one to become a greater force for good. In Dahomey, Robur disrupts a ceremony involving mass human sacrifice in much the same spirit that Phileas Fogg rescues the Indian widow from her involuntary suttee in *Around The World In Eighty Days* (1872): the technically more sophisticated are, at least potentially, more moral than

superstitious adherents to pre-industrial paradigms. Verne was not blind to the megalomania latent in this thinking. Although, in this case, the airship enthusiasts are the villains of the piece, and attempt to murder Robur and all his crew out of sheer pique, in the sequel, *Master Of The World* (1904), Robur himself comes to grief after deliberately

steering into the heart of a storm.

Other sf by Verne is rooted in the 19th-century tale of exploration and adventure in unknown places which (as he implicitly prophesied) improved technology and understanding have rendered obsolete; it is characteristic that he should write a continuation of Poe's *Arthur Gordon Pym* (*The Ice Sphinx*, 1897). His early *Journey To The Centre Of The Earth* (1864) was written in terms of hollow-Earth theory, not then wholly discredited, so it could rank as a travel tale.

Other writing is only marginally sf; there is a steam-driven elephant in *The Demon Of Cawnpore*, and *For The Flag* (1896) features guided-missile technology. A more serious example is his minor *Propeller Island* (1895), in which civil strife aboard a floating city leads to its being literally torn apart – a more credible outcome than the mechanism used in *From The Earth To The Moon* (1865), a giant cannon which shoots the protagonists into orbit and which, as any contemporary scientist could have told him, would have killed them instantaneously. A recently discovered MS describing 20th-century Paris in pessimistic (and at times surprisingly accurate) detail, lends weight to Verne's prophetic status.

Sirens Of Titan (1959) is a wide-ranging satire, directed principally at science-fictional tropes and the norms of capitalism. *Slaughterhouse-5* (1969), the author's most famous novel, also contains sf elements, although to many sf readers it is not as satisfying as the three titles mentioned above.

HOWARD WALDROP

AMERICAN NOVELIST

BORN: 1946

In the main a short-story writer, Waldrop's few novels include the engaging time-travel tale *Them Bones* (1984). His zany, pop-culture-influenced stories have been collected in the omnibuses *Strange Things In Close-Up* (1989) and *Night Of The Cooters: More Neat Stuff* (1991). He has been silent in recent years, but everyone wishes he would write more.

PETER WATKINS

BRITISH FILM DIRECTOR

BORN: 1935

One-time *enfant terrible* of British television, Watkins was driven into the cinema by the forces of censorship. His powerful vision of nuclear holocaust, *The War Game* (1965), was banned by the BBC and released as a theatrical movie two years later. His other films with futuristic settings are *Privilege* (1966), *The Peace Game* (1968) and *Punishment Park* (1971).

IAN WATSON

BRITISH NOVELIST

BORN: 1943

Relished by sf fans for their liveliness and provocative ideas, Watson's early novels include *The Embedding* (1973), *The Jonah Kit* (1975), *The Martian Inca* (1977) and *Miracle Visitors* (1978). They combine politics, international settings and speculative notions drawn from many branches of the "softer" sciences such as linguistics and psychology. Later novels like *The Gardens Of Delight* (1980), *Chekhov's Journey* (1983), *The Fire Worm* (1988), *The Flies Of Memory* (1990), and the big two-parter *Lucky's*

Harvest (1993) and *The Fallen Moon* (1994), have tended to be still more various in their subject matter and effects (a number of others are classifiable as fantasy or horror).

His many short stories have been collected in *The Very Slow Time Machine* (1979), *Sunstroke* (1982), *Slow Birds* (1985), *Evil Water* (1987), *Salvage Rites* (1989), *Stalin's Teardrops* (1991) and *The Coming Of Vertumnus* (1994): despite his large body of novels, these shorter pieces, all alive with ideas, form a very important part of Watson's output.

STANLEY G. WEINBAUM

AMERICAN NOVELIST

BORN: 1902 DIED: 1935

A short-lived writer of great charm. In 'A Martian Odyssey', life on Mars is discovered by

 JAMES WHALE *HIS TRAGIC END SOMETIMES OVERSHADOWS THE FACT THAT, IF NOT GREAT, HE WAS AT LEAST TOUCHED BY GREATNESS ON OCCASION*

IAN WATSON *IDEAS-BUBBLER; OCCASIONALLY ACTIVE IN BRITISH LOCAL POLITICS, HE USUALLY HAS HAD SOME CAUSE TO PROMOTE — ALTHOUGH HIS FICTION IS NOTABLE FOR ITS BREADTH OF MIND AND RANGE OF REFERENCE*

H. G. Wells — British Novelist — Born: 1866 Died: 1946

Herbert Wells was renowned for the prophetic power of many works, including 'The Land Ironclads' (1903; forecasting the tank), *The War In The Air* (1908; large-scale bombing), *The Sleeper Awakes* (1899; suspended animation) and many others. Yet he is now best remembered for works of far wider-ranging imagination, most notably *The Time Machine* (1895), *The Invisible Man* (1897), *The War Of The Worlds* (1898) and *The First Men In The Moon* (1901).

Of these, *The War Of The Worlds* stands apart. The basic idea, not far removed from current thinking, is that Mars, being smaller than Earth, cooled more quickly, evolved life earlier and became de-natured sooner. Now its inhabitants turn their "vast, cool and unsympathetic" attention enviously towards the Earth, and launch a war of territorial aggression, quite overwhelming Victorian military technology. They even begin to terraform their conquest, spreading a characteristic red weed, before succumbing to terrestrial bacteria, the only enemy for which they are unprepared. The Martians, having eliminated their own diseases aeons ago, have forgotten what they were like, and have no natural immunity. The "moral" sometimes drawn, that we should not disregard even the humblest of our fellow species, is jejune; regardless of human attitudes, had the Martians considered and allowed for germs the story might have ended differently.

The other three form more of a group, since all reflect the impact of technology on those who use it. The invisible man of the title, having invented and swallowed a drug which confers permanent invisibility, sets out to take criminal advantage of his condition. He fails, for a variety of reasons which he might have anticipated, including his need to wear clothing against the weather and the need, before he can enjoy the proceeds of theft, to find people willing and able to deal with him. The moral has to do with human interdependence, and appears

H. G. WELLS WAS A *FORMER DRAPER'S CLERK, LEADING* FABIAN *INTELLECTUAL, AND NOTORIOUS LOVER OF WOMEN WHO WERE SUPPOSEDLY ATTRACTED BY HIS HONEY-SCENTED BODY ODOUR*

yet more strongly in the other two. In *The Time Machine*, the world of the 803rd millennium is divided between elfin Eloi and brutish Morlocks, descended from the leisured and working classes of Wells's day. They no longer perceive each other as human, and the Morlocks emerge at night to take Eloi for food.

Most interesting is *The First Men In The Moon*, which represents in Selenite society an extreme form of the socialist/eugenist/utilitarian ideals which Wells himself propounded. There people are raised from birth to their pre-ordained functions. Cavor, the scientist who tours this world, is horrified yet fascinated; his soul revolts at the ugliness,

while he is unable to deny the logic behind every procedure, as when he notes a Selenite lying about in a form of suspended animation, and is told that he is redundant, but being maintained in that state against future need. Better, perhaps than leaving him to starve in the streets, but no less a denial of his individuality. Wells's later scientific romances, from *The World Set Free* (1914) to *The Shape Of Things To Come* (1933) and beyond, have less literary merit and yet still, in many cases, are of profound interest — as are his numerous non-fiction works and mainstream novels. In the view of many critics, he remains the genre's greatest author.

humans, and it proves to be friendly, but sadly incomprehensible; in 'The Adaptive Ultimate', a woman cancer victim is cured but later becomes an amoral siren; and 'The Lotus Eaters' features an intelligent plant that is unfortunately not blessed with a sense of self-preservation.

JAMES WHALE

BRITISH FILM DIRECTOR
BORN: 1896 DIED: 1957
A London stage director, summoned to Hollywood to direct British-oriented material, Whale will be remembered forever by cineastes for his two sf-horror movies inspired by Mary

Shelley's gothic novel: *Frankenstein* (1931) and *The Bride Of Frankenstein* (1935). The latter, in particular, is a comic masterpiece. He also directed *The Invisible Man* (1933; from H. G. Wells's novel).

His death was sad — he was found drowned in a Hollywood swimming pool.

JAMES WHITE

BRITISH NOVELIST

BORN: 1928

White is a Northern Irish writer best known for his Sector General series of stories, set in a gigantic orbital hospital, and for his novel *The Watch Below* (1966). Their humane assumptions are underpinned with strong feelings for medical procedures and ethics. In both, the writing is sufficiently assured to allow suspension of disbelief, necessary as both are highly contrived.

Sector General is designed to handle a huge variety of intelligent species, often inhabiting mutually lethal environments, a factor which contributes many plot-lines but fails to bear close examination — one feels that other, more specialized and less grandiose structures, would have served better. The idea that medical ethics should be universal is attractive, but the arrangement frequently requires staff to tackle problems for which they are inadequately briefed and unsuited by training and temperament no less than physically. The theme of *The Watch Below* is the triumph of the spirit over adversity, and mainly concerns the lives of a small group (five, originally) trapped in the hold of a submerged tanker. They contrive a workable ecology, wherein they live and breed. Meanwhile intelligent fish (!) have launched a colonial fleet towards the Earth, and conflict seems certain until they discover the tanker and its inhabitants.

KATE WILHELM

AMERICAN NOVELIST

BORN: 1928

Wilhelm's fictions have the deceptive strength and contours of a primed bear trap partially hidden under a fresh snowfall. Never showy or grandiose, always craftful and frequently brilliant, Wilhelm and her four decades of stories and novels occupy an important place in one of sf's lineages: that of subtle, strong, undernoticed female writers such as Leigh Brackett, Kit Reed, Lisa Tuttle and Carol Emshwiller.

Beginning to publish in 1956 with 'The Pint-Size Genie', Wilhelm turned out entertaining if unexceptional stories later collected in *The Mile-Long Spaceship* (1963). An early novel in collaboration with Ted Thomas — *The Clone* (1965) — continued this pattern. But Wilhelm was soon to be energized by her marriage to Damon Knight and by the ambient swell of the New Wave. Her future collections from the point of *The Downstairs Room* (1968) onward would contain elegant, sometimes elusive stories such as the Nebula-winning 'The Planners'. At this point, one could detect Wilhelm's preference for a certain powerful strategy: domestic and near-future settings would be lovingly and brightly delineated, only to be disrupted and/or redeemed by an intrusion of the fantastic. This tactic was perhaps best illustrated by the Hugo-winning *Where Late The Sweet Birds Sang* (1976), which speaks softly of a post-apocalyptic world.

Around this time, Wilhelm began to spread her wings with a series of non-sf novels. (In fact, her very first book was a mystery, *More Bitter Than Death*, 1963). These books were not unsympathetic to sf concerns. The series featuring Danvers and Meiklejohn as protagonists frequently played with genre trappings. But this movement away from pure sf somewhat diluted her presence within the field, although she was honoured with Nebulas in 1986 (for 'The Girl Who Fell Into The Sky') and 1987 ('Forever Yours, Anna'), stories that showed her still at the top of her form. In 1991, she successfully combined her interest in sf and detective fiction with *Death Qualified: A Mystery Of Chaos*, which melded chaos theory and murder. Wilhelm seems like some Fifty-Foot Woman who has burst the confines of her ranch house to wear its shattered roof like epaulettes.

PAUL O. WILLIAMS

AMERICAN NOVELIST

BORN: 1935

Known solely for his Pelbar cycle of novels, beginning with *The Breaking Of Northwall* (1981): a millennium after the great nuclear war, scattered settlements of Americans are groping their way once more towards civilization, but numerous conflicts mar the progress. Rich in detail, it draws fruitfully on the author's knowledge of the North American past and Amerindian cultures. Sequels include *The Ends Of The Circle* (1981), *The Dome In The Forest* (1981) and *The Fall Of The Shell* (1982).

WALTER JON WILLIAMS

AMERICAN NOVELIST

BORN: 1953

A very capable writer who first came to prominence by riding on the coat-tails of the cyberpunk movement: his *Hardwired* (1986) was regarded as being rather similar to the work of William Gibson and others; nevertheless, it was popular. His many novels since then have run a gamut of themes.

In one of the best, *Aristoi* (1992), a future society of technological abundance is controlled by the elite *Aristoi* who spend much of their time in the virtual-reality realm known as the "Oneirochronon".

JACK WILLIAMSON

AMERICAN NOVELIST

BORN: 1908

To summarize Grand Master Williamson's heroic, record-breaking career in less than a monograph is gross injustice. From the dawn of genre sf (his first story appeared in 1928) right down to his thrilling *Demon Moon* (1994), he has kept pace with every development of sf. With his *Legion of Space* books, he pioneered space opera. With his *Humanoids* series, he investigated the pitfalls of artificial intelligence in still-relevant depth. Like his frequent collaborator Frederik Pohl, Williamson has been there and done that — twice over!

CONNIE WILLIS

AMERICAN NOVELIST

BORN: 1945

Willis won awards for *Lincoln's Dreams* (1987) and *Doomsday Book* (1992), both of them very accomplished time-travel novels, as well as for a number of short stories.

Her novella *Remake* (1994) takes a sharp look at the future of Hollywood.

ROBERT CHARLES WILSON

CANADIAN NOVELIST

BORN: 1953

A quiet writer of growing reputation, Wilson began with the parallel-world novel *A Hidden Place* (1986). Later books, *Memory Wire* (1988), *Gypsies* (1989), *The Divide* (1990), *A Bridge Of Years* (1991) and *The Harvest* (1993), all add to the impression that he is a major talent of the more traditional sort.

DAVID WINGROVE

BRITISH NOVELIST
BORN: 1954

Wingrove's single immense (eight volumes, still incomplete) novel, *Chung Kuo* (from 1989), features a world dominated by Chinese neo-Confucianism and plagued by overpopulation (mitigated in later volumes by large-scale civil war). Its most successful aspect is the emotionally charged character studies of youthful geniuses of both sexes.

ROBERT WISE

AMERICAN FILM DIRECTOR
BORN: 1914

It may seem incongruous for the director of *The Sound Of Music* (1964) to be associated with science fiction — but that's Hollywood! Wise's sf movies, at least the first of which may be reckoned a classic, are *The Day The Earth Stood Still* (1951), *The Andromeda Strain* (1971; from Michael Crichton's novel) and *Star Trek: The Motion Picture* (1979).

DONALD A. WOLLHEIM

AMERICAN EDITOR
BORN: 1914 DIED: 1990

Less frequently mentioned than Gernsback or Campbell, Wollheim is one of the most important figures in the history of sf publishing — as significant in the development of the paperback side of the genre as the other two were for magazines. He edited some of the earliest anthologies, such as *The Pocket Book Of Science Fiction* (1943), then went on to do solid work for Avon Books in the later 1940s, before joining the newly-formed Ace Books in 1952. At Ace, he reprinted vast quantities of old pulp material while simultaneously encouraging newer writers:

Gene Wolfe — American Novelist — Born: 1931

Wolfe is distinguished in many fields, but in sf renowned for his four-volume far-future novel 'The Book Of The New Sun', consisting of *The Shadow Of The Torturer* (1981), *The Claw Of The Conciliator* (1982), *The Sword Of The Lictor* (1982) and *The Citadel Of The Autarch* (1983), plus a sequel, *The Urth Of The New Sun* (1987). The series features an interesting use of language: unfamiliar everyday objects are given names which have already been adopted into English from other tongues, but with their meaning subtly distorted, as if by the billion-year history of Urth, where the more durable products of the 20th century and later can appear as low-strata fossils. On much the same principle, well-known stories are re-told in distorted forms, preserving their spirit but suggesting that they have been filtered through many tongues and the folk memory. Some which receive this treatment are Chaucer's 'Nun's Priest's Tale', Theseus and the Minotaur and the Parable of the Wicked Tenants. It is a measure of Wolfe's skill that his versions do not suffer by comparison with the originals.

But the principal character, Severian, focuses the book and confers its classic status. Superficially Severian is a standard enough hero — handsome, brave, serious-minded, kindly and highly sexed. On the other hand, he has from earliest childhood been apprenticed to the Torturers' Guild, and has sedulously acquired the skills of that profession. The tensions which arise between his intellect, his emotions and the rationale wherewith the Guild justifies its activities, inform a long, episodic novel which culminates with Severian installed as Autarch with a war-torn world to remake. In the fifth book, he begins that task.

Another four-volume work, 'The Book Of The Long Sun', is set on a run-down, multi-generation starship, now nearing its goal. Beginning with *Nightside The Long Sun* (1993), it also uses mythic analogues, but the general

 GENE WOLFE *CORRESPONDED WITH* **J. R. R. TOLKIEN** *ON LINGUISTIC TOPICS*

effect is less good. The central character is the celibate priest of a fatuous and repulsive religion (it involves blood sacrifice, and he regards a bird of sufficient intelligence to plead for its life in simple, two-word sentences as a particularly desirable victim).

Among Wolfe's shorter fiction the linked stories collected as *The Fifth Head Of Cerberus* (1972) are especially worth noting. Set on a human-colonized world, they explore the questions of identity and individuality which inevitably arise in a culture where cloning is practised and where deceased personalities are downloaded to computers. There is also the question of the autochthons, who may be extinct, but who may in fact have taken over the lives and identities of the colonists, extinguishing them. If that is the case, where should the ancestral loyalties of a "colonist" lie vis-a-vis a surviving group of autochthons?

Philip K. Dick, Samuel R. Delany, Ursula Le Guin, Thomas M. Disch, Brian Stableford and a host of others all got their start in book publishing thanks to Wollheim. Sometimes a sharp practitioner, he was also personally responsible for initiating the Edgar Rice Burroughs and J. R. R. Tolkien publishing booms (in 1962 and 1965, respectively), with vast consequences for the emergence of fantasy fiction as a separate market-place category. In 1972, he left Ace to found his own imprint, DAW Books, where he pursued similar policies for the next 15 years or so, on the one hand reprinting ancient pulp such as William L. Chester's *Kioga* books, and on the other encouraging the emergence of major new talents like C. J. Cherryh and Tanith Lee. Although he was no great shakes as a critic of sf — as his book *The Universe Makers* (1971) reveals — no one did more to form the reading tastes of several generations. His achievements should not be underestimated.

JACK WOMACK

AMERICAN NOVELIST

BORN: 1956

Womack is known for his loosely affiliated New York sequence, the first of which, *Ambient* (1987), is a competent near-future horror story of corruption in corporate high places — written in the cyberpunk idiom. Quasi-sequels include *Terraplane* (1988), *Heathern* (1990) and *Elvissey* (1993).

PHILIP WYLIE

AMERICAN NOVELIST

BORN: 1902 DIED: 1971

As well as much polemical non-fiction and some film screenplays, Wylie wrote many novels of ideas which may be classified as sf. They range from *Gladiator* (1930), an early "superman" tale, through *When Worlds Collide* (1933; with Edwin Balmer), which was filmed in 1951, to the posthumous nightmare of environmental pollution, *The End Of The Dream* (1972).

JOHN WYNDHAM

BRITISH NOVELIST

BORN: 1903 DIED: 1969

A writer of variable quality, Wyndham is chiefly remembered for his classic *The Day Of The Triffids* (1951), in which a synthetic species of quasi-intelligent, venomous mobile plants decimate humanity and dominate the landscape once almost everyone has been blinded in the mysterious "night of the green flashes". The story concerns the efforts of the hero and his girlfriend (both sighted) to establish a home for themselves and a little girl whom they "adopt", to keep it secure against both the plants and other, less humane survivors and to sustain civilized values.

Another admirable book, *The Chrysalids*

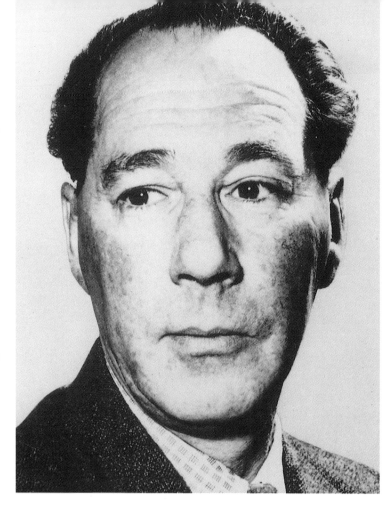

(1955), is set in a grim post-debacle world where much of the land is radioactive and mutants of all species, especially the human, are rooted out with cold fanaticism. There the hero loses his childhood sweetheart when, her damning extra toes being discovered, she is sterilized and exiled into the badlands. He himself is a mutant, having telepathic powers, and the later chapters concern his struggles, first to disguise that power (shared by his latter girlfriend and his sister) and then to escape once it is recognized. The closing chapters feature a brief and poignant encounter with his lost love.

CHELSEA QUINN YARBRO

AMERICAN NOVELIST

BORN: 1942

Her early short sf, collected in *Cautionary Tales* (1978), includes some excellent work, notably 'Un Bel Di', in which the story of *Madame Butterfly* is re-enacted in a yet crueller context. By contrast, 'The Generalissimo's Butterfly' makes its point by an ostentatious avoidance of

sensationalism. Most of her later work is historical horror fiction rather than sf.

ROBERT F. YOUNG

AMERICAN NOVELIST

BORN: 1915 DIED: 1986

Young's short stories are his best work. Many of them express contempt for American materialism, especially as typified by automobile worship, and are written from the viewpoint of that society's losers. Typical are 'Thirty Days Had September' and 'Emily And The Bards Sublime'.

TIMOTHY ZAHN

AMERICAN NOVELIST

BORN: 1951

A scientifically trained short-story writer for *Analog* magazine, whose 'Cascade Point' (1983) won a Hugo award, Zahn entered the book market with militaristic space opera about cyborg soldiers of the 25th century, in novels such as *Cobra* (1985) and its sequels *Cobra Strike*

(1986) and *Cobra Bargain* (1988). Later, he found his metier with *Star Wars* spin-off novels which have sold in spectacular quantities.

YEVGENY ZAMYATIN

RUSSIAN NOVELIST

BORN: 1884 DIED: 1937

An Anglophile and H. G. Wells-admirer, Zamyatin is remembered for his powerful dystopian sf novel, *We* (1924) — a book long banned in the Soviet Union though published freely in the West. George Orwell acknowledged that it was an influence on his own *Nineteen Eighty-Four* (1949).

GEORGE ZEBROWSKI

AMERICAN NOVELIST

BORN: 1945

Zebrowski's big book is *Macrolife* (1979), a grand vision of humanity's future in space. Other novels preceded and have followed, but latterly he has been less active in the field.

ROGER ZELAZNY

AMERICAN NOVELIST

BORN: 1928 DIED: 1995

One of Roger Zelazny's last works of fiction before his sorrowful, untimely death was not sf but an adventure set in America's Old West. *Wilderness* (1994), written with Gerald Hausman, recounts the parallel and intersecting true stories of two mountain men as they surmount incredible dangers and trials with almost superhuman efforts of muscle and will. Reminiscent of a Philip José Farmer World of Tiers adventure (Farmer and Zelazny held each other's work in admiration), the book is a testament to the huge spirit and heart of its author, whose best sf always promulgated a jaunty, droll, unbeaten demeanour even in the face of incredible challenges and assaults. (One thinks of a blinded, imprisoned Prince Corwin of Amber patiently plotting while awaiting the regrowth of his eyes ...)

In 1962, still at his civil service job, a young Zelazny began to utter on paper those mythic narratives which soon earned him recognition as one of sf's brightest stars. Ransacking old cosmogonies for figures with shoulders broad enough to carry his plots, Zelazny took Sturgeon's poetic sensibilities and married them to Bester's violent energies, pouring the resulting compound into a mould of modern, musical plainspeech. With stories such as 'The Doors Of His Face, The Lamps Of His Mouth' (collection of the same name released in 1971) and 'A Rose for Ecclesiastes', Zelazny gave the field both stirring adventures and mature characters fully enmeshed in adult responsibilities (sometimes to the point of regarding all humanity as their rambunctious progeny!). With his first two novels — *This Immortal* (1966) and *The Dream Master* (1966) — Zelazny proved he could deliver the same jolts at longer lengths.

But it was with *Lord Of Light* (1967) that he truly came to resemble one of his own demi-gods. Telling the story of a world where high tech allows the donning of celestial identities taken from the Hindu and Buddhist pantheon, the novel delivered spiritual parables along with the thrills of a war amongst godlings. The books that followed seemed unable to recreate this exact blend. They erred either on the side of too much mythos (*Creatures Of Light And Darkness*, 1969) or too much action (*Damnation Alley*, 1969). While always captivating, they no longer seemed to embody the best of their era. With later works such as *My Name Is Legion* (1976) and *Eye Of Cat* (1982), Zelazny came close to his best effects. In the arena of shorter works, he came even closer with award-winning entries like '24 Views Of Mount Fuji' and 'Permafrost'. Much of his energies in this period were devoted to his popular Amber fantasies. Now we will be graced with no more Zelazny stories. Instead, we can picture him in some heaven as he was fictionalized by his friend Samuel Delany in the story 'We, In Some Strange Power's Employ, Move In A Rigorous Line': a laughing jetcycle outlaw, his wings burning like those of some techno Icarus.

ROBERT ZEMECHIS

AMERICAN FILM DIRECTOR

BORN: 1951

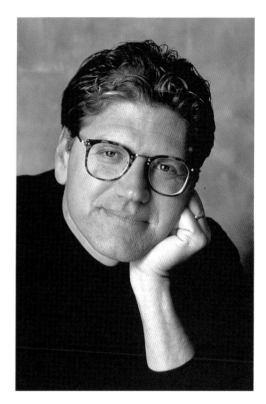

 ROBERT ZEMECKIS *AS A FILM-MAKER HE HAS SHOWN EVERY SIGN OF BEING QUITE AT HOME IN SF*

A Spielberg protégé, Zemeckis made his name with the adventure comedy *Romancing The Stone* (1984), then went on to direct the movies' three finest time-travel comedies, *Back To The Future* (1985), *Back To The Future Part II* (1989) and *Back To The Future Part III* (1990), all co-scripted with his usual working partner Bob Gale. They display a complete ease with the conventions of the sf time-paradox story, rare in cinema. His other big success was the semi-animated fantasy *Who Framed Roger Rabbit?* (1988; based on a novel by sometime sf writer Gary K. Wolf).

DAVID ZINDELL

AMERICAN NOVELIST

BORN: 1952

Zindell's output to date is all set in the Shanidar universe, with its pseudo-Neanderthal atavists and its cold city of *Neverness* (title of his first novel, 1988), seat of an exclusive order of space pilots. The plot-lines of his big books verge on the mystical, and the writing is notable for its brilliant ornamentation.

A-Z of Heroes & Villains

THE CHARACTERS AND ENTITIES OF SCIENCE-FICTION LITERATURE AND FILM: HUMAN AND ALIEN, ROBOTIC AND TRANSHUMAN

PROBLEM CHILD
ALEX (MALCOLM MCDOWELL) IN STANLEY KUBRICK'S FEROCIOUS, STYLISH ANTI-UTOPIA, A CLOCKWORK ORANGE

Adam Adamant

CREATORS: TONY WILLIAMSON
AND VERITY LAMBERT
SOURCE: ADAM ADAMANT LIVES! (BBC TV)
DATE: 1966
Gerald Harper played this Edwardian dandy, who is frozen in a block of ice in the year 1902 – and thawed out in the Swinging Sixties. A gentlemanly hero, his crime-busting adventures were attractively tongue-in-cheek.

Aelita

CREATOR: ALEXEI TOLSTOY
SOURCE: AELITA (NOVEL)
DATE: 1922
Daughter of the chairman of the Martian Supreme Council, the beautiful Aelita is, in all but title, a princess of Mars; but it takes an Earthman to teach her how to kiss. The Russian silent film version (1924) starred Yulia Solntseva.

Genly Ai

CREATOR: URSULA LE GUIN
SOURCE: THE LEFT HAND OF DARKNESS (NOVEL)
DATE: 1969
An envoy of the Ekumen to the planet Gethen, whose inhabitants may become either male or female at the critical point of their breeding-cycle. Ai's mission proves problematic, involving him more intimately than he initially desired with the exiled Gethenian Estraven.

Alex

CREATOR: ANTHONY BURGESS
SOURCE: A CLOCKWORK ORANGE (NOVEL)
DATE: 1962
Ultra-violent, juvenile gang-leader who rules the streets of dismal near-future Britain. Alex is a 15-year-old mugger, rapist and killer, and he tells his story in the blackly-humorous, futuristic slang called "Nadsat", full of Russian loan-words. The police are the "millicents", Alex's gang-members are his "droogs" and "horrorshow" serves as their all-purpose term of praise and/or disgust. Paradoxically, Alex happens to be a lover of Beethoven's symphonies. After his arrest, the authorities use scientific conditioning techniques to make him behave meekly; but an unforeseen side-effect is that he loses his ability to enjoy classical music. Forced to be "sociable", Alex becomes the impossibility of the book's title: a clockwork orange, or programmed man. He is deprived of the finer things in life along with his urge to violence. Malcolm McDowell starred as Alex in Stanley Kubrick's film of the book (1971), memorable for its scenes of rape and grievous bodily violence performed to a soundtrack of Singing In The Rain. There was also a stage musical version of Alex's adventures, written by Burgess and produced by the Royal Shakespeare Company in 1990.

ALF

CREATOR: PAUL FUSCO
SOURCE: ALF (NBC TV SERIES)
DATE: 1986
An obnoxious, furry Alien Life Form who moves in with the Tanner family, causing farcical disruption. The Tanners exhibit awesome grace under fire, using ALF's antics as a launching-pad for a series of sickly moral lessons.

Aliens

CREATORS: DAN O'BANNON AND RIDLEY SCOTT
SOURCE: ALIEN (FILM)
DATE: 1979
Creatures first manifest in the form of a claw-like entity that clings to the face of a crewman from the starship Nostromo. An egg laid within the body of the crewman hatches into an insectile beast, which bursts out of his belly before going into hiding. It grows spectacularly into a slavering monster, at first seen only in glimpses until it has killed all of the crew, save the infinitely resourceful **Ellen Ripley**, who manages to dispose of it. The last scene of the first film and the two subsequent sequels offer ample scope for observing that the creature resembles a cross between a crocodile and a locust. It belongs to a hive species whose queens are even nastier than the standard model; one of them fights a memorable duel with a massive humanoid machine controlled by Ripley in the climax of Aliens (1986), after hundreds of her offspring have been annihilated. Alien3 (1992) reverts to small-scale conflict. A determined attempt to produce the ultimate race of bug-eyed monsters, although – like all monsters – they are more effective while kept teasingly off-stage. There have been spinoff series of "Aliens" comic books (as well as paperback novelizations derived from these).

Alley Oop

CREATOR: V. T. HAMLIN
SOURCE: NEWSPAPER COMIC STRIP
DATE: 1933
America's favourite caveman had a girlfriend called Oola and a pet dinosaur called Dinny. Occasionally, he would go time-travelling to later eras. Hamlin drew the strip until 1971; Alley Oop was perpetuated by other hands thereafter.

Alyx

CREATOR: JOANNA RUSS
SOURCE: PICNIC ON PARADISE (NOVEL)
DATE: 1968
An assertive, time-travelling female soldier-of-fortune, capable of getting by as a mercenary, outlaw or tour-guide. She has abandoned many lovers and several children, thus qualifying as a true female counterpart to the stereotyped male sf hero. She also appears in a few other stories by Russ, and all of them are collected, together with the original novel, in the book The Adventures of Alyx (1976).

CURTAIN CALL ONE OF THE MONSTERS FROM ALIEN3, IN A PARODY OF THE SHOWER SCENE FROM HITCHCOCK'S PSYCHO

John Amalfi

CREATOR: JAMES BLISH
SOURCE: *EARTHMAN COME HOME* (NOVEL)
DATE: 1953

The immortal mayor of New York, who cleverly helps the computerized City Fathers to govern while the domed city roams the galaxy in search of work. He eventually witnesses the cataclysmic destruction of the universe, hoping in his own optimistic and pragmatic fashion to play a key part in a new Creation.

Telzey Amberdon

CREATOR: JAMES H. SCHMITZ
SOURCE: *THE UNIVERSE AGAINST HER* (NOVEL)
DATE: 1964

Young, female, non-white protagonist of an engaging space-opera series. She discovers she has psionic powers and becomes quite a superwoman. Follow-up volumes featuring the same heroine are *The Lion Game* (1973) and *The Telzey Toy* (1973).

Captain America

CREATORS: JOE SIMON AND JACK KIRBY
SOURCE: MARVEL COMICS
DATE: 1941

Mighty superhero clad in a Stars-and-Stripes costume and a snug-fitting hood with a big letter "A" on the forehead. He began life as an average joe called Steve Rogers: injected with a wonder drug by Professor Reinstein, he grew enormous muscles and set about winning World War II almost single-handed. He had help from a teenage sidekick named Bucky, and their main enemy was the Red Skull, a mutant Nazi spy. After the war, Captain America ceased to have a purpose and the comic book's popularity declined. But the "greatest champion of democracy" was revived in 1954 to fight communists; and he came to life again during the nostalgic superhero boom of the 1960s. The cinema serial *Captain America* (1944) starred Dick Purcell as the hero. Much later, two TV movies, *Captain America* (1978) and *Return Of Captain America* (1979), starred Reb Brown as the original Captain's otherwise-identical son. Captain America also appeared in spinoff novels, *The Great Gold Steal* by Ted White (1968) and *Holocaust For Hire* by Joseph Silva (Ron Goulart, 1979).

Andromeda

CREATORS: FRED HOYLE AND JOHN ELLIOT
SOURCE: *A FOR ANDROMEDA* (BBC TV SERIAL)
DATE: 1961

A beautiful young girl (Julie Christie) created by a supercomputer assembled by scientists according to instructions transmitted from the Andromeda galaxy. Her desire to be free of the machine's control leads her to participate in its destruction – at which point its dangerous nature becomes obvious.

PATRIOT GAMES *CAPTAIN AMERICA, WIMP TURNED SUPERHUMAN AVENGER, BESTRIDES THE RUINS AND SEES THAT JUSTICE IS DONE*

Paul Atreides

CREATOR: FRANK HERBERT
SOURCE: *DUNE* (NOVEL)
DATE: 1963

Alias the Kwisatz Haderach, alias Muad'Dib, an interstellar prince, expert in martial arts and various skills of the mind, who inherits the planet Arrakis (also known as Dune) from his assassinated father and undertakes a long, hard struggle to win his birthright. Assisted by the tough desert-dwellers called the Fremen, and the Sandworms, mysterious creatures that are the source of the drug ("melange") that confers longevity, Paul becomes a charismatic war-leader. The complex story is told in Frank Herbert's hugely bestselling novel *Dune* (1965; originally serialized in two sequences in *Analog* magazine from 1963). Paul's later career as Emperor is described in the sequel *Dune Messiah* (1969), and the centuries-long saga of the Atreides family and the planet Arrakis is spun out over four more books: *Children Of Dune* (1976), *God-Emperor Of Dune* (1981), *Heretics Of Dune* (1984) and *Chapter-House Dune* (1985). Detailed biographies of Paul, his son Leto Atreides and many others are given in a massive secondary work, *The Dune Encyclopedia* compiled by Willis E. McNelly (1984). The David Lynch film of *Dune* (1984) starred Kyle MacLachlan as Paul, but was generally received with disappointment.

Steve Austin

CREATOR: MARTIN CAIDIN
SOURCE: *CYBORG* (NOVEL)
DATE: 1972

A "bionic man" with vast strength, an all-seeing artificial eye and the ability to run like the wind: in effect, he is a latter-day **Superman** whose powers are depicted with a slightly greater degree of scientific credibility. Steve Austin is a test pilot who is seriously injured in a plane crash and then reconstructed by scientists as part-man, part-machine. Coming to terms with his newly made-over body, he finds that he has wonderfully enhanced physical abilities, and soon he is using his unique skills to pursue villains on behalf of the US government. Sequel novels, also by Caidin, are *Operation Nuke*

A STING IN THE TALE *Paul Atreides (Kyle MacLachlan) duels with Feyd Rautha (Sting) in David Lynch's film of* Dune

(1973), *High Crystal* (1974) and *Cyborg IV* (1975). The first book formed the basis of a very popular juvenile-oriented television series, The *Six Million Dollar Man* (1973-78; so titled because that sum of money is what the hi-tech operation to create the cyborg hero is supposed to have cost), with Lee Majors as Austin; and this led to an equally successful spinoff series, *The Bionic Woman* (see **Jaime Sommers**). There was also a *Six Million Dollar Man* comic book in the 1970s.

Ayla

CREATOR: JEAN M. AUEL
SOURCE: *THE CLAN OF THE CAVE BEAR* (NOVEL)
DATE: 1980
Blonde, stone-age girl raised by a tribe of

WE CAN REBUILD HIM *Steve Austin (Lee Majors) in the telvision cyborg show* The Six Million Dollar Man

Neanderthals. Her adventures continue in *The Valley Of The Horses* (1982), *The Mammoth Hunters* (1985) and *The Plains Of Passage* (1990). The film *Clan Of The Cave Bear* (1986) starred Daryl Hannah.

Barbarella

CREATOR: JEAN-CLAUDE FOREST
SOURCE: *V MAGAZINE* (FRANCE)
DATE: 1962
Beautiful spacewoman whose saucy comic-strip adventures on other planets were collected in the book *Barbarella* (1964). In the film of the same title (1967), co-scripted by the satirist Terry Southern, Barbarella was embodied – rather memorably – by Jane Fonda.

Batman

CREATORS: BOB KANE AND BILL FINGER
SOURCE: *DETECTIVE COMICS*
DATE: 1939
Sinister-seeming costumed superhero of American comic books, second in fame only to the great **Superman** himself. Batman's real name is Bruce Wayne; he is a Gotham City socialite and philanthropist who dons his grey-and-blue bat-suit (with cape and mask) in order to fight villains incognito. His assistant is Robin the Boy Wonder, alias Dick Grayson. These energetic vigilantes use a range of marvellous vehicles and technological gadgets in their struggle against such baddies as the Joker (who "smiles a smile without mirth, a smile of death"), the Penguin, the Riddler and the sexy Catwoman. From 1940, Batman had his own comic book, and before long he was appearing in the cinema. The film serial *Batman* (1943) starred Lewis Wilson, while the later *Batman And Robin* (1949) had Robert Lowery as the hero. A distinctly tongue-in-cheek television series (1966-68), starred Adam West as Batman and Burt Ward as Robin. It was a considerable success, and a feature film, *Batman* (1966), used the same cast. There have also been several TV cartoon series of Batman adventures. A spinoff character is Batgirl, alias Babs Gordon, who appeared in *Detective Comics* from 1967 and also featured in later episodes of the 1960s TV series. Two novels by Winston Lyon, *Batman Vs. Three Villains Of Doom* and *Batman Vs. The Fearsome Foursome*, were published at the time of the hero's peak popularity on television. Latterly, Batman has been given a whole new lease of life by the talented comic-book artist and writer Frank Miller: in the graphic novel Batman: *The Dark Knight Returns* (1986), he re-imagined Batman as a rather sad, superannuated (but still powerful) figure in a world that no longer has a place for costumed superheroes. This inspired many other graphic novels and comic-book imitations, including, most significantly, Alan Moore and Brian Bolland's *The Killing Joke* (1988) and Grant Morrison and Dave McKean's *Arkham Asylum* (1989). Since Miller's revival of the character, three mega-movies, owing much to latter-day graphic-novel visual styles, have kept the hero in the forefront of popular consciousness: *Batman* (1989), *Batman Returns* (1992) and *Batman Forever* (1995). Michael Keaton played Batman in the first two of these, and Val Kilmer played him in the third. The astonishing success of these films led to a plethora of spin-off novels and anthologies, including *The Further Adventures Of Batman*

HOLY CAPED CONUNDRUMS *DC Comics's Batman meets another version of himself. This latest cartoon incarnation has proved a very popular addition to the Dark Knight's canon*

edited by Martin H. Greenberg (1989), *The Batman Murders* by Craig Shaw Gardner (1990), *The Further Adventures Of The Joker* edited by Greenberg (1990), *Batman: Captured By The Engines* by Joe R. Lansdale (1991), *Batman: To Stalk A Specter* by Simon Hawke (1991), *The Further Adventures Of Batman 2: Featuring The Penguin* edited by Greenberg (1992), *Catwoman: Tiger Hunt* by Lynn Abbey and Robert Asprin (1992), *The Further Adventures Of Batman 3: Featuring Catwoman* edited by Greenberg (1993), *Batman: Knightfall* by Dennis O'Neil (1994) and *Batman: The Ultimate Evil* by Andrew Vachss (1995). Perhaps Batman really is forever.

Elijah ("Lije") Baley

CREATOR: ISAAC ASIMOV
SOURCE: *THE CAVES OF STEEL* (NOVEL)
DATE: 1954

A troubled but persistent detective who slowly comes to terms with having robot R. Daneel Olivaw as a partner; they bring a murderer to justice in a claustrophobic future New York. Baley went on to solve more mysterious murders in otherworldly settings in *The Naked Sun* (1957) and *The Robots Of Dawn* (1983).

John Barr

CREATOR: JACK WILLIAMSON
SOURCE: *THE LEGION OF TIME* (NOVEL)
DATE: 1938 (BOOK 1952)

A boy wandering in an Arkansas field in 1921, who must pick up a magneto from a model-T Ford instead of a stone if he is make the crucial scientific discovery leading to the establishment of utopian Jonbar. He remains blissfully ignorant of the fact that vast time-travelling armies are fighting to determine what he does.

Jack Barron

CREATOR: NORMAN SPINRAD
SOURCE: *BUG JACK BARRON* (NOVEL)
DATE: 1969

Hard-driving American TV interviewer of the near future who exposes a businessman's crooked research into longevity. A creature of the media landscape, Jack is notably foul-mouthed and highly sexed, and is at his most intense when "on air".

Oswald Bastable

CREATOR: MICHAEL MOORCOCK
SOURCE: *THE WARLORD OF THE AIR* (NOVEL)
DATE: 1971

One of E. Nesbit's Bastable children, now full-grown. His fighting skills having been honed in the 53rd Lancers and the Special Air Police, he becomes a "nomad of the time streams", fighting for multiversal liberty against a host of enemies. The prototype steampunk hero, he reappears in *The Land Leviathan* (1974) and *The Steel Tsar* (1981). The three books have been combined as *The Nomad Of Time* (1984; later revised as *A Nomad Of The Time Streams*).

Sam Beckett

CREATOR: DONALD P. BELLISARIO
SOURCE: *QUANTUM LEAP* (TV SERIES)
DATE: 1989

A time-slipping scientist played by Scott Bakula, Dr Beckett is a physicist whose arcane experimentation has allowed him to move around in the time-continuum represented by his own life-span. The catch is that, when he materializes at a new date, he always does so in the body of another person. His companion in these adventures is the sardonic Al Calavicci (Dean Stockwell), who appears as a hologram invisible to all except Sam. Puzzling stuff, but it succeeded in making sufficient sense to its many keen viewers – the one thing insufficiently explained, to the best of our knowledge, is just why this fictional hero bears the name of an eminent Nobel Prize-winning Irish playwright and novelist. Timeslip Sam has also appeared in a series of spin-off novels by Ashley McConnell and others.

Zaphod Beeblebrox

CREATOR: DOUGLAS ADAMS
SOURCE: *THE HITCH HIKER'S GUIDE TO THE GALAXY* (BBC RADIO SERIAL)
DATE: 1978

A two-headed confidence trickster, master of the stolen starship *Heart Of Gold*. Mark Wing-Davey played him with admirable gusto on radio and in the TV version of 1981 – in the latter case, with the assistance of a rather uncommunicative plastic twin mounted on his shoulder.

Doc Benway

CREATOR: WILLIAM S. BURROUGHS
SOURCE: *THE NAKED LUNCH* (NOVEL)
DATE: 1959

Sinister doctor in Burroughs's grotesque satires, including *The Soft Machine* (1961) and *Nova Express* (1964). He is said to be "an expert on all phases of interrogation, brainwashing and control". Roy Scheider played him in the film *Naked Lunch* (1991).

The Berserkers

CREATOR: FRED SABERHAGEN
SOURCE: *BERSERKER* (STORY COLLECTION)
DATE: 1967

Heavily armed and armoured spacefaring machines programmed to annihilate all living creatures that they encounter. They have been carrying out this mission – virtually unopposed – for thousands of years by the time they meet the expanding interstellar empire of humankind. Although most starfaring races have become too refined to be effective fighters, human beings

I AIN'T GOT NO BODY AL *(DEAN STOCKWELL)* AND SAM BECKETT *(SCOTT BAKULA)* IN TV'S QUANTUM LEAP. *THE FAST-PACED DIALOGUE THESE CHARACTERS MAINTAIN KEEPS THE SHOW LIVELY*

have retained all their barbaric virility: their centuries-long war against the Berserkers is a series of hard-fought victories. The phases of the war are chronicled in five further novels and five more collections, one of them including material by other authors. The Berserkers are the ultimate symbols of mechanical "otherness". Their efficiency and implacability are awesome, but their inflexibility is continually exploited by adversaries who possess cunning as well as courage, and a better kind of intelligence. In the end, therefore, they serve to glorify the things we humans value in ourselves.

Big Brother

CREATOR: GEORGE ORWELL
SOURCE: NINETEEN EIGHTY-FOUR (NOVEL)
DATE: 1949
Dictator of the future state of Oceania, who **Winston Smith** learns to "love" – i.e. to obey. Big Brother is never actually seen in the novel, but he is a looming presence in everyone's mind. A sequel by another hand, *1985: A Historical Report* by Hungarian writer Gyorgy Dalos (1982), provides a description of Oceania's history after the death of Big Brother.

Bill and Ted

CREATORS: CHRIS MATHESON AND STEPHEN HEREK
SOURCE: BILL & TED'S EXCELLENT ADVENTURE (FILM)
DATE: 1989
Dopey, slang-spouting teenagers (Alex Winter and Keanu Reeves) whose blithe innocence allows them to meet all challenges effectively – including, in *Bill & Ted's Bogus Journey* (1991), an encounter with Death. The dependence of the laid-back people of the future on the as-yet-unrealized achievements of their band Wild Stallyns is an amusing conceit.

Bill The Galactic Hero

CREATOR: HARRY HARRISON
SOURCE: BILL THE GALACTIC HERO (NOVEL)
DATE: 1965
A hapless farm boy shanghaied into the Imperial Space Corps to fight the reptilian Chingers. He endures a series of blackly comic catastrophes, losing his foolish ideals and various body-parts, ending up as the kind of hard-bitten hero who would sell his own brother for a month less service-time. His scathing satirization of the kind of starship trooper previously glorified by

various other sf writers gave way to rather aimless slapstick when his career resumed in 1989 in a series of calculatedly silly sequels by other hands.

Roj Blake

CREATOR: TERRY NATION
SOURCE: BLAKE'S 7 (BBC TV SERIES)
DATE: 1978
The leader of a resistance movement against an oppressive interstellar Federation, who is put aboard a prison ship after being framed by his adversaries. After escaping with other prisoners in an alien starship, which he renames *Liberator*, Blake – gruffly played by Gareth Thomas – becomes a kind of interstellar Robin Hood: a man of stout heart and infinite resource (the latter aided in later adventures by the supercomputer ORAC). He was, alas, constantly upstaged by the cold-hearted cynic Avon, who was much sexier. Blake's removal from the series at the end of its second season was suitably heroic, but his brief reappearance in the final episode was murkily ambiguous. Perhaps he really had become a ruthless and cynical bounty-hunter, but anyone with an ounce of sensitivity would far rather believe that it was merely a cunning ploy that went tragically awry.

THE MAGNIFICENT SEVEN *THE CREW OF THE LIBERATOR IN BBC TV'S BLAKE'S 7, WITH ROJ BLAKE (GARETH THOMAS) IN THE CENTRE*

The Blob

CREATORS: THEODORE SIMONSON AND IRVIN S. YEARWORTH, JR.

SOURCE: *THE BLOB* (FILM)

DATE: 1958

A treacly mass that grows by absorbing the flesh of any and all victims after arriving on Earth in a meteorite. It is vulnerable to extreme cold – a weakness which allows its career to be cut short. It was recast as a biological warfare experiment-gone-wrong in the 1988 remake.

The Body Snatchers

CREATOR: JACK FINNEY

SOURCE: *THE BODY SNATCHERS* (NOVEL)

DATE: 1955

Alien vegetables whose "pods" are somewhat reminiscent of giant marrows until they turn into replicas of human beings, after which they are distinguishable from the originals only by their dispirited lack of emotion. Don Siegel employed the motif as the ultimate allegory of Cold War paranoia in the film *Invasion Of The Body Snatchers* (1956).

Brick Bradford

CREATORS: WILLIAM RITT AND CLARENCE GRAY

SOURCE: NEWSPAPER COMIC STRIP

DATE: 1933

Red-haired spaceman hero (one of the rivals to **Buck Rogers**) who enjoyed a vigorous space-operatic career for many decades, syndicated to American papers. The cinema serial *Brick Bradford* (1947) starred Kane Richmond.

Professor Branestawm

CREATOR: NORMAN HUNTER

SOURCE: *THE INCREDIBLE ADVENTURES OF PROFESSOR BRANESTAWM* (CHILDREN'S BOOK)

DATE: 1933

Crackpot inventor who builds impractical machines (famously illustrated by W. Heath Robinson). The Professor was still causing merry mayhem in books such as *Professor Branestawm's Perilous Pudding* (1979) and *Professor Branestawm's Hair-Raising Idea* (1983), and he has also appeared on BBC radio and in a television series (1969).

Nathan Brazil

CREATOR: JACK L. CHALKER

SOURCE: *MIDNIGHT AT THE WELL OF SOULS* (NOVEL)

DATE: 1977

Master and sole crew-member of the starship *Stehekin*, who enjoys a hectic series of adventures on the enigmatic Well World before discovering his true nature – and then has to go through it all over again in a later volume in the series before coming into his astonishing heritage.

Captain Nathan Bridger

CREATORS: ROCKNE O'BANNON AND TOMMY THOMPSON

SOURCE: *SEAQUEST DSV* (TV SERIES)

DATE: 1993

Master of the super-submarine *SeaQuest DSV*, played by Roy Scheider with the earnest intensity appropriate to the educational sub-texts which were added to the first season scripts. His perplexed expression may have reflected the show's development problems, but he stayed with his ship for the revamped second series.

—◦◦◦—

Calhoun

CREATOR: MURRAY LEINSTER

SOURCE: 'RIBBON IN THE SKY' (NOVELETTE)

DATE: 1957

A doctor in the Interstellar Medical Service, which provides a tenuous link between the squabbling worlds of a galactic civilization. With the aid of his inarticulate alien partner Murgatroyd, he brings an unfailing ingenuity to the solution of problems in which the political and the medical are inextricably entwined.

Callahan

CREATOR: SPIDER ROBINSON

SOURCE: *CALLAHAN'S CROSSTIME SALOON* (STORY COLLECTION)

DATE: 1977

The amiable proprietor of a bar whose clientele includes time-travellers, aliens, telepaths and anyone else who might have an interesting tale to tell. Like all good bartenders, he is a constant source of moral support for the deserving but is not a man to get on the wrong side of.

Susan Calvin

CREATOR: ISAAC ASIMOV

SOURCE: *I, ROBOT* (STORY COLLECTION)

DATE: 1950

A pioneering robopsychologist whose account of the evolution of positronic robots governed by the famous three laws of robotics – in which she played a leading part – forms the frame-narrative of the classic collection. Her inability to form rewarding human relationships is more than compensated for by her empathy with robots, whose cause she champions tirelessly.

Jake Cardigan

CREATORS: WILLIAM SHATNER AND RON GOULART

SOURCE: *TEKWAR* (NOVEL)

DATE: 1989

A private eye in 22nd-century Los Angeles who displays the conventional virtues of his species, while pursuing justice through the mean streets, aided by a wisecracking robot. He survives being fitted up and sentenced to four years in coma to undertake further knight-errantry in further volumes.

Jherek Carnelian

CREATOR: MICHAEL MOORCOCK

SOURCE: *THE DANCERS AT THE END OF TIME* (NOVEL SERIES)

DATE: 1972

A holy innocent among the immortal inhabitants of a far future, when everyone must find ingenious ways to stave off the ennui of absolute power. He carefully cultivates an obsession with the morals and manners of the distant past, which provides temporary distraction by allowing him to taste the bittersweetness of humanity.

John Carter

CREATOR: EDGAR RICE BURROUGHS

SOURCE: *A PRINCESS OF MARS* (NOVEL)

DATE: 1912

Nineteenth-century Confederate army officer, a

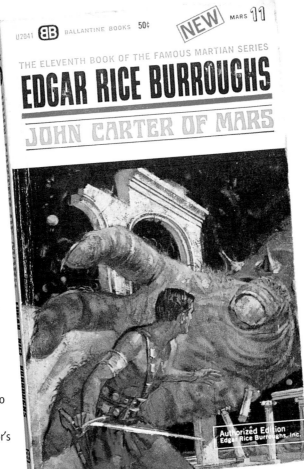

LIFE ON MARS *John Carter takes sword against an archetypal menace in the final volume of the famous series of planetary romances by Burroughs*

perfect Southern gentleman, who is waylaid by hostile Indians in the American West but suddenly finds himself transported by magical means to Barsoom (which turns out to be the planet Mars). There, among the evocatively described canals, rotting cities and dead sea-bottoms of an ancient world, he fights giant green men and other monstrosities, and falls in love with a beautiful, red-skinned, egg-laying princess, **Dejah Thoris**. At the cliff-hanging climax of the tale, he is returned to Earth again, much against his will. This swashbuckling planetary romance, its author's first attempt at fiction, was originally published in the legendary *All-Story* pulp magazine and eventually reached book form five years later (1917). Its immediate sequels, *The Gods Of Mars* (1918) and *The Warlord Of Mars* (1919), tell of Carter's return to the red planet and continue to chronicle his rise to power in Barsoomian society. The later novels in the series often relegate him to a secondary role, although he does come to the fore again in a number of them: *Thuvia, Maid Of Mars* (1920), *The Chessmen Of Mars* (1922), *The Master Mind Of Mars* (1928), *A Fighting Man Of Mars* (1931), *Swords Of Mars* (1936), *Synthetic Men Of Mars* (1940), *Llana Of Gathol* (1948), and the posthumously published *John Carter Of Mars* (1964; one of the two stories in this volume is probably not by Burroughs). Strangely enough, there have been no cinema or television adaptations of John Carter's adventures (although a film has been rumoured for years), but he has had several incarnations as a character in newspaper strips and comic books. Burroughs's son, John Coleman Burroughs, drew a strip version of *A Princess Of Mars* in 1941, and this was followed by a comic book in the 1950s. After the great revival of Burroughs's popularity in the 1960s and 70s, Marvel Comics launched their *John Carter, Warlord Of Mars* in 1977.

Case

Creator: William Gibson
Source: *Neuromancer* (novel)
Date: 1984

An outlaw who recovers the precious ability to plug himself into the worldwide computer network and launch a simulacrum of himself into the cyberspace where data are lodged. A loner who cannot hack it in the mundane world, he becomes superhuman in his preferred environment – a capability which made him a vivid role model for countless computer-nerd wannabes.

Catwoman

Creator: Bob Kane
Source: DC Comics
Date: 1940

Originally called the Cat, Catwoman became the most ambiguous of all **Batman's** opponents: an incarnation of the dangers of female sexuality which might woo Bruce Wayne away from his mission. Julie Newmar played her stylishly in the

1960s TV series, and Michelle Pfeiffer added a wonderful intensity to her dual personality in *Batman Returns* (1992).

Mr Cavor

Creator: H. G. Wells
Source: *The First Men In The Moon* (novel)
Date: 1901

"Short, round-bodied, thin-legged little man, with a jerky quality in his motions," who chooses "to clothe his extraordinary mind in a cricket cap, an overcoat, and cycling knickerbockers and stockings". He is the inventor of "Cavorite", a substance which counters gravity. By enclosing themselves in an airtight sphere which is coated with this remarkable material, Mr Cavor and his friend Mr Bedford are able to fly to the Moon. Bedford eventually returns to Earth, but Cavor is stranded in caverns beneath the Moon's surface where he confronts the Grand Lunar, ruler of all the Selenites. The unsatisfactory film of the novel (1964) starred Lionel Jeffries as Cavor. A sequel by another hand is the novella 'The Ant-Men Of Tibet' by Stephen Baxter (*Interzone*, May 1995), in which we learn how Cavor comes to a sticky end on the Moon.

George Edward Challenger

Creator: Arthur Conan Doyle
Source: *The Lost World* (novel)
Date: 1912

Black-bearded British scientist of ferocious temperament. Together with the eminent explorer Lord John Roxton and the young newspaper reporter Edward Malone, Professor Challenger goes in search of "Maple White Land", a mysterious plateau in South America. There, they discover living dinosaurs and ape-men. Doyle revived the irascible and opinionated Professor for two later novels, *The Poison Belt* (1913) and *The Land Of*

Sir Arthur Conan Doyle
THE POISON BELT
Together with 'THE DISINTEGRATION MACHINE' and 'WHEN THE WORLD SCREAMED'

A PROFESSOR CHALLENGER STORY

Mist (1926), as well as a couple of short stories – all of which are collected in the omnibus volume *The Professor Challenger Stories*. The silent-movie version of *The Lost World* (1925) starred Wallace Beery as Challenger, and was celebrated in its day for its advanced special effects. The remake (1960), with Claude Rains, was less impressive.

Chocky

CREATOR: JOHN WYNDHAM
SOURCE: *CHOCKY* (NOVEL)
DATE: 1963

Friendly alien invader of a young boy's mind. Originally a story in *Amazing* (book form, 1968), it was adapted by Anthony Read for Thames TV (1984), with Glynis Brooks providing Chocky's voice. The sequels, *Chocky's Children* (1985) and *Chocky's Challenge* (1986), were also by Read.

Malachi Constant

CREATOR: KURT VONNEGUT
SOURCE: *THE SIRENS OF TITAN* (NOVEL)
DATE: 1959

An exceedingly fortunate man who believes that somebody "up there" must like him. He is shanghaied to Mars and spends time in the caves of Mercury before arriving on Titan to discover the awful folly of his – and humankind's – delusion.

Dr Conway

CREATOR: JAMES WHITE
SOURCE: *HOSPITAL STATION* (STORY COLLECTION)
DATE: 1962

A doctor attached to Sector General, a galactic hospital that treats members of countless alien species, known and unknown. Often in collaboration with the psychologist O'Mara, Conway brings affectionate sensitivity and clever rationality to the tricky business of diagnosis and treatment.

Dr Coppelius

CREATOR: E. T. A. HOFFMANN
SOURCE: 'THE SANDMAN' (STORY)
DATE: 1816

Sinister master of a beautiful female automaton.

The ballet *Coppélia*, by Léo Delibes (1870), was based on the tale, as was the opera *Tales Of Hoffmann* by Jacques Offenbach (1881) and the film of the latter (1951).

Tom Corbett

CREATOR: ROBERT A. HEINLEIN (INDIRECTLY)
SOURCE: *TOM CORBETT – SPACE CADET* (TV SERIES)
DATE: 1950

The heroic young pioneer of TV's pioneer sf series for young viewers, loosely based on Heinlein's *Space Cadet* (1948), played by Frankie Thomas. Keen, clean-cut and broadcast live, the hero was popular enough to give rise to eight spin-off books.

STRANGE FRUIT *JERRY CORNELIUS (JON FINCH) IN THE STRANGE FILM VERSION OF MICHAEL MOORCOCK'S EVEN STRANGER NOVEL, THE FINAL PROGRAMME*

Jerry Cornelius

CREATOR: MICHAEL MOORCOCK
SOURCE: *THE FINAL PROGRAMME* (NOVEL)
DATE: 1968

Chameleon-like anti-hero of a series of Pop-Art sf novels. A long-haired, pill-popping young man of ambivalent sexuality, he has the ability to travel through the many parallel worlds of the "Multiverse". Later Cornelius titles by Moorcock are *A Cure For Cancer* (1971), *The English Assassin* (1972), *The Adventures Of Una Persson And Catherine Cornelius In The Twentieth Century* (1976), *The Lives And Times Of Jerry Cornelius* (1976), *The Condition Of Muzak* (1977; winner of

the Guardian fiction prize), *The Great Rock 'n' Roll Swindle* (1980; in which Jerry meets the Sex Pistols), *The Entropy Tango* (1981) and *The Opium General And Other Stories* (1984). A number of short sequels by other hands are collected in the anthology *The Nature Of The Catastrophe* (1971), edited by Moorcock and Langdon Jones. The character also makes guest appearances in some of Moorcock's 'Eternal Champion' fantasies. Jerry's Cockney mother, the redoubtable Honoria Cornelius, reappears in Moorcock's most ambitious novels, *Byzantium Endures* (1981), *The Laughter Of Carthage* (1984) and *Jerusalem Commands* (1992). Moorcock's work is exceedingly complex; characters recur and series overlap with joyous abandon. Jerry Cornelius has also featured in a comic strip, initially drawn by Mal Dean, later by R. Glyn Jones, which was published in the "underground" paper *International Times*, circa 1969-1970. The film *The Final Programme* (1973), which was released in the US as *The Last Days Of Man On Earth*, starred Jon Finch as the mercurial Jerry.

Mitchell "Mitch" Courtenay

CREATORS: FREDERIK POHL AND CYRIL M. KORNBLUTH
SOURCE: *THE SPACE MERCHANTS* (NOVEL)
DATE: 1953

An ambitious advertising executive who is kidnapped and stripped of his identity after his agency lands the Venus Project account. He is forced to learn what life as a mere consumer is like, and becomes severely disenchanted with his profession and the world which it has helped to create.

The Creature

CREATORS: HARRY ESSEX AND ARTHUR ROSS
SOURCE: *THE CREATURE FROM THE BLACK LAGOON* (FILM)
DATE: 1954

Also known as the Gill Man, an aquatic monster found far up the Amazon. The first film was made in 3D and given an adults-only certificate. Played by various stuntmen in rubber suits, the Creature spawned two sequels in *Revenge Of The Creature* (1955) and *The Creature Walks Among Us* (1956).

Croyd

CREATOR: IAN WALLACE
SOURCE: CROYD (NOVEL)
DATE: 1967

A vanVogtian superman who is continually forced to stretch his extraordinary mental powers to the limit in saving galactic civilization – of which he is effectively the ruler – from a series of apocalyptic threats. The ultimate power-fantasy protagonist for readers with a sense of style.

Cthulhu

CREATOR: H. P. LOVECRAFT
SOURCE: 'THE CALL OF CTHULHU' (STORY)
DATE: 1928

Alien god of the elder days, centre of the so-called "Cthulhu Mythos", elaborated after Lovecraft's death by August Derleth and others in anthologies such as *The Mask Of Cthulhu* (1958) and *The Trail Of Cthulhu* (1962).

The Daleks

CREATOR: TERRY NATION
SOURCE: DOCTOR WHO (BBC TV SERIES)
DATE: 1963

Tin-can aliens on wheels whose monotonous voices, threatening to "exterminate" all who cross their path, became one of the most familiar sounds on British television. According to Nigel Robinson (*Time Out*, 1 January 1982), "the Daleks were

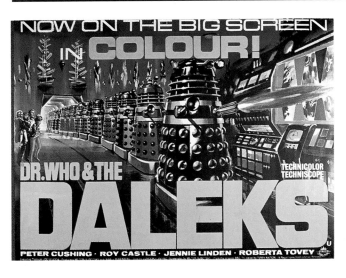

WE WILL EXTERMINATE *THE DALEKS APPEARED ON THE CINEMA SCREEN AS WELL AS ON TV – AS SEEN HERE IN A POSTER FOR THE FILM STARRING PETER CUSHING AS DR WHO*

WHERE EAGLES DARE *FRANK HAMPSON'S DAN DARE STRIP WAS AMONG THE FINEST COMIC ART OF ITS DAY, PROVOKING A GREAT SENSE OF NOSTALGIA IN OLDER READERS*

not the sole reason for the show's early success, but they did push the audience from three million to eight million."

Dan Dare

CREATOR: FRANK HAMPSON
SOURCE: *EAGLE* (COMIC)
DATE: 1950

Heroic space pilot featured in the lead comic strip of the British boys' paper *Eagle* until 1967. Dan is a wholesome, strong-jawed hero with rather Satanic eyebrows: in effect, he is an updated version of the ideal Battle of Britain pilot. He serves as a colonel in the Interplanetary Space Fleet, and, with his "batman" Digby, he has adventures on the planet Venus and further afield. His arch-enemy is the dome-headed **Mekon.** The strips were conceived, drawn and written by Hampson, and later carried on by other hands. Dan Dare proved extremely popular, and his adventures were adapted for the radio and children's books. Noel Johnson played Dan Dare on Radio Luxembourg, 1951-56. According to James Slattery, in his introduction to the reprint volume *Dan Dare, Pilot Of The Future* in

The Man From Nowhere (1979), "everybody read Dan Dare – Cabinet ministers along with Rhondda Valley schoolboys. And in the 50s, the exploitation of the characters and craft in the strip by commercial concerns was almost ridiculous – the young fanatic could skip out of his Dan Dare pyjamas, into his Dan Dare slippers and dressing gown, brush his teeth with Calvert's Dan Dare toothpaste, all before checking that it was time (on his Dan Dare watch) to kit up in his Dan Dare T-shirt, belt, scarf, spacesuit, etc..." There were attempts to revive a Dan Dare strip in the 1970s (in *2000 A.D.* comic) and in the 1980s (in a new *Eagle*), but, lacking the visual flair of Hampson, Dan's later adventures have proved disappointing.

A book, *The Man Who Drew Tomorrow* by Alastair Crompton (1985), tells the story of Hampson's career; it is amusing to note that the *Eagle*, begun by the Rev. Marcus Morris, was intended as a Christian propaganda comic. Whatever the intentions of his creators, Dan Dare is recalled nostalgically by many British sf readers of a certain age as their first and most reliable fictitious guide to the marvellous world of the future.

Davy

CREATOR: EDGAR PANGBORN

SOURCE: *DAVY* (NOVEL)

DATE: 1964

A runaway stableboy who grows to maturity as an outlaw in a post-holocaust world. He is a typical picaresque hero – pugnacious, randy and generally irrepressible – whose hard-won understanding of himself and the folkways of his misfortunate world serves to dramatize its awful tragedy.

Rick Deckard

CREATOR: PHILIP K. DICK

SOURCE: *DO ANDROIDS DREAM OF ELECTRIC SHEEP?* (NOVEL)

DATE: 1968

A bounty hunter for the San Francisco police whose job is "retiring" rogue androids. As the androids he hunts become less easily distinguishable from human beings, he is thrust into a turmoil of doubt as to the morality of his work, the significance of the empathy he feels for his victims and the value of his relationship with his wife as well as his involvement with a commercially-marketed messiah. The unmarried and unreligious Deckard of Ridley Scott's film *Blade Runner* (1982) has far less depth than the novel's protagonist, although Harrison Ford tried hard to seem sufficiently tortured – and the

MAN AGAINST MACHINE *A GRIM-FACED RICK DECKARD (HARRISON FORD) IN RIDLEY SCOTT'S BLADE RUNNER, BASED ON PHILIP K. DICK'S RATHER DIFFERENT CHARACTER*

teasing possibility that he might be an android himself is retained. The recent production of a spin-off book by K. W. Jeter has put the movie version of Deckard into print for the first time, and the resultant confusion about which Deckard is the real one, and which is not, has a certain ironic propriety.

Dejah Thoris

CREATOR: EDGAR RICE BURROUGHS

SOURCE: *A PRINCESS OF MARS* (NOVEL)

DATE: 1912 (BOOK 1917)

A red-skinned, egg-laying Martian princess whose narrative function is to be continually threatened by fates worse than death, so that she can be rescued by the heroic **John Carter**. Other heroines relieved her of this burdensome duty in some of the later sequels, but she was special because she was the first.

Arthur Dent

CREATOR: DOUGLAS ADAMS

SOURCE: *THE HITCH HIKER'S GUIDE TO THE GALAXY* (BBC RADIO SERIAL)

DATE: 1978

A bemused Englishman who becomes the involuntary hero of a space epic when the Earth is threatened with demolition in order to make way for a hyperspace bypass. Dent was played by Simon Jones. Other notable characters from the series are **Zaphod Beeblebrox, Marvin the Paranoid Android**, and the unfortunately-named Slartibartfast – not to mention a mighty computer called Deep Thought. Douglas Adams went on to write a bestselling book, also entitled *The Hitch Hiker's Guide To The Galaxy* (1980), which was followed by several sequels: *The Restaurant At The End Of The Universe* (1981), *Life, The Universe And Everything* (1982), *So Long, And Thanks For All The Fish* (1983) and *Mostly Harmless* (1992). A BBC television series

JUDGE, JURY AND EXECUTIONER *JUDGE JOE DREDD, THE MOST BAROQUE AND ORNAMENTAL LAW-ENFORCER EVER CONCEIVED*

(1981) was based on the radio serial, with Simon Jones repeating his role as Arthur Dent.

Judge Dredd

CREATORS: PAT MILLS, CARLOS EZQUERRA AND JOHN WAGNER

SOURCE: *2000 A.D.* (COMIC)

DATE: 1977

Joe Dredd, a heavily-armed, helmeted law-enforcer of the futuristic Mega-City One. His adventures are recounted in a British comic strip which has been reprinted in numerous large-format paperback books. Many artists have worked on the strip over the years, including, most notably, Mike McMahon and Brian Bolland. The ultra-violent Judge Dredd has become the most admired of contemporary comic-book characters in the UK, a cynical **Dan Dare** for the 1980s and 90s. A series of spinoff novels began with *The Savage Amusement* by David Bishop and *Deathmasques* by Dave Stone (both 1993). The long-awaited movie *Judge Dredd* (1995) starred Sylvester Stallone.

Jason dinAlt

CREATOR: HARRY HARRISON
SOURCE: *DEATHWORLD* (NOVEL)
DATE: 1960

A wandering gambler and spaceman of fortune whose readiness to meet new challenges is tested to the full by a series of commissions that take him to some extremely hostile environments. His ability to judge risks always allows him to stay alive, albeit by the narrowest of margins.

W. H. Donovan

CREATOR: CURT SIODMAK
SOURCE: *DONOVAN'S BRAIN* (NOVEL)
DATE: 1943

Kept alive as a disembodied brain after suffering terrible injuries in a car crash, mail-order magnate Donovan becomes more domineering than ever, achieving telepathic dominion over a young scientist. In the 1953 film (the second of three), the possessed scientist was memorably played by Lew Ayres.

The Dragonriders of Pern

CREATOR: ANNE MCCAFFREY
SOURCE: *DRAGONFLIGHT* (NOVEL)
DATE: 1968

The Cinderella-like Lessa and her male counterpart F'lar became the prototypes of a whole series of similar characters who stock the individual works in the long-running Pern series. She is feminine and intuitive, while he is masculine and logical, but their developing relationship makes them both better-balanced. Their relationship with one another is, however, far less important than their empathy with the psychically gifted alien dragons they ride: an intimacy far deeper than anything possible between human beings, forged by bonding immediately after their dragon partners hatch. Later volumes in the series replace Lessa with a variety of other initially unassuming heroines, who are by no means mere clones. She made occasional further appearances, playing a more maternal role.

Earl Dumarest

CREATOR: E. C. TUBB
SOURCE: *THE WINDS OF GATH* (NOVEL)
DATE: 1967

Dour space-opera hero who searches for his long-lost home-planet, Earth, through a very long series of repetitive adventures. Later 'Dumarest' novels include *Derai* (1968), *Toyman* (1969), *Kalin* (1969), *The Jester At Scar* (1970), *Lallia* (1971), *Technos* (1972), *Mayenne* (1973), *Veruchia* (1973), *Jondelle* (1973), *Zenya* (1974), and many more up to the mid-1980s.

E.T.

CREATORS: MELISSA MATHISON AND STEVEN SPIELBERG
SOURCE: *E.T.: THE EXTRA-TERRESTRIAL* (FILM)
DATE: 1982

A "little squashy guy" from outer space who is befriended by the children of a Californian household. E.T. is a gentle soul who has come to Earth in search of plant specimens; he gets stranded and is afraid. Given refuge by the children, he returns their kindness by showing them how to fly. Eventually, he jury-rigs an apparatus which enables him to phone home. He falls ill, apparently dies, and is reborn shortly before the spacecraft returns to carry him away. It is a remarkably moving story, perhaps the only film of recent times that has reduced a large proportion of its worldwide audience to tears. "E.T. phone home" became a catch-phrase of 1982-83, when the movie rapidly established itself as the most commercially successful in Hollywood's history. E.T.'s grotesque but endearing looks were designed by special-effects man Carlo Rambaldi. The script was novelized by William Kotzwinkle, who later wrote a sequel, "based on an original story by Steven Spielberg", called E.T.: The Book Of The Green Planet (1985).

TELEPHONE MAN
SPIELBERG'S E.T.: THE EXTRA-TERRESTRIAL – *A RARE COMBINATION OF ENDEARING AND REPTILIAN*

Palmer Eldritch

CREATOR: PHILIP K. DICK
SOURCE: *THE THREE STIGMATA OF PALMER ELDRITCH* (NOVEL)
DATE: 1965

A cyborg merchant adventurer who returns from an expedition to Proxima Centauri with a lichen whose hallucinogenic derivative Chew-Z seems to be powerful enough to warp reality and impose his personality on its users. His prosthetic arm, jaw and eyes give him a sinister appearance, which is by no means misleading.

The Ethicals

CREATOR: PHILIP JOSÉ FARMER
SOURCE: *TO YOUR SCATTERED BODIES GO* (NOVEL)
DATE: 1971

The mysterious designers of the Riverworld, a vast stage upon which the entirety of humankind is reincarnated. Richard Francis Burton tries to figure out the truth of conflicting rumours by confronting them, after a trip on the "suicide express", but they remain stubbornly elusive through several sequels.

Manse Everard

CREATOR: POUL ANDERSON
SOURCE: *GUARDIANS OF TIME* (STORY COLLECTION)

DATE: 1960

An ex-serviceman and mechanical engineer recruited as an agent by the Time Patrol, whose job is to protect history from chaotic disruption. He is resourceful and tough-minded, as one might expect of a man whose every success really does prevent the end of the world as we know it.

The Ewoks

CREATORS: LAWRENCE KASDAN AND GEORGE LUCAS
SOURCE: *RETURN OF THE JEDI* (FILM)
DATE: 1983

Teddybear-like aliens with squeaky voices, native to the forest-world of Endor, who help **Han Solo** storm a heavily-defended Imperial base. They were popular enough to return as central characters in TV movies and an animated series, proving that "too cute" can be added to "too rich" and "too thin" on the list of things you can never be.

Mr Fantastic

CREATORS: STAN LEE AND JACK KIRBY
SOURCE: MARVEL COMICS
DATE: 1961

Real name Reed Richards, a bendy superhero with enormously stretchable limbs, thanks to the regulation bombardment by cosmic rays. He is the leader of *The Fantastic Four* (the others are the Invisible Girl, the Human Torch and the irascible Thing).

Paul Janus Finnegan

CREATOR: PHILIP JOSÉ FARMER
SOURCE: *THE MAKER OF UNIVERSES* (NOVEL)
DATE: 1965

Better known as Kickaha the Trickster, PJF (note the initials) was a World War II veteran going through college on the G.I. Bill before he gave it up to live a life of adventure in the World of Tiers and the other pocket universes to which it is connected. He is laid-back, streetwise and promiscuous: the 1960s version of **John Carter**.

Dominic Flandry

CREATOR: POUL ANDERSON
SOURCE: 'HONORABLE ENEMIES' (NOVELETTE)
DATE: 1951

An agent of the Terran Empire, equally able to function as soldier, diplomat or spy. The galactic civilization in which he features is modelled on the Europe of Ruritanian romance rather than ancient Rome, and he is strongly reminiscent of the stiff-upper-lipped heroes of that typically British genre. Books in which he appears include *We Claim These Stars* (1959), *Flandry Of Terra* (1965), *Ensign Flandry* (1966), *The Rebel Worlds* (1969; published as *Commander Flandry* in the UK), *A Circus Of Hells* (1970), *The Day Of Their Return* (1973), *A Knight Of Ghosts And Shadows* (1974; published as *Knight Flandry* in the UK) and *A Stone In Heaven* (1979).

The Flash

CREATOR: GARDNER F. FOX
SOURCE: ALL-STAR COMICS
DATE: 1940

A lightning-fast member of the Justice League of America, originally equipped with a tin hat with wings, but reincarnated for the 1960s in a sleek crimson one-piece outfit. His tendency to dissolve into a blur when going into action challenged the ingenuity of his artists, if not their drawing abilities.

The Flintstones

CREATORS: WILLIAM HANNA AND JOSEPH BARBERA
SOURCE: THE FLINTSTONES (TV ANIMATION)
DATE: 1960

Fred and Wilma, stone-agers who lead a typical suburban life amid palaeolithic automobiles and dinosaur-powered appliances. Fred was voiced by Alan Reed and Wilma by Jean Vander Pyle. The live-action film (1994) starred John Goodman and Elizabeth Perkins.

Flinx

CREATOR: ALAN DEAN FOSTER
SOURCE: *THE TAR-AIYM KRANG* (NOVEL)
DATE: 1972

Full name Philip Lynx, a street-urchin from the planet Moth who gets caught up in a madcap scheme to capture an ancient alien superweapon called the Krang. Sequels include *Bloodhype* (1973), *Orphan Star* (1977), *The End Of The Matter* (1977) and *Flinx In Flux* (1988).

The Fly

CREATOR: GEORGE LANGELAAN
SOURCE: 'THE FLY' (SHORT STORY)
DATE: 1957

A hybrid creature produced by a botched experiment in matter-transmission. Al Hedison did his best with very limited resources in the 1958 film, but Jeff Goldblum's fabulously gruesome metamorphosis in David Cronenberg's 1986 version remains unforgettable.

Phileas Fogg

CREATOR: JULES VERNE
SOURCE: *AROUND THE WORLD IN 80 DAYS* (NOVEL)
DATE: 1872

English eccentric who circumnavigates the globe. David Niven starred in the film (1956). An sf sequel is *The Other Log Of Phileas Fogg* by Philip José Farmer (1973), in which Fogg has dealings with aliens from outer space.

Gully Foyle

CREATOR: ALFRED BESTER
SOURCE: *THE STARS MY DESTINATION* (NOVEL)
DATE: 1956

A futuristic version of the Count of Monte Cristo, the violent, vengeful and enigmatically haunted Foyle disguises himself as the effete Geoffrey Fourmyle while plotting to bring down his enemies. His eventual success is a painful but glorious metamorphosis into a strange superhumanity.

Victor Frankenstein

CREATOR: MARY SHELLEY
SOURCE: *FRANKENSTEIN, OR THE MODERN PROMETHEUS* (NOVEL)
DATE: 1818

Eighteenth-century natural philosopher (that is, a scientist) who creates an artificial man, or monster, which he disowns – and which then turns on him, killing those he loves and ruining his life. This fable of over-reaching ambition and

IT'S A WRAP *Victor Frankenstein, played by Peter Cushing, in a Hammer Films version of the story which has little in common with Mary Shelley's original. Films differing wildly from the book have been very popular at the cinema where spoofs such as Abbott And Costello Meet Frankenstein thrived*

fatal retribution was invented by the 19-year-old wife of the poet Percy Shelley. The name "Frankenstein" has become part of modern mythology, and in popular parlance the scientist, Victor Frankenstein, is often confused with his creation, **The Monster** sewn together from bits of various corpses. The macabre story of Frankenstein's hubris and its monstrous nemesis has been immensely influential, and indeed Brian Aldiss and others have claimed it as the inspiration for most subsequent science fiction. Within a few years of the book's publication, it had become a favourite in the form of sensationalized stage adaptations, and such 19th-century melodramas are the direct forbears of the 20th-century movie versions of the story. Modern sequels by other hands include the novels *Frankenstein Unbound* (1973) by Brian

Aldiss (about a 21st-century time-traveller who visits both Mary Shelley and her fictional characters); *The New Adventures Of Frankenstein* (1977) by Donald F. Glut; *The Frankenstein Papers* (1986) by Fred Saberhagen; *Brittle Innings* (1994) by Michael Bishop (a Frankenstein baseball novel, which sounds a weird mixture but was highly praised by critics); and *Frankenstein's Bride* (1995) by Hilary Bailey (an attempt at a "straight" sequel to Shelley). There are also novelizations of many of the films listed here. Early film versions of the story were made in 1910 and 1915, but it seems these no longer exist. Our latter-day conceptions of Frankenstein and his monster owe almost everything to the first Hollywood talkie version, James Whale's *Frankenstein* (1931), which starred Colin Clive as the scientist and Boris

Karloff as his creation. The movie has spawned countless sequels – *The Bride Of Frankenstein* (1935), *Son Of Frankenstein* (1939), *The Ghost Of Frankenstein* (1942), and so on. More recent examples are the British Hammer Films remakes, beginning with *The Curse Of Frankenstein* (1957), which starred Peter Cushing as Frankenstein and Christopher Lee as the monster. Later entries in this series, all with Cushing as the scientist but with various actors standing in as the creature, include *The Revenge Of Frankenstein* (1958), *The Evil Of Frankenstein* (1964), *Frankenstein Created Woman* (1967) and *Frankenstein Must Be Destroyed* (1969). There have also been many spoofs, ranging from *Abbott And Costello Meet Frankenstein* (1948) to *Young Frankenstein* (1974) and far beyond. Two American TV-movie versions of Shelley's novel were made in the same year, 1973; one of them, benefiting from a script by Christopher Isherwood, was rather inaccurately titled *Frankenstein: The True Story*, and had Leonard Whiting as Victor and Michael Sarrazin as the monster. A British independent television version (1984) had Robert Powell as Frankenstein and David Warner as his creature. The most recent filmic attempts to grapple with the material are Roger Corman's *Frankenstein Unbound* (1990), based on Brian Aldiss's sequel, with Raul Julia (scientist) and Nick Brimble (monster); *Frankenstein – The Real Story* (1992), with Patrick Bergin (Victor) and Randy Quaid (creature); and *Mary Shelley's Frankenstein* (1994), with Kenneth Branagh as Frankenstein and Robert De Niro as the pathetic monster – here more closely resembling the depiction in the novel than in most other films.

Captain Future

Creator: Edmond Hamilton
Source: *Captain Future* (pulp magazine)
Date: 1940
Alias Curt Newton, a spacefarer who pursues interstellar bandits and is accompanied by his three weird assistants – a robot, an android, and a "living brain". The magazine ran until 1944, and a number of the novellas were reprinted as paperbacks in the 1960s, when the bold Captain proved popular once again.

THE MOST COLOSSAL CONFLICT THE SCREEN HAS EVER KNOWN!

JOHN BECK
presents

KING KONG
VS.
GODZILLA

PRINT BY
TECHNICOLOR

CERT X
ADULTS ONLY

AND WILD BILL HICKOK...
CALAMITY JANE...BUFFALO BILL... THEY FOUGHT THEM ALL!
THE RAIDERS U

PRINT BY TECHNICOLOR

ROBERT CULP · BRIAN KEITH JUDI MEREDITH JAMES McMULLAN

BEASTLY BEHAVIOUR *The Japanese dinosaur Godzilla had many adversaries, one of the most popular being the giant ape from American movies of the 1930s. The meeting of such great crowd-pulling behemoths obviously seeming a sure-fire hit to the Hollywood moguls*

The Fuzzies

CREATOR: H. Beam Piper
SOURCE: *Little Fuzzy* (novel)
DATE: 1962

Teddybear-like inhabitants of the planet Zarathustra whose intelligence and self-consciousness are in doubt until sunstone prospector Jack Holloway proves the point, saving them from the exploitations of a mining company. They are wise after their own particular fashion, as various sequels set out to demonstrate.

Galloway Gallegher

CREATOR: Henry Kuttner
SOURCE: *Robots Have No Tails* (story collection)
DATE: 1952

A slapdash inventor capable of extraordinary creative feats when drunk, who is usually incapable of understanding what he has wrought when he sobers up – an unfortunate tendency, given that his inventions invariably have problematic bugs that need ironing out.

Garth

CREATORS: Steve Dowling and Don Freeman
SOURCE: *The Daily Mirror*
DATE: 1943

Comic-strip muscleman who enjoys extravagant adventures in time and space, often accompanied by his genius friend Professor Lumière. Talents who worked on the strip in later years include Peter O'Donnell (writer) and Frank Bellamy (artist).

Godzilla

CREATORS: Inoshiro Honda and Takeo Murata
SOURCE: *Gojira* (film)
DATE: 1954

Enormous fire-breathing dinosaur, which threatens to destroy Tokyo, in the Japanese movie released in English as *Godzilla, King Of The Monsters*. The creature is awakened from its sleep, deep in the primordial ooze, by an H-bomb test. (An earlier American film which used a similar idea is *The Beast From 20,000 Fathoms* [1953], based on a story by Ray

Bradbury.) Godzilla has appeared in many subsequent Japanese films and television cartoon series. Movie sequels include *King Kong Vs. Godzilla* (1962), *Godzilla Vs. The Thing* (1964) and *Destroy All Monsters* (1969). An odd spin-off in book form is the seriously-intended novel *Gojiro* (1991) by American writer Mark Jacobson.

Charlie Gordon

CREATOR: Daniel Keyes
SOURCE: 'Flowers For Algernon' (story)
DATE: 1959

Dim-brained man whose intelligence is enhanced to genius level by surgery. Keyes's tale was expanded to book length under the same title (1966). The film *Charly* (1968) starred Cliff Robertson, and was followed by a stage musical featuring Michael Crawford.

Flash Gordon

CREATOR: Alex Raymond
SOURCE: Newspaper comic strip
DATE: 1934

Fair-haired and fearless spaceman hero who has adventures with his girlfriend Dale Arden on the planet Mongo and elsewhere. The cinema serial *Flash Gordon* (1936) starred Buster Crabbe as the hero and Charles Middleton as his arch-enemy, **Ming the Merciless**. Crabbe perpetuated the role in two further serials, *Flash Gordon's Trip To Mars* (1938) and *Flash Gordon Conquers The Universe* (1940). Flash also appeared in an American television series (1953-54), where he was played by Steve Holland. The extravagant feature film *Flash Gordon* (1980) starred Sam J. Jones and featured a soundtrack by the band Queen. An earlier movie, *Flesh Gordon* (1974), is a well-made and quite funny pornographic spoof. There has also been an animated TV movie of Flash's exploits (1981). A series of Flash Gordon novels appeared with Alex Raymond's name on the covers (presumably adapted from the original comic strips); these were the work of "Con Steffanson" (Ron Goulart and Carson Bingham) and included such titles as *The Lion Men Of Mongo, The Plague Of Sound* and *The Space Circus* (all 1974).

SAVIOUR OF THE UNIVERSE
Flash Gordon (Buster Crabbe) with the beautiful Dale Arden (Jean Rogers) in the fondly-remembered cinema serial of the 1930s

Gilbert Gosseyn

Creator: A. E. van Vogt
Source: _The World Of Null-A_ (novel)
Date: 1945 (book 1948)

An amnesiac who quickly learns that he has several bodies and many other superpowers. His burgeoning enables him to play a crucial role in preserving humanity's utopian civilization against invaders from beyond the solar system, but his initial confusion is never entirely cleared away, even in the sequel.

Donal Graeme

Creator: Gordon R. Dickson
Source: _Dorsai!_ (novel)
Date: 1959 (book 1960)

A young cadet in the Dorsai mercenaries whose tactical brilliance and innate sense of responsibility – which makes him into a moral as well as an intellectual superman – win him rapid promotion. He remained the presiding genius of the ensuing series although his personal appearances were infrequent.

Grainger

Creator: Brian Stableford
Source: _Halcyon Drift_ (novel)
Date: 1972

A pilot recruited to operate a prototype starship that can overcome many of the hazards of navigating a problematic hyperspace. A scathingly sarcastic undeclared pacifist, he struggled churlishly but manfully through a whole series of awkward situations in a six-book series.

Green Lantern

Creators: Martin Nodell and Bill Finger
Source: DC Comics
Date: 1940

Alias Alan Scott (later Hal Jordan), a superhero whose amazing "power ring" enables him to fly and to call on forces that can defeat all villainy.

A member of the "Justice Society of America" (along with the Flash, Hawkman, etc), Green Lantern was remodelled in 1959.

Lt. John Grimes

CREATOR: A. BERTRAM CHANDLER
SOURCE: 'TO RUN THE RIM' (NOVELLA)
DATE: 1959

A long-serving officer in interstellar equivalents of the Merchant Navy, ending up in the Rim Worlds Naval Reserve after a stint with the Federation Survey Service – a career whose structure reflects his author's own. He is something of a loner but stays fiercely loyal to the various causes he espouses in numerous sequels.

Lemuel Gulliver

CREATOR: JONATHAN SWIFT
SOURCE: GULLIVER'S TRAVELS (NOVEL)
DATE: 1726

English surgeon aboard a ship wrecked off the coast of Lilliput, an island where the natives are six inches tall. He awakes from his sleep on the beach to discover he has been tied down by the frightened Lilliputians. He befriends his captors, who call him the "man mountain", and later visits Brobdingnag, a land of giants, and Laputa,

SF SATIRE TODAY SWIFT WOULD MAKE GULLIVER A TRAVELLER TO OTHER PLANETS

an island of impractical scientists. Swift's satire, superbly realistic in manner and clearly ancestral to modern sf, has been read widely. It has become a children's classic: bowdlerized and abridged, Gulliver's adventures have been presented to the young in countless editions. Adult sf sequels include two novellas by Hungarian writer Frigyes Karinthy, *Voyage To Faremido* (1917) and *Capillaria* (1921): in the first, Gulliver visits a planet of machines where organic life is regarded as an abomination; in the second, he finds himself in a land where women rule and men are eaten. Films include the animated *Gulliver's Travels* (1939) and the live-action *Three Worlds Of Gulliver* (1960), starring Kerwin Mathews.

Ragle Gumm

CREATOR: PHILIP K. DICK
SOURCE: TIME OUT OF JOINT (NOVEL)
DATE: 1959

A well-meaning man who makes a living using his intuition to solve a daily newspaper puzzle. He eventually finds that his life is a comforting delusion sustained by military men using his talent to anticipate enemy bombings, thus encountering the urgent problem of acute reality-decay.

HAL 9000

CREATOR: ARTHUR C. CLARKE
SOURCE: *2001: A SPACE ODYSSEY* (NOVEL AND FILM)
DATE: 1968

A spacecraft's computer intelligence which malfunctions and murders two of the crew. The surviving human dismantles the computer's memory, and HAL regresses to mental infancy, singing "Daisy, Daisy..." In the sequel, *2010: Odyssey Two* (1982), HAL is reactivated by the crew of another spaceship.

Gil Hamilton

CREATOR: LARRY NIVEN
SOURCE: THE LONG ARM OF GIL HAMILTON (STORY COLLECTION)
DATE: 1976

A psychically talented officer in a global police force who retains an effective "phantom arm" in spite of the fact that the lost limb has been replaced. It is, however, his intelligence and ingenuity which enable him to solve the intricate puzzles that confront him.

Hammer's Slammers

CREATOR: DAVID DRAKE
SOURCE: HAMMER'S SLAMMERS (STORY COLLECTION)
DATE: 1979

A corps of space mercenaries licked into fearsome shape by Colonel Alois Hammer, who is an odd combination of cynic and idealist. The conflicts in which they become embroiled are exotic, but the starkly realistic treatment of combat situations draws on the author's own military experience.

Jeff Hawke

CREATORS: SIDNEY JORDAN AND ERIC SOUSTER
SOURCE: THE DAILY EXPRESS
DATE: 1954

Brave astronaut hero of a comic strip which ran for two decades. A British equivalent of **Buck Rogers** or **Flash Gordon**, Hawke became embroiled in much derring-do on the space frontier.

Max Headroom

CREATORS: GEORGE STONE AND STEVE ROBERTS
SOURCE: MAX HEADROOM (TV FILM)
DATE: 1985

Disembodied pop-video presenter played by Matt Frewer in Channel 4 Television's *The Max Headroom Show* (1985). Supposedly a computer-generated image, Max has "a permanent suntan, improbably white teeth, the squarest of jawbones, a high forehead and the bluest of eyes". He also stutters. A picture book about the character is entitled *Max Headroom: 20 Minutes Into The Future* (1985). Max was repackaged for an American TV series in 1987-88, with Matt Frewer reprising the role.

Robert Hedrock

CREATOR: A. E. VAN VOGT
SOURCE: THE WEAPON MAKERS (NOVEL)
DATE: 1943 (BOOK 1946)

 RUBBERHEAD *MAX HEADROOM (MATT FREWER), THE COMPUTER-GENERATED MAN, A CULT SUCCESS ON BOTH BRITISH AND AMERICAN TELEVISION*

An immortal superman who creates the Weapon Shops as a means to secure individual liberty against government oppression. He is forced to defend them against the hostility of Isher Empress Innelda, and does so with the awesome competence of a typical van Vogtian hero.

The Heechee

CREATOR: FREDERIK POHL
SOURCE: *GATEWAY* (NOVEL)
DATE: 1977

The skeletal alien Heechee, who have gone into hiding because of the threat to all life posed by the mysterious Assassins, do not actually appear on stage until *Heechee Rendezvous* (1984), but they are present in spirit throughout the series in which humans use their hazardous abandoned artefacts to expand into interstellar space.

He-Man and She-Ra

CREATOR: MATTEL TOYS
SOURCES: *HE-MAN AND THE MASTERS OF THE UNIVERSE* AND *SHE-RA, PRINCESS OF POWER* (TV ANIMATION)
DATES: 1983, 1985

He-Man, alias Prince Adam of Eternia, heir to the secrets of Castle Grayskull, uses his magic sword to thwart the plans of the evil Skeletor. She-Ra is his twin sister Adora, raised in ignorance of her identity on the planet Etheria, who is briefly his adversary before taking her place alongside him. Dolph Lundgren played He-Man in the 1987 film.

Dominick Hide

CREATORS: ALAN GIBSON AND JEREMY PAUL
SOURCE: *THE FLIPSIDE OF DOMINICK HIDE* (BBC TV FILM)
DATE: 1980

A prim young pilot from the staid London of 2130 (Peter Firth) who time-warps his flying saucer back to the present day and is affectionately loosened up by a girl (Caroline Langrishe). She enables him to become his own ancestor. He revisited her in *Another Flip For Dominick* (1982).

Howard The Duck

CREATOR: STEVE GERBER
SOURCE: MARVEL COMICS
DATE: 1973

Rebellious intellectual duck from another dimension of space and time. An unlikely superhero, Howard quickly became a cult figure. He was even thrust forward as a prospective candidate in the 1976 Presidential election. The comic-book series was discontinued in 1979 when Gerber left Marvel, and a revival of Howard the Duck in 1985 was generally deemed less successful. Howard has been described as "the single most anarchic and essential character ever created in mainstream comics" (Mick Mercer, *New Musical Express*, 26 October 1985). He has since featured in his own movie, *Howard The Duck* (1986; also released as *Howard – A New Breed Of Hero*), where he was played by a whole succession of midget actors in duck costumes.

Hope Hubris

CREATOR: PIERS ANTHONY
SOURCE: *BIO OF A SPACE TYRANT* (NOVEL SERIES)
DATES: 1983-86

An archetype of ruthless ambition, who rises to power without the merest trace of a scruple but is ultimately forced by his position to make the uncomfortable moral choices that temper his fiery character.

The Humanoids

CREATOR: JACK WILLIAMSON
SOURCE: 'WITH FOLDED HANDS' (NOVELETTE)
DATE: 1947

Robots created with a prime directive "to serve and obey and guard men from harm" who take the latter part of the instruction to extremes at the expense of the former. The conclusion of *The Humanoids* (1949) – originally titled "...And Searching Mind" – addresses the issues raised with unusual even-handedness.

The Incredible Hulk

CREATOR: STAN LEE AND JACK KIRBY
SOURCE: MARVEL COMICS
DATE: 1962

Also known as Dr Bruce Banner, a meek scientist who every now and again metamorphoses into a huge green-skinned

GREEN GIANT MARVEL COMICS'S MUSCLEBOUND INCREDIBLE HULK ATTRACTS MANY CHALLENGERS, DESPITE THE BLATANT WARNING SIGNS (AGGRESSIVE BEHAVIOUR, GREEN SKIN, DISTRESSED CLOTHING...)

humanoid, apparently brainless and ravening (but curiously law-abiding, since it is usually villains that he stomps on). Banner's career as a part-time monster began during a bomb test when he found himself accidentally "bathed in the full force of the mysterious gamma rays". Now, whenever he is possessed by anger, he turns into the Hulk, and on reverting to normal shape he has no memory of his actions as the green brute. This modern variation on *Dr Jekyll And Mr Hyde* is one of the most absurdly memorable characters to have sprung from American comic books. The Hulk also appeared in the animated television series *Marvel Superheroes* (1966-68), and subsequently in his own live-action series which commenced with the TV movie *The Incredible Hulk* (1977). The latter series, which ran until 1982, starred Bill Bixby as Dr Banner (his forename changed to David) and muscleman Lou Ferrigno as his green alter ego. One critic has described the TV Hulk in memorable terms: he "has the standard body-builder's physique, with two sets of shoulders one on top of the other and wings of lateral muscle that hold his arms out from his sides as if his armpits had piles. He is made remarkable by his avocado complexion [and] eyes like plover's eggs." The series was

very popular with kids the world over, a fact reflected in the successful merchandising of Hulk dolls, Hulk T-shirts, and other trivia. There have been several Incredible Hulk novels, including *Murdermoon* (1979) by Paul Kupperberg – in which he meets **Spider-Man**. Recent "come-back" TV movies featuring the character include *The Incredible Hulk Returns* (1988), with Bill Bixby and Lou Ferrigno reprising their roles, and *The Death Of The Incredible Hulk* (1990), with the same cast.

David Innes

CREATOR: EDGAR RICE BURROUGHS
SOURCE: *AT THE EARTH'S CORE* (NOVEL)
DATE: 1914

American action-man who journeys deep under the Earth's surface in scientist Abner Perry's wonderful Iron Mole: "a steel cylinder a hundred feet long, and jointed so that it may turn and twist through solid rock if need be. At one end is a mighty revolving drill..." Innes and Perry discover the hidden land of Pellucidar, a place of everlasting daylight (radiated by a central "sun"), where time seems not to exist and prehistoric beasts still roam. Their exciting adventure story was serialized in *All-Story* pulp magazine, and eventually published in book form in 1922. Burroughs's sequels are *Pellucidar* (1923), *Tanar Of Pellucidar* (1929), *Tarzan At The Earth's Core* (1930; in which David Innes meets another of his author's creations, Tarzan of the Apes, far from his African jungle), *Back To The Stone Age* (1937), *Land Of Terror* (1944) and the posthumously published *Savage Pellucidar* (1963). The author's son, John Coleman Burroughs, drew a newspaper comic-strip entitled 'Dave Innes Of Pellucidar' (from 1940). The hero also appeared in a British-produced film, *At The Earth's Core* (1976), where he was played by Doug McClure.

The Invisible Man

CREATOR: H. G. WELLS
SOURCE: *THE INVISIBLE MAN* (NOVEL)
DATE: 1897

Dr Griffin, an over-reaching English scientist who discovers the secret of invisibility, tests the result on himself, and is driven mad by the

consequences. The celebrated film of the book (1933) starred Claude Rains, for the most part swathed in bandages, his face becoming visible only at the very end of the picture. A number of films followed the success of this adaptation, including *The Invisible Man Returns* (1940), *The Invisible Man's Revenge* (1944) and such spoofs as *Abbott And Costello Meet The Invisible Man* (1951). There have been two television series called *The Invisible Man*: the first, made in Britain in 1958-59, perhaps owed a little to Wells's story; the second, made in America in 1975-76, certainly owed nothing at all. The latter series starred David McCallum as an invisible secret agent, and after a season it was retitled *The Gemini Man* with Ben Murphy taking over the lead. A reasonably faithful version of Wells's novel has since been serialized on BBC TV (1984), with Pip Donaghy as the unhappy Dr Griffin.

═══◦◦◦═══

Professor Jameson

CREATOR: NEIL R. JONES
SOURCE: 'THE JAMESON SATELLITE' (NOVELETTE)
DATE: 1931

A dead scientist whose uncorrupted body oulasts the human race in an artificial satellite. Following his resurrection by the robotic alien Zoromes, who place his brain in a mechanical body, he becomes an inquisitive immortal wanderer touring the universe in their company.

Captain Kathryn Janeway

CREATORS: RICK BERMAN, MICHAEL PILLER AND JERI TAYLOR
SOURCE: *STAR TREK: VOYAGER* (TV SERIES)
DATE: 1995

Gravel-voiced commander of a Federation starship rather less grandiose than the Enterprise. Kate Mulgrew plays her with a somewhat martyred air, as befits the master of a vessel accidentally transported halfway across the galaxy that continually runs into more trouble while trying to get home.

Jasperodus

CREATOR: BARRINGTON J. BAYLEY
SOURCE: *THE SOUL OF THE ROBOT* (NOVEL)
DATE: 1974

A robot gifted with self-consciousness by its creator who struggles to cope with the curse of existential angst. His quest for a way to prove that he alone out of all robotkind is an authentic individual was still unended at the conclusion of the sequel.

Adam Jeffson

CREATOR: M. P. SHIEL
SOURCE: *THE PURPLE CLOUD* (NOVEL)
DATE: 1901

A survivor of the near-extinction of mankind by a cloud of cyanogen gas, modelled on Job rather than his namesake. He wanders the world for 20 years before finding a female survivor, and is at first perversely determined that he will not allow her to become his Eve.

Dr Jekyll and Mr Hyde

CREATOR: ROBERT LOUIS STEVENSON
SOURCE: *THE STRANGE CASE OF DR JEKYLL AND MR HYDE* (NOVEL)
DATE: 1886

Henry Jekyll, a high-minded man of medicine, concocts a chemical potion that has the unintended effect of transforming him into the villainous Edward Hyde, haunter of London's night-time streets. This pre-Freudian fantasy of a split personality has become one of the great modern legends. Sequels include *Dr Jekyll And Mr Holmes* by Loren D. Estleman (1979), wherein Jekyll meets a famous fictional contemporary; *Jekyll, Alias Hyde: A Variation* by Donald Thomas (1988); *The Jekyll Legacy* by Robert Bloch and Andre Norton (1990); and, best-received of them, *Mary Reilly* by Valerie Martin (1990), which retells the story from the point of view of Jekyll's maid-servant. There were seven silent-movie versions of Stevenson's story made between 1908 and 1921 (the last starred John Barrymore). Sound films include *Dr Jekyll And Mr Hyde* (1931), with

THE ENEMY WITHIN *SPENCER TRACY AND INGRID BERGMAN IN HOLLYWOOD'S 1941 VERSION OF DR JEKYLL AND MR HYDE*

Fredric March; a remake of the same title (1941), with Spencer Tracy; *Abbott And Costello Meet Dr Jekyll And Mr Hyde* (1953), with Boris Karloff; *The Two Faces Of Dr Jekyll* (1960), with Paul Massie; and the trans-sexual *Dr Jekyll And Sister Hyde* (1970), with Ralph Bates.

Jenkins

CREATOR: CLIFFORD D. SIMAK
SOURCE: *CITY* (STORY COLLECTION)
DATE: 1952

Robot manservant of the Webster family who remains unfailingly faithful to his programmed ideals, acting as mentor to the intelligent dogs who inherit the Earth when humankind moves on. He valiantly stays behind when the dogs leave too, abandoning Earth to the ants.

The Jetsons

CREATORS: WILLIAM HANNA AND JOSEPH BARBERA
SOURCE: *THE JETSONS* (TV ANIMATION)
DATE: 1962

A futuristic family designed as a slick and gadget-ridden counterpart to **The Flintstones**. Amiable head of the household George worked for Spacely Space Sprockets; his whizzkid son Elroy helped to establish the propeller beanie as the badge of the cartoon sf fan.

Joenes

CREATOR: ROBERT SHECKLEY
SOURCE: *JOURNEY BEYOND TOMORROW* (NOVEL)
DATE: 1962

American raised on a remote Pacific atoll who returns to the land of his forefathers in search of enlightenment. A typical innocent abroad, he finds the world of civilization a lot less easy to understand than he had hoped, but half-deserves the saintly role thrust upon him by founders of a new religion.

Cirocco Jones

CREATOR: JOHN VARLEY
SOURCE: *TITAN* (NOVEL)
DATE: 1979

Female spaceship captain who is recruited by the living world Gaia as a sort of internal policeman, wandering that entity's huge body.

The story is continued in *Wizard* (1980) and *Demon* (1984).

Halo Jones

CREATORS: ALAN MOORE AND IAN GIBSON
SOURCE: *2000 A.D.* (COMIC)
DATE: 1984

Punkette heroine of *The Ballad Of Halo Jones*, a strip – later reissued as a three-volume graphic novel (1986) – about a very lived-in future, full of outrageous argot, menacing street-gangs and alien monstrosities.

Waldo F. Jones

CREATOR: ROBERT A. HEINLEIN
SOURCE: 'WALDO' (NOVELLA)
DATE: 1942

Sick young engineer who is obliged to live in the weightless conditions of an orbiting satellite in order to compensate for his wasted muscles. But from there he is able to solve several of Earth's problems. (Real-life remote-control manipulation devices were named "waldoes" after this character.)

Tabitha Jute

CREATOR: COLIN GREENLAND
SOURCE: *TAKE BACK PLENTY* (NOVEL)
DATE: 1990

Owner-operator of the Alice Liddell, whose own wonderland is an overpopulated solar system dominated by Capellan conquerors. A natural survivor who continually escapes from tight spots by the skin of her teeth, she eventually finds her way to an even larger stage with even tighter corners.

≈≈≈

K9

CREATORS: BOB BAKER AND DAVE MARTIN
SOURCE: *DOCTOR WHO* (BBC TV SERIES)
DATE: 1977

Robot dog K9, whose voice was usually supplied by John Leeson, joined the cast of *Doctor Who* in its 15th season and remained until the 18th (1980/1). In spite of its relatively short tenure and limited manoeuvrability, it remains one of the series's most memorable inventions.

Kemlo

CREATOR: E. C. ELIOTT
SOURCE: *KEMLO AND THE CRAZY PLANET* (NOVEL)
DATE: 1954

A refreshingly ordinary but quietly heroic youth born on a space station where everyone has the same initial. His remarkable ability to survive in airless space proved useful when he and his two friends became involved in a long series of strange adventures.

Craig Kennedy

CREATOR: ARTHUR B. REEVE
SOURCE: *COSMOPOLITAN* (MAGAZINE)
DATE: 1910

American "scientific detective" who used technological gadgetry as well as new-fangled psychological methods to solve his cases. His adventures were collected in *The Silent Bullet* (1912; also known as *The Black Hand*), *The Poisoned Pen* (1913) and two dozen later books which appeared before the author's death in 1936. Kennedy was played by Arnold Daly in the silent cinema serial *The Exploits Of Elaine* (1915) and its sequels *The New Exploits Of Elaine* (1915) and *The Romance Of Elaine* (1916). (The "Elaine" of these films was played by Pearl White, most famous of the early serial actresses.) Herbert Rawlinson took on the lead role in another serial, *The Carter Case: The Craig Kennedy Serial* (1919). The character was revived in the sound era for *The Clutching Hand* (1936), a 15-parter which starred Jack Mulhall; and again in the television era for an American TV series, *Craig Kennedy, Criminologist* (1952), which starred Donald Woods. During the second and third decades of the century, Craig Kennedy was the best-known fictional detective in the United States, sometimes referred to as "the American Sherlock Holmes".

Dr Robert Kerans

CREATOR: J. G. BALLARD
SOURCE: *THE DROWNED WORLD* (NOVEL)
DATE: 1962

British biologist who, influenced by the waterlogged jungle landscapes of a flooded 21st-century London, experiences strange dreams: it seems that part of his mind is descending on a

Night Journey into the deep wells of humankind's prehistoric past.

King Kong

CREATORS: MERIAN C. COOPER AND EDGAR WALLACE
SOURCE: *KING KONG* (FILM)
DATE: 1933

Monstrous ape discovered on a Pacific island and shipped to America as a circus attraction. Kong runs wild in New York, climbs the Empire State Building and is eventually killed by the machine-guns of fighter planes. The film is the most famous beast-fable of the 20th century. It starred Fay Wray as the lovely girl who softens Kong's heart – he carries her to the top of the skyscraper in his hairy fist. The animation of Kong himself was achieved by special-effects man Willis H. O'Brien. The movie inspired several sequels and remakes, such as *Son Of Kong* (1934) and the Japanese films *King Kong Vs. Godzilla* (1962) and *King Kong Escapes* (1967). There has also been an animated TV series about Kong's adventures (1966-68). The original movie was remade in colour (1976), with Jessica Lange in

SCARY MONSTER *THE ONE-AND-ONLY KONG – COOPER AND SCHOEDSACK'S MYTHICAL BEAST WHO TOUCHED THE HEARTS OF MILLIONS DESPITE HIS FEROCITY*

CAPTAIN CLICHÉ *ALL-AMERICAN HERO: CAPTAIN JAMES T. KIRK (CANADIAN-BORN WILLIAM SHATNER); LATER CAPTAINS IN STAR TREK SPINOFF SERIES HAVE BEEN A BALD BRITISHER, A BLACK MAN AND A WHITE WOMAN – WHO WILL BE NEXT: A BLACK WOMAN... OR AN ALIEN?*

the Fay Wray role, and the remake was followed by an inferior sequel, *King Kong Lives* (1986). The sf author Philip José Farmer wrote a moving short-story sequel, 'After King Kong Fell' (1974). The oft-reprinted novelization of the first film was by Delos W. Lovelace (1933).

Kimball Kinnison

CREATOR: E. E. "DOC" SMITH
SOURCE: *ASTOUNDING SF* (MAGAZINE)
DATE: 1937

"Lensman" hero of the ultimate series of extravagant space operas. Kinnison is a human member of the Galactic Patrol, an elite military force that has been bred and trained by the alien Arisians to aid them in their cosmic struggle against the evil Eddorians. Each Lensman wears a super-technological lens on his wrist; this conveys wonderful abilities (rather like The Green Lantern's power-ring). The early Lensman stories were serialized in sf magazines during the 1930s and 40s, then republished in book form (with added material) as follows: *Triplanetary* (1948), *First Lensman* (1950), *Galactic Patrol* (1950), *Gray Lensman* (1951), *Second-Stage Lensman* (1953) and *Children Of The Lens* (1954). The novels

proved enormously popular when they were reprinted in paperback during the 1960s and 70s (and it may be that they had a strong influence on George Lucas's *Star Wars* films – see **Luke Skywalker**). Sequels by other hands are *New Lensman* by William B. Ellern (1976), and a trilogy by David A. Kyle: *The Dragon Lensman* (1980), *Lensman From Rigel* (1982) and *Z-Lensman* (1983).

Captain James T. Kirk

CREATOR: GENE RODDENBERRY
SOURCE: *STAR TREK* (TV SERIES)
DATE: 1966

Brave captain of the *Starship Enterprise*, in command of a crew of several hundred persons engaged on a five-year interstellar exploratory mission. Kirk was played by Canadian-born actor William Shatner. Among the more notable members of the crew are his deputy, the cool **Mr Spock**, Dr Leonard "Bones" McCoy, and the sexy communications officer Lieutenant Uhura. It is their task "to boldly go where no man has gone before" (or to boldly split infinitives no man has split before, as the British sf writer Bob Shaw once said). The series and the characters it created have proved remarkably durable; the whole thing was the brainchild of writer-producer Roddenberry, though "the Star Trek universe" has long since taken on an unstoppable life of its own. A series of animated *Star Trek* adventures was first broadcast on US television in 1973-74. Numerous novelizations, of both the live-action and the animated TV series, were written by such sf authors as James Blish and Alan Dean Foster. Moreover, a large number of "original" novels and stories about Captain Kirk and his crew have now been published; some of them are by amateur writers who are avid fans of the series, an early example being the book *Star Trek: The New Voyages* (1976) edited by Sondra Marshak and Myrna Culbreath. There is even an underground pornographic literature, known as "K/S" (for Kirk/Spock), produced in duplicated fanzine format and sold by Trekkies (or "Trekkers" as they prefer to be known) at their numerous conventions around the world. After rumours of a new TV *Star Trek* proved unfounded in the late 1970s, a series of cinema feature films was initiated: *Star Trek: The Motion Picture* (1979), *Star Trek II: The Wrath Of Khan* (1982), *Star Trek III: The Search For Spock* (1984), *Star Trek IV: The Voyage Home* (1986), *Star Trek V: The Final Frontier* (1989) and *Star Trek VI: The Undiscovered Country* (1991). William Shatner continued to play Captain Kirk in these big-budget films. When the first one was released, one critic remarked on the ageing of the familiar actors' faces, but added that Shatner seemed "oddly youthened" by contrast: perhaps this was a sign that the character he embodied would be with us for a long time to come. Indeed, even after the much-delayed launch of a new TV series, *Star Trek: The Next Generation*, with a new captain (see **Jean Luc Picard**), Kirk still popped up now and again, most notably in the film *Star Trek: Generations* (1994).

Klaatu

CREATOR: HARRY BATES
SOURCE: 'FAREWELL TO THE MASTER' (STORY)
DATE: 1940
An alien visitor who arrives on Earth, accompanied by a huge robot, to deliver a warning message. He was memorably portrayed

by the earnestly sensitive Michael Rennie in Robert Wise's classic film version of the story, *The Day The Earth Stood Still* (1951).

Michael Knight

CREATOR: GLEN A. LARSON
SOURCE: *KNIGHT RIDER* (TV SERIES)
DATE: 1982
Handsome driver of an electronic car with a mind of its own – a black Pontiac, equipped with weapons and a built-in talking computer called KITT. Michael was played by David Hasselhoff, and the series ran until 1986.

Lois Lane

CREATORS: JEROME SIEGEL AND JOE SCHUSTER
SOURCE: *ACTION COMICS*
DATE: 1938
Feisty girl reporter, unaware that her meek colleague Clark Kent is really **Superman.** Lois was played by Margot Kidder in four *Superman* films (1978-87). The *Lois & Clark* TV series (from 1993), has Teri Hatcher in the role.

The Last Men

CREATOR: OLAF STAPLEDON
SOURCE: *LAST AND FIRST MEN* (NOVEL)
DATE: 1930
The last of the descendant species of *Homo sapiens* who live on Neptune following the expansion of the sun. They are the products of design rather than natural selection, formed of "artificial atoms" which make their bodies exceedingly resilient; they are immortal and telepathic. Adapted to the physical environment of their new world, they look very different from their ancestors – but they preserve a similar sense of beauty, intimately linked with sexual attraction. Having discovered that a further change in the sun will destroy the solar system, they undertake a systematic study of human evolution, reaching back mentally in time to examine their various ancestors. Sometimes, they become detectable as disturbing phantoms, thus maintaining a continual but problematic presence within the human imagination, which functions uneasily as a visionary goal towards which their parent races may strive. A more intimate linkage of this kind is described at greater length in *Last Men In London* (1932).

FALLING IN LOVE AGAIN *LOIS & CLARK, 1970S STYLE: MARGOT KIDDER AS LOIS LANE AND CHRISTOPHER REEVE AS CLARK KENT (AKA SUPERMAN). WHILE INVESTIGATING STRANGE GOINGS-ON AT THE HONEYMOON HAVEN OF NIAGARA FALLS LOIS THINKS SHE HAS TUMBLED THE INEPT KENT'S TRUE IDENTITY*

Isaac Leibowitz

CREATOR: WALTER M. MILLER
SOURCE: A CANTICLE FOR LEIBOWITZ (NOVEL)
DATE: 1960

The founder of a monastery which provides a focal point for the slow rebuilding of civilization after a nuclear holocaust. The few homely relics of him which remain are not what his devout followers think they are; in transforming him into an abstract object of worship – as Christ was earlier transformed – they are paving the way for history to repeat itself.

Silence Leigh

CREATOR: MELISSA SCOTT
SOURCE: FIVE-TWELFTHS OF HEAVEN (NOVEL)
DATE: 1986

An ambitious would-be space-pilot who eventually qualifies for a series of space-operatic adventures, which are eccentrically enlivened by her dabblings in alchemy and astrology.

Otto Lidenbrock

CREATOR: JULES VERNE
SOURCE: JOURNEY TO THE CENTRE OF THE EARTH (NOVEL)
DATE: 1863

German professor who descends into an Icelandic volcano, discovers a subterranean world inhabited by prehistoric beasts, then returns via an eruption in Sicily. In the 1959 film his name is anglicized as "Oliver Lindenbrook".

The Lilliputians

CREATOR: JONATHAN SWIFT
SOURCE: GULLIVER'S TRAVELS (NOVEL)
DATE: 1726

Miniature inhabitants of Lilliput. A sequel is T. H. White's Mistress Masham's Repose (1947): the heroine finds Lilliputians living in England. Another is Henry Winterfield's Castaways In Lilliput (1958): Australian kids rediscover a Lilliput which has become ultra-modern.

Adam Link

CREATOR: EANDO BINDER
SOURCE: 'I, ROBOT' (STORY)
DATE: 1939

A well-meaning robot falsely blamed for the death of its creator by people who insist on seeing "him" as a Frankenstein monster. He was even nobler in the version of his story presented in the revived Outer Limits TV series in 1995.

Dave Lister

CREATORS: ROB GRANT AND DOUG NAYLOR
SOURCE: RED DWARF (BBC TV SERIES)
DATE: 1988

A lowly technician on a huge mining spaceship who awakes from suspended animation after a catastrophe to find himself alone, save for his mutated cat, an annoyingly well-meaning robot and a hologram of his officious superior **Rimmer**. Craig Charles plays him convincingly as the ultimate cheerful slob. Thanks to a successful merchandising campaign the self-professed smeg-head is emblazoned upon many household items.

The Lithians

CREATOR: JAMES BLISH
SOURCE: 'A CASE OF CONSCIENCE' (NOVELLA)
DATE: 1953 (EXPANDED AS A BOOK 1958)

Kangaroo-like aliens whose life-cycle recapitulates their evolution from sea-dwelling ancestors. They live in sinless harmony with their Edenic world but have never been Saved, so a Jesuit observer naturally concludes that they must be a Diabolical trap set to tempt humankind from the True Faith.

Logan

CREATORS: WILLIAM F. NOLAN AND GEORGE CLAYTON JOHNSON
SOURCE: LOGAN'S RUN (NOVEL)
DATE: 1967

A policeman in an overcrowded world, whose job is hunting down people who refuse to submit to compulsory euthanasia on their 21st birthday. His dutiful conformism melts away when his own time lapses, and his adventures sustained him through two tamer sequels. Michael York played him in the woeful film version of 1976.

Lok

CREATOR: WILLIAM GOLDING
SOURCE: THE INHERITORS (NOVEL)
DATE: 1955

The last surviving Neanderthal man, a powerful but sweet-natured individual who is hurt and baffled by the deaths of his relatives, one by one, at the hands of the incoming Cro-Magnon people (the "inheritors" of the title). Lok dies; the reader weeps. This was the Nobel Prize-winning author's own favourite among his novels, and his most science-fictional.

Lazarus Long

CREATOR: ROBERT A. HEINLEIN
SOURCE: METHUSELAH'S CHILDREN (NOVEL)
DATE: 1941

A grizzled American hero with remarkably lucky genes. He is extremely long-lived, an early-20th-century rugged individualist who survives into the 21st century, when he leads a revolt of long-livers and succeeds in becoming a space colonist, taking his people out to the stars. This wish-fulfilling tale was first serialized in Astounding SF, then revised for book publication in 1958. Heinlein took Lazarus even further into the future (and into the past) in the much later and more complex novel Time Enough For Love, Or The Lives Of Lazarus Long (1973), which, as its title suggests, is a time-twisting yarn. A number of would-be wise and witty apothegms from this book were republished separately in a small illustrated volume called The Notebooks Of Lazarus Long (1978). The near-immortal Lazarus is nothing if not a mouthpiece for Heinlein's often cranky social and political beliefs. Talkative and opinionated, he reappears in smaller roles in still later Heinlein novels, The Number Of The Beast (1980), The Cat Who Walks Through Walls (1985) and To Sail Beyond The Sunset (1987; the author's swan song).

Lylda

CREATOR: RAY CUMMINGS
SOURCE: 'THE GIRL IN THE GOLDEN ATOM' (NOVELLA)
DATE: 1919

The beautiful girl who tempts the unnamed Chemist to make his pioneering journey into the microcosm and befriends him on his arrival there. She is less passive than the heroines of many similar romances, displaying considerable enterprise in the sequel novel, People Of The Golden Atom (1923).

M

McAndrew

CREATOR: CHARLES SHEFFIELD
SOURCE: THE MCANDREW CHRONICLES
(STORY COLLECTION)
DATE: 1983

An inventive genius whose early adventures take him out of the solar system and into the cometary Halo beyond Pluto. His career reaches its peak with the development and gradual perfection of a drive for use in interstellar spaceships, whose theory is painstakingly explained to the reader.

Rod McBan

CREATOR: CORDWAINER SMITH
SOURCE: NORSTRILIA (NOVEL)
DATE: 1964 IN TWO VOLS.; RESTORED TEXT 1975

A young man who buys the Earth in order to continue an intellectual mission to rediscover the psychological roots of human nature. Hardened by the challenging Norstrilian rites of passage, he is further tested when his brain is transplanted into another body but he never really capitalizes on his experience.

Marty McFly

CREATOR: BOB GALE AND ROBERT ZEMECKIS
SOURCE: BACK TO THE FUTURE (FILM)
DATE: 1985

A personable teenager (Michael J. Fox) driven to despair by his awful parents, who musters all his resourcefulness and wit to the project of ensuring that they meet when he is thrown back in time to 1955. He copes manfully with the Oedipal challenge of his mother-to-be's infatuation and the necessity of helping his nerdy father-to-be cultivate a little moral fibre, and changes his family history for the better. His character is allowed to develop further in the single story formed by two sequels, confronting another self who has gone off the rails and finally bringing a much-needed non-confrontational maturity to his incarnation as "Clint Eastwood" in 1885. He remains one of the most interesting, endearing and competently-constructed characters ever featured in mainstream cinematic sf.

THE OLDEST TEENAGER IN TOWN *THE EVER-YOUTHFUL MICHAEL J. FOX AS MARTY MCFLY IN* BACK TO THE FUTURE — *A TIME-TRAVELLER WITH PRESSING FAMILY BUSINESS TO TEND TO, WHO MANAGES TO SAVE THE WORLD AND INVENT ROCK AND ROLL WITH THE AID OF A SKATEBOARD AND A SOUPED-UP DELOREAN*

Connor MacLeod

CREATORS: GREGORY WIDEN AND RUSSELL MULCAHY
SOURCE: HIGHLANDER (FILM)
DATE: 1985

An immortal with a magic sword (Christopher Lambert) who must fight a similar adversary for the privilege of being last of their line. *Highlander II: The Quickening* (1990)

reinterpreted the two as aliens from the planet Zeist, but the subsequent TV series reverted to a fantasy premise similar to that of the 1985 film.

Dr Mabuse

CREATOR: NORBERT JACQUES
SOURCE: DR MABUSE, THE GAMBLER (NOVEL)
DATE: 1920

Scientific mastermind played by Rudolf Klein-Rogge in Fritz Lang's two-part film *Doktor Mabuse* (1922). Although he originated in prose, the villainous Mabuse made more impact in films, including *The Testament Of Dr Mabuse* (1933) and the much-delayed *The Thousand Eyes Of Dr Mabuse* (1960).

Mad Max

CREATORS: GEORGE MILLER AND JAMES MCCAUSLAND
SOURCE: *MAD MAX* (FILM)
DATE: 1979

Full name Max Rockatansky, a handsome, heavily-armed, taciturn ex-cop played by Mel Gibson in three futuristic Australian movies directed by the talented George Miller. In the debut film, Max pursues a gang of bikers who are responsible for the road-death of his wife. In the oil-thirsty world of the next movie, *Mad Max II* (1981; also known as *The Road Warrior*), he drives an armour-plated automobile and fights off attacks by bands of motorized barbarians, eventually becoming a saviour to a community of relatively civilized folk. In the third, *Mad Max Beyond Thunderdome* (1985), the roving hero has a bad time in ramshackle Bartertown, a post-disaster settlement ruled by a formidable woman known as Aunt Entity. Max escapes to the desert, where he rescues a tribe of children and leads them to their promised land. This last adventure was novelized by sf writer Joan D. Vinge. The role of Max made Gibson a superstar, and the films, though basically "road movies", were praised for their style – particularly the middle one, which was described by sf writer J. G. Ballard as "punk's Sistine Chapel".

The Man From Atlantis

CREATOR: LEE KATZIN
SOURCE: *THE MAN FROM ATLANTIS* (NBC TV SERIES)
DATE: 1977

A vividly green-eyed "castaway" with gills and webbed fingers, recruited as an agent for the Foundation for Oceanic Research (under the pseudonym Mark Harris). Actor Patrick Duffy reproduced the same dazed innocence in Dallas, so it wasn't just the contact lenses.

The Martians

CREATOR: H. G. WELLS
SOURCE: *THE WAR OF THE WORLDS* (NOVEL)
DATE: 1898

Countless imaginary inhabitants of the planet Mars have been described in science fiction, but there is one particular species who forever will be thought of as the Martians. These are, of course, the monstrous aliens who invade Earth (or, more precisely, England's leafy Home Counties) with their three-legged fighting-machines and all-destroying heat-rays, in Wells's splendid novel: "Those who have never seen a Martian can scarcely imagine the strange horror of their appearance. The peculiar V-shaped mouth with its pointed upper lip, the absence of brow ridges, the absence of a chin beneath the wedge-like lower lip, the incessant quivering of this mouth, the Gorgon group of tentacles, the tumultuous breathing of the lungs in a strange atmosphere, the evident heaviness and painfulness of movement, due to the greater gravitational energy of the earth – above all, the extraordinary intensity of the immense eyes – culminated in an effect akin to nausea. There was something fungoid in the oily brown skin, something in the clumsy deliberation of their tedious movements unspeakably terrible." These highly-evolved but frightful beings, with their vast, cool and unsympathetic intellects, are eventually defeated by God's humblest creatures, our planet's disease bacteria. Wells's book is one of the great, fundamental tales of science fiction, and it has been emulated by many later writers. Sequels by other hands include *Sherlock Holmes's War Of The Worlds* by Manly Wade Wellman and Wade Wellman (1975), *The Second War Of The Worlds* by George H. Smith (1976), and *The Space Machine* by Christopher Priest (1976). The most famous adaptation of the

THE ROAD WARRIOR *A MAN OF FEW WORDS BUT SUCH STYLE:* MEL GIBSON AS MAX IN GEORGE MILLER'S *EXCITING AUSTRALIAN MOVIES*

 MARTIAN ON TO VICTORY *The Martians: in the 1953 movie they had flying machines, but in* **H. G.** *Wells's original novel they walked on tall tripods; both versions carried devastating "heat-rays"*

original story, and one which caused a major public panic in America, was Orson Welles's radio version (1938): when broadcast, its verisimilitude caused many listeners to believe that the United States really was being invaded by monsters from outer space (and this "phantom invasion" itself inspired a much later TV movie, *The Night That Panicked America*, 1975). The Hollywood film version, *War Of The Worlds* (1953), was rather less effective, though adequately exciting. A later American TV series (1988-90) used Wells's title but had little to do with his story: it did not even refer to its alien invaders as Martians.

Uncle Martin

CREATOR: Jack Chertok
SOURCE: *My Favorite Martian* (CBS TV series)
DATE: 1963
A Martian with various mental powers (Ray Walston) stranded on Earth and passed off as an eccentric uncle by Bill Bixby. Walston made the character thoroughly likeable, although the only truly memorable thing about him was his retractable antennae.

Captain Marvel

CREATORS: Otto Binder and C. C. Beck
SOURCE: *Whiz Comics*
DATE: 1940
Affectionately known as "the Big Red Cheese", Captain Marvel's real name is Billy Batson. A scrawny youth who sells newspapers for a living, he meets a wizard who promises him "the wisdom of Solomon, the strength of Hercules, the stamina of Atlas, the power of Zeus, the courage of Achilles and the speed of Mercury". All he has to do is pronounce the word which is an acronym of these heroes's names – SHAZAM. This he does, repeatedly transforming himself into the red-suited, mighty-muscled Captain Marvel. As one of the most popular of all the costumed superheroes who have appeared in American comic books, at times his adventures used to outsell **Superman**'s, and indeed the owners of the latter character, DC Comics, brought a lawsuit against Fawcett, Captain Marvel's publishers, which succeeded in banning the character for many years. It was alleged that the Captain was altogether too similar to the Man of Steel. From 1941 to 1953 (when he was

suppressed), he had his own comic book, *Captain Marvel Adventures*. The character was revived (by his old enemies, DC Comics) in 1972, and has pursued his colourful crime-fighting career ever since. A movie serial, *The Adventures Of Captain Marvel* (1941), starred Tom Tyler as the Captain. A much later television series, *Shazam!* (1974), had Jackson Bostwick as Marvel (later replaced by John Davey). There has also been a TV cartoon series based on the character.

Marvin The Paranoid Android

CREATOR: Douglas Adams
SOURCE: *The Hitch Hiker's Guide To The Galaxy* (BBC radio serial)
DATE: 1978
A melancholy robot much given to proclaiming mournfully that nobody ever listens to him even though he has "a brain the size of a planet". Stephen Moore's mogadon-slow baritone (re-used in the TV version) was much imitated by nerdy teenagers who felt exactly the same with far less justification.

The Mekon

CREATOR: Frank Hampson
SOURCE: *The Eagle* (comic)
DATE: 1950
A "Treen" from the planet Venus, deadly foe of spaceman **Dan Dare**. The Mekon is green-skinned, slit-eyed, small of body and vast of head. Like most villains of space opera, he is intent on conquering the human race. He became so familiar to a generation of readers that, as late as the 1980s, British Tory members of parliament used "the Mekon" as a nickname for one of their cabinet ministers (Angus Maude).

Mike Mercury

CREATOR: Gerry Anderson
SOURCE: *Supercar* (TV series)
DATE: 1961
The first stringy superstar of SuperMarionation, trusty pilot of Professor Popkiss's marvellous invention and heroic adversary of Masterspy. Graydon Gould supplied the voice, Gerry Anderson the movable eyes and versatile mouth, which were lifelike by the standards of their day.

The Mesklinites

CREATOR: HAL CLEMENT
SOURCE: MISSION OF GRAVITY (NOVEL)
DATE: 1954

Natives of the huge and rapidly-rotating planet Mesklin, who live near the poles where gravity is 700 times greater than Earth's. Physically and psychologically adapted to these conditions, they resemble giant centipedes and are paranoid about falling objects. The party who go to the rescue of a stranded Earthman exhibit great courage and enterprise.

Metal Mickey

CREATORS: COLIN BOSTOCK-SMITH AND MICKEY DOLENZ
SOURCE: METAL MICKEY (LWT TV SERIES)
DATE: 1980

An incompetent household robot with magic powers and an annoying habit of saying "Boogie Boogie", improbably built by a teenage whizzkid. Because he was almost as charmless as his American counterpart **ALF**, he was popular enough to last four seasons.

Laurent Michaelmas

CREATOR: ALGIS BUDRYS
SOURCE: MICHAELMAS (NOVEL)
DATE: 1977

A TV reporter who secretly rules the world with the help of his trusty computer sidekick Domino. By comparison with other instruments of vicarious teenage power-fantasy, such as **Kimball Kinnison** and **Ender Wiggin**, he is reasonably urbane but not very likeable.

The Midwich Cuckoos

CREATOR: JOHN WYNDHAM
SOURCE: THE MIDWICH CUCKOOS (NOVEL)
DATE: 1957

Alien children planted in the wombs of women in an English village by a UFO, who develop mental powers and a collective consciousness as they grow to maturity. The children who played the characters in the film version, *Village Of The Damned* (1960), did an excellent job with the help of wigs calculatedly mismatched to their eye-colour.

The Mighty Morphin Power Rangers

CREATORS: SABAN ENTERTAINMENT AND TOEI PRODUCTIONS
SOURCE: MIGHTY MORPHIN POWER RANGERS (JAPANESE/US TV SERIES)
DATE: 1993

Six colour-coded teenage superheroes who are equally adept at martial arts and manning huge Transformer-like fighting-machines. In the "real life" sequences of the version shown in the US and the UK, Jason, Zack, Kimberly, Billy and Tommy substitute readily enough – in spite of being somewhat overweight – for the Japanese originals, but poor Trini has to change sex every time she dons her costume.

Ming The Merciless

CREATOR: ALEX RAYMOND
SOURCE: FLASH GORDON (SYNDICATED COMIC STRIP)
DATE: 1934

Villainous ruler of the planet Mongo, diehard adversary of the clean-cut **Flash Gordon** and mad scientist Hans Zarkov. In the cinema serials of 1936 and 1938, the archly sneering Charles Middleton created the definitive Ming, which Max von Sydow tried in vain to recapitulate in the 1980 film.

Johnny Mnemonic

CREATOR: WILLIAM GIBSON
SOURCE: 'JOHNNY MNEMONIC' (STORY)
DATE: 1981

A "very technical boy" with an exceedingly good head for data and the ambition to become even more technical while remaining ready, willing and able to be crude whenever the situation warrants. The prototype of all cyberpunks, played by Keanu Reeves in the 1995 film version.

Mustapha Mond

CREATOR: ALDOUS HUXLEY
SOURCE: BRAVE NEW WORLD (NOVEL)
DATE: 1932

Piercing-eyed, hook-nosed World Controller, known as "his fordship", in the biologically-engineered, euphorically-drugged and efficiently-

THE EYES HAVE IT *IN THE AGE OF THE TEDDY BOYS (THE 1950S) JOHN WYNDHAM AND HIS FILM ADAPTERS CAME UP WITH AN EVEN MORE EXTREME VERSION OF THE GENERATION GAP – BEAUTIFUL BUT DEADLY CHILDREN "FATHERED" BY UNSEEN ALIENS*

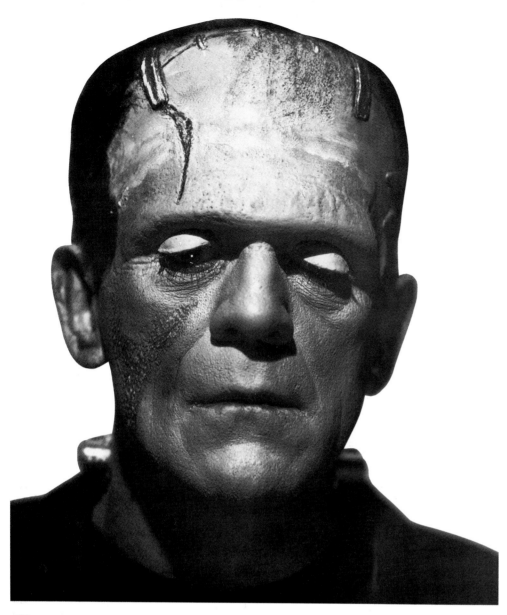

 IF YOU WANT TO GET A HEAD... *THE MOST FAMOUS MAKE-UP JOB IN MOVIE HISTORY: FRANK PIERCE WAS RESPONSIBLE FOR THE APPEARANCE OF FRANKENSTEIN'S MONSTER (BORIS KARLOFF)*

automated Europe of 600 years hence. A relatively benign equivalent of Orwell's **Big Brother**, he was played by Ron O'Neal in the TV mini-series version of the story (1979).

The Monster

CREATOR: MARY SHELLEY
SOURCE: *FRANKENSTEIN, OR THE MODERN PROMETHEUS* (NOVEL)
DATE: 1818

In a genre that has featured countless monsters (often of the bug-eyed variety), Victor Frankenstein's creation, a patchwork of dead human parts vivified by electricity, remains *the* Monster. Boris Karloff starred in the most famous film version, *Frankenstein* (1931). Karloff's shambling creature, both menacing and pathetic, has never been forgotten: it is part of the indelible visual iconography of the 20th century.

Guy Montag

CREATOR: RAY BRADBURY
SOURCE: *FAHRENHEIT 451* (NOVEL)
DATE: 1953

A "fireman" who is occupied in burning the books which some obstinate members of an orderly society stubbornly refuse to give up. He begins to doubt the wisdom of this attempted thought-control and eventually becomes an outlaw custodian of literary lore. Oskar Werner put in a dignified performance in the 1966 film.

Dr Morbius

CREATORS: CYRIL HUME, IRVING BLOCK AND ALLEN ADLER
SOURCE: *FORBIDDEN PLANET* (FILM)
DATE: 1956

A futuristic version of Shakespeare's Prospero, who eventually is forced to confess that his invisible and extremely unruly Caliban has been dredged up – by means of alien technology – from his own id. Walter Pidgeon played the role in suitably tortured fashion.

Dr Moreau

CREATOR: H. G. WELLS
SOURCE: *THE ISLAND OF DR MOREAU* (NOVEL)
DATE: 1896

Scientist who endeavours to turn animals into men, by gruesome means. A sequel is *Moreau's Other Island* by Brian Aldiss (1980). In the film entitled *The Island Of Lost Souls* (1932), Moreau was played by Charles Laughton. A later version, under Wells's title (1977), starred Burt Lancaster.

Jet Morgan

CREATOR: CHARLES CHILTON
SOURCE: *JOURNEY INTO SPACE* (BBC RADIO SERIAL)
DATE: 1953

Intrepid and authoritative spaceman voiced by Andrew Faulds in the popular British radio show and its two sequels. The serials were sold to 58 countries, and Chilton based three novels on the scripts: *Journey Into Space* (1954), *The Red Planet* (1956) and *The World In Peril* (1960). There was also a Jet Morgan comic strip in *Express Weekly* (1956-57).

 **DOC SAVAGE** *BURT LANCASTER AS THE BEAST-TORTURING DR MOREAU IN THE 1977 FILM VERSION OF H. G. WELLS'S CLASSIC*

Mork And Mindy

CREATORS: GARRY K. MARSHALL, DALE MCRAVEN AND JOE GAUBERG
SOURCE: MORK AND MINDY (TV SERIES)
DATE: 1978

Derived from a *Happy Days* parody of *My Favorite Martian*, Robin Williams shot to stardom playing the hapless Mork from planet Ork. He was a misfit on his own world before becoming the ultimate misfit on ours, sent to study the folkways of Earth – each episode ends with his report home. His trusty native guide Mindy (Pam Dawber) exhibited astonishing patience.

The Morlocks

CREATOR: H. G. WELLS
SOURCE: 'THE TIME MACHINE' (NOVELLA)
DATE: 1895

Hairy dwellers in a far future underworld, who tend the machines which sustain the effete Eloi and emerge by night with the apparent intention of cannibalizing them. The highly unflattering description of an alien species offered by Wells's time-traveller is questioned in belated sequels by David Lake and Stephen Baxter.

The Mother Thing

CREATOR: ROBERT A. HEINLEIN
SOURCE: HAVE SPACE SUIT – WILL TRAVEL (NOVEL)
DATE: 1958

An alien policeperson whose "beat" includes the region into which the young human protagonists accidentally launch themselves. She is small, furry, warm and protective: a sort of cross between British TV's Dixon of Dock Green and a security blanket.

Mulder & Scully

CREATOR: CHRIS CARTER
SOURCE: THE X-FILES (TV SERIES)
DATE: 1993

Fox Mulder and Dana Scully, special investigators of the far-out and the paranormal on behalf of the FBI. David Duchovny was Mulder (the credulous one) and Gillian Anderson was Scully (the sceptical one). Playing on the public's love of paranoid conspiracy theories surrounding unidentified flying objects and the like, the show swiftly became a cult success. A series of spin-off novels featuring Mulder and Scully began with *The X-Files: Goblins* (1994) and *The X-Files: Whirlwind* (1995), both by Charles Grant.

Chad C. Mulligan

CREATOR: JOHN BRUNNER
SOURCE: STAND ON ZANZIBAR (NOVEL)
DATE: 1968

A lapsed sociologist and cynical commentator on the follies of overcrowded humankind in such works as *The Hipcrime Vocab*. He is dried out in order to make a constructive contribution to the analysis of society's problems and turns out to have a soft centre after all.

Roy Neary

CREATOR: STEVEN SPIELBERG
SOURCE: CLOSE ENCOUNTERS OF THE THIRD KIND (FILM)
DATE: 1977

A power-company technician who develops an obsession with UFOs after a series of sightings, having subconsciously received a telepathic summons to a mountain in

NO SEX, PLEASE – WE'RE FBI AGENTS *MULDER (DAVID DUCHOVNY) AND SCULLY (GILLIAN ANDERSON) IN THE X-FILES, PART OF THE CHARM OF WHICH IS THAT THE PLOTS ARE FAR TOO BUSY TO ALLOW TIME FOR ANY HANKY-PANKY*

Wyoming. He is the fortunate one chosen to be taken aboard the alien mother ship, hand-in-hand with an **E.T.**-clone.

Admiral Harriman Nelson

CREATOR: IRWIN ALLEN
SOURCE: *VOYAGE TO THE BOTTOM OF THE SEA* (FILM)
DATE: 1961

Master of the experimental submarine *Seaview*, forced to take personal responsibility for the world's salvation when the polar ice-caps start to melt but equal to the task. Walter Pidgeon was replaced in the role by a suitably stern Richard Basehart in the popular TV series (1964-68).

Captain Nemo

CREATOR: JULES VERNE
SOURCE: *20,000 LEAGUES UNDER THE SEA* (NOVEL)
DATE: 1870

An Indian prince turned super-technological pirate, and master of the wonderful submarine *Nautilus*. Nemo was embittered by Britain's crushing of the Indian Mutiny in 1857, and he used his immense wealth to build his submarine in utmost secrecy; he now roams the seas, occasionally surfacing to sink an "enemy" warship. In one encounter, he picks up three involuntary passengers: the learned Professor Aronnax and his manservant, and the bold harpooneer Ned Land, and takes them on a fabulous undersea voyage. In Verne's semi-sequel to this story, *The Mysterious Island* (1875), the Nautilus is crippled and Nemo hides away in a cavern beneath an uncharted island. He becomes a Prospero figure for the castaways there, working scientific miracles that enable them to survive. At the end of the novel, he drowns in the sunken *Nautilus*. A modern sequel by another hand is *The Secret Sea* (1979) by Thomas F. Monteleone, in which Nemo sails his fantastic vessel into parallel worlds. The Captain has appeared in many films, including *Mysterious Island* (1929), in which he was played by Lionel Barrymore; *20,000 Leagues Under The Sea* (1954), starring James Mason; *Mysterious Island* (1961), with Herbert Lom; and *Captain Nemo And The Underwater City* (1969), with Robert Ryan. There has also been an American

television series, *The Return Of Captain Nemo* (1978), which starred José Ferrer.

Joe 90

CREATORS: GERRY AND SYLVIA ANDERSON
SOURCE: *JOE 90* (TV SERIES)
DATE: 1968

A nine-year-old boy whose brain plays host to patterns lodged there by his scientist father, enabling him to assume various adult roles while serving as an agent for the World Intelligence Network. The last but least successful of the SuperMarionation puppet characters.

Lafayette O'Leary

CREATOR: KEITH LAUMER
SOURCE: *THE TIME BENDER* (NOVEL)
DATE: 1966

A self-taught psychic whose imperfect command of Professor Schimmerkopf's mesmeric techniques precipitates him into the first of a series of parallel worlds, where he undergoes farcical adventures. He is sustained through three sequels – *The World Shuffler* (1970), *The Shape Changer* (1972) and *The Galaxy Builder* (1984) – by his talent for improvisation.

Helen O'Loy

CREATOR: LESTER DEL REY
SOURCE: 'HELEN O'LOY' (STORY)
DATE: 1938

The perfect robot woman, constructed by male artifice. The unsatirical prototype of the Stepford Wives, who gladly submits to being switched off when the husband whose lifelong servant she has been finally dies. An earnest testament to the necessity for feminism.

Jimmy Olsen

CREATORS: ROBERT MAXWELL AND JACK JOHNSTONE
SOURCE: *THE ADVENTURES OF SUPERMAN* (RADIO)
DATE: 1940

Cub reporter on the *Daily Planet* newspaper, city of Metropolis. After his debut on radio, he appeared in DC Comics, gaining his own title,

Jimmy Olsen, in 1954. His vivid orange hair was untransposable to other media. Marc McClure played him in four recent **Superman** films (1978-87).

Casher O'Neill

CREATOR: CORDWAINER SMITH
SOURCE: *QUEST OF THE THREE WORLDS* (FIX-UP NOVEL)
DATE: 1966

A mystically-inclined soldier of fortune, nephew of the ruined ex-ruler of Mizzer, whose adventures have a significant spiritual dimension that comes increasingly to the fore in the build-up to his penultimate adventure, when he achieves a kind of personal salvation.

The Overlords

CREATOR: ARTHUR C. CLARKE
SOURCE: *CHILDHOOD'S END* (NOVEL)
DATE: 1953

Mysterious aliens whose arrival on Earth – prompted by the imminent development of space travel by human beings – is the prelude to the establishment of a peaceful utopia. They use their superior technology unselfishly, to the

THE OVERLORDS *THESE BEINGS FEATURE AS MIDWIVES TO A COSMIC REBIRTH IN CLARKE'S MEMORABLE NOVEL*

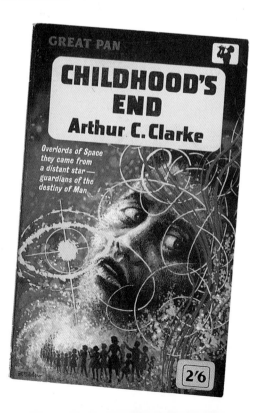

GREAT PAN

CHILDHOOD'S END
Arthur C. Clarke

Overlords of Space they came from a distant star— guardians of the destiny of Man

2'6

apparent benefit of humankind – but in so doing they remove the circumstantial challenges which have inspired human creativity. Their initial refusal to reveal themselves is explained when they turn out to resemble medieval images of the devil. They are indeed "fallen angels" in a metaphorical sense: their fate is to serve as midwives for the metamorphic collective "apotheoses" of other races – transcendent evolutionary leaps to a new phase of existence, which they cannot achieve themselves.

Warren Peace

CREATOR: BOB SHAW
SOURCE: *WHO GOES HERE?* (NOVEL)
DATE: 1977
An amnesiac recruit to the Space Legion, having joined it in order to win the privilege of forgetting his past, becomes insatiably curious about what it was that he needed to forget so completely. His quest to find out involves him, hilariously, in time-paradoxes and other tricky plot-twists.

Lady Penelope

CREATORS: GERRY AND SYLVIA ANDERSON
SOURCE: *THUNDERBIRDS* (TV SERIES)
DATE: 1965
Full name Lady Penelope Creighton-Ward, plummy heroine of the British TV puppet show. She works for International Rescue, a hi-tech aeronautical outfit operating from a secret island base, and she has a pink Rolls Royce driven by a Cockney chauffeur, the ex-convict Parker. The glamorous Lady Penelope's voice was provided by Sylvia Anderson. She also appeared in two feature films – *Thunderbirds Are Go* (1966) and *Thunderbird Six* (1968) – and in comic strips that ran for several years beyond the initial life of the TV series (which itself has been very popular in re-runs and video releases).

The People

CREATOR: ZENNA HENDERSON
SOURCE: *PILGRIMAGE* (FIX-UP NOVEL)
DATE: 1961

TO BALDLY GO
PATRICK STEWART AS CAPTAIN JEAN LUC PICARD *BROUGHT HIS STAGE-TRAINED ACTING ABILITY TO* STAR TREK: THE NEXT GENERATION

Psi-powered human-seeming aliens shipwrecked on Earth. They hide their powers lest they suffer persecution from their unwitting hosts, while nobly and subtly using their skills to help the unfortunate, the downtrodden and the lonely.

Jean Luc Picard

CREATOR: GENE RODDENBERRY
SOURCE: *STAR TREK: THE NEXT GENERATION* (TV SERIES)
DATE: 1987
Spaceship captain played by the authoritative British actor Patrick Stewart. At the helm of a new, larger *Starship Enterprise*, and in the manner of his distinguished predecessor **Captain James T. Kirk**, Picard boldly (and baldly) goes where no one has gone before (note, the word "one" has replaced "man" in these more politically correct times). His helpers include an android crewman named Data, played by Brent Spiner, and an alien Klingon lieutenant called Worf, played by Michael Dorn. As a follow-up series, *The Next Generation* proved very successful, with a substantially longer TV life

than its forebear. Initiated by Roddenberry, it was produced in the main by newer talents Rick Berman, Michael Piller and Jeri Taylor. Patrick Stewart's Picard reached the big screen in the movie *Star Trek: Generations* (1994), where, thanks to some time-twisting shenanigans, he meets the venerable Captain Kirk (still played by William Shatner). In addition to various novelizations of scripts, a spinoff series of original novels about the adventures of Picard and crew, written by authors such as Michael Jan Friedman and Carmen Carter, had reached nearly 50 volumes by the end of 1995.

Billy Pilgrim

CREATOR: KURT VONNEGUT
SOURCE: *SLAUGHTERHOUSE-FIVE, OR THE CHILDREN'S CRUSADE* (NOVEL)
DATE: 1969
A battered innocent who shuttles backwards and forwards in space and time between the fire-bombing of Dresden in 1945 and the planet Tralfamadore in the far future. Billy is a great fan of the seedy sf writer Kilgore Trout. In the film

Slaughterhouse Five (1972), Pilgrim was played by Michael Sacks.

Pirx

CREATOR: STANISLAW LEM
SOURCE: *TALES OF PIRX THE PILOT* (STORY COLLECTION)
DATE: 1968

A trainee space pilot who rises by degrees to the top of his profession, becoming wiser and more competent as he negotiates his way through a whole series of petty catastrophes, most of which involve wayward and unreliable machinery.

The Predator

CREATORS: JIM & JOHN THOMAS AND JOHN McTIERNAN
SOURCE: *PREDATOR* (FILM)
DATE: 1987

An alien hunter with near-perfect camouflage who picks off members of a special-forces team until neutralized by Arnold Schwarzenegger. The 1990 sequel reveals that he and his ugly pals have been using Earth as a safari park for some considerable time.

Dray Prescot

CREATOR: ALAN BURT AKERS
SOURCE: *TRANSIT TO SCORPIO* (NOVEL)
DATE: 1972

Earthman who enjoys colourful adventures on the planet of another star, much like John Carter of Mars. The formulaic sequels include: *The Suns Of Scorpio* (1973), *Manhounds Of Antares* (1974), *The Tides Of Kregen* (1976), *Secret Scorpio* (1977), *A Life For Kregen* (1979), *Beasts Of Antares* (1980), *Delia Of Vallia* (1982), *Seg The Bowman* (1984), and many more. The British author, real name Kenneth Bulmer, eventually dropped the "Akers" pseudonym and it was simply replaced on the books' covers by the character's name.

The Prisoner

CREATORS: PATRICK McGOOHAN AND GEORGE MARKSTEIN
SOURCE: *THE PRISONER* (TV SERIES)
DATE: 1967

NOW YOU SEE ME *THE ALIEN PREDATOR ARRIVES IN LOS ANGELES, WHERE PERHAPS HE SHOULD HAVE BEEN ALL ALONG IF HE'S IN SEARCH OF PLENTIFUL HUMAN PREY*

Known as "Number Six", a nameless hero played by Patrick McGoohan, who also devised and co-wrote the series. Number Six is a former secret agent who awakes to find himself a prisoner in a strange environment resembling a luxury holiday camp. He makes repeated attempts to escape, but is thwarted by hidden surveillance, technological gadgetry, brainwashing techniques and the like. His captors remain mysterious, their almost disembodied malevolence lending an air of Kafkaesque nightmare to the entire series. The first of several novels based on the scripts is *The Prisoner* by Thomas M. Disch (1969). The series was not a popular success on its first airing, but it has been repeated many times and has gained a cult following.

Qfwfq

CREATOR: ITALO CALVINO
SOURCE: *COSMICOMICS* (STORY COLLECTION)
DATE: 1965

A childlike observer whose origin predates the Big Bang. He is capable of assuming many guises in order to make the best use of the giant playground

which is the universe, taking temporary delight in all its phases and productions.

Professor Bernard Quatermass

CREATOR: NIGEL KNEALE
SOURCE: *THE QUATERMASS EXPERIMENT* (BBC TV SERIAL)
DATE: 1953

Brilliant scientist who made a speciality of tackling threats from outer space, in three hugely successful serials (the others were *Quatermass II,* 1955, and *Quatermass And The Pit*, 1958-59). Most definitely intended for adults, though no doubt watched by children cowering behind the sofa, they were discussed in bus queues throughout the UK. The actors who played Quatermass in these productions were Reginald Tate, John Robinson and André Morell. In the first, the professor tackles the case of alien spores which transform a returned astronaut into a vast vegetable monster that ensconces itself in Westminster Abbey; in the second, he investigates a chilling mystery involving alien invaders at a governmental scientific base in the North of England; and in the third and best of them, he is called into action when an ancient space vehicle is discovered during builders' excavations in London. All three stories were subsequently filmed: *The Quatermass Xperiment* (so-spelled; 1955; known in America as *The Creeping Unknown*), with Brian Donlevy; *Quatermass II* (1957; known in America as *Enemy From Space*), with Donlevy; and *Quatermass And The Pit* (1967; known in America as *Five Million Years To Earth*), with Andrew Keir. In all cases, the scripts were shortened considerably from their original lengths, and therefore purists regard the films as inferior to the TV productions. Nigel Kneale revived the Professor for a new television serial titled simply *Quatermass* (1979; also called, in shorter form, *The Quatermass Conclusion*). This starred John Mills, but was received with less enthusiasm than the classic serials of the 1950s. Kneale also turned his script, which had been written in the 1960s and shelved for a decade, into a novel (1979). It is perhaps to be regretted that the author never saw fit to novelize his three previous serials: such books could have been among the best-ever TV spinoffs (in fact, the un-novelized scripts were published by Penguin Books in 1959-60 and went through several printings). Although embodied by so many different actors, Professor Quatermass retains a distinct identity in a generation's memory as a pillar of scientific rectitude and as the character at the heart of Britain's finest media sf.

R2-D2 & C-3PO

CREATOR: GEORGE LUCAS
SOURCE: *STAR WARS* (FILM)
DATE: 1977

Two robots which continually have greatness thrust upon them by the plots in which they are caught up. The unobtrusively heroic R2-D2 resembles a mobile whistling pedal bin, while the well-spoken C-3PO is a gilded whinger, but they both have a certain stubborn charm.

Ralph 124C 41+

CREATOR: HUGO GERNSBACK
SOURCE: *RALPH 124C 41+* (NOVEL)
DATE: 1911 (BOOK 1925)

A clean-cut young genius whose remarkable inventiveness is put to the test when his sweetheart is kidnapped by a lovesick Martian. He rises magnificently to the challenge, as befits a demigod of the Atom-Electronic Age.

Frank Reade

CREATOR: HARRY ENTON
SOURCE: *FRANK READE AND HIS STEAM MAN OF THE PLAINS* (DIME NOVEL)
DATE: 1876

Resourceful engineer protagonist of a long series of adventure stories published under the byline "Noname" in American boys' papers and dime paperbacks. The inventive hero, who was soon replaced by his almost indistinguishable son, Frank Reade, Jr, appeared in over 180 novellas published between the 1870s and the 1900s. In terms of its central sf gimmick, the first of these was actually a plagiarism of an earlier dime novel, *The Steam Man Of The Prairies* by Edward S. Ellis (1868); and wonderful steam-driven machines of various types featured in many of the later yarns, as did airships, submarines and even spacecraft. Although Harry Enton is the writer credited with the creation of Frank Reade (for publisher Frank Tousey), most of the later tales were written by Luis P. Senarens, an extremely prolific hack sometimes dubbed "the American Jules Verne": he took young Frank on exciting trips to darkest Africa, to the poles, under the Earth, to the bottom of the sea, and into outer space.

Ben Reich

CREATOR: ALFRED BESTER
SOURCE: *THE DEMOLISHED MAN* (NOVEL)
DATE: 1953

An entrepreneur troubled by disturbing visions, whose attempt to commit the perfect murder in a world of telepathic policemen comes close to succeeding. After being forced to confront his criminal proclivities, he must suffer the demolition of his warped personality.

Jaime Retief

CREATOR: KEITH LAUMER
SOURCE: *ENVOY TO NEW WORLDS* (STORY COLLECTION)
DATE: 1963

A skilled operative in the Corps Diplomatique Terrestrienne, who copes with all manner of delicate situations in a long-running series of comedy thrillers. He usually finds his stupid, stuck-in-the-mud superiors as problematic as his sly, warmongering adversaries.

Perry Rhodan

CREATORS: CLARK DARLTON AND KARL-HERBERT SCHEER
SOURCE: MOEWIG-VERLAG (PUBLISHER)
DATE: 1961

Space-conquering hero of a vast series of novellas published in Germany. Rhodan's adventures span the galaxy, "the ultimate series incorporating everything that was ever thought of in science fiction written into one interminable sequence" (according to critic Franz

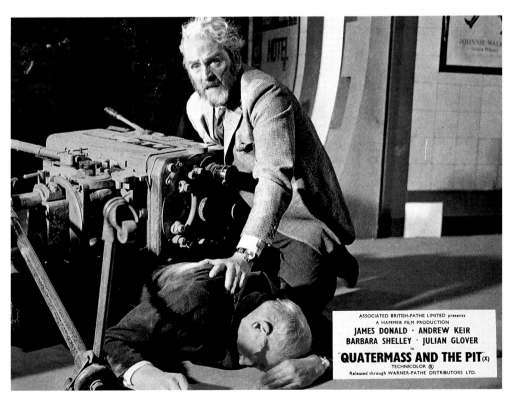

DON'T LOOK NOW *ONE OF THE MANY FACES OF PROFESSOR QUATERMASS, ANDREW KEIR PLAYS THE SCIENTIST IN THE THIRD HAMMER FILMS PRODUCTION AND IS SUITABLY AGHAST AT WHATEVER ALIEN LIFEFORM IS COMING HIS WAY*

ASSOCIATED BRITISH-PATHE LIMITED presents
A HAMMER FILM PRODUCTION
JAMES DONALD · ANDREW KEIR
BARBARA SHELLEY · JULIAN GLOVER
in
"QUATERMASS AND THE PIT"(X)
TECHNICOLOR ®
Released through WARNER-PATHE DISTRIBUTORS LTD.

Rottensteiner). There have been many hundreds of episodes, making this one of the longest fictional series of any kind ever penned. Other authors who have contributed to the saga include Kurt Brand, H. G. Ewers and Kurt Mahr. The stories have been translated widely, and appeared in English from 1969. By 1981, it was claimed, more than 750 million copies of the Rhodan tales had been sold in German.

Arnold J. Rimmer

Creators: Rob Grant and Doug Naylor
Source: *Red Dwarf* (BBC TV series)
Date: 1988
An archetypal loser, who converts his despairing self-loathing into snide officiousness and various other kinds of obsessive behaviour. Initially incarnate as an immaterial hologram, he eventually becomes the beneficiary of "hard light" solidity. Chris Barrie plays the part with uncanny conviction.

Ellen Ripley

Creators: Dan O'Bannon and Ridley Scott
Source: *Alien* (film)
Date: 1979
Tough spacewoman played by Sigourney Weaver in the celebrated Ridley Scott movie, and its sequels, James Cameron's kinetic *Aliens* (1986) and David Fincher's dour *Alien3* (1992). A role-model for feminists the universe over, she battles the vilest of extra-terrestrial menaces, a creature which secretes itself aboard a spacecraft (and similar enclosed environments, in the later films) and eventually kills all but one of the crew. Ripley is a splendid survivor – at least up until the last moments of the grim third movie. Novelizations of the screenplays were written by Alan Dean Foster.

Robby The Robot

Creators: Cyril Hume, Irving Block and Allen Adler
Source: *Forbidden Planet* (film)
Date: 1956
Vaguely humanoid electro-mechanical entity that resembles a 1950s jukebox on bulbous legs. Robby is servant to **Dr Morbius**, who presides like Prospero over the lonely planet Altair-4 (in this refashioning of *The Tempest*, Robby plays the part of Ariel). He helps Morbius and a party of explorers from Earth to fight the local equivalent of Caliban, the Monster from the Id. The novelization of the film was written by W. J. Stuart. Robby proved popular, and he was brought back as the "star" of a later film, The *Invisible Boy* (1957). This is not really a sequel to *Forbidden Planet*, but an entirely different story about a boy who builds his own robot.

RoboCop

Creators: Edward Neumeier, Michael Miner and Paul Verhoeven
Source: *RoboCop* (film)
Date: 1987
A cyborg enforcer built from the body of an honest cop who was betrayed by his corrupt

superiors and horribly mutilated by a criminal gang. He is intended by his makers to be an efficient automaton but he gradually recovers a ghostly consciousness of his lost identity, which equips him with a healthy measure of his former compassion and idealism. This device, cleverly extrapolated with minimal resources by actor Peter Weller, added a curious poignancy to the stereotyped search-and-destroy revenge plot, and gave the character a vital ambiguity which justified the sequels. A similar ambiguity helps to sustain the spinoff TV series in spite of the fact that the less comprehensively-costumed RoboCop is no longer allowed to do anyone any serious harm.

Robur

CREATOR: JULES VERNE
SOURCE: *ROBUR THE CONQUEROR* (NOVEL)
DATE: 1886
Inventor of a very advanced airship, with which he holds the world to ransom. At first a benign aeronautical version of **Captain Nemo**, Robur develops into a dangerous madman during the course of Verne's extravagant tale (also known in English as *The Clipper Of The Clouds*) and its late sequel *Master Of The World* (1904). Vincent Price played Robur in the Hollywood film entitled *Master Of The World* (1961).

Roderick

CREATOR: JOHN SLADEK
SOURCE: *RODERICK* AND *RODERICK AT RANDOM* (TWO-VOLUME NOVEL)
DATE: 1980
A robot made in the image of a teenage boy who is stolen from his human foster-parents and forced to embark upon a long odyssey through the hostile and puzzling human world. A delightfully pathetic and magnificently scrupulous modern Candide.

NUTS AND BOLTS POLICING *ROBOCOP (PETER WELLER)* – A POPULAR FILM-AND-TV IMAGE OF THE CYBORG AS LAW-ENFORCER WHO PATROLS THE STREETS OF A CORRUPT, NEAR-FUTURE METROPOLIS

Buck Rogers

CREATOR: PHILIP FRANCIS NOWLAN
SOURCE: 'ARMAGEDDON 2419' (NOVELLA)
DATE: 1928
American scientist, initially known as Anthony Rogers, who accidentally time-travels from the 1920s to the 25th century, via suspended animation, and finds himself embroiled in a revolution against Asiatic tyranny. He made his debut in *Amazing Stories* magazine; a second novella was combined with the first in the belated book *Armageddon 2419 AD* (1962). But, long before it reached book form, cartoonist Dick Calkins took this rather unpromising material as the basis for his newspaper strip *Buck Rogers In The 25th Century*, which, in addition to changing his forename from Tony to Buck, soon carried the hero off-Earth and into the wilder realms of space opera. The strip was an immense success, running continuously from 1929 until the late 1960s, and becoming so well-known that at one time the entire sf genre in America was stigmatized as "that crazy Buck Rogers stuff". In 1932, Buck made the transition to the radio: "While planets waged war against each other with death rays, gamma bombs, incendiary missiles, and massed flights of space ships, Buck, his lovely co-pilot Wilma Deering, and the brilliant Dr Huer spent week after week trying to save the universe from total destruction" (according to R. W. Stedman). Later, the space hero appeared in a cinema serial, *Buck Rogers* (1939), which starred Buster Crabbe (who had already played the similar character **Flash Gordon**). A cheaply-made television series of the same title (1950-51), starred Ken Dibbs. Nearly 30 years later, an elaborate TV movie, *Buck Rogers In The 25th Century*, also released as a cinema feature film (1979), had Gil Gerard as Rogers, and this gave rise to a new TV series which ran for two seasons in 1979-81. This occasioned a number of paperback spin-offs; but that was not the end for Buck: a few years later the games company

THE ORIGINAL SPACE COWBOY *BUCK ROGERS*, ARCHETYPAL HERO OF SPACE OPERA – AND AN AMERICAN FORERUNNER OF BRITAIN'S DAN DARE. HIS CAREER HAS SEEN HIM TRAVEL ALL THE WAY FROM THE 1920S TO THE END OF THE MILLENNIUM. ANOTHER 300 YEARS AND HE'LL CATCH UP WITH HIMSELF

TSR began publishing a quite unrelated series of new Buck Rogers novels, their titles including *Rebellion 2456* (1989), *Hammer Of Mars* (1989), *Armageddon Off Vesta* (1989) and *Prime Squared* (1990), all written by Melinda S. Murdock.

Rossum's Universal Robots

CREATOR: KAREL CAPEK
SOURCE: *R.U.R.* (PLAY)
DATE: 1920
Race of artificial humans made from synthetic protoplasm, intended to serve as slaves while true humans employ their leisure for the pursuit of spiritual perfection. Having acquired souls, they rebel against this destiny and destroy their makers. They are the source of the word "robot".

Rotwang

CREATORS: THEA VON HARBOU AND FRITZ LANG
SOURCE: *METROPOLIS* (FILM)
DATE: 1926
The evil scientist-cum-magician who superimposes upon a remarkably curvaceous robot the image of the saintly Maria, so that it may go forth and incite the downtrodden workers to disastrous rebellion. He is a symbolic figure of remarkable unclarity.

THE ANGRY GHOST

 MAN OF BRONZE *Doc Savage, the pulp-magazine hero extraordinaire*

Jane Saint

CREATOR: JOSEPHINE SAXTON
SOURCE: 'THE TRAVAILS OF JANE SAINT' (NOVELLA)
DATE: 1980

A feminist revolutionary sentenced to "total reprogramming" in a sensory deprivation tank, who undertakes a bizarre tragicomic dream-odyssey which serves in the end to confirm her ideals, and perhaps to return her to a better world.

Langdon St. Ives

CREATOR: JAMES P. BLAYLOCK
SOURCE: *HOMUNCULUS* (NOVEL)
DATE: 1986

An archetypally aristocratic scientist-detective in a mock-Dickensian 19th-century London, who is continually called upon to thwart the schemes of the evil Ignacio Narbondo, aided by his fellow members of the Trismegistus Club.

Sapphire & Steel

CREATOR: P. J. HAMMOND
SOURCE: *SAPPHIRE AND STEEL* (TV SERIES)
DATE: 1979

Elementals who assume human form in order to combat chaotic forces disrupting the continuity of history. The psychically-talented Sapphire (Joanna Lumley) and the broodily resilient Steel (David McCallum) are a very strange team who do a very weird job in a very bizarre fashion.

Doc Savage

CREATOR: LESTER DENT
SOURCE: 'THE MAN OF BRONZE' (NOVELLA)
DATE: 1933

Full name Clark Savage, Jr., a brilliant young scientist who is trained by his father to become the ultimate crime-fighter. Doc has the benefit of a perfect physique and a sharp, analytical brain. He uses many technological gadgets in his fight against villainy, and he is assisted by a team of comrades who include the enormous engineer Col. John Renwick ("Renny"), the thickset chemist Lt. Col. Andrew Blodgett Mayfair ("Monk"), and the well-dressed lawyer Brig. Gen. Theodore Marley Brooks ("Ham"). He also has a lady friend, his cousin, the resourceful Patricia Savage. Normally, Doc resides in a vast apartment at the top of New York's tallest skyscraper (presumably the Empire State Building), though he also has a "Fortress of Solitude" on an Arctic island (where he is wont to perform brain surgery on criminals). One of the best-known pulp superheroes of the 1930s, he appeared in 181 issues of *Doc Savage Magazine*, published between 1933 and 1949. All of the magazine's novellas carried the house byline "Kenneth Robeson", but in fact 165 of them, including the first, were written by the expert pulpsmith Lester Dent. Most of the stories were reprinted in paperback books during the 1960s and 70s, and met with considerable renewed success: many of Doc's adventures are fantastic in the extreme, and some of the evocative titles of these slim volumes are *The Thousand-Headed Man* (1964), *The Mystic Mullah* (1965), *Land Of Always-Night* (1966) and *The Czar Of Fear* (1967). In addition, Doc Savage appeared briefly on the radio (1934) and in comic books (1940-43; and again in 1972-75). The film *Doc Savage: The Man Of Bronze* (1975) starred Ron Ely (a former television Tarzan) as the well-muscled hero. Savage also appears, under the pseudonym "Doc Caliban", in two novels by Philip José Farmer, the pornographic *A Feast Unknown* (1969) and the more straightforward *The Mad Goblin* (1970; also known as *The Keepers Of The Secrets*). Farmer has also written a detailed biography of the character, *Doc Savage: His Apocalyptic Life* (1973), in which he describes the golden-eyed hero as "the Archangel of Technopolis". A further lease of life for Doc Savage came in the early 1990s, when Farmer's original novel *Escape From Loki* (1991), an extravaganza about Doc's adventures as a boy during World War I, heralded a renewed series of his adventures in paperback. Apart from Farmer's book, these have been written by Doc Savage enthusiast Will Murray, initially drawing on rediscovered outlines by Lester Dent, and published under the traditional house name of Kenneth Robeson. Titles include: *Python Isle* (1991), *White Eyes* (1992), *The Frightened Fish* (1992), *The Jade Ogre* (1992), *Flight Into Fear* (1993), *The Whistling Wraith* (1993) and *The Forgotten Realm* (1993).

Captain Scarlet

CREATORS: GERRY AND SYLVIA ANDERSON
SOURCE: *CAPTAIN SCARLET AND THE MYSTERONS* (TV SERIES)
DATE: 1967

An almost-indestructible, colour-coded agent of Spectrum, dedicated to saving Earth from the body-snatching Martian Mysterons and the machinations of the traitorous Captain Black. An oddly ambiguous puppet character, continually dicing with death.

Hari Seldon

CREATOR: ISAAC ASIMOV
SOURCE: *FOUNDATION* (FIX-UP NOVEL)
DATE: 1951

The great pioneer of psychohistory and presiding genius of the original Foundation series is represented therein solely by his works, although the oft-quoted *Encyclopedia Galactica* briefly summarizes his career. He appears in *Prelude To Foundation* (1988) as a modest but ambitious young theoretician who attracts the unwelcome attention of the Emperor after arriving on the planet Trantor to deliver a paper on psychohistory at an academic conference. His later career, when he has fully realized the vital part that he must play in securing the future of civilization, is described in *Forward The Foundation* (1993) – at which point, Asimov confessed, surely to no one's surprise, that he regarded Seldon as his very own alter ego.

David Selig

Creator: Robert Silverberg
Source: *Dying Inside* (novel)
Date: 1972

A telepath whose ability to eavesdrop upon the thoughts and feelings of others has alienated him from human society. As his power gradually wanes, he realizes that mental isolation may be the first step on the road to authentic community.

Severian

Creator: Gene Wolfe
Source: *The Book Of The New Sun* (four-volume novel)
Date: 1980

An orphan raised as an apprentice torturer in a far-future city from which he is banished for an act of mercy. His subsequent wanderings allow him to become the heir of the Autarch who rules the world and the messianic Conciliator who will welcome the rebirth of the sun.

Shevek

Creator: Ursula Le Guin
Source: *The Dispossessed* (novel)
Date: 1974

A brilliant physicist born and raised in the straitened communist society of Anarres, who visits the neighbouring world of Urras – where an ethic of individualistic enterprise prevails – after formulating his General Temporal Theory. Although he is a creative individual himself, he finds it a very discomfiting place.

The Silver Surfer

Creators: Stan Lee and Jack Kirby
Source: Marvel Comics
Date: 1966

Silver-coated alien being who rides a thought-controlled flying surfboard. An ally of **Mr Fantastic** and the Fantastic Four, the Surfer is probably the weirdest of the superheroes unleashed on the world by Marvel Comics. He had a reputation in the late 1960s as "a popular philosopher on matters of war, peace, and power".

Sirius

Creator: Olaf Stapledon
Source: *Sirius* (novel)
Date: 1944

An Alsatian dog whose intelligence is artificially augmented. He grows up with Plaxy, the daughter of his creator, and forms a uniquely intimate relationship with her – but the world of men has no place for him and he cannot entirely transcend his "wolfish" instincts.

Commander Benjamin Sisko

Creators: Rick Berman and Michael Piller
Source: *Star Trek: Deep Space Nine* (TV series)
Date: 1992

Officer in charge of an ex-Cardassian space station located close to a strategically-important wormhole, and played by Avery Brooks. As a black single parent, he has a natural sympathy with minority groups and has a relentlessly suspicious mind. His sterling qualities were rewarded with a promotion to captain at the end of the third season.

Luke Skywalker

Creator: George Lucas
Source: *Star Wars* (film)
Date: 1977

Youthful hero of the most successful space-adventure story of recent decades – the

---

CAN YOU FEEL THE FORCE? *Luke Skywalker (Mark Hamill) sets out on a great adventure in* Star Wars

Star Wars trilogy. Luke grows up on a far planet, and on reaching manhood finds himself sucked into a revolutionary war against the interstellar Empire. He trains to become a "Jedi knight", and meets the beautiful Princess Leia Organa, the roughneck space pilot **Han Solo**, and the comical but talented robots **R2-D2** and **C-3PO**. Eventually, by using his Jedi skills and by tapping "the Force" (a sort of spiritual ether), he overcomes his arch-enemy, the black-clad and heavy-breathing **Darth Vader**. *Star Wars* achieved phenomenal popularity, a success which was helped by superb special effects and a rousing musical score by John Williams. The sequels, *The Empire Strikes Back* (1980) and *Return Of The Jedi* (1983), were just as popular as the original. Mark Hamill played Luke Skywalker in all three. A publishing and merchandising industry has grown up around *Star Wars*. As well as the bestselling novelizations of the film scripts, there have been other novels about Skywalker and his confederates: an example is *Splinter Of The Mind's Eye: From The Adventures Of Luke Skywalker* (1978) by Alan Dean Foster. There have also been several American radio serials and many comic books devoted to the saga's characters. This spin-off industry gained its second wind in 1990, when Lucas gave permission for a further novel series by various hands; the first of these to appear was *Heir To The Empire* (1991) by Timothy Zahn, which took up the interstellar action some five years after the events of *Return Of The Jedi*. The book sold extremely well, as did the sequels by the same author, *Dark Force Rising*

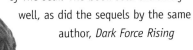

(1992) and *The Last Command* (1993). Other novels have followed, by writers such as Roger MacBride Allen, Kevin J. Anderson, Barbara Hambly, Vonda N. McIntyre, Kathy Tyers and Dave Wolverton.

The Slans

CREATOR: A. E. VAN VOGT
SOURCE: *SLAN* (NOVEL)
DATE: 1940 (BOOK 1946)

A psychically-gifted mutant race engineered by ordinary humans but jealously persecuted. They are stigmatized by tendrils growing on their foreheads, but a new strain of tendril-less Slans, capable of hiding among humankind, dramatically alters the balance of power.

Michael Valentine Smith

CREATOR: ROBERT A. HEINLEIN
SOURCE: *STRANGER IN A STRANGE LAND* (NOVEL)
DATE: 1961

A human child born and raised on Mars, equipped with psychic powers acquired from the Martians. He returns to Earth and founds a cult based in the Martian philosophy of "grokking", eventually suffering the fate typically allotted to messiahs. Contrary to rumour, he had no influence on Charles Manson.

Northwest Smith

CREATOR: C. L. MOORE
SOURCE: 'SHAMBLEAU' (NOVELETTE)
DATE: 1933

The hard-bitten hero of a lively series of interplanetary adventures, which involved him with various alien femmes fatales and other subtle menaces. He extricated himself from their clutches with more than a little difficulty, but always with a certain rakish aplomb.

Winston Smith

CREATOR: GEORGE ORWELL
SOURCE: *NINETEEN EIGHTY-FOUR* (NOVEL)
DATE: 1949

Unhappy minor bureaucrat in the future totalitarian state known as Airstrip One (actually Britain). He rebels against the Thought Police, but eventually his spirit is crushed by the interrogator, O'Brien, and he learns to "love" the state's unseen leader, **Big Brother**. In Nigel Kneale's famous BBC television adaptation (1954), Smith was played by Peter Cushing. In the subsequent feature film (1955), he was portrayed, rather less satisfactorily, by Edmond O'Brien. In the remake (1984), John Hurt took the part.

Dr Zachary Smith

CREATOR: IRWIN ALLEN
SOURCE: *LOST IN SPACE* (TV SERIES)
DATE: 1965

Cast away with the Robinson family as a result of his own incompetent sabotage, the cowardly and perpetually-whingeing Dr Smith (Jonathan Harris) remained the perennial fly in their ointment, whose hypocritical machinations added an extra twist to every plot.

Han Solo

CREATOR: GEORGE LUCAS
SOURCE: *STAR WARS* (FILM)
DATE: 1977

Rough, tough space pilot, played by Harrison Ford, who assists **Luke Skywalker** and Princess Leia in their struggle against Darth Vader and the evil Empire. Solo's further adventures have been recounted in a series of novels by Brian C. Daley: *Han Solo At Star's End* (1979), *Han Solo's Revenge* (1979) and *Han Solo And The Lost Legacy* (1980).

Jaime Sommers

CREATORS: HARVE BENNETT AND KENNETH JOHNSON
SOURCE: *THE BIONIC WOMAN* (TV SERIES)
DATE: 1976

Super-lady played by Lindsay Wagner in an adventure series spin-off from *The Six Million Dollar Man*. Like **Steve Austin**, she is "rebuilt" after an accident and hence is able to run like a cheetah, lift huge weights, and hear at a distance – all in the cause of catching various crooks and spies. Over a decade after the series ended, Jaime and Steve returned in the TV movie *Bionic Showdown* (1989).

Garry Sparrow

CREATORS: LAURENCE MARKS & MAURICE GRAN
SOURCE: *GOODNIGHT SWEETHEART* (BBC TV SERIES)
DATE: 1993

Nicholas Lyndhurst played the TV repairman who becomes an inadvertent time-traveller, from the 1990s to the Blitz-torn London of 50 years earlier, in this engaging sitcom. He ends up wooing a cockney barmaid while posing as a great songwriter, most of his "compositions" being stolen from Lennon and McCartney or Elton John.

Spider-Man

CREATORS: STAN LEE AND STEVE DITKO
SOURCE: MARVEL COMICS
DATE: 1962

Real name Peter Parker, one of the best-known costumed superheroes of the 1960s and since. A diffident bespectacled youth, Parker is bitten by a mutant spider which imparts its arachnid skills to him. Discovering that he now has enormous strength and awesome climbing ability, Parker decides to become a crime-fighter and to that end adopts the persona of Spider-Man. Clad in a red and blue outfit decorated with black webbing, and armed with a "webshooter", he pursues baddies wherever they may lead him – which usually means up and down the sheer faces of city skyscrapers. "Spidey" has appeared in various Marvel Comics titles, in animated television series, and in the live-action TV movie *Spider-Man* (1977) and the subsequent series, where he was played by Nicholas Hammond. Spider-Man's exploits have been recounted in the novels *Mayhem In Manhattan* (1978) by Len Wein and Marv Wolfman, and *Crime Campaign* (1979) and *Murdermoon* (1979) by Paul Kupperberg.

DOES WHATEVER A SPIDER CAN *THE IMMENSELY STRONG (BUT CURIOUSLY INTROVERTED) SPIDEY, ALIAS PETER PARKER*

Mr Spock

CREATOR: GENE RODDENBERRY
SOURCE: *STAR TREK* (TV SERIES)
DATE: 1966

Pointy-eared, supposedly emotionless and highly "logical" alien crew-member of the **Starship Enterprise**, played by Leonard Nimoy. He hails from the planet Vulcan. Apart from **Captain James T. Kirk**, he became the most famous character of the series, much loved by the "Trekkers" who regularly hold conventions to honour *Star Trek*. (One of their amusements in the 1980s was the performance of an illicit comic-pornographic play, *Spock In Manacles*.) Mr Spock features prominently in the novelizations of the series by James Blish (who wrote 11 volumes between 1967 and his death in 1975) and many other writers. Blish's book *Spock Must Die!* (1970) is an original novel about the character (not based on a script). *Spock, Messiah!* (1976) by Theodore R. Cogswell and Charles A. Spano is another such original book –

Sphere Science Fiction
Harry Harrison
THE STAINLESS STEEL RAT

THE ADVENTURES OF SLIPPERY JIM *FIRST IN A SERIES OF POPULAR SF NOVELS BY HARRISON*

its title is perhaps revealing of many fans's attitude to Mr Spock. Leonard Nimoy continued to play Spock in the feature films based on the TV series: *Star Trek: The Motion Picture* (1979), *Star Trek II: The Wrath Of Khan* (1982), *Star Trek III: The Search For Spock* (1984), *Star Trek IV: The Voyage Home* (1986), *Star Trek V: The Final Frontier* (1989) and *Star Trek VI: The Undiscovered Country* (1991).

The Stainless Steel Rat

CREATOR: HARRY HARRISON
SOURCE: *THE STAINLESS STEEL RAT* (NOVEL)
DATE: 1961

An interstellar crook-turned-policeman, alias Slippery Jim DiGriz, who appears in a series of humorous sf yarns. Later titles include *The Stainless Steel Rat's Revenge* (1970), *The Stainless Steel Rat Saves The World* (1972), *The Stainless Steel Rat Wants You!* (1978), *The Stainless Steel Rat For President* (1982), *A Stainless Steel Rat Is Born* (1985), *The Stainless Steel Rat Gets Drafted* (1987) and *The Stainless Steel Rat Sings The Blues* (1994).

CAPTAIN'S LOGIC *THE POPULAR MR SPOCK (LEONARD NIMOY), COMPLETE WITH BEATLE HAIRCUT AND FLAME-TIPPED EARS*

Eric John Stark

CREATOR: LEIGH BRACKETT
SOURCE: 'QUEEN OF THE MARTIAN CATACOMBS' (NOVELLA)
DATE: 1949

A swashbuckling soldier of fortune and interplanetary outlaw, a gritty paragon of all masculine virtues. His principal stamping ground was Mars, but he also visited Venus and he was revived for a new series of adventures outside the solar system, in the world of *The Ginger Star* (1974).

The Starman

CREATORS: BRUCE A. EVANS, RAYNOLD GIDEON AND JOHN CARPENTER
SOURCE: *STARMAN* (FILM)
DATE: 1984

An alien visitor to Earth (Jeff Bridges) who incarnates himself as a replica of the heroine's dead husband, pursuing a rather problematic relationship with her before unequivocally demonstrating his niceness and exiting, pursued by smokey bears. He came back (as Robert Hays) for a short-lived TV series.

Dr Strangelove

CREATORS: TERRY SOUTHERN AND STANLEY KUBRICK
SOURCE: *DR STRANGELOVE, OR HOW I LEARNED TO STOP WORRYING AND LOVE THE BOMB* (FILM)
DATE: 1963

Weapons technologist, a former Nazi now working for America, played by Peter Sellers in Stanley Kubrick's definitive satirical film about the nuclear threat. Strangelove, inventor of the ultimate doomsday bomb, is a complete madman who cannot prevent his right arm from rising in an involuntary Nazi salute. The script was based on the novel *Two Hours To Doom* by Peter Bryant (1958; also known as *Red Alert*). Strangelove does not appear in the original novel, which is a sober, admonitory work; however, he does feature in Peter George's wholly rewritten version of the book, *Dr Strangelove* (1963).

Sub-Mariner

CREATOR: BILL EVERETT
SOURCE: MARVEL COMICS NO. 1
DATE: 1939

Prince Namor of sunken Atlantis, an aggressive superhero who is able to swim at speeds of 60 miles an hour (and fly through the air). Sub-Mariner was the very first hero of the Marvel family, and he has continued to lead a healthy existence ever since. Like many of the great comic-book figures, he appeared in an animated television series during the 1960s.

Supergirl

CREATORS: MORT WEISINGER AND OTTO BINDER
SOURCE: ACTION COMICS
DATE: 1959

Real name Kara, alias Linda Lee Danvers. Like her cousin, **Superman**, she hails from the planet Krypton, has immense strength and super senses, and can fly. In the film *Supergirl* (1984), she was played by Helen Slater.

Superman

CREATORS: JEROME SIEGEL AND JOE SCHUSTER
SOURCE: ACTION COMICS
DATE: 1938

Space-born hero who can fly, is invulnerable, has x-ray vision, and is capable of moving mountains. A refugee from the planet Krypton, he is raised on Earth by loving foster-parents. In daily life, he is the "mild-mannered" reporter Clark Kent; but when occasion demands he removes his suit and glasses, and soars into the sky resplendent in blue tights and red cape. Superman is the most omnipotent hero ever (although he can be weakened by the mysterious element Kryptonite), and the most famous character to emerge from American comic books. He was created by two young sf fans who planned the character in the early 1930s: a prototype of Superman appeared in their fanzine, but when they tried to sell the concept they met with failure. It was in June 1938 that Superman found a home, with the company that was to become DC Comics. He was a huge success, and the progenitor of a whole line of outlandishly costumed heroes. From 1939, Superman had his own comic book, and before long the Man of Steel was a considerable hit in other media. Siegel and Schuster lost control of their creation, and the individual most responsible for developing Superman, over several decades, was comic-book editor Mort Weisinger. One of his innovations was to give the character the power of time travel; he also rewrote the story of Superman's origins, introducing super-villains from the planet Krypton, alternative time-lines

and other refinements that helped keep the saga from becoming too predictable. As well as the multiplying comic books, there have been occasional novels about Superman; examples are *The Adventures Of Superman* by George Lowther (1942), *Superman: Last Son Of Krypton* by Elliott S. Maginn (1978) and *The Death And Life Of Superman* by Roger Stern (1993). An anthology containing all-new stories is *The Further Adventures Of Superman* edited by Martin H. Greenberg (1993). Clayton "Bud" Collyer was the actor who gave voice to Superman on radio, from 1940 (he indicated the character was taking flight by the repeated phrase "Up, up, and awa-a-a-ay!"). Collyer also worked on the soundtracks of short animated films about Superman produced by Max Fleischer (1941-43). Others who have incarnated the hero include Kirk Alyn in the film serials *Superman* (1948) and *Atom Man Vs. Superman* (1950); and George Reeves in the feature film *Superman And The Mole Men* (1951) and the television series *The Adventures*

Of Superman (1952-57). The big-budget feature films *Superman* (1978), *Superman II* (1980), *Superman III* (1983) and *Superman IV: The Quest For Peace* (1987) all starred Christopher Reeve as the Man of Steel: he made a good-looking hero – even if he was most effective when he played the diffident Clark Kent. Another TV series, *Lois & Clark: The New Adventures Of Superman* (from 1993), has brought the character into the 90s, with Dean Cain in the lead.

Tom Swift

CREATOR: EDWARD L. STRATEMEYER
SOURCE: *TOM SWIFT AND HIS MOTOR-CYCLE (NOVEL)*
DATE: 1910

Inventive boy-hero of a long series of books for kids, continuing with such titles as *Tom Swift And His Electric Rifle* (1911). Obsessed by wonderful machines, he is very much in the mould of his dime-novel predecessor **Frank Reade**. Produced by Stratemeyer's fiction factory, all the stories appeared under the house name "Victor Appleton", although most of the early books were written by Howard R. Garis. That original series came to an end in 1938, but from 1954 to 1971 a second series appeared: these concerned the adventures of "Tom Swift, Jr" and they were overseen by Harriet S. Adams (Stratemeyer's daughter). Further series have appeared in the 1980s and 90s, mainly by professional sf writers using the Appleton name.

Tank Girl

CREATORS: JAMIE HEWLETT AND ALAN MARTIN
SOURCE: *DEADLINE* (COMIC)
DATE: 1988
A foul-mouthed Australian superbitch with a fondness for graphic violence and a mutant kangaroo for a boyfriend. The 1995 film version starring Lori Petty gave her a name (Rebecca Buck), a really neat tank and a Mad Max-ish setting, but softened her up considerably.

Teenage Mutant Ninja Turtles

CREATORS: KEVIN EASTMAN AND PETER LAIRD
SOURCE: SMALL-PRESS COMIC BOOK
DATE: 1984
"Cowabunga!" they cry: comic-strip turtles, mutated by effluents in the New York sewers where they dwell, and expert in the martial arts. The green-skinned, pizza-loving, streetwise foursome are named after Italian Renaissance artists – Raphael, Michelangelo, Donatello and Leonardo. Originally intended as a spoof, the Turtles swiftly became an enormous craze, inspiring an animated television series of the late 1980s in addition to toys and spinoff books and a run of live-action films: *Teenage Mutant Ninja Turtles* (1990), *The Secret Of The Ooze* (1991) and *Teenage Mutant Ninja Turtles III* (1993).

Troy Tempest

CREATORS: GERRY AND SYLVIA ANDERSON
SOURCE: *STINGRAY* (TV SERIES)
DATE: 1964

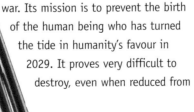

TEEN DREAM *TANK GIRL, THE ULTIMATE PUNK SF HEROINE AND EVERY TEENAGE BOY'S FANTASY*

Agent of the World Aquanaut Security Patrol and pilot of the submarine *Stingray*. More inclined to fits of bad temper than the other heroes of SuperMarionation, perhaps because of his simultaneous involvement with the boss's daughter, Atlanta, and the mutely enigmatic Marina.

The Terminator

CREATORS: JAMES CAMERON AND GALE ANNE HURD
SOURCE: *THE TERMINATOR* (FILM)
DATE: 1984
A cyborg killing-machine sent back in time from a future in which humans and machines are at war. Its mission is to prevent the birth of the human being who has turned the tide in humanity's favour in 2029. It proves very difficult to destroy, even when reduced from

HARD ON THE INSIDE *THE TIME-TRAVELLING HUMANOID ROBOT KNOWN AS THE TERMINATOR (PLAYED BY ARNOLD SCHWARZENEGGER)*

the musclebound bulk of Arnold Schwarzenegger to a mechanical skeleton. Schwarzenegger returned in the 1991 sequel as an altruistic convert to the human side, sent to defend the boy who will – if allowed – grow up to be humanity's leader against a new attack by a more advanced and rather mercurial model. Magnificent special effects elevated both Terminators to the ranks of cinematic sf's most convincing non-human villains.

The Thing (From Another World)

CREATOR: JOHN W. CAMPBELL, JR.
SOURCE: 'WHO GOES THERE?' (NOVELLA)
DATE: 1938
Shape-shifting alien capable of mimicking and replacing its victims, identifiable only at the level of molecular analysis. The film version of 1951 was in the forefront of the Cold War monster-movie boom; John Carpenter's 1982 remake was truer to the original and had some brilliantly nasty special effects.

Algy Timberlane

CREATOR: BRIAN W. ALDISS
SOURCE: *GREYBEARD* (NOVEL)
DATE: 1964
Former soldier and sometime member of DOUCH(E) – Documentation of Universal Contemporary History (English branch) – who is now going grey, although he is one of the youngest people remaining in a world where no children have been born for many years, due to the aftermath of a series of nuclear tests.

The Time Traveller

CREATOR: H. G. WELLS

SOURCE: 'THE TIME MACHINE' (NOVELLA)

DATE: 1895

An unnamed man of science who builds his own machine for travelling the time-stream. He visits the year 802,701 AD, where he finds a society divided into two: the peaceful but aimless Eloi live in the sunlight, and the dangerous **Morlocks** lurk below ground. The Traveller returns to recount his frightening experiences to a group of friends, then disappears once more into far futurity. The open ending has inspired a number of people to write sequels. The German writer Egon Friedell published his *The Return Of The Time Machine* in 1946; later efforts include *The Space Machine* (1976) by Christopher Priest (in which the Time Traveller visits Mars); *Morlock Night* (1979) by K. W. Jeter (in which the Morlocks from 802,701 invade the London of the 1890s); and *The Time Ships* (1995) by Stephen Baxter (the most complex and fully worked-out sequel of them all, published in the centenary year of Wells's masterpiece). A film, *The Time Machine* (1960), starred Rod Taylor as the Time Traveller. The American TV movie of the same title (1978), with John Beck, bears small resemblance to Wells's story. On BBC TV, a 60-minute adaptation appeared as early as 1949, with Russell Napier as the Time Traveller. Nicholas Meyer's cinema film *Time After Time* (1979) imagined H. G. Wells himself as the Traveller, played by Malcolm McDowell: he pursues Jack the Ripper to late-20th-century America.

The Transformers

CREATOR: PALITOY

SOURCE: *TRANSFORMERS*

(TV ANIMATION AND COMIC BOOKS)

DATE: 1984

Articulated humanoid robots that can be reshaped into various kinds of vehicles. The good Autobots are continually locked in combat with the evil Decepticons. In the 1986 movie, Orson Welles provided the voice of a megalomaniac planet. The media manifestations were glorified ads for the toys, and caused some controversy among anxious parents for that reason.

The Triffids

CREATOR: JOHN WYNDHAM

SOURCE: *THE DAY OF THE TRIFFIDS* (NOVEL)

DATE: 1951

Large ambulatory plants equipped with lethal stings, featured in Wyndham's bestselling book (published in America as *Revolt Of The Triffids*). After the majority of the human race has been blinded by mysterious lights in the night sky, the Triffids come into their own, driving the hero and his small group of friends to a refuge on the Isle of Wight. The novel has been filmed (1963) and serialized on BBC television (1981).

The Tripods

CREATOR: JOHN CHRISTOPHER

SOURCE: *THE WHITE MOUNTAINS* (NOVEL)

DATE: 1967

Conquering aliens whose "capping" technique controls adults and re-medievalizes human society – but they fail to quell the rebellious spirit of the uncapped heroes. The TV version of 1984-85 was unfortunately axed before reaching the concluding volume of Christopher's initial trilogy.

Kilgore Trout

CREATOR: KURT VONNEGUT

SOURCE: *GOD BLESS YOU, MR ROSEWATER* (NOVEL)

DATE: 1965

Under-appreciated, penniless sf writer who has pretty neat ideas even though he can't write for sour apples. He first appears as a minor character, "the author of 87 paperback books ... unknown outside the science-fiction field". He reappears in Vonnegut's best-known work, *Slaughterhouse-Five* (1969), where he is the favourite living author of that novel's hero, **Billy Pilgrim**. He goes on to play a leading role in *Breakfast Of Champions* (1973) and a more retiring one in *Jailbird* (1979). In *Galapagos* (1985) – which is narrated by his son, Leon Trout – he features briefly as a ghost. In 1975, there appeared an amusing novel, *Venus On The Half-Shell*, which carried the byline "Kilgore Trout". Some readers believed this to be by Kurt Vonnegut, but in fact it turned out to be the work of literary trickster Philip José Farmer. The latter has also published an "interview" with the great man, 'The Obscure Life And Hard Times Of Kilgore Trout' (1973). The name echoes that of sf writer Theodore Sturgeon (publicly admired by Vonnegut), though in other ways the description does not fit.

Tweel

CREATOR: STANLEY G. WEINBAUM

SOURCE: 'A MARTIAN ODYSSEY' (STORY)

DATE: 1934

An intelligent but very strange bird-like alien who helps two stranded humans in spite of the fact that they can only communicate by dubious sign language. Often hailed as the first real alien to be featured in pulp sf.

—◦◦◦—

V

Darth Vader

CREATOR: GEORGE LUCAS

SOURCE: *STAR WARS* (FILM)

DATE: 1977

Heavy-breathing, black-clad villain of the space-opera saga that continued with *The Empire Strikes Back* (1980) and *Return Of The Jedi* (1983). Formerly a Jedi knight, Annakin Skywalker (and, as it turns out, father of the young hero **Luke Skywalker**), Vader has been seduced by "the dark side of the Force" and now serves the evil Emperor. He was played by stuntman David Prowse, although his deep voice was provided by James Earl Jones.

Nicholas van Rijn

CREATOR: POUL ANDERSON

SOURCE: 'MARGIN OF PROFIT' (NOVELETTE)

DATE: 1956

An overweight trader blessed with vast and varied appetites, sometime head of Solar Spice & Liquors. He is a significant "merchant prince" of the Polesotechnic League, whose commercial activities loosely unite a string of worlds destined to be the nucleus of a fledgling galactic empire. Later works featuring van Rijn include the novel *War Of The Wing-Men* (1958; revised as *The Man Who Counts*), the collections *Trader To The Stars* (1964) and *The Trouble Twisters* (1966), and the novels *Satan's World* (1969) and *Mirkheim* (1977).

possibly stand against him for long is his confused clone-brother Mark. His adventures have won lots of awards, as befits a perfect role-model for bright and reasonably buoyant kids.

The Vril-ya

CREATOR: EDWARD BULWER-LYTTON
SOURCE: *THE COMING RACE* (NOVEL)
DATE: 1871
A society of superhumans living in a secluded underworld. They are physically magnificent even though they have no need of muscle-power, all work being done by means of vril: a kind of atomic power administered by magic wands. They are not entirely happy, however, because life holds no challenges for them.

TALL, DARK AND CONSUMMATE EVIL
DARTH VADER (DAVID PROWSE) IN STAR WARS PROVED AN EFFECTIVE FOIL TO THE YOUNG LUKE'S RIGHTEOUS QUEST TO BECOME A JEDI KNIGHT FIGHTING FOR GOOD

Captain Video

CREATOR: LARRY MENKIN
SOURCE: *CAPTAIN VIDEO* (TV SERIES)
DATE: 1949
Spaceman of the 22nd century, in a very early and extremely low-budget American TV show. With his Video Rangers, he patrols the solar system in a spaceship called the *Galaxy*. The first actor to play the Captain was Richard Coogan, but he was soon replaced by Al Hodge, who took the part for the bulk of the series. The hero was also embodied by Judd Holdren in a cinema serial, *Captain Video* (1952). There was a Captain Video comic book in the early 1950s, and an animated TV series, *Captain Video's Cartoons* (1956-57).

David Vincent

CREATOR: LARRY COHEN
SOURCE: *THE INVADERS* (ABC TV SERIES)
DATE: 1967
An ordinary man who stumbles upon a dark secret – Earth is being invaded by aliens who can mimic humans perfectly save from their inflexible little fingers – but cannot convince anyone else (because dead aliens always disintegrate). Roy Thinnes was the definitive justified paranoid, who spent what seemed like years trying to warn the world.

Lorq von Ray

CREATOR: SAMUEL R. DELANY
SOURCE: *NOVA* (NOVEL)
DATE: 1968
The obsessive heir to the commercial empire constituted by the Pleiades Federation, who requires a massive supply of the psychomorphic power-source Illyrion if he is to wrest control of interstellar transportation from his arch-rival Prince Red. He goes after it with splendid recklessness.

Miles Vorkosigan

CREATOR: LOIS MCMASTER BUJOLD
SOURCE: *THE WARRIOR'S APPRENTICE* (NOVEL)
DATE: 1986
A highly-motivated military genius who becomes a charismatic leader – in spite of his very short stature and awkwardly brittle bones – and contrives to lead a complicated double life as an officer in the Barrayaran Navy and the commander of the Dendarii Mercenaries. This enables him to combine the uses of legitimate and illegitimate authority, rather as if the Scarlet Pimpernel had turned out to be the Duke of Wellington, or the Sheriff of Nottingham had been Robin Hood's secret identity. He is witty as well as clever and he eventually finds a perfect mate in Elli Quinn; the only adversary who can

Riddley Walker

CREATOR: RUSSELL HOBAN
SOURCE: *RIDDLEY WALKER* (NOVEL)
DATE: 1980
Youth who lives in a post-nuclear England, thousands of years hence. In the debased but strangely poetic language of a barbarous future, he narrates his meagre life-story. His account forms the text of the novel. Hoban has since written a stage version of this cautionary fable (1986).

Enoch Wallace

CREATOR: CLIFFORD D. SIMAK
SOURCE: *WAY STATION* (NOVEL)
DATE: 1963
Mid-West farmer, a fabulous hermit, who turns out to be 124 years old and a veteran of the American Civil War. His longevity has been conferred by aliens, who have appointed him as keeper of their secret galactic way station. Wallace, with his old-world virtues and love of the land, is the archetypal Simakian hero, fondly remembered by all the author's readers.

Nigel Walmsley

CREATOR: GREGORY BENFORD
SOURCE: *IN THE OCEAN OF NIGHT* (NOVEL)
DATE: 1977

An astronaut and space scientist who has an interesting encounter with "the Snark" – an alien machine intelligence – which proves to be the first step of a journey that takes him into the distant future and deep into the wonderland of esty (solidified spacetime). While there, he plays a key role in deciding the ultimate fate of all life in the universe.

TIN CAN ALLY *Perhaps the best-loved incarnation of Doctor Who, Tom Baker, with a tame Dalek*

The Watchmen

CREATOR: ALAN MOORE
SOURCE: *WATCHMEN* (GRAPHIC NOVEL)
DATE: 1987

The second-generation vigilante guardians of an alternative Earth where costumed superheroes have been maintaining law and order for half a century. They are confused and confounded by an enemy whose machinations they are ill-equipped to combat. They represent a further evolution of the problematic Marvel superheroes of the 1960s.

Herbert West

CREATOR: H. P. LOVECRAFT
SOURCE: 'HERBERT WEST – REANIMATOR' (STORY-CYCLE)
DATE: 1922

A mad scientist, protagonist of an unsuccessful series of horror-comedies by Lovecraft. He was spectacularly revived to star in a magnificently nauseating movie, *Re-Animator* (1985), in which Jeffrey Combs played the lead. The repetitive 1989 sequel proved that there's no point in flogging a dead horse twice.

Julian West

CREATOR: EDWARD BELLAMY
SOURCE: *LOOKING BACKWARD, 2000-1887* (NOVEL)
DATE: 1888

A rich Bostonian who goes too far in seeking a cure for his insomnia and sleeps until 2000, waking into an egalitarian utopia which he slowly grows to like (with the assistance of Edith Leete, the great-granddaughter of his former fiancée). Several sequels by other hands confused him with very different schemes of enlightenment.

Doctor Who

CREATORS: SYDNEY NEWMAN AND DONALD WILSON
SOURCE: *DOCTOR WHO* (BBC TV SERIES)
DATE: 1963

A benign, but often crotchety or eccentric, "Time Lord". He was hero of the children's

GREAT GRAPHICS *With its sophisticated text, The Watchmen became the most famous of all sf "graphic novels" (comic books with thick spines)*

series which ran until 1989 and became the best-known science-fiction phenomenon in Britain. The otherwise nameless Doctor travels through time and space in a vehicle known as the *Tardis* (disguised on the outside to resemble an old-fashioned London police telephone box), and is capable periodically of renewing his own face and body. The most celebrated of the show's scriptwriters was Terry Nation, who introduced the Doctor's deadly enemies, the alien Daleks. The series was astonishingly long-lived, and a number of actors played the Doctor over the years. The first was William Hartnell, who portrayed the mysterious Time Lord as a rather irascible old man. He was followed by several younger actors – Patrick Troughton, Jon Pertwee, Tom Baker (whose characterization was the most memorable: he played the Doctor as a tousle-headed weirdo who sported a very long scarf), Peter Davison, Colin Baker and Sylvester McCoy. At the height of the series's popularity, "the youth of Starship Britain would watch Hartnell or Troughton or Pertwee or Baker – the loner, the individualist, the eccentric – triumph over pan-galactic evil armed only with the eccentricities of the wardrobe department, his brains and a sonic screwdriver" (comedian Alexei Sayle, in an article entitled 'Why I Should Have Been The New Doctor Who: The Case For A Marxist In The

Tardis', 1984). The Doctor appeared in two cinematic feature films: *Doctor Who And The Daleks* (1965) and *Daleks: Invasion Earth 2150 AD* (1966), both of which starred Peter Cushing. Although he originated on TV, *Doctor Who* has been especially popular in book form, with more than eight million novelizations of scripts in print by 1985: the 100th account of his adventures, *Doctor Who: The Two Doctors* by Robert Holmes, appeared in that year. The preceding 99 volumes included many titles by Terry Nation and Terrance Dicks, and there have been over 50 more by various authors since. In addition, there are numerous non-fiction books such as *Doctor Who: The Key To Time – A Year-By-Year Record* by Peter Haining (1984), published to celebrate the 21st anniversary of the character's first appearance. A serious critical study of the TV series is *Doctor Who: The Unfolding Text* (1983) by John Tulloch and Manuel Alvarado. Since the show finally went off-air, the Doctor has become even more prodigiously visible on the bookshelves. A series of all-original spinoff novels, 'The New Adventures Of Doctor Who', began with *Timewyrm: Genesis* by John Peel (1991) and has been followed by several dozen more titles.

Ender Wiggin

CREATOR: ORSON SCOTT CARD
SOURCE: 'ENDER'S GAME' (NOVELETTE)
DATE: 1977 (EXPANDED VERSION 1985)
A young boy recruited to a military academy who demonstrates unique tactical skills in a series of war-games, only discovering belatedly that the last of them was for real and that the icons he controlled on his VDU really were spaceships battling alien invaders. A perfect juvenile power-fantasy for the age of computer games, for whose cynical composition Card tried to make amends in the expanded version and its sequels, making the hero into a genetic experiment who suffers terrible guilt after his genocidal act. In *Speaker For The Dead* (1986) and *Xenocide* (1991), Ender becomes an itinerant minister conducting funeral services while trying to find a way to resurrect the alien species whose slaughter he contrived. His journey is a time-consuming one, involving

Einsteinian time-dilatation, but his partial abstraction from the galaxy's time-scheme helps fit him for his quasi-messianic role.

Colonel John Wilder

CREATOR: RAY BRADBURY
SOURCE: '...AND THE MOON BE STILL AS BRIGHT' (STORY)
DATE: 1948
The commander of an expedition to Mars which ends in poignant tragedy. A mere captain in the story, he was promoted to colonel and established as the central character of the TV mini-series version of *The Martian Chronicles* (1980). Rock Hudson wrestled heroically but ineffectually with the impossible task of translating Bradbury's lyricism to the small screen.

Peter Wilkins

CREATOR: ROBERT PALTOCK
SOURCE: *THE LIFE AND ADVENTURES OF PETER WILKINS, A CORNISHMAN* (NOVEL)
DATE: 1751
Shipwrecked sailor whose adventures resemble Robinson Crusoe's and Lemuel Gulliver's. He is an early hero of sf because he discovers a lost land in the Antarctic which is inhabited by flying people, one of whom he marries.

Isherwood Williams

CREATOR: GEORGE R. STEWART
SOURCE: *EARTH ABIDES* (NOVEL)
DATE: 1949
American student who survives a plague that kills almost everybody: he and a handful of others attempt to rebuild society, with unexpected but logically persuasive results. As his name hints, Ish's moving tale is an inversion of the true-life Californian story of Ishi In Two Worlds (see the 1962 book of that title by Theodora Kroeber).

Wonder Woman

CREATORS: CHARLES MOULTON MARSTON AND HARRY PETER
SOURCE: *ALL-STAR COMICS*
DATE: 1941
Also known as Diana Prince, a stunningly beautiful Amazon from Paradise Island in the Bermuda Triangle. Clad in a star-spangled

costume, and armed with various super-powers, a magical lasso, and a pair of "Feminium" bracelets which repel bullets, she goes to the USA in order to help that country win World War II. Wonder Woman has been the most successful of all the comic-book super-heroines, pursuing a steady career as a fighter for peace, justice and a kind of feminism. From 1960, she was a member of the Justice League of America, along with Batman and Superman. She appeared in the animated television series *Super Friends* (1973) and its various follow-ups, and as a live-action character in the TV movies *Wonder Woman* (1974), starring Cathy Lee Crosby, and *The New Original Wonder Woman* (1975), with Lynda Carter. The subsequent popular TV series (1976-79) also starred Carter. A redesign of the DC Comics Wonder Woman title in the late 1980s, under artist George Perez, reduced the sf elements.

—⟨ø⟩—

The X Men

CREATORS: JACK KIRBY AND STAN LEE
SOURCE: MARVEL COMICS
DATE: 1963
Mutants assembled by wheelchair-bound fellow mutant Professor Xavier to fight crime as Cyclops/The Beast, Iceman, Angel and Marvel Girl. They remained defiantly noble in spite of the naked prejudice directed against their kind by ordinary humans. Revamped versions became even more popular as *The Uncanny X-Men* in the 1980s.

—⟨ø⟩—

Steve Zodiac

CREATORS: GERRY AND SYLVIA ANDERSON
SOURCE: *FIREBALL XL-5* (TV SERIES)
DATE: 1962
A pilot for the Pacific Ocean-based World Space Fleet, the pioneer who took SuperMarionation into space and engaged it with the full spectrum of space-operatic cliché. An adult version of Mike Mercury, whose replacement was the grumpy ocean-bound Troy Tempest was not universally welcomed.

Propaganda

science-fiction magazines

THE SCIENCE FICTION MAGAZINE IS THE ARENA OF THE NEW, IT KEEPS TALENT ALIVE AND ENCOURAGES OTHERS TO CARRY THE TORCH — HERE WE LOOK AT THE MOST INFLUENTIAL.

Amazing Stories was the magazine whose launch by Hugo Gernsback in 1926 established sf as a separate literary category or a despised ghetto — depending which sf historians you read. *Amazing* grew out of Gernsback's "educational" use of sf in his popular science magazine *Modern Electrics* (first published 1908), which in 1911-12 serialized his own novel *Ralph 124C41+*. This was full of clever and even prophetic ideas for gadgets, but virtually unreadable as fiction. Similar fact-crammed stories dogged *Amazing*'s earlier years, eked out with reprints from Poe, Verne and Wells. But new space-opera writers like Edmond Hamilton, E. E. "Doc" Smith with his *The Skylark Of Space*, and Jack Williamson also began to

appear, and these were wildly popular; some oldsters reckon that the heart of sf's Golden Age was *Amazing* in the late 1920s and early 1930s, under Gernsback and his successor T. O'Conor Sloane.

Amazing's fortunes varied markedly under several publishers and many editors. By 1938, following sharp competition from *Astounding*, the magazine was flagging and changed hands. The new editor Ray Palmer boosted circulation with fiction from Edgar Rice Burroughs, and then with Richard P. Shaver's Shaver Mystery stories, based on a "true" conspiracy theory of evil underground

 WAR STORIES *To counter* Astounding *and boost circulation* Amazing *turned to Burroughs's tales*

beings called "deroes" who secretly controlled the world. Shaver actually believed this; Palmer just pretended to. Many readers were outraged.

Mechanically written hack fiction dominated *Amazing* in the 1950s, some by writers who ultimately earned fame, such as Harlan Ellison and Robert Silverberg. The 1958-1965 editorship of Cele Goldsmith produced better stuff, including early work by Marion Zimmer Bradley, Ursula K. Le Guin and Roger Zelazny. *Amazing* wobbled on through the 1960s and 1970s under various editors (including, briefly, Harry Harrison), always chronically short of funds to buy top-notch stories. The games company TSR acquired it in 1982 and installed George Scithers as editor, but seemed uninterested in seriously promoting the magazine. A 1991 relaunch in large, "slick" format looked attractive but had little commercial success, and the magazine quietly subsided in 1994.

Astounding Science Fiction (later *ANALOG*) emerged in

1930 to challenge the then four-year-old *Amazing*. The first editor Harry Bates had two powerful cards to play: *Astounding Stories Of Super-Science* made no pretence of being educational and concentrated on action-adventure hokum with strong reader appeal, while its high rates of payment attracted authors who could deliver the goods. When the publishers went bust in 1933, Astounding was quickly revived with F. Orlin Tremaine as editor, and established itself as the leading sf magazine. Authors like E. E. Smith were lured from *Amazing*; Tremaine also published L. Sprague de Camp, Murray Leinster, H. P. Lovecraft, C. L. Moore, Eric Frank Russell, Stanley G. Weinbaum and many others.

One such author was John W. Campbell, who took over *Astounding* in 1937 and imposed his own powerful personality, retaining control until his death in 1971. Through the 1940s and 1950s, Campbell was the most influential editor in sf magazine history, coaxing memorable work out of Isaac Asimov (including the Robot and Foundation series), Robert A. Heinlein, E. E. Smith once again (the Lensman stories), A. E. van Vogt and more. Campbell was also a highly controversial figure, who would jolt readers with plausibly argued editorials defending slavery or cannibalism, and who — despite his magazine's reputation for hard sf with equations and rivets — repeatedly fell for pseudoscientific ideas like "psi machines" and reactionless space drives. It was *Astounding* that in 1950 gave L. Ron Hubbard (another regular author) his platform to launch Dianetics, which later became Scientology, and which Campbell relentlessly touted to his readers.

In 1960, the magazine title became, eccentrically, *Analog Science Fact — Science Fiction* (in 1965 the words Fact and Fiction were exchanged). Throughout the 1950s and 1960s, it had won eight Hugo awards, and in 1964-5 Campbell serialized one of the most popular sf novels ever, Frank Herbert's *Dune*. The last years of the Campbell era were anticlimactic.

Ben Bova succeeded Campbell as editor, and loosened *Analog's* policy by allowing a little healthy sex and swearing; though some long-time readers protested, Bova won six 1970s Hugos as Best Editor. In 1978, he resigned and was replaced by Stanley Schmidt, who still edits Analog. It

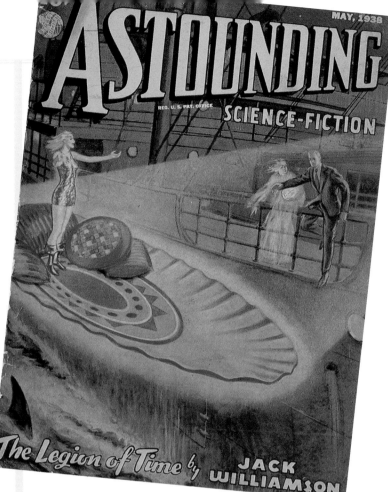

remains relatively successful and still features award-winning stories, but its influence has lessened owing to competition and the market's continuing shift of emphasis from magazines to original books, and away from hard sf.

Unknown was *Astounding's* sister magazine, devoted to fantasy rather

than sf. Its influence was far greater than suggested by its brief lifespan from 1939 until wartime paper shortages halted publication in 1943. Under John W. Campbell's determinedly rationalistic editorship, writers were encouraged to produce light or humorous "rationalized fantasy" which applied scientific thinking to the supernatural — as summed up in L. Sprague de Camp's and Fletcher Pratt's title 'The Mathematics Of Magic' (1940; incorporated into *The Incomplete Enchanter*, 1942). Such humorous and anachronistic fantasy was eventually to become a best-selling publishing category in the hands of Piers Anthony, Terry Pratchett and others.

The Magazine Of Fantasy And Science Fiction

first appeared in 1949 and from its outset was consciously more upmarket and "literary" than the sf pulp magazines: C. S. Lewis himself was twice persuaded to contribute. Its initial editors were Anthony Boucher — himself a distinguished writer — and J. Francis McComas; others followed, including the fine writer Avram Davidson in 1962-64. The longest-serving editor was Edward L. Ferman, from 1966 to 1991; F&SF won eight Best Magazine Hugo awards between 1958 and 1972, and Ferman received three Hugos as Best Editor in the early 1980s — reflecting the decline of *Analog*.

F&SF could always be relied on for stylish and haunting short stories (serials appeared more rarely than in other magazines): the gentle sadness of Zenna Henderson's People series was a characteristic example, and Walter M. Miller's classic *A Canticle For Leibowitz* was built from novelettes published in *F&SF* during the 1950s. The downside was an occasional weakness for dire folksiness — fortunately rare. Sober covers and a lack of interior illustration made *F&SF* visually as well as stylistically respectable. Many stories from its pages have won major sf awards.

Notable *F&SF* features included the Special Issues which showcased particular authors with new stories, essays and bibliographies: Theodore Sturgeon was the first to receive this treatment, in 1962. Isaac Asimov contributed nearly 400 monthly science essays from 1958 to 1992, the year of his death. With Ferman's retirement as editor, the much younger writer Kristine Kathryn Rusch has taken over; her inevitable changes to the magazine's tone have been criticized by some, but she took the Hugo Award for Best Editor in 1994.

Galaxy Science Fiction

began in 1950 and had its great days under the editorship of H. L. Gold (1950-61) and Frederik Pohl (1961-69), scoring an early success with the 1952 serialization of Alfred Bester's novel *The Demolished Man* — subsequently a 1953 Hugo winner, as was *Galaxy* itself. The editorial tone was sparky and fizzy by comparison with the sometimes dour *Astounding*; it was happy to deal in soft sciences like psychology and sociology, and actively encouraged humour. Robert Sheckley's dotty short stories were entirely at home in *Galaxy*, as were the sharply satirical collaborations of Frederik Pohl and Cyril Kornbluth (e.g. *The Space Merchants*, serialized as *Gravy Planet*). Further Hugo-winning stories were contributed by Avram Davidson, Gordon Dickson, Harlan Ellison, Fritz Leiber, Robert Silverberg, Clifford Simak and Jack Vance. Algis Budrys's 1965-1971 book review columns were another highlight, and have since been collected as *Benchmarks: Galaxy Bookshelf* (1985).

Under later editors, the magazine generally declined, though towards the end of James Baen's 1974-77 stint there were signs of improvement: Pohl's Gateway, one of the finest sf novels of the 1970s, was serialized and later picked up both Hugo and Nebula awards. But when Baen left, *Galaxy*'s decline accelerated; the schedule faltered, there was no money to lure big-name authors, and the end came in 1980. A 1994 revival of the title as a small-press magazine,

though well intended and having the founder H. L. Gold's son E. J. Gold as editor, bore no real resemblance to *Galaxy* in its heyday.

If was founded in 1952, but its early life under such editors as James L. Quinn is largely forgotten despite the appearance of one classic story, James Blish's 1953 *A Case Of Conscience* (expanded into a Hugo-winning novel in 1958). Damon Knight was also briefly an editor. *If* reached fame after its 1959 acquisition by *Galaxy*'s publishers, which led to its appearing as a theoretically complementary but in fact largely indistinguishable sister magazine to *Galaxy*, under the same editors — especially H. L. Gold and Frederik Pohl. Pohl's reign was the most successful, with the magazine winning three Hugo awards from 1966 to 1968 after the 1965-66 coup of serializing *The Moon Is A Harsh Mistress* — Robert Heinlein's long-awaited return to something like peak novel form.

Despite its similarly distinguished record, If's fortunes declined with *Galaxy*'s, and it was eventually merged with *Galaxy* in 1975.

 BEST FOOT FORWARD *Bester's follow up to* The Demolished Man *was another success and was snapped up by* Galaxy

New Worlds

is the best-known British sf magazine, generally associated with its most flamboyant editor Michael Moorcock — though it was founded by John Carnell in 1946, and edited by him for 141 issues to 1964. The Carnell incarnation of *New Worlds* is often underrated despite its 1957 Hugo: there was much good fiction by British authors such as Brian Aldiss, J. G. Ballard, John Brunner and James White; Philip K. Dick also appeared. Ballard was not yet writing such creatively deranged material as he would for Moorcock, but the magazine was already growing hospitable to avant-garde and psychological sf.

This was the aspect which was force-fed under the editorship of Michael Moorcock from 1964 to issue 194 in 1969 (various colleagues like Charles Platt edited the "final" issues, to 201 in 1971). *New Worlds* became the flagship of "New Wave" sf, whose writers revolted against the deadened, boilerplate prose and narration of — in particular — traditional "hard sf" as found in US magazines. Experimenting with prose techniques produced some powerful and effective fiction, such as J. G. Ballard's "condensed novels" and works by Samuel R. Delany, Thomas M. Disch, John Sladek and Norman Spinrad. But, in less talented hands, the results could be disappointing: slack prose poems decorated with would-be shocking imagery, larded with drugs, pop-culture and trendy pessimism ("entropy" was the great *New Worlds* catchword) and desperately lacking in substance. More traditional sf also featured, such as Harry Harrison's satire *Bill, The Galactic Hero*; meanwhile, *New Worlds* and the New Wave helped change the nature of sf tradition. It seems bizarre today that a few rude words in Spinrad's Bug Jack Barron (serialized 1967-8) should not only have prompted a question in Parliament about the UK Arts Council funding of this wickedness, but also — more damagingly — caused the major UK retailer/distributor W. H. Smith to ban the magazine.

New Worlds reappeared as a 1971-76 series of paperback anthologies variously edited by Moorcock, Platt and Hilary Bailey — ten volumes corresponding to issues 202-211 and including the debut columns of the fine sf critic John Clute. It was a small-press magazine from 212 to 216 (1978-79), and continued as four UK anthologies edited by David Garnett (217-220, 1991-94). Further Garnett-edited volumes are expected from a US publisher, beginning in 1997.

Science Fantasy

, a sister magazine to the original *New Worlds*, began in 1950 and like *New Worlds* went through various editors and publishers. Most issues were edited by John Carnell, succeeded in 1964 by Kyril Bonfiglioli (now best known for his blackly comic thriller novels) and finally Harry Harrison and Keith Roberts as joint editors. The title changed to *Impulse* in 1966, and again to *SF Impulse* in the same year. This reflects the fact that the magazine carried sf as well as fantasy, and is historically important for housing the first stories of Brian Aldiss, J. G. Ballard, Christopher Priest and Keith Roberts — who contributed the fine long stories later assembled as his classic novel *Pavane*. Roberts also provided distinctive cover art from 1965 until *SF Impulse*'s death in 1967.

Locus

, which carries no fiction, is generally accepted as the trade newspaper of sf; it began as a fanzine in 1968 and its original co-editor Charles N. Brown still presides over what is now called a semi-professional magazine or "semiprozine". The semiprozine Hugo category was instated after annoyance that *Locus*, which by the late 1970s was a commercial source of income for Brown, was still winning the Best Fanzine Hugo from traditional hobby fanzines done for love: it had won eight times as Fanzine and proceeded to win the Semiprozine award nine years running, 1984-92. *Locus* is probably indispensable.

Science Fiction Monthly

was, from 1974 to 1976, the most visible sf magazine presence in Britain, thanks to a giant tabloid format which reflected its orientation towards pull-out posters. These were generally of paintings done for book jackets (especially books from SF Monthly's publishers, New English Library), many of them singularly unsuccessful when seen at many times the intended size. The inexperienced editors Pat Hornsey (1974-75) and Julie Davis (1975-76) seemed to mix good and bad stories and reprints almost at random; the interviews and other non-fiction features contributed by sf fans were more consistent in quality. An attempt to relaunch the magazine as the more sensibly sized *SF Digest* in 1976 was effectively abandoned before the sole issue appeared.

Isaac Asimov's Science Fiction Magazine

began in 1977, titled by analogy with the long-running crime-fiction outlet *Ellery Queen's Mystery Magazine*, from the same publisher. Isaac Asimov was billed as Editorial Director and contributed many editorials in his usual essay vein, though these tended to be over-brief; the actual editor's job was performed by George H. Scithers (1977-82; he then moved to the revived *Amazing*) and, after a short interregnum under Shawna McCarthy, the established writer Gardner Dozois became editor from late 1982 to the present.

At first, Asimov's tended to focus on rather lightweight fiction; Scithers detested downbeat endings, and stories which sounded deeper notes tended to be bounced with "futile" ticked on his notorious check-the-boxes form letters of rejection. Nevertheless he bought some notable fiction — including Barry B. Longyear's award-winning 'Enemy Mine', later a movie — and won two Hugos as Best Editor. McCarthy brought the magazine a third; under her editorship and then Dozois's, a wider spectrum of fine fiction appeared, and the magazine's popularity expanded beyond its initial fan audience.

Dozois in particular seems unconcerned about whether stories are hard sf, fantasy, or indeed barely sf or fantasy at all: his main criterion is excellence, and it has paid off. He collected seven Best Editor Hugos in the period 1988-95 (missing only one year), and has published a quite extraordinary number of award-winning stories. Asimov's is now the most widely respected of commercial sf magazines, by both readers and writers.

Omni was founded in 1978 by Bob Guccione of *Penthouse* soft-porn fame, as a glossy sister magazine of popular science with a couple of sf stories (in later years, just one) appearing per issue. The science has sometimes trailed off into pseudoscience and ufology, but despite occasional poor work by "name" authors like Isaac Asimov, the stories were kept to a high standard by *Omni*'s fiction editors Ben Bova (1978-89 — formerly of Analog), Robert Sheckley (1980-81) and especially Ellen Datlow (1981 onwards). *Omni*'s fees for fiction were phenomenal by sf standards, enabling it to snaffle more award-winning material than one would expect from its relatively low fiction content — although sf authors have also been encouraged to contribute non-fiction articles. Perhaps the most influential stories published there were William Gibson's original cyberpunk shorts, including the quintessential 'Burning Chrome' and — later to become a movie — 'Johnny Mnemonic'. ("I'm never going to reject a Gibson story!" Datlow once said to a rival editor who hoped to publish him.)

In 1996, *Omni* reacted to the recent world-wide rise in paper prices by cancelling its print edition and going on-line; it became available only through Internet's World Wide Web.

Science Fiction Chronicle, first published in 1979, is a

New York rival to the US West Coast sf newspaper *Locus* and is still edited by its founder Andrew I. Porter. In 1993 and 1994, it broke *Locus*'s traditional lock on the Best Semiprozine Hugo.

Interzone, the one commercial magazine now regularly publishing sf

in Britain, was founded in 1982 by an editorial collective with eight members. This has dwindled over the years: since 1988, the one active editor has been David Pringle, who is also the magazine's publisher. Early issues seemed rather overshadowed by the memory of the Moorcock *New Worlds*, but distinguished writers were featured — Moorcock himself, Angela Carter and, perhaps inevitably, J. G. Ballard. As time passed, a wider and more varied range of narrative styles was welcomed to the magazine's pages. *Interzone* "discoveries" include Stephen Baxter, Greg Egan and Geoff Ryman; John Clute's erudite book reviews, Nick Lowe's witty movie column and David Langford's more recent gossip page are also popular.

Interzone continues with some assistance from the UK Arts Council, but has cheeringly many genuine devotees — who voted it a 1995 Hugo award as Best Semiprozine. After *New Worlds* and possibly *Science Fantasy*, it is the most important British sf magazine.

 GLOSS *It appears that letters* **SFX** *don't stand for anything, but do look a bit like* **SEX**

 THE LAST PLACE *The only commercial magazine to publish science fiction in the UK is* Interzone *which gained recognition with its* **1995** *Hugo*

SF Age, a promising new slick magazine, first appeared in 1992 and rose rapidly to a US circulation level comparable with much longer established sf magazines; its original editor Scott Edelman is still in charge. Good fiction has appeared, along with broad non-fiction coverage of books, movies, art, comics and games. Further recognition will surely come if *SF Age* can stay in the market for a few more years.

SFX, launched in 1995, is the latest commercial magazine about sf to appear in Britain. The editor is Dave Golder, the production is glossy, with almost painfully eye-catching covers. Despite its subtitle "Adventures in Science Fiction", *SFX* includes no fiction; it recognizes the size of the media sf market and runs major movie and TV features, but is also sympathetic towards sf's fictional roots. Book reviews feature in every issue, there are regular "literary" columnists, and *SFX* honours the dead with substantial memorial tributes to — for example — John Brunner in 1995 and Bob Shaw in 1996. There is a cheering readiness to be rude about dreadful spin-off products trading on media successes or cult interest.

Glossary

Science fiction is notorious for its jargon — but any good sf novel or movie will take care to explain the words you need to know, either directly or indirectly. The following are the most popular

ALTERNATIVE WORLD — a version of Earth where history took a different turn, as in Keith Roberts's Pavane, where Elizabeth I was assassinated and Britain fell under Spanish rule.

ANSIBLE — faster-than-light (ftl) videophone communicator, so named in Ursula K. Le Guin's novels.

ANTIGRAVITY — an impossible (so far as we know) but fictionally useful counteracting of gravity. In Bob Shaw's Terminal Velocity, wearers of antigravity outfits can fly.

ANTIMATTER — "inverted" matter built of antielectrons and antiprotons, which on contact with normal matter's electrons and protons goes off in an annihilation reaction far more efficient than a nuclear bomb. Possibly a good fuel for spaceships (as in Star Trek), but for obvious reasons it has been produced only in invisibly tiny quantities.

BEM — Bug-Eyed Monster, a joky name for the standard villainous aliens in early space opera. For political correctness, we now say "extra-terrestrials" or ets.

BERSERKER — not a chap with horns on his helmet, but the common sf name (coined by Fred Saberhagen) for a hostile, spacefaring machine intelligence.

BIONICS — short for bioelectronics, the building of power-assisted enhancements or replacements into human bodies (familiar from TV's The Six Million Dollar Man). See also cyborg.

BLASTER — slightly outdated word for a hand-held energy gun; space opera equivalent of the six-shooter in Westerns.

BOBBLE — a particular kind of stasis field described in Vernor Vinge's Realtime books.

CETI — Contact with Extra-Terrestrial Intelligence.

CONTRATERRENE — early sf word for antimatter. Jack Williamson's Seetee Ship features an alien antimatter vessel: Seetee equals CT equals Contra-Terrene.

CORPSICLE — by analogy with "popsicle" (US for "lollipop"), a body frozen by cryonics.

CRYONICS — deep-freezing human bodies to preserve them, either as a form of suspended animation or (as is already happening) in hope that future medicine can use nanotechnology to restore life and health to the dead.

CYBERPUNK — sf sub-genre defined by William Gibson with his 'Burning Chrome' and Neuromancer: a sort of sf film noir generally featuring drugs, alienation and cyberspace derring-do in a world dominated by giant, unpleasant multi-national corporations.

CYBERSPACE — the glowing,

hallucinatory, virtual-reality view of Internet data transfer and data crime described in William Gibson's novels and seen in the movie Tron.

Cyborg — short for cybernetic organism, a blend of man and machine. Often electronically enhanced good guys are called bionic, while "cyborg" is reserved for more sinister examples.

Dyson sphere — a shell of matter completely surrounding a sun, to make maximum use of its energy output and provide hugely expanded living area (as compared with planets). Larry Niven's Ringworld is a partial Dyson sphere; Bob Shaw's Orbitsville is a full-sized one.

Dystopia — a politically nasty place to live (opposite of Utopia, a good place). Nineteen Eighty-Four is set in a dystopia.

Entropy — the general tendency (enshrined in the Second Law of Thermodynamics) for things, including the universe, to run down; a new wave fad.

ET — extra-terrestrial, i.e. not from Earth; an alien.

FTL — Faster Than Light, as in space travel and communication that defies Einstein's speed limit.

Force field — a solid physical barrier composed of pure energy. The "force fields" known to puny Earthling scientists (such as magnetic fields) are hopelessly inferior to the sf version.

Generation ship — one possible route to the stars if ftl is impossible is to send a vast, self-contained vessel (perhaps an entire hollowed-out asteroid) whose passengers will live and die aboard until, generations later, their descendants reach a new world.

Hard sf — stories strictly plotted to focus on science which is consistent with known physical laws. Good hard sf is mind-expanding; bad hard sf resembles engineering manuals. Hal Clement is the patron saint of this sub-genre.

Hive mind — ants, bees and termites seem individually very stupid, but as a whole an ant-colony or beehive operates with strange intelligence. (Human neurons have little individual computing power, but in bulk make up our brains.) Many creepy sf aliens have hive-mind intelligence; Frank Herbert's disturbing Hellstrom's Hive features humans adapted as hive creatures.

Hugo Award — the most prestigious sf award, voted on by members of each World SF Convention. Named after Hugo Gernsback.

Humanist — sf sub-genre apparently invented for debating purposes as the opposition to cyberpunk; defined chiefly by not being cyberpunk. Kim Stanley Robinson and Lucius Shepard have been given this label.

Hyperdrive — sf jargon for any kind of magic engine that drives a spaceship faster than the known laws of physics allow.

Hyperspace — imaginary region "outside" normal space, providing short cuts that make ftl travel possible without "really" going faster than light.

Jaunte — verb meaning "to transport oneself by teleportation", coined by Alfred Bester in Tiger! Tiger!

L5 — the gravity and motion of the Earth and Moon lead to points of "balance" called Lagrange points, numbered L1 to L5. Large space stations or colonies would be particularly stable if positioned at L4 or L5.

Mutant — nuclear radiation can damage human DNA and cause the genetic copying errors known as mutations, almost always damaging if not fatal. Sf mutants resulting from the aftermath of nuclear World War III tend to form a repulsive, mis-shapen underclass, or to have psi powers, or both.

Matter transmitter — gadget that does away with traffic jams by projecting you like a radio message; step into a booth near home, step out in Australia or on the Moon.

Multiverse — a super-universe including all possible alternative worlds of sf and fantasy. Used by Michael Moorcock to link all his books, however seemingly incompatible.

Nanobots — microscopic robots constructed by nanotechnology, small enough to (for example) patrol your bloodstream destroying hostile bacteria.

Nanotechnology — a proposed technology of tiny machines the size of large molecules, working together in huge swarms to manufacture almost anything by building it atom by atom. Currently sf's technological flavour-of-the-month.

Nebula — the second most prestigious sf award, voted on by members of sffwa. Also a cloud of stars or interstellar gas.

Neurojack — nerve/electronic connection enabling futuristic hackers to plug their nervous systems directly into cyberspace.

NEW WAVE — the late 1960s "revolution" in sf, largely associated with New Worlds magazine under Michael Moorcock's editorship, which reacted against hard sf with doses of pop-culture, anarchy, consciously experimental writing, and obsession with entropy.

ORGANLEGGERS — illicit traders in human organs for transplant surgery (based on "bootleggers"); Larry Niven popularized it as an sf term, but organleggers now exist....

PARALLEL WORLD — same as alternative world, though usually with less emphasis on the link of shared history.

POSITRONIC BRAIN — jargon invented by Isaac Asimov for the artificial intelligences in his famous robot stories. Positrons, also known as antielectrons, are real particles but unlikely to be useful in computers: see antimatter.

PSI — generic sf name for a range of probably imaginary mind powers like psychokinesis, telepathy and teleportation.

PSYCHOHISTORY — invented science used in Isaac Asimov's Foundation series to predict large-scale social and political trends centuries ahead with uncanny accuracy.

PSYCHOKINESIS — manipulation of matter by mind power; the posh name for bending spoons.

SCIENCE FANTASY — a halfway house between fantasy and sf. Anne McCaffrey's dragon books have a fantasy feel but some tenuous scientific justification, so we call them science fantasy.

SETI — Search for Extra-Terrestrial Intelligence, usually by listening on likely wavelengths using radio telescopes.

SFWA OR SFFWA — Science Fiction (and Fantasy) Writers of America, the writers' organization that selects the nebula awards.

SHARED-WORLD SF — story sequences produced by different writers using a common background, like the Man-Kzin Wars series set in Larry Niven's Known Space universe or the Berserker Base collection set in that of Fred Saberhagen's berserkers.

SINGULARITY — the point where a mathematical function zooms off to infinity. Black holes may contain gravitational singularities with weird wormhole properties. Some sf writers imagine a singularity of evolution or technological progress, at which point humanity goes off all past scales of measurement to become like gods.

SOL — slightly upmarket Latin name for the Sun.

SPACE ELEVATOR — literally an elevator cable strung from somewhere on the equator to a synchronously orbiting satellite, allowing payloads to be winched into orbit without wasteful rockets: see Arthur C. Clarke's The Fountains Of Paradise. Unfortunately, the cable demands an (at present) impossibly strong material to support even its own weight.

SPACE OPERA — large-scale, fast-moving sf that emphasizes action-adventure rather than making any particular sense. Examples: E. E. Smith's Lensman books and Star Wars.

STASIS FIELD — imaginary force field which preserves anything inside it, completely immune to time or decay.

STEAMPUNK — "retro" historical sf or science fantasy set in Victorian times, usually an exaggeratedly Dickensian London. Examples: Tim Powers's The Anubis Gates, William Gibson's and Bruce Sterling's The Difference Engine.

SUSPENDED ANIMATION — another way for space travellers to tackle journeys lasting decades or centuries, drugging or freezing them for revival at journey's end. Slightly more plausible than a stasis field.

TELEPORTATION — moving objects (including oneself) more or less instantly from place to place, usually by psi power. If you use a machine, it's matter transmission.

TERRA — slightly upmarket Latin name for the planet Earth.

TERRAFORM — to reshape another world's climate and ecology until it's enough like Earth that we Earthlings can live there unprotected.

VON NEUMANN MACHINES — hypothetical space probes that can build copies of themselves using raw materials mined from comets or asteroids, aiding either active seti or the exploitation of our solar system's resources.

WORMHOLE — another name for a short-cut route outside normal space/time, like hyperspace.

ZERO GEE — zero-gravity or free-fall, allowing astronauts to "float" in space.

Index

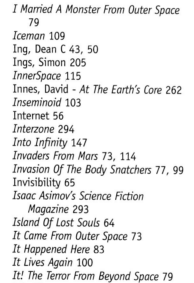

Acknowledgements

The Publishers would like to thank the following sources for their kind permission to reproduce the pictures used in this publication:

3 UFA/Ronald Grant Archive
4 **TC** Babylon Productions Inc./Corbis/Everett
4 **CR** Warner/Alexander Salkind/TMs & ©Copyright DC Comics/Corbis/Everett
4 **BL** Greenaway for 20th Century-Fox Television/Kinema Collection
4 **CLB** Fox/Corbis/Everett
4 **BC** TCF/Ronald Grant Archive
4 **BR** Paul Jackson for BBC North West (Seasons 1-3), Grant Naylor for BBC North (Seasons 4-6)/Ronald Grant Archive/M Vaughan
5 Desilu in association with Norway Corporation (Seasons 1-2), Paramount in association with Norway Corporation (Season 2-3)/Corbis/Everett
6/7 Universal/Joel Finler Collection
8 **L** Bantam Doubleday Dell Magazines
8 **R** Mary Evans Picture Library
9 **T** Tor Books
9 **B** Warner/Ladd/Blade Runner Partnership/Ronald Grant Archive
10 ICC/Cine Trail / Belstar / Stephan/Ronald Grant Archive
11 **T** 20th Century Fox/Ronald Grant Archive
11 **B** Hulton Getty
12 Hulton Getty
13 (artist Antonio Cabral-Bejarana)/La Rabida Monastery, Palos/AKG London Ltd.
14 Hulton Getty
15 **T** Mary Evans Picture Library
15 **B** Mary Evans Picture Library
16 **T** Mary Evans Picture Library
16 **B** Hulton Getty
17 **T** Columbia TriStar/American Zoetrope/Japan Satellite/Indie Productions/Ronald Grant Archive
17 **B** Hulton Getty
18 Baen Books
19 Paramount/George Pal/Ronald Grant Archive
20 (artist Hubert Rogers)/ Bantam Doubleday Dell Magazines
20 (artist George Barr)/Underwood Miller
20 (artist Peter Gudynas)/Grafton
20 Bantam Doubleday Dell Magazines
20 Vintage
20 W R Chambers
22 (artist Howard Brown)/ Bantam Doubleday Dell Magazines
23 Ace
24 W R Chambers
25 **T** (artist Solonevich)/ Bantam Doubleday Dell Magazines
25 **B** (artist H.W.Wesso)/ Bantam Doubleday Dell Magazines
27 T Chatto & Windus
27 **B** (artist Trevor Denning)/Michael Joseph
28 Berkley
29 (artist Emsh)/Galaxy Publishing Corp.
30 Hamilton & Co.
31 Thornton Butterworth
32 Ace
35 (artist Emsh)/Galaxy Publishing Corp.
36 (artist Peter Cross)/ Harmony Books
37 Lancer
38 Ace
39 New English Library
40 Victor Gollancz
41 Tor Books
42 (artist Frank R. Paul)/ Continental Publications Inc.
43 (artist George Barr)/ Underwood Miller
44 (artists Jack Rubin & Irving Freeman)/Harper & Row
45 (artist Lionel Dillon)/ Gnome Press
46 **T** Ace
46 **B** HarperCollins Science Fiction & Fantasy
47 Ace
48 **T** Bantam Books
48 **B** Vintage
49 HarperCollins
50 (artist Alex Schomburg)/ Edward L. Ferman
51 Dutton
52 Scion
53 (artist Ron Dilg)/Nelson Doubleday
54 (artist David Mattingly)/ Bluejay
55 Bantam Doubleday Dell Magazines
56 **T** (artist Don Bolognese)/ Arbor House
56 **B** (artist Peter Gudynas)/ Grafton
57 Reader's Library
59 (artist Brian Lewis)/Nova
60 **T** (artist Keith Parkinson)/ Baen Publishing Enterprises
60 **B** Victor Gollancz
61 (artist Romas B. Kukalis)/ Morrow
62 20th C Fox/Brandywine/ British Film Institute
63 UFA/Kinema Collection
64 Universal/Joel Finler Collection
65 Universal/Joel Finler Collection
66 RKO/Joel Finler Collection
67 **T** London/Ronald Grant Archive
67 **B** Universal/Joel Finler Collection
69 Universal/George Pal/Kinema Collection
70 TCF/Joel Finler Collection
71 **T** RKO/Winchester/Joel Finler Collection
71 **B** Ealing/Ronald Grant Archive
72 UA/Dowling/Ronald Grant Archive
73 Paramount/George Pal/Joel Finler Collection
74 **T** Ronald Grant Archive
74 **B** Warner/Joel Finler Collection
75 Exclusive/Hammer/Ronald Grant Archive
76 **T** U-I/Ronald Grant Archive
76 **B** MGM/Ronald Grant Archive
77 Allied Artists/Walter Wanger/Joel Finler Collection
78 Hammer/Joel Finler Collection
79 United Artists/Stanley Kramer/Ronald Grant Archive
80 **T** MGM/Kinema Collection
80 **B** MGM/Galaxy/Ronald Grant Archive
81 **T** AIP/Ronald Grant Archive
81 **B** British Lion/Pax/Ronald Grant Archive
82 Columbia/Stanley Kubrick/Joel Finler Collection
83 Paramount/Devonshire /Ronald Grant Archive
84 Filmstudio/Ronald Grant Archive
85 **T** Paramout/Joel/ Gibraltar/Ronald Grant Archive
85 **B** Rank/Anglo Enterprise/Vineyard/ Joel Finler Collection
86 **T** Hammer/Anthony Nelson Keys/Ronald Grant Archive
86 **B** Marianne/Dino de Laurentiis/ Joel Finler Collection
87 **T** Selmur/Robertson Associates/Ronald Grant Archive
87 **B** TCF/Apjac/Ronald Grant Archive
88 MGM/ Stanley Kubrick/Joel Finler Collection
90 Universal/Robert Wise/Ronald Grant Archive
91 Warner/Polaris/Ronald Grant Archive
92 **T** Universal/Michel Gruskoff/Douglas Trumbull/British Film Institute
92 **B** Mosfilm/Ronald Grant Archive
93 UA/Jack Rollins, Charles Joffe/Ronald Grant Archive
94 MGM/Ronald Grant Archive
95 **T** Saltpan/AFDC/Royce Smeal/Joel Finler Collection
95 **B** Jack H. Harris/Ronald Grant Archive
96 British Lion/Ronald Grant Archive
97 Columbia/EMI/ Ronald Grant Archive
98 TCF/Lucasfilm/ Corbis/Everett
99 UA/Robert H Solo/Ronald Grant Archive
100 Warner/Alexander Salkind/Joel Finler Collection/DC Comics
101 Mosfilm Unit 2/Ronald Grant Archive
102 Paramount/Ronald Grant Archive
103 TCF/Lucasfilm/Ronald Grant Archive
104 Filmplan International/ Kinema Collection
105 **T** Warner/Kennedy Miller Entertainment/Corbis/Everett
105 **B** New World/Android/ Kinema Collection
106 Warner/Ladd/Blade Runner Partnership/Ronald Grant Archive
107 Universal/Joel Finler Collection
108 **T** Lisberger-Kushner/ Ronald Grant Archive
108 **B** Filmplan International/ Ronald Grant Archive
109 **T** Umbrella/Rosenblum/Virgin /British Film Institute
109 **B** TCF/Lucasfilm/Kinema Collection
110 Columbia/Delphi/Kobal Collection
111 **T** Universal/Steven Spielberg/Ronald Grant Archive
111 **B** Orion/Hemdale/Pacific Western/ Corbis/Everett
112 **T** Kings Road/TCF/ Ronald Grant Archive
112 **B** Embassy/Ronald Grant Archive
113 TCF/Brandywine/ Corbis/Everett
114 TCF/Brooksfilm/ Joel Finler Collection
115 ICA/Akira Committee/ Joel Finler Collection
116 **T** TCF/Lawrence Gordon/Joel Silver/John Davis/Corbis/Everett
116 **B** Rank/Orion/Joel Finler Collection
117 **L** Fox/De Laurentiis/ Kestrel Films/ Ronald Grant Archive
117 **R** Fox/Rex Features Ltd.
118 **T** Warner/Doric/Ronald Grant Archive
118 **B** Warner/Ronald Grant Archive
119 Hollywood Pictures/ Amblin/Tangled Web/Ronald Grant Archive
121 **T** Guild/Carolco/ Pictorial Press
121 **B** Guild/Carolco/Pacific Western/ Lightstorm/Ronald Grant Archive
122 UIP/Universal/ Amblin/Pictorial Press
123 Alliance Communications/ Corbis/Everett
124 NBC TV/B & B Productions Inc./Corbis/Everett
125 DuMont Television Network/Corbis/Everett
126 BBC/Ronald Grant Archive
127 BBC Television/Ronald Grant Archive
128 BBC/Joel Finler Collection
129 BBC/Ronald Grant Archive
130 Cayuga (filmed at M-G-M)/Corbis/ Everett/CBS
131 ABC Television/Pictorial Press
132 BBC/Ronald Grant Archive
133 Jack Chertok/Pictorial Press
134 **T** Daystar-Villa di Stefano for United Artists Television/ Ronald Grant Archive
134 **B** Arena for MGM Television/Ronald Grant Archive
135 Irwin Allen for 20th Century Fox Television/ Kinema Collection
136 **T** CBS/Irwin Allen with Jodi Production Inc/Van Bernard Productions Inc for 20th Century Fox Television/Corbis/Everett
136 **B** AP Films for AV/ITC/ Pictorial Press/Polygram
137 **T** Michael Garrison with CBS/Corbis/ Everett
137 **B** Greenaway for 20th Century Fox Television/ Corbis/Everett
139 Desilu in association with Norway Corporation (Seasons 1-2), Paramount in association with Norway Corporation (Seasons 2-3)/Corbis/Everett
140 Quinn Martin/ABC/Pictorial Press
141 **T** Everyman Films for ATV/Pictorial Press/Polygram
141 **B** BBC Television/Ronald Grant Archive
142 Paramount Pictures TV/Corbis/Everett
143 Century 21 Pictures for ITC Worldwide Distribution, Pictorial Press/Polygram
144 Universal Television/Corbis/Everett
145 **T** Thames Television/Pictorial Press
145 **B** Harve Bennett/Universal/ NBC/ Corbis/Everett
146 Pictorial Press/Polygram
148 BBC Television/Ronald Grant Archive
149 **T** Glen A Larson in association with Universal Television/Corbis/Everett
149 **B** BBC Television/Ronald Grant Archive
150 **T** Miller-Milkis Productions Inc. and Henderson Production Co Inc. with Paramount Television/Corbis/Everett
150 **B** BBC Television/Ronald Grant Archive
151 **T** Mark VIII Ltd with NBC TV/Corbis/Everett
151 **B** Glen A Larson/Universal Television/Corbis/Everett
152 ATV Network/ Pictorial Press/ Polygram
153 **T** WNET/Thirteen/Ronald Grant Archive
153 **B** Charles Fried/Corbis/Everett/NBC
154 **T** BBC Television/RCTV Inc./ Australian Broadcasting Corp./Corbis/Everett
154 **B** BBC
155 ABC Motion Pictures/Corbis/Everett
156 BBC/Ronald Grant Archive
157 **L** Kenneth Johnson with Warner Bros Television/Corbis/Everett
157 **R** Chrysalis Visual Programming Ltd. for Channel Four/Corbis/Everett
158 Atlantis Films Ltd. with John Wilcox Productions Inc./Corbis/Everett
159 Paramount Pictures/Corbis/Everett
160 **T** BBC Television/Corbis/Everett
160 **B** BBC North /Ronald Grant Archive/M Vaughan
161 Kenneth Johnson/Corbis/Everett
162 Bellisarius Productions with Universal Television/MCA/Ronald Grant Archive
163 **T** Zenith/Corbis/Everett
163 **B** GranadaTelevision/Corbis/Everett
164 Babylonian Productions Inc./Corbis/Everett
165 Roundelay Productions/Corbis/Everett
166 Paramount/Corbis/Everett
167 Ten Thirteen Productions with 20th Century Television/Corbis/Everett
169 Trilogy Entertainment/ Corbis/Everett
170 Paramount Network/Ronald Grant Archive
172 Corbis/Bettmann
174 Victor Gollancz
174 Rex Features Ltd.
174 Victor Gollanz
175 **T** HarperCollins
175 **B** Corbis
177 HarperCollins
178 HarperCollins
179 **T** Little Brown/S Denton
179 **B** HarperCollins
180 Legend
181 M Bishop
183 HarperCollins
184 J K Klein
185 Corbis/Bettmann/UPI
186 **T** HarperCollins
186 **B** Rex Features Ltd./Fotos International
187 Corbis/Everett
188 Victor Gollancz
189 Blunck Studio of Edmond
190 Rex Features Ltd.
191 Century/J Exley
192 Corbis/Everett
193 **T** University of Massachussetts Photo Service
193 **B** L Sprague de Camp
195 Jamie Spracher
196 Mary Evans Picture Library
198 Corbis/Everett
199 Penguin UK
201 Pictorial Press
202 Jerry Bauer
204 Penguin UK
205 HarperCollins
206 Victor Gollancz
207 Kinema Collection
208 **T** Pictorial Press
208 **B** Pictorial Press
209 M Wood Kolisch
211 **T** Dr F Rottensteiner
211 **B** Hulton Getty
212 Pictorial Press/J Mayer
213 **T** Rex Features Ltd.
213 **B** Victor Gollancz/ S Earnshaw
214 Belfast Telegraph Newspapers Ltd.
216 **T** The Orion Publishing Group Ltd.
216 **B** Rex Features Ltd.
217 Mirror Syndication International
218 Del Rey/Valada
219 Corbis/Bettmann
220 K Bubriski
221 Hulton Getty
222 **T** Fred Fox Studios Ltd.
222 **B** Bloomsbury
223 HarperCollins
224 Rex Features Ltd./Sipa-Press/K Rano
225 Maggie Noach
226 Rex Features Ltd.
227 **T** Corbis/Everett
227 **B** Victor Gollancz
228 Hulton Getty
229 HarperCollins
230 Rex Features Ltd.
231 **L** Legend
231 **R** Penguin UK
232 Penguin UK
235 John Vance
236 Corbis/Everett
237 **T** Corbis/Bettmann/UPI
237 **B** Hulton Getty
238 **T** Corbis/Everett
238 **B** Victor Gollancz
239 Hulton Getty
241 Gene Wolfe
242 Penguin UK
243 Rex Features Ltd./Sipa-Press
244 Warner/Polaris/Corbis/Everett
245 TCF/Brandywine/Corbis/Everett
246 Captain America Vol. 346 October 1988. Marvel Comics 1988. © Marvel Entertainment Group Inc./Kinema Collection
247 **T** Ronald Grant Archive
247 **B** A Universal Television Production /Rex Features Ltd./Fotos International
248 Batman, Trademark and Copyright © 1994 DC Comics. All Rights Reserved.
249 **T** Bellisarius Productions in association with Universal Television /MCA/Ronald Grant Archive
249 **B** BBC/Ronald Grant Archive
251 **T** Ballantine Books/Kinema Collection
251 **B** © Berkley Medallion Edition, 1966/Kinema Collection
252 Goodtimes/Gladiole/Kinema Collection
253 **T** The Eagle 2.11.55, vol. 6, No47 © Fleetway /Kinema Collection
253 **B** British Lion/Regal/Aaru/Kinema Collection
254 **T** Judge Dredd © IPC Publishers 1986-87/Kinema Collection
254 **B** Warner/Ladd/Blade Runner Partnership/Corbis/Everett
255 Universal/Corbis/Everett
257 Warner/Hammer-Seven Arts/Ronald Grant Archive
258 Toho Productions/ Universal /Kinema Collection
259 Universal/Ronald Grant Archive
260 Bruce Publishing Company Ltd./Kinema Collection
261 Chrysalis Visual Programming Ltd. for Channel Four/Rex Features Ltd./M Frewer
262 The Incredible Hulk ®, Vol 1, No.258, April, 1981. Marvel Comics Group. Copyright © Marvel Comics Group, a division of Cadence Industries Corporation. All rights reserved/Joel Finler Collection
263 MGM/Ronald Grant Archive
265 **T** Paramount in association with Norway Corporation /Ronald Grant Archive
265 **B** RKO /Joel Finler Collection
266 Warner /Alexander Salkind/ Ronald Grant Archive/DC Comics
268 Universal/Steven Spielberg/Kinema Collection
269 Warner/Kennedy Miller/ Entertainment/Kinema Collection
270 Paramount/George Pal/Kinema Collection
271 MGM/Ronald Grant Archive
272 **T** Universal/Joel Finler Collection
272 **B** AIP/Cinema 77/Kinema Collection
273 Ten Thirteen Productions, in association with 20th Century Television/Corbis/Everett
274 Pan Books Ltd./Kinema Collection
275 Paramount Pictures/Ronald Grant Archive
276 Fox/Lawrence Gordon/Joel Silver/John Davis/Ronald Grant Archive
277 Hammer/Anthony Nelson Keys/Ronald Grant Archive
278 **T** TCF/Brandywine/Kinema Collection
278 **B** Rank/Orion/Kinema Collection
279 Buck Rogers Annual 1984. © Copyright 1983 Western Publishing Co. Inc. All rights reserved./Kinema Collection
280 Bantam Books/Kinema Collection
281 TCF/Lucasfilm/Rex Features/Fotos International
282 Spiderman, Marvel Comics 1988 © Marvel Entertainment Group Inc./Kinema Collection
283 **T** Sphere Science Fiction/Kinema Collection
283 **B** Desilu in association with Norway Corporation (Seasons 1-2), Paramount in association with Norway Corporation (Seasons 2-3)/Rex Features Ltd.
284 Superman ®, Vol42, No. 345, March1980. DC Comics Inc. Copyright © 1979 by DC Comics Inc. All rights reserved./Joel Finler Collection
285 **T** Deadline, iss. 69, June/July 1995, Deadline Publications Ltd. 1995.
285 **B** Guild/Carolco/Pacific Western/ Lightstorm/Joel Finler Collection
287 TCF/Lucasfilm/Joel Finler Collection
288 **T** Watchmen, Trademark and Copyright © DC Comics. All rights reserved.
288 **B** BBC/Ronald Grant Archive
291 SFX Magazine March 1996/Future Publishing
294 Interzone Magazine/© Interzone 1995

Every effort has been made to acknowledge the pictures in this book correctly. We apologise for any omissions which will be added to any further editions.

Acknowledgements

The Publishers would like to thank the following sources for their kind permission to reproduce the pictures used in this publication:

3 UFA/Ronald Grant Archive
4 **TC** Babylon Productions Inc./Corbis/Everett
4 **CR** Warner/Alexander Salkind/TMs & ©Copyright DC Comics/Corbis/Everett
4 **BL** Greenaway for 20th Century-Fox Television/Kinema Collection
4 **CLB** Fox/Corbis/Everett
4 **BC** TCF/Ronald Grant Archive
4 **BR** Paul Jackson for BBC North West (Seasons 1-3), Grant Naylor for BBC North (Seasons 4-6)/Ronald Grant Archive/M Vaughan
5 Desilu in association with Norway Corporation (Seasons 1-2), Paramount in association with Norway Corporation (Season 2-3)/Corbis/Everett
6/7 Universal/Joel Finler Collection
8 **L** Bantam Doubleday Dell Magazines
8 **R** Mary Evans Picture Library
9 **T** Tor Books
9 **B** Warner/Ladd/Blade Runner Partnership/Ronald Grant Archive
10 ICC/Cine Trail / Belstar / Stephan/Ronald Grant Archive
11 **T** 20th Century Fox/Ronald Grant Archive
11 **B** Hulton Getty
12 Hulton Getty
13 (artist Antonio Cabral-Bejarana)/La Rabida Monastery, Palos/AKG London Ltd.
14 Hulton Getty
15 **T** Mary Evans Picture Library
15 **B** Mary Evans Picture Library
16 **T** Mary Evans Picture Library
16 **B** Hulton Getty
17 **T** Columbia TriStar/American Zoetrope/Japan Satellite/Indie Productions/Ronald Grant Archive
17 **B** Hulton Getty
18 Baen Books
19 Paramount/George Pal/Ronald Grant Archive
20 (artist Hubert Rogers)/ Bantam Doubleday Dell Magazines
20 (artist George Barr)/Underwood Miller
20 (artist Peter Gudynas)/Grafton
20 Bantam Doubleday Dell Magazines
20 Vintage
20 W R Chambers
22 (artist Howard Brown)/ Bantam Doubleday Dell Magazines
23 Ace
24 W R Chambers
25 **T** (artist Solonevich)/ Bantam Doubleday Dell Magazines
25 **B** (artist H.W.Wesso)/ Bantam Doubleday Dell Magazines
27 T Chatto & Windus
27 **B** (artist Trevor Denning)/Michael Joseph
28 Berkley
29 (artist Emsh)/Galaxy Publishing Corp.
30 Hamilton & Co.
31 Thornton Butterworth
32 Ace
35 (artist Emsh)/Galaxy Publishing Corp.
36 (artist Peter Cross)/ Harmony Books
37 Lancer
38 Ace
39 New English Library
40 Victor Gollancz
41 Tor Books
42 (artist Frank R. Paul)/ Continental Publications Inc.
43 (artist George Barr)/ Underwood Miller
44 (artists Jack Rubin & Irving Freeman)/Harper & Row
45 (artist Lionel Dillon)/ Gnome Press
46 **T** Ace
46 **B** HarperCollins Science Fiction & Fantasy
47 Ace
48 **T** Bantam Books
48 **B** Vintage
49 HarperCollins
50 (artist Alex Schomburg)/ Edward L. Ferman
51 Dutton
52 Scion
53 (artist Ron Dilg)/Nelson Doubleday
54 (artist David Mattingly)/ Bluejay
55 Bantam Doubleday Dell Magazines
56 **T** (artist Don Bolognese)/ Arbor House
56 **B** (artist Peter Gudynas)/ Grafton
57 Reader's Library
59 (artist Brian Lewis)/Nova
60 **T** (artist Keith Parkinson)/ Baen Publishing Enterprises
60 **B** Victor Gollancz
61 (artist Romas B. Kukalis)/ Morrow
62 20th C Fox/Brandywine/ British Film Institute
63 UFA/Kinema Collection
64 Universal/Joel Finler Collection
65 Universal/Joel Finler Collection
66 RKO/Joel Finler Collection
67 **T** London/Ronald Grant Archive
67 **B** Universal/Joel Finler Collection
69 Universal/George Pal/Kinema Collection
70 TCF/Joel Finler Collection
71 **T** RKO/Winchester/Joel Finler Collection
71 **B** Ealing/Ronald Grant Archive
72 UA/Dowling/Ronald Grant Archive
73 Paramount/George Pal/Joel Finler Collection
74 **T** Ronald Grant Archive
74 **B** Warner/Joel Finler Collection
75 Exclusive/Hammer/Ronald Grant Archive
76 **T** U-I/Ronald Grant Archive
76 **B** MGM/Ronald Grant Archive
77 Allied Artists/Walter Wanger/Joel Finler Collection
78 Hammer/Joel Finler Collection
79 United Artists/Stanley Kramer/Ronald Grant Archive
80 **T** MGM/Kinema Collection
80 **B** MGM/Galaxy/Ronald Grant Archive
81 **T** AIP/Ronald Grant Archive
81 **B** British Lion/Pax/Ronald Grant Archive
82 Columbia/Stanley Kubrick/Joel Finler Collection
83 Paramount/Devonshire /Ronald Grant Archive
84 Filmstudio/Ronald Grant Archive
85 **T** Paramout/Joel/ Gibraltar/Ronald Grant Archive
85 **B** Rank/Anglo Enterprise/Vineyard/ Joel Finler Collection
86 **T** Hammer/Anthony Nelson Keys/Ronald Grant Archive
86 **B** Marianne/Dino de Laurentiis/ Joel Finler Collection
87 **T** Selmur/Robertson Associates/Ronald Grant Archive
87 **B** TCF/Apjac/Ronald Grant Archive
88 MGM/ Stanley Kubrick/Joel Finler Collection
90 Universal/Robert Wise/Ronald Grant Archive
91 Warner/Polaris/Ronald Grant Archive
92 **T** Universal/Michel Gruskoff/Douglas Trumbull/British Film Institute
92 **B** Mosfilm/Ronald Grant Archive
93 UA/Jack Rollins, Charles Joffe/Ronald Grant Archive
94 MGM/Ronald Grant Archive
95 **T** Saltpan/AFDC/Royce Smeal/Joel Finler Collection
95 **B** Jack H. Harris/Ronald Grant Archive
96 British Lion/Ronald Grant Archive
97 Columbia/EMI/ Ronald Grant Archive
98 TCF/Lucasfilm/ Corbis/Everett
99 UA/Robert H Solo/Ronald Grant Archive
100 Warner/Alexander Salkind/Joel Finler Collection/DC Comics
101 Mosfilm Unit 2/Ronald Grant Archive
102 Paramount/Ronald Grant Archive
103 TCF/Lucasfilm/Ronald Grant Archive
104 Filmplan International/ Kinema Collection
105 **T** Warner/Kennedy Miller Entertainment/Corbis/Everett
105 **B** New World/Android/ Kinema Collection
106 Warner/Ladd/Blade Runner Partnership/Ronald Grant Archive
107 Universal/Joel Finler Collection
108 **T** Lisberger-Kushner/ Ronald Grant Archive
108 **B** Filmplan International/ Ronald Grant Archive
109 **T** Umbrella/Rosenblum/Virgin /British Film Institute
109 **B** TCF/Lucasfilm/Kinema Collection
110 Columbia/Delphi/Kobal Collection
111 **T** Universal/Steven Spielberg/Ronald Grant Archive
111 **B** Orion/Hemdale/Pacific Western/ Corbis/Everett
112 **T** Kings Road/TCF/ Ronald Grant Archive
112 **B** Embassy/Ronald Grant Archive
113 TCF/Brandywine/ Corbis/Everett
114 TCF/Brooksfilm/ Joel Finler Collection
115 ICA/Akira Committee/ Joel Finler Collection
116 **T** TCF/Lawrence Gordon/Joel Silver/John Davis/Corbis/Everett
116 **B** Rank/Orion/Joel Finler Collection
117 **L** Fox/De Laurentiis/ Kestrel Films/ Ronald Grant Archive
117 **R** Fox/Rex Features Ltd.
118 **T** Warner/Doric/Ronald Grant Archive
118 **B** Warner/Ronald Grant Archive
119 Hollywood Pictures/ Amblin/Tangled Web/Ronald Grant Archive
121 **T** Guild/Carolco/ Pictorial Press
121 **B** Guild/Carolco/Pacific Western/ Lightstorm/Ronald Grant Archive
122 UIP/Universal/ Amblin/Pictorial Press
123 Alliance Communications/ Corbis/Everett
124 NBC TV/B & B Productions Inc./Corbis/Everett
125 DuMont Television Network/Corbis/Everett
126 BBC/Ronald Grant Archive
127 BBC Television/Ronald Grant Archive
128 BBC/Joel Finler Collection
129 BBC/Ronald Grant Archive
130 Cayuga (filmed at M-G-M)/Corbis/ Everett/CBS
131 ABC Television/Pictorial Press
132 BBC/Ronald Grant Archive
133 Jack Chertok/Pictorial Press
134 **T** Daystar-Villa di Stefano for United Artists Television/ Ronald Grant Archive
134 **B** Arena for MGM Television/Ronald Grant Archive
135 Irwin Allen for 20th Century Fox Television/ Kinema Collection
136 **T** CBS/Irwin Allen with Jodi Production Inc/Van Bernard Productions Inc for 20th Century Fox Television/Corbis/Everett
136 **B** AP Films for AV/ITC/ Pictorial Press/Polygram
137 **T** Michael Garrison with CBS/Corbis/ Everett
137 **B** Greenaway for 20th Century Fox Television/ Corbis/Everett
139 Desilu in association with Norway Corporation (Seasons 1-2), Paramount in association with Norway Corporation (Seasons 2-3)/Corbis/Everett
140 Quinn Martin/ABC/Pictorial Press
141 **T** Everyman Films for ATV/Pictorial Press/Polygram
141 **B** BBC Television/Ronald Grant Archive
142 Paramount Pictures TV/Corbis/Everett
143 Century 21 Pictures for ITC Worldwide Distribution, Pictorial Press/Polygram
144 Universal Television/Corbis/Everett
145 **T** Thames Television/Pictorial Press
145 **B** Harve Bennett/Universal/ NBC/ Corbis/Everett
146 Pictorial Press/Polygram
148 BBC Television/Ronald Grant Archive
149 **T** Glen A Larson in association with Universal Television/Corbis/Everett
149 **B** BBC Television/Ronald Grant Archive
150 **T** Miller-Milkis Productions Inc. and Henderson Production Co Inc. with Paramount Television/Corbis/Everett
150 **B** BBC Television/Ronald Grant Archive
151 **T** Mark VIII Ltd with NBC TV/Corbis/Everett
151 **B** Glen A Larson/Universal Television/Corbis/Everett
152 ATV Network/ Pictorial Press/ Polygram
153 **T** WNET/Thirteen/Ronald Grant Archive
153 **B** Charles Fried/Corbis/Everett/NBC
154 **T** BBC Television/RCTV Inc./ Australian Broadcasting Corp./Corbis/Everett
154 **B** BBC
155 ABC Motion Pictures/Corbis/Everett
156 BBC/Ronald Grant Archive
157 **L** Kenneth Johnson with Warner Bros Television/Corbis/Everett
157 **R** Chrysalis Visual Programming Ltd. for Channel Four/Corbis/Everett
158 Atlantis Films Ltd. with John Wilcox Productions Inc./Corbis/Everett
159 Paramount Pictures/Corbis/Everett
160 **T** BBC Television/Corbis/Everett
160 **B** BBC North /Ronald Grant Archive/M Vaughan
161 Kenneth Johnson/Corbis/Everett
162 Bellisarius Productions with Universal Television/MCA/Ronald Grant Archive
163 **T** Zenith/Corbis/Everett
163 **B** GranadaTelevision/Corbis/Everett
164 Babylonian Productions Inc./Corbis/Everett
165 Roundelay Productions/Corbis/Everett
166 Paramount/Corbis/Everett
167 Ten Thirteen Productions with 20th Century Television/Corbis/Everett
169 Trilogy Entertainment/ Corbis/Everett
170 Paramount Network/Ronald Grant Archive
172 Corbis/Bettmann
174 Victor Gollancz
174 Rex Features Ltd.
174 Victor Gollanz
175 **T** HarperCollins
175 **B** Corbis
177 HarperCollins
178 HarperCollins
179 **T** Little Brown/S Denton
179 **B** HarperCollins
180 Legend
181 M Bishop
183 HarperCollins
184 J K Klein
185 Corbis/Bettmann/UPI
186 **T** HarperCollins
186 **B** Rex Features Ltd./Fotos International
187 Corbis/Everett
188 Victor Gollancz
189 Blunck Studio of Edmond
190 Rex Features Ltd.
191 Century/J Exley
192 Corbis/Everett
193 **T** University of Massachussetts Photo Service
193 **B** L Sprague de Camp
195 Jamie Spracher
196 Mary Evans Picture Library
198 Corbis/Everett
199 Penguin UK
201 Pictorial Press
202 Jerry Bauer
204 Penguin UK
205 HarperCollins
206 Victor Gollancz
207 Kinema Collection
208 **T** Pictorial Press
208 **B** Pictorial Press
209 M Wood Kolisch
211 **T** Dr F Rottensteiner
211 **B** Hulton Getty
212 Pictorial Press/J Mayer
213 **T** Rex Features Ltd.
213 **B** Victor Gollancz/ S Earnshaw
214 Belfast Telegraph Newspapers Ltd.
216 **T** The Orion Publishing Group Ltd.
216 **B** Rex Features Ltd.
217 Mirror Syndication International
218 Del Rey/Valada
219 Corbis/Bettmann
220 K Bubriski
221 Hulton Getty
222 **T** Fred Fox Studios Ltd.
222 **B** Bloomsbury
223 HarperCollins
224 Rex Features Ltd./Sipa-Press/K Rano
225 Maggie Noach
226 Rex Features Ltd.
227 **T** Corbis/Everett
227 **B** Victor Gollancz
228 Hulton Getty
229 HarperCollins
230 Rex Features Ltd.
231 **L** Legend
231 **R** Penguin UK
232 Penguin UK
235 John Vance
236 Corbis/Everett
237 **T** Corbis/Bettmann/UPI
237 **B** Hulton Getty
238 **T** Corbis/Everett
238 **B** Victor Gollancz
239 Hulton Getty
241 Gene Wolfe
242 Penguin UK
243 Rex Features Ltd./Sipa-Press
244 Warner/Polaris/Corbis/Everett
245 TCF/Brandywine/Corbis/Everett
246 Captain America Vol. 346 October 1988. Marvel Comics 1988. © Marvel Entertainment Group Inc./Kinema Collection
247 **T** Ronald Grant Archive
247 **B** A Universal Television Production /Rex Features Ltd./Fotos International
248 Batman, Trademark and Copyright © 1994 DC Comics. All Rights Reserved.
249 **T** Bellisarius Productions in association with Universal Television /MCA/Ronald Grant Archive
249 **B** BBC/Ronald Grant Archive
251 **T** Ballantine Books/Kinema Collection
251 **B** © Berkley Medallion Edition, 1966/Kinema Collection
252 Goodtimes/Gladiole/Kinema Collection
253 **T** The Eagle 2.11.55, vol. 6, No47 © Fleetway /Kinema Collection
253 **B** British Lion/Regal/Aaru/Kinema Collection
254 **T** Judge Dredd © IPC Publishers 1986-87/Kinema Collection
254 **B** Warner/Ladd/Blade Runner Partnership/Corbis/Everett
255 Universal/Corbis/Everett
257 Warner/Hammer-Seven Arts/Ronald Grant Archive
258 Toho Productions/ Universal /Kinema Collection
259 Universal/Ronald Grant Archive
260 Bruce Publishing Company Ltd./Kinema Collection
261 Chrysalis Visual Programming Ltd. for Channel Four/Rex Features Ltd./M Frewer
262 The Incredible Hulk ®, Vol 1, No.258, April, 1981. Marvel Comics Group. Copyright © Marvel Comics Group, a division of Cadence Industries Corporation. All rights reserved/Joel Finler Collection
263 MGM/Ronald Grant Archive
265 **T** Paramount in association with Norway Corporation /Ronald Grant Archive
265 **B** RKO /Joel Finler Collection
266 Warner /Alexander Salkind/ Ronald Grant Archive/DC Comics
268 Universal/Steven Spielberg/Kinema Collection
269 Warner/Kennedy Miller/ Entertainment/Kinema Collection
270 Paramount/George Pal/Kinema Collection
271 MGM/Ronald Grant Archive
272 **T** Universal/Joel Finler Collection
272 **B** AIP/Cinema 77/Kinema Collection
273 Ten Thirteen Productions, in association with 20th Century Television/Corbis/Everett
274 Pan Books Ltd./Kinema Collection
275 Paramount Pictures/Ronald Grant Archive
276 Fox/Lawrence Gordon/Joel Silver/John Davis/Ronald Grant Archive
277 Hammer/Anthony Nelson Keys/Ronald Grant Archive
278 **T** TCF/Brandywine/Kinema Collection
278 **B** Rank/Orion/Kinema Collection
279 Buck Rogers Annual 1984. © Copyright 1983 Western Publishing Co. Inc. All rights reserved./Kinema Collection
280 Bantam Books/Kinema Collection
281 TCF/Lucasfilm/Rex Features/Fotos International
282 Spiderman, Marvel Comics 1988 © Marvel Entertainment Group Inc./Kinema Collection
283 **T** Sphere Science Fiction/Kinema Collection
283 **B** Desilu in association with Norway Corporation (Seasons 1-2), Paramount in association with Norway Corporation (Seasons 2-3)/Rex Features Ltd.
284 Superman ®, Vol42, No. 345, March1980. DC Comics Inc. Copyright © 1979 by DC Comics Inc. All rights reserved./Joel Finler Collection
285 **T** Deadline, iss. 69, June/July 1995, Deadline Publications Ltd. 1995.
285 **B** Guild/Carolco/Pacific Western/ Lightstorm/Joel Finler Collection
287 TCF/Lucasfilm/Joel Finler Collection
288 **T** Watchmen, Trademark and Copyright © DC Comics. All rights reserved.
288 **B** BBC/Ronald Grant Archive
291 SFX Magazine March 1996/Future Publishing
294 Interzone Magazine/© Interzone 1995

Every effort has been made to acknowledge the pictures in this book correctly. We apologise for any omissions which will be added to any further editions.